D0852966

Renner Learning Resource Center
Elgin Community College
Elgin, IL 60123

American Mythologies

American
Mythologies

MARSHALL BLONSKY

New York   Oxford
Oxford University Press
1992

RENNER LEARNING RESOURCE CENTER
ELGIN COMMUNITY COLLEGE
ELGIN, ILLINOIS 60123

Oxford University Press

Oxford   New York   Toronto
Delhi   Bombay   Calcutta   Madras   Karachi
Kuala Lumpur   Singapore   Hong Kong   Toyko
Nairobi   Dar es Salaam   Cape Town
Melbourne   Auckland

and associated companies in
Berlin   Ibadan

Copyright © 1988, 1989, 1990,
1991, 1992 by Marshall Blonsky
Appreciation © 1992 by Umberto Eco
Foreword © 1992 by Ronald Weintraub

Portions of this book were previously published
in *The New York Times Magazine, The Washington Post,
Vanity Fair, Harper's, Lear's, Advertising Age, Seven Days,
Graphis,* and *ID Magazine.*

Published by Oxford University Press, Inc.,
200 Madison Avenue, New York, New York 10016

Oxford is a registered trademark of Oxford University Press

All rights reserved. No part of this publication may be reproduced,
stored in a retrieval system, or transmitted, in any form or by any means,
electronic, mechanical, photocopying, recording, or otherwise,
without the prior permission of Oxford University Press.

Library of Congress Cataloging-in-Publication Data
Blonsky, Marshall.
American mythologies / Marshall Blonsky.
p. cm.   Includes index.
ISBN 0–19–505062–2
1. United States—Popular culture—History—20th century.
2. United States—Social life and customs—1971–
I. Title.
E169.12.B58 1991
306.4'0973—dc20
91–7940

306. U
B 654a

096019

1 2 3 4 5 6 7 8 9

Printed in the United States of America
on acid-free paper

Contents

The Key to the Magic Kingdom

UMBERTO ECO

Marshall Blonsky mentions Barthes often enough in this book that it is perhaps worthwhile to tell a story that our author did not know until now. A bit of his prehistory.

Milano 1974. First Congress of the International Association for Semiotic Studies. Twenty minutes before the opening ceremony. We had planned the Congress for two hundred people. In the course of the last months, we had realized there would be more, but we were not expecting the more than eight hundred people who materialized that morning. And among them were an impressive number of Big Ones. Somebody said that the floor looked like a Who's Who.

And there, patiently waiting, a moustached man who introduced himself as Marshall Blonsky. I felt embarrassed (you'll see why) and I looked for Roland Barthes, who was the most distinguished member of the Reading Committee. We had spent the previous year in evaluating the papers we received, and they were so many that the Committee was obliged to split into subcommittees. Every group accepted the papers of the acknowledged leaders in our discipline, rejected the blatantly crazy ones, and the whole committee met only to discuss the dubious cases. While shaking hands with Blonsky, I realized that his case had remained unsolved because at a first reading, his paper had looked to me so linguistically coiled upon itself that I was not sure it would have been understood by normal human beings.

Now, reading Blonsky's preface to this book, I understand why. He was "probably one of the first semioticians teaching in New York City . . . [managing] to impregnate [his] students with French ideas," and he was doing so by inventing an intricate French-like

English which in its turn was trying to imitate the German-like French of Lacan or, at least, of many Lacanians. We all have to start somewhere, and the American making love to his students with *la jouissance* (I remember that part) was the prototype Blonsky before he got to us. Thus I had put his paper apart for a further discussion with Barthes and other members of the Committee. And then I forgot it (believe me, the last two months before the opening of an international congress always are a damned mess, and I won't repeat such an experience again).

I realized that Blonsky did not know as yet whether he was admitted or not; but, a man of faith, our Pilgrim had sailed from the East Coast to reach the Semiotic Eldorado.

So (the secretary of the Congress, Doretta Gelmini, being a genius) I retrieved in five seconds Blonsky's paper, I found Barthes at the bar sipping a mineral water, and I told him my problem. Barthes took the paper and disappeared for fifteen minutes. Then he came back and said: "It's true, it is awkward, but there is something intriguing here . . . Let him speak."

End of story. With this writing, Marshall is also paying a tribute to the Magic Donor who gave him the Key to enter the Enchanted Palace of All Mythologies.

Worldliness

RONALD WEINTRAUB

Marshall Blonsky is not a businessman. The reader will better understand what I intend if I say it in French: *"Il n'est pas un homme d'affaires,"* he isn't a man of affairs. Or he wasn't. And therein lies a tale of how this book's language came into being. In 1987 when Blonsky was beginning the project—in homage to his inspiration and teacher, the late Roland Barthes—he intended an "armchair" book, as they say, although no one really writes in armchairs. He intended a word-processed artifact modeled after the master's *Mythologies.* The idea, as I remember it, was that Blonsky would transplant over here that book's compulsion to know what things mean. He would of course update its gesture of regarding a landscape or a phenomenon as a text to be read. Barthes' "Toys" would become "The International Toy Fair"; "Striptease" would become, I suppose, "Billy's (Jimmie's/Charlie's/fill in the name) Topless"; "Steak and Chips" might become "Steak going, going . . ." in this health-obsessed age. He could have done it in a year and taken his chances as yet another American epigone of the French, a story we know only too well.

It's sad to repeat it—the American hijacking of some of the most tragic ideas to come out of postwar Europe. The idea, for example, that given the absurdity of war, slaughter and despotism, you could no longer seriously believe that the individual ego had been or was in control of its individual choices. Because they *had* to, the Europeans replaced the philosophy of the ego or consciousness with that of codes, unconscious systems of meaning that were held to structure what individuals thought, perceived, said—and, God forgive them, did. The American fate of this idea has become clear over the past twenty years. It became a packaged product. When, in 1966, the new French philosophy came to America by way of Baltimore—its port of entry through Johns Hopkins University—the Americans turned it into an instrument for dazzling the crowd, for tenure and other academic perks. They cleaned it up, dispensing with some of the more spectacular and melancholic European elements: for example, the idea of a death drive or that consciousness flickers on and off even as we talk. Deconstruction, an exquisite philosophical procedure, weighed upon by the tragedy of modern European history, became homework.

The world doesn't need another *Mythologies,* and my friend doesn't need to make Lite Semiotics or any other product. Using my best motivational skills, I shoved him out the door to Tokyo, proposing he start there, talking to the people who make some of the myths—be they cars, computers, cassettes—that constitute our desiring selves. He never stopped going after that, except to return to New York where he allowed no secretary to transcribe the interviews, preferring instead to stay up all night, doing the job himself, recapturing the rarefied, seamy, elegant affairs into which, by now, he had insinuated himself.

I'm not sure we have anyone else like that here. And for good reason. Although I didn't know it when I gave the shove, what Blonsky would find within himself while on his travels is akin to what is currently being articulated in a manner part journalistic, part literary by a younger generation of European intellectuals who are attempting to articulate a thoroughly modern (even, to use that too-much-used term, postmodern) ethical and social democratic vision. The intellectual procedures of this generation (names like Bernard-Henry Levy, Alain Finkielkraut, Jacques Attali should be mentioned) are founded on a double rejection. On the one hand, the rejection of the Sartrian or Malrauxian—the engaged—intellectual, who, no matter how suave his discourse, always turns out to be the mouthpiece of a Cause or the supposed "meaning" of History. In Levy's lovely remark, given when he founded his new journal *La Regle du jeu* (*Rule of the Game*), the engaged intellectual "suspends for long intervals both his work and his judgment in order that, perched on his barrel or slave to his ideal, he can measure himself by values of which he is no longer anything but the figurehead." That model is exhausted. The death of European communism confirmed it.

On the other hand is the inverse model of the disengaged intellectual, "the man of science, the adept of pure forms and of an indifferent knowledge," as Levy called him, adding bitterly—"the one who will never interrupt his work to take the least part in anything." That model *was* Blonsky's, as it was that of the academic structuralists and semioticians with whom he trained. It was the model of the "human sciences," which, from the 60s to the 80s, dominated thought by its certainty of a decipherable world, by its promotion of linguistics as the master form of decoding and by the hegemony of Marxism, psychoanalysis, and the various *cenacles* of structuralism. That model is dead, too, at least in its pure form. It has become subsumed in the poststructuralist theorizing that drives today's political correctness—or, as it is so inelegantly and smugly put in PC's higher reaches—"oppositionality" and "criticality."

These models are no longer Blonsky's, although he has learned from them what he had to. Like the contemporary European development, the discourse here is that of a writer taking on that part of himself which is driven by the world. This discourse has a care for the world. The writer works, eats and banters with Ted Koppel—moments of cameraderie that give way to a glimpse of Koppel's contempt and undemocratic motives. In a dressing room, the author watches Pat Sajak swoop onto Vanna White's neck; the writer makes us smart with the condescension that follows. He watches Jeff Koons triumphantly hang and analyze a pornography show—on the eve of its destruction by revolted critics. He wears the suit as he interviews its designer, getting Armani, Ferré, Missoni to explain, using his body, the significance of changes to shoulders, gorge, and the rest. A spark of affect connects him to each of his subjects, producing a language in contact with the materiality of things. As a prototype of the intellectual journalist, even the novelistic journalist, he goes beneath the surface to explain the superficial—and a quickening antipathy to it.

In a world where there is mostly style and little substance, Blonsky gives us substance wrapped in style, irrigated by his own desire. Assimilating his experiences, we witness this book rather than just read it. The power of the anecdotes helps us remember. The writerly in it frames the ideas, it gives a preservative benefit. The journalism gives the value of the illustration to the work. It sticks to the mind, stays in the imagination. I suppose what sticks most is the very genre—elaborated, I think, unconsciously by the author. And that genre is the quest narrative. The semiotician in blue velvet, as Blonsky called himself in the early 70s, has given way to the rootless cosmopolitan, the citizen less of a country than of his language and of ethical project.

Ronald Weintraub is chief executive officer of Harmon Publishing

Mea Culpa

For over a decade I was ensconced in the academic ghetto. Suddenly one day, feeling dusty and moth-eaten, I decided to answer the call of the American road. I wanted to discover the topography of this vast mythical land. This book is the result of my first cross-country voyage from the subways of New York to the game shows of Hollywood, passing through my native Kansas City, with its personal demons. As an escape for perspective and because the idea of America has become a planetary phenomenon, I went to London, Paris, Milan, Moscow, Tokyo, and Hong Kong to hear and to read Europeans and Asians reading our myths.

During the 70s I was probably one of the first semioticians teaching in New York City. I managed to impregnate my students with French ideas, from Roland Barthes' Cartesian approach to Greta Garbo's face, and from the Eiffel Tower's steel transparency to Michel Foucault's labyrinthine weaving through the secret and aphasic ways of our supposed subjugation.

I was left with the babble of tongues in a circular library biting its own tail. Instead of looking at the world through French eyes, I wanted to remove from it the costumes of rhetoric and address the living body of the country with native eyes and the scalpel of semiology, which had become second nature to me now.

This book began with the ambition of writing an American *Mythologies* in the style of Roland Barthes. A loving disciple saluting the dead master.

The project sickened.

Some years ago, Barthes wrote a tiny analysis, very clever. On sitting at home with his mother watching TV, encountering the news flashes of the People's Temple suicides in Guyana. In a single paragraph Barthes took you through the history of semiology, talked about why he sat with his mouth agape watching television. Suicide is usually a matter of one or two; this, however, was monstrous—it broke the code of suicide. Since excess, produced by the code breaking, always produces stupefaction, I, Roland Barthes, sitting with my mother, couldn't write a semiotics of what I saw.

Still in that single paragraph, he continued: "For me myself, I am embarrassed given the present state of my knowledge, not to know more about what these poor bastards believed, as if the attempts at interpretation today are so concerned with forms (such as fascination, hypnosis, etc.)"—a reference for the learned to psychoanalyst Jacques Lacan—"that we feel it is unnecessary to consider the contents."

And I, who am American, when I read that micro-essay, wrote on its margin this little shout: "But you could have found out! You could have gotten on an airplane and joined the press corps and interviewed the survivors and could have married your interpretive strategies to empirical news-gathering technique." This small rebuke requires an explanation.

Barthes was obviously a leader in his field when he wrote those words on the People's Temple massacre. At the time of his death in 1980 he was professor at the *Collège de France* in Paris, and, for a number of years already, had enjoyed—and suffered—the status of white statue. Every day at lunchtime, upon his return home, he would turn off the phone to savor solitude. I and others felt that had he lived on, he would have slipped out from under the ecstatic apprehension of his last years as he did from under all the other apprehensions, whether they were structural or subjective. Little matter that. For those with a taste for irony, within the apparently irresponsible esthete of the last five years he was a tormented man who believed his relations with reality were imaginary and could at best be hypothetical.

The imaginary: for Barthes, a noun not an adjective, it is to images what bestiary is to beasts. It is the image system, the varied, reflexive, always deceptive modes in which one imagines oneself, or even, as Barthes said, in which one wants to be loved. The imaginary is the system of the mirrors we hold up to ourselves. "You are that," says the mirror. That of Barthes was the novel. In 1978, in a lecture called "Proust and Me," given at New York University, he said:

> If I desire to make a novel, and that's what I'm talking about, I do not aim to rewrite *À la recherche*, no? . . . simply, to identify myself with Proust wanting to write it, wanting to write the work. I identify myself with a project, I don't compare myself with the author of a work.

Only a fragment of this lecture has been published (in *Le bruissement de la langue* [*The Rustle of Language*], 1984, 1986). What we have has been so *fignolé,* as the French say, so polished and overdone that the profoundest meaning of the lecture has been excised. For good reason. In the audience I could hear the lecture strewn in French with the untranslatable phrase *''n'est-ce pas''* (which I just translated as ''no?''—meaning: ''isn't it so?''). There was nothing didactic about the talk. The *n'est-ce pas* was a sigh, a fading, a conscious questioning of the speaker's remarks. Barthes more than anyone knew the contingency of mirrors. They can break. They can fall from the hand. They lead to an identity that endlessly undoes itself, for, in the end, it is anchored in no referent. We say that sitting in front of the mirror, there where we imagine ourselves, we mistake ourselves. But Barthes, who had never stopped denouncing the ''natural,'' never could trick himself into the jubilation said to come with that mistake. ''So I'm *that!*''—end of anxiety.

Whence the hypothetical in his life. Here is the close of ''Proust and Me,'' an awkwardness you must not take as modesty:

> A question, to end with: Does this mean that I'm going to write a novel? Well, I don't know anything about that. That is, I don't know if I'll have the force, the talent for it. I don't know what form of novel I could produce. I don't even know if it's actually possible, that is, in current history, in the actual state of literature, to produce a novel. I don't know anything about it. But what matters for the moment, and the lecture here, is the witnessing of this immediate moment . . . what matters is to act *as if* I could write one. I am placing myself in effect in the position of the one . . . no? *n'est-ce pas?* . . . in deciding to write a novel, even if I don't do it or not right away. . . . That's the very definition of the hypothesis, isn't it, ''as if, as if.'' Well, I place myself in the hypothesis of the novel.

He didn't plan to renounce teaching right away, he said in the seminar that followed the lecture. Rather, in his course at the *Collège,* he planned to teach the very novel he fantasized and hypothesized—surely a method so unusual, one shouldn't expect to find it in some how-to on writing. ''I'm going to place the emphasis on theoretical reflection for the preparation, without touching the preparation itself. But,'' he confessed, ''I risk relapsing into the meta-novel. Effectively, I am menaced by this.''

Why such agony over a novel that some say he had already written? ''Its characters are Sade, Fourier and Loyola,'' said his friend Umberto Eco, referring to Barthes' 1971 *tour de force* by that name. The answer is the following, Barthes' fantasy of the novel in its great historic moments, *War and Peace,* the *In Search,* and so on: The novel is an act of love that can triumph over death and over the drought of the heart, the latter being the most terrible thing we have to endure; Barthes thought of the difficulty of loving, which he traced to the Middle Ages and which was called *acedia* by the monks, the impossibility of investing, the impossibility of loving. ''In the face of this drought, the very great novel, we receive it as something . . .'' Barthes faltered, resumed: ''the word is idiotic, is it not, as an act of love. There is no other way of saying it.'' The novel is an activity that brews up a storm, as we say; brews up a world, embracing the world, loving the world.

Each person who was at that lecture can choose his or her own most pathetic moment. For me, it was hearing:

> In *War and Peace* Tolstoy paints those that he loved, his family, his mother, Princess Marie who was his mother, etc., his father, his grandfather. And Proust too, you know, painted those he loved, Albertine, *n'est-ce pas*, his mother and grandmother. And at that moment, the novel permits the one who writes it to say that these beings that he loved, that he loves, have not lived for nothing, that they have been welcomed, that they are welcomed, and justified, *n'est-ce pas,* a little as Michelet thought to justify the innumerable deaths of history precisely by writing history. And the novel permits saying affect fully but indirectly. You know that today there is an enormous super-ego, notably in the intelligentsia, which devalorizes the expression of the affective, the expression of sentiment, the expression of tenderness, and which devalorizes either to the profit of the politically rational or to the profit of the instinctual, that is, the sexual. Well, the novel, it seems to me, postulated here, permits turning away this superego. By the mediation of the novel, all the affects are enunciable. I can announce all my affects. I have the possibility of saying *everything,* even tenderness.

So Barthes had a reality-ache, and he had to act *as if* he could assuage it. And that is why I took offense when he wondered what those ''poor bastards'' believed. The novel is writing placed under the instance of reality, not truth, and had Barthes traveled in reality and to Guyana (understand, Guyana is a metaphor), perhaps *he* could have justified those innumerable deaths there. Perhaps he could have enunciated an affect more tender than ''poor bastards'' (*ces malheureux,* before Richard Howard and I translated it).

At a conference at Cerisy-la-Salle in Normandy, Barthes once joked that he had crossed the river Memory, and arrived at this village, Cerisy, which he called *Brume-sur-Mémoire* in the style of French villages: Fog-on-Memory. He retained that image in the latter part of his life because, he said, he felt foggy all of the time. He had so little confidence in his memory, he had such a sentiment of the precariousness of ideas, such fear of aphasia, that he carried a little notebook and jotted down everything, ideas, perceptions, but mostly ideas. What he didn't grasp was that it wasn't just his problem, it is ours—and I want to stress the perceptual part. To access our physical and psychic present—in a time of numbness and drought of spirit—may be impossible. But I wanted to try for the sake of this book. Not to write a novel, not to stage a world, for I am no demiurge and find very little will to power over being. My metaphysical impulse is weak, and I have little talent to overwhelm you with the novelist's almost unbearable accumulation of props and people, the rich and multiple furniture of his or her world. But I too have a reality-ache, and I wanted in mid-life to place myself under the sign of the real and forget the arrogance of telling truth for a while. And besides, in the United States, even more than in Europe, to be an intellectual (which means to be a professor) means that you are making a living by speaking in a coded language with its jargon. It is not a truth you speak, it is a profession that you practice Where? On the margin of the nation, writing in your journals for the 3000 or so other teachers, talking to the nation's children. I wanted to hit the road, to try to become an intellectual in action. Like most Americans I like to walk my talk.

And if I failed? Eco tells the story of Mario Missiroli, former editor-in-chief of *Corriere della Sera*, "dead since aeons but the Walter Cronkite of Italian journalism, able to survive with every regime," Eco says. "Allegedly, he complains: 'I'm up at six, I have no time for breakfast with the family. I'm at the office at seven, dispatches, wire reports, pictures—I can barely find room for my doughnut on my desk. And I never go out for lunch, and the sandwich is so hastily eaten, even if it's gourmet I can't taste it. And I'm lucky to eat slightly better when dinnertime comes. Always at the desk, of course, doing still some interviews. And when the others are with the family or the girlfriend, here I am under the harsh light over my desk, reading, reading, editing, editing.'

"'Then why do you do it?' asks a colleague.

"'*Sempre meglio che lavorare,* always better than working,' says Missiroli."

On the occasion of an apartment renovation, I dismantled my library, putting all my books into boxes, classified according to the position they had occupied in the shelves covering the four walls of my study. I could find my way in the dark to the four corners of my world—Lacan on the northeast corner, Lévi-Strauss to the southeast, Derrida in the west, not to mention Wordsworth, Coleridge, and Mallarmé at the northwest, the corpuses and corpses I had dissected for my doctoral thesis.

Most of my books are still in boxes. And all of my experiences come no longer only from books but from the shapes, sounds, and sights of all the figures I have come upon in the landscape. I no longer study artifacts, corpses, but have gone to the living sources of American myth. I went to Bangor, Maine, to see Stephen King; L.A. to interview Vanna White, who in her dressing room sweetly asked if she could hold my tape recorder; Hugh Hefner in the same city meantime declining an interview—too busy playing with his animals in preparation for his upcoming wedding. Refused by the once-and-never-again king of promiscuity, I was fraternally embraced in Beverly Hills by 60s ideologist Timothy Leary, after admitting positive inclinations toward hallucinatory experience. I went to Washington to contend with Ted Koppel; to New York, to discover Milton Glaser's latest permutation on pleasure; to New York again, to witness columnist Jimmy Breslin sardonic on bigotry, American and otherwise:

Vladimir Dounaev, Moscow TV's man in America, has just interviewed Breslin on racism in Reagan's time. It'll play well on Vremya—*Vlad's licking his chops. The camera stops but Breslin, who can't, says:*

In 1980 Reagan made his first major speech of his campaign in Philadelphia, Mississippi, the scene of the civil rights murders in the 60s. He made the speech in favor of states' rights, which is an old code word meaning keep the blacks out. And that went out all over the country, and the whites deserted the Democratic Party because they were afraid of blacks.

In Breslin's kitchen, Sergei the cameraman has the Sony on his shoulder again. Maybe another morsel . . .

Let me tell you a story—I don't think we're the only ones afraid of blacks. I still treasure an evening spent in Havana at the 20th anniversary of the Cuban Revolution when they had the blacks, when the whole Third World came, and the Russian military was there, and Americans were not there of course because we're so brilliant we will not associate with these people. I was there as a reporter. Now Castro came out and he

Vlad is beaming in fraternal reflex as the friend he calls Jim . . .

had his entire Central Committee with him, one black out of 25 [blacks constitute a significant percentage of the Cuban population of ten million], and the guy was about 90 years old and he kept saying "yes sir" whenever Castro talked.

. . . and now James treats him to a preview of what his bosses will before long be doing to the dinosaur of communism

Now the Russians are sitting there. There was a general and his wife, she was wider than he was, she looked like she could punch him out. There were about four of them in a row. And here came the blacks in the flowing robes and

	they were sitting on each side of them. And here go the Russians. [Breslin draws in his paunch, tries to draw his chest in, too.] Terrified. I said, "They look like guys from the Bronx, they're just as afraid." I says, "Look at them, they're going to do as well in Africa as the United States will." It was 1974. You had one black on the Central Committee. I started the clock on the countdown then. I said, "This fuck is a liar like everybody else."
ha ha	
heh	
hack	
Vlad:	You know, you can say what you want about the Soviet Union because we haven't got an experience. I can't tell you what would happen . . .
Breslin:	I think if you put Harlem into one side of Moscow . . . you'd have a lot of trouble if you put two million blacks all of a sudden.
Thirty years of imaginary fraternity is moving Vlad's lips:	Could be, a problem of adjustment. But Cuba, they have their fair share of blacks [laughs] and they solved their problem, I was there, everywhere. They're probably not very good at other things but as far as blacks and whites . . .
Breslin:	Yeah. It was the same middle class shit heels that we have in this country.

I did not rely on the published books of King, the television programs of Koppel, or the XXX-rated videos of Annie Sprinkle. I followed one of the seven dwarfs during the '88 presidential race (Richard Gephardt asking me over and again if Gorbachev was for real). And maintained my affiliation with the losers, joining the campaign of Pat Robertson as unlikely pseudo-advisor . . .

Pat (on bus with me during New Hampshire primary):	I'm not getting any analytical advice at all [testily]. I'm getting a few lines from time to time.

. . . deconstructing, or maybe disinforming as I got close, this theocrat who, for a few and a time, sang seductively of an eternity in order to shame us for our ephemeral attractions. Playing the Dark Doctor from New York in my anthracite suit, I flew with him in the eye of his hurricane to Baton Rouge to forgive Jimmy Swaggart:

Pat on his plane (his pilot, Don Miracle!!), sitting in a green armchair, hands me a yellow pad on which he has written:

Jimmy has confessed to me his moral problem. He has asked for forgiveness and I believe that God has forgiven him. And today I publicly take this opportunity to extend Christian love and reconciliation to Jimmy. I've talked to him twice today at his home . . .

You bet he has. Jimmy wants to show up for the appointment for his forgiveness but the family won't have it. The Swaggart home's too palatial—if the network reporters in the back of the plane get a look . . .

. . . and I have expressed my love to him and my support for him. I take this same opportunity to address all of those in our nation who feel rejected and alienated. There is love and forgiveness and hope and reconciliation . . .

This is too drippy, I can't go on.

Dark Doctor:

The press is going to say it's drippy, icky, a ploy. You know, there's symbolism in your favor. You're like a god—excuse the blasphemy, I refer to Greek antiquity—who drops from the clouds.

More likely, a lord from a feudal land visiting another, on his knees.

You've declared a parenthesis in your voyage. Do you like it?

He writes, and Jimmy doesn't show, and reason doesn't yet produce monsters offering reconciliation, and I continue on my way, forgetting to enroll in the British Air Frequent Flyers Program—

"Marshall! Marshall! Marshall!" said my editor on hearing it. I could have taken a couple of friends or sympathetic critics on a free trip to Paris. I'm sorry, I got too excited.

Also fat. Milton Glaser says in these pages that for many, the restaurant is the social center of life today. "The restaurant is where you tell people you're breaking up," he says, "but you also tell them there you love them, or you make a proposition." Or you interview them there. That is why there's a whole lot of eating going on here. I am twenty pounds overweight—oral indulgence, compensation for living in hotel rooms for four years. I'm glad this is a book, not a TV

Figure "Preface.1" Pat has invited me to watch him tape "Face the Nation" with Leslie Stahl. I stand on the CBS stage in New Hampshire right behind the cameraman. Stahl has just sprung on him. "Do you believe in the Armageddon?" she said. Pat is smiling: "Well, the word *Armageddon* means Mount Megiddo. . . . There is a place that was called the Via Marius in Israel where the Assyrians and the Egyptians used to go up and have at each other." Connie Snap, his Communications director, is shaking her head, putting it down on the table before her. Pat just blew it. The answer Stahl's code required was very simply: No. Pat is continuing: "and the thought was that one day at the conclusion of everything, there would be one big battle."

show—you can't see the author in a book. My sympathies for fat Merv in chapter 11.

But I did not rely solely on America's views of America. I traveled to Tokyo to hear Naohiro Amaya, president of the Japan Economic Foundation, predict a metastasis of ego from now to the twenty-first century; to the foot of Mount Fuji, to the Fanuc plant, to watch robots make robots to replace American workers; to Moscow, to watch Yevgeny Yevtushenko struggle to defend perestroika, trying to cope with American dynamism; to Paris, to hear Jacques Attali, then Mitterand's special advisor, declare the "amortization" of America and the rest of the world. In Paris I also heard Costa-Gavras angrily tell a secret or two about Anglo-American advertising. In Milan, a few months before the Wall Street crash of '87, Giorgio Armani sketched for me a few designs to signal contrition for the shameful eighties. And a little later in New York, I observed from behind the camera as a Moscow TV team tried to find greed on the sidewalks of New York.

Vladimir Dounaev had promised me a "vox pop" for this book, a *vox populi*, a man-in-the-street interview to reveal our greed and gluttony, appetite and ambition; so following his own interview of Breslin for *Vremya*, the three of us plus cameraman Sergei walked to get Breslin a cigar, then stationed ourselves outside the Lincoln Center subway exit at 4:30 P.M. of a workday.

"I'll get them," says Breslin, dressed in a suit and black loafers. "They come up by the dozen. Ask them anything you want."

"I mean, uh, shall I, shall I," says the suddenly shy anchor, "introduce from Moscow?"

"I'll tell 'em Soviet television. Don't worry, they love it," says Breslin, leaning on the iron balustrade, puffing, waiting, the lure for the trap.

Breslin (*nodding at a man who's just climbed up the steps*):	Let's ask him. Moscow Television: want to go on?
Dounaev (*in blue pants and beige sport coat of unknowable origin*):	How it goes for you, you know? Have you achieved something today?
Man (*suspicious*):	Or what?
Dounaev:	Or what are your priorities in life? Is it a happy day for you?
Man:	Yes, I am more happy than the Russian people are.
Dounaev (*agitated*):	How on earth do you know? Have you been to Russia?

Oops, he has.

Dounaev (*disappointed*):	Oh, I see. And what are your priorities in life?	*Mea Culpa*
Man:	In New York?	
Dounaev:	What you would like to achieve?	
Man:	My achievement? To have the happiest life, a better life, everything better than the Rus- sian people. They don't have it.	
Dounaev:	No, no, what you would like, forget about Russian people. What you would like? Money?	
Man:	No, money doesn't bring happiness.	

An NBC tour guide, an accountant, two students, a freelance writer, an ABC producer, a recovering alcoholic . . . After an hour, we couldn't find a greedy person. Breslin was certainly doing his part ("HEY, WANNA BE ON TV?"), but the tour guide hoped to raise a nice family, the alcoholic helped others by night, the freelance writer said, "Oh, I love the people of the world, man," and Vlad got more and more disgusted. What nobody told him (and nobody can now: he died of a heart attack a few months later) was that when the market fell and a month later, Tom Wolfe lit his bonfire; when Boesky pled guilty and Michael Douglas played Boesky (in *Wall Street*, of course), it was obvious to the sensitive (although not to Merv Griffin, who was ogling Resorts) that immense infra- and superstructural bills were coming due. The newspaper, magazine, novel, film and television writers, the managers of the superstructure, were signaling the end of what was called the 80s. Whether speaking as Vance Packard (isn't he dead?) in *The Ultra Rich: How Much is Too Much?* (even the dead were admonishing) or *Dynasty* producer David Paulsen announcing that poor people would now be part of the show's story line, the handlers of the culture were *periodizing*: causing the national conscience to refuse itself, to break up from itself.

As if by magic we suddenly knew Reagan had been all along acting. And who would dream of wearing oversize jackets and where did all the yuppies go? Part of a Moscow TV crew—

Woman (*addressing me*)	Your accent is so American.
Me	I studied at Moscow U.
Woman	It's wonderful.

—and on my own, I researched this book as the culture convulsed and trashed itself to restore a sense of normalcy; then innervated all over again in the Quincentenary of 1492, which, like a funeral, is serving only to assemble the living and act as the occasion to speak of the present. "Can you believe it? In those days they found it normal to issue junk bonds." Greed, business, Reagan, Giorgio of Beverly Hills, all of it became retro. The newly discovered—the turn-of-the-decade, turn of the Quincentenary, discovered—abnormality of yesterday props up the normality of the present. But the present of what story? Which, in its turn, will be trashed. And oh, will it be trashed as we really hit a turn-of-the-decade in a few years! I logged my air time without bonus miles in order to glimpse that story and the coming shape of the world.

We all believe in the existence of an economic superstructure, and of a political one. I flew hither and yon to find a cultural superstructure, a power structure attached to the surfaces, to the signs this book brings forward. We don't ordinarily associate such surfaces to a shaping function. We think of them as objects of mass desire, as responding to taste. No, subjects are creating our ideas of taste, and I flew to convene, as it were, a kind of global town-meeting in which the *nomenklatura* of our culture, the taste makers of the 90s, would reveal something of themselves. These anchors, directors, designers, writers, models, porn stars, and politicians are like a fourth estate; in practical terms, a hidden order. They create and manage the signs and myths that ignite our desire and make us who we are. Comprising an international power structure of culture, they are arguably as important to our lives as those who operate the international economy.

And they talked. About what they do and what others among their ranks are doing. As I traveled to meet them, I tried at first to be impersonal. Somewhat foolishly perhaps, I wanted something like a "truth" about America from them. Or at least I wanted to give them every opportunity to express such truth as they knew. But in the course of time I realized I was influencing the way they responded. I didn't stop myself, when it seemed relevant, from telling this one what that one had said. I told Costa-Gavras that TV commercial director Terry Bedford had said, it's a convention to use red and blues in supersaturation. "It's not a convention," Costa-Gavras said angrily, "they are the colors of rapid perception." They are too fierce to fight. And when I told Yevtushenko, he loved it: "An injection for the eyes," he exclaimed.

I found myself not saving for later my responses. A remark would suggest something—I interpreted it on the spot. I found myself changing the direction of the conversation irretrievably. (To the annoyance of several: "Are you interviewing me or is it vice-versa?" said philosopher Roger Scruton in London.) I was more than a genial master of ceremonies at the town meeting. And I certainly wasn't just a journalist bringing back the news from this poet in Moscow or that counselor in Paris. Maybe I erred on the side of brattiness from time to time. The very word "brat" suggests what I was turning into: a student. I was receiving a high, a super-education from the world's best teachers.

As you read this book you might think of it as a picture painted by the collaboration of a little community of quirky, talented people. Perhaps it's a good picture, but don't believe that it shows you reality. A picture shows you what the artist thinks is reality. A little band of talents made a picture of America in a global culture, but not in the classical mode; rather, in the impressionist. Composed of many small dots, the vision is made misty in order to signify: this is a vision of America, perhaps even hallucination. This is art more than truth.

It changed me, I think, and I might hope that it would change you, too. On the first night of my return from Moscow, I was physically revolted by the would-be actor waiters at a chic Soho restaurant: their all-white attire above the waist, black below it, their "Hi, I'm . . ." and explosive seductiveness. Say what you want about the deficits in Moscow, the waiters there keep self-respect and thereby respect you. I did not feel like an American on my return from Moscow.

After the interview with Yevtushenko (three hours from "your tragic eyes" through lunch to "God bless you"), I walked a little in the woods where he lives—Peredelkino, the writer's colony. Peredelkino, a suburb of Moscow, doesn't share Moscow's climate. It enjoys its own micro-ecology, and I had never seen such light as the light I saw and saw through as I walked in the woods on my way to the train home to Moscow. Distant foliage *was there* for my eyes so neatly outlined it was as if presented between dotted lines. I could distinguish three, seven, a dozen shades of green and yellow. The sun was bright but not in the least oppressive on this June Saturday. I thought such a stupid thought: God, this is what it must be like no longer to be anxious (will I get the interview or not?), to be flying hither and yon. Just to be at peace. I felt for an instant not a foreigner in Moscow. So I thought.

The next Monday, in Oxford, telling historian Theodore Zeldin this small, strange experience, I was jolted by his response. "It had nothing to do with Moscow," he said. "You felt good because you saw Yevtushenko, who is a foreigner in Russia obviously. You just said that he lives in an artist's colony divorced from the world. And when you say you're worried about being a foreigner, I think it relates very closely with your subject. The majority, not just of Americans, of everybody, are terrified of being foreigners, which means terrified of existing on their own."

The place where I felt I found peace is a place sequestered from mass media and mass men and women, and where I was beckoned by forms that never had interested me. I have no interest in nature—but for the first time I had.

"Perhaps you never noticed nature because you were so conscious of the human eye looking at you," Zeldin wondered.

I had come to Oxford from Russia, on my way home to talk about reading America. Zeldin was directing the conversation to the concept of the one who would utter any reading of America. The two hours we spent together were not some therapy nor confession nor advisory from a don, but they were very personal, and it is important, as you will see, to share a bit of them with the reader.

In Tumbledown House, his home, I had made a small confession. The most profound experience I have had, I think, was that of being a boy and a hyper-serious violinist. For years I stayed in my room and played Bruch, Paganini, Lalo. Second most profound experience: the same period, Talmud reading, weekly seminars with a rabbi. My problematic relation to nature derives from this, I told Zeldin. But at Yevtushenko's something happened, the problem wasn't there. And it was pleasurable.

"Listen to me," said Zeldin, an Oxford don continuing my education.

> You're beginning to reach an essence of your book. Because *American Mythologies* simply means I, Blonsky is looking around himself, has taken his nose out of his violin, and is looking around. Stopped reading Barthes and is beginning to look around a bit. In the process of looking, you're beginning to see that you're looking. And then you say, "God, I can't be a foreigner here." You're saying it worries you to think of yourself as a foreigner. Borges was once asked, "What are you? Are you a Latin?" He answered, "No, I'm not a Latin, I'm a cosmopolitan." Now it seems to me that this sort of high super-education that you are receiving turns you into a cosmopolitan. Not the education of Roland Barthes but the education of your travels. You're a bit French, you're a bit Talmudic, you're a bit this and that. You've got many things in you. That makes you inevitably not an American. It makes you beyond an American.

All nations are taught to despise their neighbors, Zeldin, author of the multi-volume *France 1848–1945* reminded me. The essence of a nation is to say that the people on the other side of the fence are no good. It's the most elementary law of the neighbor. "The experience has made you aware," said the don, "that a visit to a Moscow wood can stir you more than a visit to a Brooklyn eating house. That's why I was interested by your saying that you like certain people you're meeting more than you miss the friends you're going back to. There you touch on something. You like certain people because they make some kind of contact with you. The problem is to discover what contact. There is something in you which is feeling that which is the opposite of what it is to be an American. To be an American means to eat hamburgers or whatever the supposed things that Americans are supposed to like, watch television and go on vacation, whatever it is. But you have in the course of your travels found certain things that appeal to you and seem to be much more important. And *American Mythologies* therefore turns out to be a kind of reflection in which you discover yourself. Discover what it is in the world that harmonizes with you in some way that gets you out of the particular jackets which you happen to be wearing."

Aren't we all condemned to watch the other world, the world of others, on our televisions? That's why I was so angry with the Barthes seated with his mother: He was one of the few who could have joined the "great" world and brought it back to share with you. Not everyone gets to travel around the world and sit with Constantin Costa-Gavras as his son sleeps on his lap. You have the opportunity through this book to become, through him and the others here, a bit French, a bit Talmudic, a bit this and that. And thereby to become less American. In French, we could speak of a *dépaysement,* a decountrifying, if such a word existed; an alienation by which to see better, to know better America itself. I traveled to discover my America without European navigating charts and topographic maps. These are some of the rapids I tried to defy, some of the mountains in which I lost my way, some of the caves through which I groped. Here, in this book, you will find some of the mythological creatures I came across.

M. B.

Acknowledgments

This is the page read only by a few, the friends who, as Barthes used to say, think in my head and for whom I think. It's like a secret place in this book. Within it, I'm permitted a small amplitude, I think.

Therefore, a word first on Chantal Cinquin, French cultural counselor in Chicago, who, at the beginning of the project, wrote letters to Jacques Attali, to Costa-Gavras, to others in Paris, requesting they receive me. In the pre-history of the project, I couldn't offer anything but appearanace on these pages; later, I could tender *The New York Times Magazine, The Washington Post Outlook* and the other publications that commissioned early and short versions of some of these chapters, opening otherwise closed doors. But to Attali, to Costa-Gavras, to Jean Baudrillard, Louis Marin, Alain Finkielkraut, Paul Virilio, and Stephen Frears—who wanted nothing but a conversation—the thanks of someone who knows that the beginning is the best part. And to Daniel Dayan and Rachel Rosenblum, counselors at the fragile moment, the beginning, my gratitude. As well to Ino and Annamaria Cassini, subtle interpreters of European sensibility, ever welcoming hosts and guides. Thanks as well to Masashi Miura who opened Tokyo doors; also to Masao Yamaguchi who, sensing the need for yen to supplement the publisher's advance, arranged for the author to make joint appearances at Hakuhodo's Institute for Life and Living (fifty executives eating sushi from lacquered bowls around a SMERSH-like circular table, nodding as Yamaguchi and the author talked Lacan and the imaginary). Everywhere Yamaguchi and this writer went on the cash-producing, impromptu lecture circuit, the interlocutors bowed low to a national treasure of Japan. And thanks of course to

Ronald Weintraub, the friend who, in an initiatory stroke, talked me into the trip to that land.

To David Ignatius, foreign editor of *The Washington Post,* who as editor of *Outlook* encouraged me to think of myself as "Marshall in Wonderland"; to Bruce Wolmer, savviest of editors, recipient of many an urgent phone call starting in Tokyo and continuing to today; to Edmundo Desnoes, who taught me there was another path; to Denise Shannon, muscle and strategic brains of this project; to Daphne Merkin who keeps on reminding me that one cannot read the signs without an ethics; and to Geroge Szamuely, the bulldog on my right, Iago to the picador I became. My understanding of the Former Soviet Union was greatly enhanced by the generous discussions of Ronald Fagan and Berel Rodal; their grasp of geopolitics is but one aspect of their polymathic intelligence. Thanks as well to Michael Brainerd of the Citizen Exchange Council. Now is the time to remember the late Janet Hobhouse whose wit and sharp eye put me on notice and made me a better writer. To Sondra Farganis, colleague, booster, friend. To my former student Margaret Willig-Crane, whose thoughts on televangelism taught her teacher. To Mary Murphy, my Vergil to Los Angeles. To Richard Lerner, who took me on the road to Jack Kerouac. To Gabriella Forte of Giorgio Armani and Luisella Givigliano of Givi, whose sense of style is only matched by their tact and accessibility. To the elegant Renate Eco, who, merely by hosting a dinner party, created an entire chapter of this book. To Elizabeth Maguire and Ruth Sandweiss, loyal editors without whom this book would not be. And, finally, to Bill Sisler, whose idea this book was; its every page witnesses his editorial imagination and honors his patience and faith.

Reading over this list, it's humbling to recognize how many others are the self.

American Mythologies

Figure1.1 Safe in its sanctuary is vitamin-enhanced Barbie in the hands of new convert to capitalism, 6-year-old Anika Polzin of Schwenefeld, once East Germany. The end of her first day of shopping in Helmstedt, then West Germany. *Courtesy Reuters/The Bettman Archive.*

Introduction

The Berlin Wall was a futile attempt to stop the infectious spread of American mythologies. The stuff that dreams are made on—objects, ideas, and values—had been treated as an illness by the socialist world, to be quarantined, kept in abeyance by atomic weapons, tank and artillery divisions, ideological indoctrination, Big Brother's watchful eyes, and travel restrictions. To no avail. When the Berlin Wall came crumbling down after 28 years, the world discovered that everybody was already contaminated by American myths.

When the masses could move freely, they did not liberate a prison, storm a palace, or try to execute their oppressors. Instead, they wanted to see, touch, and buy the icons of postmodernity. Anika Polzin, a six-year-old East German girl from Schwanefeld, rushed across the Wall and after a sensuous day of touching, looking, and shopping, bought a Barbie doll. The next day, under the title "A Culture of Spies Vanishes," the *New York Times* carried a photo of a smiling, ecstatic Anika holding the blond Barbie in its packaged altar, apparently untouched by history and sealed in Mailbu gold. Another East German child, Gregor, spotted a familiar figure. "Das ist Batman," he screeched, pointing to an array of Batman replicas. "Batman und Batman und Batman!" he pointed out as he hummed the tune from the movie and walked along a row of blue and black, sharp-eared Batmen on display.

And these myths not only stormed Eastern Europe but have seduced the rest of the world. Elvis and Madonna have joined the sumo wrestler and the samurai in the Shinto temple. In China, the spread of American myth was so swift after Nixon reestablished diplomatic relations in 1976 that Deng Xiaoping was forced to look up from his bridge game and smother it in blood. In the middle of Tienanmen Square, at the Gate of Heaven, the students had erected a modified replica of the Statue of Liberty in porous Styrofoam. If Confucius had given China a sense of social responsibility and hierarchy, now the New York green lady had added a vision of change and contemporary individualism.

How naive, therefore, were those who muttered "How could they!"—how could the French in 1992, in the very year of Europe's own quincentennial introspection (expulsion in 1492 of the Jews from Spain, massacre of part of Europe by another, appearance of syphilis in Geneva, arrival of the potato, tobacco, corn, sugar), how could the French have allowed the Walt Disney Corporation, on 5000 acres of Marne La Valée Renoirscape, to turn the image of America into a mega-resort, EuroDisney, that one ducketeer thinks will be a cultural Chernobyl. "You know what?" Tony Anselmo, the current voice of Donald Duck, told me in the Roy O. Disney Building overlooking Mickey Avenue in Burbank. "In Europe thay have more of a culture for art than here. I'm sure they're going to laugh at us."

Laugh at you? Listen. "You know, there's a town next to Disney which is called Meau," EuroDisney graphic design chief Paul Prejza is drawling. "They make the best brie in the world, something called Brie de Meau. I thought they should make a Mickey Mau. They could make a special box with ears on it and sell it to Disney."

Actually, they're doing something more audacious, Prejza informs me in his airy loft in Culver City, Los Angeles. "There's one town [among the five around which Disney has built] that's gearing up for the onslaught of Disney," he says. Adds associate Robert Cordell: "They closed their streets and put in malls. It's a medieval town"—mutating into modernity for Disney.

And thereby we know better what EuroDisney's about. Postmodernity, which is our modernity, is the name for the condition in which the last residues of the past have been swept away without a trace. More brilliant than any of us have thought him, Michael Eisner came up with this idea: Where but in Old Europe with its quaint peasants, peti-bourgeois commerce, and narrow, ancient streets could there be a better market *for their elimination.* Following an idea of critic Fredric Jameson, EuroDisney shall be then the triumphant blotting out of a piece of European culture and history, namely the Renoirscape. The Valley of the Marne shall be renovated and transferred to the present as that very different and postmodern thing called *simulacrum,* very much the subject of this book.

Disney is in Europe to sell the American message of gigantism. "Just wait till they see those hotels in EuroDisney," Prejza's partner Deborah Sussman laughs as she projects images of the hotels. "They're bigger than Versailles."

Each—there are five of them—will be the biggest hotel in Europe.

4

Together, they'll symbolize what may be Eisner's grandest ambition: to be and be known world-wide as the ultimate patron of the millennium's architecture. To this end, old collaborator Michael Graves built Hotel New York, a Dick Tracey-fied simulation where pretty pink takes the place of our dirty red brick and where barrel vaults pretend to be high rises. "It's weird," Sussman says, "it doesn't look a bit like New York, not in any way."

So? It's a simulation but scarcely less a myth. Now there is Antoine Predock's Hotel Santa Fe before us. Predock is building a flying saucer supposed to have landed. A volcano will erupt every whatever, the smoke forming a huge Indian face. To get to registration you'll pass under an immense drive-in movie screen. Only there won't be a movie on it. It'll be a billboard. Only . . . "They're having considerable problems with determining the image, Cordell says, "because John Wayne's estate would not allow them to use John Wayne. They got Clint Eastwood to agree to let them use his image but nobody feels Clint Eastwood is quite the right image. He doesn't speak to the old west the way John Wayne did."

"It's so anti-France in a way," Prejza's telling me, "a permanent circus, another New Town." Before Disney, in the 60s and 70s, the French built what they called New Towns, eventually four of them, on the outskirts of Paris. Ghettos. "In a way the Disney development is the last of the New Towns in quotes one worse than the other. When you go there and you think of those Renoir paintings of all those people sitting on those little boat docks and having fun with paper lanterns hanging above and then you see what the hell's out there now, it's really discouraging."

What he doesn't get is that the French leaders know this, and are willing to sacrifice a little Renoirscape in aid of a glorious vision that makes Disney, all $6 billion of it, a piece in a set of moves.

EuroDisney is intended as a magnet to draw in the Germans, the British (London to EuroDisney: 3 hours by nonstop TGV), and soon, the people from the former socialist countries; it is intended to be one more institution in making Europe a vast economic and political unity of some sort. With Paris as its core, of course. "If Europe doesn't realize its continental unity, then its economic vassalization with respect to the Pacific is certain," Jacques Attali, former Mitterand aide, said apocalyptically. Europe has a trump, he thinks: its geography. "700 million inhabitants since Europe goes from Ireland to Russia, 700 million inhabitants capable of assembling on a territory practically entirely accessible by road, with total cultural proximity since European culture goes from Dickens to Tolstoy and from Cervantes to Kafka"—and now Disney.

Which may act as a kind of melting pot, erasing differences among the nationalities housed in "Santa Fe," "New York," or "Newport." Those hotels and theme parks become one more instrument by which cosmopolitan European leaders are trying to suppress the dream in the different nationalities of finding one's roots and singular destiny. "If each seeks his destiny alone, it can only be found in violence, xenophobia, the refusal of others," Attali told me. Let's say that EuroDisney—housed among the quasi-slums of Paris—will be a useful tool but only one more tool in attenuating national memory. Eisner dreams of being Medici and the French dream of forgetting him. New World ambition and Old World cunning.

Don't take myth lightly. Behind it is the enormous power of modern industrial production coupled with a formidable myth-generating communication industry that is bringing about a new, planetary culture system whose core regions are a unifying Europe, a Japan organizing the Pacific, and a United States whose role in the system is still to be determined. The collapse of the Wall, the crisis in the formerly socialist world, and the failure of Third World wars are rooted not only in economic and political reality, but in a myth-ological impotence, an inability to produce personally felt icons and objects. Next to Barbie and Batman, Madonna and EuroDisney, there seems to be nothing comparable in the culture of the peripheral regions. And that's to mention only a handful of western myths.

The socialist myths were purely political and short-lived. The hammer and the sickle, Lenin and Che were myths of struggle and war, not of pleasure and play. Not even Yuri Gargarin, the Soviet cosmonaut, had the right stuff. Although many might question the value and depth of contemporary western myths, like it or not, they have shown their world appeal and tenacity, in spite of the mystery of their surface and their plastic, nonbiodegradable power, their smoke-and-mirror nature. It's not an Orwellian nightmare or a Renaissance ideal, but we must recognize their promiscuity and, for a moment, withhold judgment, the better to analyze the phenomenon.

This book is an attempt to decode a series of American myths. I have not only seen these myths on stage, I have gone backstage to interview the creators and to study the mechanics that set in motion this monstrous dream factory.

The global market order is the support system for American mythologies. The two together function like the systole and diastole of our heartbeat. They are interwoven and operate as a unity. The myths of adolescence, for example, did not appear until after World War II, when American industry could dedicate resources to a new market, teenagers. Deanna Durbin, Mickey Rooney, and Archie with his saddle shoes were the Hollywood faces of this budding myth, finally flowering into, at the time, disturbing figures such as James Dean and Elvis Presley. Like all incipient myths, they were nurtured by death and fear. In the process of creating this new space, Dean pushed it to the limit, colliding his Porsche Spyder with a station wagon, mangling "Little Bastard" (as he called it) against a telephone pole. Elvis was constantly being curbed, repressed, and attacked for his naive and outrageous pelvic sexuality. Both are now immortals, one roaming the planet, the other making special appearances in full regalia at his Memphis, Tennessee, Graceland shrine. The space now is seething with outfits and stars. Prince, Madonna, and Michael Jackson are the new faces of this postwar myth that had its sweet origins in Judy Garland's pilgrimage to Oz and Elizabeth Taylor's canter to national velvet. Today American myth is a multi-billion-dollar global industry with its own music, MTV iconography, matinee horror films, L.A. Gear, Reebok, spandex, and a garment industry that serves a rigorous and changing dress code. When Madonna decides to turn her cuffs on a pair of cut-off jeans, industry mass-produces the whim.

Every aspect of the new order's socioeconomic life is constantly producing its own icons, objects, values, and patterns of behavior. This is impossible in a planned economy and defies all preconceived ideological world views. "Teachers and utopian thinkers," Yuri Afanasyev, the Soviet historian, said, in the throes of perestroika "used to believe that a society of universal justice and prosperity could be built simply by thinking it out. But the epoch of conscious construction of ideal societies died in Western Europe a long time ago. Even with the French Revolution there was an attempt to take deliberate action, but it failed disastrously. And they went back to their normal course of development. But we [the Soviet Union] have been in this state of deliberate, conscious construction for 70 years. It has to be given up." Myth cannot be generated by state planning. It doesn't happen by deliberate, conscious construction. It only happens in a pragmatic, open society.

Even a Renaissance scholar such as the late Bart Giamatti was wide open to the American myths, such as baseball, which he saw as part of the mythology of homecoming. He rejected the rationality of research and investigative reporting. "All those who will not accept precooked releases, the myths we make for ourselves, these people dismay me," Giamatti once said. "How else will progress be made unless artifice be encouraged. My gosh, what would happen to a society in which reality got loose? Look what has happened in the past. So to the banquet of communication, let others bring the granola and raw carrots; just send me the Fritos."

On a recent trip to Tokyo, where I was invited by the American Center of the U.S. Embassy to talk about American signs and symbols, in a reference to American fashion I mentioned Madonna. "Did you interview her?" the Japanese scholars besieged me. "Does she have sympathy for the Ku Klux Klan?" one said. "I saw 'Like a Prayer.'" After a while they stopped talking to me and discussed among themselves, starry-eyed, their own vision of Madonna.

When I heard "nothingness nested inside nothingness," I knew that Madonna had been assimilated into the pantheon of Japanese Zen Buddhism.

When I visited the Russian poet Yevgeny Yevtushenko in Moscow he was constantly answering challenges posed by western mythology. Suffering blood poisoning after a recent trip to Italy, dressed in American jeans and a Russian shawl, in subtle ostentation he had strewn the current *Newsweek, Time,* and other western publications over his VCR. Challenged by the dynamics of western film—he had just screened some Michael J. Fox films—he felt compelled to take a Russian stand, as if everything American were a challenge to his identity. "Good actor, he creates energy," Yevtushenko flourished, overrating this mini-myth of the 80s before confronting him with superior Russian culture: "Nekulturny," he added. He was struggling with the Laocoön of American mythologies. I encountered the same ambivalence when interviewing Umberto Eco. His *Foucault's Pendulum* is many things, including a European version of *Indiana Jones and the Last Crusade,* an ambiguous mixture of medieval European scholarship and modern American comic strips. Eco's a monk who wants to make love with Wonder Woman.

"Superman is late for an appointment with Batman at a bar," Eco's telling me. "'I was on my way here,' he says to Batman, 'but flying on the way I saw Wonder Woman lying naked sunning herself on a cliff.'"

"'So?' says Batman.

"'So,' says Superman, 'I did what any gentleman would do, I flew down and obliged the lady.'

"'Was she surprised?' Batman asks.

"'Not as surprised as the Invisible Man,'" snaps Superman Eco.

French rationalism has spent the last 35 years trying to digest American mythologies. Roland Barthes' *Mythologies* throughout the years sought to explain in European terms American cultural artifacts from plastic and detergents to Avedon, Humphrey Bogart, Warhol, and Superman. Barthes developed *la sémiologie,* to a great extent to interpret and digest the postwar Americanization of Europe—what the French went through then, we had already experienced in the 20s, according to many historians. Today, Jacques Attali—when I first met him, François Mitterand's special advisor—continues the wrestling match with the evil angel, America. I cancelled an interview with Claude Montana to visit the Elysée Palace—

(Attali having cancelled the previous night, then rescheduled in Montana's time . . . "I'm sorry, but it isn't my fault; it's the fault of the President of France," I said to a Mr. Amr, Montana's assistant—who said to me coldly: "The President of France is never at fault.")

When I drew Attali out on Americanization, he answered imperiously:

> In terms of intellectual concepts there is no real concept coming from America. None. In economics, sociology, anthropology we can name some people, of course, but there is no one great social thinker of whom you can say: "Coming from nothing, there is a leap forward after him." It's very strange but I would be happy if you could name one. It's very strange in view of the numbers, mass capacity, the amount of money which is made and so on. I cannot name one American—I mean, of a great level. Whoever you name, they are followers. That's a very important aspect of a lack of America, worldwide.

Don't look to us for intellect—look, instead, to the blind, nearly hysteric way we live, producing a myth of global attractiveness:

> The influence of America is mainly in daily life culture, the way of living. The movement of technology is leading to the fact that amortization of tools, goods, and concepts is going quicker and quicker. You change your cars, you change your ideas, you change your wife, you change your friends quicker and quicker.

It is speed itself we worship and our lives shout out:

> You lose your roots. And it's clear that the American society which is by definition without roots—the nature of the way the country was built, without roots—is in advance, first, because it's easier to lose your roots when you haven't any or don't know where they are, 5,000 miles away, than to lose your roots when you have them, fathers and countries around and so on. America is going faster and faster on the route where everybody is going in terms of increasing the speed of amortization of ideas, signs, and goods. This is not really Americanization, this is swallowing one's own traces, cancelling, deleting one's own steps.

It's Americanization only if we choose to hate you for it; but we in Europe are going your way, too, . . . Attali disdainfully told me. And another intellectual, Alain Finkielkraut, more gently made the point:

> European television is taking on a voice which is that of the most vulgar, the most facile divertissement and it's this moment, in my opinion, that has produced a phenomenon of Americanization. Put differently . . .

Frenchmen and women can actually talk as if writing:

> the Americanization of Europe exists, I believe, but it is not the American responsibility. It is not, if you will, a plot, a conspiracy of the American multinationals. We shouldn't draw a diagram researching

who in New York, who in the White House, who at the Pentagon, who I don't know, *je ne sais pas, moi,* in the great apartment houses and skyscrapers of ABC or CBS or NBC is guilty. No one is guilty. The Americans aren't guilty. There is Americanization but the Americans aren't guilty in the sense that there was a particularly clandestine American brain which, in shadow, organized the domination of the world. Let's not apply the schema of the Protocols of the Elders of Zion.

That's what the Europeans are doing, he thinks, when they denounce the Americans, supposedly innundating the world with their products, homogenizing the planet, deracinating tradition, blah blah blah.

It isn't true. What is true, what is produced is a mimetism of America. That's to say, Europe itself, to compete with America, becomes American. And me, *et moi, je crois* [to us, bizarre accentuation of the ego], I believe that television is the most massive, most truly spectacular loss of the difference between Europe and America. Advertising all the time, ads in place of films, spectacles of distraction, soap operas melanged with news, total euphoria. That's America, that's the western world today, Europe become identical to America, the differences absolutely eradicated.

I knew enough not to be complimented when he speculated that the American model of euphoria, of amusement, had pushed to its paroxysm a trait of human nature—America revealing something of human nature itself:

That's to say that America is nothing other than the name—the metonymy, if you will . . .

The figure of speech by adjacency, as a glass stands for whiskey, a cup for coffee—

of technical modernity. And this technical modernity is incarnated in America and realized quicker, more completely than anywhere else. But America is nothing other than an incarnation of a tendency of acceleration, movement, dynamism, which is that of modernity itself. We see these things in America, quite simply, because America isn't a traditional country. There is less resistance in America to this dynamism of modernity, to things happening faster, but if you will, the movement of the other western countries has to be understood as a sort of general dynamism which is that of the technical age of which America is the avant-garde.

The Disney conundrum is child's play, then. If "America" is simply the name of modernity, Disney-on-Marne is giving to Europe a name. Arriving in Europe, Disney endorses Europe, signs it with the name "America," which means the New.

There is a general dynamism, which is that of modernity, and America pushes it farther than the others. Therefore the others can only follow because they are driven from the inside by this dynamism, which is that of technique, image, television, satellites, thus of the order of leisure, generalized consumption, that's to say, every form of leisure being transformed into consumption, the definition of leisure being consumption.

My old prof Louis Marin had introduced me to Finkielkraut, and a mere hour earlier had told me:

If you go to the stadium you participate in a ceremony, a sporting ceremony, a kind of feast. But you see much better the match, the meeting, on TV because you are everywhere. You are everywhere and nowhere at the same time on the TV.

What does that mean? I had asked.

Look, the other day we had the birthday party for myself and my grandson, and a friend of my daughter's came with a little video machine and then filmed the dinner, the candles and everything, and then ten minutes after, on our TV screen, we were looking at us laughing and singing. That for me is almost incredible because almost in the moment when we were living this marvelous and very rare moment of love and family, all convivial society, almost at the same moment we were seeing us as if we were playing the role, as if I—*comme si on me volait* [the difficulty of the analysis makes him shift to French]—as if I were robbed, as if the TV image were stealing the very living content, the lived content of my own life. At the very moment when I am filling my present with feelings and emotions and thoughts and so forth, at this very moment it became an image, a past.

I would relate the sporting event you watch on TV not in terms of time but in terms of space. What I said of my present, *je suis volé de mon présent*, I would say of my place. You know, I used to say to my students, one of the most beautiful definitions of self-identity is: Tell me *where* you are, I will tell you *who* you are. That's a beautiful definition of identity by location in space.

Who am I then? I asked. ''I am in Paris in the office of Louis Marin, I am . . .''

You have this relationship, making a book, interviewing me and in this place which is Francastel Library and so forth. And you are visiting me and so forth. We observe certain series of rites of—I don't say hospitality, our lunch was poor, but you know this kind of process. I enjoy to ask you to come in this office. And you, too. Really, we are exchanging something very important of our persons and identity through this place you visit. And you are sitting in this armchair in front of me and we are looking at us with this machine between us [my Sony pro] registering, that's a part of the process, too. But in front of the TV, you are participating in being everywhere and nowhere. You are at the top looking at the face of some people and then suddenly with the goalie. Everywhere, that is, nowhere. So it seems at first glance that your identity is expanded to the dimension of the world, but in fact it's nowhere. You vanish.

"Voilà!" said Finkielkraut when of course I relayed the message:

It's the apotheosis of consumption. This is consumption: you are filled without having anything to do. And technique gives you power, technique which is completely extraordinary. That is to say, with a null effort an unlimited power, and equally with more and more reduced knowledge and with greater and great possibilities of acting on the world. Thus, if you will, consumption is . . . His Majesty the Baby. That is, one is at once a baby, since one knows nothing and can do nothing, and at the same time a majesty, a king, since one can do everything. And I believe that in a certain manner the world of consumption makes of us His Majesty's a Baby. In my opinion that's the true name of the modern subject, His Majesty's a Baby, and America incarnated it, realized it more quickly than the others, once again, because America was the laboratory of modernity. Thus it is necessary at the same time, if you will, to recognize the Americanization of society and to defend America from accusation. Let's not make America the scapegoat for Americanization.

Utterly gorgeous French . . . sophistry? Not wholly. And not just French. When film director Wim Wenders went to Tokyo to make his 1985 *Tokyo-Ga* (Tokyo Images), he took a taxi back to his hotel one evening, filming the TV set that extends from the rear-view mirror on every Tokyo taxicab that he (and I) saw. Sitting in the back seat, he flips among the channels with his remote, watching for an instant baseball games, Crazy Eddie-like ads, pantie ads ("I like short shorts, you like short shorts"), game shows, cooing *chanteuses.* At first you don't realize the set's a part of the cab—it looks like a giant screen somehow suspended in night sky. Utterly catastrophic image of the Great God TV presiding over his Night-realm. Wenders himself speaks the voiceover:

The more the reality of Tokyo struck me as a torrent of impersonal, unkind, threatening, yes, even inhuman images, the more I longed for the loving and ordered world of the mythical city of Tokyo I knew from the films of Yasujiro Ozu.

An homage to Ozu, *Tokyo-Ga* is an attempt to see how much has changed since Ozu's death 20 years ago.

Perhaps that was what no longer existed: a view which still could achieve order in a world out of order, a view which could still render the world transparent. Perhaps such a view is no longer possible today, not even for Ozu, were he still alive. Perhaps the frantically growing inflation of images has already destroyed too much. Perhaps images which are at one with the world are already lost forever.

As he speaks these last words, you can't tell if your eye isn't trained, but the TV set isn't in the taxi, it's in Wenders's hotel room, oddly clunky fake wood thing with yellow lamp glow on the edge of the image. It's a western he's watching:

> When John Wayne left, it wasn't the Stars-and-Stripes that appeared but rather the red ball of the Japanese flag.

Unmistakably the imperturbable Wayne face; uncannily, Japanese is issuing in a low voice from it.

> And while I was falling asleep, I had the craziest thought: Where I am now is the center of the world. Every shitty television set, no matter where, is the center of the world.
> The center has become a ludicrous idea and the world as well; an image of the world a ludicrous idea, the more television sets there are on the globe.

The red ball now replaced by an image of the globe, a good-night from NTV to all you out there:

> And here I am in the country that builds them all, for the whole world, so the whole world can watch the American image.

Masterminded perhaps by Sony and Matsushita.

But whether you like us or not (and Wenders deplores us, and Tokyo as well), we *are* ahead (at least in the mode of life Attali describes), and peering at us are the French, looking at us for the signs, at once infatuated and repelled. They study us to read some of their own future, powerful in their misreading, not understanding because they are—French. "In today's world you can have only two images of a promised land," Umberto Eco told me, "either America or if you radically change your world view, some parts of Europe—Tuscany in Italy, some parts of Scandinavia—with a less hectic life, with contact with nature. But there are no other strong images." For the moment we produce the myths (but as you'll see, we're joined in this by Europeans and others), and Europeans, Russians, and Japanese are eager to interpret, reject, or assimilate them. In Tokyo recently, 36-year-old Nakachiko Tani, a government economics planner, proudly told me this story: Because of a mistake in myth selection, the Suzuki Motor Car Company, a few years earlier, had failed utterly in introducing its motorbike into Europe. Suzuki advertised it as an advanced bicycle capable of slipping through European cobblestoned defiles. But the Europeans associated the bicycle with outworn icons of elderly, bereted Frenchmen, peddling home baguettes; also to anonymous, underdeveloped, ageless Asians, wearing glasses and correct and dull clothing—the bicycling little people of teeming lands. Only when Suzuki hit on a substitute myth did its bike boom in Europe. The bike became a horse of the American west. The European buyer now was invited to imagine himself a cowboy and his overtilled, unabundant land a vast, undeveloped nineteenth-century American plain. Even the Japanese, when selling bikes to Europe, have to use an American myth to sell. The cowboy is a Trojan horse concealing Japanese goods. Postmodernity—our modernity, for now—plunders a vast reserve of values and myth without any concern for accuracy, consistency, or national culture and pride.

America has difficulty competing with Japanese cars, French theory, and Italian design. But our society is an indisputable creator of twentieth-century mythology (especially now since the Communist utopia inaugurated by the Russian Revolution of 1917 came to an end with the death and dismemberment of the Soviet Union in 1991).

Myths are strong sign systems. When Barthes wrote his *Mythologies* in 1956 (published in 1957) it wasn't by accident that his first, the most famous, was on wrestling as spectacle and not sport. It has villains more than heroes, *le salaud parfait,* the perfect bastard, totally unstable, who breaks the rules when it suits him but claims their protection when it is in his interests to do so. "He is unpredictable, therefore asocial," Barthes wrote. When his defiance of society's rules is finally overwhelmed and he lies, forearm-smashed and exhausted, the mob hollers ''*salope*'' at him—*salop* being a variant of *salaud.* In our language, "bitch" or even better: "bastardette." He is castrated for teaching the French—whose society was not and is not as flexible as ours—that you can be a cork in the bottle of life.

What is myth? Narrative writ large. That is why Barthes wrote of wrestling: "What is thus displayed for the public is the great spectacle of Suffering, Defeat, and Justice. Wrestling presents man's suffering with all the amplification of tragic masks." Amplification: That is why Barthes said that the wrestler "holds out his cards clearly to the public"; why he said that in the forearm smash, "Catastrophe is brought to the point of maximum obviousness"; why he said that "everyone must not only see that the man suffers, but also and above all understand why he suffers." As important as the concepts it produces is the enunciation of this language. The mode of telling is histrionic in *Mythologies,* which Barthes began in 1952 and completed in earnest in 1956 as "little mythologies of the month," each month a new one in the *Lettres nouvelles* of Maurice Nadeau. "He lit up in the presence of signs like a field of halogen light bulbs," his friend and elegant translator Richard Howard said of him. One day in this period he surprised a friend, the diplomat Philippe Rebeyrol, by the unseriousness of a planned afternoon. He was going to watch the Tour de France, Barthes said.

"What do you have to do with that?" Rebeyrol said.

"It impassions me, it's extraordinary, it's very interesting from the sociological point of view," Barthes answered.

The postface to his *Mythologies,* "Myth Today" "marked his entry into semiology as one enters into religion," writes his biographer Louis-Jean Calvet (*Roland Barthes, 1990*). He was a man in love with seeing signs not only, let's say, because he was 40 in '56, 40 teaching in a minor post in the provinces (Alexandria, Egypt). Semiology wasn't only a kick out of midlife torpor, it was a response to a French-specific historical moment.

I have already indicated that France was not a modernized society, at least in a way recognizable to Americans, until the 1950s. Unlike the States, French modernization on a broad level did not begin until after the Second World War. Paradoxically, while Paris experienced modernity in some respects earlier than did American cities, France nonetheless had remained a traditional society generally far longer than had America. *Mythologies* is thus a late encounter of traditional culture, of which Barthes is a representative, with forces of modernity that seemed violently original in a way they could not have to Americans. "I glimpsed with astonishment," Barthes wrote in *Le Monde* in June 1974, "while reading Saussure (it was in 1956) that there could exist an elegant method (as one says of the solution of a mathematical problem) which permits analyzing the social symbols, the class marks, the ideological wheelworks." Some of the energy of the book, some of its oddness, even some of its usefulness comes from the naive glee of a European esthete in front of what, to Americans, had become very natural, *naturalized*. Barthes saw his America, his new world in the signs with which Americans were beginning to rock-or-reject.

To this man of the left, semiology was a salvation, a new language for a politics whose speech had become blah-blah. "The origin of semiology was for me political," Barthes writes in that *Le Monde* article. "Tired of the immobile, oratorical character of the ideological denunciations," he glimpsed his Saussure who taught him that wrestling, toys, soap powders and detergents, steak and French fries, striptease, Billy Graham, the Algerian War press releases, the Tour de France, all of it and everything could be signs, endowed with meaning, interpolating us without our awareness. He confessed:

> Doubtless I would have been done better calling this science (or this discourse) a 'signaletics,' for it concerned describing how class society produces signals (more than signs), 'advertisements' that it craftily turns inside out into traits of nature; I nevertheless kept the word 'semiology,' found in Saussure, and I keep it still, since it is with him that I have continually worked. This semiology—or this signaletics—I would thus conceive as the extension of a vast project of ideological criticism whose major figure was, in my eyes, Brecht.

And as Brecht produced the famous *Verfremdung,* the alienation or distantiation, so Barthes played the alienated role of bystander at culture. "Such would be semiology's function," he wrote in *Le Monde:* "to be the zero degree of every science, the 'empty' space (it's necessary to insist on it) from which the meaning (the law) is 'regarded.'" A point death, like the place by the gate where the picador quietly watches the bull charge out; a point discharging the clamor of the world and from which are seen the follies of the others and of oneself. But as Brechtian theater shows, we never arrive there except by first plunging in, imbibing all the signs, the better to understand their contamination of the subject we are (doubtless from the first moment of speech, if not before). Before *Verfremdung,* before the characters stop and analyze, they mimic the real, they act. In what emotion, then, shall the 40-year-old Barthes act? Borrowing from his existential master Sartre, Barthes sucked in the culture to the very point of vomiting. The philosopher's tree root, that is, nature could no longer disgust; it was the culture that did. One of Barthes' metaphors for culture was a torture practiced at the time by the French army in Algeria. Wrap a towel around the Arab's head—plunge him or her into water until the victim almost suffocates. France was this suffocating textile. Brecht, Sartre, Saussure. An odd threesome whose coupling, or tripling, made a science (or a discourse).

Producing along the way a larger-than-life mythologist. Barthes, who knew he couldn't efface the signs, defaced them. Those sentences that wouldn't end, which, everywhere a period sought to be, produced a semi-colon or a colon, were like the throw of paint by a hand trained in Abstract Expressionism, covering over with its force the face of Garbo, the bodies of toys, the language of Jules Verne. Read the *Mythologies* less for their tales than their telling, a Gallic force designed to upset, even to introduce catastrophe into the law of the signs.

From a comment on his own writing by a contemporary of ours we can better grasp the behavior of Barthes's. Talking of the American myth that produced his writing, Stephen King told me: "It's full-scale, full-drive narrative. It has these huge characters that cast these long Gary Cooper shadows." And of his own mythologies, he told me: "I am screaming at the top of my voice most of the time in the fiction. Even the set-ups are just set-ups so that I can start to really scream and speed rap. It's off the scale emotionally." This is why his fiction tortures animals. "It really grosses Americans out to put pets . . ." he pauses. He means put them at risk. "Somehow pets are even worse than children, if you do something terrible to pets. So *The Dead Zone* starts off with this Greg Stilson kicking a dog to death in the doorway, and there you are. Everybody knows he's anti-American at that point, kicking a doggie to death in a midwestern farmyard." Through gross-out, King breaks and makes myth, as did Barthes.

Myths don't imitate life, they make it intelligible. In the famous formula by which semiotics is known, theirs is not a mimetic art but a semiotic one. The sign systems of myth instantly make sense and they make the world immediately meaningful. "What is portrayed by wrestling is therefore an ideal understanding of things," wrote Barthes; "it is the euphoria of men raised for a while above the constitutive ambiguity of everyday situations and placed before the panoramic view of a univocal Nature, in which signs at last correspond to causes, without obstacle, without evasion, without contradiction."

Forget the advertisingese of Barthes's prose. Myths are huge and they distort—terribly distort—they are dangerous. It's difficult enough, as I said, to access the here and now. To give up even the attempt in myths is perhaps disgraceful.

The first thing a myth does is appear. It shows its face, we see ourselves in its features, we identify with it, and it inhabits our fantasies and conditions our behavior. American myths are easily recognized, but their inner mechanics are hard to identify, describe, and replicate. The chapters in this book are groping toward the inner workings and guiding principles of this world of fluid images and patterns of behavior. One of the most insistent objections to American life has been its lack of depth, when—the American in me says—this trait is actually a characteristic of our fast-flowing time, where everything has to communicate fast and move on. Let me say, polemically and only provisionally: Let's forget depth, this European obsession with the face behind the mask. Depth is a category that pretends to penetrate surface and find gravity, marshes, passions, history, conflict, soul, compartments, origins, hidden motives, density, evil, sin, and abysmal precipices. Surface, as an organizing category of the early 90s, is choice, speed, irreversible, aleatory, euphoric, flighty, cool, rootless, visual, sentimental, comfortable, detachable, fun, well-being, changeable, and ahistorical. Let the realm of the mask, for the moment, assert itself.

The first two chapters, "In Search of the Fountain of Looks" and "Portrait of the Model as an Endless Woman," are an attempt to deal with the phenomenon of surface. First impressions are decisive. You're hired, fired, you buy or throw away, you love or reject on the power of first impressions. Let's go into the surface. And surface appears individuated by apparel. The nude is not important, the clothes are. Up to now, everybody wanted to undress reality, find the naked truth, the body behind the trimmings, what lay behind Salome's seventh veil. Apparently very little.

"The human body is not very attractive compared, for exanple, to a cheetah—that's why we have fashion," says Alexander Liberman, Condé Nast editorial director and the attorney general of image power in magazines such as *Vogue* and *Vanity Fair*. Our forefathers and mothers concentrated on undressing the other. We value dressing up. The search for interiority merely created more surface.

The nude, celebrated first by painting and then by photography, only creates another garment, one slightly boring after a while. All attempts at depth end up in surface. Whether male or female, you'll have to look as if you have on flesh-covered spandex or you won't cut it in the 90s. I don't wish it, I observe it. The spandex-like skin, the spandex over it, the Nikes, the cut-offs, the halters are a uniform to signal, as Attali puts it, that you're in shape, *en forme et informé,* in form and informed—a kind of fascism fallen over us. Nudity has become the order's dress, one glistening part leading to the other, a wash of skin, the final adornment of the body. And dress is nudity, the skin of desire, the shape of pleasure.

Together with the end of depth, the search for the hidden, comes the end of consistency and character, nineteenth-century virtues. Clothes should not be sought to define your true identity, to express your values and be consistent either with your personality or your station in life. Clothes allow you to change with the seasons, express different moods, and be different people. Like most American myths, clothes as costume found full expression in Hollywood. Nathanael West in 1933, writing about Hollywood in *The Day of the Locust,* identified this new phenomenon:

> He left the car at Vine Street. As he walked along, he examined the evening crowd. A great many of the people wore sports clothes which were not really sports clothes. Their sneakers, knickers, slacks, blue flannel jackets with brass buttons were fancy dress. The fat lady in the yachting cap was going shopping, not boating; the man in the Norfolk jacket and Tyrolean hat was returning, not from a mountain, but an insurance office; and the girl in slacks and sneaks with a bandana around her head had just left a switchboard, not a tennis court.

The power of image and surface extends surprisingly to food. We tend to eat with our eyes. Our appetite is sated by the visual contemplation of the raw and the cooked. In "Underground Gourmet" I try to explain the apparent contradiction between the abundance of visual food in America and the weakness of appreciation once the eyes give way to the taste buds. Every bookstore prominently displays cookbooks. As other areas such as poetry, classics, and philosophy shrink, this one, together with health and other forms of self-help, becomes conspicuous. At the same time, magazines dedicated to refined eating, such as *Gourmet* and *Bon Appetit,* are objects of constant perusal but seldom materialize into a feast of taste. Instead, we indulge in the coarse wafer of the pizza washed down by the holy beer in the sacrament of Monday Night Football. Our taste buds only react to shock. Instead of reacting to a range of flavors, textures, and temperature, we go for impact and abundance. The steak has to be humongous, carbonized on the outside and bleeding on the inside. Pastry is usually presented in outrageous closeup both in magazines and TV commercials. It has to be good (sweet) and plenty (large). Brillat-Savarin, the French philosopher of taste, believed that one of the cues of enjoyment is always to leave the table with a tinge of hunger. Most odd to an American.

Having been born in Kansas City, once the country's meat-packing center, I am accustomed to ballparks of barbecue. Even to this day, my father sends me from home the "WORLD FAMOUS Arthur Bryant's ORIGINAL BARBECUE SAUCE." Even with that ancestry, I was surprised by my reaction to the abundance of lobster and beef in New York's Spark's Steak House (where mob boss Paul Castellano didn't have his last supper—he was shot walking in, propelling John Gotti to stardom, unlucky chapter 13). As I sat waiting for my steak, waiters like hospital orderlies wheeled gurneys of pig-sized orange lobsters. Even I, trained to eat in steak houses in the shadow of the slaughterhouses, lost my appetite watching the gastronomes at Spark's. I felt turned off like a viewer before the gross display of flesh in porn videos.

Our eyes are subtle, our taste is coarse. We can enjoy the visual nuances of exquisitely displayed food, feel gentrified as we glance through *Gourmet* magazine, yet somehow this does not spill into our practice. It remains a visual idea. The Puritanical respect for food as simply a necessity, not a pleasure, became clear to me when I interviewed Ted Koppel and nightly suffered Chinese takeout ($4.95 per plate, I seem to remember) when we could have as easily, on ABC's resources, enjoyed a civilized French meal. But enjoyment of gourmet food in mythical America is alien to our daily experience. When I complained about the fare to Koppel, he snapped: "Marshall, as we age, our taste buds deteriorate." Taste buds don't wither, as do sex and muscle tone. In America they are never developed properly. Sophisticated people know the name of the right wine, the label on the bottle, but not the taste in their mouth.

Erotica is an area that has changed even more radically than our new myths regarding food.

Sex was always sin—until *Playboy* appeared. America has taken the sin out of sex and turned the sex into a surface commodity. It's insinuated through advertising and made explicit in hard-core, an endless proliferation of skin-to-skin videos, from *Coming in America* to *Pornocchio* to *Fatal Erection,* quasi-underground flicks that ape Cineplex and Loews' feature presentations. This endless tapestry of flesh, these openings and erections, never bring about intimacy, always slide and rub off your consciousness. So many positions, so many partners, so many moans and groans are not meant to penetrate; they are meant to clear the slate and ready you for the next product. Speed is a guarantee of emptiness and emptiness is a guarantee of new pleasure.

The porn industry is a pure postmodern product. It reached its apogee in the 80s. Gone, the pretense of naturalness, the need to couch intercourse in a romantic story, a run along the beach. Instead of *Taboo,* a film, effectively of the 70s, that showed incest and redemption, that is, depth, today we have *One Wife to Give* and *Naughty Cheerleaders,* where both infidelity and child molesting are legitimate fun activities. Sin is erased in *Good Girls Do* because to do it is no longer sinful. Depth as passion and conflict is a joke in the numberless videos titled *Inside Ginger Lynn, Caught from Behind, The Fire Inside,* and *Deep Desires.* Inside stories are not revelations but surface contacts. And men's and women's bodies, in conformity to the age of fitness, have become gleaming skin on lightly bulging muscle. "At the heart of the sequences of a porn film," wrote the French critic Jean Baudrillard, "one of the girls suffers all the positions without a change of expression. A blonde revealing black roots at the nape. Her indifference is seductive" (*Cool Memories,* 1987). Surface is fundamental for enjoyment, just as sin and corruption were in the past. One does not want today to be distracted by sin or corruption in the pursuit of pleasure; one wants to enjoy fully without having to think of the other. And porn videos guarantee that your partner will never demand, make you feel guilty, or impose any passion or complexity. It's an endless, almost religious experience of sexual beatitude. Instead of the other body or God, we have the machine image.

Even in the castle of respectability, *Vogue* magazine, European twisted pleasures become sophisticated elegance in the glossy detachment of Helmut Newton's imagery. Sin is therefore an expensive attribute of high fashion and wealth. Helmut Newton ("The Courtier's Contempt") enriches the world of fashion with German sadomasochism domesticated for consumption.

The media amplify and redefine the myth; they do not create it. Television, film, and printed matter detect new values in the environment, then send them back to the audience as the final test of operative success. "Let's run it up the flagpole and see if anyone salutes," as advertisers once said when struck by a new idea. "Let's run it past them." There is always, in American theory, an empirical verdict. The final outcome hinges on the test of the market and not on the triumph of rationalist discourse, as with the French, or of ideology or planned production, as in the dialectical model.

The production-consumption system detects a nascent myth in the environment, records it, shapes it, produces it, and if the audience confirms it, it snowballs. This doubling effect creates a new, strengthened myth. And we never know which is the strongest in this relationship; it is difficult to establish the strongest pole in the relationship. Often the media detect something that quickly disappears. Other times they merely suggest something and the society strengthens it. It can change directions, like a living organism. The Hegelian assumption of the supremacy of the idea as well as the Marxist determinism giving material production primacy are both moot in our time.

Once the acting theoreticians of the system (whether in industry, advertising, publishing, or television) detect a mythical trend, they give it shape. This process is not a passive reflection of what the chief executive officers find in the environment. They give it a voice and a shape in agreement with the changing environment, the production of goods, and the myth machine.

Game shows, for example, do not create myth but are the loudspeakers for myth clusters. On closer look, game shows ("Outrageous Fortune") reveal much about our values. They cannot be dismissed as mindless entertainment; they are actually an index of our changing values. The original game shows, such as "The $64,000 Question," were displays of knowledge and culture. Today, only "Jeopardy" continues to operate within this format. The accumulation of fragments of cultural knowledge and fact have lost their centrality in the postmodern discourse. Most shows today operate within the dreams and realities of a mass democratic audience. "The Price is Right" relies on our sensitive knowledge of consumer price points. In "Family Feud" you succeed when you show knowledge of the preferences, behavior patterns, likes and dislikes of the society. "The Wheel of Fortune" is a crossword puzzle of our linguistic proficiencies in contemporary phraseology, gnomes, pop culture, and barbershop wisdom. The social mores of our contemporaneity run through the nightly game shows.

It is no accident that Vanna White became a household image. She's not a ravishing beauty, she's a friendly, neighborhood beauty; something hard and tender at the same time. For years she didn't utter a single word, yet everybody was waiting for her daily surface: "What will Vanna wear next?" Even President Reagan, explaining to the press his decision to veto a law, said that he was going to veto it as fast as Vanna White turned the letters on the board of "Wheel of Fortune."

The power of the Vanna White myth is her very emptiness. Everybody can identify with her, it is said, as a sister, Barbie mother, friend, lover, wife, mistress. But the Vanna myth is actually more than this. One of the basic principles of the contemporary media is their rich surface and enormous space for identification.

This is the Vanna Factor, a concept precisely defined by Ted Koppel:

> We don't hear Vanna. She speaks only body language, and she seems to like everything she sees. No, "like" is too tepid. Vanna thrills, rejoices, adores everything she sees. Therein lies her particular magic. We have no idea what, or even if, Vanna thinks. Is she a feminist or every male chauvinist's dream? She is whatever you want her to be. Sister, lover,

daughter, friend, never cross, nonthreatening and nonjudgmental to a fault.

The viewer can, and apparently does, project a thousand different personalities onto that charmingly neutral television image, and she accommodates them all.

Address to 1987 graduating class, Duke University

Koppel feels himself both the beneficiary of the principle as well as its victim. "In theory," he tells me, "I am equally tough on everyone; therefore viewers can project on me their own politics, their own views, their own predisposition. That makes me the beneficiary of a certain public acceptance that I would not have if I were, let's say, a commentator that expressed his own views on subjects or a politician." Koppel unwittingly has discovered the theory of relativity for the social mores of the 90s, a theory I would call the empty vessel.

Oriental philosophy uses the concept of emptiness as a creative force. Lao-Tzu, in *The Tao, the Way of Life,* stated:

> Thirty spokes unite in one hub;
> It is precisely where there is nothing, that we find the usefulness of the wheel.
> We fire clay and make vessels;
> It is precisely where there's no substance, that we find the usefulness of clay pots.
> We chisel out doors and windows;
> It is precisely in these empty spaces, that we find the usefulness of the room.
> Therefore, we regard having something as beneficial;
> But having nothing as useful.

Four years to prepare this book—to make myself postmodern— and one of my biggest gaffes: forgetting that the Vanna Factor applies everywhere in media life, even behind the scenes. I had been interviewing at NBC "Nightly News" for months; the producers and vice presidents accepted my low-profile, observational presence. All was going well, and yet when the "News" agreed to let me cover it covering the first Reagan-Gorbachev summit, as if an old academic demon possessed me, I had to call an old professor for advice. Where else? Paris. Louis Marin, excited over my next day's trip to Washington, told me I had to, *had to* specify my relationship to the network. "You are an operator of the network but at the margin," he said. "You are not neutral, as if any observer could be neutral. Your relation to the network is like that of Racine to Louis XIV, like that of the historian to power. Inside the network, on the side of the network, you'll write its power applied to the power of the two kings."

Shrugging off casual greetings from producers the next morning in Washington, I sought out Bill Wheatley, then executive producer of the "Nightly News." News to tell him from Paris semiology. "I need to specify our relationship," I began. And ended staring at a disbelieving American telling me how can I think I'm a member of the network? What, I'm not neutral, what kind of reporter am I?

I'm the banished kind of reporter—sitting alone for two hours by a nonworking computer, while Wheatley, in the best American manner, simply lets the turgid French theory evaporate from his mind. I had forgotten—and Wheatley forgave me—that in America we're fluid, undefined, we don't caption our behavior like the still acutely class-conscious Europeans. I had learned, at not too large a price, that only by remaining fluid can you function within a system that abhors theory and precision. You don't position, define your-self at every point of a discourse, like the French do; you let things shape you. If the Europeans are always after a precise definition, the French especially, one that allows for barely any space, the Ameri-cans, on the other hand, given the dynamic nature of the society, prefer to flow like a river. And that flow takes you from here to there, places you and defines you. Not the other way around.

The media are volatile given their lack of electoral constituency, direct governmental, legal power; they are forced constantly to be aware of their limits. By amplifying the voices of business, govern-ment, and academia, the media hear and help shape what is called the mood of America. The rules the networks play by, for instance, call for them to mediate among power groups including the strong force of public opinion. In the Third World, the media are intensely manipulated. In France and England, the press has often abused its privileges. In America, people depend on the media for direction, given the weakening of the family and the size of the country. The media display and discuss changing values.

American mythology is incomplete without its dark side. The upbeat mood, the need to promote well-being, has displaced evil, hell, suffering, and death from American mythologies. The hell that has virtually disappeared from the pulpit has reappeared in the form of horror. Horror is secular hell, the other side of the goodness, the well-being of America, the consumer paradise that the country, until recently, has been building for two hundred years. "There is a superstitious, knock-on-wood feeling in a lot of horror fiction," Stephen King told me for the chapter on horror in this book, "the idea that we have lived so well for so long that there must be dues to pay. We have a puritanical, Calvinistic side to our nature that suggests that if we do very well we must be doing something wrong and there must be dues to pay. A lot of horror provides us with this secular vision of hell."

Horror, precisely because it is not taken seriously, is the permitted place for exploring society's secrets, its taboos. Another form of evil in America is found in our Third World: the subway system. When people think of New York, they see danger and evil in the subway system. It's the underground world where the beast lurks. It's dark and the middle class enters it with discomfort, afraid to stumble into a sleeping homeless person, be approached by a disturbed pan-handler, or be mugged and raped by the lurking figures of the dark. In the big cities of America, the homeless are the zombies, part of the mythology of the forces of Lucifer.

The virus of evil moves and mutates into different forms. It appears in an innocent painkiller like Tylenol contaminated with cyanide, forcing the retrieval of millions of capsules. It reappears in a roaming band of giggling teenagers pricking passersby with needles suspected of AIDS contamination. An arrested prostitute bites a policeman and shouts: "I've got AIDS, you're dead, man." The virus surprises you one sunny afternoon in a deranged drug addict who assaults you in the marble lobby. It takes the form of "wilding" youth that could shatter in a minute the fitness of a female or male jogger.

Our new man and woman slide over the surface of what was once a Pax Americana, move and live on trust that Rosemary will not give birth to the Devil and that the Plymouth Fury will not start running over innocent pedestrians; that the space and objects around us will not be inimical. This peace is constantly being threatened. Our rich surface is precarious but it has created a whole new outlook. The new philosophy includes our new views of nudity, home, energy, health, history, and passion.

Although this world we have been choosing to call "post-modern" might rest on a California fault, it has been a dazzling oasis in the turbulent history of western culture. The word itself had a triumphalist feel now embarrassing (end of history and all that blah blah). That world will be played out by the turn-of-the-millennium, and all the planners I visited on my trip were squinting to see the new order in the making.

In Tokyo, Naohiro Amaya, former vice minister of the Japanese Ministry of International Trade and Industry (MITI) and president of the Japan Economic Foundation, when I first met him, reminded me that every period's hard technology required an adequate soft technology at the level of the nation. In the nineteenth century the leading hard technology was the steam engine, each nation well or badly establishing economic and political systems, ethics, and values compatible with steam engine technology. The United King-dom was the best at it, Amaya said; that's why the U.K. was a leading nation of the nineteenth century.

But in the twentieth, this changed. The dominant hard technol-ogy became the internal combustion engine and the electric motor. The nineteenth-century British system wasn't compatible. That of the U.S. was. "You developed the social softwares," Amaya said, by which he meant the social, economic, political, and ethical systems that were somehow compatible with internal combustion engines and electric motors. Because of this, he told me, the United States became the leading nation in the first half of the twentieth century.

Relaxing on the couch in his modest office, sipping green tea (every interview in Tokyo starts with tea), I just didn't get it. Democracy and the automobile engine? Was he putting me on? So I asked, what ethical component did we develop to make ourselves compatible? Amaya answered disarmingly: "You believed in the value of democracy whereas the British believed in aristocracy and class-distinct society." Get it? In this rather novel theory, we developed democracy and gave it a content—freedom conceived spatially—to permit the consumption and production of cars, and the transfer to labor of machines formerly monopolized by capitalists. Amaya continued his lecture:

> In the nineteenth century the machine was monopolized by the capitalists. Labor was not in a position to own and make use of the machines. It was a sort of slave of the machines. But in the twentieth century the ownership and utilization of machines got more and more democratic. Before Henry Ford, cars were owned and utilized only by the rich. But Ford reduced the price to $900, which meant the democratization of motorization went on drastically in the United States.

The car and democracy? Freedom conceived spatially? Scarcely as odd as it seems. Amaya was doing nothing more than telling of our own Jack Kerouac, who crystallized such experience in his tortured life. Here is Kerouac in 1959 reading from *Visions of Cody* and *On the Road* to that other hipster, he of mass TV, Steve Allen.

Allen (at the grand piano on the set of his show):	And right now we'll look into Jack Kerouac's *On the Road,* and he'll lay a little on you. I'll play the blues as we did [in the rehearsal].
Kerouac (as Allen plays gently):	Well, a lot of people have asked me why did I write that book or any book. All the stories I wrote were true because I believed in what I saw. I was traveling west one time at the junction of the state line of Colorado, its arid western one, the state line of poor Utah, and saw in the clouds, huge and massed above the ethereal golden desert of evenfall, a great image of God with forefinger pointed straight at me. Through halos and rolls and gold folds of the light existence of the gleaming spear in his right hand which sayeth: "Come on, boy, go thou across the ground; go moan for man; go moan; go groan; go groan alone."

RENNER LEARNING RESOURCE CENTER
ELGIN COMMUNITY COLLEGE
ELGIN, ILLINOIS 60123

The phonic displacements giving an aural image of arterial motion. A motion at whose source is pain. Emptiness.

"Go roll your bones, alone; go thou and be little beneath my sight; go thou and be minute and as seed in the pod; go thou, go thou, die henst. Of this world, report you well and truly." Anyway, I wrote the book because we're all going to die— In the loneliness of my life, my father, dead and my brother dead, my mother far away, my sister and my wife far away, nothing here but my own tragic hands that once were guarded by a world, a sweet attention, that now are left to guide and disappear their own way into the common dark of all our death, sleeping in my raw bed, alone is stupid: with just this one pride and consolation: my heart broke in the general despair and opened up inwards to the Lord.

Here is a postwar discovery of the nullity of American vehicular freedom, of life absent "beatitude, pleasure in life, and tenderness," as Kerouac told Bill Buckley in 1968 on "Firing Line." "They called it in the papers Beatmutiny, Beat insurrection, words I never used being a Catholic. I believe in order, tenderness, and piety." I think his vision was a ghastly preview of limitless motility in a closed chamber next to vacuous mom and dad, date and spouse. Kerouac scarcely intended to look with horror on the beginnings of the 50s. At the start of *On the Road,* he writes:

A western kinsman of the sun, Dean. Although my aunt warned me that he would get me in trouble, I could hear a new call and see a new horizon, and believe it at my young age; and a little bit of trouble or even Dean's eventual rejection of me as a buddy, putting me down, as he would later, on starving sidewalks and sickbeds—what did it matter? I was a young writer and I wanted to take off.

Somewhere along the line I knew there'd be girls, visions, everything; somewhere along the line the pearl would be handed to me.

Kerouac: a guy who will not settle down after the war. Most people would take the car and move it into the suburbs. Kerouac kept on going, reinventing the open road—the frontier—myth. Just before suburbanization was in place; before the malls; before the golden age of the golden arches; before cruising and dating and the commodification of adolescence; at a moment of social exhaustion when we became a tamed organizational society; right after the war, Jack Kerouac made of his life an avant-garde of a mega-system to come. "Mallarmé said that poetry is the language of a state of crisis, and each novel of Jack's," said poet Michael McClure, "has to be an act of vision and an act of desperation. It's an act of bravado. He really is an outlaw of the sensorium."

The car is still—as Stephen King will tell you here—a myth of freedom; maybe a myth precisely because motorized freedom is dying, starting to end in the 70s as there emerged a new hero of the roads, the long-distance trucker of myth whose existence in song and film served to mask a crisis shaking that sector of the economy: the strikes, take-overs, moves toward monopolization, resulting in violence on the Pennsylvania Turnpike. The larger crisis was that of the Arab oil embargo, the ensuing failure to find an energy policy, the decrepitude of the highway and related infrastructure of the U.S., especially in the Northeast. You may own a gleaming car today, you may be indebted up to your eyeballs to experience *Fahrvergnügen;* effectively, you go nowhere, stuck in immanent gridlock, choking in thy neighbor's gas fumes—and in California, supposedly the way of the future, some of us ever ready to reach for the gun.

This is only another way of saying our hard technology is no longer that of the car. We are no longer the oil and electricity civilization, but the telematic, the culture of will projectible over distance. And given the advent of "nomadic objects," as Attali calls our Faxes and cellulars, laptops, ATMs, CDs, and self-diagnostic medical devices, we possess the power as never before to forage far from our roots, in his words, to subvert our links to family, culture, and nationality. Space is becoming irrelevant although we can traverse it for our pleasure. "Japan is also working on a hydrogen-powered motor that promises, within the next 15 years, to place all cities in Japan within one hour of Tokyo," Attali observes in his recent book *Millennium,* an apocalyptic translation of the 1990 French title, *Lignes d'Horizon* [Horizon Lines]. "This development [part of what he calls the hyper-industrialization of our age] will transform the Japanese archipelago into a unified metropole of a scope that can anchor the vast Pacific prosperity." To the telematic nomad, a car is pure nostalgia, a sign of lost time. As car designer Giorgetto Giugaro tells you later, maybe the Americans are the last to be told: Mighty Car, the Phallomobile, is finished.

Let's say we are searching out the ethical, cultural—the soft—system most compatible with the utterly untrammeled egos many of us are becoming, hurling our bytes worldwide. What is the shape of this system? Amaya was optimistic, strangely bullish on America. What is that soft system? I asked.

Nobody knows, you see. It is very difficult to answer. What is quite clear is that the Russian system is the worst—

hence, the ill-fated perestroika:

because according to that system, information is monopolized by Kremlin or KGB. That is the worst system for the information civilization. I think the core of the information civilization is democratization of ownership and utilization of information. From now to the twenty-first century, I think the essence of civilization will be democratization of access to and utilization of information. I think the roles and activities of individuals will increase, and human capital will be more important than physical capital. And of course the essence, the last unit of human capital is an individual. So the creativity of the individual will be the most important thing in the next century. From that viewpoint, I think America is most compatible with this requirement.

Was he being discreet? Offering the visitor a final compliment of no greater status than the initiatory tea?

At the elevator after the interview he came up to me, oddly smiling given the following P.S.: "The community's authority is declining very sharply here, and Ego is getting bigger and bigger. The accelerator is on and there's no brake," he laughed. I should have asked him, what's so funny? but the elevator door shut on him, and I was soon back on the street next to the imperial palace where, the night before, inept terrorists had lobbed unexploded missiles into the Emperor's gardens.

Without the laughter or anti-Americanism, but without that patriotism thing, either—without wrapping up in the American flag of Bush or Madonna—we shall try to test the shape of American soft technology. Is it apposite to the new age? Have we begun the adjustment to the economic dynamisms in the wings? Is our future increasing democracy or something more . . . administered? Let's look at some signs. And ask their creators. Why not just ask: what's the new order in the making?

In Search of the Fountain of Looks

1

I have always wanted to dress the way I thought I should be seen. My first conscious attempt was to look like a French semiologist. In 1970, still in my pre-history when I embraced the stuff in France, I would see the French with their slight bodies wear these incredibly fitted clothes, talking Lacan (*le sujet profond,* the deep self, *c'est un pur trou,* he's pure hole—everything was "pure" then, pure chance, pure war) and I *qvelled,* as they say in Yiddish. I fell for the look. Being an American I knew that it wasn't only the ideas you spouted, you had to look the part. I didn't want to affect an Oxford don. I didn't want tweeds. I didn't want to wear a soft sweater like Einstein. I wanted to be . . . sharp. The French intellectuals looked so elegant compared wtih us! And I then thought elegance was French, all the way from Louis XIV to Chanel and Jacques Lacan (who, four years later, was escorted to the First Semiotic Congress in Milan by his *dames de compagnie,* one in black and one in white).

I became part of the peacock revolution of the 70s. There I was teaching semiotics myself in New York, wearing blue velvet suits, even blue shirts inside them. Or brown velvet, beige shirt. Or a gray flannel suit with lapels so wide, my friend and professor Geoffrey Hartman couldn't help himself once: "You look like a businessman, for Christ sake!"

No, businessmen then were peacocks, too.

I wore Pierre Balmain blue velvet, clothes so tight I looked painted into them. I didn't mind. I was slim. We were always dieting, torturing our bodies to make them as little as the Europeans', for whom these clothes were cut. Our American chests were the insoluble problem. The weight lifting we did to make our hips slim for the penis-binding trousers—unhappily, it expanded the chest to the point that we could never close the jacket with agenda or wallet or anything inside it. We couldn't put glasses in the breast pocket because they would upset the delicate balance. And our ties, of course, were wide as bibs, the peacock spreading its tail.

So a decade and a bit later, when the publisher of this book told me to go see Italian designers and ask them what men's clothes mean, I decided not only to quote them, but to look like them. A more studied reason: When I interview I don't present myself as antagonistic. I am not Oriana Fallaci. Or Ted Koppel. I am sympathetic, not polemic (except in the Koppel case, where he rubbed me the wrong way and I, him). I am in the place of the other, first to perceive, to learn; and only in a quiet later moment to analyze, to criticize, to puncture and establish a distance from the viscous, affective, human specificity in order to reveal its structures and dynamics.

Therefore, while interviewing, I exploit a personal trait: a certain wonderment at or freshness to the world, a presentation without excessive ego, as if the outer skin of ego had been shed, exposing naive sensibility merely *registering*—a surface to be written on. So I wanted to dress in a way the Italians would like. I didn't want to present to them another school—that of American power dressing, for instance. The brutal, sharp, stiletto look, say, of Michael Douglas in *Wall Street*. To do so would have been to say: "I don't buy your look. The proof is the way I'm dressed." I wanted the Italians to like me and talk to me, that I might learn.

The world's an enormous shopping catalogue. Anything can be bought, any place. Ireland, if you do its jigs. The Chinese, if you buy their silks, applaud their acrobats. Japan? Go to martial arts class. Indonesia? Get into their rhythms. The Middle East? Cuisine. Always cuisine. We eat every country there is and the intrinsic value of that food . . . isn't. For the sake of instant acceptability, local traditions—like the vein of the shrimp we savor—have been removed by the merciful gods of marketing. The real place, the origin of the sign we munch, would be "icky" to us. We are like curators who know the origin of the art work is extinct. We are collectors of a real we think vanished, and we proliferate names in our lives— place and brand—as if to compensate in costume-, in image-change for a world and world tour we're sure we can't take. Or wouldn't want to, if we could. That is why in America we can take on any look we want, I had taught and thought. That is why—piece of cake, as Ted Koppel would say—I opted for *a l'italiano* for the Italians.

So the pleasure of repackaging myself to signify solidarity with my subjects—plus the fact I'd run down all my suits! I'd be embarrassed appearing in tatters at the Elysée of Design—shot me out of the house to . . . the Armani boutique. At 815 Madison

Avenue in New York, a postmodern Medici palace in huge upper stories of glass to let the masses on the street see the wonders inside. There were few wonders when I got there. All that was left was a single-button, pale, bullet-gray model, uplifted shoulders trying to give me lift-off, it seemed; plus lowered lapel to expose more chest in order to give me a puffed-up "fight or flight" look to ape the higher primates. Along with striped Armani shirt and faded red you-know-whose tie, I thought I cut quite a sight as I wore my new suit to via Borgonuovo 21 to meet—whom? Why, Himself— Giorgio Armani, of course.

It's Sunday at 7 P.M. Armani has interrupted his weekend to redo our interview. Yesterday, at Milan Central Station, while I was arguing with a cashier over a refund, my briefcase was stolen—"by a gypsy," the cop tells me. The Armani interview tape was in that briefcase. Now, he and I are playfully redoing the interview. *"Vous avez dit,"* I say (we're talking in French—"then you said . . ."), and he: *"Oui, oui . . ."*

"Will you say it again?"

And I, a half hour later: "And then you drew . . ."

"Oui, oui, oui, oui."

"Will you do it again?"

Because he has rushed into Milan from his country house in Sant'Ambrogio, he is dressed in a blue T-shirt exposing a muscular torso. He sits behind a marble desk. Atop it a delicate lamp illuminates his tanned face capped by pure white hair (impossible to dye hair that color). He is more serious than he was in the prior interview. He tells me again that the president of Fiat, Cesare Romiti, has just given a speech deploring "capitalismo selvaggio," wild capitalists, the new breed of chief executive who will do anything to fulfill his financial aims—to show more money—rather than broaden his industrial base. "He will eat his mama, if he has to," Armani says—use any financial gimmick, because money wizardry has been fashionable. It brings immediate results and applause from the crowd. Armani feels personally implicated by Romiti's address. The uplifted Armani shoulder—recalling the epaulet of the soldier, even the silhouette of the samurai or Florentine knight—played its part, he thinks, in the world of grab and greed that industry itself, not only finance, became in the 80s. In a stroke of colored pencil on a piece of paper, Armani slashes in the famous square shoulder line. "The jacket shoots out from the shoulder," he says, demonstrating his signature shape. "That's not something that goes with man. I agree with Romiti, we became too hard." Little did I know it, but my trip would take place under the aegis of the couple he just set in place: *hard/soft.* Drawing his new, softer shoulder for winter, he says: "You see? It falls naturally on the body, a second skin." Armani wanted you to wear this jacket like a pullover. "I want to eliminate the jacket's being a formal feature," he says. The formal banishes the viscous, anything having to do with feeling. "I want to render it very casual, very true, like a sweater. At this moment of the world, one has to rediscover a little heart, and fashion can help. One has to have the courage to show oneself a little bit as one is"—a beat—"inside."

It was getting late, dark, relaxed. In that palace of cool elegance it was easy to bring up the topic I had dared to bring up before. I had asked him about myself. I of course had on the Armani. He didn't like what he saw.

"I see you dressed in a certain way," he's saying circumlocutiously. "Probably because you wanted to be elegant . . . for me, *pour moi*"—hearing those soft words (in French the mouth opens to say "me"), I felt like a young woman before her first lover—"dressed in Armani" . . . a pause . . . *"en face du créateur,"* in front of its creator.

Figures 1.1, 1.2 His and her "schlep" suits. Armani's new sincere look.

"You aren't twenty years old," he's saying, "you aren't a man of fashion." Who am I, then? I ask, feeling rebuked when first I heard it. Read my (poor) substance, I tell him.

He did. "You look like a country gentleman," he says, but doubtless seeing surprise in my face (he has just told me I'm not fashionable), he adds: "country gentleman *un peu suède*. It's Ingmar Bergman I see. You have a kind of melancholy of Bergman. You have the look of *penseur*." What does a *penseur* wear? "I would have preferred," God said, "that you dress in a sweater, with pants in black cotton and a blue T-shirt."

"But Signor Armani," I sort of cry, "that's *you*. That's what you're wearing."

"No matter, that is you also."

Everyone dreams of being dressed by Armani. To have come so high and to be told wear a blue T-shirt—is he mad? Mocking me? No, here in a land perhaps less postmodern than my own, Armani's apparently essentialist. He seems to believe a soft essence is exteriorizing itself on the face he sees. A modernist believes in the profound subject, a deep person demanding *its* manifestation, not the playful one I sought to deploy. In courteous but serious tone, a prince of postmodernism is atavistically telling me I can't feign corporate prince because I'm an intellectual. I can't wear old Armani hard because I am soft.

You are free to assume any image you want, but you also have to sell it to others. This other wasn't buying. I had come to Italy somatically coded (melancholy eyes, no longer twenty). From the moment I opened my mouth I was linguistically coded (talks in paragraphs, soft voice). What's a code? A rule that correlates expression with content, first impressions with lasting ideas. Armani knows the interview's for Oxford University Press. He sees the bald head, hears the whole paragraphs—bango, he sees melancholy eyes and attaches the content "soft" to me. A code's a machine: Throw in a signifier, it'll spit out a signified. A code's relentless; never will it alter the ticker tape of meaning. Whatever land you're in, whoever you're before, it snaps together whole paragraphs with "professor." It's an instantaneous operator for a culture that long ago made up its collective mind about things. Here, intellectuals. If they're American, they're on the margin—code them harmless.

When the briefcase was stolen, my surface of suit failed me. I reverted to Age of Anxiety type, unable to dismiss the event with comfortable or mocking irony. I might as well have been wearing an academic tweed jacket as I tried to recall the playful first interview, looking for something lost, looking for meaning, on a weekend in a room where Armani could have been next to a stylish Italian or American acolyte looking for nothing, for whom the surface play of lapel and line would have sufficed. A code, worldwide, labels such intensity. *You can trust your daughter with this man of the mind* was doubtless the slip of meaning that fluttered through Armani's mind.

Perhaps I unconsciously accepted the creator's rejection of his pseudocreature. Because when I saw Gianfranco Ferré shortly thereafter, I made a confession, thereby coding myself as sensitive. "I wore your leather trench coat in London—I was shamed," I tell him. In January '87 I went through Heathrow in a brown greatcoat given me by Ferré's New York distributor to ward off Europe's great cold that year. Huge shoulders, chocolate leather, a volume of butter leather down to my ankles, a belt with no holes to buckle— you had to twist the belt ends around on each other. Gesture of the hand, of the casual. The Pakistani customs officer bowed to me, gestured me through while stopping yobs and oiks dressed in denim.

London is part poor now. Shabby. The wealth the City has made hasn't made jobs. They're at subsistence, below it, the blacks, the Pakis, the poor whites, the kids. I wore the coat twice in London. Once at MGMM, a big music video production house in Golden Square—the G in the name, Brian Grant, saying: "I covet that coat." The second time: at a working-class comedy and sing-along club. I was so embarrassed to look rich, I folded the coat in halves, folded it once, folded it again to make it half the size, then again until I could hold it, two feet by two, no more, behind my back as I laughed and drank beer and made nice with the poor set. I disgusted myself, for here I was, in appearance a Ferré burgher—Ferré designs for a haute bourgeoisie that spits at the poor. Here I was, in appearance a prince among wretches in London to sniff out the life the moneyed set has decreed for these subsisters. I told Ferré what I had endured when it came my time to interview him.

"I think that outfit was not belonging to you," he says. "I remember that season I was showing the long brown leather coat, very rich, like something that reminds me of 30s richness." And something else from the 30s, very Italian. Fascism—fashion will quote anything. No wonder the bowing at Heathrow, the surprised looks at the door of the club, the exclamation of mega-time Grant. Rock-'n-roll's kind of fascist and I was dressed as a slick movie version Gestapo officer. Ferré is continuing:"At the same time I was showing a more simple, less opulent outfit." Had he dressed me for London, that would have been his choice. Which? "I will never suggest to you a coat in that leather. I will suggest a more simple coat. In suede. With softer lines, less outstanding. Because of you." I think he meant because I'm a *penseur*. Since I think, I think not to offend the poor of London. I wear suede to assuage them. Let them wear suede.

In suede, back in London, I wore . . . what? . . . to see designer Katharine Hamnett. Savvied by my Milan interviews, a smart but not shouldered, anthracite Italian suit, a Ferré tie, of course-gorgeous *vieille rose* and blue flowers on it.

Figure 1.3 Dressed by Ferré in a long leather greatcoat, a slick movie version of a Gestapo officer.

"We brought back the whole big tits thing, didn't you know?" says Hamnett.

I didn't.

"Oh yes, after us it was like, tits are back. *What's that?*"

She at last had noticed my tie.

"It's Ferré," I said.

And suddenly, from across the workroom she calls her cave, Katharine Hamnett is running at me, a scissors in her hand. *"I'm going to cut that thing off,"* she cries in jest (but all of me doesn't know it's jest). "I want to get you in something fabby," she says. And six-foot-tall Hamnett is guiding five-foot-nine me to a rack on which is her James Bond suit. "I wanted to give this suit to all the Greens," she says, "because in Germany they look like such woolies. They have terrible haircuts. One of them even wears a lace collar. I mean, who's going to take them seriously? The smarter your clothes, the more people take you seriously." So she wants to give the Greens—and me—"the ultimate smart suit, the suit that Holly Johnson in *Frankie Goes to Hollywood* has. There it is."

I am fondling it. It is silk. It is rich. It is me?

"Try it on," my new friend says. "You have to look terribly Oxford, don't you think?"

Do I? And Oxford and James Bond?

"I think that will be your killer stance," she says.

A little shame in my voice, I tell her: "You know, I'm not conservative in the slightest. I'm rather . . . eccentric, I don't know if you can tell it."

It's as if she were a psychoanalyst, so strong is the lure of the Great Designer.

"I think you're great," Katharine Hamnett says (she met me yesterday). "I think you're this natural survivor." How can she have read me thus? I thought I was tranquil, a *penseur*. "How you survive in America, I don't know. It's a frightening business over there. No bottom line on behavior. I think a bigger one."

"I'm forty-two."

"I'll have it made for you. Yeah, that's too tight."

But already falling in love with the silk, I suggest . . . "if I take off my sweater, Katharine?" Mm, it's Katharine now.

"Yeah, take your sweater off."

Something comforting, maternal, yet erotic is in this cave as we undress me to redress me. At this instant, from outside, a woman's cry. "My God, somebody's having a mortal crisis," I say.

"I thought so, too," says . . . Katharine. "Yeah, just one size bigger, I think. Come, look in the mirror."

Jacques Lacan said that we acquire the "rootstock" of our egos when, between six and eighteen months, our mothers show us our image in the mirror. "That's you," mother says, and we who were dribblers, spastic, unable to form a sense of self inasmuch as we hadn't been able to act like solid selves . . . upon hearing the coo of mother's "that's you," we think "that's me." We identify with the image before us, for us. Next to big Hamnett who shows me me, I feel like an infant again.

"Hmm, you could do with a bit more width in the back. An Englishman would wear it loose," Mother tells me.

But I'm not an Englishman! I hear inside myself. No matter—

"You have to wear it the way an Englishman . . . one size up. Now turn around. You see?"

I'm malleable substance in her hand.

"Hmm, it's quite nice, isn't it?" from her voice.

"It's lovely," I say.

"I think it's a bit short, too." She has shifted to the High Designer mode, the Fitter. I'm a model, feeling for myself the warmth of being molded by her hand.

"Whatever you want," I say.

"I'll get you a size bigger. A cardigan as well. You've got to have the Oxford cardigan, the most beautiful English wool." I am being made soft again, simulated Oxbridge. When, that afternoon, I actually get to Oxford, actually ring the bell at Tumbledown House, the home of Professor Theodore Zeldin, I am shamed again. Zeldin, the real, is in baby-blue wool sweater, roseate of skin—no gray cardigan for him!

Who knows? Maybe I was obsessed by power, given that the European designers had made me soft, not hard. I told the *New York Times* about the wild capitalist Armani wanted to soften, the high-flyer along the Moscow–Bonn–London–New York–Tokyo lane. The venture capitalist, the investment banker, the high-powered lawyer, the man who specializes in those major, megaworld deals that so upset Romiti. Armani had called for him to have the courage to show himself as he was, inside. I felt more strongly now that Armani wasn't *simply* postmodern, hadn't accepted the triumph of surface over depth (surely hadn't in my case). Because I was sure that on the corporate fields of Milano, New York, and Paris, no one was interested in your supposed inside; nor are you, in theirs. We don't approach one another with . . . sincerity, the chastened Armani notwithstanding. Romiti, I felt, had bared a dark side of postindustrial wealth, the aggression driving managers to hurl themselves anywhere at the speed of the jet or electronic transfer to fight for and defend territory. "They want to leap up the steps of the stairway of success, without worrying too much about the methods used," Romiti had said drily, his image exposing a paleocapitalist world, including many more than chief executives, much more than money gimmickry.

Claude Montana must have thought so, too, and here I pause for a confession of personal failing. When I was in Moscow, Yevgeny Yevtushenko told me a long, elegant story about ties (see chapter 17), and I promised him that I'd give him a Claude Montana tie showing . . . a Gentleman, Victorian, with striped pants and long coat. Ascot. He stands, rigid, seeming to be suspended, on a middle step of a green staircase, the lower part of the tie. Or is it an escalator? Impossible to tell which. The Gentleman holds a red railing, a European stripe, southwest-to-northeast, a railing unattached to any structure—precarious support for the ascent. The background, electric blue; the red railing stripes go up the tie at large intervals to the neck. If our Gentleman is on an escalator, suggested by his handhold and inert stance, perhaps he thinks that merely by dressing well, and being white, his rise will be assured, mechanical. I loved this inspiration of Montana, this visualization of Romiti's words: loved it so much I couldn't part with it. Thank God Yevtushenko (I hope) never remembered my promise! He said, by the way, that being a capitalist I wouldn't do the tie justice. On me, it would be pastiche, dead mimicry of the corporate hierarchy. On him, it would be parody, with its ulterior motive of jamming the escalator. He swore he'd wear it at a future mass poetry reading—in an *un*postmodern place like Budapest, or a Buenos Aires slum, where the satire would produce anticapitalist conviction. Sorry, Comrade Yevgeny, as I return to Romiti, who often fashions himself into a scourge of Italian inequity.

In the speech that so pricked Armani, he continued, on the cavemen: "[Their] ambition has become almost a style." Not almost—*a* style. Greed has to out and signify itself. A style of managing, a style of clothing—both are parts of a system, I thought after visiting Armani. Armani thinks that Jean-Paul Gaultier originated the epaulet shoulder, but it was Armani, ten years ago, who made it commercial. A decade ago, as the raiders, mergerers and other wild capitalists decreed a new code for business conduct, Armani sent a message on the shoulders and on chests of his clientele (everyone knows he's famous for dropping the lapel and front buttons, enlarging the chest). Armani, yes, did give vestimentary cudgel to the managerial elite who wore his clothes. But by the ruse of his obviousness, his exaggeration, he also signaled "to whom it may concern" the long, unhappy, harsh lives inside the terrorist corporate tower. "Society is strong, hierarchical, organized, and structured," Attali said à propos Armani. "So fashion has to hide it. And Armani will hide it through destructuration and very vague dress. It is also a way of rebelling against the nature of society." Armani, he thinks, is proposing to the executive class another way, a softer way, "and maybe it will be not only a way of hiding the truth," said Attali, "but of creating a new truth." When I met Armani, as the vicious 80s were ending, the once and future innovator and cultural reader was ambivalently retreating from an aggression even mainstream American television was sensing to be extant, growling not cowering.

A few weeks after my return from Europe, I was asked to read "power ties" on ABC's "Good Morning America." Why did executives then favor miniature polka dots on fields of yellow? asked the associate producer. Why did the Irangate Senators all wear red? I asked Gabriella Forte, Armani's assistant, then in New York, to choose an Armani that I could read on the show. She asked me to come to the boutique. "I hope you won't be insulted if we change your look?" she said when I arrived. I was half afraid she would ask me to go on the show sincerely, in T-shirt and "pull." She chose instead an oversize, one-button, white cotton jacket. Of the new, softer shoulder. (It was to be the source of continuous irritation along a quest about to begin.) New jacket plus new everything: pants, belt, shirt, and oh those pants! Doubly pleated baggy pants, inside of which I thought I felt drafts, and my God, that jacket, so long I felt I was in the overcoat of a clown. I thought the master had gone crazy instead of being grateful to be among the first of his new penitents. The "me" Gabriella and Giorgio had found was nothing other than his image—not of himself, God forbid—but of a stance for the early 90s. Instead of shop til you drop, it would be abase thyself and keep on shopping. Knowing little of this in Forte's hands, I put on the Master's pants, belt, shirt . . . and tie. Its design? Almost none. From two feet away, it read plain navy blue. Silk, of course. "Armani says," Forte told me, "that amidst all these ties that speak and speak vulgarly, he chooses to remain mute." Or talk softly. Which I told Charlie Gibson on-air, when we said good morning to all those power-grubbers Duke of Windsoring their ties. The little semiotic collaboration between the designer and the professor was to have aired June 23. The night before, however, Jackie Gleason died, and I and Armani's message remain to this day "in the can."

So it should hardly surprise the reader that my idea caked. I had become structuralist. Prompted by Romiti and Armani, I saw system in the erratic parts. A style of managing, a style of dress. Absolutely. I thought the young and not-so-young striders on the stairway were seeking out the designers, tailors, and authorities who provide vestimentary shield and cudgel.

The man at the top of the stairs—waiting to welcome you or throw you down them—this man I called "Paleo-man," and the *Times* said yes to my idea. It sent me to search out his style (to get a glimpse of him also, if I could). What is the banner, the flag, of International Man? This would be the quest that would substitute for my own recent search.

Want to take a lunch at the Four Seasons? said the *Times* editor. Sure.

Do it in the Grill Room. Dinner at Le Cirque?

You bet.

And take a peek inside Hermès (supposedly exclusive fashion accessories store).

Absolutely.

Look for the Lord of the Airs there. But above all, go to the people who design for him.

Having exhausted and been exhausted by Europe, I turned to the American designers. They were only too pleased to tell me how they dress my international traveler.

"The leaders have to look and have always looked different from the followers," *Dress for Success* author John T. Molloy tells me over the phone. He is, in his own happy words, "the best in the world at what I do—even the K.G.B., I hear, uses my information." He tells me he dresses politicians, performers, executives, whole sales forces in the intimidation suits, sincerity suits, whatever uniform their success requires. "No matter what environment you're in, there's a uniform of power. Hell's Angels and top executives are both wearing power outfits. The only difference is, one group plays rough."

Yes, to be sure. But shoving aside the smug wit in my face, I tell myself that my assignment is to find out how they show themselves, these roughhousing boys and girls of greed, reaching out to deal God himself.

(A broker from a major U.S. firm telephones me urgently: wants me to call an Italian friend who knows an *éminence grise* cardinal at the Vatican; she got the idea of modernizing the cardinal's money management. As many of the cardinals as she can hook! European, backward, they rely on hidden, trustworthy friends to manage their investments. She, instead of that, proposes her firm and herself as a safer, more direct, more profitable, more *modern* way to growth and greed.)

The first designer I met emphatically told me what the uniform *wasn't*. Joseph Abboud is talking to me about ugly Americans. "From their thick-soled loafers to their center-vented jackets to their blue button-downs, you can always pick those guys out, the Americans in Europe," he says. He seems to be saying he's culturally superior and putting *you* down, if you're wearing a button-down, because you're a slob, not Euro-cultured. All of the designers I met were like intellectuals; they postured, each trying to unify, to encompass our inconsistent, multiform world in a single theory, a kind of fishhook in the market of the powerful. Each is selling his point of view as if it were total. Each is ideologizing his Look. Abboud, the day I met him, was trying to impose "Europe" on men he first shamed for being American.

He continued: "We can't be the big American abroad, a lot of dollars in our pocket, because the dollar doesn't speak the way it spoke twenty years ago." It's as if he were angry at our deficits. "We aren't the heavies any more, so we can't stand out abroad." Maliciously, he drew me this word portrait of the American abroad: "those guys with the red striped ties and the chinos—they're grotesque! They signify nothing but American provinciality. They might as well be in Nantucket red or Kelly green."

Why such vigor, passion, *ressentiment?* Because he's describing the competition, Brooks Brothers. And there's a war on.

Abboud was angry at these men for another, more intelligent and less selfish reason. By reading their clothes, he has understood that their vision and business dealings enact themselves only in America. I think they are late capitalist losers to him; they are not multinational men. To grasp this, to save him from himself and his line (both senses), I tricked him, softly, out of his anger.

"How would you dress *me?*" I say, wearily anticipating the words I'd hear. "I hope you don't think *I'm* a dumb American," I add.

"I really see your character, your face, your mustache, with a richness to them," he says. "If you take that and put it into clothing it interprets into beautiful, brown, rich tweeds." He was doing beige and brown that season. "I don't see you in dumb business suits. You're a writer."

In short, I'm not powerful.

"You're a writer": it means you're an intellectual, ergo should be soft. Marshall in Wonderland: maybe, but he came back bored. To live by a code is to be like everyone else. At bottom, no originality, no spontaneity. You appear to be playful but something is dead in you. From every star in the Designerland I toured came the naive construct: the intellectual cloaked in soft things, sweaters, tweeds, corduroys.

A few days later Alexander Julian will say it yet again. He opens a closet, takes a suit off its hanger. "This is the suit [of the international man]. Blue, slight chalk stripe. But before I can grasp its type, he's whisked it away, gone to the closet . . . got *my* suit. A bolt of herringbone cloth. "It's soft," he says, unrolling it. "It looks intellectual. Alludes to Yale 1930s."

Grossly anti-Semitic in the 30s, Yale wouldn't have let me be a student then.

As he walks back to that closet of uglies (to me), he says over his shoulder: "The herringbone gives you a little of that professorial injection." And here he is returning with "my" tie. "It has a little bit of that amethyst and turquoise in it that says you're not dealing with the average person," he says. "It comes off as intellectual and approachable. You want to elicit information from people and a true reading by making them comfortable."

In these designers' heads must be Professor Einstein, he of the goofy hair and sweaters. The characters they think with must go further back to "Oxford"—there's Huxley! Hullo. There's all the intellectuals of the British establishment. Dressed in tweeds, slightly crumpled. This is a European idea, that of the Campus, a space whose nature is safe from city corrpution (La Sorbonne shares the rats of Paris). It is a Euro look from the outside at the Anglo world, mistaking it to be stylish. Recall what Tom Wolfe said on the publication of *Bonfire of the Vanities*. Asked why he dresses in exquisite whites, he answered in effect: not to ape that twisted soul, Baudelaire, to evoke the beginnings of modernity. Rather, in order *not* to dress in the drab simplicity of a Ph.D. I'm a dandy, ergo you can't consider me an intellectual. I'll be a dandy *and* be a good writer, his clothes say. *You are spouting platitudes from outer space . . .* his clothes shout at the power that tries to soften, to marginalize the intellectual.

So Abboud softens and sees me in browns and:

"That'd be great," I tell him, "but what about the Suits—how would you dress *them?* In ties, say?" And he starts to tell a fiction:

> Ancient madders because money has never been newer. A lot of wines and navies mixed with old gold that bring the tie down, that give it some sense of tradition. As you print one color on top of another, you bury the colors little by little to achieve a certain muddiness.

He picks up a foulard:

> See how easily you can read the foulard? How clear and hard and defined the colors are? Ancient madder tends to be more muted, less readable. Wearing it I'm the guy with great taste, but you don't know where I come from. You don't know anything about me, finally.

Except for this:

> In the clothes I design for you, whoever looks at you will feel a gesture toward a traditional somewhere. They won't be able to say where that is. And they'll feel of that tradition, it evolved into something new. You.

This beautiful language evokes Ted Koppel's formula for power conquest (page 301): Don't be on the record, be an empty vessel. Now from Abboud comes: Let no one know what is inside you—the contrary of Armani. Unlike the clerks of the system, the writers and intellectuals, you are to have no character, no richness to your looks. But as you craft your image, suggest the traditional and you will appear to be power, which of course legitimates itself through tradition. But in all this be unreadable: No one must ever name your tradition. You yourself may not even remember it, for you have evolved from it. You are something new and no one knows what it is yet.

You are unreadable, you are unlocalizable. And you will never wear a red striped tie, explains Fred Pressman, president of Barney's, New York. "This club [multinational men] crosses borders, whereas the rep speaks of national history," Pressman tells me.

Fashioned upon the British regimental tie, the stripes of the rep were originally flags, indicators of belonging—first, to a military unit, but finally, to a nation. "The clothes of the aggressive, of the worldly traveler, are ideology-free," says John Molloy. They make you nationally invisible.

We seem to be talking then of businessmen, centered in the homes of world capitalism, New York, Paris, London, Berlin, Beverly Hills; cosseted by states that serve them; world travelers driven by a principle of border-free reach. Fiat USA president Furio Colombo is chatting with me: "Einstein once said, 'You will never resist what is technically easy.' We are traveling"—the day before, he was in Rome—"because it is easy to travel." In an older era, that of the rep tie, shall we say, each firm was conceived as a state within a state. Today's huge auto corporations, oil firms, engineering concerns, are subjects of no states. They seek and are producing the whole globe as an "ideologically homogeneous market where life will be organized around common consumer desires." The words are Attali's, and he ought to know. As president of the new EBRD, he's charged with helping privatize Eastern Europe. Now that Disneyland has opened outside Paris, don't expect to see Babar. Because it has become easy, in the delicious phrase of Colombo, Paleo-man's reach has become imperial.

Look at the most expressive part of the top man's costume, the tie, the most individualistic utterance in the language of men's clothes. Look there and see, in the madders and paisleys, not the slightest interest in indicating any belonging to any tradition (Abboud notwithstanding). For a time in the late 80s, large paisleys were popular. Thus, Gianfranco Ferré designed a tie of giant paisleys swirling—blue and red rivulets inside them—to the very edges of the tie and beyond. One could say that wearing his tie, you signified that you knew no boundary, that you could spread anywhere; or rather, you barely signified it: the muted green and purplish paisleys almost can't be seen. I don't want my will known, said the tie, another empty vessel.

On my trip to Italy to see Armani and the others, Rosita Missoni— deliciously treating me, not as an intellectual but as if *I* were a top man, a conquering American—had sent to my hotel room, one night, a gift. Opening the box, I discovered a sweater I'd admired earlier that day in her Sumirago factory. Inside it was a multicolored shirt, and inside its neck was a red-watch tie she had created of red so vibrant it seemed to pulse before me. ("Did I go too far?" the note inside the box said.) As if not to be outdone, Ferré's people gave me a red satin tie—little blue stars on it—the red so intense I have always been too embarassed to wear it. The one time I wore the Missoni outfit in Manhattan a hairy athlete in luminous jogging shorts slyly smiled, and his girlfriend in spandex made no attempt to hide her snicker. Like many Upper East Siders, their preoccupations were local and they couldn't recognize globalist dress. Still

. . . my closet is replete with Missoni Uomini, and there they shall stay.

These are traces of a sensibility in touch with internationalist ideology. I believe it's reasonable to analyze these fashion bits as sign. You can spread anywhere, say the ties, consolidating the egos of those who wear them. They, *trans*national managers, want to go their way around the world, unimpeded by liberationist, reactionary, or any local ideology. There really is a mother-eating multinational man. And if it's a matter of his dealing with the infidel himself, he'll do it.

It doesn't matter if there's a cold war on or not. Toshiba, before perestroika, sells a submarine machine tool to Russia (forget the sensitive transfer of technology—it didn't respond to the company's higher, business interest). Several years before the cold war ended, his aide Gerard Dufour, for medical reasons unable to drink, embarrassed about the matter, asks how to (or must he) conceal this from the real Stoli downers, mythological as quasi-beasts, residual Russians, a minor impediment to doing business globally. I overheard Young & Rubicam chairman, Alex Kroll, describing a vision that will, a few days following his remarks, take him to Moscow. There, he plans to beat out other American ad agencies. He hopes to conclude a joint venture, a monopolistic U.S.–Soviet ad agency to represent all American firms doing business in Russia. Forget it.

Or, again, listen to investment banker Felix Rohatyn give some of the theory of Y & R's move (which in no way foresaw the end of the cold war):

> The only way we can begin to think of reducing our trade deficit as we reduce our budget deficit is . . . some overarching political negotiation with the Soviet Union, disengagement in central Europe, and a shift of the argument from a military one to one of economic development. It's clear to me that the western world has too much capacity that has been built up all over the world. Technology is so available that the only way for us to continue is to create a lot of demand, not only in the Third World, but in the Soviet Union and China. Unless those countries themselves become more prosperous and there is economic demand there, we have built such tremendous capacity in the western world—too much to sustain our own growth unless that growth comes from those other parts of the world.
>
> *Remarks at Asia Society, New York, 20 October 1988*

The loyalty of Kroll, Dufour, and Rohaytn is to the United States—not of America—but of Capitalism. An archipelago including Berlin, Tokyo, and Singapore but scarcely West Virginia, the Bronx, the inner cities, or the *Gastarbeiter* of Germany. Dufour, in a different, more global interpretation, was ashamed that he wouldn't be adequately New Capitalist: You swill vodka in Moscow, sing along with Sinatra, *karaoke*-style in Tokyo, and mourn the passing of Balinese culture while doing textile deals in Indonesia.

All these fashion traces I touched, from the spreading paisleys to the killer suits, gesture toward this real, toward this new world system of capitalism. But the error I made on my trip was to take the Designerspeak I heard for fashion—for world capitalist—reality. 'I, Armani—I, Abboud—I, Missoni—craft the Look for the New Capitalist.' It was a mistake intended by the various speakers themselves. To speak of a Look is perhaps, through publication, to be the promoter of that Look—and bear in mind that to arrive at this, the first chapter, I had to prepublish in the *New York Times Magazine* fashion supplement. The culture craves new looks, new names— and who knows, by talking about it we may bring it to be. The designers were like Quixotes in my presence. I experienced no interiority, no doubt. They were full of fixed ideas they were overeager to transmit. And if some stubborn fact didn't correspond to the Look, they would ignore it and, I think, if need be, invent to complete the system.

A little Quixotified myself, I went to see Furio Colombo, president of Fiat USA, clearly an international manager. He manages all Fiat interests, financial to PR, in America.

How does the international man show himself? I ask him. "By an intriguing exchange of signals," Colombo answers. "He wears something European and also something American. Shoes still tend to be Italian, but whereas they used to be glove leather, perfect and smooth—the Gucci style—now they recall American shoes, which are harsher, larger, more manly" [bear in mind, this long, lovely, seemingly never-ending sentence wasn't written; it's being crafted, orally, on the spot—no wonder he's the PR chief!], "with an element of remembering New England boats and walking on the beach." But these shoes are too fine and too soft to be strictly American—"too tender," says Colombo, poetically. They are for a First World constituency that wants to signify Americanness but still enjoy and evoke the "softer, sweeter, more complacent life of Europe," in his words.

Thus, even as the idea of Manly America dominates the First World, American (or other First World) top men, if you accept these admissions, don't live wholly by U.S. codes. Our food isn't good enough; perhaps our women aren't complacent enough. Colombo is telling you what Fellini showed, years ago: for their advanced cuisine and gadgets, soft clothing and women, charming chatter, promenades and other perks of the good life, the Top Guns of America most easily reach for the *dolce vita* it may be Europe's destiny to provide.

Because the Americans are seen as the ones with planetary vision (a more attractive model than the Japanese); because the Europeans have only in the 90s begun to see a total market without nationality; for these and other reasons, European managers no longer dress in the style the Italians call *spezzato,* divided—sport coat and pants, "a style that signified our freedom from the uniformed American managers," Furio Colombo says. "You don't go to the office like that"—pointing *to me*—"any more." I have on . . . of course, Armani. Blue blazer, gray slacks. "Nowhere." With vehemence. "Not in Paris, not in Rome, not in Milano, not in Stockholm. There used to be a margin for intellectuality, for a freedom that European managers wanted to have and to show when compared to the more uniformed American managers." Colombo ends abruptly: "Now the American managers took over."

He is of course dressed in today's undivided style, wearing (because it's summer) a khaki linen three-buttoned suit—"three buttons because it's a little old-fahsioned"—he purchased off the rack "from the Torino shop called Olympics. No, no, no," he corrects himself. "It's a Cenci suit from Rome"—whose pants will take from an hour to half a day to be altered, I'm told. "American corporate organization is stronger than European," he says, "therefore Europeans appreciate it and imitate it, therefore they appreciate the style, too." But the cut of the suit and its cloth are different from a middle American, middle-class uniform—let us say, "sweeter."

The Americans also will wear a version of his suit, he thinks. They are attracted by Euro-life, by the idea of a quality of life that, in Europe, traditionally has been "softer, sweeter, more complacent"; therefore it's natural, Colombo thinks, that one may want to incorporate, even in one's working day, something softer and sweeter. "We work harder, maybe with better results, but with harsher life, and we want more compensation. There is a limit on how much you can compensate yourself with money so you want to compensate yourself with fringe benefits. Luxury is such a benefit."

This is not about Ferragamo shoes or Missoni ties. The deliberate melange of your clothing seems to be a recognition marker. It says of you that whatever your supposed home country and continent, you're part of a global class whose members are linked by borderless mass media, by an omnivorous consumption of *dolci,* and by first- or business-class travel made easy by your secretary. Space is not real to you, which we said in the introduction.

Clothing designer and author Allen Flusser, who dressed Michael Douglas for his *Wall Street* role, should know a few things about the world of corporate appetite and ambition. In his New York studio, between fittings of Concorde-flying publicist John Duka, former *New York Times* society writer, now deceased, Flusser treats me to a little discourse on world-class clothing:

> The people who write about clothes would say that there is a confluence of ideas that transcends national boundaries, an international thinking about what is a proper cut—

The proper, the only—the scholars call this logocentric thinking. To turn the world's diversity into a one. A *mine*.

> —an amalgam of English and American. These are the most elegant clothes that have ever been made, the silhouette known in the 1930s as draped clothing, popularized by the Duke of Windsor, Fred Astaire, Doug Fairbanks, Jr.

Two of those are actors. Which tells . . . ?

> The shoulders are a little wider, the chest has a breaking effect. It drapes in front and back. Look at the back of the coat.

He turns around for me. Duka has just said of Flusser: "Allen is very designed. From the tips of his black-and-white tie shoes to the bar in his collar and that black-and-white tie, he's a symphony of black, white and gray today."

> *FLUSSER*   It should break. I can move with complete freedom.

The look isn't exactly English, Flusser tells me. He thinks England doesn't have a national style any more, that the Savile Row tailors exert greatly reduced influence. In this, he is joined by Joseph Abboud, who, with more American bravado, says:

> We are seeing the influence from America creeping into English fashion just as it creeps into European and Italian fashion. We, the fashion leaders in this country, have taken the sensibilities and reinterpreted what we thought was English and given it back to them better than they gave it to us. If I saw, and you'll excuse the expression, a pee-green—

Since he's talking and I can't know the spelling of the word, he feels obliged to spell it out in words, not letters, for me:

> —and I don't mean the vegetable—urine-green tweed jacket, which is this yellowy-green shade which never sells, there's something that we could take and soften and make a little browner and make it more khaki, because the roots of something really great are there. As it exists in its purest form, it is not salable, but in the hybrid we create, it becomes more English than English. It's realer than English.

I mentioned earlier that these designers resembled intellectuals. Abboud is a half-step away from saying the word "hyper real," a key construct of postmodern theory.

> If we could see someone at his country home in England, reading the paper by a fire, his collie at his feet, we'd want to see him in the softened, browned pee-green, because that's how we visualize him.

Let's say straightaway: Current fashion wants nothing to do with a real, "pee"-green Englishman, if that's what he looks like. (Flusser also seemed offended by the real of Englishmen: "The well-dressed English," he told me, "tend to wear very dark suits, a bit strong shirt, and solid tie. Americans' ties are a little bolder"—as if

47

signifying, by contrast, the power depletion of the English.) Abboud is telling you that those who made planetary capitalism have made for its clothing—drawing from an England that is little more for designers than a museum, a depository of style—something realer than the real British, something more perfect than the real, a sort of utopian Englishness that short-circuits reality. If we were speaking in a technical language, we'd say that in the circulation of images of England, the referent, the thing itself, disappears. Only the hyped (up or down) images matter to us.

Everything Abboud just said to us tells that he considers himself a special-effects artist of clothing. And if he is right in judging his success, his effects destroy the cause. Which means that we are no longer interested in England, in origin. For the consumers of fashion, nothing seems to lie beyond the interpretation, its vision, of England. This means that if you wear one of these suits, or behold one, you'll never have the sense that it's a lie or a weak imitation. Since you'll never feel there's a "behind" to it, a depth or origin of it, it will be pure surface.

Pure surface, simulacrum, that you not only enjoy—you're euphoric over it.

> *Abboud* *Young Sherlock Holmes* was a wonderful movie to give a certain inspiration of a mood, a color, a tone. They had dinner. It was almost amber. Everybody was in their navy blazers. That's what we envision England as. We envision it as the most beautiful handknit sweaters and tweed pants, when you're up in the islands.

Little matter that you never go to the English isles.

But hand-knit sweaters aren't for the traveling men of this chapter. Let us return to Flusser. The elements that are common to all the men "who are now beginning to dress better," in his circumlocution, are suits with more ease to them "than Savile Row clothes." And with more shape, more architecture. Their shoulder, arm, and side lines seem to cut through the air. Fabric as knife. Whether they have vents—one or two—"or none at all, that's irrelevant." The suits are hard, not soft, in their evocation. Armani seems to be a dinosaur: You are not sincere in business dress; you are brutal.

> *Flusser* The best-dressed people in London, Paris, Milan, or New York all dress more or less in the same way. The international style is nothing more than powerful clothes, as I've described them, and powerful clothes are judged powerful in any of the countries, even if in Milan they're a fraction more square-shouldered and nonvented and the line a bit more linear. The man I'm talking about can jump on the Concorde and go anywhere and be recognized in certain circles as a guy who comes from money or has money.

And here is how money looks at you.

I had come before these arbiters in Armani jacket, the old broad-shouldered, gorge-lowered, chest-expanding power model, a Saks Fifth Avenue shirt under it. The shirt was about the only acceptable thing I had on. "The collar's not bad for you," Flusser says. "It has a certain amount of length, which is good for your face, which is soft."

There they go again!

He adds:

> Ferré and Armani correspond to what you call "in style," but to be in fashion doesn't mean you dress well. To be acceptable in a store, to wear the latest design from Armani, does not mean you dress well.

I am a New York Jewish intellectual, who, postmodern, wanted to assume another image. Why not? What stops me? This stops me—Flusser stops me:

> His [Armani's] clothes are obsolescent.

And Duka adds:

> As a person of any taste or intelligence or as a gentleman, you can't wear those clothes. They're clothes for hustlers. That's why they were given to Richard Gere to wear in *American Gigolo*. It's a California way of dressing. He's dressing these young guys that he knows or sees on the street, fantasizes about, or has working for him. He's dressing some sexual fantasy. It has nothing to do with being a man. It's some awful travesty.

Joseph Abboud, too, had chastised me: "I don't want a guy to look like he's got a coat hanger in his coat still." He had added of me: "We'll get you in our point of view. We should try to do something with you. I mean, one button has always been synonymous with being sharp clothing, a little fast. These guys are never fashionable."

I remember this as Flusser continues to fuss over my sleazy look:

> Fabric-wise, the Italian suit still tends to be, by American standards, a little faster fabric, a little slicker, shinier, not traditional by standards of English-American herringbones, classic fabrics. We have always associated more "creativity" with the Italian fabrics. There's more of a softness through the fabric.

As I begin to relax, thinking it was a compliment, looking me right in the shoulder, Flusser adds:

> But those are suits Sid Caesar would wear. We're talking wide shoulders. In those days when you made a lot of money, the idea in the late 40s, the early 50s, was the bigger the clothes the more you could afford. Think of Desi Arnaz. The shoulders would be out to here.

His arms outstretched.

Basically Armani is a women's wear designer.

No, he's a men's tailor who *then* began to design. He didn't feminize men, he virilized women. Armani: he armed women. He is famous, lest we forget, for the androgynous look, for the unifying constructedness he gave the sexes. But Flusser's not having it:

> *Flusser* His clothes drape off square shoulders very easily, like women's clothing. Europeans, who tend to be more narrow, squarer shoulders are fine on them. Americans with already broad shoulders, athletically oriented with big chests, need a softening effect. Therefore you make the shoulders more natural.

Armani and the Europeans are unnatural for us. And a suit's not culture, not a sign, it's another skin "that molds to your body and takes on your personality," says Flusser. We are full of signs, but the designer of some of them won't assume these signs, *as* signs. He is elaborating an ideology guaranteed by Nature, the Body, the Person, alibis functioning as a disguise, a mask imposed on the signs. Which ideology? A sales pitch for America. Flusser wants to take business from the Europeans. A major arena in which the American image isn't supreme is design. America struggles with Europe. New York with Milan, Paris, London.

When Flusser told me that "great clothes"—not the travesty I have on—"mold to your body, take on your personality," he revealed himself as modernist. High modernists believe in the ideology of style—what is as unique as your own fingerprints, as incomparable as your own body. By contrast, postmodernism—an attempt to grasp more recent sensibility—sees nothing unique about us. Postmodernism regards "the individual" as a sentimental attachment, a fiction to be enclosed within quotation marks. If you're postmodern, you scarcely believe in "the right clothes" that take on your personality. You don't dress as who you are because, quite simply, you don't believe "you" are. Therefore you are indifferent to consistency and continuity. Jean-François Lyotard, postmodern theorist, has written: "One listens to reggae, watches a western, eats McDonald's food for lunch and local cuisine for dinner, wears Paris perfume in Tokyo and 'retro' clothes in Hong Kong." Or Armani in the classroom. You self-consciously splice genres, attitudes, styles. The Intellectual as Italian Sharpie? Why not?

I first noticed the Italian look in the 70s, when there was more flexibility than today. I cling to it. It is coherent with my persona, which never wanted to be fully integrated into academia or accepted its styles of behavior, thought, and therefore dress. The Italian look is L.A.? I identify with L.A. With Nathanael West, who, as I remarked in the introduction, saw the fluidity of the person that would only in recent years become generalized across the States.

Let us say I admire the Angelinos for starting on that path where everybody walks now. But we have changed from their time. In Italy I told fashion ad man Nando Miglio why Hamnett designed uniforms—slick lycra body suits that make women look like reborn Emma Peales from the 60s British television hit "The Avengers." Hamnett told me: "Because [the body suit] is the perfect military blouson. Soldiers are powerful. Soldiers can tell people what to do. Like the perfect businessman. It's to do with an obsession with power because right now people have never felt less powerful and more threatened in their lives."

"I don't believe in those words," Miglio's telling me. I was in a James Bond suit, and Miglio, "Mr. Look," as he is called in Italy, was a study in beige: even beige "pull" (pullover to you and me) was on his back, the arms knotted loosely over his chest.

"I'm not the age any more to wear an officer's jacket," he says. "Well, maybe I do in summertime. But even in the past, when I was wearing something inspired by the military, I didn't feel different at all. I felt just . . ." His search for the *mot juste* is cut short by his assistant:

"He feels strong," she says.

> *Miglio*   No, no, no, I don't feel strong. If I wear safari jacket—
>
> *Assistant*   But if he don't feel it . . .
>
> *Blonsky*   So what is an outfit, then? What does it do? How does it make you feel?

What was I indeed feeling at that instant costumed as James Bond? What had I felt in the one-button Armani? In the great leather trench coat?

> *Miglio*   I never felt different. I felt just . . . okay.

Fashion makes you feel . . . okay? What does that mean?

> *Miglio*   It's a *clin d'oeil,* a wink—
>
> *Blonsky*   Just a gesture toward something?
>
> *Miglio*   Exactly.
>
> *Blonsky*   Never anything more?
>
> *Miglio*   It is nothing but that.

Fashion never does anything but make you feel okay, that is, coded, a member of a community. You spend hundreds on a costume, you cut off your old image and put on a new and do it all again, in order just to feel all right and keep inside a community that keeps shedding its second skin to put on a new one and whose members never feel powerful, rebellious, or any positive attribute at all. Nathanael West's "girl in slacks and sneaks with a bandana around her head" would today be winking at her costume, and so would we, watching her. And don't worry. No problem. We'll accept the artifice. Since many of us don't believe in jungles or any nature at all, since we don't believe that you've the soul of a hunter or any depth at all, how could we not wink back at your surface for a day?

If I admire the Angelinos, then all the more reason *for me* to take on their look, assuming I want a life adequate to postmodernism. But every designer I met, Armani included, told me, give it up. Each used different words for me—each, proposing a style for me, called me the same: American/Intellectual/Academic/Jewish. "Your face is a little soft"—"It's a California way of dressing"—here it is happening again in America. Rebuffed in my image construction. The conservative world of this chapter can't abide it when you step out of a character you never identified with to begin with.

Armani is not unmanly, but his softness is effeminacy to power back here. A tailor of the powerful and a former chronicler of their soirées are telling me that, teaching me the values of the American corporate elite. "Armani": Although his name suggests power, arms, armor, protection, he told me he didn't want to give an armor to impress, to show power and shout success. He told me he felt that there was a change taking place, in Europe but also overall in the industrialized world. "They'll eat their mama," he said, implicating the very Americans I am studying here. He thought that in the current doubt about the future, this was a moment to ponder—and he translated into fashion in front of me, by sketching, the texture and the style adequate for this ambiguous period. He showed me his cubist palette and I watched him draw his *griffe*, his line. "It runs down the body without sticking to it, giving the idea of a uniform, a second skin," he said. A softening of his already soft style. Clothes you want to enjoy, caress, and move in. Introversion. Style of pause and pondering as we thread our way into the 90s.

Not for the Americans who can't afford to pause, for whom pondering, that is, intellectuality, would be an unwanted brake. It's Flusser who's Armani, the armorer, and Duka, his friend, is now grounding this style in the nature of an epistemology:

> More men know about clothes these days—

That is, know what Flusser just told me:

> —but still nowhere near as many men who knew about clothes prior to World War II, when there was more of a sense of how to dress.

When there was a canon that hadn't yet broken. But then it split, creating numerous spaces for other images, for the fashion Other. It's this history Duka obscures, using historicity itself as his means:

> My father was an immigrant from Greece, and the clothes he wore were fabulous. He had wonderful, pale suits. There was more of a sense of how to dress prior to World War II.

Repetition in the service of nostalgia—postmodern trait.

Everything got destroyed.

No, it fragmented. From the viewpoint of the very rich, it became confused. Flusser and Duka are trying to impose coherence, impose their codes on me and the designer I came to admire.

Who, in his own way, imposed a point of view by saying we have to dress honestly. Why? What's honesty? A running line? A second skin? There is no reason to believe that one style is superior to another. To be postmodern: It means also to be sensitive to the chaos of our style ecology.

But fishing in the upmarket waters, the great designers can't afford to be pluralist. And neither can the corporate ruling elite. Here is designer Alexander Julian, picking up a bit of its uniform, a plain charcoal-gray square of wool. Like a salesman showing his wares, he crumples it, then opens up his hand. The cloth springs back into a square, not a wrinkle on it. "That's Tasmanian super-100 wool," he says (how much an inch?)—"which is that guy's [the top man's] suit. This megaworld deal maker is signifying that he is in command and control and that he is comfortable within his world. It is not possible to show comfort in anything that is tight. That is why there'll be movement in the silhouette of his luxury fabric."

Maybe he won't want to show comfort. Maybe he'll signify the sheer tension of colossal egos. Despite his attempt to stop time, Julian is only telling me that this is now, and tomorrow will be some other, and five years ago the crumpled look of cotton was classy.

Julian is telling me now "he'll wear fabrics that read 'not hard-edged'—like flannels rather than worsteds or serges. He'll want materials that absorb light rather than reflect it," because power absorbs everything, like a black hole. "He'll present a parodox, a direct and forceful unobtrusiveness." Paradoxes are for literature, not clothes, I think. Hasn't my quest all along been narrative? Who'll best fabulate? "The collar will look both pointed and spread—" Is it possible? Like those illustrations that blink as you pass—the eyes now open, now closed—now it's pointed, now it's spread. "—the dark silk handkerchief, you almost won't see." Because it's an empty vessel? Come on, Julian, he's a mythic vessel. We'd especially see his hanky if it tried to hide. We see *everything*. A surface is prey to our animal eyes—Ted Koppel teaches us that (chapter 12). "His look is between custom-made and old, off-the-rack clothes. It's studied, but the study was done offstage and you'll never realize it."

"His look is between" . . . "you won't realize": Julian is saying, with Koppel, that power wants to discharge all predicates. It would like to be hypnotic. After being with the top gun, you are not to remember the nature of his fabric or any of his details—he will present you with one, monumental, forceful Gestalt. Who is this archetype? Not once did a designer mention a proper name.

The writers of the historically important television series "L.A. Law," although creating some debonair figures, hadn't (for good reason) written in such a multinational prince when I interviewed for this chapter. What if they were to? I asked Shelly Levine (he picked the men's clothes for the show). How would you dress him—this man soon to be a major character in a CBS series?

"The men in this position would be too wrapped up in more important things to have their suits custom-made," he says. But Flusser told me, absolutely, custom-made. But then Colombo buys off the rack. My head's getting abuzz from Designerspeak. "A number of designers have come up with their look, Brioni, Armani, Cerutti." Am I hearing straight? Duka told me the Italians were unmanly. "They won't be dressed in the new British style with its dark gray colors, its stripes, its Prince of Wales plaids," he adds. There goes Julian's gray Tasmanian. There goes Flusser's Duke of Windsor. "He'll be in blue or black by way of establishing authority. Single or double-breasted, his suit will definitely have a vent. No vent would mark him as European, Italian."

But Armani doesn't usually like vents. An Armani that hides its Armaniness? Delicious. At last. The design concept starts to come apart at the seams.

Vent or no vent? I asked Anthony Merlino, Cerutti vice president. "A vent encourages you to use your hands to spread the back of the jacket. It tells you to put a hand in your pocket, strike a pose—what the French call *désinvolture,* ease. This man is too taut for that."

Julian said he was comfortable.

"His tie will be a foulard, or a very subtle stripe," Levine is telling me. Then what about Abboud's madder?

What about his shoes? I asked Merlino. Simple black lace—a cap toe, not a wing tip, rarely a loafer. "Same reason as refusing the vent." Then what of Colombo's loafer recalling New England?

Enough of this game. The designers had to contradict each other. Their mythic Top Man had to fly apart. Bonn-Tokyo Man was an invention, a groping toward a definition, a consolidation of something in the air; maybe even the creation of a new image with its sales and prestige value. Every designer claimed to be the One Who Knew. But each of these butlers of the rich, these servants who brush the shoulders of the rich as they travel the world, made a proposal to me. Offered a fictional code. Alexander Julian himself once winked in language and revealed it: "It's 30s and 40s Hollywood," he said, "which has a slight exaggeration and glamorization of the jacket silhouette."

So it's not true Brit, it's Hollywood Brit.

"So are we involved yet again in one more postmodern nostalgia, reviving the 30s, the 40s?" I asked.

"It's a factor, it's part of it," Julian said. "Brokered Brit. The broker is the American socioeconomic tradition of the last 50 years."

He means of course American economic and cultural power, which has been able to ransack the world for legitimation and chose "Britain" for awhile. Suddenly he says: "That frightened me. I don't want people to suddenly overanalyze what it is."

Cat's out. What it is *is* idealization. As Julian himself says in a moment: "You can't buy a type A suit." Type A is his name for my man.

I went to New York's Hermès to look for him. The month was August. The manager kept saying, "No, no, no," as men passed by her as we circulated in the store. "Don't they work in New York in August?" I asked. "Apparently not," she answered. Rubbish. Type A doesn't exist.

"There's not many of them on the street," Julian's telling me. "They're in an office or in a limo. There aren't many of them on the street. Come to think of it, there aren't that many of them around."

Julian and company are designing for a fashion show of power. I see them on the stage of my mind—the male models, terrifying black holes absorbing power. What you've been given is the prehistory of some look that doesn't exist, that may never exist. The designers are groping toward a code for those who would like to be powerful and can only afford the image. But there are no permanent and definite images or concepts of fashion. They are fluid, like postmodern society. The search coagulates every few years before it proceeds. In fashion as in postmodernity, you cannot hold onto anything. You have to flow and slide on the surface of this endless world, like an empty vessel of sorts, playing with different roles. All of these people who claim to be on top of it are simply trying to get hold of the market for a while. Sales as well as PR values.

But high-consumption capitalism requires a ceaseless transformation of style. Constant turnover. What is good today *mustn't* be tomorrow. As Christian Lacroix's short, happy life at the top teaches, styles have to be short-lived to make room for new styles, new consumption. (He made women baubles—even into the Grave 90s—sprinkling them with sweet-sweet smelling "C'est la vie!" in bottles whose stoppers are little red hearts.) Second law: The fashion of the day must be multiform. Styles, not style. All must be possible. No hegemony.

Although each of the designers I spoke to tries to dominate the market, none ever will. This is why Armani is called effeminate. The system gives him a space *but*—not, heretofore, too large a space. In the democracy of our advanced capitalism, everyone has a small room for a time. Except Armani, who is being given the house. Made Jesus Giorgio. Wait and see in these pages.

Portrait of the Model as an Endless Woman

2

Back from the road, I had an utterly clashing wardrobe, impossible to mix and match. Where was me? I wondered. What if there weren't one? What if I were a pure semiotic product? Or more than one?

Character and consistency were once the most highly regarded virtues to ascribe to either friend or foe. We all strove to be perceived as consistent and in character, no matter how many shattering experiences had changed our lives or how many persons inhabited our bodies. Today, for the first time in modern times, a split or multiple personality has ceased to be an eccentric malady and become indispensable as we approach the turn of the century. You can be conservative and circumspect, dressed in Chanel as a young woman. (And I want to speak now only of women—you'll see why.) In your middle years, you can become outrageous and wear a ten-gallon hat with your Chanel, or tattered jeans under your Russian sable. And when you're three times thirty, you can dress like a pre-Raphaelite virgin, hiding in paisley shawls and veils under a soft velvet hat.

Or even within a day, you can assume many authentic roles. In the morning, you can dress in Ralph Lauren, sipping your coffee in the manicured garden of your country manor. You can go to work in a Calvin Klein, all American crisp simplicity. In the evening, you can go to a dinner, dressed as a femme fatale looking like a bonbon wrapped in a Christian Lacroix. And you can slide into bed dressed in Helmut Newton, German expressionist lingerie, a promise of unbearable pleasures.

Models, given their mimetic ability to adjust to time, place, and interlocutor, are the forerunners of one of the most highly appreciated skills of our era: role playing. We're all expected to play roles in this postindustrial world, men as well as women. But women, because of history and experience, are the highest seeded in the game. And among women, models have made role playing a profession—and in some extraordinary cases, an art form. "In my 43 years in the business," said Ford Agency president Eileen Ford, "I don't think I can name you forty-three great models. They would have to be mind readers or emotion readers or probably both," she told me, defining the characteristics of a successful actor or role player.

In the fashion world, Dovima, Lauren Hutton, China Machado, Sunny Harnett, Dorian Leigh, and Suzy Parker would be at the top of this short list, together with figures such as Jean Patchett, Donna Mitchell, Carmen dell'Orefice, and Lisa Fonssagrives-Penn. These women have played different roles and have been different people at different stages of their lives. Some have continued modeling and others have become sculptors, executives, fashion designers, and family cornerstones. "A great model," Ford told me, "is a chameleon. She will respond to a different thought today and a different environment tomorrow. Their success, as a rule, has been predicted on their skills, not only on their beauty." "Irving Penn gave me a little story I would act out," said Jean Patchett of her early modeling in the 50s. "It was according to what the outfit was. Once I was in a Dior suit, holding an umbrella, standing on a street corner—Penn told me to hail a cab. It would be just a piece of white paper passing by that I hailed. I would be there trying to get the cab and looking for the cab. In another instance, I was in a theater and it was intermission. I was dressed in a Balenciaga, and he told me that my young man had gone out to get us an orangeade and hadn't come back. So I went out and I was looking for him, and there I was straining my neck and looking and looking and couldn't find him. Another day, I was at Cartier's looking at jewelry and there wasn't any there, but I was gazing intently as if at pearls and diamonds. Or I was in a restaurant and there was no young man, but I was making love to a young man in this restaurant."

Ms. Patchett is now happily married to a banker; they live half the year in Long Island and the other half in the California desert. They have adopted a child.

Carmen dell'Orefice has been a successful model for the last 45 years. In each stage of her life, she has played different roles according to both her looks and her moods. Nearing sixty, she is still a statuesque dream, posing with hieratic gestures. "I don't want to be a man," she said over lunch at New York's La Goulue, her silver mane slightly bobbing as she gestured over salmon *fumé*. "I don't want his job and I like to be responsive. I express all my creativity in being responsive." From the age of seventeen, she has played many roles before the eye of Norman Parkinson's camera. "While he was alive we always created a fantasy, which was either witty, funny, loving, plebian, abstract. I've had so many sittings with him over the years . . . we went through all the expression and development of a relationship that two people have who've lived together most intimately. There are many ways of making love."

Woman as the artist's model has been with us since the Renaissance, the beginning of the modern age. The artist and his model have a long relationship. Within that dynamic relationship, women have played that role consciously or unconsciously, deliberately or passively. Today, male and female alike must assume it consciously. We must learn the language of our times, the language of role playing. "A woman must continually watch herself," wrote the perceptive British critic John Berger in *Ways of Seeing* (1972). "She is almost continually accompanied by her own image of herself. Whilst she is walking across a room or whilst she is weeping at the death of her father, she can scarcely avoid envisaging herself walking or weeping. From earliest childhood she has been taught and persuaded to survey herself continually." This self-awareness today has extended to both sexes. No longer is a paunch acceptable in a man as a sign of *ventripotence* (belly power), nor is the stink of cigar easily forgiven or appreciated. Gigi, in Colette's novel, not only has to enjoy the cigar smoke as a sign of wealth, but also must be able to choose the cigar appropriately, in her role as a demi-monde beauty. Today we must all conform to the demands of physical beauty and have the intellectual ability to respond promptly to the demands of the social environment.

"One might simplify this by saying *men act* and *women appear*," wrote Berger, defining something that today has merged into a single androgynous identity. All of us today must both appear as well as act. "Men look at women. Women watch themselves being looked at. This determines not only most relations between men and women, but the relation of women to themselves. The surveyor of woman in herself is male; the surveyed female. Thus she turns herself into an object—and most particularly an object of vision: a sight." We are all sights in the modern world, which, as Lacan said, is omnivoyeur but not exhibitionist.

(But we're not all in the modern world. Those who are old, poor, infirm, unhip, deindustrialized, considered nerds or failures—you get the idea—need not apply. Jacques Attali alludes to them at the end of this book when he contemptuously dismisses St. Louis, Missouri, as another country, not a part of the America dreamt by Europeans (p. 470). St. Louis, metaphor of the other America—it, not a part of the United States of Capitalism. we've only begun to discuss).

In the archetype of the couple, both the observer and the observed are one and the same. The photographer and his model, in the fashion world, are an androgynous reality. In the beginning,

Plato saw man and woman as a single unity that only later was severed into separate sexes. The photographer and model exemplify the Platonic model. They bring each other to life in the photographic intercourse. In Antonioni's *Blow-Up,* the photographer and his model, Veruschka, the model née German princess, reach an artistic and erotic crescendo.

"He is my photographer but I am his model," Carmen explained, "and therein lies the truth of it. There is a healthy symbiosis and you use other senses besides the body." She is fully aware of the nature of the event. "There is a camera and a lens, which is the extension of the photographer's brain and what's in the photographer's psyche, and I'm in front of the camera and I'm looking and feeling and listening to the direction. I'm fitting into the landscape he has put me in and I become something within something."

Cecil Beaton was one of the early masters of fashion photography, a man whose camera was rather obtrusive in a European, British manner. It established too strongly a relationship of power in which the model did not see or feel herself. "I can remember a session with Beaton, being photographed for a cover with Carmen," said Patchett, talking to me from her Long Island residence just back from a golf game and remembering with a certain nostalgia her path-breaking career. "We got dressed up in these beautiful Norman Norell dresses and we went out and Mr. Beaton was there with a large eight-by-ten camera. He took three pictures and said, 'Ta-ta.' But Penn took about five hundred pictures and he used a Rolleiflex. This camera is rather intimate, a little camera. You look down into it and he sees you standing the way I'm actually standing, not upside down as in the eight-by-ten that Beaton preferred. I liked the Rolleiflex because it was small and not as intimidating as an eight-by-ten standing up there on a pedestal. I just felt very close to the Rolleiflex. I loved Penn for what he was and how good a photographer he was. He made me feel pretty. We had a communal relation but it was through the camera. It was like making love to a camera, not really to the photographer."

The patriarchal image of the artist, the photographer, has dominated the history of photography, an image originating in the magisterial role painters claimed over their models. Here is photographer Victor Skrebeneski as demiurge: "They [models] need directions and I'm here to direct, to see that they do what I think is visually correct for me. But it's my photograph. Iman gave what she always gives," he said, referring to a lingerie shot, "presence, beauty, posture, the reasons I work with her, mainly for the presence. She's statuesque, she fits my idea of Hellenistic sculpture, which is a favorite sculptural period of mine."

The fashion photographer Hiro, on the other hand, is fully aware of the other side of the coin—the model—without whom photography would not exist. "It's not just me saying I'm going to do this so

Figure 2.1 Donna Mitchell photographed by Hiro in the Craters of the Moon, Utah. "She reflected the landscape," Hiro remembers. "Look at her eyes. They seem to be moving back into the shell of her. Look at her mouth. She looks wasted." © *1968 Hiro. Donna Mitchell, Craters of the Moon, Idaho, 1968.*

you do that," Hiro told me. "I am waiting for what the model feels. I'm the one beginning the whole process but something has to come back. Back and forth, back and forth it goes. I'm watching them being made up, I'm watching them get their hair done, that's where I get the information. Each model is different, uniquely so, but even the same model is different at different times."

Hiro here is playing a passive, receptive role, one usually attributed exclusively to the model. "I am always watching very very carefully when I work with a model, even off the camera when we are having dinner together or getting ready. I watch very very carefully through the corner of my eyes. She starts posing. I get a lot of ideas from them. I'll think, 'That's interesting,' and I incorporate it."

Donna Mitchell, Hiro's favorite model, discovered for him the vastness of the Craters of the Moon in Utah. "It was a very difficult, desolate place to work. It's a volcanic wasteland. Standing there is like standing on a sponge. The earth has an enormous power of taking the energy out of you, and Donna immediately reflected the landscape, expressed the scene. Her eyes picked up the topography. Look, her eyes, she looks wasted," he says, pointing to the Mitchell photo he has found. "It's not the lighting, it's not the nose, nothing to do with the detail of an eyebrow, it's the eyes. Eyes have enormous expression and hers seem to be moving back into the shell of her. And look at the mouth. The two lips have lost their resilience, seem wasted.

"Something was happening between Donna and me. It wasn't conscious in my head. It's something like when you throw a ball and she throws it back, very quick. In a matter of five minutes it's all over. And the model has to carry half of the ball." The model, contrary to what most photographers claim, is not a passive object, not a thing in itself but a thing in relationship to the photographer, often breathing life into a fictional arrangement. Models bring photographers to life as much as they are brought to life by the Camera. "Finally one day I was standing in a street in Lima, Peru," Patchett told me, "and my feet hurt and I took my shoe off." At that point her photographer, Irving Penn, came to life. "He said, 'That's terrific.' Another time I had a big leghorn hat on and it happened again. I just sat back and took the pearls I was wearing in my hand put them in my mouth and I took my shoe off again and that picture won him an award." That happened 25 years ago and keeps happening every day. Model and photographer are the two poles of an electrically charged field.

The person holding the camera plays a male role, but sometimes you find a woman behind the camera. "Donna Mitchell understood my fantasies even before I did," said photographer Barbara Bordnick. "She was more experienced than I when I first worked with her. She was remarkably intuitive, she was brilliant. In the early 70s

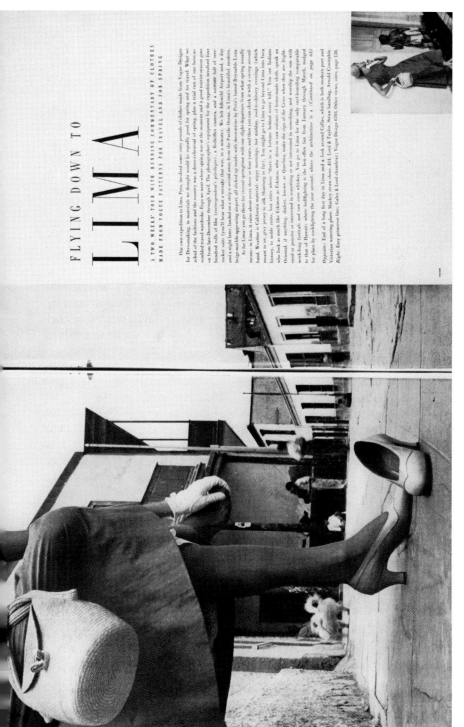

FLYING DOWN TO
LIMA

A TWO WEEKS' TOUR WITH RUNNING COMMENTARY OF CLOTHES
MADE FROM VOGUE PATTERNS FOR TRAVEL AND FOR SPRING

Our own expedition to Lima, Peru, involved some sixty pounds of clothes made from Vogue Designs for Dressmaking, in materials we thought would be equally good for spring and for travel. What we asked of the fashion and the country was a dress-rehearsal of spring, plus a trial run of our forear-rusabled travel wardrobe. Ergo we went where spring was at the moment and a good-natured helpful crew on from late-December through April. The photographer's assistants, a camera, and expedition-load of two hundred rolls of film (correspondent's privileges). A stateless... eighty-nine items, a wardrobe full of seer-sucker suits (you'll hear what a mistake that was)... the Pacific Ocean in Lima's beautiful, modern, and a night later, landed on a strip around sixteen, with decorations by Peru's famed Reynaldo Luza, large-marble-appearing airport, all decked up snugly with one-night departures from what spring usually means: in Lima, it rains about every three or four years, and then you can deck it with a creepy second-hand. Weather in California mysticale: nippy mornings, but midday, cool-to-breezy evenings (which meant to us, grey jersey in silk. Slumming, by fact). You might go to Lima to go beyond Lima into Inca history, to noble ruins, but cities where "there is a fortune behind every hill." You see Indians who look as much like Eskimos as Quechua, make the sign of the Cross when they are fright- Oriental, if anything, in their dialect, known as Quechua, make the sign of the Cross when they are fright- ened or genuine and raw corn whiskey. You go to Lima for the only surf-boarding comparable week-long festivals where bullfighting is the box-office lure from January through March, nudged to that of Hawaii; where the architecture is a *(Continued on page 65)* for place by cockfighting the year around; where the architecture is a *(Continued on page 65)*

Opposite: End of a long first day in Lima and a look around Callao, which is both modern port and Victorian watering place. Monkey straw shoes, $18. Lord & Taylor. Straw handbag, Arnold Constable.
Right: Easy princesse line. Galey & Lord chambray. Vogue Design #703. Other views, view, page 126.

Figure 2.2

Figure 2.3 Donna Mitchell, seated, with a little help for her friends. If this scene were synesthetic, you might be hearing Ravi Shankar on the sitar and Ala Rakha on tabla. An icon of lost time. *Courtesy Barbara Bordnick.*

Donna, two other models, and I were on the beach for a *Harper's Bazaar* shooting for which the editor and I had decided on an East Indian theme. So we got the kind of Indian jewelry made of gold pieces that, when banged against one another, make wonderful, light, musical noise. Donna, sitting on the sand, shook the jewelry and began to hum. Carol and Eva, the two other models, began to dance. They were all wearing long billowy skirts and tops. Everything was moving in a slow rhythm, the models' arms at the right time photographically. Donna's tinkling sounds set the pace and mood I needed. It was perfect fashion for *Harper's Bazaar* editorial."

Some models, like the late Lisa Fonssagrives-Penn, consciously contribute to the mood and accuracy of the fashion photos. "I would look at myself in the dressing room mirror before going on the set and instinctively try to solve the photographer's problem," Fonssagrives-Penn said, referring to a shooting session for *Vogue* in Paris in the late 30s. "I would look at the cut of the dress and try different poses to see how it fell best, how the light would enhance it, and basically try to create a line the way one starts a drawing. I would objectify myself and become more of a director than an actress."

The model assumed both sexes, was both the observer and the observed, became her own photographer. "I became this girl and not Lisa Fonssagrives. So that when I saw the contacts I would think: 'There that girl stands correctly, there she looks awkward . . .' It was a kind of game, the exchange that takes place through the lens. This is why I hate the word 'shooting.' It implies something so one-sided and impersonal. It was never a 'shooting,' but a sitting or a séance.''

Fonssagrives-Penn, during her career, has played several roles. She has been a dancer, a director, a model, and a sculptor, not to mention her creative relationship, on and off the stage, with Irving Penn, her husband.

A genius, Scott Fitzgerald once wrote, is one who can hold two contradictory ideas in the mind and not go crazy. Today, one can hold not two but four or more contradictory roles in one's life and not go crazy. Quite the contrary: live a much fuller life. Hollywood, like most things American, is the forerunner of change in social mores, and was even in Nathanael West's time in the early 30s.

Photographers' models have been playing this game for over a century, a game that only now the rest of us are beginning to understand and play. Models such as Carmen, Jean Patchett, Lisa Fonssagrives-Penn, or China Machado have been changing role skins for half a century. In one of her earliest roles, Jean Patchett takes us back to the 50s, when models were not celebrities as they are today, but were often perceived as glorified call girls.

''I was studying at Goucher College in Maryland, when a friend of mine told me, 'Why don't you go to New York and be a model?' I went home and talked it over with my parents. The glamour attracted me more than my studies. Modeling, quote unquote, in the little town on the eastern shore of Maryland where my parents lived, was not very well looked upon. They never thought of it as being a very good profession. My family thought that all models were really call girls. I think that was what the connotation was of that word on the eastern shore of Maryland or in New York City. And I remember one thing, there was a young girl who came to New York and she got herself in trouble.''

Jean Patchett and the other models of the period were creating a space for professional modeling in this country, what has become a respected and highly paid career in the 80s. They broke ground for models like Paulina Porizkova, Isabella Rossellini, and Cindy Crawford, all celebrities of the 80s. Today, a model like Jerry Hall both poses for fashion and entertains British royalty in her Chateau de Fourchette in the Loire Valley, quite different from the life of most postwar models. ''When we first started out in 1949,'' said Patchett, ''we were only paid $12.50 an hour for editorial work. Commercially, if we were doing an ad, let's say for in the front of the book, we were paid $60 an hour. And finally, four or five years after I started, *Vogue* got up to being $25 an hour, which we fought for.''

She also fought for a respectable model image. ''You'd go to work and you were ready to be put in front of the camera in a very reasonable time and not have them pay you for the time which you should have been at home putting your hair up and getting your makeup on. Today, I gather that part of the sitting is for makeup artists and hairdressers to fix the girl's hair. I guess they don't mind paying all that money. It's such an expensive business today compared to back then. We were paid very well but we weren't paid what the girls are being paid today. Even so, I did not wear dungarees and tennis shoes. Our hair was coiffed and our makeup was on and we were ready to go. I felt that if I was going to be a model, I should look like a model at all times, dress and wear white gloves, wear my shoes, my high-heeled shoes, go to work looking like a model."

"Well, that had to do with their class demarcation, white gloves basically were a class symbol," Alexander Liberman, editorial director of Condé Nast Publications, told me. "It meant gentility and that had a lot to do with early fashion magazines. Condé Nast himself had to check if somebody was in the *Social Register*. If the names were in the *Social Register*, it was okay to photograph them for *Vogue*. Ladies in finishing school or young girls were taught to wear white gloves. Correctness, manners, all of this has been erased. Of course there are other manners that exist but the kind of manners that demanded the string of pearls, white gloves, the little black dress, have been erased. This was the correct behavior that separated you from other classes, frankly aping aristocratic manners. The queen of England, who has to shake a million hands, always wears gloves. You seldom see the queen of England with no gloves. You don't sully yourself basically. It's a status symbol. *Vogue* editors had to wear hats, but the secretaries were not allowed to wear hats. The war changed everything. Women had to work, they had to take men's jobs, and some went into factories and in general the whole concept of the unsoiled hand that went with the white glove is finished.

"Democracy does not want anything to stand out," Liberman insisted. "Today, readers and editors resent strangeness, affirmation of difference. So we are back to a sort of cultural leveling in many ways." A cultural leveling that allows us today in our open society to go from one class or professional outfit to another. This breakdown of class dressing is also evident in male fashion. In a recent exhibit at New York's Fashion Institute of Technology, a rainbow of male roles was displayed, independent of income or social position. The show, entitled "Jocks and Nerds: Men's Style in the 20th Century," offered a typology of ten different clothing styles from the worker and the rebel to the cowboy and the dandy, passing through the businessman and the hunter. The appearance, the surface, of America has become more democratic, independent of the number of digits of your income.

In less than five years, Jean Patchett played different roles and traveled extensively. In 1949, dressed in black—black gloves, black hat, and black dress—she sees her future unfolding in a pack of tarot cards. A year later, she poses menacingly, doing her best not to smile and reveal her youth. In that same year, we see her in a Peruvian cafe in the Andes munching her pearl necklace, apparently bored or coquettish next to her wine-sipping escort. From there she flies to colonial Trinidad in Cuba, where she ambles in a Panama hat surrounded by enormous flowers. Back in New York, wearing a sacerdotal hat, her face covered in a net and a scarf around her neck, she readies herself for a night at the theater.

Carmen, her contemporary, has never stopped traveling or changing outfits. When she was in her early teens, Salvador Dali was the first to use her as a model. "He was at the St. Regis and he would take me to Pavillon for lunch after he would paint me or draw me. I saw him a year and a half before he died, and we remained friends right to the end, even through all the terrible things that went on." Her early career in modeling began with Cecil Beaton, and she has been the model of photographers such as Horst, Avedon, Victor Skrebenski, Scavullo, and Norman Parkinson. Parkinson, who had worked with her in her early career, rediscovered her at fifty. "In 1978, Parkinson remembered that I was alive. We had dinner one night at the Colombian Coffee House on Fifty-seventh Street. And he said: 'For an old bag you don't look so bad. I think that we ought to do something together.' And I said: 'Well, listen, you're such an old fart, if you can still get it up, I'm up for it.' And that's how we always talked with each other. Until he died, I didn't stop working with him, for French *Vogue*, *Town & Country*, and for cosmetic and fashion ads."

In 1985, at the time of the Claus von Bulow scandal, *Vanity Fair* had von Bulow play the role of the rebel in the leather jacket, photographed by Helmut Newton. Von Bulow later appeared next to Arnold Schwarzenegger in the "Jocks and Nerds" catalogue. That very year, *Town & Country* sent Carmen and Parkinson to Newport, Rhode Island, for a photo session at a von Bulow–like mansion. "I lay on the steps with my head down as if I had fallen down the stairs," Carmen told me, remembering the scene with amusement, "and Parks had people drop this coat as if I had fallen and the coat were falling after me. It looked like I had just fallen down the stairs. It was really too much. They couldn't publish it politically, because this man was accused of murdering his wife and was still on trial."

Carmen has played many roles, has been a nymphet for Dali, a powerful Roman matron for a high-fashion display in an Italian rotunda, a grande dame for *Town & Country*, the Mad Woman of Chaillot for French *Vogue*, the innocent debutante for *Harper's Bazaar*, a gracefully aging beauty for Revlon. She has been, like the phoenix, reborn from her own ashes a dozen times in her lifetime. She has been a woman for all seasons. "At fifty I went to French

Figure 2.4 "I help to create a fantasy. It can be witty, funny, loving, plebeian, abstract. I become something within something else." *Carmen Dell'Orefice.*

Vogue and of course the French, thinking that a woman, whatever her age is, if she is right in her skin, has integrity, it shows. It doesn't matter the age. If you're right at five years old, it shows. That's all we can do. . . . I know people my age who look like Methuselah. We cannot change our genes, but we can do with them and our mind what science helps us to do with our bodies. I do things intuitively and not architecturally, not figuring out how I put my elbow on the table and my finger in my mouth, but using you as the mirror for myself. A woman knows at a certain point not to wear a décolleté, I know I wouldn't expose my flesh the way I did when I was young, because I have a different view of the parts of me that are attractively exposable today, not by anybody else's standards but by my own. We are designing ourselves constantly, and if we could do it with some creativity and excitement and fun, then women wouldn't feel so awful about aging. They never lived enough and enjoyed their flesh when younger and they don't enjoy the aging flesh. Mine ages like everyone's. Everybody says, 'Oh gosh, you look so wonderful and you don't look your age.' I am my age, I've had a lot of experience, I've had three marriages, one child, some other experiences along the way, a mother and a father and responsibilities and death and dying and aging and I am me.''

Age is just another role, not a catastrophe. We can be reborn again and again, men and women alike, as long as we change with the seasons and act to fulfill our fantasies. This is the American in me speaking. In the next chapter, our European eyes look apalled at how we eat.

My Life
3
as an
Underground
Gourmet

One summer evening not long ago, I rang the Greenwich Village doorbell of a woman who had been the Underground Gourmet of a popular magazine, and is now doing important other things. I had an appointment to interview her about American attitudes toward the trinity of gourmet appetizers—caviar, smoked salmon, and, third in rank, foie gras.

The woman (whom we'll henceforth call UG) had entirely forgotten the appointment, and when I showed up at her door, was eating dinner with her husband. Embarrassed and irritated, she half-welcomed me inside, offering me a place at the table that soon reminded me of Peter Sellers's in *The Party*. In that movie, Sellers plays an Indian in La La Land who, arriving at a star's dinner party uninvited, finds no room at the table nor even a chair available in the dining room. No problem—the exuberant blond male star installs him on a child's chair at the corner in front of the swinging door to the kitchen. Sellers's chin is barely above the tablecloth, and every time the servants enter with a new dish he is shoved, face and chest on the table, apologizing profusely to the profuse and beautiful women right and left.

"There's no dinner for you, but sit down, I can find soup," UG motioned to me and I did. I knew it would be an evening in which my American values would clash with French arrogance and sensuality. The arrogance in the form of rude honesty was already there: forgetting I was coming, depriving me of a share in the meal I never expected to join. On the little breakfast table for two was my bowl of lentils near her husband's plate of steak with peppercorn sauce, a little sausage for piquancy by its side. I was mildly shocked and amply pleased to see her come my way with a plate. "This is all there is," she said, as I dismissed the soup bowl. On the plate was a junior steak, also with a bit of peppercorn sauce, and I was happy as any traveler at a mealtime inn. Maybe it wouldn't be a clash after all.

Dinner over, her husband retired, and the elegant, forty-something gourmande and I retired as well—to her living room of marble fireplaces and parquet floors, their grandeur warmed by lacquer bowls of fruit and the right flowers clustered hither and yon as if arranged in fidelity to some *HG* layout. An ample bar near the mantel testified to the concern for the comfort of guest and host alike. God was in his heaven and not unpleased with this tasteful woman. We began the interview, seated on a decorative sofa, the two bodies turned toward each other to discuss luxury number two, smoked salmon (a topic that would have been humiliating, had I a belly only full of soup).

"You don't chew salmon, you squeeze it between your tongue and your palate," UG is telling me. "It has to disintegrate in your mouth, melt away. And the taste has to linger. It's like drinking a very good glass of Bordeaux. Once you've drunk it, it's not gone—you still feel it in your mouth. The taste is still excited by the encounter with this wonderful fish. But the incredible lingering of taste should be faint. You have to go"—she makes the sound of unseen saliva gobs as she opens her mouth, demonstrates the tongue-salmon-palate sandwich from which you only suck the salmon juice. "It's something you want to recall rather than something you actually taste. If you taste, it's cheap salmon," she says.

I was having cheap ideas. There was too much intimacy in her description of food, too much erotic saliva for one trained mainly in visual sensuality, from luscious food to shining bodies, but removed from touch and oozing liquidity that reminds one of idiots dribbling, or the saliva between two mouths after a kiss. But I refrained from polarizing the interview. I wanted to appreciate salmon. I wanted to learn how to suck it and how to recall its essence.

Now I remembered my semiotic master Louis Marin, in Paris, telling me what the present is, for Aristotle: "It's the invisible, ungraspable limit between past and future, it's nothing." The salmon pops in and I never even tasted it; it's a remembrance. To an American, trained for sharp, pungent, explosive, sweet and sour tastes, that's unthinkable. For us, the pleasure is one of being overwhelmed by flavor, not teased by subtleties.

"Salmon's a tissue," UG is saying. "Do you know what a clementine is?" I shake my head. "A clementine is one of those extraordinary, magnificent tangerines. The skin is a membrane so delicate that the juice of the inside of each little segment of it can go through. It's like a net." I couldn't stop making the wrong associations: membrane, to me, was the hymen of virginity. I began to think of the deflowering of a virgin.

"I want an orange," she says, interrupting, her desire imperious.

What American would announce desire so emphatically? But apparently oblivious of any reading I'm doing, my host and inductress walks to the fruit bowl at the other end of the long room and, as if I needed another metaphor, over her shoulder throws: "It's like good poetry."

Something about the sweet smell of the clementine—my sense of smell seems never to have been so acute—is troubling me as she slowly peels the outer skin away. That smell and the mouth that never stops talking of salmon are like a double stop in violin playing, like a fourth, which is the virtuoso's ever so vulgar way to evoke the *dolce,* the sweetness of life. An American in the Paris of Greenwich Village is beginning to die of duration and *dolci.*

"I did a story on smoked salmon and somebody introduced me to a young lord, this third or fourth son, impoverished, who had gone to Oxford and come back and decided he wanted to smoke salmon. And he brought this plate of thin but roughly cut salmon and I put it in my mouth and I thought, 'My God, I never knew what smoked salmon tasted like before!'" Her voice is hushed. "It was so delicately smoked, so transparent, so"—seeking the word—"soft." She has a husband upstairs, I'm costumed in tie, chinos, yellow foolscap, and pen. I'm a man of the tape recorder, if not cloth, and, *tant pis,* I hadn't come prepared for this transmigration into . . . *it.* The American I was had forgotten that food is the Great Metaphor, able to transport us to the sexual. Why? Because, after all the joys of this or that sex, the act remains a tad or more embarrassing. Genitals and nether parts still surprise—creatures from some deep—as they emerge from spandex, Calvin briefs, and other l.a.wful gear. No Pill or shrink has borne us to an *ars sexualis,* sex remaining a parallel world, as distant and near as those Territories you'll meet in Stephen King's chapter 15. Therefore, to get there, we have to "flip," as in King's Talisman, drink the equivalent of his "magic juice." Which is . . . food. Dinner ("Hi, it's Jim, Jane, Don, Donna, I'd like you to have dinner with me next . . .") is the Great Pretender, the Naturalizer, the Metonymy that absorbs our lust into this okay activity ("I mean, you've got to take a break for dinner, right?") which is a step in a narrative requiring resolution, a consequence, an end ("Boy, wasn't that shrimp something?"—"Would you like a drink at my place?"). Disguise, disguise, disguise until one of the two summons the courage for . . . not a kiss but the head brought close to the other's, made a close-up, an emboldened message (OKAY OKAY OKAY?). It tricks the superego, flipping us into Territories in which one wonders, 'How did we ever take so long to get here!' Convivial eating, that Grand Deception, Deferrer of the Unsayable, becomes because of that—from appetizer to dessert and passing through shared forks—the vibrant metaphor of crawlly flesh we do everything to conceal.

Whence the jokes, oh, the sexist jokes. Take Rodney Dangerfield:

"My wife heard that food is a substitute for sex—she put a mirror on the dining room wall."

"You know," UG is saying, "the softness wasn't a disintegrating softness. It was a softness that has some texture to it. It was as if you ate every thread of a loom, as if somehow you could distinguish all the elements that made that piece of cloth and all the elements that made this thing were disintegrating in your mouth to give this sensation. It was the best salmon I've ever had in my life."

I was beginning to feel uncomfortable. The Puritan and the glutton within me found it too much indulgence in the idea of food. To me, a good meal is steak and spaghetti sauce with a scotch. I have barely and with revulsion learned to refer to spaghetti as pasta. I wish I could discourse on food like the great ideologue of food, Brillat-Savarin, when actually I can only appreciate the prose of Roland Barthes. I remember late at night in my apartment ordering greasy obnoxious Chinese takeout food while enjoying the subtleties of Barthes on BS, as he called him: "True to his philosophy of essence, BS attributes to ozmazome a sort of spiritual power—it is the very absolute of taste, a sort of meat alcohol, as it were; as a universal (demonical?) principle, it takes on sundry and seductive appearances; it is ozmazome that produces the very *roue* of meats, the browning of roasts, the gamey scent of venison; most importantly, it makes the juice and the *bouillon*, direct forms of quintessence (the word's etymology refers to the joint notion of smell and *bouillon*)." Only now can I admit to myself that I belong to a different cosmology of taste.

I pretend I understand French food but I really only love meat and new potatoes. The other day, when I was with a young lady careful about her figure and diet at the French-owned *Le* Parker Meridien in New York, I couldn't keep my eyes off those glittering nickled orbs that contained fowl in white sauces and veal in brown juices, crude American forms of medieval gourmand pleasures. Like one of those grotesque monks in *The Name of the Rose* whose sexuality could only be fulfilled in food, I kept returning for seconds of meat and potatoes while she munched endives.

Heedless of my invisible meat and potatoes, my hostess continues: "The white chevrons are fat, like veins of fat in beef. The taste of the tissue . . . we say *onctueux* in French."

"Unctuous? Oily?" I couldn't help going back to my ancestral Jewish cooking.

"No." Impatient with the literal translation. *"Onctueux* is to slide. It's so smooth that there's not a ridge, not a ripple in the texture. And that's why I'm saying, when you put this salmon in your mouth and it melts, it's as if you're going back to the simplest element."

And to my shame I invoke the Master: "The maternal suck, as Barthes would have said."

"I know. If it were an atom, you would go back to the single atom that made that salmon. But this is very rare," she sighs.

It all seems like poetry to me, abstracted from my America of Stephen King sucking his vomit back up again (page 364), so I ask, concretely, how do you accomplish all this?

"You feel it between your tongue and palate. You go—"

I: "Between your tongue up he-e-uh—" Because my tongue is at the roof of my mouth, I'm losing articulated language.

She: "Go li-i-ke th-i-th." She is talking with Proustian recollection. I see her mouth full of imaginary food.

"You press your tongue against your palate"—it's as if she's commanding a penetration—"and somehow it's the contact of you with you, and the salmon in between—"

!

"—that makes it. Uhm," she grunts softly. "It's like eating caviar."

Why do I keep feeling uncomfortable? Why can't I surrender to the taste, the imagery, and the remembrance of the gourmet pleasures?

"The greatest joy of eating caviar is to take a spoon and dip it in a bowl of caviar," she's saying, "and put it in your mouth, and then crack all the eggs under your teeth. One by one. That is the most sensual thing that can exist."

"The most sensual?" I say.

"Uh huh."

"More sensual than sex?"

"Um, yeah."

"Why?" Almost a yelp from me.

From UG: "The pleasure can be very long. Did you ever try it?"

I could have tried it at her place, she having been a food critic and all that. We thus return to the idea that caviar served to a guest is the opposite of the experience that I, a pseudo-guest, endured in her home. What we discussed, I regret to say, was the idea of caviar, not caviar. There I was with a princess of gastronomy and what I imbibed was the sign of caviar, not caviar; the sign of hospitality— bean soup and a bit of meat— scarcely hospitality in that rich house. For the function of caviar, about which we were speaking at table, is to salute one's guests, to include them in a tiny community of the unique where they can imagine themselves stars, celebrities, top of the heap, the very content of American desire. Bring out little pups in a blanket and watch the expression of your guests. Bring on the beluga, the sevruga or the osetra, and it will be a consecrating gift, silently coding your guests as American royalty. I was at table, superficially included, in fact excluded, as I watched her husband eat serious steak and drank my little porridge, talking caviar.

No sour steak from this quarter. After all the restaurant meals I had eaten, interviewing, before coming to this house (only to mention lunch with the models and dinner with the designers) meals had come to seem to me like an endlessly repeated affair. Sex with a spouse, a porn tape viewed for the fiftieth time. I had no desire for yet another meal, even that of a gourmet. The pleasure of food was no longer mine, talking overriding tasting. Which made the ritual potential of food all the more acute.

So there I was in the Village, ready to discuss salmon, caviar, and foie gras, three foods about nothing *but* salutation to guests, their inclusion in communities of desire, beneficence, *luxe*. There I was, given the *signs* of these delicacies—a crust of bread, so to say, floating in soup next to He Man steak. (It goes without saying, it would have been a feast in the Third World.) Might as well, like Peter Sellers, be sitting in a chair four inches too low, slapped in the head with the kitchen door every time a waiter goes by. Since, on my chair, I was in the realm of signs, I crazily started rewriting the script of *The Party:* Put the Other, the excluded Sellers, in a chair six inches too high—he'll eat stooped over in perpetual supplication.

"The pleasure can be very long," she had said, connoting sexuality. For extravagant food, like sexual refinement, is a perversion. And this, perhaps, is another source of its metaphoric power. Perversion is the exercise of a desire which serves no end, like that of the body given over to lovemaking without any idea of procreation. In his 1825 *Physiology of Taste,* Brillat-Savarin, remarked that on the one hand there was natural appetite, of the order of need, and on the other, appetite deluxe, which is of the order of desire. We have a *need* for procreation to survive, the individual has a *need* to eat to subsist; and yet the satisfaction of these two needs doesn't suffice us: we have to stage the luxury of desire, amorous or gastronomic. Again I think of Roland Barthes, the phantom to whom this book is secretly dedicated, who wrote of Brillat-Savarin that *luxe* is an "enigmatic, useless supplement," that desired (versus needed) food is "an unconditional loss, a kind of ethnographic ceremony whereby man celebrates his power, his freedom to burn his energy 'for nothing.'"

So, muted by the eroticism in the room, when UG, my personal BS, asked, had I ever cracked each and every caviar egg, I softly said no.

"You should try it. Take a teaspoon—you have to have it for breakfast."

Is she mad? Breakfast after you stumble out of bed, weak from sleep's psychosis, the more excessive amongst us feeling like dragons throwing flames of whiskey at the image in the mirror about to brush its teeth? Caviar certainly is not my idea of breaking the fast at sunrise.

Sunrise, *American* sunrise: breakfast pleasures echoing through years of magazine ads of steaming coffee, crispy bacon (today, bacon substitute), and enticing eggs with their sunny side up—still lives reinforced and given the prestige of motion pictures by television commercials in supersaturated moving color.

"You roll the caviar in your mouth and, one by one, you crack those eggs. It's incredible," she says.

The obvious question:

"What happens when you crack the eggs?"

"There is a great sensation of achievement. Glory. Magnificence."

Her way of telling you that caviar punctuates the present—it was an expostulation of triumph. Breaking the eggs objectifies this meaning.

I ask: "Is there anything inside the eggs you're—"

"Oh yes! I mean, there is an explosion of taste. Of life that never shall be born."

She laughs and I say: "One more sturgeon that won't—"

"Uh huh."

"—come into being."

"Ye-ep."

Later, trying to use the experience to teach French culture through the culinary, I find my students revolted. It's icky, it's ugly, they say. "That's gross!" a woman expostulates.

It's ugly because interiorized. American taste is dominated by advertising, and advertising appeals to the visual and the social. The gorgeous red lobster and the black pearls of caviar, surrounded by ice nesting in a silver bowl, have more to do with wealth, status, and conviviality than with our taste buds and the remembrance of things eaten.

The French love the idea that they're crushing every caviar ball, that it's like chewing newborn sturgeon. The French not only are visceral, they're intellectual—like doing it, love talking about it. They love their tongues so much they can't decide whether to taste or talk with them. Think about our food critic on the sofa with me crushing the little balls. Her language now is very little sensual; it has more to do with a conception of caviar, as unborn sturgeon. If you're a real sensualist (something I learned to be much later), you don't as you chew sense anything unborn. The impression is entirely actual, present, a slightly salty earthy taste, like the sea but like the mother earth below the sea, the marinely telluric. Even we Americans can train ourselves to imbibe its unique texture, smooth yet with little moments in it. For sure, eating caviar isn't downing white bread or chocolate pudding—through and through smoothness absent punctuation.

My students, on the other hand, believed in the exquisite beauty of caviar; the idea that it's prestigious, that only the rich have it, that you put it in a silver bowl on ice, that it's lustrously gray like tiny pearls. (The good stuff isn't black.) But once it enters our body and I gave the other part of the idea, once I *deepened* the idea, once the image disappeared because it was inside the mouth, it was then that my students expelled the idea. Let's be outrageous and say: Americans can't stand the idea of profundity. If it's not superficial, the stuff of image, we reject it. Because once it's in your mouth, why of course there's no more image; nothing for an American to love. Everything to hate. Once the caviar left the visual world it became offensive to Americans, who, had they been French, would have been enriched by the tale. Americans live in movement, driven to action by advertising imagery, whereas the French still sit back and ponder, that is to say, talk.

Two codes, the American visual and the French linguistic/ sensuous. Still today, the French are more sensuous than we. They enjoy food more, therefore have to ponder it; they have long hours for lunch and like to talk and drink as they eat. Americans buy French wines and foods but don't enjoy them; don't have the palate or vocabulary by which to enjoy. Anyone old enough to have lived here when Americans didn't drink wine, when they didn't take brie, might have said—noticing the recent advent of French wines and foods—"Oh, we're having more wine, we're having cheeses. How relaxed we're becoming, how civilized."

Not so. Our problem is, we don't enjoy our wine. We have only seen it in elegant environments and thus think it's sophisticated; and are competing with one another to see who knows more about wine. But we cannot really taste it. We Americans eat with our eyes and react to crude overdoses: ice cream, potato chips, chocolate.

Our hostess is saying to me: "Did you ever have salmon caviar?" and I shake my head. "I'll give you some," she says and walks to the end of the room where the orange was and returns. "Then you can tell me how it tastes." Big shining orange balls in front of me, a film on them. "Try it. Salmon caviar is starting to become the caviar—"

"Here I go."

"—of the poor as leek is the asparagus of the poor."

"I bite into each?"

"Uh huh," she says.

I'll say. But I don't say, out of politeness. It's fishy tasting, and there's a stickiness in-between and over the eggs. I am puncturing, not the eggs at first, but this film as if, in a horror film, protecting the alien hatchlings.

So I sit there with my fingers in my mouth, ashamed to retrieve the cracker on which are the shining, orange—God knows what they look like now—balls. Since I am unable to bite, swallow, or expel, they remain suspended in mid-Atlantic between France and America.

The unexpected contact with the real and not its sign taught me that, in fact, it wasn't the real thing at all. For most Americans, as for my students, caviar is a myth of inclusion amongst the ever evolving Ralph Lauren set; it's a door slammed on failure and relapse. All your appetite and ambition, your search for an image succeeded, says that luminous lump on the plate; now it's caviar not Miller time. Given our need of myth, our appetite for signs, our (forgive me) palate illiteracy, we Good Housekeepers and Gourmets can save our dollars. We can give a substitute, a sign for caviar: orange balls. And no one's to know that the only thing worse we could do is give our guests lumpfish eggs, those little things that you get, seventy-nine cents a jar, at the supermarket. The jar says "CAVIAR" and then: "Made from lumpfish eggs," in tiny letters. It has nothing to do with caviar, and once again we learn that a sign can be used to lie. It's a splendid way to deceive.

So, with a mouthful of signs, that is to say, nothing, I boarded the subway in search of dinner. New York is intense and unremitting. Even in the winter it feels hot with fever and delirium. Tonight it was a frenzied jungle. Shrieking, the E train was boiling us, garish shades, glancing at all costs at the billboards and not one another. Shoved out the door by the press of people behind, I heard the train clank and whistle away, and glanced back where it had been, and I thought I was looking at the sufficient sign of the subway. As you look across the tracks, you see four ranks of pillars cutting the space, forming what looked like a penitentiary cellblock. Under harsh fluorescents, past the empty whiskey and Coke bottles that tell how lazy some of us are, I gratefully climbed up the steps of the Fifty-ninth Street stop, Columbus Circle. Outside, the space was packed with strollers, hustlers, card cons, cops, sleeping bums, and cautious dealers. The head filled up with intruders, yelping, yapping—all dense materialism. You could easily see the clarity of the dividing line between making it and not; it was everywhere apparent. As you walked, you could hear for the thousandth time the different little cautionary tales of what happens to you if you make it and what happens if you don't. There you could be, lying by that statue of Columbus guarding Central Park, or asleep outside the Port Authority Terminal past which my train had just fled. If you open your eyes, you see the commuters stepping over you, on the verge of shuddering, holding their noses, disappearing.

Rome, Paris, Tokyo by night distend themselves. In Rome in summer, the strolling men wear their jackets, like capes, over their shoulders. In Tokyo, knots of students clog a sidewalk, laughing in front of a yakatoria. Passersby thread their way through, no one cursing. In Paris, immense, well lit cafes disgorge well-fed patrons onto the *boul.* where, briskly, without rushing, they connect themselves to another little night adventure. In New York, although we put tables and chairs on the sidewalk, the agitation and appetite are still palpable at night. Black and white, singles and couples, New Yorkers grimly push past as if on a high wire, everyone thinking he or she will make it here, as Frank Sinatra encourages.

"Unbearable agitation, I feel it actually when I go over there, especially if I've got a book coming out," novelist Martin Amis said of New York when I met him in London on my way back from seeing Armani and company. "I can feel my head load up with junk. The first time it happened to me I found I was doing all those things that writers are meant to do, or are assumed to do, like peering abjectly into book stores to see how the pile was doing. And I thought, 'Oh Christ, I've turned into this sort of person. For the rest of my life I'm going to be peering abjectly into bookshops and wrenching open the daily paper to see if there's a review.' The minute I got back to London it lifted, and with incredible relief I went back to being English again. Tom Stoppard told me he had exactly the same experience. The frenzy takes you over, you can't resist it. I'm amazed that New Yorkers put on such a good act of even pretending to think about anything else other than making it."

Of course, most don't make it. And then the rage takes over. I see a young black who isn't going to make it, any more than that secretary—pardon me, assistant. Their fierce ambition joins that of almost all the rest of those around me this night, converted first into frustration and then hostility all the way to rage—especially in those ghetto youth who, in irony they may not realize, call themselves the "left," the left-behinds. Said Amis: "If a reasonably cultivated English writer is completely, irresistibly swamped by New York ambition within about twenty minutes of getting off the plane, what's it like if you've lived and breathed that stuff?" The people seemed wired so tight this night that I had need of a calm companion, so I got "street smart" (as the New York Telephone ad instructed) and shouted through the phone at a friend "You'll meet me there?" Unhinged by this former Rome in devolution and unable to make myself exquisite, that is French, a lover of caviar and salmon, I relapsed. I arranged for dinner *en forme de* Big Mac. And, oddly, kept doing so for months after that Village dinner of damned signs. It didn't matter if it were night or day, summer or winter, it was a *konstante Kraft,* as Freud says of the drive, a constant force that American advertising had pumped into me, moving my legs and my mouth. I seem to be able to do nothing about it, whether I feed alone or, more likely, with a companion: I have a Mac-ache.

Twenty-five years ago when I arrived on Fifty-seventh Street wet from Kansas City, starry-eyed, I used to nurse a cup of coffee at the Automat, near the corner of Sixth Avenue, not far from Carnegie Hall and the galleries. I came for the culture of Fifty-seventh Street and not for the shopping mecca. the Automat was a landmark then, as McDonald's is today. The Automat, misnamed in anticipation of the computer age, had only a surface of automation. Those endless pigeonholes that proffered sandwiches and pies were actually fed from behind by people—newly arrived Puerto Ricans and blacks from the south. This elegant art deco building now houses the New

York Delicatessen, and as we walk east, into the shopping area—
Henri Bendel, Bergdorf Goodman, and Tiffany—we discover a new
icon of *gourmandise,* the new McDonald's Museum, 47 West Fifty-
seventh Street, a late-twentieth-century piece of Americana. The
tinsel **M** of McDonald's is an anomaly in this top-drawer area.

Today, the Puerto Ricans are out in the open. Barely a few strides
past the arch, Hispanic hands and smiles ushered my friend and I
forward to the shortest of ten lines before cash registers, alongside
the slumming executives, late from work, the clerks of the system,
the passersby, the wide-eyed tourists from Toledo and Teaneck.

The dark lady was waiting for our order. My companion said:
"Un momento, por favor," being Cuban-born, and turned to me.
"To order knowledgeably, I need more time." To abate the server's
impatient, midnight-black eyes, I turned to my friend Edmundo
and suggested: "Would you like mustard, barbecue, sweet-and-
sour, or honey with your Chicken McNuggets" ($1.99)? He said:
"You have the McNuggets, I want the classic, the Big Mac"
($2.49—20 cents more than elsewhere to defray the estimated
monthly rent of $67,000). I turned to the dark lady, who was
circling the preprinted form, and said: "Cokes for both. And make it
two Big Macs."

She said: "What size Coke?"

Confused by choice, I said: "How many sizes are there?"

"Small, medium, large, and extra large," she said.

"Don't you see? My friend is tall," I said. "He wants large, I'll take
medium."

In less than a minute, give or take a few seconds, we received our
bag of goodies. We ascended a staircase encircling a red, blue, and
yellow glowing McDonald's column. Upstairs, our paper bags in
suspension, we discovered a woman with two children about to
leave her place by the large plate-glass window overlooking Fifty-
seventh Street. As we moved in, one of the kids screamed: "Where's
the gummi bear?"

"Excuse me," she told us, and picked up an F.A.O. Schwarz bag.

"Classy kid," I said as we displaced them. The crumpling of the
bags as we unpacked played solo to the Mozart string quartet in the
background. "Presto," I remarked.

A Puerto Rican with a smashing **M** baseball cap rushed up to wipe
the table. "It's all right," I told her.

But she said, "I have to."

So Edmundo said, in Spanish: "Are people afraid of getting AIDS
here?"

"Oh no," she smiled, "AIDS is history. People who come here are
very *decente.*"

In the best of all possible worlds there is no AIDS, and
McDonald's *is* the best of all possible worlds.

Opening the mini-sarcophagus, we unpacked a timeless bit of

Americana, the Big One, and the gloriously crisp McNuggets, served on a bed of plastic. Looking for the sauces, I found I had only been given the barbecue—a little ungenerous, I thought.

But I covered my McNuggets with a swirl of the sauce, a taste of which proved pungent and fetching. Edmundo took a french fry and dipped it into the Fancy Ketchup as an appetite awakener, and also applied the Fancy Ketchup to his old-fashioned Big Mac.

I looked out of the window giving onto the Frumkin/Adams gallery across the street, exhibiting—in *its* second-floor window—a big William Beckman drawing of a sullen nude couple idly overlooking the gridlocked traffic below, in the merchandising center of the world. I turned my head back to the freshly wiped tables in a murky, neon-blue-lit, kidney-shaped space that turns five hundred people per hour over and out at lunchtime.

The stainless-steel eatery—the steel of the ceiling and walls so polished it's a giant mirror throwing the blue neon light dazzlingly every which way—is the culmination of an idea that began more than 30 years ago, when Ray Kroc started the first "fishbowl" restaurants. The decor was that of your own car—for you drove into a lot, walked to a glass window, and gave your order as, through the window, you witnessed boys and girls tossing the burgers and frying the potatoes, the eats that you brought back to the Chevy to feed the wife and 3.1 kiddies. The outfit that had the genius to serve automobiling America today operates more than ten thousand restaurants in the U.S. and worldwide and has served, as of this writing, 70 billion burgers to a world that consumes the burger, like blue jeans, as an arch-sign of America herself.

"Imagine, Marshall, those billions of mouths chewing McDonald's in Tokyo, Tijuana, Trafalgar Square, and Topeka," said Edmundo. "It's hallucinatory."

McDonald's has become the largest restaurant company in the world, with multi-billion-dollar sales per year and with marketing spending in multi-million dollars. Not satisfied with this preeminence, president/CEO Michael Quinlan told his shareholders in the summer of '88: "We see as our competition anyone who sells food. . . . Our goal is to be dominant." And already, McDonald's is in Europe, including Russia, Latin America, and Asia.

Meanwhile, in New York, the little eight thousand-square-foot temple on Fifty-seventh Street is a consecration, and, like all consecrations, a sort of demise, a sacred point where nothing can be changed, where one is dead, as if McDonald's had at last reached its level of incompetence. Like Venturi's Las Vegas, McDonald's, which became emblematic of postmodern populism, is an antique in America, as happily hollow as Sammy Davis, Jr. used to be singing at the Sahara. Entering the place on the edge of the 90s is like entering the Whitney Museum of the twenty-first century to find not Warhol's coffin-like cans of soup but a happening in a

Figure 3.1 McNightmare on 57th Street. *Courtesy of Catherine Smith.*

blue so cold it's as if we were inside a mortuary. But the sights here don't overly threaten. These people around me are not the *Nosferatu,* the undead. They are the unliving. McDonald's on Fifty-seventh Street is a living Eating Museum of America. The blue neon on the ceiling snakes kidney-like around the eating area, mirrored by a slate snake on the tiled floor. You are in a murky pool, underwater, half easeful and half about to choke.

"How do you find your Big Mac?" I asked my dining companion.

"It didn't come out quite right. The sesame-seed bun has absorbed too much blood," he answered. "How's yours?" It had been lying all this while in its styrofoam (shortly thereafter abandoned, environmentally unfriendly), still warm in its plastic environ. I had the craziest impulse at this moment. My tongue pushed the Big Mac against my palate. Juice, that's to say blood and not ozmazome, dripped down my gorge. Rejoicing in the American plenitude of the experience, I rolled the bite in my mouth, seeking the flavors. There weren't any. The only thing I could taste was the pickle. The rest was texture. The tastes have canceled themselves out. I can palpate, of course, feel the shredded lettuce between my teeth, already forming plaque. At McDonald's Central, they shred the bland leaves because larger pieces would give too much lettuce flavor (a contradiction in terms?). The McDonald machines dice and compact lettuce, cheese, onion, pickle, tomato, sesame seed bun, homogenizing everything. Nothing shall be in a large enough piece to allow you to taste its flavor. You can't taste meat in a Big Mac because the patty's canceled by the special sauce canceled by the lettuce, cheese, onions, sesame seed bun. A Big Mac, the icon of one of the addiction industries—like crack, liquor, gambling, anything video, as Amis says—is just one stiff gummy mass. The only thing crisp, the only thing with any taste, is the pickle. And it's not even a Jewish pickle.

In his novel, *Money,* Martin Amis renamed U.S. fast-food chains. He set his stage with Burger Den, Burger Hutch, Burger Shack, Burger Bower, Furter Hut, Donut Den. Falling asleep after a dinner of burgers slopped down with gin, virgin film director né ad man John Self, the novel's hero, awakens most mornings vomiting into his Melitta filter. Over coffee in his Leamington Street flat, I asked Amis why. "I don't know if John Self is a representative figure, but he suspects he is," Amis answered, "and it's self-destruction, it's self-cramming. One morning he wakes up and says, 'What did I do to myself last night? I didn't mean me any harm. All I wanted was a good time.' In America everyone's so sold on the good you wonder how all the evil gets done."

Amis, "nasty, British, and short" (as more than one London literary wag has described him), reminds us once again that we buy products less to imbibe than to mean. And what they mean—a single signified, a million signifiers—is the Good, that is, Fast, Life.

In our hutches and bowers, slurping and munching, we meet again and again the Great, the Unique Metaphor, which says tirelessly, "Have fun," and thus establishes America's lyric discourse.

"Pepsi is water, sweeteners, and flavorings," said Allen Rosenshine, chairman of BBDO worldwide, one of the world's largest advertising agencies, creator of the celebrated Pepsi Generation campaign, the very one that enabled the Baby Boomers to define themselves for almost thirty years now. "If you're really bone-dry thirsty, you don't drink Pepsi," he added, moving his lips like a parched man. "You drink it because of what it signifies." And every season or so, BBDO changes that signification. When I sat with Rosenshine, at the beginning of this project, asking him who to see for the advertising chapter, he told me that BBDO was niche-marketing Pepsi, appealing to the avant-garde impulse—doing so as Coca Cola continued seeking all America as a market. "There you see him in the Coke spots, the adorable kid à la Twain, running along the white picket fence, his dog Spot right behind." Doubtless he never masturbates. I say this to echo Rosenshine, who told me, *au courant* postmodernist theory, that our age had reached a moment of crisis, the sense that the past is restricting, smothering, blackmailing us. The cute kid, the suburban house, good old Dad, all of it, he thought, was the stuff of tired clichés for enough of us that Pepsi could prosper by mounting a polemical campaign whose form was "down with." "Down with moonlight," the futurist motto, is a statement typical of any avant-garde. As novelist/semiotician Umberto Eco told me in the interviews for chapter 16, "you need only to substitute something appropriate for the moonlight, which for the futurists was the Romantic tradition. The avant-garde destroys the past, it disfigures it."

"Down with suburbia" was Pepsi's attack on what it regarded as defunct myth. Calling its strategy leading-edge, headlining its spots with Michael Jackson, BBDO advertising tried to capture, according to Rosenshine, "the most *au courant* people, the people who were current with the contemporary movies, including what was happening in science fiction, all of that defining the leading edge." Coke's response was almost to agree that its product was out of date. The company introduced what came to be known in the trade as New Coke. Coca-Cola said in effect: "We are changing Coca-Cola. It will now have a new appeal and a new taste," in fact the sweeter taste of Pepsi. The result was a nation-wide product repudiation whose meaning was: "Don't mess with our icon." The repudiation was the contrary of the avant-garde impulse. The nation, at least in the soft drink universe, wasn't ready to give up old Coke, wasn't prepared to give up what that sign stood for. Whatever it was, America as it were said: "No way do we want your new Coke, Coke." But the problem was that Coke had already introduced it, and now there were two Cokes, new Coke and a renamed Classic

Coke. Telling me the story when I paid a call near the end of this project, Rosenshine continued:

> Coke now announced: "Okay, you can have your old Coke back and it's now called Classic Coke." It was a marketing fiasco.

Which became a semiotic or public relations bonanza, because it:

> regenerated tremendous interest in Coke per se, which the company could not have regenerated with the normal marketing and advertising channels. It was Coke's blunder that forced America to say to it: "What a great product"—meaning symbol—"you have in Coca-Cola. "And we don't want it changed." When America said that, if our theory is correct, the country was endorsing the cute kid—all the old icons. I mean, is America hungry for those old icons? What the hell is Norman Schwartzkopf?

And when I say he's Bubba from Alabama, he says:

> He's a palatable Patton, a Patton who doesn't beat up his soldiers. A Patton who knows how to talk to the media. I just heard on the air, the other night, one of these direct response recordings, all the great old songs of World War II.

As it were, on 1–900–OLD–HITS:

> Can you imagine that? That's how they position them, the great love songs of World War II—talk about an oxymoron! It comes from our success in the Gulf—now we can relive the good old wars, we've washed Vietnam, which was a disaster, we've washed Korea, which was a stalemate. And by virtue of our success in the Gulf, we now have legitimacy to go back to World War II and relive its great old love songs.

What did Coke (not to mention its rival) willy-nilly discover? A residual wellspring of white picket fences, a portion of the American populace crying: "We won't give it up! Whatever your New Coke is, we don't want it!" Meaning: "We want our white picket fences, we want our little dogs, Spots; we want that little non-masturbatory kid—we want to be that kid." Only telling us and Rosenshine all over again, given the drag of regressivist America, how lustrously different, how semiotically salient can be the positioning of the avant–garde.

The dynamic marketer who saw me off and saw me return and who, for four years, struggled to keep his massive client supposedly existential, on the edge—Rosenshine, who was oddly my alpha and omega, a lifetime in advertising—has been playing Mayakovsky. Or if you prefer, Picasso. Or early Cage. From first to last he he's been growling "Down with. . . ." In this sense, BBDO, an ad agency—like all agencies, reviled by cultural critics—finds itself in the company of a closet cultural critic like novelist Stephen King (see p. 352). Both are mythoclasts.

So for the last four years, clutching your can of Pepsi, you have signified the good life of the avant-garde. Of course Coca-Cola retorted—its image of a swimsuit-clad beauty slapping her suitor booted up America.

"Yes, Coke has moved evolutionarily along with the times, reflecting changes you just simply can't ignore any more," Rosenshine observed. "But the basic core value of Coca-Cola is what it always was, whereas Pepsi still wants to be leading edge, still wants to be offset from Coke by being seen as the more modern, more hip badge, recognizing that Pepsi can't go over the edge, either. No product, no advertising can lead society. It can only reflect."

"A brand is a style, a way of expressing a character," said Jacques Séguéla in Paris, where I saw him on my way to the Milanese designers of chapter 2. This master ad man was one of those responsible for managing François Mitterand to the presidency of France. A *"force tranquille,"* a tranquil force, he called him—rhetorically speaking, an *impossibilia,* an impossible thesis, utterly unrealizable, thus the luxurious denial of reality. "If Coca-Cola hadn't a character, it would never have become the favorite drink of the world," Séguéla told me. "The character of Coca-Cola is eternal youth. The character of Pepsi is American youth"—failing from the other side of the Atlantic to discern the Pepsi-Coke wars, although dead-on about immortality. Translated for the Thai market, Pepsi's slogan—"Come alive, you're in the Pepsi generation"—became: "Pepsi brings your ancestors back from the dead."

"And the character of Marlboro is serenity, a kind of virility," Séguéla continued. "The Marlboro cowboy is fifty years old. He's got blue eyes the color of jeans. Little wrinkles of age. He's completely master of himself. He's passed through the years of desire to the other side. It's security, serenity he signals." For those who light up precisely because of stress.

Séguéla told me to think of Coke, Pepsi, and Marlboro as if they were stars, today's Marilyn Monroe or Clark Gable, even more star than Tom Cruise or Matt Dillon. "The Americans invented star strategy but they never amply perceived it, never codified it," he said. "Marilyn was infantalism in perpetuity. Clark Gable was the good American—in sixty-five films, not a word against America. Everything was legendary and mythic in the Hollywood star system, and I think advertising has returned to the source of myth. It lends an imaginary value to a product. When a woman buys a pair of pantyhose, she buys a few grams of nylon and how many tons of imaginary advertising? Advertising lends a soul to the product." The Seguelas and Rosenshines have made products into souls, into depths that we ourselves aren't—and would despise if we were.

Holding a Coke in one hand, a Pepsi in another, all the while puffing the Marlboro, you swell into something that will live young forever, in serene solidarity with its brood. The Marlboro out, the

Big Mac in, you tell yourself: *"Pow!"* Because to get the Big Mac in—there are so many layers of it—you've had to open your maw wide; a gesture rewarded, if not in taste, then in stinging volume. "I'm a killer eater," says the chomping O your face becomes. Is it any wonder that John Self for the duration of *Money* suffers face-ache. Full of hysteria, you think of yourself as an original body, distinguished from other bodies, having it all. Exuding plaque for your coronary arteries, the Big Mac permits you to swell the lungs, beat the chest—and when you add the obligatory fries and shake—become the assimilatory center of your world.

Until, a plummet, it sinks in your belly, slowing your progress. I remember once giving a brief interview on fast food to *Glamour*. When the fact checker called with my quote, I heard: "Blonsky says the trend to fast foods is one way we express the energy and vitality of the 70s."

"I didn't say that," I told her. "Fast food is a *sign* of vitality, I didn't say we're vital."

"It's a sign of *vitality,* that's what the quote says," she told me. "No, a *sign* . . ."

We never could get it straight, that a sign is a presence that stands for something absent, fast food for animal high spirits. The in/out, eat-on-the-run of fast food is the way we congratulate ourselves for shaving time from all our activities—to the profit of nothing. From bedroom to boardroom, the greatest good is to save time—an orgasm or meeting, it makes no difference. Remember Attali's "You change your cars, you change your ideas, you change your wife, you change your friends quicker and quicker," as he rushed me through a thirty-minute interview at the Elysée. As a young man, Umberto Eco taught himself to cut something like 30 percent from shaving, showering, from every mundane activity, thereby to give more time for scholarship. Like Eco, we constantly search for time-savers, but unlike Eco, few of us put the added time to quality use. Indeed, the very term, "quality time," tells this writer that it's a sign simply for spending less time with the kids.

Far from a signal of our vitality, one could argue that fast food *is* laziness. How many of us declined the plastic bags enclosing each and every one of our purchases on Mall Day? How was it possible even to drive by a Fat Boy and refuse the Styrofoam coffin handed into our window? In the era of ecological vigilance, we've barely begun to meditate our convenience purchased with clutter. No matter what it does to the environment, I want it *big . . . hot . . . now.*

When I take Umberto Eco to dinner (p. 376), you'll meet him shoving away his half-eaten, still abundant plate of mixed seafood grill, growling *basta,* offended at our gigantism of eating. "The European nouvelle cuisine is superb in inverse proportion to the quantity," he'll lecture me. "A beautiful dish of nouvelle cuisine has half a finger of meat with a strawberry upon it and two little spoons of sauce and that's all. Usually an American dish must be so big that you cannot finish it." And at espresso time, toying with a little cup, he warmed to his topic: "This is not American. To be American it should be a paper cup of coffee bought, let's say, in a station. It's enormous, it slushes off because it arrives too full and it's boiling. You have to wait half an hour to drink it, and usually you don't have time to do that because if you bought the coffee at the coffee stand at the station, it means that you have only five minutes so you sip something burning out your mouth and then you throw it away." Why not half a cup at medium temperature? Because of the myth of excess. Half a cup medium would mean that you don't have the most for the cents you spend. For your change, you must have the maximum quantity, the maximum heat—even at the cost of being unable to drink the coffee.

The sign of our frenzy, the Big Mac, is also an archesign of our time. In his 1977 book *Noise,* Jacques Attali wrote:

> The repetitive economy is characterized by a mutation in the mode of production of supply, due to the sudden appearance of a new factor in production, *the mold,* which allows the mass production of an original. . . . Molds of this kind are everywhere: computer programs, car designs, medicine formulas, apartment floor plans, etc. The same mutation also transforms the usage of things. The usage to which representative labor was put disappears with mass production. The object replaces it, but loses its personalized, differentiated meaning. A paradox: the object's utility is exchanged for accessibility. Considerable labor must then be expended to give it a meaning, to produce a demand for its repetition.

Pepsi is amber fluid signifying nothing of the human, of the culture that produced it. Indeed, it signifies nothing at all. So Rosenshine has to invest it with alien myth, lavishly spend Pepsico's capital in order to produce demand for a bland, matte, inert, unattractive artifact, the production price of which is a decreasing fraction of the retail sales price. The bulk of the money you plunk down as you hurry into the 7 Eleven goes for the marketing.

> Repetition is established through the supplanting, by mass production, of every present-day mode of commodity production still inscribed within the network of representation. Mass production, a final form, signifies the repetition of all consumption, individual or collective, *the replacement of the restaurant by precooked meals, of custom-made clothes by ready-wear, of the individual house built from personal designs by tract houses based on stereotyped designs, of the politician by the anonymous bureaucrat, of skilled labor by standardized tasks, of the spectacle by recordings of it.* [Italics mine.]

Attali's harrowing America and rescuing none of us. And while, after visiting Armani, I can hardly opt for ready-to-wear, still, there's a different way to look at the Big Macification of the world—

one, shall we say, less anti-American. With *The Name of the Rose* Umberto Eco touched the pulse of our modernity, and as you'll see, he has a kind spot for popular culture and prefabrication. Eating a Reuben in Indianapolis, he told me: "This Reuben is exactly the same as the Reuben I could eat at this moment in California, while in Europe the steak I eat in Lyon is not the same as I eat in Paris. Here, everything was invented at the same time, while in Europe you had a sort of archaeology, a buildup of customs and usages. In America what the customer wants is the security to have the same, and you have made in America a unified hamburgeralization"—like generalization—"that prescribes exactly the weight and the size of any hamburger sold and cooked in any restaurant. This is due also to the fact that Americans move from city to city more frequently in their lives than the European. And so it's very normal to have a job six months in New York and then to find another job in Austin, Texas, and so you want to find the same hamburger"—pronounced hamboorger—"and the light switch always in the same place in your hotel."

Precisely because it's always the same, we never have to think about it—even when eating it. Precisely because it's so bland, there's nothing to say about it. Gone then is the language of cuisine, the science of alimentary pleasure. You're in and out so fast—impossible to constitute protocol in the Hut, the Pouch, the Bower. No Ceremony, Party, Rite, Discourse, nothing to require refinement and pay us back in the coin of difference from the others. Fast food is profoundly egalitarian, its genius that of banishing etiquette and its divisiveness.

You can look at fast food as the greasy grub foisted on the poor who never had the education to appreciate—and can't afford the expense of—nutritious food. Or you can recognize that "good food" is cheap, that "greasy food" is not cheap, and that people eat greasily because they like it and like its meaning—all manners checked at the door. Drinking tea, scarcely a shake, the English conservative philosopher Roger Scruton told me: "People are not forced to eat greasy food because they can't afford vegetables. I'm a person who eats greasy food because I like it, and I come from a working-class background where greasy food is what people 'et.'" Protesting the radical idea of a subjugation of popular taste, Scruton, sipping tea in London, anchored the function of fast food in American popular culture. "Everybody knows that American popular culture is as it is because America is genuinely democratic," he said. "And the idea of the right of the individual has penetrated right to the bottom of society. His tastes, his ambitions, his aspirations, all have a legitimacy in America and can rise to the top and dominate in a way that, thanks to our aristocracy, they have never fully done in Europe. Now I'm not a democrat in my instincts. I like the aristocratic culture. I think an aristocratic culture is necessary and that people in an ideal world should be held down, held in their social position by a properly self-reinforcing aristocracy. Then the culture of course would be far more dignified, a far more edifying thing than it is now. But the people who criticize American popular culture are bound by a huge contradiction: they always criticize it in the name of democracy, whereas it's democracy that's produced it."

Nothing could have been further from the democratic spirit than my experience in Greenwich Village with the ex-Underground Gourmet. She was the spiritual descendant of *New York Times* food editor Craig Claiborne, the voice of the American gastronomic revolution, who spoke to me about food and conviviality, a conversation (for those concerned about the movable feast of this book) in which not a single cup of coffee was offered. "At table I like to discuss current events that give one pleasure, like the theater, film, books," Claiborne said. "No weighty matters like politics. No global, no national, no local politics." Throughout the 80s, Claiborne reformulated the contents of American pleasuring. In a text of large illustrative power, he wrote of Marvin Davis, a New York ad man: "Seven years ago, his idea of heaven was a piece of beef with spaghetti and tomato sauce." Now:

> He is the embodiment of the American gastronomic revolution over the last decade. This man, who had never cooked a day in his life, has suddenly, through his own reading, discovered the joy of eating, the joy of cooking. He has a penthouse apartment with 11,000 feet, fantastic things like snow peas, romaine lettuce, thyme, sage, tarragon, parsley, peppers, Japanese eggplant, cucumbers, basil, oregano, four kinds of tomato, eggplant—

More and more, Claiborne is saying—an orgasm of vegetables:

> Portuguese peppers, Japanese eggplant, cucumbers.

Producing ever more refined categorizations, Claiborne through the pages of the *Times* has caused a proliferation of signs, made an extravaganza of the culinary code. Take it as a sign of the American way of life, one version of it, top of the heap. The Underground Gourmet had been half-trying to turn *me* into a Marvin Davis (if she'd really wanted to, she wouldn't have stuffed me with signs); in displeasure, I had fled underground to this venue of the masses.

"The bun absorbed too much blood," Edmundo had said. "How's yours?"

"Doesn't matter now," said the sterile American in me, wounded by the image of the body's insides. But the European esthete in me, offended by the lurid sterility all around, urged my dining partner up, and we put into the bag we had brought to the formica the carcass of our meal and, walking a few steps, mailed it away in the garbage slot.

Since Edmundo and I had been chilled (rhymes with . . .) by hygiene, he decided to recoil home and I, *a contrario,* thought to soil the experience with the oily, scented antipasto at the Milton Glaser–designed Trattoria dell'Arte, two blocks away on Fifty-seventh Street, where the decor stresses the importance of breasts, ears, and especially noses, all the most famous noses in the world from Dante to Jimmy Durante. I needed the sweet smell of terrestrial nourishment, but I needed a friend even more. Matthew, however, declined the invitation to peasant fare.

"You don't exchange one grease for another," he lectured over the phone (he's a food specialist, photographer of it). "I'll meet you at Petrossian. I hear Christian's in town, he's a friend."

Christian Petrossian, whose restaurant was a block away, is known as one of the great purveyors of gourmet delicacies, of Russian caviar, smoked Atlantic salmon, foie gras, truffles, and other products from the Périgord. Petrossian's more adept clientele know that his salmon is always line-caught to avoid the damage that can occur in seine-caught fish; that his is one of the few companies allowed to participate in the sturgeon catch on the Caspian sea. Matthew on the phone is extolling his friend and his company. The only firm allowed to export caviar from the Soviet Union during the cold war, Petrossian had the monopoly on the high-standard product.

And since we're in the enthusiasm phase, Matthew Klein is one of the world's leading food photographers. He's photographed Petrossian for *Connoisseur* magazine, photographed a book for Perrier, plus almost fifty cookbooks; in addition, he's written his own cookbook, *The Joy of Ice Cream,* a bestseller in its genre. Matthew loves food so much his cholesterol level is in four digits, he tells me.

"You're in and you're out at McDonalds," said Matthew at Petrossian, "five hundred chairs, no waiting."

"No digesting," I groused my experience around the corner.

"There's no decision you have to make," he continued, before swerving: "Yeah, you have to make a decision. Is it going to be a McDLT or a Big Mac or Chicken McNuggets? And which sauce am I going to ask for? It's not threatening. It's not risky. You don't have to read a menu. Believe it or not, a lot of Americans don't know how to use a menu. At McDonald's there's no need for one."

Which, come to think of it, may not be such a bad thing. For a menu, in the great gastronomic tradition, is an incitement of desire, its ribbons of language coming from a patrimonial hoard of gustatory experience. But on today's fashion-driven menus, the last fad's cuisine has had to be obliterated to make way for the utterly new, expressed in jerry-rigged language falling inertly on one's desire center. I look at a menu—*blackened buffalo wings, perch-raised, cous-cous-fed, honey guinea hen*—I am helpless before it, I cannot

Figure 3.2 Matthew and me at Petrossian. *Courtesy Catherine Smith.*

find desire. The words on the menu have nothing to do with my structure of taste, everything to do with this moment's food fashion. After even a partial lifetime of such linguistic and not lingual fare, of pseudo-gourmet and not gustatory experience, of the joy of adjectives ("Monterey Jack, 100% steer") more than nouns ("burger"), one's desire will have been beaten down. I don't know what I want, one says before a menu in Atlanta, Chicago, Philadelphia, Phoenix, it makes not the slightest difference. I don't know *if* I want.

Life's like that for many of us. But others, fearful of eating words, threatened even by the factitious fantasy of that poor fowl, honey-drenched on her perch, opt for the Big One, the Whaleburger, the Heap of Meat. Fleeing from the indefinite, the undecidable, they find refuge in the rigid and safe territory of McDonald's. Every Big Mac I've ever eaten tasted the same as every other one. And so did yours. You don't enter McDonald's and ask for a Big Mac and hear: "Well done, medium, or rare?" producing the possibility of the too-red, the unjuicy. McDonald's eliminates the transgression of or failure to read boundaries. To the profit of what we think is the good taste.

For in America, God forbid you should have one bad meal. Millions of us—enough to scarf down 70 + billion burgers—never think that if this meal came out too dry or too red, well, there's always a good morning to another nice day. McDonald's always gives you the taste that's good enough.

So rigorous is food-industry competition, so difficult to find an edge—given how little we stray from the center of the taste palette—that if you arrive at a difference, you vaunt it, contaminate it with no other meaning, and make a fetish of it in your advertising. A fetish is a part taken for a whole; say, a pump loved as if it were a woman. A fetish appears to its voyeurs as if inside dotted lines, calling upon them to cut it out and clutch it to their chests, take it home and let themselves go with it. The photo for a food ad, like the woman's shoe, is supposed to make you burn with desire. "The idea is to get someone to salivate over paper and ink," Matthew once told me. On the day of the night I met him, he had—successfully, he thought—photographed a pie for Crisco. Actually rephotographed it. Crisco, you see, had apparently come up with a recipe for a *very* flaky pie crust. "The subject of the first shot [Fig. 3.3] isn't the home, isn't the cherries, isn't the pie, isn't the environment, it's flakiness," said Matthew, unaware at that moment, as was I, of the absurdity of talking pie at Petrossian.

The layout of the ad was to require his photo to be printed the size of a page and a third, double life-size, $8^{1}/_{2} \times 11$, and Matthew sought artistically to take advantage of this gigantism. He thought to move the spectatorial eye instantly to the vast flakiness of the pie, to create the effect of being an eye at crust level. The copy line: "For a light and flaky pie crust your family will gobble up." And thereby hung the little tale he told me, the Petrossian menus by our hands disdainfully closed amidst such banality. Yesterday, his candidate for the Crisco shoot had been rejected. "The art director and I think it was one hell of a lot stronger [than today's shot]. Imagine that blown up for a page and a third."

"I bet I know why the client didn't buy it," I said, about to spring some jargon onto my vis-à-vis. "It's not as phenomenologically stable as the other."

"Right," said Matthew, not missing a beat, "you don't read 'pie' as quickly. You read 'flaky' there, but flaky what? You'd be surprised by the image, and then you'd have to translate it, and you'd say: 'Wow, that's one hell of a flaky pie crust!'"

But this is a logocentric country, as learned discourse puts it. We're centered on the logos, the word, and our belief in its stable meaning, instantly given, impregnably enduring. The image must instantly produce a name in response to the viewer's and to society's "What's that?"

"We thought we got enough meaning out of the picture, that there would be enough there to read 'pie,'" said Matthew, "but the client didn't. And the dialogue was something like this, the client saying, 'Well, I like it but. . . .' And the art director said: 'Puts you on edge, doesn't it? Gives you butterflies.' And the client said: 'Yeah, it does.' And the art director said: 'Great advertising does that to you.' The client said: 'Yeah, but I still can't get over the butterflies.' So they didn't go with that idea—too bold for them."

On the cutting edge of marketing, Crisco had sought the Platonic

Figure 3.3 Today the semiotic burden is lightened, but this Crisco image has too little—or too much—meaning. "What am I looking at?" you could ask. In this era of instantly graspable figures, that's not acceptable. Crisco's ad agency rejected it.

form of Flakiness. When Matthew delivered—Flakiness unburdened of all material objectivity and the spirit-crushing weight of banal artifacts and brand names—Crisco balked. The adjectival noun flowing from the image had to be anchored in a common noun, flakiness in *pie,* to combat the dysfunction we feel in the presence of an uncertain image, the dysphoria we feel adrift from the nameable (Fig. 3.4). The client had told Matthew, without saying so, to limit the polysemy of his image, to fasten down the "floating chain" of meanings around it, to fix on one in order to combat the terror of uncertain signs.

"Is Petrossian here?" I asked Matthew, who called for the maitre d', who told us he was, now he wasn't, but would be later. Matthew ordered salmon, and I, freed of material need by the Big Mac, ordered up words.

In Matthew's practice, as he had just related it, I thought I had discovered the possible obsolescence of traditional semiotic anal-

For A Light And Flaky Pie Crust
Your Family Will Gobble Up...

...Here's Your Recipe
for Success.
The Crisco Crust.

Crisco is the Recipe for Success.
With 50% less saturated fat than butter
and no cholesterol.

Figure 3.4 So photographer Matthew Klein reshot. "Oh, that's a pie," you say now. The happy client accepted it.

ysis, so I asked my friend: "Do you ever load your food pics with signs like Panzani?"

In 1964 in the journal *Communications,* to which he was a major contributor, Roland Barthes published the canonical "Rhetoric of the Image," the analysis of an ad for Panzani, a downmarket French pasta manufacturer, like our own Ronzoni (Fig. 3.5). Barthes thought that, for his scholarly clientele, he was discovering, perhaps for the first time, not that images bore symbols, but that the symbols were ordered in a language, associated, "spoken" by a rhetoric analogous to that of a natural language, French, English, whatever. What Barthes didn't know was that from the instant he published this path-breaking demonstration, his audience included French admen and women. "At the moment when Barthes criticized advertising, he directly inspired advertising," said his first biographer, Louis-Jean Calvet. "When [Georges] Péninou, who already worked in ads, brought him to Publicis [Péninou's agency] for a lecture before the creatives, he went a bit bluffing. Péninou even

Figure 3.5 The famous Panzani ad.

gave him a commission on the discourses vaunting cars for Renault. That's to say at the very moment when he was perceived as a destroyer of the system of objects, he in fact formed people who held an opposite discourse." Through an irony that perhaps would have amused him, *la sémiologie* has been taught for more than two decades, thanks to Barthes, in the advertising schools, and the students know by heart his analysis of the Panzani ad.

Reading its image, Barthes discerned a series of discontinuous signs in the represented scene. In no particular order, one of them produced the idea of a return from the market, implying euphoric values, that of the freshness of the products and that of the purely managed preparation to which they were destined. A second was almost as evident, its signifier being the "reunion," as he put it, a party of the tomato, pepper, and mushroom, plus the tricolor hue (yellow, green, red) of the ad; its signified, its content, being Italy, or rather *Italianness,* also the signified of the linguistic message, the legend and the labels.

Continuing to explore the image, he discovered, "without trouble," he said (without trouble for him—remember, in those days people didn't read the connotations of imagery), at least two other signs. In one, the tight mustering of different objects transmits the idea of a total culinary service, as if Panzani furnished all the housewife needed for a nutritious meal. Scarcely true; she's being flattered by the subliminal use of a cornucopia, which even Barthes didn't name. And she's also being flattered by the fourth sign, the composition, evoking the memory of so many alimentary paintings and referring to an esthetic signified: "still life." She is flattered all over; for she is not standing in some market line, glancing through the French equivalent of *Family Circle.* She's a woman of leisure at the Louvre, ravishing a work of art, as the Europeans put it, promoted in social standing.

These four connotations Barthes called the cultural message; and he was led to another, the natural message, formed by the literal image, that which I'd see if I had no cultural knowledge but only the anthropological knowledge of a child: the tomato, mushroom, net shopping bag, et cetera, an image of identifiable, nameable objects. Nature seems to have spontaneously produced the represented scene, and this natural message not only ties and "speaks" the four signs of connotation, it plunges them into a "lustrous bath of innocence." The general scene, the nature before you, the denoted image naturalizes the symbolic message, "it makes innocent the very dense (especially in advertising) semantic artifice of the conno-tation." It is precisely because the universe of connotation is so replete that advertising has to "disintellectualize" its appeals.

Barthes hated these "loaded" signs; Panzani's was exemplary of mass cultural signs. For Barthes they were today's tree root, which so filled Sartre with disgust, and from that moment the younger

Barthes' vocation was stabilized. He pursued overloaded signs, excesses of meaning, in a language of disgust. "What is sickening in myth," he wrote, "is its resort to a false nature, its superabundance of significant forms." He spoke, in an interview in the 70s, of the "somewhat dense and heavy, not to say overbearing and a little nauseous layers" of a literary text, intending it as a model of mass cultural signs. Removing the existentialist nausea from the instrument Barthes had developed, a generation of French sign makers packed a profundity of meaning into an advertising that some of us blithely analyzed as if it had come from some evil empire and not our own.

It all seemed threatened now. Matthew had already given me the answer to my question: "Do you load up with connotations?"

"When I'm given the opportunity," he answered. Matthew, I should add, was my first student before he professionalized. I taught him Panzani. Now most of his work is national consumer advertising in food and still life. "The problem is," he continued, "that in advertising most of those decisions are already made before the client comes to me, and the clients come with single concepts that don't permit the loading of the shot."

Dense semantic artifice isn't wanted now, and a brief history of marketing since the 50s tells why.

In the 50s, marketing conventional wisdom held to the notion that if one were a merchant and if a hundred people walked past, one of them would come in and buy something. If 1000 people walked past, ten of them would come in and buy. If you showed your product to a million, perhaps a thousand would buy it; if you showed it to ten million, ten thousand et cetera. Thus companies advertised to the ten million, appearing in the great national magazines, *Life, Look, The Saturday Evening Post,* that sought to reach the entire nation. The end of the 60s, however, saw the beginning of what today we call niche marketing. "We're selling tennis rackets," said marketers, "who buys them? Young professional men, aged twenty-four to thirty-six. How do we reach twenty-four- to 36-year-old professional men earning $60,000 to $80,000, 30 percent of it is disposable income?" The *Life* magazine of those days would have told them that perhaps 5 percent of its audience fit the profile, requiring the manufacturer to advertise to some twenty million other people to secure the 5 percent, wasting substantial capital in the process. "We're not looking for young mothers," the marketers would have said, "we're not looking for high school students, poor people, or those who already have all the tennis rackets they're going to buy." Why not advertise in a magazine of only 30,000 subscribers, a tennis magazine obviously, but also *Scientific American,* for example, given that although it only has, say, 100,000 readership, most or 100 percent of them fit the profile. Suddenly the cost effectiveness problem is solved. And with the solution, the end of the national—and the advent of the special interest—magazine. That trend has run now through several generations: narrowcasting, not broadcasting.

"In the days of Roland Barthes, you would try to make a sign that had the greatest number of connotations," Matthew told me, "the greatest number of meanings for the greatest number of people. Now you want to narrow that beam of meanings down and focus it to a very very narrow segment and aim it like a laser right between the eyes of the people that are in the position to buy your product and are considering it." Suddenly Barthes is radically historicized.

And suddenly the length of the evening, the weight of the conversation in this palace of palm fronds, crystal, and Russian caviar, the continuing absurdity of talking Crisco, Panzani, and residual Barthes for the 90s, all of it and that McCannon ball rolling in my stomach sap my desire for the life of underground gourmet. Matthew having finished his salmon snack, I call for the check.

"Wait, I know Christian's here," he tempts me.

You know those evenings where (a social situation) you long to leave and can't leave? Where, at your limit, you think you'll crack—but don't crack? Where your humble pillow is the idea of heaven to you? This was mine now, even though Himself, Christian Petrossian, was now sitting at our table, Matthew-procured—doubtless a great honor to this fast-retiring underground gourmet.

"First of all, did you like it?" Petrossian is asking me, a great platter of smoked salmon before me (I wasn't conscious of its arrival). "We shall start at the beginning. . . ."

I snap to as Professor Petrossian continues, cathechizing: "It's a little bit like the caviar we import. You know, we have the privilege of going to the Russian fisheries ourselves to choose our caviars. Nobody else in the world has this privilege. For the salmon, it's a little bit the same thing. We go to Norway, all over the North Atlantic coast, to choose our salmon. Then we fly them to Paris."

Once in Paris they are killed (excuse me), or having flown dead to Paris, they join the salmon raised and retired on farms, Petrossian tells me. "Farm salmon is of course different from wild salmon, which exercise in the ocean, cross the ocean, have a lot of *gymnastique*—exercise. He visits exactly what he needs, instead of living in a little place and turning around and around and opening his mouth to be fed," says Petrossian in praise of the more muscular, ocean-going salmon. I don't know if it's my fatigue or his mythology, but I think at this moment that he's deriding his "farm" salmon: lazy. But lazy or not, their deaths are not only painless, I'm hearing, they live on after death, as pampered as in life. "When we salt the salmon by hand, we leave it for hours in this salt," says Petrossian. "Then we take it out and wash it. And we brush—with a brush. And the salmon rejects the salt that it doesn't need to keep"—still alive, cooperating in his perfection—"so you have to brush the salmon. But the salmon keeps the salt it needs." For America, for the realized utopia where animal death is painless, where animals go happily to pouty mouths like the schmoos in the old "Li'l Abner" comic strip, Petrossian's salmon spend hours being groomed.

It's as if, addressing Americans, even the cynical French use the discourse of cheer. In America (and more and more, over the "civilized" world), to die is sick, it's an error—even for animals bound for the table. So we *ex*-inscribe death; in great ways and small, perform a symbolic lockout.

"Salmon is a wonderful fish, a wonderful personality," Petrossian continues. "From one salmon to another salmon, there are always little differences, because that is the life of the salmon."

"What's his personality?" Matthew plays naif.

"Okay, it's *onctueux*, unctuous," he answers.

Here we go again.

"When I first touched your salmon," I say, "it was like a tissue, a membrane." Life with UG had taught me something.

"Right," says Petrossian. And whether Matthew and I have led him or not, I realize that he's telling a sexual story.

"When you eat Petrossian salmon, do you experience it in the cheeks, at the tip of the tongue, or at the back?" I ask, restored to vitality by this sexy little mythology.

"I think it's a full mouth," the charming Petrossian obliges. "And it's a feeling also, not only a taste, I think—a feeling and a taste. A taste and a feeling." We're getting giddy. "A feeling of unctuosity— *l'onctuosité*—a thing *qui fond dans la bouche* [which melts in the mouth]—you feel it in your mouth, on your palate. You don't have to chew it, not really. If you left it, it almost could melt."

I could melt with pleasure, we say. And we know to what that refers. Even in the age of AIDS, sex remains legal and death pornographic. Society shall never interdict sex, which it liberated for consumerist as much as social reasons, filling its former hiding place with death in its function of secret rite and fundamental interdiction. The sexy salmon membrane is happy to slide down your throat and become liquid. And we—from those of us who sit at Petrossian's feet to the readers of Craig Claiborne or my underground gourmet—joyously planting, slicing, munching, noshing, we answer the great injunction to forget death and eat. The joy of eating is a perpetual motion function to which many of us are slave, bound to its naivete, its pathos, and its sentimentality.

Save, that is, for the McDonald's eaters among us, who are perhaps the only ones free from the terrorism of good eating.

4 *The Switch of Pornography*

. . . As the porn people are saved from the terrorism of good sex.

At the Kitchen, one of New York's chicest avant-garde theaters, Annie Sprinkle, performance artist, née Ellen Steinberg, née porn star (150 feature films, 50 loops), née and still golden shower specialist, is accepting an Aphrodite Award "for sexual service to the community," she tells me later. "This really means so much to me," she gushes in a candylike Barbie voice, thanking the audience of two hundred hip critics, artists, and intellectuals alert to the fashion of pornography, made sweet for the night out of the mouth of this five-foot-four ("five-foot-seven or eight in heels," she says), mega-buxom Goldie Hawn of triple X.

"But I really have to accept this on behalf of all sex professionals everywhere all over the world, and all sexual outcasts," she adds, "and all sexual adventurers, too," she says coyly, "because they really all deserve it, and now if it's okay I want to thank just a few people personally," she pastiches the Academy Awards. "Gerard Damiano for giving me my first starring role in a porno feature, *Teenage Deviant.* . . .'' Impossible, hearing her, watching her in glittery evening gown, to rail in the manner of the *New York Post* which, in an editorial, recently denounced the Kitchen for allowing Sprinkle (yes, she took her name from her specialty) to engage in "various acts of crude sexual exhibitionism, all the while boasting that her 'performance' is 'government-funded.'" It was less a boast than a joke between skits: "I usually get paid a lot for this, but tonight it's government-funded," launching her into the rare and turbulent air where the dead Robert Mapplethorpe suffers the blasts of conservatives certain that "pornographic artists" are the avant-gardes of the great culture war on decency. The Kitchen, recipient of

Figure 4.1 Annie Sprinkle about to strip and then some at New York's Kitchen. *Courtesy Dona McAdams.*

National Endowment for the Arts funding, answered that it used "generated income," not NEA money, to fund Sprinkle; its critics naturally cried accountants' tricks. Whoever paid for the Aphrodite and the gown and the thirty-odd dildos and love incense and oils and other scenery, I doubt whether the *Post* editors, any more than conservative columnist Pat Buchanan, also throwing verbal stones at the *putain noir,* any more than Orange County Congressman Dana Rohrbacher, reading her into the Index of the *Congressional Record,* had actually seen the performance. Or, for that matter, much porn.

For Sprinkle, strange perhaps to say, sanitizes the erotic of its convulsions and expostulations. In her films, as in all adult film and video, the big bodies are made almost like bouncing balls, accompanying the plastic rock that makes watching porn about as interesting at first glance as a piano bar for anonymous employees of a great corporation. Pornography is sex drained of its sweat, its labor, its apogee and nadir. It is a realized dream of our time: to produce a body without a soul, without a center, without a dense source of pleading, supplication, astonishment, indecent pathos, the entire repertory of emotion elaborated shamelessly by a body, especially by a body in heat. Pornography excludes innovation—improvisation—which Freud held to be the condition of orgasm. Entirely adequate to the spirit of America, pornography is just . . . fun.

"And all the porn fans and tricks out there for really supporting me over the years," Sprinkle exhausts you with her thousand thanks, even as porn exhausts with its endless decouplings and recouplings. "To my New York healing circle for getting me through the AIDS crisis, to . . . uh . . . there are so many people, my porn star support group, Club 90, we've been meeting for seven years now and their support has been invaluable and that's Candida Royale, Gloria Leonard, Veronica Hart, and my beloved Veronica Vera and the staff of the Kitchen have all been just wonderful and Scott McAuley, the curator here, for really taking a chance on me and I want to thank my favorite artist Linda Montano for making me what I am today"—a pause—"a performance artist."

And after the two hundred ho ho's and hah hah's: "I thought now I'd like to show you all my cervix. But before I'm going to show you my cervix I want to take a little bit of a douche first. [Nervous laughs.] It'll just take a second. I'll go to the bathroom. Don't get the wrong idea. I mean, I love all my pussy juices and smells and flavors and tastes but not everybody feels the same way"—going into a little bathroom onstage, about to offend conservative America—"we'll just take a quick rinse, hope it's not too cold. There"—inserting a little nozzle into her vagina—"you aren't getting embarrassed, are you?" to the audience.

For this chapter I made myself lovable to Sprinkle's New York feminist wing of the pornographic business. I took Sprinkle and Vera and Royale to dinner. Sprinkle on our first date told me she had "fucked half the state of Arizona as a teenager." And Vera, on ours, took me as an honored guest to New York's Show World, where in a parody of Dante, we ascended circle after circle of nether delights, pausing in the "booths"—on a phone to her, you direct a woman behind glass—for this little epiphany of shame:

Mulatto, nude, her feet on the glass, legs splayed to give the best possible view:	Jerk him off.
This author:	*Excuse me!*
Veronica Vera:	He's embarrassed.

With apologies to all the porn fans out there, the wankers who've wet-dreamt of personally being inducted by a porn queen, I had been *épaté*'d. And that, these stars and directors think, is their social function, to surprise and stupefy the bourgeoisie by nourishing their difference from the straight world. In Los Angeles, where I heard the "big" directors put down the New York actresses as "neurotic, wan, bad-bodied man haters," I was surprised to hear director Ron Sullivan, aka Henri Pahcard (*Babylon Pink, Viva Vanessa, Power Blonde, Outlaw Ladies, Hot Wire*, et cetera), tell me the women of porn "can tell themselves that since they're uttering lines as they suck cock, they're not prostitutes." Sullivan—"but it's their mind, because the day before or the next day, they'll have their favorite John come by to give them two hundred dollars for a quickie" (later, he tried to reclaim this assessment)—has only a slightly less scathing characterization of himself. In speedy bullets he tells me he makes only a little more than $100,000 a year; only now after 20 years in the business, drives a Nissan Maxima; disdains Beverly Hills, where he could propose himself as director of unprestigious horror or slasher films for which he could double or triple his income—the reason for all of which, he says, is his relative lack of talent and a rejection of the bourgeoisie generalizable to all the industry.

"There's a publisher of an adult magazine who takes anything I want to write as long as it's X-rated, so I write little short stories," he makes a figure of speech of his hobby. "He pays me $250 for five typed pages, whatever I feel like saying, sometimes based on actual events, sometimes totally fantasized. I write and make one pass. I don't rewrite anything, and of course the discipline of a good writer is how well he rewrites, as you know," he adds allusively. "That a person like myself can do something on a whim," referring to more than short stories, "and make an unfair amount of money for something so trite and trivial and insignificant—that might be the one thing obscene about our industry."

Serving me vegetable soup in his small apartment (rent: $450 a month, phone: $100) that doubles as editing room, Sullivan easily admits, when I ask him why he cuts away from erotic full-body shots to genital close-ups ("the plumbing shots," he laughs): "because I don't think we ever take the time to question what do we like to look at. We probably are too jaded." In his brown-wall-to-wall carpeted apartment in Van Nuys (the middle-class L.A. suburb, home to a large part of the porn business), Sullivan, forty-seven, tells me he's one of the top five directors in the business, happy to be "a big frog in a small pond. I'd much rather be on a set shooting a porno movie than in a meeting in Beverly Hills at the Polo Lounge"—oblivious that the seedy Polo Lounge, hangout of prostitutes, isn't where the meetings happen any more. Sullivan, whose wife lies abed (her back injured) during the interview, used to enjoy the sexual perk in his younger days; instead of "fucking those gorgeous girls on camera," he's content today to be an "old veteran" making "elite product." "We're having too much fun resting on our laurels," he says of the old vets, five out of some fifty porn directors. "Sleepy creatures tend not to get up." Two bowls of soup later, Sullivan introduces me to his lanky teenage son, then takes me into the adjoining room to watch him edit and hear him make a derisory crack about his penis to his colleagues at the Steenbeck editing machine.

Hunkered in their Van Nuys trenches, the soporific creatures of porn throw the poison gas of their product over the land, offending the Rorbachers and Jesse Helmses, guardians of American morality. "We do seem to, if not march, at least respond to a different vibration from the bourgeois world," Sullivan adds. "At the same time, we try to identify with it. We try to behave and look the same but we almost tend to caricaturize it. I compare us to the Mexican-Americans of San Diego and L.A., the zoot suiters protesting in the 40s during the war."

Caricature, like parody, mimics a language, exaggerates and makes abnormal what it regards as a disease of that language. Annie Sprinkle, finishing her douche in the Kitchen, is about to parody a major trait of postmodernity.

"I use only straight water, I don't use any chemicals, do you use chemicals?" she says to a woman in the audience. "What a mess, oops," as water drips down her leg. "Okay, we're almost done. There. That's about it. Thank you for being patient." And patting herself dry with toilet paper—"Does someone want to keep that?"—she offers: "You're probably wondering why am I going to show you my cervix? Well, there are several reasons. Oops, I didn't get all the water out—" she singsongs.

It's a game of parody on parody, caricature interrupting caricature, making it all the sharper when finally it will come (no pun intended).

"Why am I going to show you my cervix? Well, I sort of devoted my life to breaking taboos, especially sexual taboos. . . ." But that isn't why at all. She doesn't intend to reveal a depth under the taboo but its contrary. Read what her audience will find when the veil of the taboo is lifted.

"What I'm going to do . . ." Seated on a chair, the gown hiked up, spreading her legs as at a doctor's office, she inserts a gynecological speculum—"Let's all say that, *speculum*"—and invites the audience to come up and look inside. And it does, by twos and then clumps of people until there is a queue as at a Moscow meat market, a block long, along the stage apron, one entire side of the theater, even rounding into the back of the theater, women as well as men, spelunkers ready for an exotic cave. An attendant hands each a flashlight upon arrival.

"Hi, can you see the cervix?" she questions a visitor.

"Is there a cervix charge?" he says.

"Hello, okay, oh wow, oh I love this, hello, okay, oh wow," she encourages the successors. "Can you see it?"

"A little dot," says a woman.

"Do you see the whole circle?" Annie asks.

"Is it edible?" as if talking of candy.

"Looks like a tick on a dog's ass," says a southern voice.

"Step right up," Annie says. It's a circus. "Isn't this better than Santa Claus?" she burbles. "Wow, this line keeps growing!"

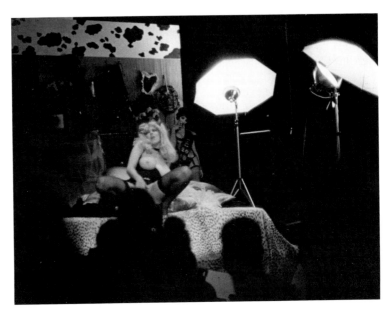

Figure 4.2 "Post-porn performance," Annie Sprinkle, above, called this show. So those staring eyes are ravishers of art, not flesh. *Courtesy Dona McAdams.*

It's a circus inside whose rings are . . . a little dot, nearly nothing. It's a visit to Macy's Santa during which the Fat One yawns and shrugs you off his lap. The hundred-odd campers eager to penetrate the feminine surface find a dot with all the status of a gumball or a tick. With good humor, Annie, who earned her reputation by expressing—literally, pressing out—her interior, teaches the troops that beneath the surface is just more surface.

In the "Post-porn performance" of Annie Sprinkle (title of the show), the speculum plays at satisfying the lust to see all. What it zooms in on and signifies is put off as the amateurs of spelunking struggle with the unfamiliar instrument. (Whence Annie's "do you see it?") And when at last the viewer has it in gaze, it appears insignificant, derisory. The manipulation of the speculum at the surface has itself become the object of desire, an ultimate surface that has triumphantly succeeded in drawing the thing beneath it out onto a banal plane where it loses its darkness, mystery, depth, and value to be consumed in its own right as image and surface—a tick on a dog's ass.

This is how all pornographic imagery works.

When one looks at sexually explicit video (film is outdated, photographs outpaced by the VCR), one intermittently has the sense that the woman, the lure of the system, has been *forced,* even when she appears most complaisant. This one has such an exquisite face but botches her lines so, the image of failed actress wafts from her: she is here because she can't be legitimate. Cast an eye over the women of pornography: Almost without exception they look subtly deformed, like Andy Warhol silkscreen figures, like Judy Garland, whose lipstick is displaced some millimeters above and below her lips. A nose on these stars twists down or up when it should be straight; an eye is pinched at the end; lips are too thin; hair, too bleached. Forgive me, ladies, they are not pretty enough to be straight.

Candida Royale, director of "couples' movies," formerly porn star (everybody's a star in this business) is talking to me over drinks in a New York bar favored by the biz. She has just told me that for 15 years, including the entirety of her career as a sex-film actress, she had waist-length hair. "I just came from my hairdresser, it's severely cut right now. It took me a long time to get up the guts to cut it off this short. I feel it's integral to how I'm just coming out as a person and feeling better. I came out from behind the hair and I came out from behind the porn-star image to feeling, being who I really am." She now directs "couples'" films—"for the last four-and-a-half years of my life trying to create nonexploitive, nonsexist erotica." I hadn't asked for anything personal, but toward the end of a two-hour conversation, she told me about the shearing of the hair, her penitential break with and of herself, and she said:

> I had a tremendous future ahead of me in the legit show-biz world and I just [she pauses] suffered a lot of [pause] confused feelings because of my involvement in the sex industry.

She was a dancer and singer in San Francisco. Her greatest success was "a lot of underground stuff in San Francisco with the Angels and the Coquettes, and I was in a play with Divine which was an equity production and I was singing in jazz clubs. I was called the little white Ella Fitzgerald because I was so good at scatting."

Let's understand that we are dealing with the commodification of some humans' misery. "In California"—where her own films are unpopular, not "raunchy"—"they call Gregory Dark brilliant," Candice (her real first name) says. Dark, whose real name is Brown and who is since retired, was a "hot" director (*New Wave Hookers, Let Me Tell You About White Chicks, Black Bun Busters, White Bun Busters* . . .).

> The Dark brothers make the most male-dominated, sexist, degrading, racist sex available. It's all interracial, it's all these "Hey, mama!," getting white girls like Ginger Lynn and doing anything they want to them and these girls just go wild, loving every minute of it.

109

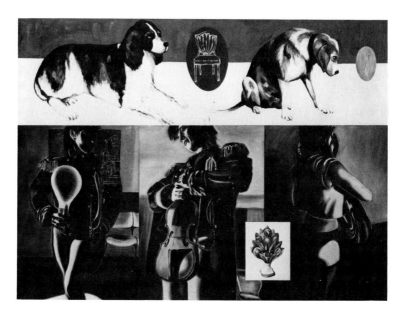

Figure 4.3 The absence of pornography. In a military jacket *sans culottes,* the woman presents a cabaret image nuanced by sadness (the lighting and color play a role in it, but especially the gaze). She is in three poses, not in the same picture plane but in three panels: holding a huge lightbulb, almost like a black hole, giving no light; covering her nudity with a violin, in no way holding it as would a violinist; lastly, partially undressed, hefting a big metallic tuba, the light glinting off it, turned away from the viewer. Above, two dogs, one dejected, one placidly alert, painted in naturalistic style, cousins of Courbet canines. Self-possessed, slightly lost, the dogs mirror the woman, conferring on her their bifurcated quality.

"Intervals." Salle is in front of the unfinished painting. "If you read from left to right, there are maybe a score of them that split the field. They go from dark, light, dark to light. It goes from here, one, two, three, four, five"—he's at the left end of the canvas—"fifteen, sixteen, seventeen, eighteen. There are eighteen changes of value from the left end to the right. It changes at a rate over an area. You could think of it as music."

The intervals draw attention to their play, they dephenomenalize the figures. Salle goes further in such derealization. He could have had such a rhythm in a single field but believes it would have been "wrong. Then you'd say, 'This painting depicts the passage of time'—a visual cliché. Putting these three views in one panel would have been like early modernism, old fashioned." Salle feels strongly that one "dies a bit" between the panels. He calls the panel demarcation "an interval of death": the image, he thinks, evanesces there, then returns in the next panel. "I think all of my paintings that work work on this same principle; they create an image and then take it away briefly so that you can feel its death or its passing, and then they bring it back."

Look at the second panel. The frontal plane is the violin; all the more so the elbow, which seems literally to be elbowing its way to the edge of the picture. Meantime where is the point of focus? Salle, touching now this,

(Figure 4.3 continued) now that part of the panel, cannot find it. "You're wandering around, you touch this, this, that," he says, "and that wanderingness, the lack of focus after two very strong focal points (the violin and the elbow) is interesting." It precedes and parallels the tuba player's turnaway. "It's because she's turned around and is less there that makes it interesting"—a word again charged with meaning, that of deconstruction. By withdrawing focus and face, in a hundred other ways, too, Salle withdraws presence without eliminating it altogether. He reveals a suppressed category of being, the neither-present-nor-absent; in no case, the exuberantly real of contemporary imagery and expectations. "You don't know how real this woman is. She's painted just real enough that she could be real but she's painted not real enough." In many ways large and small, Salle withdraws the presence of the happy, that is erotic body, to reveal as it were a secret that life itself seeks to maintain. No matter the position, the endearing words, the clasps, the other is Other, that is impossible, inaccessible, retractile. This is what you would experience in sex, what we'd all experience, were the culture not to lie to us. This is the essentially anti-erotic nature of life that pornography—not Salle—denies. David Salle—anti-pornographer.

A sense of a debased world from which one can exit at will, a glimpse into the margin, always and still emanates from these materials, relayed by "Royale"—"It's made primarily by white trash," painter David Salle told me; Salle, who has himself been regarded by some critics as a pornographic painter. "That's one of the things that's compelling about pornography, if it is compelling." Salle is still talking: "It's just such human misery, but no one's miserable particularly." Or as Baudrillard said in *Cool Memories*, recall: "At the center of a porno film, one of the girls suffers all the figures without changing expression—a blonde with black hair at the neck. Her indifference is seductive." Turned every which way, by one and by two, the Nordic blond's expression never changes. Cool misery. It's happy, easy, cool there.

A party inside the industry. At an annual Critics Adult Film Association Awards, Gloria Leonard, editor of the magazine *High Society*, verbally duels with *Screw* magazine editor Al Goldstein: a back and forth of insults, and then Leonard: "Al Goldstein, a legend in his own slime." She has incorporated the "straight" world's acceptance of "porn" or "porno"—inside the industry, one rarely says "pornography," for that word means dirty, in both senses.

I walk into a porn postproduction house, bearing for repair and resplicing a rare old eight-milimeter film *in a Glad bag*—am I mad? I didn't think—that's to say I unconsciously thought—porn was trash and so signified by putting the bits and pieces of the film into the black plastic bag . . . offending the head of the house, who had wanted to help me. "I wouldn't touch it with a ten-foot pole," he told me. It's filth, it's misery. But no one seems to be miserable, said Salle. Candice is talking:

I became someone else. I was Candida Royale, I wasn't Candice. It was like having two characters inside of me, and Candida was someone who was paid to go and make believe she was having a lot of fun. I wasn't receiving pleasure. I was just given and I was someone else. They wanted it so bad.

"She was so hot, she used to fuck the pizza delivery boys," a California director told me so long as I wouldn't use his name. "She was very young and slender and sweet-looking with this heart-stopping long raven hair, and she was drugged all the time," said another director—"she didn't know what was happening to her."

In a dismissive marketing aside, Ron Sullivan evokes the ferocity of her past and of porn: "I don't think her product is attractive to the consuming market. Candida is just trying to make a product that she herself can live with. Like, she'll cut the edges to make it more palatable for herself—perhaps to give justification to her past behavior as a performer."

We, on our side of the porn screen, haven't contact with the preparation of the cool image. Three-dimensional beings, composed of feelings, suffered for us, as perhaps Candice suffered—suffered acting failure, suffered the publicizing of the most private bodily movements. Says Sullivan: "Many of them do it so they get an opportunity. They're very serious about their acting. And they want to make some money. They'd rather act in a porno movie—they don't have anything against sex, they enjoy it—for $600 than be a waiter for $60." Next time you watch, think of that mild, sexually explicit body on the video as the stakes of a prior struggle. The force of ferocious competition exercised itself on that body, traversed it in order to make it that Face, that Hand, that Buttock. (Porn parts became standardized in the 80s: Breasts surgically became prominent; buttocks, muscular, depimpled; hair, whitely blond.) Just as the civil state drafts the civilian and imposes on him the form of a soldier; just as the nation converts the individual into a national, eventually a nationalist—so the market system forms a portion of its females into soldiers of pleasure. Annie Sprinkle and friends even call themselves, humbly, sex workers. Our pleasure, their misery. And it is possible, looking at porn, to hear the sighs of that misery, the sighs of that handmaid's tale of a destiny as cooer, sigher, dynamo, slut, oozer of sexuality—these aren't my nouns; they come from the Adam Director of Adult Films to characterize female "stars" and "superstars" of adult video.

The force of pornography: A man behind a kneeling woman pushes against her with such power that she loses her grip on the ground—has to shift her center of gravity. A double penetration: You witness as it were a greediness of man, as if those two—behind her, beneath her—were a single man wanting to occupy too much space. A stud slaps a woman on the buttocks, leaving after the second blow a strawberry, the tatoo of his libido. A man having performed the requisite outdoor "cum shot"—"I know, I know it's outmoded," says Sullivan, "we're trying to get away from it"— beats his organ, like a truncheon, on buttock or belly, ostensibly to squeeze every last drop out, to show you as much from his insides as your heart may desire.

Or you hear the director tell his actress, push her breasts together or leave them alone or move this way or that: Although those in the industry say the commands should have been cut out, *would* have been had time not been so tight and budgeting so strict, I do not think it is a matter only of incompetence, as Sullivan wants me to think—it is a code at work on the directors. They tell me they're just the porn equivalent of country boys: big frogs in little sex ponds. He doesn't know it, but that pleasant-sounding director giving orders is the Marquis de Sade for our time.

He never says, "Raise your voice," or "Pant more," or "Scream for me." Unlike the other Marquis, he not only doesn't want the feminine scream, he doesn't want her voice in any way at all. Have you ever wondered why, the instant penetration occurs, so does that bad "Saturday Night Live"–like music? Or that gushy pop Liberace score? *To-night we l-o-ove.* . . . Or all that bad rock that you hear? It occurs in order to repress, to obliterate the voice of the actor. The Marquis de Sade thought the scream was the victim's mark; his characters rigged up helmets over the women, "arranged so that the screams drawn from her by the pain inflicted on her resembled the lowing of a cow" (Barthes, *Sade Fourier Loyola*). The value of the helmet machine was to isolate the scream and deliver it to the libertine as a delightful part of the victim's body, a sonorous fetish.

But the voice, which is much harder to train than the body, is a rasping, grating thing, full of regional accent and the ugliness of contingency (squeaky, nasal, unmelodious, etc.). The voice bears the materiality, the individuality of the body. High-pitched or low, it seems to have come from deep down in the cavities, the membranes, the cartilages. It jars your fascination with the well-sculpted flesh on muscle (just enough fat between to produce the Jiggle, beloved of porn fans). What you want, on looking at porn, is the smooth finish of a surface, and a voice, very precisely, is deprived of finish.

So, if you're an actor or actress, the directors don't want your voice, and they'll coat it with music; what they want is your body on camera—in the men's case, erect.

"If we hire six men and six men are working that day, it's inevitable that one of those men will have trouble when the week before," says Sullivan, "the *day* before, he was fine. It depends on how much is going through your head that day, if you have some emotional attachment for somebody not on the set, or on the set. You've got to get like a robot to do this."

He's thankful even for a minute's, a few seconds' worth of erection. "You're spending eighteen cents a second waiting for a guy to get his dick up, and if it's weaving up and down, I may have to shoot it for an hour and a half just to get ten minutes of screen time. Quite often, I can shoot a few seconds of hard-core penetration—all the actor may be capable of—and use the footage over and over again within that close-up."

The woes of a porn director: He has to worry, not only about the origins but the end of the process. "Quite often we lose time waiting—it's hard for the actor to come," says Sullivan. "They're worn out and they're tired of the girl they're working with, and they've twenty guys watching them. One actor out of a hundred can do this; you and I couldn't do it. They are the unheralded heros of our industry."

Whose anxious bodies, like those of their distaff counterparts, the director has to trick. "There are many people in the business who aren't sure why they're doing it and don't want to be doing it," Sullivan instructs me. "It takes a long time to get them on the set. For various reasons they find little ways not to be there, and they find ways to get off the set. If I say cut, they'll get up and run and get a cigarette, so I tend not to cut, just keep the cameras rolling because there's part of them that's saying, 'I shouldn't be doing this, I don't want to be doing this, I don't like doing this.'"

These unsung heros and heroines are sports of nature. They Nautilus-train and California-bake their surfaces, leaving bra and underpant patches of white; surfaces on surface, pseudoclothing the voyeur tries to strip off with the eyes—one more vain attempt to arrive at something, at *anything* beneath the surface.

But the actors rise to the top precisely because they've made of one or more superficial traits a fetish. The women: each manipulates a somatic schtick: Christy Canyon,* a virgin look atop "enormous breasts," says Candice in disdain; Ginger Lynn, next door's blond with hangover eyes and cantilevered rump, an engine all apart from the rest of her; Taija Ray, her mouth a perfect O, a pout atop a compact, waistless body able at even and rapid speed to move up and down, a perpetual motion machine.

---

*"Even in bed they keep the ornament on or the shoe—it rarely fails. I think the crudeness of the sexual act demands an opposition of refinement. You get a kick out of the jump between the suggestion of maybe elegance and the bestiality of the act portrayed, because the sexual act involves destruction of image, transformation of the image of perfection and purity, literally getting under the skin of the image and suddenly distorting a mask that becomes uncontrollable in passion. In pornography it's acted out—pornography is a parody of love. It's game playing with certain signals, sounds, words. My wife said to me, "Why do they say yes all the time?"
ALEXANDER LIBERMAN, *editorial director, Condé Nast publications.*

And the men: As Sullivan told you, they're fetishized much more ruthessly, they're merely sticks, penises; the rest is refuse. Little Tommy Byron, as he's called: unstately, unplump, a small slender muscleless body, a rickety frame to hold a multi-inch, megathick member; thuglike Frank James, sweating like a summertime Central Park buggy horse over tiny, svelte, buttocky, sixteen-year-old-looking Nikki Charm, despoiled by this flesh mass. Or all-over-hair-bearing, fat Ron Jeremy, former English prof, barely a patch of white skin showing, dubbed Round Jeremy, who—remembering his ex-profession—can't stop talking; who orders the women atop him or kneeling: "All yours now" . . . "ride it" . . . "up to you" . . . "you're an animal" . . . "all yours now" in a pseudoparoxysm of license. He's like a three-foot-high Bugs Bunny doll, a lot of gray fuzzy hair on its chest—you pull a string and out comes: "Want a carrot?" . . . "What's up, doc?" Round Jeremy is replete with pillow talk: "Up to you, doc" . . . "want a carrot?"

Is it or isn't it porn? A test: If this man will defend you—lawyer to the industry, John Weston, partner in the L.A. firm of Brown, Weston & Sarno—then congratulations, you're a porn star or producer or director. Weston proudly gave me porn rental figures for 1991 and the three years before; around 400,000,000 per year, "just in the general video stores, not counting the all-adult stores." Each rental, he admits, doesn't correlate with one person; you can have rented ten or a hundred films in a year, but he insists: "Censorship people will say that ten people, ten perverts rented ten million films to arrive at my figure. But the figures have a built-in error factor: Very seldom is an X-rated tape viewed by one person alone. When rented, it is watched by two people or more." A few minutes later in the interview, he described the consumption of this tape: "By people who have VCRs and can't wait to get home and get it on fifteen minutes later." As if this were the industry line, Sullivan, too, told me: "I think that as soon as the tape gets into the first sex scene, the couple gets diverted. They'll start talking to each other about sex, the tape will continue playing, they'll pay less and less attention to it, they'll start communicating better than they ever have before, and they will end up having sex and giving credit to the sex tape when all it was, was merely an ice breaker." As if an X-rated tape could as well be blank after the first fifteen minutes; as if it were but a stimulant or a signal to leave it for another order of thing, lived experience.

Forgive me, Ron: "Our heavy consumer is men in their forties and lonely women in their thirties," he contradicts himself a few minutes after the ice-breaker image.

"Experience is," Weston continued, "that after a tape is watched, it is given to a neighbor to watch"—it's passed around like tomatoes from a back yard—"or to one's aunt." Sure: ". . . pornography, a form in which masturbation was the *only* subject," says Martin

Amis (*London Fields*). Porn as good neighbor policy—that's how "normal" Weston—and Sullivan—want me, and you, to think this stuff is.

I asked Weston, how does he know that people don't watch alone? "Can you give me a sense of your research method?"

"I can't."

The words uttered very tight. Sense of suppression, defensiveness. A beat.

The porn people have hitched their wagon to the ideology of relationship. The tape in the VCR, like a martini, like a modest sex toy, like a vacation away from the kids—it's just another aid to interpersonal relations. Who in this age of sexology could object?

We think that on the sofa, before the little screen, we're having a private experience; but that privacy is public. What room doesn't have a set now? Who walks into a room and doesn't eventually turn the TV on? In the most private place, I am bombarded by images of the exterior that have the force of a redoubled exteriority: I am shown a forest fire in China, a rugby match in Australia, a bombing in the Persian Gulf, more starvation in Ethiopia—everything on the same plane as the Monaco Grand Prix. Everything is there in my private place. There is no longer any possibility of a separated place, no longer the possibility of maintaining distinctions between inside and outside, fantastic and real. My interior has been publicized, the public has been interiorized—it's all mixed up. And although many of us still make the trek to theme parks, it's a ritual, a salute to the kids. We don't need any longer to go to a utopian space that has severed its links with reality. Our world, including our living room, has become a fantastic Disneyland.

Some of whose characters are "adult." We are in our homes watching, and we get to see everything, go everywhere, even to the most intimate places in which the subgods and subgodesses shake and shout, forming configurations that, by rights, I shouldn't see or hear. Some have never been seen before, are unavailable to normal people. "We're seeing things that cannot be done," Sullivan tells me. "The performers are trained, once they get aroused, to arch their bodies back, keep their legs up, open up their bodies to the camera so we can zoom in and get the plumbing shots." We are bombarded with images that, in principle, should be so exterior to us that we should never, except perhaps in the vaguest way, form signs of them. Yet these other beings are brought to us, our privacy invaded. We share this privacy with these sexual stars; we are socialized to watch others' sex, we cannot withdraw. I am in their place, they are in my place. Everything happens as if I were in receipt of a generalized instruction to turn on the TV, and as one of its subcommands, to let these images of the others' sex into my private space. And we are everywhere—now at the genitals, now at the heads. Now they've altered position—we are at this other or newer time. The porn people participate in a generalized power to make video images go quick, quick, quick! as you can snap your fingers.

Paul Valéry described how, in his day, you went faster than the speed of horses; if you didn't have a newspaper at your doorstep every morning, you were missing out, you felt. As the rhythm speeds up, of course, it keeps speeding up. The momentum, the acceleration, has to increase until, said Valery, "we are poisoned by speed."

And by ultrarapid montage. We are hooked on video clips. We receive in a few seconds what once took hours to explain. And these intensified, compacted messages bring about the end of story, of everything that was psychologically necessary to manage the comfort of our comprehension. Instead of being installed in duration, explanation, narration, the spectator is fascinated by images that run by without stopping. One can't be installed in a sofa today, there's no longer a place for the attentive spectator; he or she has only a soft part to play in the blending of the images. We usually think of montage as one image disjunct from another; but we have learned to pass over the abrasion, the montage point; we feel the rightness of the juxtaposition, enjoy the shock of the cutaway. We're always being yanked from a picture field, thus yanked away from the rest, the pasturage for the eye that is given by the depth of picture space.

I am evoking a new modality of the person, in nervous, excitatory relation to his or her entire sensorium. Which helps account for what I kept insisting, in L.A., was a defect of the movies: Bodies are never allowed to develop their configurations, altering them, decomposing them, recomposing at the rhythm of desire and of contingency. Desire, Barthes once said—and I told Sullivan—is a movement to arrive somewhere. But you guys always cut that movement short. Cut from medium shot to the close-up; cut from that to another position we never even saw the partners enter. Never does the camera stay at a single point, like a proper voyeur on the alert to an entire desire experience.

"Good point, good point," went Sullivan. "But the cameraman has shot his thousandth picture; probably he'll think: 'I've seen enough of this, I'm going to cut.'"

Porn people poor-mouth themselves: We're incompetent, we'd like to change, we will change. A poor-mouthing reminiscent of Terry Bedford, in chapter 6: When asked why he overused the color palette of blue and red, he ascribed it to boredom: "It's a convention." Which heaped on him the fury of Costa-Gavras: "It's not convention," he told me bitterly; there is antihuman logic in that palette.

There is similar logic in porn montage.

Montage made all the quicker by your hand holding the remote control. Today, we're all Keith Talent, who can "no longer bear watching television at the normal speed, unmediated by the remote and by the tyranny of his own fag-browned thumb. Pause. SloMo. Picture Search" (*London Fields*). Precisely in order to frustrate porn's montage, you fast-forward to your good bits, rewind and go to SloMo and take a hit or two of the freeze frame near the end. Porn's remote life. With a hand on each joystick, it's a distracting exhausting effort to beat the director and find a bit of sex peace. You never get it.

I could ask you to read again Louis Marin in my introduction, but you probably wouldn't do it. So here's Louis offering this analogy:

> If I go to the stadium, I participate in a sporting ceremony, a kind of feast. But I will see the match much better on the TV. Through it I am everywhere on the field; I am nowhere and everywhere at the same time on the TV. And I am robbed of my place.
>
> I used to say to my students: "One of the most beautiful definitions of self-identity is: Tell me *where* you are and I will tell you *who* you are." That's a beautiful definition of identity by location in space and by relationship to spatially bound others.

"Who am *I* then?" You'll recall I asked. "I am in the office of Louis Marin—"

> You are making a book, interviewing me in that place which is Francastel Library. You are visiting me. We observe a certain series of rites of, I don't say hospitality: our lunch was poor [he laughs] because of your speed, your interest in coming back here for the interview. I enjoyed to ask you to come in this office. And you enjoyed coming in. Really, we are exchanging something very important of our persons and identities through this place. You are sitting in this armchair in front of me, your head tilted, at rest on your hand, whose elbow rests on the chair.
>
> We look at each other with this Sony between us, registering; that's part of the process also. In front of the TV, you participate in being everywhere and nowhere. You are at the top looking at the faces of some people, then suddenly with the goalie—everywhere. And no-where. So it seems at the first glance that your identity is expanded to the dimension of the world. In fact, it's nowhere. You vanish.

I don't want to comment now on this startling "You vanish." Instead, I present a rather dramatic intentionality to pornographic materials; an intentionality explicitly given by Will Harvis, in-tensely thirtyish, graduate of Goddard College, reader of Foucault when I first met him, pornographer, he says, because of First Amendment respect. "What I see in adult film," he said, "is that this is uncensored." In a rather passionate flow of words, he continued:

This is reality as stark as the producer or the director of the movie want it to be. It can be extremely explicit or mildly explicit in language, in the visuals, in the sound. I can do anything with my movie that I want to do.

It reminds me of Joyce talking to his friend Maria Jollas: "I find I can say anything I want with words." I can access all of the real. Even from Joyce we wouldn't today accept the claim. But as if he hadn't read his Foucault and today's poststructuralism, it's a hunger for the real that Jarvis seems to suffer. A hunger brought on by a mass culture that doesn't nourish. Says Jarvis:

> Nobody in porn is going to cop out at the last minute. They cop out in television, radio, books, advertising, reporting. You get up to a point and you can't go any further. They cut short. Rather than deliver reality, they tease.

I can imagine Jarvis with Amis's Keith Talent, watching Nicola Six on video:

> "'Slow it,' moaned Keith, as the fade began. With a soft snarl he snatched at the remote. Then Nicola's quarter-clad brown body dashed backwards, and became a clockwork mannequin, then a living statue, as Keith froze the frame of choice.
> "'That,' said Keith, and sighed, not with yearning so much as with professional sincerity, 'that is the real thing.'"

Editing his directorial debut, *Our Naked Eyes,* Jarvis points to the screen, where delicate Cara Lott has just received a gigantic bump from the flabby belly of a pornographic blob. "We deliver reality," he repeats, and I think of Sullivan, jubilant if an actor can muster a few minutes, even a few seconds of "hard-core penetration—I can use the footage over and over again within that close-up," Sullivan foams, "and use simulated footage that I can shoot indefinitely." In case you've been in awe of those unsung heroes . . . they cheat.

It bothers Will, my Vergil among the devils in Miss Jones, that TV spots for bras, until recently, only showed the cups over a sweater on a mannequin; only now can one see a live model. Disturbed, nevertheless he understands: "Television is an entertainment medium; it is not meant to deliver reality"—commercial TV/"adult" TV, that is the distinction upon which he insists.

He thinks that if he shows you his "real" he has solved the problem of commercial signification. And his real, like that of Sullivan, like all the others', is hyperreal.

Think of Abboud's pea-green jacket. Of Ferré's giant paisleys. Glance ahead at Glaser's mouse making gorgeous charcoal stripes (p. 230). At Vanna's glossy vapidity when I ask her, did she agree with Koppel? (p. 258). The hyperreal is more perfect than the real,

A Day's Work at My Research

Will Jarvis was angry at me because I came in at the end of this scene. I had rushed away from the set to the Yale Club, expecting a call from the Soviet Embassy that never came. "Set!" a gruff voice would answer every time the phone rang; I left the set afraid the Soviets, helpful in chapter 18, would read the voice and not have to interpret the "Oh God, harder!" in the background. "At least we porn people keep our word," Will reproached me on my return. (He meant, my word had been to watch the whole thing, the real thing.) During my absence, Will, who doesn't cheat you out of the real and who was on a budget, had drafted one of the crew to perform opposite actress Cara Lott ("Because she cares a lot," Will told me). So there before you is the porn star who played Melanie Griffith's body in *Body Double* (yes, Brian De Palma cheated, Melanie's body wasn't "good" enough)—and a newly born actor who's on the alert for a knock at the door. His girlfriend, also in the crew, had been sent away to buy Chinese dinner—he doesn't want her to know he's cheating.

Figure 4.4 *Courtesy of Barbara Nitke.*

realer than the real, gorgeous special effects that make you forget about drawing or real women or men. You no longer have the desire to find its origin—the system has destroyed its own causes. Something has been substituted for something else and you forgot the substitution. The prosthesis fits fine. You're happy with it. Cool.

Sullivan says he gets in there for the plumbing shots because you need verification: I see it! The absolute Particular, *that* Penis. Sullivan thinks he points a camera at a certain vis-à-vis—am I crazy? he suggests, do I think he *likes* staring an inch away from a penis? The wet shot's "the proof, it really happened—we're getting away from it more and more." No you're not. The plumbing and the wet shots abolish the real by abolishing the distance implied by its gaze. Perspectival space is gone; with it, scenery. You get sex in its pure state, sex so close it's stripped of all seduction.

Hyperreal sex is fat sex, too much sex, an overdose or over-development. Thus even when the shots aren't plumbing, you get so much that there is nothing to add, no fantasy to exchange for the shot. "Take Christy Canyon," Candice told me. "She's a girl with enormous breasts with a look they can promote like a virgin look. She's a simulation." A simulacrum. "These women are not meant to look real," said Candice. "They are not representations. They are fantasy or distortion made concrete, made material."

"Look," said Will, "it's a better-than-life situation, because a lot of the human interaction is cut out. Two people meet and you don't know whether you like that person the first time you meet him or her; maybe the relationship develops and if so maybe with difficulty. Porn is hyperreal because you cut out that stuff and go to the end product of the interaction. And that end product goes well. You know as well as I that sometimes, in fact very often in sex, all is not well."

Porn doesn't give you the *there it is,* the *yo!* of sex. It prestidigitates it. There is no malaise in porn, no light vertigo, no trouble there, nothing having to do with the body so often described in literature as a total body totally trembling, victim to light seisms. The pornographic image is tonic. The novelist Phillipe Sollers writes:

> One senses in it the very dynamism of prudery simply inverted, it has something naively 'nordic' about it, it conforms to the Protestant spirit of capitalism in expansion, middle cadres, secretaries, beginning, middle, end. Motor. Action. Sex is enrolled in the space of consumption. Its negativity is denied, it has become profitable.

The sexual body is a mistake, a slip-up, a blunder of the system, a hole in the management of physiologies, a light insult to the spirit of enterprise, a more or less violent recollection of the gravity of the organs.

Real bodies abrade one another as they try to move as one. Said Jarvis: "The woman says no, I don't like that." To be a body is to suffer materiality, contingency, negativity. "In porn everybody's willing," Jarvis continued. "The woman always sucks the man and her breasts are silicone perfect."

"This is the first time in its history." Sollers concluded, "that humanity disposes of an official 'good version' of sexuality, including its deviances, its anomalies—"

Of which porn itself is one. Everything of the difficult, the troubling, the affected itself is gone. (Maybe you *can* give it to your aunt.) Porn—we are so comfortable with it, we shorten its name, call it by a nickname—porn, as other practices, removes the self and its sticky subjectivity from the act. It is a fat abstraction from the world—whence its appeal. Today we prefer images of the body to the body. And not only do we abstract, we abstract from the abstraction and prefer that. Hence, perhaps, the advent of digital effects. Hence, the SloMo ejaculations—without your having to touch the remote.

I really wonder how many couples, on looking at pornography, overdrive into the tremble of excitation. Those "enormous" breasts, that giant penis, all that jiggle—what now when you look at an "average" breast, penis, motility? A little burst of hate? A sickening feeling? What if an ordinary (the very word comes with a fall of the stomach); what if an ordinary woman, man, said "Kiss me" or touched you urgently?

The women (it's always the women, the *girls*) of porn are automata, love dolls, abstracted from subjectivity, from somatic materiality. This is why language is minimal, why the cuisine of erotic language is reduced to the "faster, faster, harder, harder, deeper, deeper" and little but that. It's why music, usually sentimental rock, accompanies every coupling. Watching porn, it's as if we were at the piano bar of sex.

> When I got out of porn I put myself into therapy. I realized that I didn't know I had lost my original, lovely, sensual, pure sexuality. The sex that I was having, thinking that I knew so much about sex because I was in porn movies; I was having the same kind of sex at home as in the film, the same kind of opening oral sex and so on. I realized that I didn't know the first thing about making love. The drugs on the set had enhanced sexuality in a fake way and suddenly there I was with my husband, we were looking at each other; it was a look that said: "Okay, no drugs, now what?" It was starting all over again, rediscovering sensuality.
> CANDICE SJØSDEDT

Humanity: nothing impresses it any longer excessively, and this is probably the reason we live simultaneously an epoch of redoubled conformism and of benevolent, medical, formidably moral liberalism. Nudes? As many as you want. Postures? Please. Coituses, sodomizations, fellatios? Why not? Sadomasochism in ceremonies for fashion presentations? Yes, yes. What has to be avoided at all, it seems, is the *instant.* Its expense in return for nothing, its interior spasm.

PHILIPPE SOLLERS

Religion, family, work: the Nordics of porn exists to allow an escape from their discipline. Into what you think is the hidden, the forbidden. "We want to give you feelings of dirty, pornographic, rather than beautiful and erotic," Sullivan told me. "Total nudity is innocence, panties pulled down the knees is not. I'm known for shooting the obligatory sex scene in a bathroom. In *Hot Wire* we built the bathroom to great specifications including staining it with Coca-Cola. What we're looking for is the zipless, Erica Jong, instant physical thing—selfish greed. Put them in the toilet, take the seats off the commodes, add some color, add the sound of flies buzzing— and leave part of the clothes on. This is bad, nasty, evil. You see, the parents who are having children now, who were the wild radical people of the 60s, they're not telling their kids sex is bad."

So he has to. Simulation of sin in the heaven of America.

It's bedtime, porntime. A few hours earlier, you've watched Vanna White, the national icon who rarely says a word; now, in the privacy of your nice home, you think to excite yourself with almost as statuesque, almost as clean a shape that will do what Vanna White won't.

Sorry. She before you is not cold, nor unmoved, nor slow to temptation; but she approaches that state. For the icons of porn are the very ones of advertising, the art of industry. In advertising you never get a *woman*'s image; rather, that of an icon, cold. "Whenever I photograph a woman next to a car," TV commercial director Terry Bedford told me, "I have to always empty her of life. Under no circumstances can she appear to be more lively or *as* lively as the car. She is glacial." The codes of advertising passed into porn. Too much heat there would exhaust its consumer. Cool makes him buy another tape, and another. . . .

Indeed, cool makes him a good consumer in general—easily able to control himself, to calculate his purchases. To jump, to explode with passion, to become obsessed? You would be lost, you wouldn't be able to function. You would lose your consumer power. Pornography is a switch—off.

End of a weekend with Helmut Newton and entourage. Washington, 7:30 A.M., Omni hotel, checkout. Newton beside a column is idly opening a sack, thumbing through some magazines inside. Xavier Moreau, Newton's agent, points to his bill, arguing with the cashier. "Seven dollars you charge—for what?" His voice is raised, guests are staring. "There was no penetration!" he snarls, and I shrink away to join Newton. "Give him this," Newton says, hand-

123

ing me the sack. And when sanguinary portly Moreau joins us, I do as I am told. Moreau opens the sack, peers inside, humphs, and saying, "It's for you," hands it to me. "Helmut, a word . . . " he says, drawing his client away. As they chat I open my gift, magazines with titles like *The Dresden Diaries, Pinned & Smothered, Lesbian Dildo Bondage, The Training.* . . . A beady-eyed gentleman looking oddly like Martin Heidegger floats before me, held in some web, wrists and ankles in restraints, his botton covered in silk panties. A slattern, her lipstick awry, inserts ben-wa balls. . . . It was all so utterly prosaic that the Paris-born Moreau gave it to this American, supposedly slavering over the quotidian passing for porn here. Doubtless on one of his nocturnal prowls in Washington (from which I had been excluded), Newton had purchased this first matter for his fantasy.

Earlier that day, walking in the trench of the Vietnam war memorial, he had complained that porn in Europe wasn't what it used to be. You can no longer go to an elegant club, sip champagne, and watch the gorgeous have at it. It's all so American, he told me, watching relatives trace the names of deceased on the monument. Small wonder. Porn isn't about elegance over here. But Helmut Newton is.

He's also about cruelty.

The
Courtier's Contempt:
Helmut Newton's
not so Beau Monde

5

"When we at *Vogue* published the image of the woman on the sofa (Fig. 5.1), we created a violent reaction," said Alexander Liberman, editorial director of Condé Nast Publications. "To us it seemed a very natural situation. Here is a woman looking very suggestively at a man only suggested by the pants and back of torso. Her pose, her gaze, imply erotic possibilities. It seemed Newton was able to catch a moment of a reality about to happen. The adventure could go on, or not. He starts imagination—the spectator is left with desire to pursue the narrative, complete the scenario."

So Newton awakens desire, he gives the spectator an appetite for a good story. But what is the subtext of forty-some-odd years of producing editorial and advertising adventures? Why have they aroused so much controversy? What is the source of Newton's fashion and commerical power?

Death is a strong part of the story. In a photograph called *Office Love* (not shown), there's little left of her dress, the arms are submissive. Is she arching her back to complete the embrace or is her lover forcing her toward him? In full dress and bent over the side of her breast, he sends the mind to a thought of the vampire at the neck. In *Père Lachaise, Tomb of Talma* (Fig. 5.2). Thanatos becomes explicit. Holding her breasts, the woman mirrors the sarcophagus statue holding a head. A tight bodice pushes out the breasts—it can't be comfortable. Erotic perhaps, pleasant by no means. You wear the accoutrements to make yourself sexual.

And that is the fashionable woman—so many accoutrements. Such labor to her will to ignite your desire. It is this labor we call style—drained away by Newton. A labor for—naught.

Figure 5.1 Woman examining man, Saint Tropez 1975. *Courtesy Helmut Newton.*

Figure 5.2 Père Lachaise, Tomb of Talma, Paris 1977. *Courtesy Helmut Newton.*

Newton starts to tell an interesting story, the story of fashion, which you yourself must complete. There is Jenny Kapitan, in *Pension Dorian,* her leg in a cast, also her neck (Fig. 5.3). The two casts, the cane by means of which she stands, are signifiers of her pain. But look how straight she stands, how she thrusts forward her wide hips and belly and holds her head aloft. It is a poignant image, delivered in the code of sexuality, but also that of medicine. And medicine, the art of staving off death, is the contrary of sex.

Look at the proud head. She's showing off her* brace. Look at the pelvis—she's displaying the cast. As if it were stylish.

Style robs you of life, says the image. And style is violent in another way: toward the others.

The women of *Sie Kommen* (Fig. 5.4) strut their bodies so congruent with today's erotic and fitness somatotypes. A skin, muscle, bone exhibition: the hero parts. All articulated: even the pubis, ending in a point, has a life of its own. Then why isn't Eros there? Because their nudity has become dress, as said in the introduction, one lustrous part leading to the other, all prominent, fetishes. They are runway models showing this season's new look: skin. The title acts like the announcer: "Sie kommen! Here they come!" Two of them are aggressive, their hands on hips; one is defensive, arms folded over diaphragm. They are fashion warriors, not victims. They say, "Look but don't touch." But the igniter of Eros, which is language, makes another voice-over: "I'm coming! I'm coming! all four of us coming!" But they're not; and never will, for you. And so they say—fashion says—"Look and die with desire."

The philosopher Jacques Derrida has written that style is pointed, it seeks to project itself in the world in the manner of a spur, it disdains, it rebuffs, it thrusts itself into view and hurts those who encounter it. Like Derrida, Newton in a thousand ways shows that fashion style is inherently fetishistic, it is violent. "I started to work for French *Vogue* in '61," Newton says. "Right through the 60s I did my utmost to push the sexiest fashion photos on them. I was fresh from the Australian bush, totally instinctively cutting against the terrible blandness of the time."

Newton thrust himself into view when style was on the decline, when the 60s uttered the message that style kept us from our

---

*"There's something very sad about the human body. Look at all the paintings of Adam and Eve being expelled from Paradise. It's rather pathetic. Women cannot be glorious bare because that's the way God or whoever is the creator made bare human beings—they are rejected. And I think fashion is an escape from the human condition. What does Newton need? High heels. Even the projection of the body becomes different. The buttocks stand out differently. That's why high heels were invented. The slant of the buttocks, the chest, everything changes, becomes glorious instead of being humble and closer to reality and nature. Aggressiveness enters into the appearance of the body, and I think high heels have a quality of superiority through height, confidence and a certain sadism, cruelty."—Alexander Liberman.

Figure 5.3 Jenny Kapitan, Pension Dorian, in a really high heel, Berlin 1977. *Courtesy Helmut Newton.*

Figure 5.4 Newton himself captioned this photo. "Sie Kommen," he wrote. Paris 1981. *Courtesy Helmut Newton.*

authentic selves. To remove our politeness, our grooming was to show each other the deep, personal, natural selves we were. Newton is the inheritor of the modernist idea that perhaps all is style, perhaps there is no secret self aching to be liberated.

It's January, in front of the Reagan White House, the very beginning of this project. Newton on impulse stops his car, lopes out of the seat, and approaches a woman with a camera who stands next to a life-size Ronald Reagan made of cardboard. She makes her living photographing tourists with "the president." Placing his arm around "Reagan's" shoulders, Newton tells the woman: "Photograph my friend and me—from our toes to the top of our heads." Helmut "kinky" Newton has noticed that his new friend shares an interest in bondage: To keep Reagan from falling, the woman has lashed cords around his legs.

The woman remonstrates with the master of artifice. "It won't be real if I do that," she says.

"From tipee toe to top of head, I said."

She starts to raise her voice: "Are you doing this to me *because I'm a woman?*"

He drowns her out: "DON'T GIVE ME THAT RACIST SHIT!"

She appealed to him in the code of feminism that all of us have been trained to respect. He refuses to accept the code and slaps back with gratuitous authority. He breaks conventions and can be as cruel in his behavior as he is in his images. The genius of artifice has no patience with amateur realists.

But there are signs of softening around the legendary hard-core edge. "I don't deserve to be called King of Kink," Newton says. "I haven't done anything kinky for a long time." The "photo op" over, the boy in the man (who was then sixty-six) is pouring gobs of ketchup onto his lunchtime burger. "There was a big article on porn in media in *Time*," he says. "Didn't name Newton at all. He seems to be looking very acceptable these days."

The artist who didn't hesitate to be rude to the realist knows well that "acceptability" comes from being disciplined by conventions, and he refuses such civilization. Why then is he out of the gutter?

The system isn't being shocked by this once and perhaps future king because of his change of métier in the late 70s: from fashion to portraiture. "After forty years in fashion photography it was getting too much to be put on the spot monthly or weekly to dream up new ideas to please the advertisers of fashion magazines. I was worn out, exhausted trying to think up the riveting mise-en-scène that the model, the makeup and hair people—all that investment—demand."

"His fantasies are extraordinary," says photographer and author Matthew Klein, my dining companion a chapter or so back. "Anybody can have a fantasy, but not anybody can have a Helmut Newton fantasy. His are richer, more explicit, less obvious, more exotic, quirkier than yours or mine or anybody else's. He is a genius of fantasy." And fantasy, evidently, like life itself, is subject to the wear and tear of repetition.

Newton felt that the dresses, the frock coats, the made-up models, were like endlessly repeated substances dooming him to repetition. So he developed an active desire for a mutation. He decided to opt for the real and not its signs.

"We make a distinction in my business between models and real people," he says. "We never refer to models as real people. Because they are paid a high sum of money, these 'unreal' entities become whatever the photographer says. But I wanted to talk with a real person who, out of his or her desire, had designed a real life that I might control and manipulate under the constraint of the real."

Newton sought another set of constraints: that of fame or notoriety, power, and wealth. "I didn't realize until 1974, when Philippe Garner of Sotheby's pointed it out to me, that I was the portraitist of the high bourgeoisie. Philippe mentioned—it was like a jolt—that all that leather stuff, the whips, what is called my sexist world, were the keys to unlock the Paris 16th *arrondissement* apartment, the environment of the very rich."

Newton's disclosures became artifacts in the new *Vanity Fair,* when, in 1983, Liberman and former *Tattler* editor Tina Brown recreated the magazine to become the cutting edge of celebrity journalism. In 1984 the Museum of Modern Art in Paris mounted a retrospective of 220 of Newton's portraits. The idea of portraiture so obsesses him—"Portraits disappeared after the war, they've only come back over the last fifteen years"—that he became the portrait-ist of his own mortality. In 1973 he suffered a massive heart attack and shortly thereafter began a self-portrait series. There are portraits of the subject sitting on his doctor's examining table; others lying back in his dentist's chair. "I'm fascinated by the face of the famous or notorious, anybody who has astounded the world," he says. "They've written themselves on the world. Who wants to look on my or your Aunt Agatha?"

So Newton invades privacy, as he puts it. Enters the celebrity's home. He photographed David Bowie, Charlotte Rampling, and David Hockney getting out of bed in the morning. He poked his camera into the stars' night tables to find signals to the lives they led. "How orderly Bowie's drawer was," Helmut told me. "I wondered what that cigar stub in Charlotte's drawer meant?"

Look at his portrait of Regine (Fig. 5.5). Does she think she's being elegant, strutting like a chorus girl? It's German expression-ism in a crowded room: a woman in a hat and bare breast, making love to a snake lamp. This stylish person who is missing her bottoms has arched her back so acutely—look again—she has to hold onto the lamp base to keep from falling.

Look at Sigourney Weaver, who slits open her elegant dress to reveal—not an elegant expanse of nyloned leg, but the blatant place where nylon ends and constricted flesh begins. No smile, either. Suspicious eyes, too.

And Charlotte Rampling's eyes seem to slide your way sidewards in mocking suspicion (photograph not shown). And Newton him-self in *Self-Portrait* (Fig. 5.6) duplicates *Las Meninas* of Velazquez, where his wife could be the king; he, the painter; and the nude, a princess. The contrast he enforces—dressed/undressed—links him to a classical visual tradition. But in that coat, Newton looks for an instant like a flasher. Bent over the camera, his coat beginning to part, his pose sends a deconstructive frisson through that of June, his wife, posed as fashion editor, alertly leaning forward in the director's chair, palm cradling chin.

What you are seeing isn't the private self, densely subjective. You are seeing the terrible distortion, the transformation the star system has made of the self that would be king. What Newton gets is the failed emotion, the bitterness meant to be repressed by the public

Figure 5.5 Régine at home. Newton wrote the caption you just read. Laconic, no? *Courtesy Helmut Newton.*

Figure 5.6 Self-portrait with wife and models, Paris 1981. *Courtesy Helmut Newton.*

image. Newton's photographic images parallel the painterly imagination of David Salle, of George Grosz, and of course, of the master "peintre de la vie moderne," Charles Baudelaire.

Newton has an obsessive idea, the human becoming stone, a statue, being infiltrated by nonhumanity. Sucking at Nastassia Kinski's breast is the unliving, a doll of Marlene. Sometimes, when Newton couples human and mannequin, you can't tell which is which right away. Sometimes never.

To be human is of course to pulse with desire. But his eroticized beings suffer, and what they are suffering is a depletion of life force itself. He once photographed, in extreme close-up, a mouth covered by gray makeup; the exception, a red smear on the lower lip. It was scarcely a desiring, desirable woman-mouth. It was more like a mountain defaced in red. The human has calcified, and in an irony masking his lament of that fact, Newton has made a statue to calcification, has aggrandized that condition into art.

Because we feel depleted, weak, there enters into our lives an impulse to compensate for that human power failure. And there is fashion's function. Newton, like Baudelaire before him, has grasped that clothes and makeup are prostheses: they cover up, they correct for, a lack. Instead of simply playing the fashion game—proposing all manner of adornments and coverups—Newton signals the dark side of fashion.

That is why model Jenny Kapitan stands in that neck brace wearing the leg cast. "That was a real cast," Kapitan told me. "I had twisted my knee dancing rock-and-roll, and when I appeared, abashed, before Helmut for the shooting, he said: 'That fits me perfectly, I've been doing all these pictures with braces.'" He was attracted to her injury, her deficiency. So look again at her, the woman of fashion in the process of dressing up (or down). Her undergarments are braces. Her depletions are propped up in this site of enervation. Which one? The Salon Kitty, a favorite whorehouse used by the Nazis to extract secrets from gullible clients. Newton's faces, his bodies, are as much objects as the objects he photographs. See if you can decide which is more alive, more desirable: Veruschka's face, hair, pubis (she's hidden most of it), or the view from her balcony. Which do you prefer: the breasts of the passive *Woman Being Filmed* or the necklace above them? Andy Warhol's tightly closed, down-turned lips, or the tape recorder and consumer products he grasps?

"He has discovered a secret behind the erotic," says Liberman of Newton. "His observation of women is one of the most profound and scathing at the same time. He puts into play strange forces of domination, of the exploitive, of orgasm. It's a whole sexual mythology he deploys—lesbians, transvestites, hookers. His so-called low-life eroticism has to do with a certain conception of the liberated woman. Behind the apparent classiness that he conveys through his high fashion, there is another level present. He shows that desire can even flow toward a raincoat. Maybe modern desire *is* a raincoat."

Or that notorious saddle on the woman in the bed. It's cruel and refined. The hunt takes place in the bedroom. Will the horse throw the rider or will they both capture the prey?

Like all the great painters of the Renaissance, Newton works for a patron. But unlike the Renaissance painters, he's always threatening the patron's values. Xavier Moreau, one of his publishers, said: "Newton is a creative mercenary, and he requires a force to constrain him, like a Party, a Cause, an Ideology. He works best within a code, but if you constrict him with a code, make him a strong border, he decides to have his way anyhow."

Stendhal said that the political novel was like a shot in a concert hall. Newton is an erotic powder keg, a vicious knife, in the midst of the 16th *arrondissement* salon. He's about to slash or blow you to pieces.

How would you like a life without glossy image to consume? That's the precipice to which Newton takes you.

135

6

T*he* B*ritish* R*evolution* *in* A*merica*

And here we are with the prestidigitators of that gloss, the unsung cultural heroes of America—its admen and women.

America is America, and Europe is Europe—and never the twain shall advertise the same. American advertising is data-driven for the most part. A part of the marketing genius of America is its research capability. Critics of American advertising maintain that the creative is merely an afterthought, a mechanical actualization of concepts drawn from the research. European advertising, on the other hand, often comes closer to the tradition of feature films: the sensibility of the director is not overwhelmed by the agency's need to satisfy a client.

Some U.S. agencies import foreign talent to catalyze lackluster creative work. And there is where the fun begins.

Even when the Europeans speak the same language as we do, American and British directors of TV commercials find that their differences are often the source of irksome misunderstanding.

They work in the same media, yet they come from different worlds. The Americans seldom wanted to do anything *but* advertising, and the British did advertising because they couldn't do cinema.

Around 1977, a group of young, ambitious British artists, who wanted to direct film and found few opportunities, lowered their ambitions and started shooting commercials. ''In England there was nowhere to go,'' said Terry Bedford, one of the precocious talents of British image-making. ''Television was an avenue you could open to flex your muscles, experiment. You concentrated on commercials as the route through to films, and in doing so dragged a lot of people along. We built an industry, it got very glossy, it also became an art form."

Ridley Scott, Hugh Hudson, Allen Parker, and Howard Guard used television commercials to experiment and create a new, sophisticated, and powerful style of television commercials. "I loaded magazines for Ridley when I left art school," director Terry Bedford reminisces his youth. "I remember Ridley having fun one day. 'I've got a Titan crane 'cause I want to see what it can do,' he said. It was 17 feet off the ground, the largest crane available, the sort of thing you'd never see in a TV ad. He was indulging, playing.

"Another time, in Austria, on the same set where they shot *The Third Man,* he said, 'I'm going to cut a three-minute version of this. I know Benson & Hedges doesn't want it, but *I'm* telling the story, I want to see what I can tell in three minutes.' He was learning his trade." The success of British directors attracted the attention of top management in American advertising. "We were astonished in the late 70s," a Grey Advertising executive told me, "because we saw uses of color and lighting that we had never considered possible, and what we began to do was imitate these British."

And buy them.

I recently asked Philip Dusenberry, chairman of BBDO New York, *not* who he thought were the best directors amongst the British Mafia, but to whom he paid the most money. Ridley Scott, Tony Scott, Adrian Lyne, and the no-longer-apprentice Terry Bedford comprised his short list. For the Brit directors, art and style were high priorities. For the American agencies, art was the instrument to achieve impact and sales. This has been a constant element of friction in the ongoing love-hate relationship between British directors and American agencies.

I followed Dusenberry's lead to London as an American eye to study the clash. Terry Bedford, one of the leaders of the Mafia and the only one not yet a feature film director, was available and outspoken.

"Here you have control—in America you don't," he said as he treated me to a critique of his reel and revealed the nature of the Brit–U.S. misunderstanding. "In America," he continued, "they begrudingly give you a first cut—a director's cut, they call it. And often, even if you get it, you work with an editor of the agency's choice, not yours, so he's not a friend. It's very very frustrating working in America."

Understandable as his artistic frustration was, there is logic on the American side. We want to prevent the artist's "blackboxing" his final product (here it is, take it or leave it); blackboxing that would prevent the agency's input in the production, thereby control of the final product. It is a clash between the artist's interest in his work and the agency's need to partition production and thus assert its control. But control in aid of what?

A few years ago, for American Express, Bedford was given a script presenting "a young kid playing the piano and he just invents a tune and his girlfriend comes in, cooks dinner. It was written in a very lounge-lizard style. I said it couldn't be rendered in such a laid-back way." He told American Express, "it's got to be rock-and-roll, got to come at it fast or you won't have any chance of getting it in 30 seconds." Eventually AmEx agreed. Bedford pursued his own logic. "He's a rock-and-roll kid, a songwriter, make him look fast, maybe he should have an oriental girlfriend. He's in L.A., after all." The avant-garde casting, as Bedford called his idea, turned the client not just cold but morbid. It was killed at the top. "Those people just won't let that happen. So the rock-and-roller was taken out." As well as the oriental. "We ended up with somebody who didn't satisfy me but seemed to satisfy everybody else." Terry Bedford wanted to create an atmosphere of cutting-edge modernity in which orientals of the Pacific rim are central. His world was too far out for AmEx, which, citing research, but in fact as a matter of ideology, resisted allowing images of the multiracial entity America has become. Bedford was obliged to recast the spot, coating America white. "Casting is one of the areas where the interference is higher in America than anywhere else," he said.

Control in aid of what? Images of Disneyfied good cheer. Let Bedford instruct you in the World According to the Agencies:

> Recently, for Oldsmobile, I was working in a disused steel mill in Fontana, just outside L.A. It used to be an area of giant steel mills, it's a location used for gritty Blade-Runneresque movies. When you walk into it you're dealing with structures like skyscrapers. One of the big vats in which they used to melt iron ore stands, like 40 floors high, and I'm thinking of somehow or other trying to manhandle this location into a commercial for a car.
>
> Now when Oldsmobile came to me with its concept it was nothing more than pulling the drapes back—*duh duh!*—brass band, people marching, fireworks, champagne. But the automobiles of this particular year looked no different from those of the last year. Which is why I proposed, instead of the clichéd brass band, coming to the most uncosmetic location I could find; this one, the dirtiest, the most disgusting, old iron, basically; coming here and putting these pristine shiny cars into this rubbish tip, this black hole.
>
> "Yes, yes, yes, we love your ideas. Great, great, great, great, great." They buy into it but once they've bought into it they start to move back towards mediocrity, creep back moment by moment. "Well, maybe we should sweep the floor up"—that kind of thing.

The British Revolution in America

139

Only it's scarcely mediocrity, and Bedford will come in his narration to realize that.

I decided to hatch the cars out of machinery. So we built two machines that we split open. On the outside they looked like dusty old pieces of industrial waste. On the inside we placed brand-new vans and cars. And then we buried a car under scrap iron—the idea was, the scrap iron was going to blow away as though some tornado had come and picked it up to reveal a pristine car. It seemed in good contrast to the dusty old cheap metal.

Bedford was on the way toward a mythopoetics: the recrudescence of the American automobile industry. To ward away interference he focused on narrativity. "There'll always be a story to be told"—agencies are still respectful of narrative, Bedford told me. They are afraid to tamper with story for fear of destroying it.

The story line involved a night watchman whom I made the instigator of the action. He comes along doing his rounds late at night. He sees a plug lying on the floor and it's arcing, *zzzzzz*, and he thinks, "Huh! That should be plugged in." And plugging it in, he energizes the whole factory, and the show starts. Lights come up, the cranes start to move, cars hanging off them covered in sacking. Projections start, images on the walls of cars traveling, a giant face in the air, that of the female announcer, all of it done in postproduction, a mammoth show. You see, the plug is the watchman's magic wand, and whatever he touches he breaks open. Even his flashlight is magic now; he points it at industrial waste and it, too, cracks open. His breath is magic; by blowing on a pile of waste the wind carries it away to reveal a car.

It's Friday before the shoot. Casting, finished. Art direction, done. Pre-light, okay.

Phone rings, seven o'clock in the morning. Producer's on the phone. Disaster.

"The head of the agency says we can't use this cast," he tells me.

"What do you mean can't use the cast?" I say. "Everybody agreed. Guy's booked. He's on the plane, he's flying from New York to L.A."

"Can't use him, too working class."

"What do you mean, 'Too working class?' It's perfect that he's working class, it's exactly what he is."

"No way can we use this person. This is who you've got to use."
It was a bumbly old counter corner store kind of guy. Father Christmas, basically. Sweet old man, the sort of guy on whose knee you put your granddaughter. Except he was 84 years old. Couldn't remember my name from one day to another. Thought everybody was new every day

he got up. And the guy who was flying from the east coast? He was turned around when he landed. Put back on the plane and sent away. He really could act, too.

Want to know how I was going to end the script? I had a kind of goofy guy to be the assistant. He was out of it so when all the security screens were displaying this weird and wonderful party—

—a vision of an industrially awakened America—

—he's watching Bugs Bunny on the television, and he doesn't become aware of something going on until a second before it ends when he glances around and catches an image and goes, "Wow! What's this? Am I seeing things?" Gone. So he's prompted to go rushing down to the shop floor and when he arrives the party's over and the night watchman is walking around with a cheeky smile on his face, whistling the tune. And then, just as a little aside, uses his flashlight to operate the vending machine at the end of the corridor. It pours him a cup of coffee without his having to do anything. A nice little sweet touch to end on.

My guy was thin, fit, not cosmetic in any sense. His face was characterful, if anything ex-police or -service.

Bedford planned to make an image space, an ideological space in which working people might recognize themselves and be magnified. For once, let us say, the machine will act on their behalf. The producer, however, wanted them invisible. He ex-inscribed them.

I did not want a stereotype Old Man, but the stereotype is what I did give you. And that says to me a lot about this country. You go out of your way to invest in sentimentality on television. And for a lot of people and generations of them, the television set is the reality check; if you prefer, the Father that tells everyone what life should be like. And how are the young people going to find within themselves the critical faculty to decide that such and such is a true portrayal of life or is not? It's asking too much of them. And we all contribute to it. You just bow out in the end. What are you going to do? Friday before the shoot, you can't walk away from it, you're financially involved. You're crippled.

Terry Bedford, at $18,000 a day, one of the highest-paid TV spot directors in America, finds it difficult to adjust to the modernity of America, all the while contributing to it, first, in an ideological way, and then, in a formal way even he at first didn't realize. He came to the rather painful awareness of the formal imperative by way of a mild complaint. We were looking at his spot for Pepsi called "Time Machine," in which a young time traveler inadvertently takes a can of Pepsi "back in time, before television, before radio, even before soft drinks" to the year 1885. "Funny enough, on film it's not as blue as that," he uttered in mild contempt. A narcissism of small difference, I thought, recalling Freud. The ceiling lights glowed blue, the back wall was blue, the time capsule exuded blue as if Creation had been parsimonious in color. When the young traveler (his tie and collar red) stepped into the capsule, the sparks from the thrown switch were icy blue (a few, red). "The guy in the control box turns everything up," Bedford said, referring to the postproduction technician transferring film to tape. "He won't let a movie shot go out. He will turn everything up full bore, which is something that wouldn't happen here. It destroys mood. This to me is too much light," he assesses.

But far from being an aberration of "Time Machine," it's virtually inbred now, he tells me. "We certainly use cold back light, I mean, there's no doubt about it," he confesses. And suddenly, felt as in a horror film where something inside metastasizes through the skin, Bedford is fairly bursting with the technique of this color enhancement. Pointing to a frame from "Time Machine," he notes: "This has probably got half blue gel on it." He tells me he puts blue gelatin on regular lamps, he doesn't like the newer lamps his contemporaries use, HMIs, lamps that perform like the aircraft-landing lights that beckon you down, "blue by nature. If you use it straight, you will get a blue halo effect," the very effect of the ceiling lights in "Time Machine." He continues: "And/or you'll get a blue cast, a cold cast. The HMI was the beginning . . ." he muses the years, '77, '78. "They certainly seemed to coincide with the revolution. I personally didn't like them because they were insensitive, had no finesse to them. Whereas an old-fashioned lamp had a hard beam in the center and then a softness on the edge. And if you were photographing people, you could cant it off slightly and catch them in the edge of the beam and get a very very soft, gentle background light which looked like filtered sun coming through late afternoon, through a window or through some trees."

But the British revolution in advertising wasn't about people and the modulation of their moods. Bedford told you: "It destroys mood." He destroys mood. All the advertisers destroy mood.

HMIs burn at 5400° Kelvin, a little short of the temperature of the sun (its photosphere is 5780°), but their color is the contrary of the sun's. "They're so massively powerful, much more powerful than tungsten lights, much more intense," director Michael Oblowitz told me. "They pierce through anything. They are very even, very hard, sharp, and moving away from a warm source, yellow being a warm source." Bedford is unable to abandon the old-world traditions of artistry and humanism. On the contrary, Oblowitz relishes the new world's abandonment of the real. "What's nice about them is, they're cold," he says. "It's ironic. You'd expect light and hot, expect it to go red, it's so intense. But in fact it goes the opposite. It's like a cold star, cold, cold light and that's what's so sexy, the fact it's cold, dead. Necrophilia lights." As if the world they lit were dead and all its three-dimensional guts bled out on some god's embalming table. "They make everything flatter," Oblowitz relishes.

"Way back before the HMIs, even before smoke, they used to throw very fine particles of clay into the air, just like dust," said Bedford. "It settled down and it would diffuse everything. What it did was, it gave you depth, it muted color so the colors didn't jump out at you. Then came smoke, and then the revolution happened where everyone said, 'We don't want any more smoke, what we want to do is see color for what it's worth. And we won't put the lamp round the back, we'll put the lamp round the front. And we'll shoot straight on, since you get every ounce of color back into the lens.' Whereas the old technique, you more likely had the lamp three-quarters back, so everything would be a tone; so if it were a red, by the time you photographed it, it would be a brown and maroon."

In our brave new world the blue sun wipes out tonal difference, it forecloses the calling into being of distinct hues and separate sensations. "Our eyes are able to see many colors and warmths, except that our eyes are trained *not* to see them any longer," cinematographer Ed Lachman said. Trained, he told me, by today's spots and films. "The old tones had an element of smoke in them so they had depth to them," said Bedford. "The smoke would push the color back."

"The background isn't really a background any more," said Oblowitz. "It's pushing up toward the front." Today's blue light triumphantly succeeds in drawing the objects of its gaze onto a single picture plane, as if arranged under glass like a precious display at Tiffany's. Features, body parts, items of clothing, cars, cans, often colored red—this furniture of the world that otherwise would be jumbled *melds.* Heterogeneous in your life, these objects form a glossy skin for the camera lens, a single object for consumption by an eye turned away from the real in love now with pure surface. Bedford remembers his friend Howard Guard "going into the Mojave desert and paving a road in coal for a mile to give it a different texture, then spraying it all red."

Unable to restrain my interpretive mania, I asked Terry Bedford why *blue,* why *red?* "I think it's a convention, really, that your back light should be blue and your front light warm."

"No, those colors you are talking about are the rapid colors," Constantin Costa-Gavras told me in Paris when I relayed Bedford's answer. Talking to me in his house in the rue St.-Jacques, his six-year-old son asleep in his arms, Costa-Gavras was irritated at the claim of convention.

"If I ever see another film with blue in the background, I'll go crazy," I had just said. "Am I crazy?"

"You are right," he laughed.

"What's going on?"

"They are called the colors of rapid perception," he answered. "Thus they strike the eye much more easily, much quicker than the softer colors. The blue, the red, are the violent, primary colors which attract the attention. They are simple colors, like simple ideas. I think it's because of that that they are used—they are understood more easily and much more quickly." In Moscow on the next leg of the same trip, I relayed the news from Costa-Gavras to Yevtushenko, who exclaimed: "An injection for the eyes!" And when, at Moscow Central Television, I brought the Yevtushenko-enriched color-and-surface idea to commentator Vladimir Pozner, he treated me to a hip display of cunning. In his cramped office, in that mellifluous voice known to everyone, he said:

> I don't know if you saw the movie *All That Jazz,* a great movie, Roy Scheider is great. In this movie you've got things that are happening right up in front of you and then in back, subtly, there's the heart surgery going on. Okay, you watch and you're forced to look behind this thing that's up in front, and you have to put the two together. It makes you participate in what you're seeing. Television doesn't want you to do that. And it's a very subtle message. And when you're looking, you may not even be thinking in these terms but what is happening to you as a human being [when watching the scene] is that you're getting a message that says, "This picture that is so bright on the front plane is really not the story. The story is happening behind in the Bob Fosse surgery." But very often in life, all you want to see is what's up in front and that's not the story.
>
> What American television is saying is, "Don't think, take it for granted, what you see is what is." I think it's succeeded to a very large extent in making people comply to that. And I must say that Soviet television, for a host of reasons not only ideological, is not like that.

When I went back to my proletarian hotel, The Belgrade, I discovered a secret bar for the hard currency crowd. A pity I had discovered it so late in my stay. On the tube, a dance recital, red costumes against deep blue scenery. In the days of perestroika, those costumes weren't honoring Bolshevism.

Back in Paris Costa-Gavras is telling me he thinks the blue and red are used to flatten the scene, a strategy coming from a generalized disdain for depth, "probably because the products sold have no depth." A little joke. But he stops my smile. "It's true. The great drama of our era is that of the culture unifying itself completely, passing by the particularities of every culture, every country. We see the same things, all of us from everywhere. A uniformization of culture that becomes nonculture."

When I bring up Jack Lemmon to innervate him—"Look, never do you see a face as sad as Jack Lemmon's in *Missing*"—he responds with Kim Basinger's face. Shot like a monstrous commercial, *9 1/2 Weeks* isn't intense. "It could have been a great movie, about sensuality," he says. "I had the occasion to speak with Kim Basinger because she has some kind of sensuality in her face, her eyes, her mouth. The sensuality in that movie is not much." He compared *9 1/2 Weeks* to what the French Canadians call *la petite secousse,* "lovemaking done in five minutes, very stupidly, and then finished, and then, okay, you have the small pleasure, this little stupid or rapid adventure. But there could have been an extraordinary relation where one discovers the other, where one discovers oneself through food, a little violence, a little fatigue, where one is very far into sexual nature. Sexual adventure, it's one of the most profound human adventures because it's a communion of two persons who put themselves together, give themselves physically. Because, finally, they're very limited, our pleasures. Thinking, which is the most important, which is philosophy. Also eat, walk, sex, less than five. So, sexual adventure, to prolong it to its maxium for two persons who agree—it is very beautiful." But not for Adrian Lyne, director of *9 1/2 Weeks,* who got his start making TV spots. True to an imperative of the era, Lyne erased the affect from Basinger. "When Michey Rourke gives her the food, when the syrup comes down her chin, it's too much," Costa-Gavras said, "it falls very quickly into the vulgar, into uninteresting things.

"But there is a logic there," he continues. "One makes emissions to be understood by people of a certain intellectual level. Here we speak all the time of the *crémière de St.-Flourd,* the lady who sells cream in St.-Flourd, a town in the center of France in the mountains. So if *she* understands the emission, it's good for everyone. It's made for her. That means that the level of emotion, philosophy, dramaturgy, and even the play of the actor are lowered to the simplest level. It's like the blue and red, a simplifying idea. My *crémière* is much more intelligent than they think, she can understand more, she is more ambitious, she has much more curiosity. But after a lifetime of looking at emissions from that thing"— pointing to his TV—"she will find her curiosity flattened. Little by little, she doesn't have to make any effort."

Costa-Gavras, who makes morality films, scarcely surprised me by saying that little by little we're losing our capacity to be attentive. Terry Bedford had tried to place responsibility on television's ontology. He had reminded me that unlike film, which moves at twenty-four frames per second, the TV image is continually changing; by nature it has a slightly bleeding edge. "Even the act of watching a spot on film in a preview theater concentrates one's mind," Bedford said. "It's much more easy to cope with a series of still frames coming at you than it is when it's projected lights are coming at you all the time and continually changing. A flying dot where you can't see it."

But the Parisian moralist sees a politics of the TV image. "Flattening them and not teaching people to think—it's the best way of governing them, making them do exactly what we want them to do. There won't be any resistance, there won't be reflection on the way of living, the way of doing. Thus one continues at one's life while a few people make all the decisions." He mentions a Robert Scheckley sci-fi story about a planet where, when the children reach nine, "they enter a cell, a chamber, for several hours. That's all, we don't know what happens." The TV is this cell, I'm to understand. "There are no police because each is his own policeman. Each does exactly what has to be done. *Tout va très bien,*" he ironizes, echoing the title of his friend Jean-Luc Godard, "*dans le pays plat,*" the Flatlands of America.

To a man and woman, the French intellectuals I visited sounded the Friendly Fascism theme, America the Badlands leading the way for all the civilized world.

"Ultrafast montage is a visual drug," military historian and theorist Paul Virilio told me.

Why drug people? I tried to riposte.

"Because you don't need them any longer," he answered outrageously. "When we had need of people, there was a prohibition on alcohol, on drugs, on sex, because we had need of people to work, to make war. Automation eliminates the need for people, thus the drug completes the work of automation." Coke, crack, TV—simply choose the signifier of your social class, says Virilio. "We're going to fascinate, hallucinate, the spectator by images which unfold too rapidly." He slaps his hands, snaps his fingers. "In a certain sense, we mock the spectator. Think of the spectator as a primary matter with whom we play, whom we slander, whom we triturate. He has a soft part to play from now on. He is inert."

I was so intrigued, all the while drugged myself by anti-Americanism, that I had to relay the French putdown to Bedford. I did so, when I next saw him—on a Brooklyn street chosen to look like Chicago, on a summer shoot for Miller beer.

Bedford surprised me with the religious connection. "Going back to my art school days in color theory, blue is the infinite, the wisdom, and it's always the color of Mary, isn't it? She always has a blue robe on," he told me.

And, later in his New York office, we screened two commercials. For Fendi perfume, a woman runs into a cathedral. Blue pours at you from a window high in the door, meant to evoke stained glass. In the other, a Dodge Daytona bursts through a garage door; blue light pierces the eye. Whereupon I had the craziest thought: that modern power in the form of the television image recasts a power we thought to have crushed. That of the Nazis—its rally power.

In 1934 Adolf Hitler put the architect Albert Speer in charge of the yearly party rally at the Zeppelin Field in Nuremberg, the assemblage of middle and minor party functionaries who tried to impress

Hitler by their bearing and discipline. In his autobiography, *Inside the Third Reich,* Speer drily remarks on the difficulty of this task: their paunches made the party stalwarts ridiculous. "The saving idea came to me," Speer wrote, "'Let's have them march up in darkness.'"

The thousands of flags belonging to all the local groups in Germany were to be held in readiness behind the high fences surrounding the field. The flag bearers were to divide into ten columns, forming lanes in which the ventripotent faithful would march up to greet their leader. But since all this was to take place at night, Speer would need light, lots of it. Like today's advertisers, he hit on the idea of aircraft lights. "I had occasionally seen our new antiaircraft searchlights blazing miles into the sky," he said. And because Hermann Goering made a fuss, like Amex with Bedford, he had to go over the Air Marshal's head to ask Hitler himself to lend him 130 of these lights. Luckier than Bedford, Speer won the CEO's approval:

> The actual effect far surpassed anything I had imagined. The hundred and thirty sharply defined beams, placed around the field at intervals of forty feet, were visible to a height of twenty to twenty-five thousand feet, after which they merged into a general glow. The feeling was of a vast room, with the beams serving as mighty pillars of infinitely high outer walls. Now and then a cloud moved through this wreath of lights, bringing an element of surrealistic surprise to the mirage. I imagine that this "cathedral of light" was the first luminescent architecture of this type, and for me it remains not only my most beautiful architectural concept but, after its fashion, the only one which has survived the passage of time. "The effect, which was both solemn and beautiful, was like being in a cathedral of ice," British Ambassador Henderson wrote.

It created an effect similar to the HMIs, power through ice. And more than half a decade later, it's the same, Bedford is indicating. A cathedral of blue ice—to be sure, like ice sculpture—is what he creates in your living room. A cathedral at night. "Outdoor light is blue," Lachman said. "That's why we have clichés like 'blue moon.' So another reason they've gotten into blue light is that they want to stress the nighttime." This is not the eventide of romance nor the starry night of the sublime, it is a regressive, primitive night. "Lighting in the 40s was chiaroscuro lighting, coming from *film noir* and working in black and white," said Lachman, director of photography whose most recent work is *Mississippi Masala,* Hanif Kureishi's *London Kills Me* and Paul Schrader's *Light Sleeper,* as well as the Wenders *Tokyo-Ga* which began this book. "There was detail in the lighting because you had to create space and form by the light alone," he said. "In the 50s, with the advent of color and television, there was more need for photographic speed to tell the story—there wasn't time for set-ups—so the lighting became flatter and general in its approach. That created an attitude about color. The cinematographers used bounce and flatter light to achieve photographic results. So directors and cinematographers are trying as it were to return to the 40s chiarascuro lighting with a 50s sensibility of color, which is saturated in a way that becomes abstract"—as if history had regressed to a more garish time. Perhaps to make you stare (etymological source of "garish"), Bedford made a dazzling, night-time cathedral. Let's say straightaway, power, fascist or capitalist, will always want itself expressed. In the old days, power had to get people out of their houses, it needed large areas to create images. Today, it reaches you at home.

Like Ridley Scott before him, Bedford too indulged himself, made a three-minute film for his personal reel while shooting a spot for New York Life. As aired, the commercial was tame: woman captain, first Jupiter landing, returns to earth. The insurance company told him not to waste time on the landing itself. Get to the pitch. "Outrageous," he said. "I mean, it was *Jupiter*. I wanted to show the landing from six, from six hundred angles." In his own version, the film is grim. On a vast plain in Florida, the crowd awaits her. Everyone is drawn up in lines, like the Nuremberg faithful. It's nighttime, the light is intense, the spiccato strings make your heart race. A television correspondent, a monitor in your foreground. Feeling of imminent catastrophe. It's our Nuremberg. Advertising is showing its teeth.

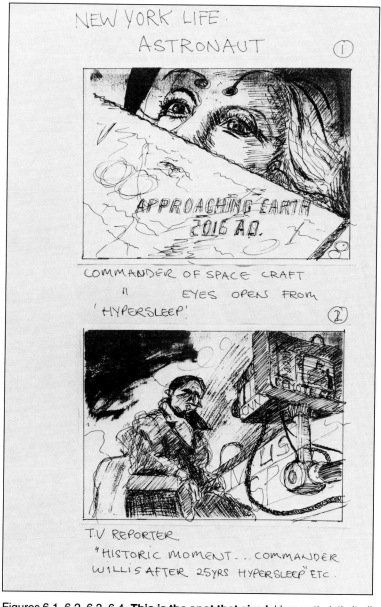

6.1

Figures 6.1, 6.2, 6.3, 6.4 This is the spot that aired. How optimistic it all is here in "Jupiter landing." The music is a lullaby as we first see the commander in hypersleep. A group of dignitaries waits to welcome her. Emergency vehicles move in place—notice the little one, R2D2. You see the landing in exactly one shot. The hatch opens and haughtily she descends. Her insurance agent greets her: "I thought you might want to get together to see how you're doing—financially." A tiny pause—involuntary?—suggesting a date. Absurd. "So all those plans you put in place 28 years ago . . ." she responds. And the voiceover, soft, conspiratorial, euphoric: "Your future is coming—get the most out of life with New York Life." Your future is coming and it's death. *Courtesy Terry Bedford.*

149

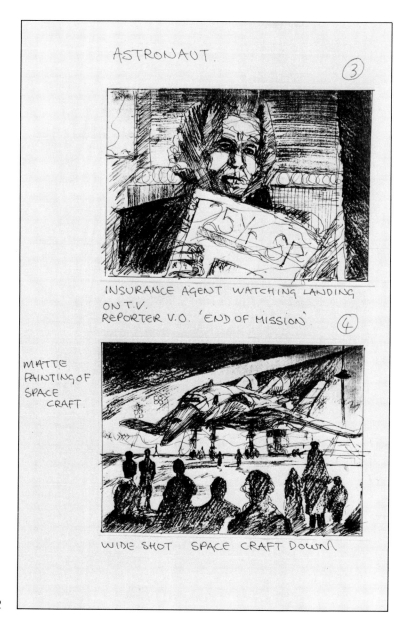

ASTRONAUT.

③

INSURANCE AGENT WATCHING LANDING ON T.V.
REPORTER V.O. 'END OF MISSION'.

④

MATTE
PAINTING OF
SPACE
    CRAFT.

WIDE SHOT   SPACE CRAFT DOWN

6.2

ASTRONAUT.

C.U. COMMANDER LEAVING SPACE
CRAFT.
T.V. REPORTER,
     "SHE HASN'T AGED A YEAR!"

6.3

GROUND SUPPORT BUS AND ESCORT LEAVE
PAD.
INSURANCE AGENT V.O. "PLANS IN PLACE
YEARS AGO".

END SHOT   COMMANDER + NEW YORK LIFE
INSURANCE AGENT MEET
AGENT "DOING FINE".
SUPER CAPTION.

6.4

Figures 6.5–6.11 **And this one never did—it never could.** Bedford used the occasion of the shoot to make a mini-film for his showreel, an evidence that he can make feature films with the big boys. Gone is the lullaby, replaced by grating, tremoloing strings. Droids on the plain await her landing, the coloration utterly, frighteningly blue, large lights in their face. The voiceover is that of a television correspondent. "There has been some concern here after an unexpected three-hour loss of transmission." The correspondent's hair is all of a piece as if synthetic, his jacket a uniform of some kind. Soldiers crouch, waiting—this is an emergency. Seven times—in seven shots—you see the descent. "This is the first Jupiter landing," Bedford told me. "Outrageous. You can't show it in one shot." Look at her coming out—she doesn't look so confident, does she? And now she's rushing on the tarmac: "Come on, let's get these tests over with," she snaps, truly a commander, Woman Empowered. Using a hand-held camera, Bedford on a motorcycle shot the emergency vehicle ahead of him. The image wobbles to rattle your insides. And R2D2 is nowhere in sight. Absurd as they may seem, the images that aired fit neatly into official American euphoric ideology. Bedford fashioned the outtakes above into his personal images: a catastrophic, nighttime view of a regimented world. It is a view of the world that Wim Wenders might cherish; for he says, in *Tokyo-Ga* (see pp. 12–13), that "perhaps the frantically growing inflation of images has already destroyed too much. Perhaps images at one with the world are already lost forever." To be at one with the world, to make the world transparent—this is precisely what New York Life or any other commercial image producer desires. In *Tokyo-Ga* Wenders tells you what the commercial image makers want:

Each person knows, for himself, the extreme gap which often exists between personal experience and the depiction of that experience up there on the screen. We have learned to consider the vast distance separating cinema from life as so perfectly natural that we gasp and give a start when we suddenly discover something true or real in a movie, be it nothing more than the gesture of a child in the background, or a bird flying across the frame, or a cloud casting its shadow over the scene for but an instant.

Or the administered world as it is.

It is a rarity in today's cinema to find such moments of truth, for people or objects to show themselves as they really ARE.

Assuming they *are;* assuming we are not by now nothing but our own external images; assuming that the self is not but an artfully constructed mask, entirely made of surfaces, a pure semiotic product.

For Wenders and for me, the commercial image is a simulacrum, a substitution for the world in which the world has been forgotten and that's okay. The title of an HBO series could well be the global name for such imagery: *Dream On. Courtesy Terry Bedford.*

6.5

ASTRONAUT. ③

T.V. REPORTER......
"HISTORIC MOMENT-.....

④

INSURANCE AGENT WATCHING LANDING
ON T.V.

T.V. REPORTER V.O.
'END OF MISSION'

6.6

6.7

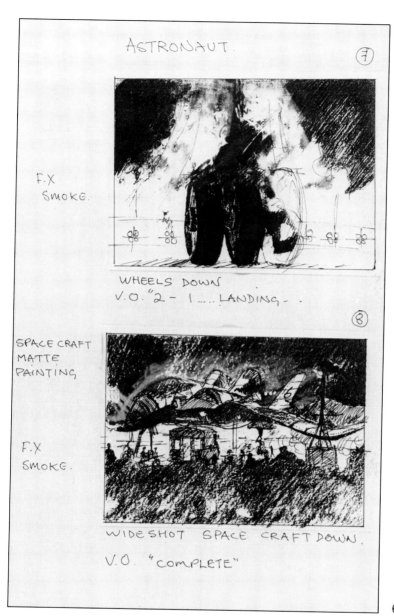

ASTRONAUT. ⑦

F.X
SMOKE.

WHEELS DOWN
V.O. "2 - 1 ..... LANDING - .

⑧

SPACE CRAFT
MATTE
PAINTING

F.X
SMOKE.

WIDE SHOT SPACE CRAFT DOWN.

V.O. "COMPLETE"

6.8

6.9

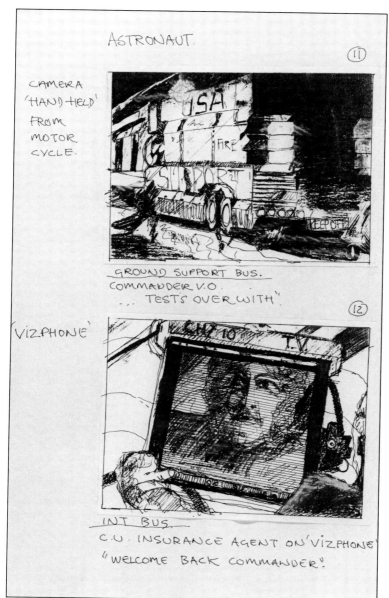

ASTRONAUT.

⑪

CAMERA
'HAND-HELD'
FROM
MOTOR
CYCLE.

GROUND SUPPORT BUS.
COMMANDER V.O.
"... TESTS OVER WITH"

⑫

'VIZPHONE'

INT BUS.
C.U. INSURANCE AGENT ON 'VIZPHONE'
"WELCOME BACK COMMANDER."

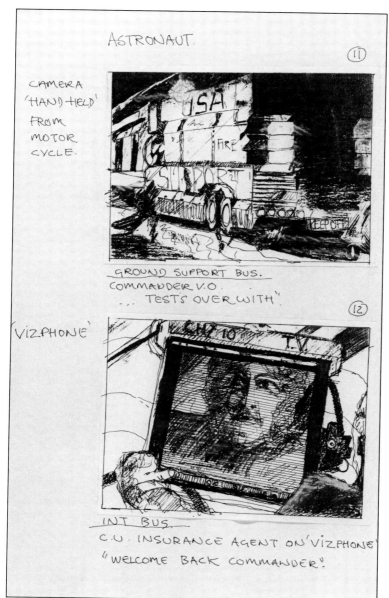

6.10

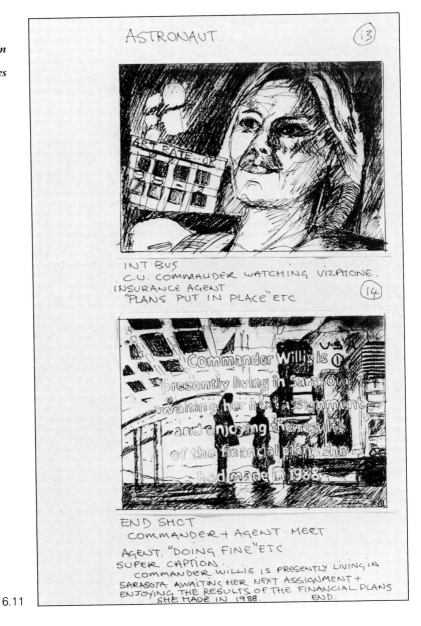

6.11

A European on Madison Avenue

A quite different case of cross-fertilization is Nestor Almendros, the cinematographer who won an Academy Award in 1978 for *Days of Heaven.* Another import from Europe, but in this case part of the French Revolution in film making. Almendros, born in Spain, has worked with most of the *nouvelle vague* French cinema directors, from Eric Rohmer to Francois Truffaut. His crossover to TV commercials, which began in the 70s, includes a spot for Giorgio Armani, and in America, he collaborated with Richard Avedon for the Calvin Klein Obsession fragrance spots. He also did a Crystal Light spot featuring Raquel Welch. His contribution, like that of the British, has been on the formal, artistic side. But unlike the British, he has found working in American TV commercials more rewarding and creative than most visual-art critics would tend to agree. He considers that television commercials allow the cinematographer a greater opportunity for experimenting and discovering new visual territories; not without disadvantages, however.

"When you do these mini-films," Almendros remarked, "you have so much money and time—for a 30-second film, two or three days in which to shoot it. In a feature the most time that 30 seconds could take up is an hour or two, otherwise the filming would be almost infinite. So you tend to do what the French call *fignoler*—do things too well, overdo them. This is fine for a mini-film because it has to be seen very quickly, things having to be very precise and very perfect. But if you were to carry that to feature films, then it would look too *léché*—another French word. It means, literally, licked with your mouth." Which is what the Brits taught the Americans to do. "Every shot in a spot is like a painting," said Almendros. "Like when the dessert is too sweet, too much sugar."

The time and money one spends on a few seconds, and the need to reach an audience effectively and fast, causes television to encourage the search for powerful, visual metaphors. In film the narrative process is more important, a process that takes time and allows discourse. Spots, on the other hand, are like Japanese haiku, the effect of which has to be achieved almost instantaneously. TV spots are like poetry and film, like prose.

Almendros gives another reason for the creative and experimental possibilities of television. "Everybody knows a commercial is a fantasy, it has nothing to do with reality. Every shot is like a painting." And since spots belong to the genre of the fantastic, no claims of realistic portrayal should be made. I can do anything I want, Almendros thinks. And there is money for it. Everything is possible and the artist can invent.

Almendros is right, but here lies a paradox. Although no claims of realism should be made on the artist, the audience relates the spot to everyday life—supposedly the opposite of the fantastic. But because we believe everyday life is a realized utopia, because everyday life is licked and glossy to us, we haven't the slightest trouble making the crossover from spot to street. The close-ups, the immediacy of the flesh and of the flesh of objects, all this is hyperrealism establishing an intimacy with the viewer, scarcely different from the hyperreal around us. Almendros told me that film was the true vehicle of realism and mentioned his own work in *Kramer versus Kramer*. But you go to the movies in the dark and sit as in a dream before their imagery. When you leave a movie theater, as if still a bit groggy from sleep, you are cleansed and emptied. But watching a TV commercial, you do not experience an Aristotelian catharsis. You are not cleansed; instead, you are driven to go outside your home and buy either the cereal, the deodorant, the jeans, the car, the evening beer, or the sleeping pill.

Television commercials go against the traditional role of art, which as Joyce said, should avoid being either didactic or pornographic. Commercials are both. They excite your prurience and they tell you what to do—the opposite of traditional art.

Almendros's work in television, on the other hand, has influenced his filmography. "When I started doing TV commercials, my films got more precise, less sloppy," he said. "Every little detail improved, and I became very graphic. The legs got important, the feet, the hands—I portrayed the whole through the part"—synedoche—"and made a graphism of the human body."

This also has a beneficial effect on the commercial possibilities of Almendros's film work. Since now one of the main markets for films is video and the small screen, close-ups, details, and precision enhance the posttheater life of the film.

In both cases—Terry Bedford and Nestor Almendros—the formal aspects of television spots have been revolutionized. The success of America, as in other areas of production, has been more in marketing and software than in the specific quality of the individual product, be it a car, a perfume, or a British TV commercial. The Japanese, the Italians, the French, the British thrive in the softer and more creative areas of style, specific objects, and artistic production. The economic power of the United States enables it to buy British and French images. The brain drain has now turned to image drain. On the other side of the 90s, America seems at the midpoint of the road of life, as Dante would put it, and must make a choice between following the path of unrivaled marketing genius or reinvigorating its basic research and object design. All this must give us pause.

7 My Dinner with the Ecos . . .

Admen don't pause. Their brains are afire to sell anything by any means.

"Can you help us sell America?"

It was December 1984. I had been invited into Warwick Advertising, a multi-million-dollar-a-year Manhattan agency to help several of its executives, who were now explaining their problem to me. Their client, Burlington, was an American textile manufacturer that, together with the other greats of the field, had formed a consortium and a war chest. The money was to pay agencies like this one to stop American clothing makers from buying their fabric offshore, usually from the Asians, often compounding the insult by signing the design of the cloth with European or Japanese names. The "Buy American" campaign was already in its first stage. I was shown full-page newspaper ads threatening the clothing firms, warning that in six months would come a groundswell of demand for American cloth, a rank-and-file roar to be caused by a second-stage campaign.

"Oh, what's the content?" I said.

"That's why *you're* here. We thought you could tell us."

They thought I'd know how to slip into the American psyche, how to cross a few wires and make a demand or desire or a wish or a want where before there was none.

I tried to explain that semiotics doesn't conjure out of whole cloth, as they say. "What if the collective unconscious couldn't care less where the cloth is from?" I said.

"Can't you change it?"

Maybe I can identify widespread needs in the culture; that much I can do, I told them—"but what if people need the European name? You know, Benetton?"

The meeting ended badly, the executives disappointed. But a month later I got a second chance, with another agency, BBDO, to offer some sound semiotics. "I really would avoid the patriotism, guys," I said to the vice president managing the interests of Dupont, another partner in the consortium. Remember, it was January 1985 now, the inauguration just over. Only a few months before, Reagan's TV commercials had been showing sunsets, a parade of flags, a high school band, a bride, picturesque landscapes, pretty faces. Accused of sleeping at cabinet meetings, Reagan had told a college crowd: "I'd love to bring you all into a cabinet meeting and we'd all nap together." The students loved it. For a generation reared on TV cartoons, Reagan fashioned the image of a kindly grandfather napping with kindergartners.

"The Republican corporate executive mood," says John Kenneth Galbraith, "was to substitute rhetoric, advertising skills for reality. There was the feeling with Reagan that here after many travails was a pleasant escape from responsibility." Reagan read scripts, acted roles for a public that knew these were roles and was well satisfied. "Most of the population knows that Ronald Reagan had only the foggiest ideas of what the policies of his Administration were," linguist Noam Chomsky told Bill Moyers on public television. "Nobody much cared. The Democrats were always surprised that he could get away with these bloopers and crazy statements and so on. The reason is that much of the population understood very well that they were supporting someone like the queen of England or the flag. The queen of England opens Parliament by reading a political program, but nobody asks whether she understands it or believes it." Queen Ronald.

"There was a certain reassurance that came from a president who was preoccupied only with Grenada, Nicaragua, and SDI," Galbraith told me. And there I was in 1985 with the admen, the scriptwriters, at the height of their prestige, sensing that they might ape their Tuesday Team colleagues who had resold us Ronald Reagan.

"Look, when it was a matter of what's distant, a president, patriotism worked," I said. "But when it concerns what's right up against your body, your precious moneymaker [I know, a little crude], your image, you don't want glory. You waved the flag for Reagan, now you shake your behind for yourself."

"We knew that," the man said emphatically.

"But you'll use patriotism anyway?" I said.

"Maybe."

"Why?"

"Ten million dollars? That an answer?"

Patriotism would play well with the client.

And that is what the consortium got, a parade of Las Vegas–style hacks, Liza Minelli, Sammy Davis, Jr., all breathless in praise of America (occasionally, you still see the spots). They are about as symptomatic of deeply felt needs as Henny Youngman's violin is. What they are about is "shtick" and nothing *but*. The product they're hawking keeps slipping from your mind. Like so many commercials whose products you never remember, these for the textile industry are selling selling, they're selling buying, they're selling consuming. What a joke on the firm that gave its agency $10 million! The commercials create a demand for consuming—be it European or Japanese or American products, no matter.

"America is only a marketing network any more," Jacques Attali told me. You'll recall his interest in speed:

> The amortization of American tools, goods, and concepts is going quicker and quicker. America is going faster on that route where everybody is going: the increase of the speed of amortization of ideas, signs, and goods. And this is the swallowing of our traces, it is the cancellation, the deletion of our steps.

The motor of this nullification is marketing, the euphoric announcer of the new. As my little visit to the textile people suggests, we are so wealthy that it doesn't matter that people buy American—it only matters that they buy.

Semiotic Survival

> "We were formed as a race that needed fantasies to survive."
>
> GIANFRANCO FERRÉ, *fashion designer*

> "We haven't a drop of oil, not a sheep extra for wool, not a single natural resource except our own people. The Italian survival strategy was to add beauty to others' natural resources, then export that added value worldwide.
>
> FURIO COLOMBO, *President, Fiat USA*

Because the agencies wanted Sammy Davis to dance away your taste for the import, my publisher a few years later asked me to turn my back on Sammy's wiles; to go to a center of export, arguably the center of design, Italy; and there look for the logic of the design that makes so many of us pulse with desire. Here is the report of what I found, here is an account of a people who are an economic force in America because of a history of oppression that made them take their semiotics seriously.

The little charade in those American agencies was about semiotics (see page 386 for definition). Here in Italy at the end of the 80s was a chance to see semiotics being acted out for real, the first scene being a dinner thrown for me in Milan by Renate and Umberto Eco.

Renate called up fashion designers Krizia, Armani, Ferré, the architect Vittorio Gregotti, the sociologist and columnist Francesco Alberoni, fashion publicist and former top model Benedetta Barzini. Renate's invitations illustrate a difference between the U.S. and Italy. European designers are validated by culture, they want it and talk it. It's not a patina—it's a part—of doing business in Europe. And so it was simple for Renate to call up these lira millionaires for a soiree. All of them have contacts with the major Italian writers, intellectuals, politicians. I can't think of a single American professor, not even a writer, who could get so many design stars to dinner. Even the best semiologist at Brown couldn't call one of them; couldn't get Calvin Klein or Geoffrey Beene to dinner, much less all our top designers at the same time.

Over a dinner of pasta fresca, scaloppine, and fresh vegetables, after Venetian berduzzo and dessert of gelatto, after Eco regaled us with a new article on fakes and forgeries, I found myself relayed from person to person, from Missoni to Bellini to Barzini, amongst fashion, car, furniture, electronic designers in Milan, Turin, Varese, Rome.

Start with the history of one man, Eco. For a quarter of a century, he has not only been an academic but a journalist for national newspapers and news weeklies, offering travel notes, thoughts about politics, denunciation of sport, meditation on television. Currently he writes the back page for the national magazine *L'Espresso*. Like the designers he had to dinner, Eco is culture-bound, and when he writes of American mass production and gadgetry, he feels obliged to attack in the mode of irony (see box). His bias is toward signs; he tries to interpret and help others interpret signs. Eco insists that if he has said some things that interest Italians, it is because he looks at the world through the eyes of a semiologist. Whereas we put on our back pages curmudgeons, quote-dropping pundits, and moralizing bluestockings, the Italians give a platform to a professor who, year by year, has changed the way Italians (and the design elite) have chosen to see and speak about their culture and the rest of the world.

A history of Italy made Eco possible. "Italy had nothing but people as its raw material," says Furio Colombo. "The Italian strategy *had* to be that of adding imagination, adding creativity, adding that added value of beauty." The practice began in the Renaissance, the English sending wool to Prato to be colored ("to become beautiful," says Colombo), the Italians returning it to England with their mark. The strategy continues to this day in numerous fields of artisanry, the most spectacular perhaps being the ornamentation of gold. According to Colombo, almost 75 percent of the world's gold intended to be ornament comes to the Piedmont, to Tuscany, to one or two other sites where hundreds of craftsmen do nothing but work the gold of non-Italians (Italy has no gold), reselling the difference at twice the original value. "The history of our people is that of being dominated," Gian Franco Ferré says. "First it was the barbarians, then the Spanish, then French, then Austrian. We had to—*come se dice . . .*" Ferré pauses. *"Sopravivere,"* he continues. Survive, it means. But Ferré insists on the etymology of the word. *"Sopra*—over, *vivere*—live," he says. "We had to live over—leap over—the present, over the invader. And that is fantasy, to imagine a future without the invader."

But why was the fantasy visual? I asked Furio Colombo.

"Because language was cut and segmented into very small regions," he answered. "Someone from Piemonte couldn't understand someone from Sicily. Someone from Tuscany couldn't understand someone from Naples. And besides this horizontal fragmentation of the language, there was the vertical fragmentation of class. The clergy spoke Latin, the common people spoke their babble of tongues." Because it was impossible to understand one another vertically and difficult horizontally, "vision became the way of communicating," said Colombo, "and that is why the role of the Italian painter has been so incredibly large."

Colombo evoked Paolo Uccello's famous painting *The Battle,* its dazzle of lances that sweep by in diagonal, the varicolored knights and infantrymen. "It's the beauty of wonderment, it can only have been the response of someone who had nothing to do with the battle." In other words, what we call beauty—a static, even vapid term—is a shock, if you can only see the painting as Ucello saw it. For him, for his audience, it was a force, a sublimation of wonder, hatred, alienation, the feelings of the conquered watching on as the incomprehensible above them played out their power game. "Even there," says Colombo, "is added value for the conquered, the redeeming feature to always being visited by the foreigner."

To be "visited," to be poor and at risk, is always to be scanning. Any seasoned traveler knows that the people of poor countries are avid with their eyes. Try to cross a poor village in southern Italy, in northern Africa, in Asia, Bangladesh, Pakistan. Immediately you see a scenography of mobile eyes, ready to catch a movement, a signal, a message that needn't be verbal but upon which survival may depend. Is this a friend or an enemy? What type of friend, what type of enemy? Meaningful or meaningless? Benevolent or malevolent? The world is pertinent for the poor through oppositions dependent on signals. "Since Italy was continuously invaded by foreigners speaking unknown languages, bringing unknown customs, to observe the foreigner, to have good eyes for him, to treat him as signal and read the signal has always been vital for us and is our legacy," added Colombo.

You read the visitor and if he is friendly, read his taste, decipher his culture, then develop the skill to add value to his products . . . *design* them.

American Gadgetmania

UMBERTO ECO

The airplane flies majestically over endless plains, spotless deserts. This American continent is still able to offer moments of almost tactile contact with nature. I am forgetting civilization but the fact is that in the pocket on the back of the seat in front of me, among the instructions for rapid evacuation (of the airplane, in case of accident) and the little bag for rapid evacuation (of my body, in case of nausea), next to the film program and the Brandenburg concertos in earphones, there is a copy of "Discoveries," a brochure that lists, with inviting photographs, a series of objects that can be ordered by mail. In the days that will follow, on other flights, I will discover similar publications, "The American Traveler," "Gifts With Personality," and other publications of the kind.

They make fascinating reading, I get lost in them and forget about nature which is so monotonous because, it seems, "non facit saltus" (and I hope neither does my airmobile). How much more interesting culture is, and as we know it serves to correct nature. Nature is hard and hostile, and culture instead allows man to do things with less effort and to save time. Culture frees the body from the slavery of work and disposes it to contemplation.

Just think, for example, how annoying it is to manipulate a nasal spray, by which I mean one of those little pharmaceutical bottles that are squeezed between two fingers in such a way that a beneficent aerosol penetrates the nostrils. No fear. Virilizer ($4.95) is a machine in which one inserts the flacon and which squeezes it for you in such a way that the jet goes directly into the most hidden crevices of the respiratory tract. Naturally, the machine is held in the hand, and altogether, to judge by the photo, one has the impression of firing with a Kalashnikov, but everything has a price.

I am struck, and I hope I won't be struck any further, by Omniblanket, which costs a good $150. It is really just an electric blanket, but it contains an electronic program in such a way as to adjust the temperature according to the parts of your body. I mean, if at night your shoulders feel cold but your groin is sweating, you can thereby program Omniblanket, which will keep you warm at your shoulders and cool at the groin. It's your problem if you're nervous and toss and turn in the bed. You'll roast your testicles or whatever you have, depending on the various sexes, in that area. I don't think we can ask for improvement from the inventor, because I suspect that he's been burned to a crisp, despite the impassioned appeals of Pope Wojtyla.

Naturally, while sleeping you might snore and disturb your partner of whatever sex. Well, Snore Stopper is a kind of watch that you put on your wrist before going to sleep. As soon as you snore, Snore Stopper, through an audio-sensor, perceives it and emits an electric impulse that goes through your arm and reaches one of your nervous centers and interrupts, I don't understand very well just what. But anyway, you don't snore any more. It costs only $45. The trouble is that it is not advisable for people with heart disease, and I have a suspicion that it can also prejudice the health of an athlete. Besides that, it weighs two pounds, which is almost a kilogram, and therefore you could use it with the spouse with whom you have been united by many decades of habit, but not with a one-night stand, because to make love with a machine weighing a kilo on your wrist could produce some collateral accidents.

We know what the Americans do to eliminate cholesterol, and that is, they run for hours and hours until they die of a heart attack. Pulse Trainer ($59.95) is worn on the wrist and is connected by a wire to a little rubber cup that you put on your index finger. It seems that when your cardio-circulatory system is on the brink of collapse, an alarm sounds. This is progress when one remembers that in underdeveloped countries, a person stops only when he is out of breath—which is a very primitive parameter, and perhaps for this reason the children of Ghana do not go jogging. It's curious, however, despite this neglect, they are almost completely devoid of cholesterol. With Pulse Trainer you can run with tranquility and, by tying to your chest and around your waist, two Nike Monitor belts, an electronic voice, informed by a microprocessor and by a Doppler Effect Ultra Sound, tells you how far you have run and at what speed ($300).

If you like animals, I advise you to get Bio Pet. You put it around the neck of your dog and it emits ultrasound (PMBC Circuit) that kills fleas. It costs only $25. I don't know if it can be applied to one's own body to kill crabs, but I fear the usual side effects. Duracel lithium batteries are not included in the package. The dog must go and buy them for himself.

The Italians became readers of culture, sensitive to systems of signs, because they had to. Not because it was semiotic and fashionable. Thus Ferré, taking the pulse of the culture, reading movies, rock musicians, and the street itself, sees a fascination with uniforms. "Look around—too many uniforms," he says. "Men, they have to be dressed in gray. Fashion people in black. Gays in no way—or sometimes obviously eccentric. Snobs—English mood but with a personal touch. Too much! We are victims of the code of the uniform." And the drab uniformity of life it produces. "The spirit of the age is drab. Fantasy is cancelled. It is the culture of the small personality."

Ferré's response was to subvert the uniform, to give a sense of furlough or respite, all the while designing inside the military code. "I play with the tradition, to remove the woman from her situation," of being put in uniform, Ferré said. He showed me a sketch. "This is a very large and simple white short for woman," he said.

"I suggest to wear it with those navy pants. Navy, but look, with this pink stripe down the side, like the gendarmes." Like and *un*like: a gendarme would be cashiered for wearing these pants. "Always I do it by opposition. I mix in a free way colors like red and pink, fabrics like matte and shiny. I make the outfit express a difference, and that's a sign. My signature."

So these designers are diagnosing the conditions shaping our lives. Can they do so early? Can they read our feelings before we can say them—even before other artists can express them? Can we see in design what our opinion and thoughts will later be? A striking example was given me when I met Giorgio Armani for chapter 1. You can reread it, if you wish, but in case you don't, merely recall that talking to me in Milan, before the Wall Street crash, before it would become fashionable to decry the masters of the universe (the phrase is a cliché now), Armani was signaling the coming denunciation of those who would know no limit. "We have to rediscover the courage to be important, to be valuable, to be managerial, all of that—but not be bandits," he said. He began his design for winter '88 months before he met me. In other words, months before the corporate conscience was pricked, Armani design signaled the coming brake of caveman capitalism. "A creator, a stylist has to be au courant the spiritual realm," he said. "For myself, I try to move with the movements around me, to be *presso della strada*—near the street—and transform its happenings so they become"—a beat—"Armani."

He feels the signs of the street in his guts when he walks and when he works. He doesn't double the experience with language. And he can express himself without words—his drawing, his design, *is* that expression. But when pressed, as on occasion he is and as he was by me, he can easily delight the interlocutor with little spoken essays. Armani is a semiotic designer not because he can talk signs. He is semiotic because he intuitively understands what semiotics should have been, but wasn't, from its modern beginnings. Semiotics isn't just the study of signs, it is the study of *me*—of what signs mean deeply for the people who make and exchange them. Armani, who says he wants to be near the street, likes the street and transforms that affection into affectionate fashion. He walks and lives driven by a sensibility of pleasure. Armani is guided by the idea that it's a pleasure to feel, to see (and be seen as) one's body. Whether the body is conventionally beautiful or not is totally beside the point. Armani is semiotic precisely because he embraces our affective part. But—my second intuition—his semiotics isn't only a way to power, any more than it is with the other designers I spent time with. When the Italians sit down to dinner, naturally the talk turns to signs eventually. The sign is a way to creation, culture and, conviviality. In France, where sign sensitivity is equally high (if colder), the French designers *have* to take a distance from their work. They have to show themselves capable of analyzing their creations. In France you gain power when you can rationalize your work. In furniture design, also, the artist can bend the codes. Indeed, the design movement called Memphis, from its beginning in 1981, was intended as a disruption of design rules. "People thought Memphis was just a game, which is absolutely not true," says Barbara Radice, writer and theoretician of Memphis. "Memphis was a dead serious attempt to break the codes, to open up the possibilities of design, introducing a new iconography which involved coloristic, decorative, and material juxtapositions that were imposing, very intense. For example, juxtapositions of very high status material—marble— with very low status material—plastic laminate."

She took me on a tour of the apartment she shares with Ettore Sottsass, guiding spirit of the movement. "Look at Ettore's bookcase, all in differently colored plastic laminate. The shelves aren't orthogonal—why should they be? Books lean, books fall down, so they may as well lie down from the start." She showed me a chair by Memphis designer Michele De Lucchi. "It's like a stool with an arm going around like the orbit of something around the earth. Very strange iconography." The world, for Memphis, offers existential happiness—were it not for codes that narrow our sight, that wring our bodies of vitality. But design can be what Memphis calls "sensorial." It can be expressive signs charged with information about the senses and all other modes of life.

"We realized that we could reconsider the old semiotic catalogue," said Sottsass, "the one bequeathed us by the so-called modernist movement, with its emphasis on function. An object was supposed to be functional to the hand, the eye, and so on. But there are other kinds of functions, political, psychological. Maybe if you have to work for eight hours writing stupid commercial letters, a functional table can become so cold it's unfunctional. Function is something that deals with your life, not only physical problems."

Mies van der Rohe was of course the master of the functionalist idea that pillars and beams, that glass, floor, and ceiling were but elements of a structure, to become merely geometric surface or line in order to indicate the structure. "Take color," says Sottsass. "It was imagined only as underlining the movement of the structure. We thought it could take on its own life, that structure is not the most important way of perception." If structure is thus an abstraction suppressing individual elements, the response of Memphis was to unbind the parts in order to let their distinct shapes and patterns and colors stimulate the viewer into life. "The whole world is fake," says Sottsass. "In America you see houses made out of bricks that are not bricks. You see green in the airport that is not verdure. The coffee is fake, the cheese is fake."

"We don't like real," added Radice. "We don't like to see, to touch. It's scary."

"This wood is fake," said Sottsass, pointing to his own table. Thus, using the fake, the laminate, Sottsass tries to return us to our reality devoid of signs. This, too, is the idea of the Missonis, famous for their riot of color in handmade textile design. "I want you to have this sweater," Rosita Missoni said as we toured her factory in Sumirago. I put on a cardigan whose pattern was like an oscillograph's, burnt red lines over brownish mustard over grayish white over blue with black in it. All the while, nubs of pale yellow, purplish red, gray-green, and electric blue aroused my eye, moving it in a score of directions. The Missonis have rebelled against the narrow coloration of the world, its texture, and its images.

My attention again was called to color a few days before in Paris by film director Constantin Costa-Gavras. We discussed the colors of commericals, music videos, commercial photography, and film. The chapter on advertising presented his ideas. Recall his conclusion. "There is no resistance to imagery and its signification. A few people make all the decisions—it's today's way to govern people."

In one way or another, resistance to code, to governance, a restoration of intensity and the life of the body underlay the intention of most of the designers I called on. Thus Mario Bellini, one of the world's foremost product designers, will tell me with zest in the next chapter the somatic origins of his cassette deck for Yamaha. In the permanent collection of New York's Museum of Modern Art, the deck (you can see it on p. 182) recuperates an ancient iconograph in order to appeal to the eyes. In a culture of fakes, as Sottsass told us, Bellini has restored a very old form that favors the body. In design after design—you'll see some of them in a few pages—he seeks to restore the sense and ease of the body to lives increasingly become abstract.

All of these designers have taken the Italian way of seeing the world and telling it to one another; they have taken their sign

Figure 7.1 (*above, left*) Armando Testa, greeting card, 1978. The easy chair. *Courtesy Armando Testa.*

Figure 7.2 (*above, right*) Armando Testa, greeting card, 1980. Table with shoes. *Courtesy Armando Testa.*

Figure 7.3 (*below*) Armando Testa, magazine cover, Easter 1991. Cover for *Famiiglia Cristiana,* Italy's largest circulation magazine. *Courtesy Armando Testa.*

systems, adapted them for export, and charmed America. The most extreme of the Italians, who is not suitable for export, is the man known as the dean of Italian advertising, Armando Testa, whose work Federico Fellini has called "triumphantly energetic" and whose clients include Alitalia, Ferré, Procter & Gamble, San Pellegrino, Pirelli, and Borsalino, making Armando Testa S.p.A the largest advertising agency in Italy. What, in this advertising, caught the fancy of the creator of *Roma?* Look at a few of the greeting cards Testa sends world-wide every Christmas. In 1978 he upholstered a chair in prosciutto, losing his prosciutto client along the way. In 1980, in a personal photograph, he covered a table in fat-marbled salami, adding some pumps nearby (doubtless Ferragamo). It's pretty easy to grasp the quality that captured Fellini's favor. It's the Felliniesque itself, corporality, which to us would appear as piggishness. No one except an Italian could have the idea that food—here, prosciutto—could become an easy chair. "The Italians have this piggish attitude, so they wallow in food," Latin American novelist Edmundo Desnoes told me. A resident in Italy in the late 70s, he doesn't intend a slander by that somatic metaphor; rather, in this time of massive superego and moralizing, he's pointing to the chair as mama, as comfort, as wonderful white fat on top of your tongue. An American might say: oh, what a good idea! But it would upset him because he or she is nutty over health, over cleanliness. The Italian would sink in the chair, try to smother himself in the prosciutto. In this way of thinking, Testa's next step has to be Laura Antonelli as the newest sex goddess mama in skin made of salami. An American seeing her salami breasts would run in horror. An unreconstructed Italian man would doubtless die of joy. "Imagine that—*two* pleasures!" he would say.

"America is famous for and is best at skyscraper specialization, the most advanced technological crafting," says Testa. "But in doing that, Americans go very far from normal reality and contact with one another. Italy, on the contrary, is such a small place, its people staying close to each other, that there is a lot of osmosis among Italians. Because we live in small cities, we're gossipy, used to talking to each other a lot."

Testa calls the osmosis *molto legato,* very easy, *una forma normale,* the most normal thing in the world—an osmosis that allows artists and intellectuals to coexist happily with business people. The exchange permits fantasy to flourish in commerce. "It's very common in Italy that many creative persons are able to bring their visions into commerce—Armani, Versace, Bulgari, Cipriani, the owner of Harry's Bar in Venice."

And Testa, of course. "I am able to flow freely from art to salami, to enjoy myself in playing with certain elements. It's no big deal, it's our country, which fortunately or unfortunately is a more humanitarian than technological society."

On Easter Sunday 1990, he added temerity to fantasy to publish his *redesign of the cross.* On the cover of *Famiglia Cristiana,* Italy's largest-circulation magazine, was the most famous commercial symbol of history, according to Testa—but Christ was gone. In his place was the cross alone, its edges in the papal color, yellow. In the iconograph, the crucified Christ's head lolls rightward—in a deft stroke resemblant of haiku's concision, the top of the cross lolls rightward. Testa no longer copies the Savior, he signifies him. For the first time in two thousand years, the graphic designer isn't stuck to his agonized model; he is detached from his signified. Crucifixion is given to be read, not seen. Audaciously, Testa dissolves the sticky substance of the most major Christian icon. Emotion no longer inundates, submerges us—it becomes reading. After two millennia of marketing Christianity, Testa told me, he thought it was time to relax the sell, to detach the form from its traditional end and thereby create, as Italian opinion quickly put it, a sublimated sign, all the more dramatic because of its new simplicity.

Testa's *Asparagus Chair* shows how the Italians see the world. "Fingers become asparagus? It's . . . *icky* to Americans, like sitting in that chair. What are we supposed to do? *Bite* the fingers? It's Magritte, it's intellectual, it's . . . European. The same European ideation that enabled Italy to survive is here seen at such an extreme as surely to be unwelcome in America (but celebrated in Italy). The Italians, since the "made in Italy" boom of the 70s, have been taking their way of perceiving and speaking about the world, much of it obnoxious to us, taming the excess and selling the residue to an elite of America as crazed over *italiano* as the Italians themselves may be over food, not even to mention ideas.

Giorgetto Giugiaro, the world-renowned car designer—he designed the Volkswagen Golf, the Saab 9000 Turbo, the Fiat Uno—has also known the experience of offending the American market. At the time when the Italian design community was elaborating its new esthetic, Giugiaro in 1976 entered a competition of New York's Museum of Modern Art called "The Taxi Project: Realistic Solutions for Today." The purpose of the project was to promote the development of design that reduced air pollution, all the while introducing new safety features and passenger comfort. Other contestants were Volvo, Volkswagen, and several American companies. In preparing his solution, Giugiaro told me, he confirmed a long-felt silliness to American car taste. "Americans, who always want a big car," he said, "also want a low car so they can pretend that they're driving sports cars." This is an absurdity to him given that we can never legally drive more than 65 mph—that our cars, in fact, haven't the power but only the sign of the sports car. "The sign is from hood to front window and rear window to license plate," he said. "The real is the space you have from the pedal to the seats behind—that is the important thing." Giugiaro's design and the prototype he built for

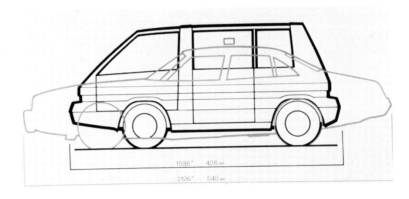

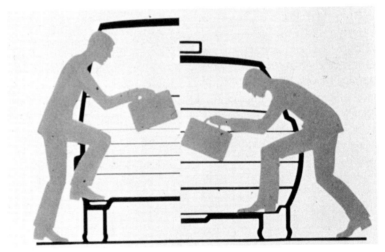

Figures 7.4 (*above*), 7.5 (*below*), 7.6 Giorgetto Giugiaro. Proposed taxi design for Museum of Modern Art (New York) competition. No elegant (or other) person will be getting out of an American cab like this soon. Giugiaro's design offended an American code.

7.6

the contest eliminates the semiotic front and boot—"they're phallic ideas, man doesn't need them," he said. "I increased the height, giving comfort to the driver, and reduced the front and back, reducing by almost 30 percent the area the taxi occupies. Now it's 6.98 square meters against the 9.72 typical New York yellow cab meters. Therefore," Giugiaro adds in a mode of glee almost, "we have a reduction of 2.75 square meters for each vehicle. Which means that 1,000 Italdesign taxis gain 27.4 square meters of space for society. This is rational." Lots of luck. Giorgetto showed his prototype *"hors concours,"* he told me, out of competition. I think he knew it didn't have a chance. He sought to educate the Americans out of their fascination with useless size, semiotic size. But Americans have no interest in European rationality. They want size, lots of size—remember that FDR's favorite song was "Give me land, lots of land—don't fence me in." What Giugiaro well understood when he entered *"hors concours"* was that America, once so abundant in everything and still abundant of space, couldn't in '76 and almost still can't manage to stop indulging its love for "phallomobiles." When he told me this story in Turin, I stupidly worried about his future, if he were to persist in working for the American car companies driven as he was by rationality. "But you don't understand," he told me, "we work for the Japanese, for the Europeans." I *am* the Japanese that have been killing your car industry!

The little charade in the agencies I visited was about semiotics, the cast of mind that sees the art, architecture, social behavior, political acts, design, and other artificial landscaping of the world as signs issuing from codes that are unwritten and usually unconscious. The advertisers trying to save the American textile industry had no interest in reading current codes of America. They had no interest in whether there was a deeply felt need for American textiles in the culture. Instead of diagnosing a condition and producing advertising to respond to that condition, the people I met wanted to use a fortune in labor and money simply to produce, to force, demand, regardless of whether American cloth has usefulness, that is, meaning, for Americans. In fact, with textiles, as with cars, electronics, sporting goods, toys, and shoes, the evidence is that Americans don't want to buy American. Indeed, they are willing to pay a premium for foreign brand names. Recall the words of Jacques Attali: "America is only a marketing network any more." What he meant by that polemical sentence is that American companies will tax their assets, grind up their productive resources if need be, to make it *appear* that there is use, to attach the most attractive face to the most banal, inert product.

I say this in neutral fashion. Merchandising is the supreme skill of America. Many foreign exporters still believe that quality sells, that if your product is good, people will beat a path to your door. Tell many a Latin American that he or she will have to invest $20 million marketing what cost only $10 million—the exporter will say you're crazy! But you aren't. That's the way of hucksterist America. My agency put me on notice: we sold the nation Reagan with euphoric patriotism—we'll sell it cloth the same way, wait and see.

The Italians I visited aren't reaching mainstream America, those who lust after the goods I saw backstage at "The Price Is Right" (chapter 10). The Italians don't want to, and they can't. What they make is crafted. Italy is hundreds of little cities whose members band into families of craftspeople. What they produce is labor-intensive and has to be expensive. Mass production in the American sense is alien to these artisans, whose work is alien to mainstream America. Ernesto Gismondi, for example, whose firm Artemide makes the Richard Sapper Tizio lamp, knows that it is so delicate, so frail, that most Americans wouldn't buy it. They couldn't throw it around. Americans have a desire to treat objects with disrespect. They have so much abundance that throwing things around, even breaking them, makes for signs of their wealth. "No problem, I'll just charge a new one." Gismondi, like the other Italians I met, wants just a sliver of the vast American market.

All these sweaters and chairs and lamps whose designers I encountered are difficult to fabricate, are delicate, require craftsmanship. The Italians, who still have artisans, as do the Japanese, can fashion them. They all have the same intentionality: they all want to steal a piece of French action. Until a mere decade ago. French was the only culture outside the Anglo world that we Anglos respected. But then came the Italians, the little wedge of mozzarella between the big cheeses. "Our success was of course due to the fact that Italian-designed objects were beautiful," says Ino Cassini, an Italian diplomat in Rome. "But let's be honest. The American taste for Italy was a falling in love with 'Italy,' with the artificially created, snobbish idea that Italian was fashionable," Cassini adds. "We fall in love, we fall out of it. It can last ten years and then the wheel of fortune will go where? To the Koreans? To the Indians?"

It depends on who does the best job of filling in the letters or playing at charades. Probably, Americans will have a smaller role in designing the game plan.

8 ... and Ice Water with Bellini

So back in New York, I went to another European to have a little chat.

I met with Mario Bellini at a Saturday night dinner in Milan, researching the previous chapter. Ernesto Gismondi, president of Artemide, was our host. Ettore Sottsass, Barbara Radice, Vittorio Gregotti, Mario, and a dozen other design stars robustly conversed. Bellini's first words to me—he was seated at my side—were intimate for a stranger: "Why are you sad?" So I told him. I had just come back from Turin, following an interview with Armando Testa (p. 174). I had overpaid on the train. I had argued, back at Milan Stazione Centrale, for a refund, my briefcase at my feet. Upon looking down, the stupid little fight over, no briefcase. Stolen. In it, the tape of my Giorgio Armani interview, conducted at his Milan studio the day before. The stolid line of twenty behind me acted as if it had seen nothing.

"Armani is a friend," said Bellini, "I'll call him for you tomorrow morning. Now join us." And the very next morning, Sunday at ten as instructed, I was on the phone with a tense Armani. "I will join you at seven tonight at Via Borgonuovo. Goodbye." And he was there, even on the street by his door, when I arrived. And, as you read in the first chapter, we redid the interview, in French as before, but this time: "*Et vous avez dit . . . et j'ai dit.*" And I was eternally grateful to Bellini, who did me the second favor of spending several hours with me a month later in New York. He was at the St. Regis, the day so hot that even the air conditioner only partly cooled the room. Throughout the interview, in overstuffed chairs, we refilled and filled all over again our ice water glasses, micro air conditioners when pressed to the temple.

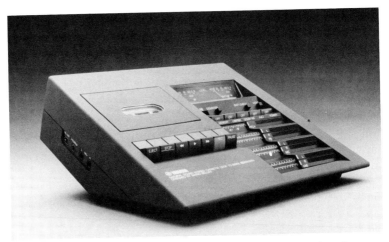

Figure 8.1 Mario Bellini. Realized cassette deck for Yamaha. *Courtesy Bellini.*

This book was then entitled *Reading America,* and I told Bellini that, when I met Armani, he had told me that he stayed *presso della strada,* near the street, looking looking looking for clues. Was Bellini like that? Could he give me an example of Bellini reading and then designing?

He told me that several years before, he was in Tokyo with Yamaha, "working since the early morning up to very late afternoon or even night," he said, "and continuously sitting on the floor without shoes, trying to solve problems, to go through details. But it has been extraordinary, this first experience with Yamaha. With three meetings we solved a very complex proposal we made to them. They had asked us to design a new cassette deck, a hi-fi cassette player and recorder, portable. And we had collected all the information, we brought them home, we set up a proposal and we brought it there with a mock-up, which was unusual for them. We had told them, 'We will never present you renderings, those nice drawings; nor we will present you several solutions, possibilities to be chosen from.' That is like being a carpet dealer. 'We will bring you one solution, the one we believe is the right one, and it will be done with a three-dimensional model—absolutely unusual for them. And we made so.'"

His syntax was awkward, his English was . . . rare trait: sincere. Listening to Bellini, it was as if you heard speech from the heart.

The Japanese apparently were astonished. The presentation and the model were so well done, they were surprised. Bellini's solution asked for spatial internal components to be custom designed; the

Japanese raised no objection. They redesigned and reconceived sliders, knobs, and elements that were out of standard completely; apparently any problem was solvable to them, Bellini remembered. His admiration for the Japanese was evident. "And so we liked them very much because they were hard workers as we like to be." And as we? I thought. The tiny comment was perhaps devastating of America. "And we discovered that the Japanese were always on time, always precise, reliable. But we, as northern Italians, were the same, always on time, always precise," he recalls. "We said, 'That day, that hour, it is finished, and that day, that hour, it *was* finished, and so we felt immediately in a good relationship."

A month before in Paris, on my way to the fashion designers of the first chapter, I had heard from Jacques Attali of such European-Japanese cross-fertilization, if not collaboration. I sipped coffee in the Elysée, listening to a monologue:

> My personal guess is that the future will be mainly based on the idea of having self-managing tools or devices which will help individuals to know more about themselves. Tools to be sort of generalized mirrors, mirrors for knowing if we are sick, mirrors informing us if we conform to the criteria of esthetics, health, or education. I think that Japan, and Europe, too, are quite well adapted to that. To take the Japanese: it is a culture totally oriented towards the idea of self-mastering or self-control of individuals. This is related to the nature of their society, based upon piling up individuals, one upon the other, and this is related to the civilization of a small, very narrow country. This leads to their culture having devices as mirrors.
>
> And mirrors also come from the fact that beauty or esthetic is more and more one of the main characteristics of rules of the future. I think that Europe and Japan are more oriented to beauty than the United States and USSR. Of course you have places like California, which are part of the world of the Continent.

Which doubtless is news to Californians. If unifying Europe is preparing to rival the Japanese, Bellini—following Attali's idea of a Euro-Japanese commonality—had been collaborating with them. He became a good friend of Hiroshi Kawakami, chairman of Yamaha. Indeed, Bellini's language was nearly reverential when he recalled Kawakami's "profound respect" for what he, Bellini, thought or what he wanted to have. "They always treated us as something like masters, as something very special. They never tried to bargain in terms of belittling what we had done and thought." Yet something in the experience had troubled Bellini, and this day, the Perrier fizzing in the heat of the room, he was trying to articulate that disquiet.

I didn't probe. I asked if his design was available in the west.

"Everywhere in the world," he answered, "in the Japanese local market and in the international market as well, United States and everywhere. It's been exported, this cassette deck, it had a tremendous success, it became immediately a symbol of something new: a kind of chisel, a cheese wedge, this square machine." In fact, it's in New York's Museum of Modern Art collection, and the Japanese advertised it, foregrounding the shape, on the subways of Japan, calling it the Bellini triangle, like a Pythagorean triangle.

But that disquiet touched his elation, he recounted. "What I always thought about them is that something of what we do escapes their understanding. They feel we are able to bring them something valuable, and they feel they can't exactly tell out of what it comes. That's why they need us."

I remember that in spring at the beginning of this research, when I was in Tokyo, just in time for the cherry blossoms, Kauhichi Tani, an impressive thirtyish senior government planning officer inducted me into something like the secret of his country's success. "The Japanese way of commercial strategy is always very timid, awkward," he surprised me. "We are always ready to learn something from abroad, from foreign markets. I suppose this is the secret of the extraordinary invasion of Japanese products in the United States and European countries." Tani gave me a striking example of this sensitivity to other cultures, which Bellini experienced as a constitutive lack of the Japanese. That example was the Suzuki motorcycle, first marketed in Europe as if it were a bicycle and then, following the failure of that, as an American horse, its driver becoming of course a cowboy (see p. 14). "We have no tradition of horse riding, but we understood that the Europeans were fascinated by the cowboy myth." The cowboy was a Trojan horse concealing Japanese goods, because the Japanese learned to survive by translating foreign cultures. And now here was the grateful, if slightly bewildered, Bellini telling of his translation by Yamaha.

"We were a little bit magicians to them," he remembered, "able to master culture which came from elsewhere in which they were, anyhow, playing an important game. That is always very delicate with this Japanese affair. They are playing what I call the western game. They dress as western people, they speak English, they read our language, they can write our writings, their writings, their language, our language, our culture, their culture. They are double, it's incredible. And they do motorcycles, which are western, better than we do. They do watches better than we do. Anything they enter, at the beginning they imitate, and then they do better."

In my Tokyo trip, Masao Yamaguchi, a celebrated cultural anthropologist, offered me the theory of what so surprised Bellini. "The whole Japanese culture has been that of simulacra," he told me. "It was a simulacrum of the Chinese culture, it was a simulacrum of the Indian culture. Repetition of Chinese civilization, repetition of Indian civilization."

184

"Simulacrum—isn't that a formula for babies?" a smart mouth once derided my penchant for jargon. No, a simulacrum is a substitution of something for something else where you forget the original; it's a repetition with a difference that doesn't matter— indeed, which you desire, embrace. Donald Trump based his Taj Mahal doormen's costumes not on Indian dress but on the costumes worn by Indian characters in old Hollywood movies. "Most people haven't been to India," said Robert Entrekin, head of the Taj's costume department. "Their perception is what they've seen on movies and TV. We had to cater to the excitement of the fantasy rather than the traditional reality of Indian culture." And when President Bush hosted the 1990 industrial summit in Houston, he offered the Japanese, German, French, and other leaders a rodeo one night, a monstrous melange of bull riding, barrel racing, the Grand Ole Opry, an Old West village, cowboys and Indians, oil rigs, square dancing, Styrofoam cacti, a model of the space shuttle, horseshoe contests, 1,250 gallons of barbecue sauce and jalapenos, 500 pounds of onions, 5,000 servings of cobbler and carrot cake, and 650 gallons of lemonade and iced tea. "We work real hard at being authentic," said Dave Higginbotham, a window-glass salesman dressed up in a sombrero and bandana and toting a rifle. "A lot of these people from foreign countries think this is still the way the South is. That's what they expect to see so we might as well give it to them."

It is the modern Japanese, before the Americans, who installed the regime of lovable fakes. The front entrance of a Seibu department store in Tokyo is many television screens, showing different scenes, then all together forming a gigantic monitor offering a gentle, vast landscape in substitution of Tokyo's. Fourteen-story-high billboards in Shinjuku (Tokyo's Times Square) sing to you. Yellow robots make yellow robots at the Fanuc robot factory at the foot of Mount Fuji. In the window of every Tokyo restaurant I saw were glossy plastic repetitions of all the platters on the menu. You cannot open or close a taxi door; it opens for you automatically. Inside the cab, you needn't be—you cannot be—separate from a TV screen: extending from the rear-view mirror, so that you never need miss a baseball game or commercial, is a small TV set right above you as if you were on a hospital bed. A simulacrum is a prosthesis and the Japanese have proliferated prostheses. They are everywhere. By techniques, machines, images, the Japanese have built a system of substitution for the body. Americans would die for (or from) it. And its origin, for Yamaguchi, is Japanese mentality itself. He told me that in Japan "is an idea called *mitate,* which is that everything which looks true is a fake of something behind it. So repetition repetition repetition is at the center of Japanese culture, see? All our poems were a kind of repetition, you see? And then by going to the extreme of repetition, we started to create something."

The Short Happy Life of Mr. Blonsky in Tokyo

Everything is imported, even to their undigested intellectual theories.

Shortly after I returned from Tokyo, I followed writer Kenzaburo Oē to Duke University and heard him deliver a devastating critique of his countrymen, starting from the idea that by 1970 that postwar literature called "junbungaku" was dead—"junbungaku" meaning a sincere, non-popular, non-mundane literature that had tried to seclude itself from the mass media. It had striven to provide a total, critical vision of the age and a human model for living it. To do this, the postwar writers had worked to "relativize" the value of the Emperor who had had absolute power; they sought to liberate the Japanese from the curse of the Emperor system which haunted their minds, even at the unconscious level. 1970 was also the year the Yukio Mishima committed his theatrical suicide, in his later years deeply lamenting the Emperor who had proclaimed he was not a deity but a human being. According to Oē, Mishima had prepared a baleful ghost to appear time and time again whenever Japan encountered a political crisis. And this is why Oē set 1970 as the year in which the curtain fell on postwar literature. Young intellectuals, who respond quickly to intellectual fads, told Oē and others that "junbungaku" was dead. This new class of intellectuals included critics, playwrights, scenario-writers, journalists, and those who, in the 80s, enjoyed the greatest popularity among the younger generation—advertising copywriters. "You may interpret the group to include almost all the cultural heroes of the grotesquely bloated consumer society of Japan today," said Oē. Starting in the latter half of the 1970s and lasting through the first half of the 80s, this vanguard of consumerism announced a new season of rationality, a trend in novel cultural ideas imported from the United States and from Europe, structuralisms, semiotics, psychoanalysis, and post-structuralisms. So bloated was Japan with and by signs that sincerity was felt to be impossible—better, grapple with the signs through semiotic discourses. Or employ the theory to write better copy or scripts, as you please. Copywriter or semiotician, they were equal in heroism.

"So great was the influx of new cultural theories that followed structuralism that it appeared on the surface that they were going to permeate through the whole of the nation's intellectual climate," Oē told his largely bored, Marxist audience. Three years before the collapse of Communism, it had come to hear of Third World struggle, and this bizarre account of fakery among First World intellectuals seemed, frankly, embarrassingly undissident. Aware or not of the restiveness, Oē continued: "An excellent summary of the new cultural theories of the West—titled 'Structure and Power'—was written by a young scholar named Akira Asada, and the book was read everywhere on the university campuses. The book sold equally as well as the most widely read work by any of the postwar writers. The book was, by no means, easy reading. However, no work of 'jun-bungaku' published in that period of time could arouse as much intellectual interest among the younger generation as this book had. After that came a time in which many new French cultural thoughts—some of which came via the U.S.—were introduced and translated, i.e., from poststructuralism to postmodernism: namely from Barthes, Foucault, Derrida, Lacan, Kristeva, and to the Yale School of Deconstructionists."

Which is why I had been so warmly received in Tokyo. My semiotic anthology, *On Signs,* comprising all those authors and more, had just come out and been imported into Tokyo from England. But even as I was being feted in Tokyo—lectures at a museum and chamber of commerce, lunch talk at a vast round table at a huge advertising agency, interview on NTV television network, pub crawling and strange encounters with latter-day geishas at nightclubs—in the midst of it all I little knew I was a simulacrum of a semiotician for these Japanese. I was a reflex of a corpse, offering nostalgia for lost cultural heroes. Oē burst my bubble. "Intellectual enthusiasm among the younger generation for new cultural thoughts had come to an end," he continued. "Not only did it end for the younger generation but it ended also for intellectual journalism, which had staged, directed, and reflected that enthusiasm."

And it was at this moment that a bomb scare stopped him; and when the drowsy anti-bourgeoisie returned to the hall, few wanted to hear Oē on faddishness any more. So I cite the paper he gave me, dedicated "For Mr. Bronsky with regards as a mutual friend of Yamaguchi": "I was, by that time, no longer a young writer and had never been part of that boom. But, as I stand amidst the rack and ruin of the voluminous introductory works and translations and look back upon that age, I notice several interesting characteristics.

"First, the young Japanese intellectuals, true to our national character, analyzed and systematized diachronically the various structuralism-based thoughts and moreover, the criticisms thereof, in order to 'accept' and—to use an antonym not quite appropriate for this word—'discharge' those thoughts. To accept Foucault, Barthes had to be discharged. Only after Lacan was discharged could Derrida be accepted—but only to await the next thinker. The shuttling of new cultural thoughts was, up to a point, an easy task for the introducers and translators who advocated their influx. Cultural heroes came and went."

The intellectual MCs used phrases like "frolicking with texts" or "the performance of thoughts" for their sport. They came to love the word "post," adding a very Japanese connotation to this prefix. By speaking of "poststructuralism" or "postmodernism," or even of cultural thoughts they felt were on the way but whose content they couldn't imagine, they set up the mechanism for ready acceptance and quick discharge, causing every theory to signal a nascent one almost ready to dethrone it. They made every cultural idea a quick consumable. Oē wrote:

> Despite this remarkable trend for absorbing new cultural theories, almost no effort was made to meticulously interpret them in view of specific situations that Japan was in. Why then did the new cultural theories from Europe and the United States become so popular among the young intellectuals and intellectual journalism? This is indeed the strange part of the story. However, I believe it can be attributed mostly to the special characteristic which our nation's intellectual journalism had nurtured ever since the Meiji Restoration. To put it very bluntly, there was an inclination for people to think that an intellectual effort had been accomplished by merely transplanting or translating the new American and European cultural thoughts into Japanese. . . . As soon as an introduction or translation was completed, the one-way flow from Europe and America to Japan was completed. That is to say, its acceptance and discharge were over. . . .
>
> This tendency has also brought about the characteristic phenomenon in today's Japanese cultural climate wherein we can see no signs of effort to accept a variety of cultural thoughts synchronically. Never have we witnessed, in intellectual journalism in our country, the synchronic existence of two adverse thoughts—for example, structuralism and deconstructionalism—jeopardizing, and at the same time complementing each other, and hence, in turn, depending on each other. . . . In the context of the cultural climate of Japan, the new cultural theories, as one organic part of literature's decline, fell prey to the general flow towards a decay faster than that of literature. I believe that the two—literature and its readers on the one hand, and, on the other, new cultural theories and the young intellectuals who accepted them—should be viewed not as adversaries in a dichotomy, but, as one entity "blended together like fresh ink spots on blotting paper." Looking at the fad in a broader perspective, we can say that the young intellectuals were not truly intellectuals as such, but merely young Japanese living a subcultural fad in an urbanized, average consumer culture.

They were simulacra of intellectuals, hollow men of theory. It was this vacuity in his world, design, that Bellini had felt and was trying ever so delicately, so as not to offend his clients, to signal to me.

Without the slightest shame he informed me that the Japanese have always believed that there is nothing that is true. Only in repetition is there anything essential. "God came in the form of a fake," he laughed. I should mention that we had this conversation on Easter Sunday.

"So the Japanese are for some reason incredible people," said Bellini, I meantime wondering who says that of the Americans today? "But then I feel they lack something," he retracted.

"What?"

"For example, when they are dressed in the western way, with few exceptions for very sophisticated people, they're always wrong. They are out of set, they put the wrong tie with the wrong this with the wrong that. They can't instinctively play with the elements. Everything is foreign to them, imported from outside."

They simulate us and are always a tad off, he thought. They do any kind of industrial design, employ ultra-modern large studios, but although Bellini conceded that the situation is changing slightly, with exceptions always, he believed that on average, "the Japanese lack the sources to understand, at bottom, what they are touching, what they are dealing with." I seriously doubted that this was a racial slur, so I sought specificity, asked for clarification in the case of the cassette deck.

Bellini was unremitting. "It was an unprecedented, unexpected solution and shape. They would never have done it by themselves," he said. "They would never have conceived something like that. Not at all. But they understood it was something new, something great." His voice was tense, not in praise of himself but in wonder at the Japanese transfixed. "They manufactured it in an incredibly nice way, as no other company would have done"—their way of saluting his transmission to them of values strange and unmanipulable. Understanding those values, we better understand Italian creativity at the end of a century no longer American.

Bellini's cassette deck was a device to record and play cassettes in a stereo mode using many sliders for control, left and right, volume and tone and balance and so on, and with meters to control intensity and power. It was conceived to be carried with a belt and to be operated while carrying it. And so he designed a sloped surface, which he drew for me (Fig. 8.2), coming out of the table surface as a chisel shape, starting from the top of the table in front of you and going backward, rising like a sloped surface. This solution enabled you to have very clearly and sharply under your eyes all that you needed to know and to see, the cassette house on the left and all the sliders on the right set in a stepped mode like the next design he drew (Fig. 8.3), progressively coming closer to you.

He derived the design from what he had studied before with Olivetti when he designed the Logos 50/60 calculator, an electronic calculating machine that was the first transversal sloped chisel

Figures 8.2, 8.3 Mario Bellini. Sketches for a Yamaha cassette deck.
Courtesy Bellini.

machine. Bellini thinks he may have invented, vis-à-vis industrial design, this sloped chisel shape, which subsequently has been imitated worldwide. The first time he used the shape, he did so instinctively somehow. Then, when he studied the reason for his work—he had been asked to do so for lectures and writings—he found that, probably, all of it had derived from the very fundamental old tablet which had been used to write and to read since Egyptian times, the *legio.* "It's like a piece of wood or something. You place it on the table, like a pulpit," Bellini told me. "It's a very fundamental old device in our culture. Everything since the beginning of our culture that has been related to reading and writing has been done in that mode." He added the note:

> Afterwards, I made an iconographical research about the form, because I was interested, because the wedge is very important in my iconography. I found many examples, paintings of the old times, the new times. There is an Antonello da Messina *Annunciazione,* which is done with a wooden chisel with arches underneath, like one of my machines; and over it, the Madonna, who seems about to touch a keyboard.

Theory today makes a "text" out of almost anything. Political power is a text to be read; daily life is a text to be deciphered; consumer goods are a textual system; also the star system, one's gender, one's body, our walking, our shopping, none of which are human nature—they are constructs. Barthes' *Mythologies* and maybe my own are demonstrations that where the others see, taste, touch, and hear, brute reality is sign and text.

Bellini, while not denying the semiotic aspect of much "reality," sought to recuperate the nature that rules us. Human and otherwise.

"If you consider your relationship with a table," he said, "it's unnatural to read or write on that flat surface. When you read, you never keep a book or a newspaper in your hands flat on the table. You do this [making the imaginary paper go up in chisel form], because it's what we call 'mathematically normal' to your eyes. As you move your eyes up and down, the distance will be averagely the same. When you do so [and he imaginarily flattened the paper toward the table], it will be too far away, and this [he seemed to bring its top closer to his eyes], it will be too close. And also when you write, it should be for the same reason at the same—the mathematically normal—angle."

"Which is?"

"About 30 degrees." He went on:

> There is another famous iconograph in painting. Very often you see a man writing or standing near a table, which is never flat, which is always in the chisel shape. That iconography is also in another An-

Figure 8.4 Antonello da Messina. *Saint Jerome.*

tonello da Messina, my favorite, *Saint Gerolamo*. It shows a little study where he has animals, a pheasant, a lion, a globe, books; it's full of symbols. You have a raised floor, like a little piece of architecture, and on three sides, shelves, and then that sloped little table and San Gerolamo, and then on two sides, a background with two arches and a landscape. It's really a symbol of the anthropocentrical position of man during the Renaissance. It's incredible, and I've often used it to explain possibly my way of thinking when designing. It's a perfect symbol of a work station, of a contemporary, open-space, office work station. And I found many other examples, incisions, *gravures,* medieval woodcuts, and I use them, too, when I do slide projections, talking about my work. And so I brought to Japan this very intense idea and projections, and the Japanese felt immediately shocked with something which they would have never been able to conceive by themselves. And what we found about the Japanese is that they lack this definite, profound possibility to conceive something out of what has already been thought and already been done in human history.

They lack, according to him, the sense of the *déjà vu,* of the *déjà fait,* the already seen, the already done; they lack the possibility of perceiving relations between the work they are doing and works that have preceded. But this lack is precisely that of the esthetic function itself, which depends on references to the already said; which depends on the possibility of integrating the work to a tradition. This cannot be. Do the Japanese lack the requisite history of art? Of literature? Of design? I scarcely believe it. Do they lack a sensitivity to the body's needs?

This last seemed to the Italians a possible reason for the lacuna they had encountered. "I think they have a sensitivity to the body's needs, but it's a very special one," said Bellini. "For example, we western people invented shoes, and the shoes we invented followed the dynamic needs of the body and of the feet. The shape they have is related to the way our foot moves and is articulated. But the Japanese traditional sandal is a perfectly rectangular tablet which has nothing to do with your foot. It has more to do with the abstract sense of the horizontal of the earth's surface. And again, we invented the . . . how do you call all this [pointing to his clothes]?"

"Suit."

"*Vestiti,* suits . . . and as you know, the western suits have always been related to the body, to its . . . how do you call this, *manicotto?*"

"Sleeve."

"Sleeves and colors and many shapes . . . to give our suits the shape of our body and to let them follow the body's behavior and needs."

"You're wearing an Armani shirt," I notice and tell him.

"Yes."

"Armani told me wants his clothes to run down the body like a second skin. Is that what's happening with your shirt?"

"The jacket is the better example."

"Armani?" I ask.

"It has varied a lot through the centuries—yes, Armani—but basically, it gives a shape to your shoulders. This is very difficult to do. Unless you're a real tailor you'll never, as a normally intelligent man, be able to cut and to put together this supposedly simple thing. It is very difficult. It has taken centuries to be invented. This and this [pointing to his shoulders, chest, collar]. If you take a Japanese suit . . . you know them?"

"No."

"Oh, they are pure geometrical shape. The normal kimono [he draws it] is a rectangular thing, too. It is an extraordinarily pure concept, but the body again plays a very strange role in it. They never try to follow your body. For some reason they try to elevate the body into purity, to that pure concept. From the religious, social, and conceptual point of view, it's a different way of seeing the world. It's very difficult to say because you need to have studied it very profoundly, but I rightly feel this, and if you take their trees, they always tried to modify the nature of the trees. You know the way they do it?''

''Bonsai?''

''Bonsai and also the way they take out sprouts, when it starts before becoming a branch. They take them out with a certain process and they leave only some of them in some cases, and so finally the pine will become as it had been drawn.''

Impossible not to recall what Barthes said in his book on Japan. In the *Ikebana,* flower arrangement, what is produced is the circulation of air, the branches, leaves, and flowers being only the partitions, corridors, baffles. It's as if the flower arrangement had been *drawn,* according to an idea of rarity.

Bellini, while not overtly disagreeing with Barthes, insisted on the idea of force. ''Yeah, rarity,'' he said, dismissively, ''but they impose the shape they have in mind onto nature. Only here and there [he draws], they allow only a few branches to spring out. They always try to give the nature a culturalized shape, a conceptualized shape. We went too far away maybe . . .''

''Sorry about that.''

''But as you asked why they are not able to do what we have done, this may be one reason. Man should be a rarity in need of no help for the hands. And then the very idea of product design is something which is more western than far eastern, I believe, and this also has to do with what I consider, from their side, a difficulty. They are extraordinary people, because, imagine writing their alphabet in our alphabet. That's what they do with ours. It is not a question of using different signs, it's a completely different concept: that of talking their language and also foreign languages. To live with a double culture like they do is incredibly challenging and that is one of the reasons they will beat out all of us because they are . . . how do you say? . . . stressing their brain, because since they are childs they are trained to do two times the alphabet, to study a few thousand Kanji to really squeeze the brain, plus the Katakana, the alphabet for our alphabet. And so they are overforced, overstressed. But for some reason they are not at ease when they have to integrate themselves to a tradition and make something new out of it, something the culture hasn't seen until now. For example, to design a chair is an incredibly mysterious, difficult kind of work.''

''For them?''

''For anybody. The chair is the most difficult item to be designed ever.''

''Tell me why,'' I ask. And realize, this is a master seminar for one. One of the world's greatest designers and his apt pupil.

"Oh, is incredible," says Bellini in that style that for us would be gushy but for educated Italians is sincerity. "A chair . . . I tell you something. To design a chair, or even a coffee cup handle, is ten times more difficult than to design a very complicated computer in terms of industrial design. That's very . . . it's not easy to explain."

He is wrought, he is moved.

"But is possible."

To ease his situation, I ask: "Do you want some paper?"

"No, no no. A chair has not been invented by any designer; by anybody, let's say. The chair sprang out of our western culture when a part of the human being decided to sit on something instead of sitting on the floor or sitting on the elbows . . . not elbow—how do you call this?"

"The heel." He's teaching design here and I, English—not a fair exchange.

"The heels. And from what I know, during the ancient Egyptian times, the chair was already perfectly defined. You can see a perfect example of a chair, a sample of chair in the Tutankhamen treasury. It was the chair of the son of Amenophus the Third or something . . . one of the nicest . . ."

He is in awe of the Egyptians, his language faltering. Obviously, I haven't the faintest will to interrupt his evocation of the sacred. I had never heard—when was the last time you heard?—such eloquence on what we take to be so banal.

"It is perfect with gently sloped and carved seat," Bellini discourses, "four legs and a very cleverly engineered structural system which allows the chair to be solid and light and then beautifully carved and decorated. And this last is the most Egyptian touch. If you take out carving and decoration, basically it was a modern contemporary, a perfect chair. If something like five thousand years ago, the chair was already perfect, it means that ten thousand years ago they had started thinking and trying . . . a lot of years. And that explains why to touch today a chair once again is so challenging, so difficult, because if something is so well and profoundly rooted in our culture, you can't joke with it. And whenever you try to design a chair basing your acts on function and technique, you are touching the 2 percent of the problem, because function and technique are obviously something you have to master to design a chair, but then what is difficult is the chair. Because finally the chair has to look like a chair. It's very banal but very profound. I believe that a chair derives from a chair from a chair from a chair from a chair. And so you will never be able to design a chair basing your design process on banal stupid things like functions. A chair is not a machine to raise your bottom. It's something, first of all, connected with your person, which means a little bit sacred. Not in the religious way but sacred because . . . look, a throne is a sacred chair, why is a chair a throne? I tell you. Your body is something very sophisticated. You are a living human being, you are not an object, a piece of something and so the chair is fitting your body, you sit on a chair. But is not a table. A table is a piece of floor, a raised piece of floor, but a chair is not as simple as a table. And due to that, anybody could be able, looking at a new chair design by somebody to say, 'Ah, what a strange chair, I don't like it, it's not a chair.' We are hyper-sensible to that. Basically, because we have been grown up understanding what a chair is."

I mentioned in the preface that I began this book with all my library in boxes due to an apartment renovation. Like numerous design victims of the 80s, I engaged designers whom I outgrew and with whose "cutting edge" taste I became uncomfortable. Throwing away the *Architectural Digests* and the books on hothouse design, I educated my taste, alas not too quickly; it took the power of periodization, the collapse of the 80s, to discredit my consultants. They had chosen for my dining room a chair of Phillipe Starck, hyper-popular, creator of the west's and far east's avant-garde hotels. They had chosen his Aleph chair. Severe. Bellini knew it.

That chair doesn't "give." It looks as if it were a Kafakaesque machine that doesn't intend you well. Impossible to avoid using a word I swore once I would never use again: The Aleph provokes a *postmodern* humiliation of the person. Ensconced within it, one doesn't experience a friendly, a human feeling. I therefore think I understand what Bellini means when he says don't tamper or touch lightly a chair. I'm not even sure, after this hot interview, that I understand what *is* a chair, merely to pursue some of the difficulty of designing a chair, according to Bellini. I tell him that I've never understood why it is that I like to put one leg over the other.

"Me as well."

"What is it one accomplishes when one at last rests the one leg on the other?" I ask. "I know that I use the chair in a very decontracted way. I seem to want my arms to . . ."

I let them dangle over the sides as if I were some Baudelairaean dandy.

Bellini says: "That's what you do in an easy chair, the gesture you just made. The chair permits it."

And I: "But there's another modality I like, which is this. If the back is straight, the chair enables this mode of sitting [I'm straight up], which is intellectual and which permits very intense communication. Without the aid of the chair, somehow conversation is much more difficult."

"To me is impossible," says Bellini. "I couldn't think of any important matter while standing."

"Why is that, do you think?"

"I don't know. Maybe because I need to decontract my muscle

and my equilibrium control system to release all my energy to the thinking process and forget my body somehow."

He can't, here, now. The ice clinks from the tongs into his glass. "When I'm standing like an animal I need to invest part of my energies and then I start feeling a little bit nervous and tired and that distracts me," he says.

The spirit to whom this book is silently dedicated once wrote that language is a screen, a veil of Maya that removes the self from experiencing the body according to *its* logic, *its* beats. Barthes said a body lives in breathlessness, haste, desire, anxiety. When we use language we forget we are bodies. (Bellini grunts very softly as I explain.) Language *is* that forgetting. And so a chair would be a kind of condition making possible this removal from the body. No? Yes? I wonder.

Yes, he agrees. And returns us to the computer, which is much easier to design, something not obviously understandable. To design a computer one needs to know many technical items overestimated, he thinks. These are easily available, whereas the proper sensibility to design a chair is not easily available. You have it or you don't. And thus we're back to the question, why a chair is so difficult.

Bellini pauses, tries again to explain: "You need to be able to finalize your designing acts in a kind of magical equilibrium. When a chair is right is an unhappy difficult equilibrium and of course there are rules by which to know when a chair is right, otherwise it would be easy. And of course the way it could eventually be right varies according to cultural variations and centuries of history. Nevertheless, I think I can feel when a chair is right and basically also common people can feel it better than saying when a computer is right. First of all, because all of us we are used to living with chairs since the beginning. They are like our arms, they are parts of our body. They're not tools like a hammer or something. They are a detached part of our bodies like the vestments, which are also very difficult to design. Many stylists make things which are taken to be vestments by the uninformed who pay dear, but very few make real vestments. The chair is even more . . . how do you say? . . . daunting? When you see somebody starting a chair, you have a kind of symbiosis of man and chair. For example, when we talk about a chair, we use the same words we use for the parts of our bodies. We say the back of the chair, the legs of the chair, the arms of the chair, which makes the chair almost like our person. We also say chairman. And the chair, as I told already, became a throne and a symbol of the power of position among others. There is something really sacred about a chair."

And like things sacred, there is something secret or unknowable about a chair. Forget my speculations about a chair. That's all they were, speculation. When I asked Bellini what is a chair? he answered in the empirical voice: It derives from a patrimonial hoard of human experiences. They can be assigned no logic other than that of the probable, of empirics, of the "already-done." The way we name the chair tells us that. Bellini thinks we name its parts "legs," "arms," "back" out of a desire for analogy, a common code. But analogy to what? What code is in play?

When we speak of the *legs* of a table or the *face* or *back* of a mountain, we are doing something peculiar and a little frightening. We are saying we don't know what nature is or even some of the artifacts that we use to stave it away. And we are doing so by employing the ancient rhetoric. The trope or turn of phrase that coins a name for a still unamed entity was and is called *catachresis*. We speak of the *wing* of a building because, strange as this may seem, it is odd to us; we don't seem to be certain what it is and we rush away absurdly to the air and ornithology to escape our doubt. But the master trope for concealing doubt is called *prosopopeia*, coining a name in order to give face, to give body, in order to fool ourselves that the thing we're struggling with is as stable as our own reassuring faces. Hence the *face* of a mountain or the *eye* of a hurricane. In studied terms, this is *catachresis* by *prosopopeia*. What is time? We don't know, so we speak of the *hands* of a clock. Indeed, we might even say that in the absence of clocks and their hands no one could be certain that such a thing as time exists. What is the mind? When Victor Hugo bizarrely writes: "The mind, this watchman made of ears and eyes," he is not making a linguistic monster, he is giving visual and human shape to something that has no sensory existence, that may not exist and whose nonexistence would be terrifying if we let ourselves think about it. But we don't, thanks to the language trick called *prosopopeia*.

Our clocks and their faces stand for time as our chairs and their arms literally stand for . . . man. Consciousness. Bellini was right to stress that we honor chairs by making a few of them into thrones. But all of them enthrone His Majesty, the Blessed Ego. Oh, really? There is so much epistemological tension about him—is he really there?—that we overdetermine the chair with our own names. The chair not only has arms, but legs and back—you can actually hear the doubt in the hysteria to call it human. But that hysteria inhabits every *prosopopeia*. We have enormous doubt about things like mind, consciousness, time, these invisibles that we strain to see signs of and for which we posit voices, faces, sensory shapes to make the unknown accessible. If you let yourself think how large is the set of vital things that we repetitively, boringly, humiliatingly name by the same small set of body parts, it might scare you how much doubt you bear. For in giving visual shape to what has no sensory existence, we are producing hallucinations—linguistic, to be sure. And whether in language or by a sorcerer's wand, making the invisible visible is uncanny. When you say all your life with the same stupid insistence that there is something sensory—a *light* of reason, the *hands* of time, the *face* of tragedy—where nothing is, the ruse can fail, the smug certainty of time and mind and the rest . . . vanish. When I heard Bellini stammer—a chair derives from a chair derives from a chair; when I heard him say the equilibrium of a good chair is "unhappy"; when I heard him say what it's not, not what it is; I think I heard a man approaching awe in the face—forgive me—of this human incapacity. But the emotion was forgotten, and he continued, telling me of his famous Cab chair, one of the most famous in history. He has designed hundreds of machines and one single chair in his life. Somehow this has to do with words. We have in English "chair" for *sedia*, "chair" for *poltracina*, "chair" for *poltrona*. We have only "chair," he has many nuances.

"This [pointing to his] is not a chair, not a *sedia* for us, this is a *poltrona*. The real chair for us is that one [pointing across the room to a four-legged side chair], that is the chair. And so I designed a few of these, the ones I sit on, but only one of that kind [pointing to it], what you call . . . I don't know how to separate them using English. The proper chair, pull . . . how do you call it? Pull up chair? Side chair? The side chair is the very difficult one, the one with four legs, while this is an historical version of that, already a little bit strange because lower. Not a proper height, not the one you would use for a dining table, is a little bit lower."

But we Americans love our recliners, our stuffed easy chairs, our poor men's thrones, our fat *meubles*, if we were reading and writing in French. *Meuble*, which means furniture and here chair, generally designates a property anything but mobile. With us, chairs, like the rest of our furniture, have an immobilizing vocation. Deep inside a pseudo-Barcelona (if we have Macy's taste) or a skin of chintz on a fat lap of foam rubber, we bless with our scepter of beer can our *stuff*. All around this fat center, our things only augment it. And our fat bodies (we're famous abroad as the land of the obese) swell more to become masters of a space. We adore centering ourselves in our easy chairs (later our beds), we little, though (forgive me) obese, proprietors of emplacement. Is it any wonder we resist the upright, the civilized position achieved by the *sedia* and by the Egyptians?

By now some will have dozed in their chairs in this endless dinner with Marshall or Mario. For my part, I was transfixed, as if something hidden since my creation were about to be revealed by this designer who hurls himself against what he thinks of as secrets, a nature to be gloriously exposed and mastered by his design.

What the two of us were sitting in at this moment had nothing to do with a chair, he told me. It was a *poltrona*, an easy chair, stuffed chair, padded chair, so much easier. He had designed many of these but only one of those, the *sedia*. It was called Cab.

"And it is done in such a way," he said, "that if you look at it from

Figure 8.5 Mario Bellini. Cab chair. *Courtesy Bellini.*

outside, immediately you feel, 'Oh, it's a chair,' as if you had forgotten what chairs were. You may have different colors of the leather, red, black, gray, and so. Real thick leather. We have in Italian *cuyo*, which is thick hair leather, and *pelle* for soft leather. You have only 'leather,' so it makes it difficult for me. The Cab is in *cuyo*, very hard one, sewed with a machine, and then you see inside, along the internal vertical lines of the four legs, you have zippers. You can open the zippers and take the chair off the skeleton, and inside the chair is a very simple metal frame which looks like a chair again. It's done with four legs. The two back legs go higher like two antennae, and then you have four sides, which connect with the four legs. That's the frame. You can't sit on it because you would fall into the middle. It looks like a chair designed by a child using four lines. It's a very simple light steel painted frame. So that steel frame without the leather jacket is nothing. That leather jacket without the frame falls down. But you cross them together and there springs out a chair. That's why I told you it is not covered with leather. If covered, you could take the leather off and still have a chair. If something is covered it means you add as a finishing the leather. But in this case the leather is acting as the skin on the cow. You have a cow, you have a skeleton inside and a thick leather skin around, and there is a tension, a pressure, and the chair lives like an organism. It's an animal. I'm always instinctively related to everything that is anthropomorphic and zoopmorphic. If you were to study all my design, it's related to that. For a reason I will tell you later. So that's the chair. And it touched something strange, and miraculously it had a tremendous success. Now it is considered *the* chair, one of the few chairs of today. And it's been sold all around the world, imitated and copied all around the world. I think it will last for tens and tens of years in the market. It is still in the market after ten years. It has sold more and more and more. And in a way, it is something which has never been done before. Never. But in a way is natural, so chair. And that's what I like in a chair."

He is telling me that in some sense he recreated the creature, the animal, the cow from whom the leather had been taken. He has always been dealing with this man-animal relationship. Much of his design, whether of furniture or machines, has a certain relationship with anthropomorphic and zoomomorphic attitudes. For Bellini, we are born structured as body, which is not something we decided to have, which is not something we can distinctively perceive outside of us. It is something which nevertheless substantiates us. We see, we recognize, by looking at, touching, feeling, tasting, and moving. And this since the beginning of our lives.

"I think it tremendously affects our way of thinking and recognizing," he naively says, "and all our culture is affected by this animal we are."

"And usually don't think we are. We usually forget."

"Oh, sure. Otherwise we would become crazy," he says. "Even our vocabulary expresses that. We talk, as I told you, about legs of this or that, hands and face and front and facade and back. Everything is done, we say in Italian, in *immagine e somiglianza del'uomo,* in the image and the similarity of man. As God created us in his image, it is said. It is nothing more or less than civilization, which has been a kind of domestication of the outside world."

As with food (chapter 3), we return to the idea of luxurious versus natural appetite. We need to eat in order to subsist, but that is not enough for us. We have to stage, as we do in sex, the luxury of desire, gastronomic in addition to amorous. And, as if we needed ever more luxury, we seem to have to add desire to our mechanisms. We need them to work in our place, but that doesn't suffice. We have to give them a useless supplement, the image of our own bodies. To make a mechanism a machine one needs to give it a body; as it were, put skin and bone on it, as Bellini did his Cab chair; as Armani, the new line he drew for me. When Armani said he wanted his clothes to be a second skin, it was an odd kind of skin he offered. It was a fat man's skin. He was giving more skin than one needed. A luxury of skin that was not mere esthetic embellishment or added value. It was something, as he himself suggested, that *goes with* man. Like a vital prosthesis, he cannot be without it. The skin he gives you is not wholly a functional skin.

"Pure function doesn't exist," Bellini exclaimed when I told him this. "Even with the body itself. What's pure function? Tell me what I need. This is not needed. Okay . . ." And he took his tie off. "This is not needed. Okay, take it off, take it out." He removed his cufflinks, and I had the craziest idea that the successor to Le Corbusier would do a strip. "Take it out, take it out. At the end, what do you do? You spray something on your body. *Shhhh.* A need?"

The young Barthes was a Marxist structuralist, dissecting wrestling, toys, steak, wine, detergents, Martians, astrology columns, ornamental cookery, electoral photography; and probing the articulations of their manipulative functions. The middle Barthes was a deconstructor, pronouncing the death of the Author, exploding his Genius into the shards of codes. The late Barthes, however, was a reconstructor, seeking diverse ways of performing *praxis*, Aristotle's practical science, his science of life, supposed to produce nothing outside of man (*poiesis* issued in poetry), but rather, man himself, happy man. Because he was one of the few in the bazaar of theorists to attempt the reconstitution, not the deconstruction of subjectivity, Roland Barthes has a place in our lives in this moment of European rebuilding and American reassessment. Chapter 15, on horror, exposes his proposal for living together. Here, we have business with the body by means of an essay called "Rasch."

It takes its title from the German word *rasch* (fast), equivalent to the Italian *presto*, because the essay is on Schumann's *Kreisleriana*, the tempo markings of which are in German. One evening, Barthes went to a Parisian concert hall with a friend, pianist Yves Nat, to hear Horowitz play the *Kreisleriana*. What he saw and heard there, he thought, was Horowitz making his fingers mimic body parts.

Our bodies, Barthes wrote, form figures, analogous to acrobatic figures; *figures du corps* in French. What is a *figure of the body*, a bodily figure? When I am in a certain humor, for example, when I'm elated, how tall am I? I am not the distance from my shin to the top of my head; rather, I am from . . .

And narrating the essay for Bellini, I got up off the *poltrona* and standing on tiptoe with arms raised, I made my right hand touch the fingers of my left hand. The heat does crazy things to us. That is how tall I am, and the reader as well. And Bellini, who told me he was zoomorphic in design, grunted in satisfaction: *''Hmmm hmmm.''* The little figure I had enacted better enables us to understand the athlete's triumphalist gesture, arms above head; he or she attains the limit of the human dimension. And when we are angry, the body feels as if it could crack, but it doesn't crack; we pound as we speak. According to our diverse humors, we mold our bodies into a rich variety of such postures.

What is a virtuoso under this concept? Horowitz is the one who is a body and who, as he plays, doesn't respect the seeming *legato* of the music. He molds his music into bodily figures starting from his own; received by the ears in the audience, these figures constitute anger, anxiety, elation, et cetera. Howowitz restores through the ear the sense of the somatic. And Bellini, through the finger.

"You see machines designed by me which make you act as a dinosaur," he said outrageously. "Or I can make you act as an animal with a tail." But touching the bulk of his design, we act as the tailless animal of opposable thumb, able to grasp his object (in both senses) because it mimics our bodies. "Understanding is affected by what we are made of," he added more reasonably. "We have two arms. It's not by chance, you know. We couldn't have three."

Eco and Bellini: Who could forget, and I especially, the passage in *Foucault's Pendulum* where Lia, representing healthy interpretation, tells her lover how the body structures meaning and design: "Pow, archetypes don't exist; the body exists. The belly inside is beautiful, because the baby grows there, because your sweet cock, all bright and jolly, thrusts there, and good, tasty food descends there, and for this reason the cavern, the grotto, the tunnel are beautiful and important, and the labyrinth, too, which is made in the image of our wonderful intestines. . . . We move on to the magic numbers your authors are so fond of. You are one and not two, your cock and my cunt is one, and we have one nose and one heart; so you see how many important things come in ones. But we have two eyes, two ears, two nostrils, my breasts, your balls, legs, arms, buttocks. Three is the most magical of all, because our body doesn't know that number; we don't have three of anything, and it should be a very mysterious number that we attribute to God, wherever we live."

Eco made Lia mythify the world, produce an artificial myth in the guise of a natural one, her body. Bellini is Lia, and the logic of his design—fast becoming extinct and rare as the dinosaur—tells how profoundly our culture rejects this mythopoetics.

"We understand by touching," he insisted, "and the arm's length distance, from shoulder to fingertip, it's a very important limit, as you demonstrated a minute ago when you got up," he reminded me. "You wanted ice that was outside that limit. Out of frustration you got up. You put the bucket here between us. Now you're reaching"—as indeed I was—"with the elbow bent." He had me half-believing his myth: the elbow bent, that is what goes with man, it's not comfortable to be at the limit with forearm and upper arm one. So I myself redesigned the room in my image. And look at Mario in the *poltrona,* treating it like a couch, almost lying down in it, one arm falling nearly to the carpet in reminiscence of the Baudelairean dandy the *poltrona* had made me only minutes ago. It was less that Mario, sympathetic, was mirroring me; more that the *poltrona,* a slave, was made to let Mario "decontract," a figure of the body.

"The doors, the windows, they are so wide, so high because of the way your body bends," he says, walking to the window. "The wall has been cut for the windowsill in relation to where your body bends. You can bend right over it but not stumble out. Everything, this proportion"—he bends in the direction of the thankfully closed window—"the tables, streets, everything has a relationship with our own body."

How easy to reconstitute such myth. The window is four feet wide so that my arms can bend at the elbow to pull the drapes. The corridor of my home, only a little wider than my waist, deliciously encloses me, providing the sense I am inside the bloodstream or intestine of my house. Bellini as Lia: we grasp how profound is this impulse to mythify, to see our houses and the furniture and objects inside them as so many signs of ourselves, chairs, beds, tables, even the walls and windows assuring my ego, making me the subject and master of a space.

The world according to Bellini: Formerly built as we are built, increasingly it mocks us. At that dinner with the Ecos, somebody mentioned Helmut Jahn's State of Illinois Center, also called the Salad Spinner, in Chicago. The noted architect Vittorio Gregotti remarked: "Why did Helmut stop? He could have made a tower of Babel."

Bellini well understands himself as an endangered species. "Due to the fact we are, let's say, intelligent people we are also perverse," he said. "Yes, we have the possibility to be against ourselves, because intelligence allows us to be perverted, and so we can do bad windows, bad doors, bad cities. And it is mostly in our postmodern time, that we experience the possibility to pervert everything." When I asked him why perversion now, he answered: "Because the links between the way things are done and the reason why they're done that way are less and less evident."

And no one cares. When, earlier, I mentioned the simulacrum, I could have added, and do now, that it's an effect, a special effect, as in film, and for us there are no longer causes. The Japanese in Houston didn't think to inquire about the real, old South. Visitors to the Taj don't ask if India was like this. The system we inhabit destroys the taste for origins, referents, reasons; they have been devoured by the image.

And of course we have become less and less physical. Everything becomes informatic, everything becomes soft. And, thinking with Bellini, you can go wrong, terribly wrong, and not really feel it. In his discourse, a hammer cannot be wrong. Everything about it, the weight, the length, the way it is crafted is physically derived, century after century, from one's hand, one's strength, how often and with what power one can beat, and so on. But imagine inventing an electronic hammer? You can be too sharp, too energetic, too fast, too slow according to our bodies.

"Is this invented correctly," I asked, "this tape recorder I'm using?"

Between us on a small glass table was my Sony "Pro," the professional Walkman that I had taken to Tokyo, Milan, Moscow (where a waiter had marveled over it), London, Paris, all the sites of research for this book. The ever-reliable Sony Pro is 11 by 4 by 1 1/2 inches, black metal covered in black plastic with red underside.

"When we enter what I call the black boxes," he answered, "it is very difficult to say what is correct. I always have been thinking over the difference between tools and machines. A tool, like a scissor, like other things, is never wrong. And then we started inventing, let's say a hundred years ago, mechanical machines like the first typewriters, at that moment the machine prevailed, because for the first time you had to let it work on its own. If you remember, before that, at the beginning of the century, we had naked mechanisms, quite visible. And then, when the difficult part of the job was over, we started putting bodies on the mechanism, what is called body work, *carosserie,* which is not a superficial thing, but rather the attempt of the human being to regain, to recover that shocking moment of the mechanism—"

"Why shocking?"

"—and to retransform it into something linked to our body."

By "recover," Bellini means cover over, and you'll recall that another of his countrymen told me of a failed attempt to ameliorate the shock of the machine. It was absurd to Giorgetto Giugiaro that Americans would lower themselves and putt-putt along their highways, producing arthritis as they bent to climb into minuscule spaces from the point of view of bodies that craved more room. American men don't have the mechanism of the sports car but live haunted by the myth of the stock car, so we cover up wimpy engines to fool ourselves we're Andreottis. We want the shock of the racing mechanism, and failing it, mythify the hood and boot to read "race car." Thinking to aid our bodies and ease our minds, Giugiaro humanized the pseudo-mechanism, displacing its hood and boot to the roof (Figures 7.5 through 7.7). This was rational, he told me. But we have little interest in rationality. To enable our brand of myth to sing in our heads, we pervert cars and torture our bodies.

For Bellini, as doubtless Giugiaro, the very word *carozzeria,* bodyworks, reveals how traumatic is the automobile mechanism; by extension, all others. So we speak of the body of the car, as our body; we build a bodyworks in a bodyshop. The mechanism has been placed into a body and that mechanism become machine.

"You remember the typewriting machine of Nizzoli in the 40s and 50s?" Bellini reminded me. "Very smoothly done, Olivetti's first famous machine. That was a body culture prevailing over the mechanism culture. Those shapes were meant to stay with our body, with our tables and furniture and cultural environments. Then we started putting power into them, electricity, making them electromechanical machines. They became faster and easier. Nothing really happened internally, but because of that possibility we tried to change those machines and we did so with more and more features. Since it was possible, we made them print faster, punch the tape, and do this and that, and they became again monsters."

He is evoking the 60s and its ideology of office mechanization. At that time it seemed that every problem could be solved with fast machines, monsters like the teletype and accounting machines. "You could write, calculate, print the paper, it wasn't yet electronic," said Bellini, "it was electromechanical. *Drrrrr,* very noisy, but mechanizing, making faster."

And then came the electronic age, which instantly cut all the mechanical interrelationships between key tops and keys. Broken were the links between hands, keys, printing units, printed paper. Now you could press a button here, have something printed there, at a distance; distance itself had become irrelevant, since transmission was now "soft" transmission, not mechanical transmission. One could even send radio information to cause a machine to print gently, noiselessly, without impact.

At that moment, the black box came into existence. Until then, the machine had been mechanism, even when powered by electricity. And even within its ameliorative body, the electric machine was more or less recognizable, given that it used a system of levers and gears. It was difficult to understand but still understandable, were you to open the machine. You could see and grasp. Its model was cause and effect.

But with electronics, everything is possible. Every strange machine could be set in a black box mode. I had asked Bellini to read my Sony Pro, and now he remarked it: "This black box [pointing to it] could be a hair dryer, why not? You press a button, you have a hole here and some warm air. It could be a radio, a cheese drainer, anything could be put in a black box. And that, I felt, should have been a terribly frustrating moment for a human being."

Listening, I smiled in pleasure at his intellect, among the most acute of all the participants in the international town meeting, which is this book.

"Because at that moment," he continued, "at exactly that moment, you felt you had lost. Something had been broken—was a tragic moment for our history. Something broken, the old, assuring, understandable, satisfying relationship with your hands and tools has gone. Completely disappeared. And a new generation of mind has, so to say, restarted our sun. You set the time not by turning something by analogy to the sun's apparent movement, but by doing *ch-ch-ch-ch* [he gently taps the table], by pressing a button. You tell the machine the time is the right time by pressing enter and then you switch the information in your display by pressing another knob. Everything is digital. It is a completely other world. And I think our generation is still frustrated and in a difficult moment by using those machines."

In preparation for the Moscow visit on behalf of chapter 17, I went to Washington, D.C., to discuss arrangements with Sergei Rogoff, representative of Georgy Arbatov's USA Institute. Yes, over another meal, Rogoff told me he'd provide some Moscow phone numbers, so I pulled out my diary, my *"Carnet d'adresses"* designed by Franco Maria Ricci. Its cover is black silk that you want to run your finger down before opening. Its cream pages let you divine their herbal origin, hinting of pale straw that ripples under your finger. Ricci produces an erotic figure of the body. Rogoff, however, surprised and instantly pronounced me a dinosaur: punching his watch, he made its face a screen, the telephone numbers appearing there like so many taunts.

"You are surrounded by junk machines," Bellini laughed, pointing to my Sony. "You have the television watch, you have everything available in shops all around, because Japanese industry has invaded all the western world. But you belong to a higher, a rather high intellectual class in this world. And you feel you can distinguish your position and your self among the mass merchandising culture by recognizing a particular value of paper, of silk, of that Ricci thing, and by handwriting maybe with a fountain pen not a ball-point pen, with special ink and then by blowing . . ." He laughed at the caricature. "But the Russian feels he would belong to the highest possible class today by having something which is newer, which is so western, that address watch." Which is Japanese, by the way.

As if nothing were the matter, the underdeveloped Russian chose the black box. But to the sophisticated Italian, something is very much the matter with the address watch and other black boxes to which we give over chunks of our lives. "Today, to design electronic machines is a semiotic problem," Bellini said, struggling with English. "To give through the design, which is an added value to that machine . . . to give that machine, which is basically software—the hardware of an electronic machine is nothing, the software is the core—to give it a body so that it can be recognizable, understandable, and to allow it to live among us in our cultural environment: this is the problem." If an electronic machine is designed into a black box shape, as so many are, it would frustrate our expectations, which are humanistic still. "I think we still deserve the human design after having lost most of our tools, which

Bellini on My Sony

I tell Bellini: "So you're saying that the problem of design vis-à-vis these black boxes is to somehow make them signify humanness?"

"Sure, sure."

I point to the Sony: "Has this one been made to signify humanness?"

"This one"—he picks it up, opens the cover—"this one is somehow half and half, you know. You have this leather jacket or seeming—"

"Plastic."

"Seeming leather plastic jacket."

"Simulacrum."

"You touched the problem," he says. "It is plastic but it seems we still need the leather sign at least. And even smell. You know, the artificial leather can have a better leather smell than the real one."

"No!"

"They put smell in," he tells me.

"Does this have it?"

Smelling, he says: "No, it doesn't but you see the grain, the texture, it's not a geometric one. It's seeming leather. They actually die copied the real leather and then the tool that does it, a cylinder, impresses the real leather feeling on the fake one." He opens the plastic leather top to look underneath it. "And then you have the inside of this which is reminding of the suede of the leather. And it seems at least for the skin of your hands, you need some natural animal-like touch. Of course you have the volume control, you have knobs and since it is considered a semi-professional machine, they made it black, the color and its regular shapes and squares recalling the professional side of something and so letting us perceive the object as serious, reliable, technically advanced. They didn't modify too much its particular shape. You're a professional, they didn't have to make it any more human for you."

Figure 8.6 Vincent Van Gogh, *The Shoes*, Paris, 1887, Baltimore Museum of Art. *The Baltimore Museum of Art: The Cone Collection,.formed by Dr. Claribel Cone and Miss Etta Cone of Baltimore, Maryland. BMA 1950. 302.*

were so understandable. Imagine nailing with a hammer, how clear, how bold. Imagine cutting something with a knife."

Imagine lacing a pair of peasant shoes, those in Van Gogh's famous *Les Souliers* (*The Shoes*) of 1887. "From the moment that these unlaced shoes no longer bear a strict relation to a wearing or worn subject, they become the anonymous, alleged, emptied support (but all the more heavy since abandoned to their opaque inertia) of an absent subject whose name returns to haunt the open form." What Jacques Derrida is evoking ("Restitutions") is the urging of the Van Gogh shoes—and of tools and texts—toward an absent self. When he comes to Van Gogh's pair of gloves (1889), Derrida deftly scorns and quotes Meyer Schapiro for considering the gloves "personal objects," for appropriating them: "The choice of objects is odd, but we recognize in it Van Gogh's spirit. In other still lives he has introduced objects that belong to him *in an intimate way* [Derrida's italics]—his hat and pipe and tobacco pouch. . . . His still lives are often personal subjects, little outer pieces of the self exposed with less personal but always significant things. Here the blue gloves, *joined like two hands* [Derrida's stress] in a waiting passive mood, are paired in diagonal symmetry with a branch of cypress, a gesticulating tree that was deeply poetic to Van Gogh . . . the gloves and the branches *belong together* [Derrida]."

It's an identity trap Derrida (but not Schapiro) sees in Van Gogh, a susceptibility to which is in all of us. We bear a hasty compulsion, pushing us to lace up the shoes and restore them, along with the gloves, to a wearer, to a subject and ego. Detachment is insupportable. We are driven by an insensate desire to attribute, which is a desire for reappropriation, for restitution. That is why Derrida mimes the sheer silliness of our restitution compulsion: "Detached, [the shoes] look at us, open-mouthed . . . sentient to the point of belly-laughing at the comedy of the thing," their non-use.

And as it is with the shoes, so it is with all tools, of which the shoe is one. A tool is a useful product, signifying its use not its inert status, interpolating the imagination, urging us to lay hands on it. The tool tells of a generalized user, of a being that says I and whose identity is given by the tool. When you peer at a tool and say "Imagine . . ." as Bellini did, you magically make it leap into your hand where it reestablishes you in your rights, in your property, in your stance and institution. You become the erect body of the master in labor. Innocent as this identity trick may appear, for Derrida it forms part of a vast system of appropriations and reappropriations in the name of which innumerable miseries have been inflicted. Derrida has made a vocation out of deconstructing—uprooting—the desire for the return, for rerooting, for common roots, for homecoming. Bellini, reconstructive not deconstructive, is telling us that, indeed, there is a state or a home or property proper to us which, all covered by black boxes, we have drifted.

Some twelve years ago, upon the advent of the Age of the Black Box, General Electric celebrated precisely what Bellini mourns. Sensing the importance of this celebration in the form of a TV commercial, G.E.'s advertising agency, BBDO, placed the spot on its show reel, which I saw in March 1979. Called "Mr. Universe," it narrated a domesticated duel between Mr. Universe, all opulent muscles, and "Ellen Walsh"—around forty and thereby, in today's mythology, without body. Meanwhile, the voice-over—which sends you to a type: crisp, executive, cute, as in "He's cute! And a earns $40,000 already!"—tells you: "Ellen Walsh has more muscle in one finger than Mr. Universe has in his whole body." And the bassoon plays this figure:

Figure 8.7 If I could make these bars synesthetic, you'd be seeing a prancing clown now.

It's a bodily figure. I have seen chorus "boys" and "girls" mime it for their pleasure (the pleasure of its difference from their sensual bodies). It's the *scarecrow* figure, limbs akimbo, mouth ajar, a kind of dribble of sound emerging from it: OOM pah oom pah OOM pah oom pah. It's the music of the clown, unserious. "There's more than a hint of Europop to it," says Martin Bresnick, professor of composition at the Yale school of Music. "It's square, corny, conservative, no aggression in it of any kind, whereas our pop is razor-edged and nasty." Of course an American wouldn't recognize it as Europop, he reminds me. "It sounds to Americans like game-show music, like the theme of 'The Price is Right.'" Which is just fine, since the commercial is a game, too, Ellen versus Mr. Universe—and Ellen is winning.

And all that followed occurred on a split screen—the primitive work on the left, the same work technologized, elevated, on the right; the system of household work, chopping, crushing, washing, drying, warming, cooling; Mr. Universe using the hand and arm, Ellen Walsh using only the finger. To press, to turn. Within the button-pressing life (hers), the finger lives meagerly.

This is no mere split screen, adjacent lives made simultaneously visible. We know very well that adjacencies don't dwell simply side by side; we search out affinities, oblige them to resemble one another. In short, impossible for Ellen Walsh and Mr. Universe merely to inhabit the same city or district; it's the same apartment they cohabit . . . only they never "get together," the consequence of which is: she goes to bed alone. The witticism of the commercial is indeed its ending. There he is peeling potatoes while she reads a book in bed. "While she reads a book": it's a marked alternative, "to read a book abed/to be in bed *with.*" Ellen Walsh sleeps alone, she lives alone, connotes the spot.

We know by now that whenever we're in the presence of an opposition—culture/nature, life/death, male/female—one of the terms is marked, is positive, the other is unmarked or negative. To put it differently, who is suffering from this partition between the two chambers of their apartment? Ellen Walsh doesn't seem to be. She goes to bed on time, enjoys a "read" (not for long, though, G.E. prescribing with much wisdom, read a passage, go to bed). You see her at the end, reaching for her nightlight. The covers are over her stomach. Underneath, she wears a nightgown. Very well protected, her body. She is, as we say, "comfy," whereas he, as she reads, has drawn "KP," that lowest of culinary acts—to peel potatoes. She goes to bed alone—and look at her smile: what a pleasure!—*while he is humiliated.* Why? Because of his maleness. And why does she sleep alone? To be maleless. His skin had glistened all along, his breasts neatly separated ("cut," as body builders call it)—pectorals, abdominals, biceps neat and pure, sensuously there. Steroid Man all pumped up. As desirous today as in 1979.

Figure 8.7a BBDO, *Mr. Universe*, New York, 1979, BBDO archives. *Courtesy BBDO.*

I told BBDO's Allen Rosenshine: "He provokes by skin and muscle—then *re*vokes by his excess." It was a life-encrypting commercial. Female life kept safe, sealed in a box—the tiniest house or apartment. Merely kitchen and bedroom. The image of the safe house, I thought then and now.

What had BBDO wrought? A powerful image of pleasure, for it united three ideas: mastery over property, the stability of the home, and the comfort of technology. It is almost sleep time, the house is safe, the lamp is lit. Here is extraordinary ego-reinforcement, the unconscious and its drives muffled. Heidegger's house of being turned into a condo banishing the body.

Many years ago, Bellini, trying to offer an enclave in this system, designed a famous yellow rubber calculating machine, now in the permanent collection of the Museum of Modern Art. He made it from synthetic rubber, somehow as soft and gentle to the touch as real skin.

It doesn't look like skin, hence the surprise when you touch it. Its keys, when you press them, are like bubbles. You touch, they depress. He avoided cylinders, those mechanical, brutal piles moving in and out of holes. The bubbles mime bodies. "You just touch them like this," Bellini said, making a poking gesture, "and it is very pleasant to keep that machine in your hands. When you put it vertically on a table, it's like a totem; it has a little bit of erotic sense. It's been seen by many commentators as an erotic object, because those bubbles remind of these parts of the body," pointing to the breast, "and when you touch it, it's soft. On the back it's got three cylindrical shapes"—not dispensing, after all, with the phallic signification. "And the possible interrelationships with the objects on it are not only the purely functional ones. It's also nice to have it under your hands or near you; it's a very light sculptural entity, a pleasure for your eyes. And that was the best example of what I designed to solve the problem of how to avoid the black box"—made adorable. Think of the G.E. music.

As the voice-over tells you, "Subject: Worksavers," as if this were as light as a memo, the woodwinds, guitar, and drum set enter:

Figure 8.8 Sent to your rest by this flute lullaby.

It's a little box step. You could fox trot to this. And now after the "cute" male, the executive announcer (so much nicer, slimmer than Mr. Universe) has said: "She can chop foods faster. She can crush ice quicker. She can wash clothes easier. She can dry clothes easier."—right at this moment the music modulates up a half-step, A-flat to A-major. It lifts us, gives a physical lift. "The music rises a half-step and goes on doing what it did before," Bresnick nuances. "It's a way of refreshing the tonal palette without doing anything." It's a safe way of letting us enter a new segment. In short, the music keeps relaying us, passing us to new blocks, each brighter, happier (with more intensity) than the previous. "She can keep rooms cooler. She can keep rooms warmer."

Cooler/warmer, wash/dry: the head spins with antithesis, the heart skips along this whistle-while-you-work music. It's idiot music, "what, me worry?" music. The music simulates the state of bliss, which the Parisian psychoanalyst Jacques Lacan characterized once in this way: If there were some Other of this state, it wouldn't be necessary to go there—that is how content I am. A single word determines the essence of this music that, for me, inaugurated the Black Box Age: the music is irresistible. The corporation is irresistible. G.E., through its agency, has made my body seem to be skipping. It's the child's body I am as I hear all the pleasures of button pressing. The ending? A gem: "Even if Mr. Universe worked all day and well into the night''—and the soundtrack proffers just a flute solo now:

Figure 8.9 As in a parody of a Beethoven symphony, three almost ridiculously final chords are strummed on an acoustic guitar.

The air is a lullaby, Ellen being sung to her sleep—''he still couldn't do what Ellen Walsh did with just one finger.'' A single bell following ''finger,'' and strummed on an acoustic guitar, the same chord, three times. G.E. *lets you hear the fingers.* ''On an acoustic guitar which has not heretofore played in the whole composition,'' Bresnick lectures. ''The chords are almost ridiculously final, like the end of a Beethoven symphony.''

And the close: ''100 years of progress for people from General Electric.''

Progress is the prosthesis, the machine in place of your body. BBDO no more than the rest of us can grasp the elusive logic of the present. But (without putting too much pressure on the little spot) I think that Rosenshine & Co. ''knew'' that something historic, be it for good or ill, was occurring. ''Progress for people'' was a way of saying something new had come into being. The Black Box era. We're all Ellen Walsh, Her Majesty the Baby—I hope you didn't forget Finkielkraut way back on page 12?

Masturbating the Mouse: Milton Glaser Struggling with Simulation

9

All his life Milton Glaser has struggled with this problem.

Now he is reading aloud the news of his premature demise. "'Bluntly put, Glaser's work isn't fashionable any more,'" he intones the London design magazine *Blueprint*. "'This isn't to deny its prodigious facility and inventiveness, or to say that some future re-evaluation won't laugh in the face of contemporary judgement. But for the time being, precisely because it answered the visual needs of an earlier period so closely, much of Glaser's work looks dated. Taste in the last decade has passed it by. What could be more sixties than his Dylan poster, or more seventies than "I ♥ NY"? His images have a largeness of spirit and, at times, a sentimentality, which is only now beginning to come back into favour.'"

Although pleased to be emerging from his eclipse, Glaser is the first to admit that his work isn't cutting edge—the edge being a formalism in which the separation of form and content is so radical that typography itself, the linguistic signifier, has become a gymnastics of form rather than the expression of a content. The spirit of our moment is, for Glaser, a nihilism aimed at meaning itself. The language we hear, the labels and magazines we read, are so much junk, choking the already overstuffed commodity landscape. And because the linguistic signs that come our way are commodities as shoddy as the phones, books, and records we throw out on the street, there is no one and nothing to believe in.

I tell Glaser that his cynicism is in line with contemporary philosophy. In my own semiotic anthology, *On Signs* (1985), I quoted Michel de Certeau as saying that sometimes belief "signifies having confidence in someone or something, sometimes believing in reality or in what one sees, sometimes trust in what is said. . . . Belief posits a relationship to something *Other*." It always implies the support of the other, who stands for what we have to rely upon. A loyalty is required of the other, presumed to be "on the up and up." But in our time we no longer have confidence in persons or institutions; we trust neither what is said or seen. None of the former explanatory systems—certainly not Marxist, not even social-democratic or educated-liberal—do we feel to be adequate; and this notwithstanding the post–Berlin Wall triumphalism of capitalist ideologues. As the French philosopher François Lyotard has argued, the master narratives have died and nothing has taken their place, although in Japan and Europe even more than here, we can discern the beginnings of the Narrative of Narcissism. For Glaser, formalism is what you indulge in, as artist or designer, when you haven't the desire or power to generate narrative or meaning.

This is why he thinks, starting about 1983 alongside the postmodern architectural boom (think of such names as Michael Stern and Robert Graves), the "fashionable" designers stressed glossy surface, the decorative, the *appliqué*. "It's understandable why if you were concerned about the meaning of things," says Glaser, "that would immediately make you old-fashioned."

When I ask him if, at the beginning of the 80s, he could have retooled and become postmodern, he answers contradictorily. He says he already was postmodern in some sense; but he was unable to alter his modernist core. "I've always been eclectic, always used parody, always been interested in corruption of purity," he tells me. "There is no purity—why, are you going to believe in style?" he challenges. Obviously not, under his pressure. He is teaching the well-known, still important lesson that what is called style is ideology. Style, if it existed in purity, would be an expression as singular as one's retina patterns; it would be a direct conduit to the artistic self and its soul. In fact, such expression is perfused by rhetoric, a code to which all of us, artists included, are in thrall. "I remember my mother reading a book," Glaser reminisces, "where it spoke of the smooth ceiling as a design decision based on a kind of morality." Even as a boy he grasped that his mother was being conned by the myth of style as nature—your own. "There's no inherent merit in having a smooth ceiling as opposed to a rough one," he says. "You make a practical decision—one doesn't get as dirty as the other—but there is no inherent morality that you can derive from that decision." In no way can you read from his decision—any of his design decisions—to a style, to an essence of Milton Glaser.

Construct that he is, Glaser nevertheless regards a part of his mind as a core, unalterable no matter if the spirit of the time has passed it by. Precisely because of this residual humanism, he has been in tension in the years since his "demise." For he well understands that he is not an artist, that his work is not esthetic, and that even painters today are not artists as philosophy has understood the term: autonomous generators of esthetic cosmologies. By ''esthetic,'' philosophy means something negative; the word points to areas supposed to resist the economic determinations of existence. ''Esthetic'' evoked our dreams that no one could manipulate our artists; that their work wasn't predictable; that this novel or that painting would not become an advertisement for the system.

We don't speak that language any more. ''Even if you're a painter, these days you have to pay attention to what's going on,'' Glaser matter-of-factly tells me. ''There's no autonomy of the work any more. It's as much market-driven as anything you do in the design field.'' And there's his problem: ''The relationship of your own voice, your own vision, your own beliefs, your own history to changes in fashion, when you are not a painter, when your own self-perception is not about being a figure who is going to produce works of metaphysical significance that transform the world. What can you give up and still retain that is unique?''

Underneath his deliberate cool, I think I hear an anxiety, which is not only his. I am not an artist, one says arily, thinking to relieve oneself of the stresses and strains of consumerism. It doesn't work. Precisely because I don't identify with a position outside the system, I am prey to the anxiety—then what liberty for me inside the system? Am I only an adman? Notwithstanding the new prestige of advertising, many of us would be crumpled if we found that we were part of a totalizing system, a sea-to-polluted-sea materialism mocking our claims to spirit. I think many of us share William Blake's self-appeal: I must create my own system or be enslaved by someone else's. Glaser's way was double: to leave whatever practice he was all too much a part of; to make himself a designer of pleasure, as if the self given over to enjoyment were somehow unburdened of the self fashioned by society.

I was deep in such speculation in an unlikely setting, Glaser's ceremonial office, meant to evoke serenity for his clients: a ficus tree there, its leaves radiantly green; an oriental rug on tile floor; a wooden table, bowl of green, yellow, red apples on it; caramel leather chairs; white tile sliding doors with stained glass windows. In this melange of nature and culture not unlike a plastic surgeon's or psychiatrist's waiting room, I had sought to provoke him a half-hour earlier with a flattery almost impossible to get past the lips. ''Most of the civilized world knows you as this deity of design,'' I had said, ''who in 35 years co-founded *New York* magazine, created the world's most famous logo''—I ♥ N.Y.—and it's less embarrassing to paraphrase. Some have said he made the word ''poster'' almost synonymous with ''Milton Glaser.'' He certainly redesigned *Paris-Match* and the *Washington Post,* not to mention hundreds of other publications. He gave corporate identities to Elektra Records, Warner Home Video and at least twenty-five other high-profile firms, along the way renovating 92 of his friend Jimmy Goldsmith's 395 Grand Unions around the country (at a ticket of $1.4 million per redesign). A few years ago *Newsweek* consecrated Milton Glaser, Inc. as a tiny empire of thirty designers and nearly a hundred adoring clients. "Is the emperor beaming in his laurels, or does he have another mutation in mind?" I had asked. "Where is—or is— Milton Glaser going?"

"I don't know where I'm going," he refused the flattery. "I have certain objectives in my life that haven't changed very much for many years. They have to do with such things as wanting to go to work in the morning because it is pleasurable and because it places me with people I like. And wanting to be well used in the sense of doing work that I think has some quality, has an effect and satisfies its objectives, both for a client—say, its functional objective—and also its imaginative potential. I like solving puzzles—professionally, in my work. Curiously, I don't like doing puzzles, although I once solved a puzzle by making a puzzle, the 'I love New York' logo."

"I" is a contained word by itself; ♥ instantly means "I love"; "N.Y." are the initials. So one has to make three quick translations to arrive at the meaning, a mild mental gymnastics in the form of a rebus. For Glaser it was the least significant thing he had ever done, but to the world at large it became perhaps his most important accomplishment—also the witty emblem of the man himself. At sixty-three, his image was that of a man afloat in the comfort of problem and puzzle solving—by appearances, the most ebullient of men. When he came striding into this little paradise of tranquility and I asked how he was, he nearly made my mouth drop by booming: "I'M TERRIFIC, HOW ARE YOU?" It wasn't a question—in his presence, you're expected to be terrific, too.

But he is not terrific, that is, happy, easy, cool. He wants to transform himself "to see how far I can go, to see how much I can accomplish, to see not merely what depth my work has, but what breadth it occupies, thus seeing if I can apply my understanding to a variety of different sorts of problems, not merely graphic ones but spatial ones, social ones, and so on. It is not unlike anybody else, who sort of wants to see how far their gifts take them. So I have made some conscious effort, although I suspect the driving impetus in my life is an unconscious one, a conscious effort to see whether I could get into areas of activity that I was not totally even familiar or competent with before I started, that is to do supermarket and interior design and more recently, the design of restaurants."

He doesn't think it's odd that he moved from two- to three-dimensional design. He learned much in the magazine business that he found applicable to supermarkets. Not directly applicable—one has to make the switch gracefully. The concept that one moves through the pages of a magazine while being entertained and informed has something to do with the idea that one moves through the aisles of a supermarket while also being entertained and informed. There are issues common to these different motions through space; for example: how does one engage people's attention? Indeed, "magazine" also means storehouse; and in French, as we know, the word for department store is "magasin." Just as a magazine in the common sense has a table of contents, Glaser gave his supermarket client, Grand Union, a table of contents over the aisles. He wasn't merely mechanically transfering a feature from the two-dimensional format to the three-dimensional. He installed a fundamental trait of the marketplace missing from American shopping sites.

"Instead of the idea of lockstep, going through the supermarket efficiently and getting it over with—which is the way most people thought about Grand Union before the redesign, or most other shopping centers—since shopping is the second largest leisure activity in the United States, shopping instead should be conceived of as a pleasurable activity," he said. "And what do you have to do to make shopping an awaited, important part of the day? You restore the marketplace to its real information resource status to people—with the tables of contents in large, attractive lettering, with promotional books, with guides, with information and ultimately with product systems down the line. People now love to shop at Grand Union."

He thinks that our malls and marketplaces are, oddly, sign-poor; dead zones of uncommunicative Muzak and the sterile sounds of water falling. He looked at the grim faces of American shoppers for whom this supposedly leisure activity was another form of work, a duty. For his client he sought to revitalize, to restore, the marketplace to its former function before the mall became media and shoppers, passive spectators who at their most vigorous "hang out." That function "isn't only the exchange of cash for product," he's now telling me—"it's also the exchange of information."

Since he was so insistent on the link between magazine and supermarket, I recalled Alexander Liberman, remarking something to the effect that in the past, his guiding concept for structuring the Condé Nast magazines was that of narrative. But today, there is a new way of telling a story, according to Liberman. One cannot get the reader involved in long text in an illustrated magazine. Liberman therefore has to use montage and collage as guiding concepts, throwing in pull quotes and captions—language used almost as concrete poetry. In an era in which people demand special effects as in cinema, he is obliged to give spectacle. I wonder if Glaser, too, hasn't experienced the need to provide montage and spectacle at Grand Union.

"A supermarket is a natural montage," he told me. "You're dealing with all kinds of different materials in a single space and accessible at once. With magazines, the very fact of having to turn the page means that a designer controls the montage, spread by spread. In supermarkets, you're walking into a montage more difficult to control." Just as with magazines, market logic requires spectacle, drama. And it is to drama and its possible place in our lives that Glaser, though I didn't know it, was leading me. "You have to eliminate anything that could function as noise in your drama," he added. "The old Grand Union had thousands of paper signs—SPECIAL SUMMER SALE, 130 YEARS OF SERVICE—all that kind of crap we took out."

Since he had moved into three-dimensional magazines, I wondered if he had given up designing the two-dimensional type. "Hardly, it's my origins," he said. "I was the Underground Gourmet, with Jerry Snyder, for the old *New York* magazine when it was the magazine of the *Herald Tribune.* My first piece was called 'Yonah Shimmel vs. the Mock Knish.'"

He chose supermarkets, whose content is food, and restaurants to design, and now placed his origins in food reportage. Why food? I wondered. "I always say it's because my mother was such a good cook," he answered, "but I wasn't particularly interested in food until I went to Italy. I lived in Bologna in 1952 and 53 when I was studying with Giorgio Morandi. Bologna has the best cooking in all the Italy, perhaps in all of Europe, and it was a real eye opener seeing how people ate outside of the Bronx, where I grew up."

Living in Italy, he was introduced to porcini and to truffles, to game. "The level of sophistication there is unparalleled anywhere in Italy. So when I came back, it was before 1966 or 67, I had this conversation about food with Jerome on the street corner— afterward, he started *New York* magazine. We were trying to up one another on our knowledge of cheap restaurants, and we realized that everybody in the city was looking for good cheap restaurants. It was an obsession. You know: 'I' got this little place downtown. For a buck and a half, you get this great steak.' So we did the piece on Yona Shimmel and the knish in the *Herald Tribune,* shortly before it folded, and it was a sensation. They got something like 35,000 requests for the Save the Knish Foundation Fund and then, when I started *New York* magazine with Clay Felker, we started writing the Underground Gourmet. It was an enormous hit in the magazine. It had a terrific effect on people's lives."

He is evoking the days when quality of life drew you to New York; when New York was the Rome of capitalism, B.A., before Armani, when your Brooks Brothers suit was your tunic, your Pucci print your *stole,* your Chanel your *palla;* New York before it became stuffed with Third World labor stuffing coffee and croissant into commuter bags, pushing clothes racks on the street, doing what former immigrants now refuse to do; New York before the occupation of the yuppies (newly sincere), helmeted in Walkmen, jack-booted in rushing sneakers; New York before it became replete with crack-high van drivers, careening taxicabs, random bullets; a New York agitated so strongly it could well crack—but doesn't crack.

"In New York the reality is so packed," Martin Amis regaled me in his London flat, "the head fills up with intruders, yelping, yapping, all dense materialism, really. Everything is mixed but mixed so tight, the old and young, ugly and beautiful, rich and poor, wedged as closely together as the two faces of a knife, the street dweller and the stretch limousine in the same frame always."

Content to play my Socratic role, I asked: "What does that do to the inhabitant who's neither a wretch on the street nor inside the limo?"

"There isn't anyone like that in New York," he answered, "only a couple of guys like you and me. In New York unless you're young and living in a studio, either you're pretty well off or you've got nothing at all. More than any other city I know, I don't see a middle class like the people who live around here, getting by, not doing very well but steady jobs, living a decent life on not very much money."

Amis told me that the novel he was at the moment writing was set in 1999, part of it set in an America in which something brutal will have happened to the poor. "I can imagine New York," he said, "with a city tax on everything that makes it just a rich person's city. Flush out Harlem. They're going to need Harlem, aren't they soon, white people. Need the real estate. There are little West Berlins in there, 105th Street and so on, where the white people have got a little bridgehead into Harlem. It's a few blocks in and it's a drag getting in and out of it, but what you get is an apartment three times the size of anyone who lives downtown for the same money."

Inspired by his sarcasm, I presumed to assist his plot. "We're going to need their space," I said, "but we don't need their bodies so much any more."

Amis said: "We don't want the bodies—well, unless they can be turned to domestic work."

"We can do our Third Economy work very nicely now without bodies," I added to the treatment.

"That's right," said Amis pre-Iraq, "and we don't need them in the army. The nuclear weapons take care of that." In the era of the Resource Wars, that's exactly where "we" do need "them."

"And we don't need them in factories because they're auto-mated," said I.

"Right," he said. "They mug you, they're dirty—in the summer-time."

"They glisten black."

"And they smell. No, New York would be much better off without them, clearly."

Such is the mentality of Bensonhurst and Howard Beach and how many Manhattanites who don't know—who never heard of—

the old New York Glaser is evoking. He and Jerome Snyder were talking then of food in the way men used to talk about the weather (before weather became theater on satellite maps). In that roomier New York, you spoke of a new restaurant find in order to tell the other: I'm speaking to you, you exist for me, I want to exist for you. Impossible words in a city where you can't even stand on a street corner to chat. People would spit at you for blocking their way.

Doubtless not even realizing the pathos of his evocation, Glaser reminisced his life as food critic: "We did the first review of a Szechuan restaurant—there was only one in those days. A couple of months later, there was a second one—we reviewed it. Then at the end of the first year there were four in New York; at the end of the second year there were twelve."

"It sounds like rabbits," I cynically offered.

"Suddenly it was like an epidemic," he refused the gambit. "Well, we had an effect. Then I started working for Joe Damm down at the World Trade Center, and I helped design some of the restaurant interiors and graphics. Joe really gave me my first opportunity to work in that area. Since then, I've always been somehow involved in food. We did the *Underground Gourmet Cookbook,* and I have designed innumerable cookbooks and books about cooking. I just like food and I know a lot about it by now.

But it wasn't just food passion that drew him to restaurant design. He loves restaurants because they involve, in ways magazines cannot, the elements of form that interest him, especially light. "I'm very interested in the effect of light on color, effects that don't exist on a flat surface. Light, space, and color: these are my subjects." He believes that he can create, through the use of space, light, and color, a site where people are transformed emotionally. "One of the things that happens when you come into the Trattoria [dell'Arte, his restaurant decorated with images of body parts] is that you get a lift, a physical lift; you suddenly feel a little lightening of your spirit. I love this social effect of restaurants: that for a brief moment you are better than you are elsewhere. Listen to the conversation, the laughter, look at the physiognomy. People in restaurants, while they're there, they're more sophisticated, they're more knowledgeable, they're better served—in the right restaurant, you feel enlarged." The diner is magnified as the outcome and finality of the social machinery, which is a design machinery. All those attractive people who make you attractive are made attractive by Glaser, that is, by the mind that installed the plates, giant body parts (breasts, arms, feet, noses) on the walls, and the terra cotta, yellow, and ultramarine taken from Italian coloring of nature. "Somebody's saying, 'I'll have a little more wine,' but it's the wine in the setting that they want. The light that's cast from the side on a woman makes her look more beautiful than she is outside. I love the idea that people, through the intervention of these elements, are

Figure 9.1 Trattoria del'Arte restaurant. Graphics and signage by Milton Glaser. Architecture collaboration with Timothy Higgins. Sculpture by Jordan Steckel.

protected from the world for the brief moment of the meal; that they're changed into another state of mind."

Hearing him, one thinks his Trattoria—where he has installed the noses of famous Italians from Dante to Durante—is today's Paradiso. But it's also interpersonal Inferno. For the restaurant today is where you tell people you're breaking up. But you also tell them there you love them, or you make a proposition, or you don't. Obviously, in a recession, you dream more of restaurants than go there, or go and guard your wine glass more. But Glaser remains adamant, recession or no, that restaurants are now the social center of people's lives. "You meet your friends in restaurants," he said. "Very often you spend the entire evening at a restaurant, which has to some extent replaced the theater in New York. You used to eat and then go to a show. Now it has become so expensive to do the two that very often people accept to go to dinner, have a conversation, and go home."

In the 80s the restaurant became media in the large cities. You were seen and you saw in restaurants. A friend across the cacaphonic room might wave as your waiter brought a bottle, his gift. You didn't go there for the flintiness of the wine or the flakiness of the salmon (perhaps you didn't even notice them). You went because your companion illumined you with beauty or prestige, because the little community there confirmed you in your status or even elevated it (or alas, decreased it). A few words from an important person in your set, the brief sit-down of the owner, the epiphanic materialization of a bottle of champagne, the roar of the music forcing you to witty sound bites seductive to your companion, the lubricious wine propelling a repressed utterance to leap like a fish into the relationship, all of it was sign and meaning and scarcely gastronomy. To Glaser the restaurant in the big cities became (and, recession notwithstanding, remains, to a large extent) the center of social life and very often the center of people's intimate lives. "To exchange intimacies—where do you do that?" he said. "On a bench? In your apartment? No, you do it in a restaurant." And woe to the one who doesn't pay the credit card bill on time.

Since more and more families are those of working mothers and fathers, or working singles, the idea of preparing a dinner became tainted, like so many other habits of the family. Dinner: one more task. Glaser told me that more and more of his friends had just stopped cooking; it's true of every friend I have. The success of people like food photographer Matthew Klein and the the advertisers that commission him shout the fact that precooked meals have replaced the large casserole where, cooking under the eyes of hearty mother and ebullient child, the meat and the vegetables lost their colors, forms, and discontinuity, softening into a thick russet sauce, which was their destiny. For better or worse, the life of the eyes, hands, and tongue have been reduced; culture itself—nature denatured—withered. One has neither time nor taste to constitute oneself as the master of the hearth, recounting all over again the triumph of human fire over nature. The proliferation of food columns; of recipes for braising, stewing, steaming, poaching; the intricate combinatories of 2/3 cup black figs, 1 teaspoon mustard seeds, 2 tablespoons finely chopped shallots, 3 tablespoons light sesame or peanut oil (take your choice), 4 medium-size cloves garlic, not only having to be peeled but sliced thin, 5 tablespoons chopped fresh cilantro—what's that?—as garnish, the final chance to cut your finger; all of it to make a sweet cranberry-pistachio chutney with black figs and eggplant slices smothered with . . . — all of it for a son or daughter with a Walkman at table and a spouse narrating the same old office intrigue? Why it's out of the question to operationalize the recipe. Food words and images have become a self-sufficient order, a symbolic realm of exotic names, often from the Third World. We consume the *image* of fine food; the reality has lost its appeal. "For many, cooking has become an ordeal," Glaser said. "They work five days a week; on the weekend, what they don't want to do is spend the day making dinner." The wealthier go to restaurants; the lucky ones, to a stage set designed by this hedonist who practices the *art de vivre,* the art of living, the least developed of the arts. "There's no payoff any more, socially or otherwise, to cooking," he said. It's no longer a sign of love for your family—your children probably don't want to eat with you anyway.

And for good reason in many instances. Eating wasn't about pleasure, it was about discipline, surveillance—"How did you do today?" "Let's face it, cooking big meals became a drag," Glaser added.

Whereupon, it being lunch time, the two of us left his offices at Thirty-second Street and Third Avenue and ran in the rain to flag a cab to his newest restaurant, Third at Sixty-fifth, formerly Fiorello's and now La Hosteria, open exactly one day.

In the cab we chat about the erosion of disciplinary America. "The era of the Big Meal, the patriarch/matriarch's way of exerting control, just ended," I offer.

"Totally," he snaps. "Obviously, there's still an impulse to hospitality, where you want to invite people to your home; but I think even that aspect of how people think about entertainment has shrunk." As if we became hostile crabs, hermits in small shells. "It's the smallest it's ever been," he adds softly.

"Restaurant going—we're talking New York, L.A., Chicago, the cosmopoli?"

"Probably. Because there aren't that many restaurants where you feel you want to take people. Here we are."

Inside, greeting the maitre d', hailing attractive young men and women waiters in black, the six-foot-two Glaser strides like the God of the Site he is, from front to the back of the Hosteria, the name he chose, approving this touch and that, now finding Burgess Meredith look-alike, owner Shelly Fireman, nervous over his new arrival. Within seconds of Glaser's appearance, he sighs into relaxation. Opening night was a success, and Glaser is ecstatic.

"I wouldn't say it was full last night, but it was three-quarters full," Fireman reports.

"That's amazing," says Glaser. He is the embodiment of American euphoria. You either feel buoyed by him or astonished at your own paucity of spirits.

"It looked wonderful, people in the room looked wonderful," burbles Fireman.

"That's the one thing that you have to plan for—what's that mirror thing?" pointing to the back wall. Glaser has tensed, seeing a detail yet to be resolved.

"Shelly," he says, "we're going to eat in the bar—see what that's like. I want to be right in the thick of it, as it were."

And Glaser and I walk back upstairs, taking a little table by the window.

"Why do you think people are beginning to turn out?" I ask. "Is it the Glaser name?"

"No, what's drawing them is in the rooms. It's complex. Go down those stairs."

And I do, retracing the steps I took to greet the owner. This time, Glaser's watchful eyes, I know, are on my back.

"There's really a stepped feeling—keep going," he shouts.

I leave the window looking onto Third Avenue, and it's as if I had left dry land. Walking down a few steps to a small dining room below the bar, its ceiling low, I have the sense of being in the lounge of an ocean-going liner. Sensuous surfaces and an atmosphere of frivolity. The light is paradoxically subdued and intense, self-referential. An eerie feeling—no one is in here, as if after last night's debauch, all the passengers had vanished. To my right, more steps down. A feeling of Dantean circles, oddly pleasant. Almost a Ship of Fools atmosphere—potential abandon. Down these steps and it's the formal dining room where I had met Fireman. Here, a captain could sumptuously spread merriment among his guests. This time, I notice the yellow pulsating from the wall, a groaning board at the entrance on which are racks of lamb, an enormous loin of veal, roast potatoes, leeks, and not a soul in sight.

"It's like entering into a piece of sculpture," he says on my return, describing my experience. "I'll have some soup today. Do you know what you're going to eat? Do you like soup?" And before I can think to answer—truth to tell, like a good American I don't care what I eat—he tells the waitress: "Artichoke soup. Then contadina salad, chicken, cabbage, black beans, and fried capers—sound interesting to you? And then we'll get a—the man likes to consume more than signs—"forcaccio for two with parma ham and fontina. What's your impression of the place?"

Said abruptly. Milton Glaser, who runs master classes at New York's School of Visual Arts, is testing his interlocutor's design sensibility.

"Uh, uh, uh. . . . You didn't alter the architecture?" I blubber.

"We made all the rooms absolutely visible so you see through," he assesses, "and you get a sense that this is one continuous room moving downward as you just moved. There used to be a pasta station—we got rid of it to open up spatially so the whole thing moves now. And we made it much airier—it used to be a dark place, dark wood, little pin lights."

Where we are is a stainless-steel-topped antipasto bar, similar to the enormous bar at the Trattoria, which has become a Glaser signature. At breakfast, the Hosteria's bar serves capuccino, rolls, et cetera to the stand-and-sip crowd. At lunchtime, it's a slower sandwich bar. Toward the "blue hour," campari and a score of other liquor bottles appear where the antipasto was. Because space was limited, Glaser had to make the bar transform itself and so reached, subliminally, to classic rhetoric and to its great trope metaphor to structure this bit of space; metaphor, which substitutes one subject for another according to the same paradigm—here, food.

A celadon green, like that of Chinese pottery, dominates the space. An off-yellow plays a secondary role, a yellow absent the stridency some artists have attributed to the color. To achieve this delicacy, Glaser perfused the yellow with White and tells me now that, above all, he sought to modulate the light to create form; to make color change in the presence of different lighting. "Look at the way the color looks at the far end," he points to the bar. "There, where it has a lot of light. You see that color underneath the sign? What color is that?" he catechizes.

"Bluish."

"Bluish green, right? Wrong, it's white," he says, delighted, although for my part I can't understand why a simple color ruse should be the source of jubilation. "It's white as this tablecloth, but in that particular location, with its spill of light and color and shadow, it turns bluish green. There's an incredible adventure that occurs as light and color change," he exults as I wonder what that adventure might be, or even if it is. "I didn't know what was going to happen in this room when these complex patterns would wrap around everything, when the dominant color was to be green and yellow. I had no idea whether it would be a pleasant experience. How could I know without building a life-scale model? Because the volume of color changes the meaning. When you have a tiny patch, it has nothing to do with having a patch at larger scale. This could have been horrible," he points to the wall pattern.

"I started out thinking about this thing I read from Ripley's *Believe It Or Not* when I was a kid. A thing called 'The Spanish Insanity Pattern,' which was supposed to be two squiggly lines and then two squiggly lines crossing—"he draws on his napkin (Fig. 9.2).

"—and the intervals filled in with alternating red and green. Prisoners during the Inquisition used to be put into a cell with the Spanish Insanity Pattern, and they used to go crazy in twenty-four hours. It's fabulous."

But I didn't express it.

"Ever since then I've had this idea in the back of my mind of taking an entire room and just wrapping this crazy pattern around. Here it doesn't quite go as excessively as it could, but I didn't know what was going to happen—might have made Shelly's patrons psychotic." Come on, Milton. "It's what we call the crazy pattern, this crazy sort of double diamond. You see"—as if he were that child Milton, reading his Ripley's—"the pattern on the floors *is the same as the pattern on the columns*"—he's excited—"except that it's enlarged on the floor."

"I have to inspect this," I say.

Had anyone overheard the conversation, I must appear as if I were already succumbing to Glaser's psychotic diamond, as if I were an Inquisition prisoner made mad by the floor of my cell. I am bent over the floor with Glaser, like an Interrogative Father, instructing

Figure 9.2 The Spanish Insanity Pattern reinterpreted by Milton Glaser. *Courtesy Milton Glaser.*

me, telling me to use my finger: "Trace that whole unit of white on the column. No, not just the one but the one next to it. And further down. Trace that shape," he insists. "Now look down at the floor. You'll see exactly that shape underneath your feet in larger scale. The whole floor pattern is exactly the same except it's enlarged."

Whereupon I realize that my vision is blurring, caused by the Glaser design or my own design of this idea: that Glaser, all along, has been telling me that he tries to design small catastrophes into the functional and figurative givens of his commissions. What I thought was a metaphoric bar is a bar that doesn't know what it is. What I thought was blue is white. The room as a whole won't stop moving. It was Cézanne who spoke of "catastrophe" and "abyss" to evoke the moment when the painter no longer sees his figurative givens and the optic organization of the canvas. Paul Klee called the experience "chaos," the "gray point." Francis Bacon calls it a "diagram," inside of which anything can be introduced; a patch of Sahara inside a head, a close-up of rhinoceros skin on part of the face. There is probably no figurative painter who doesn't experience this chaos of the visual coordinates, which opens sensuous domains, according to Bacon. Glaser, who denies he is an artist, thinks like a painter.

Since the conversation, I realize, has been about risk, I probe: "Isn't yellow a risky color to work with? I recall reading that Wifredo Lamm used to hate yellow."

"Everybody has color bias," he resists. And then: "But yeah, I think it's risky in a restaurant; but then, this green is risky. The thing you're supposed to do with restaurants, you know, is to make them pink and beige. That's supposed to be what reflects well, your complexion looks better. But I took a big chance at Trattoria, which is totally irresponsible in terms of color, and we pulled it off. The green there was supposed to be deadly, the yellow much too harsh, the terra cotta much too aggressive, but it all works," although not in the way the patrons propositioning one another may think. Look up from your mixed seafood grill at the Trattoria, at a yellow wall so intense you think it might melt. Glaser is trying to liberate the space from its official organization as restaurant. To him, all the haggling, propositioning, terminating are so many banalities, stupidities; it's all a joke as he'll tell me shortly. The Trattoria's color and light form a deconstructive design aimed at the good conscience of the ama- tory and other diners.

"It's the analogy of drawing to space that led me to the restau- rants," he says. And suddenly, after the ebullience and apparent superficiality, we start to rock and roll, as they say. "When I think of drawing, I think of it in its most primary form as an instrument of understanding," he says. "If I do a water poster, the idea of the poster as this special something that's unrelated to other things— I've never understood it. I've never understood the separation between the idea of design as an activity and our general interest in visual phenomena and the ability to draw them. Why are they separate things? Drawing is an act of synthesis as well as observa- tion because you have to decide what it is you draw, what you abstract from what's in front of you. You do the same thing when you design. Why these things became separate is very peculiar to me."

He is worked up. He wants to demystify drawing but mystifies it all over again in the process. When I ask what's up, he seems to brag a little. "Look, early on I learned how to draw and represent my ideas because I wanted to be an illustrator, and then I shifted into design, and later I learned about typography and form making and so on, and so I have the advantage of being able literally to express my ideas easily with my own hands, which is an attribute that doesn't occur so often in design. In fact, a lot of designers can't draw and have to think in another way because of that deficit."

This isn't a boast. It's a passionate defense of what's barely worth defending, that's how almost gone it is. And that is the hand. In its power to liberate the instinctual body.

"I have this ability to express my ideas easily with my own hands," he's telling me. "That's what differentiates me from a lot of other designers. They get photographs, they do collages, they use cut paper, they assemble information, they lay things out. But if you come out of the background I come out of, which has to do with making images, *physically making them yourself*"—his voice, raised—"as opposed to finding them or art directing them, it seems to me you have access to other opportunities."

"Don't you think you're fetishizing the hand?" I provoke. "The people who do these complex things in computer graphics might say so."

"I think there's a big conspiracy to convince poor designers that if they don't buy and learn how to use a computer they're out of business. I think it's a total shuck, a real manufactured panic. They've been pumping up this thing that computers are the way of the future, you can't live without them, they're a great new instrument of the imagination, get on board because the last train is leaving, if you don't learn now you can't find work—bullshit! The computer is basically a very useful instrument for certain tasks like accounting, page layouts, typesetting. As a creative instrument, it has a long way to go to prove its value, and it has some dangerous implications in terms of the removal of the creation of sensation as opposed to experience. I call it a pornographic instrument in that it substitutes sensation for experience."

When Glaser was in Israel not long ago, he was given a presentation of a new program for doing drawings in charcoal. You manipulate your mouse, and on the screen the effect is a line of charcoal. By putting pressure on the mouse, you actually change the density of the stroke, as though you were bearing down on a piece of charcoal. Little pieces of charcoal fall off on the screen as you bear down. "You get a sensation of charcoal without the experience of drawing in charcoal," he recalls. "You're fiddling with the mouse, you don't have the kinetic experience of moving your hand; you don't have the resistance of the paper; you're missing the physicality of the experience. It's like masturbating in front of a very realistic photograph and thinking that that is equivalent to making love to a woman."

Which a lot of people prefer. That's a bit what postmodernity is about, innit, as Keith Talent, Martin Amis's masturbator hero of *London Fields* would say. "While you're growing up, your television is your third parent," Amis tells me, "then, later on it becomes your lover. You're not only watching it, you're fucking it."

In *Money*, Amis's preceding novel, the film director hero, John Self, dries his hands on a fold of foliage in starlet Butch Beausoleil's "botanical laboratory or plantation hothouse"—her *HG* bathroom ruled by a "burly parrot . . . eyeing me spitefully." John's mind is empty of any thought of what led him here. It's as if the preceding sex with Butch had been excised. When he returns:

Butch was sitting up in bed watching an adult movie (silent, hard core) on a six-foot screen set into the opposite wall. I joined her. A fat pale guy was giving a bronzed blonde the treatment on a wobbly iron bed. The print was of high quality but production values were low—fixed camera, no variation or close-ups. Quite quickly I realized that the girl was Butch Beausoleil. A little later I realised that the man—the man was John Self. Me, in other words.

Butch had mounted a videocam facing the bed. For a reason she'll tell you.

> On screen the couple changed position often and strenuously. These contortions, I saw, were gauged to display the female lead to still greater advantage. But they showed you the male lead, too, this fat actor or extra or bit-part player, his pocked back, juddering beerbelly and tumescent throat. . . .

When Self in shame tells her:

> 'Okay. Wipe it.'
>
> 'Pardon me?'
>
> 'The tape. Wipe it. Do it.'
>
> 'No I won't do that, John. You see I only ball the same person once. That's why I like to keep it.'

The world according to Amis (and me): We can no longer do anything without wanting to see it immediately on video. We can no longer live at the first level, everything having to be instantly "videotized." We're in a state of reflection or better, refraction. There is never any longer an event or a person who acts for himself, in himself. The direction of events and of people is to be reproduced into image, to be doubled in the image of television. It's a little like that species of natural performance art in the desert. No one ever sees the performances, but the artist takes photos, makes videos, exposing them in a gallery. The act itself is elsewhere, forgotten. It disappears. And Amis says, and I say, that today the referent disappears. In circulation are images. Only images.

"And also when the time comes for him to have his orgasm," Amis rewrites as we talk in London, "John wonders what to think about, and then thinks he'll think about Butch Beausoleil as she might be in a magazine—even though he's actually fucking her at the time. And he once reproaches his girlfriend Selina; he says at one point: 'You're not faking it.' 'Yes I am,' she said guiltily. I wanted, with him, to create an appetitive character who had absolutely no resistance to the twentieth century, as it were—to contemporaneity." Hooked on the twentieth century. Hooked on its addiction industries. "Dope, liquor, gambling, anything video— these have to be the deep-money veins," Amis observes.

Which is why John (not to mention any *hypocrite lecteur, mon semblable, mon frère*) prefers abstraction to immediacy, images of the body to the body. In New York, in the heat of the pornographic night, as Amis writes, Self stands "davening"—ritually swaying *à la Juif*—to a photo from a mag at the Wailing Wall of Pornography. As it were, a Wapper (Woman against Pornography) accosts, chastizes him—why isn't he ashamed of himself? But he is, he tells her. Look at that, look, she says. "The girl slapped it from his hand," Amis recalls. On the floor of the store, the centerfold of his *Lovedolls* is curled over, touching the next page, the image it forms filthier by far than what's on that first page of common prayer. "Some dick is near a girl's mouth," Amis tells me in pleasure—nearer, limper than if left in peace on that centerfold. "He has no resistance to pornography or to anything else," says Amis. "French and Italian pornography comes in all gradations, I imagine, but there seems to be an emphasis on pretty pretty, frilly knickers sort of pornography. In America it's absolutely stereotyped what happens in porno loop films. She sucks him off, he fucks her, then he buggers her, then he comes in her face. Aggressive degradation. So much of it. So profitable. Doing anything on screen whether it's making love to a pig or being gang-raped."

We left Milton Glaser at the Hosteria trying not to masturbate the mouse. "You have no resistance to porn, you're not only watching it, you're fucking it," I relay Martin's message. "It gets rid of all the sticky substances of intersubjectivity—pun intended."

"It's much less complicated," Glaser plays along, "easier to deal with, less encumbering, it eases on the difficulties. Well, it's not what life's about. There's a direct relationship between that kind of experience and drug culture, addiction, dependency and the sense of isolation, withdrawal from life. Basically, everything is contained within the little dependency world; there is no other, no outside— very dangerous stuff."

Computer graphics and drug culture—quite a reach, innit. Not to Glaser, to whom pornography, a televisual sensation, is part of the larger drug culture. "It's linked to the drug culture in the way television is, by separating the ties of the family and removing the difficulty from life—you don't engage the other any more, you become autonomous. And isolated. And susceptible. And addicted," he says.

"Addicted to?"

"To your total self-absorption. The screen is another device that maintains that isolation from life. And that's what drugs do: They alienate you from life, you're only concerned with your own experience. All these constructs, from drugs all the way to the seemingly elegant computer graphics, contribute to this isolation of the person. And the consequence is the culture we now have.

Computer designers are like TV addicts. They spend eight hours in front of that fucking thing.''

So perhaps now we know why we became America the Drugged. When I was in Paris visiting the intellectuals, Paul Virilio, a sociologist of new technologies, insisted on the link between electronic speed and drugs. "Society always organizes itself according to the most rapid speed," he told me. "The quickest speed up to the 50s was still the car, the train. Then aviation. Now, since electronics, the most important speed is audiovisual, television, teledistribution, telematics, et cetera. There has been a reorganization of the social, political, cultural hierarchy around telecommunications." Hence the prestige of television, all the way from CNN's twenty-four-hour news for the elite to the "fucking" computer graphics display. Virilio thinks that we are well along the way (more so in France than here, I think) toward a displacement of investment from the market of the automobile, the motor, toward that of the audio-visual, which is going to utterly reorganize society. It took roughly a century from the invention of the steam engine to the installation of the automotive society. Perhaps it will take fifty years for society to complete recomposing itself around audiovisual speed. But happen it will, regardless of our cursing. Milton Glaser is fighting a losing battle.

Virilio reminded me that cinema has always been tied to a speed of twenty-four images per second; we rarely tampered with that speed of projection. He also recalled that the history of cinema up to the 60s was that of longer and longer films, from five- to ten-minute reels to the standard of an hour and a half. The film played in a longer and longer extensive time, which most recently has become two hours. But all of a sudden, Virilio said:

> Starting from the 60s, video appears, videography, and we are no longer in the cinema of extensive time but in the cinema of intensive time. That's to say we have passed from twenty-four images a second to thirty and even sixty, with special effects. Video is the place of special effects, the place where you can play with speed in an extraordinary way. You have the possibility of video clips, that's to say, of putting in a few seconds what formerly took hours to explain. You concentrate, you intensify the message; in place of extending it, you compact it. It's speed that dominates, no longer duration.

Hence, no longer narrative. Which is exactly what Costa-Gavras told me sadly (p. 145).

> I'll give you an example. Vis-à-vis the former spectator, film directors took time to explain the narrative to him. They felt it necessary to install him in the story—think of Orson Welles—with everything necessary psychologically to guarantee the comfort of his comprehension. Then,

233

starting from video and through video clips, you fool consciousness, you attempt a subliminal narrative, that's to say you're going to hallucinate the spectator instead of installing him in long duration, explanation, narration. You're going to fascinate him, hallucinate him by images that flow too rapidly. Look at the montage of today's films— even Eisenstein is very long beside films of Scorsese. Look at *Angel Heart,* Mickey Rourke's film.

The French are in love with Rourke; to them, a hero approaching the abyss in the era of vacuities, that's to say of Tom Cruises. Virilio snapped his fingers, clapped his hands:

> Cut, cut, cut without stopping. In a certain sense, they're mocking the spectator. He's a primary matter you play with, you make a mess of. You no longer install him in an armchair, he no longer has the place of attentive spectator. He has a soft part, he's a primary matter that you triturate. Thus we return to the fact that man no longer interests people. The telespectator is no longer a spectator, he is inert matter like plastic matter. Is this clear?

. . . he patronized. All too clear. According to this bias, we are no longer political men and women, we are already nothing but things in front of the tube. Blinded by lamps, flashes, ultrarapid montage, the shortcuts of ellipses, our very perception is mocked. Duration itself becomes more and more difficult to endure, perhaps impossible. People find it fatiguing, stressful. We are hooked on speed— both kinds. We need our speed to accelerate. They are the same: coke, crack, speed, clips. When you're going fast chewing gum playing your Watchman, you don't say: I've got my MTV, that's enough. Nothing's enough. "I want my MTV, I want my ecstasy"— that should be the slogan of our age. The culture of visual drunkeness—it's the very one of drugs. And why do we need our drugs, visual, liquid, powdery? Virilio outrageously answers: because nobody needs us.

"Why drug our people?" I asked in Paris.

"Because we no longer have need of them," he answered.

"Need of?" It had the force of *Excuse me-e-e.*

"People," said Virilio. "But of course. When we had need of people, there was prohibition—of alcohol, of drugs, the prohibition on sex because we had need of men to work, to make war. When you no longer need people, neither to work nor to make war . . ."

"You stockpile them."

"*Oui, oui* [the French we were speaking gives the sense of his speed, his excitation], the drugs complete the work of automation."

This discourse, to which I lend myself, doesn't posit "bad" leaders who have made decisions to warehouse large chunks of the population. We're not positing "bad" videographers, "bad" cinematographers. That's perhaps the problem. We can recall that Winston

Churchill, seeking the uniqueness of contemporary war in his time, said that in former wars, episodes were more important than tendencies. You could win a battle and win the war. Producing a hero—at the right moment, a Rambo, let's say—could permit winning the war. Churchill spoke of war and we can speak of political society. Today, tendency overpowers episodes. You can win many battles, have your heroes, have a reasonable politics— invent new liabilities, even new constructs like codependents— forget it, the tendencies are no longer controllable. They sweep away politics even there where it doesn't want to go. Nobody bad has said: "We're going to abandon people," it's industrial society sweeping us all along. The same for drugs as for biogenetic engineering—who can stop it? The tendencies govern, no longer human beings. Tendency is statistic, the dominant—"The tendency of man is to be unfaithful to his wife," a French wag told me at the Odéon—the inevitable. In other eras, the power of men (more than women) was so strong, there was a way of blocking tendency. But today, with science, technology, all the power of motivation, advertising, information, tendency has been stronger than Gorbachev, stronger than any political figure.

Inevitably, that's a drama of political society that will be a drama of democracy, but it's neither Milton Glaser's concern nor mine now. Glaser is a demiurge, the father of his artifacts, the absolute possessor of his form and content in the age when power has passed from illustrator and designer to the art director, the servant of corporate power who, for Glaser, has turned them almost into blue collar workers, clerks of the system. A tendency. Glaser is the hero, the captain fighting the current. But if the current is stronger than the motor . . . I ask him why he wants to save drawing.

"You have to admit the world when you draw, the world in the form of the other, the object," he responds. "You have to acknowledge it. Say you're drawing something. By the fact of drawing, *you* have to be there, have to have some understanding of your own dimensionality—you're not flat, you know, you exist in space. Whereas if I'm modeling on a flat surface, a monitor, I have to transpose the dimensionality of my two eyes and your dimensionality into a flat surface which instantly flattens a thousand decisions. When I work at the computer, everything's already flat, there is no world. It's all about what happens when you substitute sensation for experience, when you are not moving from world to the brain down the arm to the paper—what happens if you're not doing that? Nobody knows. It's really uncharted territory."

He thinks you begin to lose appetite for the world. "As with pornography—I wouldn't be at all surprised. That's what pornography is about—sensation as opposed to experience. It's a replication of sensation, that's what makes it so dehumanizing."

He said "replication" but he means simulation, a substitution for the real in which we forget the real ever existed. Every "mariachi band" in every euphoric Mexican restaurant is a simulation of a band down south that you'll never hear because you'll be too busy hiding from the natives in the Cancun Hilton. Glaser thinks the contract you make before the computer is the enhanced power of your eyes to the detriment of the hand. "I think the human hand has a greater potential," he tells me. "I'm a great believer in the idea that you start with your hand and that the distinctions you have through it are not the distinctions of thought."

And there it is, almost like a secret that he couldn't or wouldn't tell, the idea of the hand independent of mind, in the service of another force, tracing marks that no longer depend on one's will or sight. "You bring to the drawing the weights and balance of your hand," he says, as if some other world than that of the eyes were surfacing.

Glaser in the 90s is the good son of the 60s and 70s, as before him was the Parisian philosopher Gilles Deleuze. In his 1981 book *Francis Bacon: Logique de la sensation* [*Logic of Sensation,* untranslated], Deleuze wrote of the artist that the hands' marks "are irrational, involuntary, accidental, free, by chance." Even when the painting is figurative, the marks and traces "are non-representative, non-illustrative, non-narrative." They are features of sensation. Holding crayon, brush, sponge, or rag, the hand becomes independent of the eye and of the figurative. "These almost blind manual marks witness the intrusion of another world in the visual world of figuration," Deleuze writes. "They subtract the painting from the optical organization which already regulated it and rendered it in advance figurative. The painter's hand was interposed in order to shake its dependence and break the sovereign optical organization: one no longer sees anything, as in a catastrophe, a chaos."

A privileged way of this liberation was abstract expressionism, whose optic geometry collapsed to the profit of a manual line. "The eye hardly can follow it . . . the line doesn't go from a point to another, but passes *between* points, ceaselessly changing direction." Action painting, the "frenetic dance" of the painter around the canvas, upon the canvas, made visible "an exclusively manual space, defined by the 'planarity' of the canvas, the 'impenetrability' of the painting, the 'gesturality' of the color, and imposed itself on the eye like an absolutely alien power where it found no rest." So potent was the line of action painting, it not only went from edge to edge of the canvas, it began in the canvas and pursued its business outside the frame, opposing the symmetries and organic centers of the room itself.

The eye centers, stabilizes, quiesces the continuum of its gaze into the figurative, charged with domesticating the unruly drives. Demanding the rights of the hand, Milton Glaser wants to suppress the task of the eye in classical representation, that of commanding the hand. He wants to subordinate eye to hand, impose the hand on the eye. The hand holding a mouse is, for him, scarcely a hand at all. The action of the fingers approaches that of a digital code, not in the sense of the manual but in the sense of fingers that count. Giving little taps to the mouse, you construct "digits," binary bits that take you far from chance. The philosopher Deleuze and the designer Glaser were formed in the era of the great liberation wars—theirs, to shake awake the body only (Glaser is telling us) to see it confined again in the ruthless progress of technological modernity.

Glaser is talking: "There is a school of design that for any number of reasons diminishes the importance of the hand, calling it an impediment to the professional idea. You turn out to be an art director"—what scorn I hear—"getting stuff from out in the world, from illustrators, photographers, wherever. You find it and put it together." Like a jackdaw. Efficient, binary collector of other people's pieces. Quiet servant in the corporate machine. Because the machine had to triumph—that, I think, is why designers had to become clerks.

Yale literary critic Geoffrey Hartman: "I am of a generation that grew up in Germany seeing horses. Of course there were cars, more cars than horses, but they were both there. It wasn't an anachronism to see horses and cars still in symbiosis in the thirties, even in a city like Frankfurt. For me, being given a ride in a private car was an extraordinary event, and that was so even in England, in the war years of the 40s. So I suppose within me there is still some of the older ecology." I had asked him about touch, and now he said: "I find it disconcerting nowadays, and this is a pragmatic remark. . . . I've always found it disconcerting to have push buttons. I am someone who never wanted to drive a car without knowing how it works, and finally I gave in because I realized I would never know, and I would never drive a car. I've always been uneasy with the feel of pushing a button and the light going on; almost as though I should be doing more work, or there should be a greater delay time between touching and the light. Nowadays when you have cable television—I see my children do it, even I do it— even when you enjoy something, you start switching around, flipping, bringing a peculiar sense of false mastery or manipulation; maybe that's the right term, because it has the word 'hand' in it; a certain in-built nervousness overcoming you." As if the body under wraps were agitating; as if a being in some mortuarial site had suffered spasm. Reflex of the dying beast with five fingers. Hartman: "It's as if you were using the fingers on a typewriter to put letters together into words. By switching channels, you think to have put images together into some stellar product, even though it's not the case." As if we had not yet forgotten the urge to create; as if we bore deep within us the memory that you create with the hand; as if the hand were still good for a bit more than masturbating.

By day, a clerk squeezing the mouse; by night, an idle viddy watcher tapping the remote. Hartman again: "Have you ever had the experience, you read before going to bed, and after a while, you can't keep your eyes open? I noticed, to my consternation, something which is well known but I didn't know how susceptible I was to it. Just before you fall asleep, I don't know how much before you fall asleep, there is a zone in which you transit from words to the images they evoke and you think you're reading, but you're not reading; you're in the images that have been evoked. And the images unfold according to a rhythm, a principle of their own, all the while you think you're reading. Somehow the illusion that you're reading is very important for allowing those images to develop, even though you've stopped reading. Once that illusion ceases, you've passed into some other domain, call it sleep.

"My feeling is that a similar thing happens when you watch a lot of television, as you enter that habit more and more. You think you're awake, you think, 'Oh, I'm watching television,' but I'm not sure you're watching at all. I think the images take over, made innocent by the fact that you think you're in control and that you are still watching, which after all is active. In fact, something is happening *to* you. This is difficult for me, obviously, because one tends to think, 'This is what happens when the mind goes out of control; when thoughts speed up, as in certain forms of psychosis'— I forget the technical term. It's a kind of speeding up of thoughts and images, now controlled by drugs."

The world according to Hartman, Glaser, Virilio: gray spaces of small extension; within them, somnolent bodies, after-effects of accelerators, twitching now and then. The body's capture in the mega-machine of the corporation. Here is Glaser describing his own corner of this world, adumbrating his proletariat of designers. "Twenty-five years ago," he tells me, "magazines were conceptualized by their practitioners as collaborative activities. Unique practitioners, like the illustrators of the old *Saturday Evening Post,* were considered to be important contributors to the imagination and quality of the magazine. Today, magazines are 'professionalized,' the art director and editor conceiving of themselves as creators of the magazine—everybody else out there as hands hired to execute their ideas." Scarcely the hands that shake the boring figurations of the pages. "Art directors provide a complete sketch, everything worked out, and find any number of illustrators—it doesn't matter who the illustrator—to execute. In former days, the editor would highlight an area to be illustrated, then find a unique personality to perform. You'd use Robert Faucet or any of the great illustrators because they had a particular vision that wasn't duplicable by anybody else. They were celebrated for their signature."

That's it, it's precisely signature that's not wanted. Nor, thank you, typography or imagery that springs at you wriggling with desire. I am sitting with Glaser at the window of his Hosteria watching the Dantean descent, the insanity pattern, the aggression of the design. It's insistent, a design obliging my attention. Propped by the window is one of his posters we had said we'd get to. I glance at it, a poster for the city of Naples, Napoli.

Glaser has replaced the *A* with an image of Vesuvius. To change the painful subject, I ask if we can talk about the poster. "It's very important for somebody to look at this and say, 'What? I don't get it.' There's got to be that disconnection where you can't figure it out, and then the realization, the closure that comes when you go: 'Oh, that's nApoli, I get it.' That kind of interval between perception and understanding is a very critical one for design and one that I'm most interested in." It poses the deconstructive moment. It blocks the desire to "get it." You can't conclude, understand, and place your gaze elsewhere.

"The spectator will go: 'What are these dots? What are these splotches?'" he adds. "They have someting to do with the cinders of Napoli. I don't know if people get that, but it enriches the surface." His color spots without contour decompose the matter, deliver its granulations, provoke the synesthesia of feeling the fine particles between thumb and finger. The blotches just suppressed by eye to the profit of a tactile referent. At this moment I am far from a hand tapping a mouse.

I can speak in a gross way of two designers today. One type is the decorative-driven, very much fashion-related; fragmentations there, little zigzags, much coming from California, where surface, "nice" colors, "nice" shapes, pretty forms matter. Wallpapery, Glaser calls it. The other type is utilitarian. Clarity-driven, simplicity-driven, it maintains the possibility of producing a con- cept independent of the material from which it issues. I can produce a transcendental concept, rising from the system of the material, this design asserts. It's the naivest communication idea.

Each is a trap for Glaser. "The content-driven stuff can get, esthetically, very uninteresting, and the form-driven stuff can re- duce the content to banality," he says.

Why take an interest in magazines here? Because they tell us what is happening to the intelligibility of daily life in the leisure world. We peer into magazines as into crystal balls to find not our destiny but our identity. And what do we find there at bottom? Banal form and idea, says Glaser; stupidity, stereotype, a world from which the quirky person has disappeared.

"I think it's a terrible mistake," says Glaser, but it's a code, not a mistake, and he knows it. *It's a mistake* means I regret the rules of this new game. "I think it's deeply narcissistic of editor and art director. It's also why all the magazines are exactly the same these days. They all use the same cast of characters, because there is no loyalty on the part of the magazine to its contributors. Why then should there be any loyalty on the part of contributors to the magazine?''

The magazine world for Milton—a small army of the boring promiscuous—and the larger corporate world as well. Glaser finds that even when it's his own signature a client wants, that client will often allow the accomplished design to decay. He tells me: ''You remember? For Grand Union we tried to reduce the information to stuff that was useful to the pedestrian. We recommended, they accepted, we left, and now the same old stuff is all creeping back again. Working with clients makes me think of the image of a man who's lost weight, then gradually begins to fill out his old suits again.'' So strong is the rule of the impersonal that ''the old habits creep back in, if you don't have a lunatic in the center of those activities, constantly monitoring, constantly complaining.'' Isn't there a head of design? I ask. Another lunatic you can train, to be your deputy when you leave? ''Most institutions don't have such a thing. You get somebody from some place else to take it over—like a shipping clerk.''

''Hey,'' I say. It was my metaphor a few pages back. Metaphor transports to a thing a name designating something other. A ten-second English spot for wine: uncorked, the mussels in an adjacent bowl one by one applaud. To the mussels is transported the name of human hands, the spot pretending to mimic a reality, to unveil a truth (its destiny, said Aristotle). Which truth? That these lowest of bivalves are closet music and wine lovers, requiring only this wine to be revealed. Jacques Derrida taught me that such a transport can detour, not arrive, arrive and malfunction, fail to unveil, in short, deconstruct. I had used the word ''clerks'' lightheartedly, in knowledge of its deconstruction. Glaser was refusing the gambit. The name to give designers—their own, not something shipped from somewhere else—is . . . shipping clerks.

As if he had said the unmentionable. We're all shipping clerks now.

Yet said in good cheer. It's odd that the gravest things come smiling from his lips. I can't help thinking of him in musical terms. He reminds me of Nicolò Paganini, one of whose pieces I played as a child, ''Nel Cuore Piu Non Mi Sento,'' in my heart is no more feeling. A joke, given that it's one of the happiest pieces. Everybody who knows Paganini knows that it's a music of happiness. It's as if Glaser, in conversation as well as in design, were dedicated ruthlessly to pleasure, to leaving behind him the pain of experience.

''I think that, by and large, pleasure is thematically a very important strand in my life,'' he responds. ''I hope that's not the only thing my work is about, but certainly pleasure rates very high"—as it is supposed to in the profession, but doesn't. Wallpaper may soothe the eye, but that's scarcely near the springs of pleasure. "I like little jokes in the work, I like laughs, I like the pleasure of figuring things out where the pieces are not immediately obvious, where something emerges for the second look, I like little graphic games: I ♥ N.Y.

Umberto Eco said somewhere that man is the only animal that laughs—on the way to the grave. And Glaser, to whom I mention this, now laughs. I wonder aloud if there isn't a dark side to his pleasure giving.

He suspects that the impulse to engage in "creative" activities (he hates the word) originates in some impulse to create immortality. Of one kind or another, he adds. "There's a nice essay by Peter Halley in which he suggests that the impetus for portraiture in the Renaissance had to do with the idea that you could stop light. Before the Renaissance, light didn't come from outside the subject—think of Byzantine and of pre-Renaissance painting. Light was a metaphor for spirituality," he lectures, "so it came from within the painting." And I am glad to listen. "That's why they used gold leaf so much and burnished surfaces. There were no shadows in those paintings, because the light was emanating from within." Even if (it's now late in the afternoon) it *has* become my dinner with Milton.

Professor Glaser: "It was the Renaissance that discovered shadows, that you could interrupt light to create form. Actually, the interruption of light had been invented earlier—look at the paintings of Pompeii—but the invention was lost, like many other things, and then rediscovered in the Renaissance. But that discovery that you could stop light meant that you could stop time, because time is determined by the passage of light. If you're sitting in natural light, that light changes its position constantly. It moves across the heavens; thus the angle of light changes, and your face changes in response to it. But once you've stopped the passage of time—which is to say, fixed the light so that it becomes permanent—then you've stopped time. And that discovery led to the idea that through portraiture people became immortal. Which begins to explain the relationship between art and immortality. And also," he tantalizes, "explains the meaning and impulse of collecting today."

For collecting—stockpiling—is a crazy idea: why should individuals be— and be known as— collectors of painting? he wonders. "I never understood that until I realized that it is a key to immortality through the vehicle of art. The collector also stops time. After Renaissance realism, art itself became a mythic instrument for achieving immortality; whereupon the myth encompassed owning art and giving it and being represented by it in the future. If you couldn't make art and become immortal, you could at least bury it and mythologically become immortal."

It's pleasurable to be sitting here, lunching with the master, but what has the Renaissance "to do with you, Milton?"

"I suppose what you call the pleasure of my work is a means of postponing the pull toward death. At least for the moment that we're here we're experiencing the life that we're in. Causing an experience is central to the pleasure I intend. I think that the work of design is to acknowledge that we're here for a moment and that while we're alive, we want to live fully and richly and experientially—that we want to experience the life we live. The biggest fear I've always had in my life is not experiencing my own life, is becoming immune to my own life."

As if the present were inaccessible, as if the food we ate, the images we watched, the conversations we heard, the flesh we touched arrived at us empty of affect and left us numb as we were. It's easy to become immune to your own life in a culture and time, our own, where life is deflected and simulation substitutes for experience. We're all enveloped in a semiosphere—an atmosphere of signs—whose content is happiness. Simulated, of course. America is an enormous enterprise for the simulation of happiness, the simulation of welfare, of communication, of human rapport. We're happy, easy, cool, without passion, without depth.

No friend of contemporary art, Glaser reminds me that once art served to awaken us from such a state, to defamiliarize our experience of our own present. "Art said, 'You can look at a still life this way.' Or, 'This is an aspect of light you should pay attention to.' And when you went out, you saw the light that way. It made the obvious extraordinary again. You saw as if for the first time again." Art, for him, doesn't do that now. It serves another intention: more immunity. It serves itself to simulate, to reconfirm the immunity that we bring to it.

"To ask the delicate question: Does a Milton Glaser design simulate happiness?"

"Look," he says, and I hear an edge in his voice, "if you're a practitioner working in the United States today, certainly some of your work would meet your description of simulation. Why? Because that's what it's done for: to obey the logic you describe. You get an assignment and that's all that can be done within its confines. I would hate to think that all my work had that quality. Let me tell you what I'm working on now," he says abruptly. "I'm doing Falstaff for the Juilliard Opera Company, sets and costumes."

"Have you ever done costumes before?"

"No. Never done sets either, except for things like the Trattoria dell'Arte. And I couldn't figure out why we should pay attention to Falstaff himself—he's foolish and a buffoon. And then I kept listening to the opera—Verdi wrote it when he was eighty in the full possession of his powers—I realized that you could view Falstaff as

242

a kind of Sufi master, a wise man who teaches by acting the fool. The Sufis were disguised; they'd be a taxi driver or a waiter, wise people in disguise who would tell you things to do. Falstaff was that. So in the last scene there's a trick played on him, because he's a bit of a lecherous rogue and tries to have a romantic affair with the wife of an important personage in the play. She is offended by this and she figures out a way to humiliate him. The last scene is in a forest where a troop frightens Falstaff by pretending to be demons, coming to punish him for his transgressions. Suddenly he says, 'Ah, but the joke is really on you, because he who laughs last laughs best.' And then there's that fantastic aria sung with the ensemble that Falstaff leads, very Bachian, a fugue, in which he says, 'It's all a joke, folks, life is just a joke.' And I thought, that's the Sufi master speaking, right? So it's all a big joke, why don't we just enjoy it? Here, look."

We've meantime cabbed it back to his office.

Now we peer into a little model he's built: a tiny Falstaff by the side of a huge tree trunk of muted emerald, trees in the background blue, violet (see Fig. 9.3).

"I'm going to illuminate the forest so that all the trees have little points of light just like the stars behind them, and then a giant head of Falstaff comes by and fills the whole stage."

And an associate ever so gently lowers a tiny curtain almost completely filling the model stage. Falstaff's face is on it, red and yellow like the new sun.

"And I'm rigging it so that he'll wink at the audience. The whole sequence is very short, from the darkness of the woods to the troop of monsters, to his realization they're just people, to the last aria that says it's just a joke, to the explosion of this sun winking at you. Just three minutes, passing from the physical to the metaphysical—the enormous head, the wink, like God winking at you and the trees decomposing into the stars. That's it, opera ends. There's something about the opera itself that matches my own sense of what my work is about, what life is about. Since it's just a cosmic joke, you might as well laugh about it. Falstaff laughs through buffoonery and I through what you call the pleasure part of my work."

"Why buffoonery?"

"Because that's the way you can penetrate people's immunity. And that's a principle of design, incidentally. You can't say anything directly in design or in painting and still reach people any more. You have to be as oblique as Falstaff, using metaphor, comparison, irony."

As I mentioned in the introsduction, Umberto Eco says that the postmodern attitude is that of a man who loves a woman who is intelligent and well-read: he knows that he can't tell her, "I love you desperately," because he knows that she knows—and she knows that he knows—that that's a line out of Barbara Cartland. So

Figure 9.3 Milton Glaser. Set for Verdi's *Falstaff*, 1991. *Courtesy Milton Glaser.*

he says, "As Barbara Cartland would say, 'I love you desperately.'" At this point, he has avoided the pretense of innocence, he has revisited the used-up past ironically.

"That's it," Glaser (almost) enthuses. He is too sophisticated ever to yield totally to an idea. "The issue, immunity again. We are immune to our own experiences in life. So the question is: how do you penetrate? How do you make people pay attention? How do you make them believe anything?—when fundamentally, the world to us is used up. We've been lied to too much, we've experienced too much pain, so now we deflect the lie, the pain and life itself. And the laugh or the joke is a means of getting through the deflecting mechanism. Because you're unprepared for the joke, you're surprised. You've been defending yourself against something else, and the joke goes around the side. All this is very much a design matter." His design. Do not generalize. "The practice of design has many intentions, some straightforward, but a major intention has to do with penetrating people's immunity to experience, surprising them. Surprise is very much related to delight."

And also to the unconscious. Jacques Lacan observed once that the experience of the unconscious is the experience of surprise: the subject feels himself overcome, exceeded.

"I guess it's all linked to the liberation of the unconscious," Glaser says, revealing his roots. "It's our consciousness that is deflecting the world." It is our consciousness shaped by commodity culture, this culture that prefers simulation. "To get past it, we need not merely pleasure, but novelty, surprise, delight, a sense of discovery."

"Impediment, default, cracking"—this is how Lacan described the advent of your unconscious. Be it in slip of the tongue, wise-crack, or blurt. "What is produced in this gap, in the full sense of the term [in French: *se produire*] *produces itself,* presents itself as *the discovery.*" He spoke those words in his seminar of 1973 at the end of the great liberation movements.

Glaser, like Lacan, is a last vestige of such force in an era that domesticated such energies. He is a designosaur, and I say that in salute.

10 *Outrageous Fortune*

Speaking of Doritos, back in the privacy of your own home (still too early to put on the porn), there are two ways to look at game shows.

You can put them down as mindless entertainment appealing to an audience with the intellect of a thirteen-year-old—and while doing so, you can look at the household prizes offered as cumbersome and tacky. Or you can recognize that chance, games, and fortune are the stuff of mythology, a way of escaping the nightmare of history. Vanna White becomes a version of Venus, whom she portrayed in her TV movie, "Goddess of Love," berated by the critics and beloved by the ratings.

When Peter Jennings was bumped out of his 7 o'clock slot by "Jeopardy," and some months later, Dan Rather by "Win, Lose or Draw," I decided it was time to leave my semiotic ponderings in New York and get my mind tanned in L.A., the better to understand the struggle between games and supposed real-world news.

Today's successful game shows are the smooth-edged successors of the whiz-kid contests and pain-and-gain prototypes of the 50s. Gone are tearful "Queens for a Day" who earned their momentary fame at the expense of considerable indignity. (If you want self-abasement these days, you go to Geraldo Rivera, Phil Donahue, or formerly, Morton Downey, Jr.) Gone, too, are the professors, the intellectual mutants who dazzled audiences with their virtuosity or freakiness, adding three zeros to radio's "$64 Question." And gone is any interest in "What's My Line," or whether I want "To Tell the Truth," or whether "I've Got a Secret."

Today's shows are more playful, less histrionic than their forebears, but many of the same emotions and values are at work. The winners no longer faint dead away at the prospect of a trip to Rio (before a "New Treasure Hunt" winner swooned, she shouted: "I'm coming! I'm coming!"), but they still jump for joy and hug the MCs, some of whom are restrained—like Bob Barker of "The Price is Right"—and some of whom—like bantamweight Ray Combs of "Family Feud"—are sometimes literally lifted and carried away by joyful contestants.

I am on the stage of "The Price is Right." I am intimidated by the vitality of the roars and grunts of the audience. "Come on *downnnn!*' cries MC Bob Barker's crowd warmer-upper and cheerleader, Rod Roddy. I am staring at a young woman in the front row suddenly startled by my New York intrusive appearance (egghead atop black cashmere blazer), as if I were branding her mindless and the whole program lowbrow and demeaning.

"We can't be intellectually intense all day long," Merv Griffin, "Wheel of Fortune" and "Jeopardy!" creator, told me over lunch at the Beverly Hilton Hotel he now owns. "Everybody likes a little frivolous something at some time during the day. Even your William Buckleys and your Gore Vidals and your heavyweights like a little respite from all that heavy stuff, and that's what a game show is," he said, returning to his half a club salad. "I'm on a liquid diet," he told me.

"I watch news stories develop when I wake up in the morning at 7 o'clock. I scan 'Good Morning America' and the CBS news and the 'Today' show, and I rush over to CNN cable and watch them all—it fascinates me—develop a story." In the morning, news connects you to the world after a night of timeless dreams and withdrawal. For Merv Griffin, the reconnection comes through television, hot and choppy, while for others, it's through the more elaborate discourse of the morning paper. Both news and accompanying coffee are habits, drugs to plug us into wakefulness and to a day of deals and market reality. After having succeeded or avoided catastropohe, we crave the martini of a game show upon arrival *chez nous*. We relax and bask in the ahistoricity of chance and the comfort of trivial pursuits.

Griffin rises, interrupting our interview, to greet an ex–movie queen, and I contemplate his Beverly Hills image, far removed from professorial tweeds or Wall Street's subdued sharpness. He is the greedy, contemporary Sidney Greenstreet, dressed in an oversize, richly textured sweater braided with black leather. His pants are black, and I realize: This is Hollywood, Merv is entertainment royalty, and Merv is dressed in robes, then about to build his Versailles on a plateau in West L.A., a project that will collapse when, reaching for the Maltese falcon in the form of Resorts International, he finds a nasty surprise inside it (next chapter). Happily unclairvoyant, I had left the finance capital to enter the fantasy capital, two poles, flesh and fantasy, base and superstructure, content and form.

I am sitting trying to crack "Wheel of Fortune" puzzles with some seventy possible contestants. L---- N-T--N- TO C--NC- remains in front of me, as I miserably fail to figure out it's LEAVE NOTHING TO CHANCE. I even failed to complete A WALKING ENCYCLOPEDIA. Given my failure I took refuge in highbrow rage—after forty-five minutes, unable to crack the code, I consoled myself: "These phrases don't belong to my world!"

But they intimately belong to the world of what the producers call "the civilians." And they, like the rest of us, regardless of our profession or status in life, need to solve mysteries and discover the unknown. We play for the sheer joy of breaking the code, where the skill and not the result—the doing and not the meaning—compel us forward.

This is one of the basic ingredients of all game shows. "I make up the puzzles, I do a hundred at a time," Merv Griffin told me, referring to "Wheel of Fortune," "but I forget what I make up. Later, when I'm watching the airing, I'm trying—everybody in the room is trying—to get the answer before the contestants." Everybody in Griffin's home as well as every other viewer in America. Griffin says that one of the keys to game-show success is the active participation of viewers in their living room where they often answer the question ahead of the contestant. "You are a hero in your living room. The son-in-law they always thought was a dork . . . suddenly they will look at him in the living room and he gets it before the contestant."

Griffin constructed the dynamics of "Wheel" to maximize the probability that the home viewer will beat the contestant and feel proud of his or her intellectual superiority. The contestants, even while knowing the answer, instead of calling it out continue to spin, knowing they'll automatically get the next letter, adding to their money, if the wheel doesn't stop at "bankrupt."

Pat Sajak, the host with Vanna of "Wheel of Fortune," clarified the strategy: "Wheel" is structured so that virtually all the time, the viewer figures the answer out before the contestants"—never realizing he or she was intended to. "The object of our game is not to solve the puzzle, it's to solve the puzzle *and* amass money, which most people try to do. So there's that superiority thing where everybody at home feels he or she can play better than our contestants. They don't quite understand that little aspect of the game"—a built-in edge for the American home.

"What Merv Griffin did with great success was *not* to have celebrities play it," game-show inventor Mark Goodson told me. Griffin thinks the very ordinariness of the contestants adds to this edge—he doesn't care what they look like. "If they don't hurt my picture, I don't mind them being on, but they're just the catalysts to move the thing along. I don't think the people at home pay any attention to them."

"The Wheel of Fortune" mixes modern computer glitz with more conventional country-fair devices such as the heavy wheel that plop, plop, plops as the contestants bend and strain to turn it. "I'm not sure that we have in every respect improved our shows by using the latest technology," says Jerry Chester, executive vice president of Mark Goodson productions. Chester, aware of the dangers of extreme modernity, believes that if his company had produced "Wheel of Fortune," "we would have devised an electronic way to turn the letters instead of having Vanna White do it, and that would have been fatal. I think we've been guilty of being on the cutting edge of the latest video technology." "The Wheel of Fortune" strikes a perfect balance between past traditions and modern technology down to taking fortune into your hands as the contestant bends to turn the wheel physically instead of pressing an inhuman button.

In L.A., in that room with the aspiring contestants, attempting puzzle after puzzle and smarting from my failures, I had overlooked also that the phrases created by Griffin and used on the show belong to the code of the average American, phrases you hear in the office, the street, or the living room. Those who try to get on "Wheel" by decoding the puzzles affirm all over again the importance of FIFTIETH WEDDING ANNIVERSARY, IN THE PUBLIC INTEREST, BOY SCOUT LEADER, and all the other bits of national wisdom I rarely write down. In its way, this show—in their ways, all the others—appeals to a broad sector of the national audience, an audience that is the ballast of the country, the depository of the values, social behavior, and social mores of America. The "Wheel of Fortune" consolidates these values.

Another ingredient that leads educated sensibilities to underestimate the games is the nature and quality of the prizes. We all want to think that we have a singular taste, that we always choose the best and tend to reject the image of an average living room, which actually suits the prize furnishings of most programs.

When I was backstage at CBS Studio 4 in Television City, I wandered among the prizes waiting to be displayed before the covetous eyes of contestants and audience. Here is what I saw, one item next to the other: a brass bed with canopy, three candles forming the headboard; behind it, a Marantz TV-stereo, its two speakers taller than I; atop the Marantz, artificial flowers; atop the right speaker, a brass sailboat; a rose-colored sofa decorated with parrots on trees; a Hoover BrushVak; a Baldwin organ; a "classics" library (Poe, Shakespeare, Tolstoy, Jack London, Mark Twain); flowers, one, two, three, four—thirty baskets of flowers, yellow, pink, brown, orange; play money; a jacuzzi under a cupola with two folded towels on it; a flowered pitcher on the jacuzzi lip, next to it two cocktail glasses; two phone booths; a pegboard on which are hung four drills; a dining table nailed to a red carpet; a large artificial

Figure 10.1 On the stage of "The Price Is Right." So much "stuff," the intellectual in me wants to vomit. To the hard-working American, this is heaven. You judge.

Figure 10.2 "Family Feud" M. C. Ray Combs, contestant Regina Bates, and some friends dancing the hora. The semiotic Zelig goes downmarket on national TV.

tree; a hot-dog stand; a Buick Regal; and a mobile home. Enough and away! The list is exhausting and I was exhausted.

The Perezes have just beaten the Bateses in the "Family Feud." Ray Combs, the host, beckons me onstage, shouting above the hubub: "You'll never know what it's like unless you join us onstage right now." Here we go again, odd man out, attempting to dance the hora with Mrs. Bates, my mini tape recorder in one hand and Mrs. Bates in the other. "Though I'm Jewish, I can't do this!" I tell her. "I'll help you," she says. And she does. I had finally become mindless, escaped the nightmare of ideas, and enjoyed myself in the jig. Socrates didn't dance—I do, at one with the games. As my snobbishness ceased, I began to feel the warmth of participating in the celebration of an American mythology.

And this universal audience is given, through the games, a chance for its fifteen minutes of fame. "If you suddenly said to a contestant, 'Please take off your pants or dress,' they might just take it off right in front of you," Goodson told me. "I think there is a compulsion to get up and say it all on camera, just as in a more serious way, people do so in autobiographies. In game shows, little people tell their autobiography. Think of the audience as voyeurs, the contestants as exhibitionists, and the two as symbiotic." The game shows are a rare opportunity to swell and become a personality, particularly if you're inspired enough to blurt something racy.

"The voyeurs are watching, waiting for the accident to happen," Goodson added.

They are also waiting for the host—for the very structure of the show, its format—to savage the contestants. Listen to this bit of a "Wheel of Fortune" taping.

"Do you have a bus to catch?" Sajak says to an overeager contestant, awkwardly starting to walk off stage before he's lost. "$3,850 is what you won," Sajak continues, "and we're going to move right on to our second round with a $2,500 personal wheel and some sort of kitchen gizmo, Charlie."

And the announcer, Charlie, says: "It is a kitchen, Pat, featuring these Gibson appliances: a side-by-side refrigerator freezer with door ice and. . . ." My attention, having wandered, returns to Charlies's peroration: ". . . black glass oven door from Gibson, two—thousand—eight"—melifluous language—"hundred and sixty-seven dollars!"

And the man who trains the contestants, whom I now think of as weak gladiators, the man who selects them and sharpens their puzzle-solving skills, then throws them to lions of American TV watching and to the lion of Pat Sajak, Harv who stands in front of me, sitting in the first row, Harv who tells me and about fifty old ladies from San Diego when to laugh, Harv hearing Charlie perorate, cries, "*ooohhhhh!*" to stimulate applause from the San Diego ladies.

"That will be yours, if you get that puzzle now," says Sajak. Who adds: "You just got here, buddy, but so far isn't this shaping up to be the most exciting day of your life?"

Harv guffaws.

And the action stops. Lights off, Sajak relaxes. Says: "Thanks for coming, folks," to the studio audience. "When we do two puzzles in a row like this, we have to stop our tape and change the puzzle and then we edit the tape and the people at home won't know we stopped like this"—a pause—"unless you go home and open your mouths."

Harv: "*Ho ho.*" Which stimulates laughter in the audience.

"Anyway, go home and enjoy yourself, yes?" And Sajak adds, looking at Vanna next to him: "You know, what I like about the show is the low-key nature of it. And you hear we're feuding."

"I know," from Vanna.

Stage director: "All right." And lights on, cameras on.

Overeager contestant: "I'd like to solve the puzzle, please." Harv has trained the contestants to say please, to utter this formula.

"Go win," says Sajak.

"*UNITED NEGRO COLLEGE FUND?*"

"*All right,*" from Harv.

Sajak: "Nice going, guy. You're up to $9,317 in cash and prizes."

"*Cut*" from stage director.

Sajak sighs: "The little jokes, oh believe me, that's why I'm here."

"Four, three, two—"

Sajak to another contestant: "This time we're looking for a phrase. We're rolling along here, gee, you're up to round four. Awright, Frank, come on!"

"Come on, Frank," from Harv.

But Frank fails and Harv addresses: "Awright, Alfred, here we go." Harv transfers his allegiance, lightly.

Alfred: "Is there an **N**, please?" Alfred, socialized, trained to politesse.

"Alfred!" from Harv. A compliment to his charge who did well.

Sajak tells him: "Just turn your head for a moment, I have to remove the jewels."

Because the theme of the show they're taping is an Egyptian temple, and Vanna is a princess, and the temple is full of jewels you can plunder just by arriving with the right Ns and Ts. A guard from Cartier's is standing by the jewels behind Frank—and for some reason I can't figure out, Frank isn't trusted, is told not to look as the guard walks off with the jewels.

"All right, Judy, it's your turn," says Sajak.

"Pat, I think I'm going to solve the puzzle," she says.

"All right, $1650, go ahead."

Judy: *"I HAVE A CLOGGED DRAIN."*

Sajak: "Yes." Laughter. Applause from all. And Pat: "Where are we here, Fred, what's happening? Who's on first? 'Wheel of Fortune,' thanks a lot. Turn around, Alfred"—who, because Judy unclogged the puzzle, just lost. "Good luck to you." And adds, for Alfred, uncertain how to exit: "A little bit to your left. So would you classify this as the most exciting day of your life?"

"So far it is."

"Alfred goes away with twelve thousand some-odd dollars," says Sajak, who tells him as he sees the exit sign: "You have nothing to hang your head about. If you go away with nothing from this, remember: 'I have a clogged drain.'" Applause. "The nighttime show is now in its sixth season and officially that's the worst puzzle we've ever had. $1,650 is what you've won"—to Judy—"and you're up to $5,500 and you're going to win a lot of money, a lot of stuff—we'll be back to do some more in a minute."

"Cut."

Sajak: "I have a clogged drain, my pants are on fire," shaking his head.

"Ten seconds."

Sajak: "Okay, players, you can stand up now."

Game shows have been with us since the birth of television (before that, radio; before that, the importance of games is lost in the halls of history and time). And throughout all this period, they have been sytematically put down, first by churches as sinful distractions from God, truth, and work, and after that by critics as wasteful and degrading. But game shows are here to stay. Let's put it into figures. "Wheel of Fortune," to take the recent form of this timeless venture, has an annual production cost of $7 million and an annual gross revenue of $120 million. Six years ago, Griffin sold the show, together with "Jeopardy!" to Coca-Cola for what insiders think was somewhat more than $250 million. Airing on nearly two hundred stations, "Wheel" reaches 99 percent of all homes with TV—which actually means all and sundry. It is shown both during the day and during prime time. Outrageous fortune.

And it has managed to bump history in the form of the ABC and CBS News into a secondary part of the day—in the New York market, 6:30 P.M., just before the prime-time access gate of 7:00. The "Wheel" is even credited with aiding the ailing news programs. "Dan Rather was a hit because he was surrounded by 'Wheel of Fortune,'" Merv Griffin said. Preceding him before it bumped him from prime time, it created an audience for him, according to the master builder of game shows and palaces. In the cities where it followed him, it also buoyed him to the top. "Lead-in or lead-out, the 'Wheel' gave the news new vibrancy," said Bob King, an executive at King World, responsible for syndicating the show nationwide. "And on the same day it surrounded him in other cities, it destroyed him in Cleveland because it was on opposite him," said Griffin. "With 'Jeopardy!' and Peter Jennings, they took Jennings's slot away from him on ABC and put the game show in. He bemoaned the fact on his last night in the old time period. 'I'm being replaced by a game show, we really hit the low mark.' What he found was that having the show touch him afterward, putting him on earlier in New York, it made him the number-one anchorman in New York. So it's been very quiet from that news department."

Every show has a premise and a format, according to Goodson. And every show performs a different ideological function. "The Family Feud" imaginarily unifies the family as a territorial unit in competition with other territorial entities. "It's nice to be pulling together here instead of always bickering at home," as a contestant told me. And let the best family win. Second-guessing opinion polls, the contestants learn the system of population preferences and values. They're learning the importance of statistics in our society, one of the most sophisticated methods of calculating investment risks and political sympathies. The American in me says: The decline of the study of western classics, bemoaned by Allan Bloom, has been substituted for by more reliable methods of assessing the state of the world. It's more important to know the price of a beef future or the market in selling male underwear to women than Aristotle's politics or Proust's remembrance of things gone. Who needs Platonic archetypes when he or she knows the right price of a laptop computer and the favorite vegetable that Middle America likes to see as a side dish next to its steak? Potatoes, peas, or corn?

How to Prove Anything You Want

There's another way to look at "Family Feud"'s guessing game. It makes you kneel before the god Opinion Poll.

In my previous book, *On Signs,* I published these lovely words of Michel de Certeau, now deceased:

> The media change the profound silence of things into its opposite. Once constituted in secret, the real now jabbers away. We are surrounded by news, information, statistics, and opinion polls. Never has history talked so much or shown so much. Never, indeed, have the gods' ministers *made them speak* so continuously in such detail and so injunctively as the producers of revelations and rules do today *in the name* of topicality. Our orthodoxy is made up of narrations of "what's going on." Statistical debates are our theological wars. The combatants no longer bear ideas as offensive or defensive arms. They move forward camouflaged as facts, data, and events. They set themselves up as messengers of a "reality." Their uniform is the color of the economic and social earth. When they advance, the ground itself seems to advance. But in fact they manufacture it, they simulate it, they cover themselves with it, they believe in it—they thus create the stage of their law.

Look how easy it is to simulate reality through an opinion poll. Listen in to the British TV series "Yes Prime Minister" as Sir Bernard Woolley recalls being taught how to prove whatever you want with an opinion poll:

> He asked me to drop in on him in the Cabinet Office, to discuss the situation. He was most interested in the party opinion poll, which I had seen as an insuperable obstacle to changing the Prime Minister's mind.
> His solution was simple: have another opinion poll done, one that would show that the voters were *against* bringing back National Service.
> I was somewhat *naif* in those days. I did not understand how the voters could be both for it and against it. Dear old Humphrey showed me how it's done.
> The secret is that when the Man in the Street is approached by a nice attractive young lady with a clipboard he is asked a *series* of question. Naturally the Man in the Street wants to make a good impression and doesn't want to make a fool of himself. So the market researcher asks questions designed to elicit *consistent* answers.
> Humphrey demonstrated the system on me. "Mr. Woolley, are you worried about the rise in crime among teenagers?"
> "Yes," I said.

"Do you think there is a lack of discipline and vigorous training in our Comprehensive Schools?"

"Yes,"

"Do you think young people welcome some structure and leadership in their lives?"

"Yes."

"Do they respond to a challenge?"

"Yes."

"Might you be in favor of reintroducing National Service?"

"Yes."

Well, naturally, I said yes. One could hardly have said anything else without looking inconsistent. Then what happens is that the Opinion Poll publishes only the last question and answer.

Of course, the reputable polls didn't conduct themselves like that. But there weren't too many of those. Humphrey suggested that we commission a new survey, not for the Party but for the Ministry of Defense. We did so. He invented the questions there and then:

"Mr. Wooley, are you worried about the danger of war?"

"Yes," I said, quite honestly.

"Are you unhappy about the growth of armaments?"

"Yes."

"Do you think there's a danger in giving young people guns and teaching them how to kill?"

"Yes."

"Do you think it wrong to force people to take up arms against their will?"

"Yes."

"Would you oppose the reintroduction of National Service?"

I'd said "Yes" before I'd even realized it, d'you see?

Humphrey was crowing with delight. "You see, Bernard," he said to me, "you're the perfect Balanced Sample."

Humphrey really had a very fertile mind. It was a pleasure to work closely with him.

It's to mask the Humphreys of the world, able to prove anything, that Ray Combs, host of the "Feud" and narrator of the polls, is so short and so "funny." Laughing with and at him, you perform your daily stint of Poll Worship.

"The Price is Right" sharpens our consumer skills, shows us that our knowledge of right pricing is more important in our day and age than the dates of the French Revolution or the course of the Danube or how many times Texas fits into the Soviet Union. Who cares whether Americans can identify the country on a globe as long as they know it's on top. Game shows help every one of us to be on top for our fifteen minutes of fame through fortune.

In the 60s, when Griffin originated "Jeopardy!" the show slaked a thirst for knowledge among people "who didn't go to college, couldn't go to college," Griffin told me. And it does to this day, not to mention in those who did and still feel uneducated. Says Mark Goodson: "It's a rare person that can answer these questions along with the contestant. People are watching in the same way they used to watch 'Information Please,' to see how smart these people are. There's a feeling on the part of the audience that they're getting a little education." A simulacrum of education. "At first when we did it, everybody on the show looked like communists," said Griffin, "the 1960s impression of what communists looked like. The New York intellectuals. The women either had on long black dresses, no makeup, or hair tied close to their head. I used to think, 'God's sake, the show would be a smash in Russia.' I had to bring in the contestant selector one day. I said, 'God, they're all the same ilk, the New York intellectuals. They all look like Columbia University graduates who are hanging around the library."

"The Wheel of Fortune" trains you in standard America-speak. All those phrases are part of everyday life and conversation in street, office, or dining room. Vanna is Beatrice taking you through the circles of ignorance, encouraging and applauding you every time you decipher one of the riddles of the universe. "What will Vanna wear today?" is answered as she appears daily as a different bird of paradise. The day I witnessed the tapings she appeared wrapped in a gold dress and Sajak said: "Are you a leftover?" referring perhaps to gold Reynolds Wrap. She had made herself a gilt-wrapped gift. Another time she came dressed in sequined black, smiling as a merry widow.

Ted Koppel has coined a phrase—the Vanna Factor—to describe a fundamental principle of our modernity in America. Successful people are empty vessels, lending themselves to all forms of identification. Everybody sees him- or herself in the empty cipher you present. Inside the zero of Vanna you can be her friend, sister, husband, father, mother, daughter, lover, et cetera, et cetera, et cetera, as the King of Siam used to say.

I am sitting with Ms. White in the NBC hair department in Burbank. I ask if she agrees with Ted Koppel:

"Absolutely," she says quickly, spritely. "I like that." Pause. "I like that a lot."

A passive corroboration, assenting with you in sweet agreement. She Vannafied me.

Ted Koppel excoriates the Vanna Factor as a negative principle. Vanna White uses it as a democratic principle, the need to appeal to the broadest possible audience. As I interviewed her, the two of us in adjoining styling chairs, she said, referring to my tape recorder: "Can I hold it for you?"—showing the power of availability. She pleases all and everyone. Ted Koppel considers it a weakness, Vanna White enjoys and cultivates it.

"Because of the fact I don't speak on television, people are able to make me whatever they want me to be," Vanna says. "It's almost like being a puppet up there. You can make the puppet say or do anything."

"I've always thought of you as a marionette," Sajak says as he enters the room. His shirt is stained with brown powder.

"You know, I'm definitely not going to be a brain surgeon in the next few years," Vanna says, ironizing about her position. "But I have used my success to the best of my knowledge in creating other things."

"So you've definitely said no to the brain surgeon offer?" Sajak asks. And Vanna answers with a hmmm.

I mention Ted Koppel's idea to Pat Sajak.

"Yeah," Sajak says, "that's a great brain trip, but as I think about it I don't know what the hell he's talking about. That's frequently the case with him: 'Affiliates, we need to keep it for an extra ten minutes. Charo would like to do another song.' Oh, golly, that's the worst hickey I've seen," he says, bent over Vanna's neck.

Even in television you find class divisions. The game shows make a lot of money but have little prestige. Newscasting is very prestigious but occupies prime time precariously since it is less lucrative.

Ray Combs is talking to me about prestige. "Do you remember the film *C.H.U.D.?* They had some silly chemical reaction to poison gas in that film; they were mutated people, a lot like Oprah Winfrey before she lost the weight. Well, maybe I was there, my head's large for a human." As I wonder why he's telling me this, he continues: "You know, I hope Merv Griffin's theory is correct. His theory—this is the reason he picked Vanna White—he believes people who have unusually, but not grossly, large heads in proportion to their bodies, have the greatest degree of succeeding in show business. And he bases it on history, Spencer Tracy and so on. That's why he picked Vanna out of all the women. And Merv has a large head. Now my head compared to my body, it's a big head, and I don't know why he thinks that, but I hope to God he's right, because I'm going to be an Academy Award winner with this head. This ain't a game show head. This is a head that can take me to astronomical heights."

The fight for prime-time preeminence continues. A new competitor entered the prime-time arena. The news, in addition to game shows, now has to take on so-called Trash TV, *National Enquirer*—like shows ("A Current Affair," "This Evening," etc.; the titles change, the format remains) that chronicle our crime and social misdemeanor from Joel Steinberg's private life to Teddy Kennedy's drinking problem without forgetting the tatoo on Brigitte Nielsen's or some new star's buttock. If someone gets trashy you get . . . crashy. For its part, the game-show industry at the end of the 80s and beginning of the 90s had to come up with an answer to Trash TV: Crash TV. This subgenre deployed competition with names like "American Gladiators," "Roller Games," and "Interceptor." In "Interceptor," in response to the American impulse toward outdoor spirit and love of sports and action, the subgenre left the studio for the outdoors. There, the contestants met with physical obstacles and difficulties of terrain as well as the danger of symbolically lethal pursuers. But in the name of leaving the studio for the innervation of the real, the would-be action shows merely reproduced the MC-managed, bloodless performances of the conventional shows. As the American gladiators, dressed in spandex, swing from rings in the ceiling on the way to combat, they look like nothing so much as noncompetitive gymnasts. Even when it seems as if there's a buck to be made bucking fakery, you don't succeed. The culture of simulation, squeezing the life out of performance, frustrates the game-show impulse to achieve the ultimate American dream—violence. As in snuff. As in the only thing that, a few years ago, was the real thing any more. Snuff films.

The action games were a gamble, an aberration untrue to the logic "Merv" so candidly declared. Contestants of the crash games needed physical vigor, automatically excluding senior citizens. By definition, living-room watchers were unable to outwit the contestants. No chance there for the couch potato to become a living-room hero, the very essence of game shows: a chicken in every pot, a hero in every living room.

The slings and arrows of outrageous fortune are permanent fixtures in American media and consciousness. News as history will always play second fiddle—short of an economic crash or all-out war—to individual risk taking and fortune seeking. Chance, games, and fortune are the stuff of American mythology.

11

Merv Griffin
Dancing
in the Dark

"He took a chance, he played the game of the 80s, and he didn't lose much of his quarter-billion-dollar fortune."

"What is Merv Griffin?"

For Merv Griffin, 1990 began with Donald Trump MC-ing the Scopus Award Gala at the Beverly Hilton hotel. The annual dinner was being given by an American-Israeli friendship organization, and Griffin was the night's honoree. Filling the vast ballroom—at $10,000 a table—were ex-president and Mrs. Reagan, Clint Eastwood, Gregory Peck (the big Scopus medal of a past year on his red-sashed chest), Israeli Defense Minister Yitzhak Rabin, Burt Bacharach, Sidney Poitier, Eva Gabor, Marvin Davis, a thousand other friends of Israel, and the de rigueur Secret Service giants, some speaking English into their jackets, the others Hebrew. "I'm going to pay tribute to you," Donald Trump says on the dais, and then launches into a stream of ambiguous references to the art of the deal. "Tribute is money," he continues, "tribute is value, you're always thinking about money," he addresses laureate Merv. "Merv and I made a deal last year—well, don't laugh. But we did make a deal, and I want to tell you that I really didn't know Merv too well at the time. We met once or twice and everybody was fighting back and forth and I couldn't stand this guy. He was the most obnoxious, crazy character I've ever met. I really only got to know him during the Miss America Pageant, where we were judges together, and we had a helluva time—and we picked the same winner. For a change, we both were on the same side."

"I got so excited," Merv says as he stands and accepts the award, "you can't see it, I popped my button right in front, and it's a new jacket." He pauses. "I guess it really isn't from being excited—just plain fat. Since our deal, Donald, my whole body's swollen. It's true we became friends at the Miss America contest because we finally got to sit down and talk and laugh at the same things. And we got so excited, we voted for each other. But that girl won," Merv says on a down note.

He turns to Defense Minister Rabin, who a few minutes earlier had tried to link the Catholic Merv to the victory in the Six-Day War and 1981 Scopus Laureate Nancy Reagan's husband, Ronald, to the crumbling of the Berlin Wall and the democratization of Eastern Europe. "Thank you for coming tonight, Mr. Rabin, Defense Minister, and beautiful Leah [his wife]. It was great to be taken personally all through Jerusalem to the Wailing Wall," Griffin continues to explain his *liaisons amicales* with Israel. "Moments I will never forget. On my second day there, at the Sharon Hotel, it was Saturday and I came down for breakfast. It was full of little ladies on tour from New York. *'Moiv!'* That's what I'm known as in New York. A little lady came over and I thought she was going to kiss me but she said, 'Make me an egg,'" Merv says, lowering his voice. "And I said, 'Okay, you're an egg.' And she said, 'No, no.' She explained it was Saturday and it was Sabbath and I did become the Shabas goy [the gentile in charge of turning on and off the lights and stove for an Orthodox Jew, who mustn't on Saturday]. I did go behind and I made eggs for everybody and I made toast for everybody. It was my shining moment at the Sharon. Then they allowed me to conduct the Israeli Symphony and that was a really special moment, all those great musicians assembled there. I got to conduct the first movement of the Tchaikovsky Piano Concerto, which was the theme of Freddie Martin's orchestra." *Tonight we love . . .*

Another guest who came from the 60s time warp was Welsh singer Tom Jones, dressed in a double-breasted suit instead of the leather pants and ruffled shirt open to the waist he formerly wore. *''She was my woman—why, why, Delilah?''* swells Jones, and Eddie Fisher, sitting to my right, stares at the chocolate bar monogrammed with Merv Griffin's logo on his plate. The nostalgic tune brings the oldies to life. Eva is seriously swaying, Nancy is slightly smiling, and Ronald, who has been looking up at Trump like a doleful hound on the alert for supper, now listens transfixed as Jones, sans jacket, borrows a napkin—"Can I have that, luv?"—wipes his brow, and returns the new Shroud of Turin to the surprised female diner.

"These galas during the last two decades have provided scholarships for ten thousand young, bright scholars that otherwise would never have had an opportunity for higher education," intones Harvey Silbert, national chairman of the board of the Friends of Hebrew University, informing us for the first time of the nature of the Scopus Award. Everybody around me at the table—Frank Swertlow, gossip golumnist of the L.A. *Daily News,* Mary Murphy, *TV Guide* reporter, Andrea King, *Hollywood Reporter* reporter, not to mention Eddie and his singer daughter Joey—has been asking why Merv and what's Scopus. "Now I'm pleased to say," continues Silbert, "that this evening we are adding the Griffin Scholars, five hundred young people who will attend one of the five campuses of the university in the applied sciences, the social sciences, the graduate schools of medicine or law or possibly the School of Agriculture. I must tell you, in passing, that the students and professors of the School of Agriculture many of them each year go to Third World countries; they're working there now trying to help educate the people in the Third World."

"Merv, we have a very special surprise for you this evening," Silbert continues. "They're planning the erection—"

"Erection?" Frank Swertlow asks.

"—on Mount Scopus campus of the university—"

General laughter builds and interrupts him. Merv fans Eva with his napkin. Trump breaks up. Even Nancy smiles.

Ronald Reagan is toastmaster. "As Henry VIII said to each of his six wives," Reagan quips, "I won't keep you long. May I ask you to join a toast to our honoree, Merv Griffin, whose charitable good works make him the most deserving recipient of the Scopus Award of the Hebrew University, and to the enduring friendship between the people of the United States and the people of Israel. *L'chaim.*"
And all of us stand and raise our glasses.

A half hour later, I am walking immediately behind Trump's bodyguard along a corridor packed with dignitaries. "Stay close to me," Trump says as we slowly make our way to the porte cochère. The paparazzi shoot and the crowd shouts as we slide into his limousine. "How do you rate that evening, Marshall?" Trump asks as we drive away toward the Hotel Bel-Air. "Success for you," I say, appealing to his vanity. "You were edgy," I add.

"Who was edgy?" Trump seems interested.

"I don't think Donald was sharp, no," then-consort Ivana says, diluting the exchange with the rhetoric of platitude. "Donald was appreciated—it was a wonderful evening."

"Well, that's why Marshall said . . ." and Donald trails off, agreeing with my assessment. "Merv just has some sterling thoughts," he continues. "He was very down-to-earth, though," he says. "It's a nice attitude, actually. It's a good attitude now."

Donald Trump, not known for beating around the bush, was being atypically coy. He was referring to the fact that he could now exult in the outcome of the takeover war over Resorts International, which began five years ago and ended in 1990 with Griffin perceived as the loser (before Trumps's own troubles, of course.) For that gala evening, Donald Trump—who had just bought L.A.'s Ambassador Hotel, where Griffin got his big start—had flown west to humor, to content, the battered Merv Griffin.

He first came to national attention in 1950 singing "I've Got a Lovely Bunch of Coconuts," and during the 60s as the main national network talk-show host to interview the likes of Bertrand Russell, Allen Ginsberg, Jane Fonda, and Abbie Hoffman. He continued on through the 70s and 80s, one of the nation's most famous talk-show hosts, interviewing everyone from Gore Vidal to Leon Spinks to Charo. Through the years, he made investments in close to a dozen radio stations in New York and New England, in VideoPatrol and Teleview Racing, the country's largest suppliers of closed-circuit TV systems, and in Beverly Hills and northern California real estate. He also created "Wheel of Fortune" and "Jeopardy!," the two most successful game shows in television history.

Then, overnight, Merv Griffin became a mogul. His economic position leapt from small fry to great white shark with one astonishing deal: in 1986, with the help of his canny president at the time, Murray Schwartz, Merv sold Merv Griffin Enterprises, including its two all-important game shows, to Coca-Cola for more than $250 million. (Some say that if he had waited a little longer he could have gotten $1 billion.)

"I was riding in my car listening to this newscast," Merv explained to me naively, "and they said a *Forbes* report just came out on the forbes Four Hundred and it names the richest performer/businessman Hollywood has ever known. And I thought, 'Oooh, Eastwood did it!' Right? Because he's my pal and he makes all those movies and he must have an enormous—I don't even know how much money he has in percentage deals. And I can't wait to hear it." To his surprise, he heard his own name. "I almost drove over the curb. Then I started looking. I found myself looking, I hoped that nobody had heard that and was looking at me." He had almost driven off the road; he was so overwhelmed, he could not continue driving. It was as if the trees, the curb, the other cars had heard of his ascent to power.

Driving his Mercedes in the glow of his "small" fortune (he had been worth $35–40 million the day before), he suddenly heard the radio press call him ten times that wealthy. "It was a quantum leap in wealth," he told me. "Suddenly he was one of the richest men in America," said his long-time friend, gossip reporter Rona Barrett. "He was on a real high. So few people had achieved what he had, and now he had been recognized. He was flushed to the point of boiling-hot red. He thought he could do no wrong."

He also thought he could do without Schwartz, who "wanted to get off the merry-go-round, whose Coke share was more than enough and who wanted to prove he could be independent," said

Barrett. Schwartz had started as Merv's William Morris agent, and over seventeen years had guided Merv Griffin Enterprises, playing the deal-making, wealth-producing bad guy to Griffin's lifelong role of nice guy, ''*making* that whole organization,'' according to Barrett.

''Irish charmers like my father, like Merv, they're affable, they're charm machines,'' novelist Patti Davis tells me in a yuppie spaghetti joint in Santa Monica, smiling and self-assured. Her father is of course Ronald Reagan. ''And they have luck. It seems amazing, but what's called luck is smart people gravitating to people like that. Smart business people do what people like my father and Merv Griffin can't do for themselves. It's like, Holmes Tuttle was a smarter business person than my father. I mean, Tuttle and Justin Dart—he was Rexall Drugs—all these guys at that point in time, when my father was getting ready to run for governor, they could have bought half this city. Those guys helped ease his financial problems, they made a nice cushion for him. And Merv, who's not real good at business any more than my father, had the same sort of dumb luck to be in the right place at the right time.''

''Successful people are pulled along by the half dozen, sometimes three people responsible for their success,'' Barrett added. ''In the case of Merv, it was Murray Schwartz. Murray was always the support system.''

''Merv was in Rio all the time I was negotiating with Coke,'' Schwartz recalled. ''He acts as if I didn't exist. See if he mentions my name on his own all the time you're with him,'' Schwartz told me without rancor. Merv never did. ''I don't want to say what I did,'' Schwartz coyly added. ''It would be self-aggrandizing, and Merv, not me, needs the credit now. I don't want to say much more, either, because if you ask me, and you will, 'So why aren't you guys together any more?' the answer wouldn't be good for him,'' he said.

When, months into the interviewing, in Atlantic City, I brought up Schwartz's name with Merv, he stammered. ''No, no, you're trying to trick me, which, uh, which, uh. . . .'' Then out it came. ''I took Murray Schwartz, he was an agent's assistant, and I made him head of my company and taught him everything he knows. Did he invent 'Wheel of Fortune'? No. Did he invent 'Jeopardy'? No. He never had the experience to negotiate a deal like Coke. Murray Schwartz was with me for a passing time, that's all.'' (Feeling guilty, Griffin later called me through his publicist to give Schwartz his due: ''Merv wants you to know, Murray was in the room during the negotiating,'' PR man Warren Cowan told me over the phone.)

After the Coca-Cola deal, without Schwartz but with his own spot in the Forbes Four Hundred, Merv decided to do it his way. So when takeover attorney Morris Orens tempted him with Resorts International in March of 1988, Merv quickened. It was an opportunity to own the dream of Atlantic City, where the wheel of fortune takes the place of hard work and special skills, where clocks have no face, and singing and dancing are vital experiences. Hotels are "everything I love, ballrooms, bands, singing, entertaining," he had exulted upon buying the Beverly Hilton Hotel in 1987. But his second love was to be a harder acquisition. Donald Trump was about to take Resorts private; he already owned 95 percent of the vote in the business but only 12 percent of the equity, and had tendered an offer of $22 a share for the remaining stock. No one wanted to challenge Trump, the fastest gun in the east. "They just wouldn't take on Trump," Orens said. "They didn't want a lot of dirt thrown on them unless there was a better-than-even chance to succeed."

Enter Merv, the new fastest gun in the west with an unlikely Tonto, one Fedele Scutti, a disgruntled shareholder and former Philadelphia car dealer. Scutti had hired Orens to search for a buyer, convinced that Trump had artificially driven the stock value sharply down. One day, in a Showboat hotel room overlooking Resorts' uncompleted Taj Mahal, Scutti doubted Trump's claim that completion required another $500 million. He remarked that it was "a bunch of bullshit." "He didn't look inside of the computers and the ceilings that are loaded with computers," Donald Trump later told me. "He didn't look inside the building at the computer systems and the restaurants and the complicated structures that were inside. All he did was look at the shell, and the shell is the least expensive thing. He's the one that convinced Merv to do the deal [through Orens]. He's a good salesman," he added drily. It took Merv only ten minutes, listening to Orens on the phone from the east, to say yes.

What followed was a clash of two styles. It was a clash of two ways of making it c. 1980s. The West Coast versus the East Coast. Merv, post–Resorts disaster, gave me an interview by the pool of the Hilton, eating cookies, dressed in a black track suit and accompanied by an echo man. Trump, pre–Taj Mahal disaster, received me in his office, impeccably dressed in a charcoal-gray suit. Alone. He didn't even shake my hand. He went straight to business. Merv, on meeting me, exclaimed, "Oh, my biographer!" Merv tries to make you feel important and special; he dangles the lure of money, a best-selling biography. Prelapsarian Trump tries to charm you with facts, wicked quotes, and aggressive honesty. One is the art of the deal, the other is the deal of fantasy. "If you call me, I'm behind this desk or I'm walking around a job. I'm not out playing tennis, I'm not out relaxing," Trump faux-humbly remarked. "I don't do those things very well, I'm a worker."

"There's an East Coast arrogance," Griffin told a reporter at the time of the deal. "They think this is La La Land out here. But there is a very important financial community that you cannot underestimate in southern California. They probably think we're doing this interview in a Jacuzzi." Which isn't very far removed from the pool-side interview he gave me.

The first time I met Merv Griffin, in February 1989, I was surprised to see the Merv face I remembered from the talk-show 70s as if it were in some monster movie, trapped inside a larger, blotchy face, the eyes bright, intelligent, the lips thin, bitter.

Almost a year later, the blotchiness had given way to a suntan, but the lips were still bitter and the eyes were the same. Merv was munching sweets at Mr. H., as it were, for Help Yourself), an egregiously gourmet buffet in the Beverly Hilton. I couldn't stop myself from scarfing down its foot-long crab legs, New Zealand mussels, giant clams, lobster tails, *gefilte* fish—and that, just for starters. After a half-week's tenure, I was beginning to approximate Merv, who bulged in (and out of) a black track suit, most of the time accompanied by his supporting actor, Warren Cowan, the publicity czar, dressed in a slim Italian blue blazer, which accentuated Merv's informality. Merv elaborated this metaphor for his life: "I really think I'm like those people who live in big houses and have a different book in every toilet. No matter where they go to the bathroom, they can pick up the last story they were reading. I kind of like that whole thing. I probably have the most enviable job in the world. I can wake up on Monday and go work on "Monopoly" [his then newest game-show venture], I can wake up on Tuesday and go work on "Reach for the Stars" [a 60s game show he'd like to see revived], or I can work on a new special here in Hollywood or work on some crazy wild idea for marketing Paradise Island in the Bahamas. My God, it's a symphony of projects out there, and I love to put obstacles in front of myself. My ex-wife always said, 'Oh, Merv is at his best when he is out of work.'"

It's hard to imagine Merv Griffin out of work, since during his five-decade career he's been a band singer, a grade-B movie star, a Broadway actor, a game-show host, a syndicated-talk-show host, an entrepreneur, and now, with Resorts, a hotel and casino honcho. But he always ends up second best and moves on to another—lucrative—phase. Griffin's life is almost, but not quite, an American success story; perpetually on the verge of total success, he consistently falls short, if only by a notch. "I never wanted to be Perry Como," Griffin says. "See, I became a singer and didn't want to be a singer. I got in the movies and didn't want to be in the movies. I got caught in things I never wanted to be in. It wasn't until the first night I sat down for Jack Paar that I knew—that's what I wanted. I'm not a genius at game shows—I fall short in game shows all the time, I have disasters. But I am very good at entertainment."

"For Merv to have made it to the top is like a professional plumber becoming a best-selling novelist," says Mike Dann, who worked with him at CBS in the late 60s. "Merv has been out of his

267

league all of his life." But Merv claims that he doesn't care, that "the battle is the fun," that failing "was wonderful." "God, was failing great! Because failing told me to get out of that, that's not for you.

"Certainly, there are many facets to my abilities, but my personality is something else entirely. I wish I could take something serious in life. I just can't. I laugh at the wrong times. I always have. People cry at funerals; I tend to get the giggles and can't stop. I don't think the business community has ever seen a businessman like this."

He was born in 1925 and grew up in San Mateo, California. His father was a tennis pro who lost the family home in the Depression. "I remember sitting on the front stairs crying while we were being taken over to my grandmother's house," Griffin recalls.

When his father taught tennis to the affluent, Merv went along and saw the life of the rich. "He had eyes," his biographer, Peter Barsocchini, says. "Always has, still does." At five feet nine and 240 pounds in a jock high school, Merv couldn't compete in conventional ways, and dealt with that by becoming entertaining. He played the piano to ingratiate himself with the wealthy. According to Barsocchini, he was often a pretend guest at socialite parties, to whom hostesses would turn and say, "Oh, Merv, how about playing the piano?" Once, fed up with being treated as the entertainment, just a step above the bartenders, the sixteen-year-old Merv appeared at the doorstep of a leading Hillsborough hostess— "a social climber," Merv remembers—with his arm in a sling, even though his tendons weren't in the slightest pain. "She said, 'Merv! What's the matter with you? You can't play the piano?' I said no. She said, 'Oh well. Come in anyway.'" And Merv did, wanting to be with the rich but not be their buffoon. ("When Merv made it in a big way," Barsocchini elaborates, "he went right back there and bought the biggest house in Pebble Beach, where a lot of these people live. He thought, 'I'll go beyond where they ever went.'")

By 1948, Merv was making $1100 a week as a San Francisco radio crooner. "It was an enormous sum," Griffin told me, "my father thought I was selling dope." (Merv makes you laugh, is utterly charming.) After hearing Griffin on the radio, Freddie Martin, one of the great bandleaders of the day, offered him a thousand-dollar-a-week pay cut and the chance of a lifetime. Griffin was dubious. "I make $1100 a week here—why would I want to go to work for $150 a week?" he asked Jean Plant, the orchestra's road manager. "And she said, 'Oh, you want to stay and be San Francisco's favorite singer?' And I said, 'What do you mean by that?' And she said, 'Well, with the deal, you know, comes RCA Victor Records, the Waldorf Astoria, the St. Francis Hotel in San Francisco, all the great ballrooms of America.' And I said, 'But I would have to take almost a thousand-dollar-a-week cut.' She said,

'I guess so,'" and Griffin remembers her singsong answer, "'I guess so.' And then she named a couple of San Francisco radio people who'd been there for 40 years and still were in the same hole. And God, I slept on it and called her the next day and I said, 'Yeah, I like that band, I think I'll go with that band.'"

Merv went on to stints in Hollywood and on Broadway. Soon he got a call from his agent. "'Goodson-Todman [the country's top game-show producers] want to see you.' I walked into this room and a man said, 'Here's the host of *Play Your Hunch,* Merv Griffin.' There were contestants and I started ad-libbing, and it was insanity, and they said, 'Isn't he terrific!' And I thought, these people have got to be out of their fucking minds. Then this little man came forward and said, 'Well, you're terrific.' It was Mark Goodson, and I was hired." (His Donor, his Benefactor—listen to the venom of his telling of the tale.)

Thus began his career as a television host. Soon he syndicated his own "Merv Griffin Show" through Westinghouse Broadcasting, and in 1968 he came to the attention of Mike Dann, the chief programming executive for CBS at the time. The network picked Merv to launch its new talk show to compete with Johnny Carson; CBS installed Griffin in the Cort Theater, hyped him for months as Mr. CBS, and fired him after two years. He wasn't a failure, exactly, but he hadn't been able to dethrone Johnny. "He appealed to an older, middle-class audience, while Carson was a more sophisticated kind of a guy," Dann says. "Merv was more of a nice old shoe. I had hoped Merv's demographics would give him a locked-in audience. I couldn't have been more wrong. Merv had to be not equal to Carson, but better. He wasn't. He didn't have the harshness, the edge, a talker had to have even then. When you worked for William S. Paley, you had to be first," Dann remembers. "When we made the decision to take Merv off, it was a very sad day for him, but I think he forgot it very quickly." There wasn't anything to forget. Merv told me he only feigned sadness. (Pay attention to the Merv behind the Merv, so to say.) "When he told me, I looked down, I said 'Oh' in a soft voice, 'Oh,'" remembering his fine acting. Dann didn't know it, but Merv already had a contract to take the talk show to Metromedia on the first Monday after any day he was fired. In love with the buck, Merv was delighted to get fired, because by getting the boot he also got a quarter of a million 1971 CBS penalty clause dollars. The minute Dann left, he called Murray Schwartz, exultant: "We just made $250,000!" So Merv was on the road again, and at the Metromedia stop, with the new show out of the night and into the day of 4:00 or 5:00 P.M., he finally came into his own as a national figure.

On the way up, Merv's personal life—"It was atypical," Dann laconically says—had suffered. Married in 1958 to Julann Wright, a comedienne and actress, he was divorced in 1976, having in the

Intellectual

"I love ideas," Merv reminisces about his time as talk-show host.
It was the early 70s and Johnny Carson had ignored writers and rad-
icals. "When I started doing my talk show," Merv tells me, "the rule
was anybody who had written a heavy book, put them at the end of
the show, the last eight minutes. They were called heavy furniture.
After a while I realized they were major stars and the people wanted
to hear a lot more from them. Then came the days when we could
introduce them first on the show and it thrilled me." It was not so
much Merv's doing, however. Rather, it was the Vietnam War, the
student movement and the antiestablishment feeling that came rag-
ing from the 60s. It had created a generation of national dissident
figures and focused attention on intellectuals in general. Merv recognized their possible mass appeal and began inviting them onto his
show.

"My best interviews were authors. My most thrilling show
was . . . hmm, hmm, he wrote *South Pacific* and *Poland*. . . ."

"Michener," I help Merv.

"James Michener. And next to him was James Jones and next to
him . . . hmm hmm hmmmmmmm, I still have a tape of it, *Bury
the Dead, Not Far From the Madding Crowd*—that's Hardy—oh,
that great playwright who paced the floor. . . ."

He can't remember.

"And Jimmy Jones gave me my first party in Paris. His wife is in
the publishing business with Jackie Onassis in New York."

In his farewell program, nevertheless, he failed to include any dissident writer, artist, man or woman of ideas. The times they are
a-changing, they have changed. Merv preferred to begin his recol-
lections with Jerry Lewis running around the studio spouting water at
Merv and other guests. Merv idem. And the young Richard Pryor
stuffs his mouth with pie, wipes his hands on his hair, and ends up
eating the napkin. There was Reagan in the White House and the
young Nixon and Bobby Kennedy and Gerald Ford and Jimmy Carter and Prince Charles. Then came the superstars. Sophia Loren,
Burt Reynolds, Bob Hope, Jack Benny, George Burns, John Wayne.
And at the end, the heavy furniture, unidentified Gore Vidal and a
glimpse of Jane Fonda.

Once again, his lack of rigor, his unseriousness, helped him trip
into second place in my eyes.

meantime moved the show and his family to L.A. (Julann reportedly received $5 million to $10 million, half of his fortune, considered extraordinary at the time.) "They even announced our divorce
on airplanes. It was like the Good Housekeeping Seal of Approval
was caught with his pants down," Griffin chuckles, cynical about
the myth he has all his life promoted.

Ten years later, Merv became simultaneously involved in the
game-show business, managing to revitalize that genre.

His genius for game shows was unquestioned until his most
recent venture. Griffin relies on having one foot in the 50s and the
other in the 90s, and it works. Or did. "'Wheel' is the most
successful game show in the history of game shows," Bob King,
who syndicated the show in '83, told me. "Jeopardy" is number
two. They even bumped the nightly news out of its 7 P.M. (EST) slot.
Griffin's brain children monopolize the top spots of the most
profitable programs of our moment.

Even today, after waking up at seven with the *New York* and *Los
Angeles Times* crossword puzzles, Griffin enjoys devising his own
phrases and proper names for the contestant to guess and Vanna to
reveal in "Wheel of Fortune." "I do, like, a hundred at a time and
they're taped way in advance so by the time they're on the air and
I'm watching the show, I'm like everybody in the room, trying to get
it before the contestants." Merv's a puzzle freak, always has been. "I
used to play Hangman [the children's game that became "Wheel']
in the car when my parents drove to L.A.," he reminisced. Merv is
good, really good, at his professional distortion, the games. "I
remember shouting to staff, 'Get more puzzles!' on 'Wheel.' So I
devised 'Front and Back': Tinker Bell Ringer," he tells me and when
I blankly look at him: Tinker Bell, Bell Ringer," he explains. Merv
wakes and sleeps the puzzles and tells me with relish, "On the
afternoon of the day we sold to Coke, I was down on my hands and
knees with the sleeves rolled up trying to figure out the next game
show. Gary Lieberthal, who heads Embassy"—now he's playing
the name dropping game—"walked into my office and we were all
down on the floor playing a game. He couldn't believe his eyes."
Games, ballrooms, and big-band music are different names for
Merv Griffin's dreams, lodged in the 50s. They are his gift and his
limitation.

His recent foray into game-show territory was a pilot for "Monopoly," where originally a midget in tails was going to dance
across the properties along Boardwalk. "Hi, it's Merv Griffin, here
in the control room, putting the final touches on the most exciting
project I've ever worked on and probably—no, not probably, *the*
most valuable license in the world, 'Monopoly.'" These were the
words of the Merv image on the pilot, wearing a baggy casual red
Shetland sweater, supposed to signify "Beverly Hills-ness," an
image splendidly indifferent to political correctness. Merv, c. 1990,

Figure 11.1 Merv has always moved through life wearing and detesting masks. In Atlantic City, in his white-furnished Resorts suite, Merv tells me: "I had a couple of records that went to the top ten and I thought, 'This is the worst business I have ever been in in my life and what am I going to be—standing up here ten years from now still trying to sing?' I mean, I've gone downstairs to my lounge and seen an old singer still snapping [he does so] his fingers like Sinatra and I think, 'Oh, thank God I chose to go elsewhere.'" But a few minutes later, here he is in the casino blessing the slot players, for the most part old. Horns are blowing. "How you doing?" shouts Merv. Big applause. "Hi ya. I love you, too. There's a lot of love. My word, I'm going to get in trouble with the gaming commission—too much love! Feeling good! *How is everybody today?*"

"Fine!" they shout.

"You're all staring. My pants aren't open, are they?" He turns to pick a slip of paper from an urn: "Pardon me for showing my back." And turns

272

(*Figure 11.1 continued*) back: "This is for two free tickets: *Mr. Harry Ginzburg!* Where are you, Harry? You have free tickets to the Superstar Theater. Tom Jones is there this weekend and Barry Manilow and a whole bunch are coming, Dean Martin, Jackie Mason, Zsa Zsa is coming. She's working with a new policeman, they have a new act." Big laughs. "She has a new perfume, you know. Called Citation. You don't spray it, you slap it on."

Snap, snap, like that oldster doing Sinatra. It's the weight of this mask the art of Risko renders.

Figure 11.2 The blessing continued, Merv pulling another name, doing a little selling as he does: "Resorts is famous for its gourmet restaurants, we have La [sic] Palais, the great French restaurant on the second floor. Tonight, Capriccio reopens, more beautiful . . . *dinner for two, Mr. Joseph Catanese, Jr!* Are you there, Joe? I see your hand waving. Oh, he's tall." And skinny. "Way above the ground. You can use a good dinner. God, I hate people like that. Hi ya, Joe. Have you eaten here? I mean, what is he eating? Look at him! Geez, that's disgusting. Probably he's sick or something—I'm only kidding, Joe." Back in the white suite, Merv is telling me some of his loves: "It is the most fantasy place you've ever seen in your life [his Moroccan palace in La Quinta], and I love water so I love the lake out in front and then I want to live with my babies, all my horses, and so I moved all my baby Arabs there, and I love looking at trees, I have this passion for trees. If anyone ever cut down a tree on my property I would probably cut *them* down. If a gardener would tell me, 'Merv, the beetle has infested our pines'—in my Carmel Valley home which is all trees—I would

(*Figure 11.2 continued*) kill him." He starts to tell me this story: "I had a tree that was the centerpiece of my property . . ."

I interrupt him: "Merv, you don't mean that, that's a figure of speech."

"What?"

"You're not capable of killing anyone."

"Oh, of course not," he soothes. "If I can't kill a tree, am I going to kill a human being?"

But the logic of what he's just said is different: If I'd kill a gardener for killing a tree, if I loved trees that much, how could I kill a human being?

"In Hollywood Hills where I lived," he's continuing, "the centerpiece of a three-acre place was this great eucalyptus. You couldn't get three people to get their arms around it. And one day the gardener knocked on my door and said, 'Mr. Griffin, the tree died. And I said, 'The tree died? You don't mean my eucalyptus?' 'It drowned.' *'It drowned? How could it drown?'* He said, 'Eucalyptuses are short-rooted systems, they die, they drown.' And I went out and he dragged some holes in it and the damn thing was dead. It was almost like a funeral to me. So one day I said, 'We'll have to take it down'—it had gotten very porous, like balsa wood, and if it fell it would knock the whole house down, it was so big. So I'm looking out the kitchen window and I see all these Spanish people going up to my tree. They're cutting it down with buzz saws and I think, 'Oh, God, it's like cutting its arms off'—it was about thirty feet high and it had two arms sticking out like a crucifixion. And I ran outside and I said, *'Estope! Uestede!'* I didn't know what the hell I was saying but the contractor heard me and he said stop and I said, *'No mas, no more, finished, terminata!'*"

I myself heard this thirty foot No when I mentioned the $5 million "sue Donald Trump fund" he gave Resorts' bondholders. "That is not me," he shouts. *"I didn't put a $5 million figure. Those are the bondholders. I had nnnnothing to do with that. Natha."*

It is this fierce *Natha* (forgive me, Spanish speakers) that Risko has also rendered—look at the eyes behind the mask. Merv puts on the mask, the myth, of bonhomie and with the aid of Risko, I have sought to rob that myth. "Truth to tell," Barthes once wrote, "the best weapon against myth is perhaps to mythify it in its turn, and to produce an *artificial myth:* and this reconstituted myth will in fact be a mythology." By his own words under a monstrous image as this one, above, Merv has made himself something like the Baron in David Lynch's *Dune.* There he is, running then activating his jet pack, flying to the top of the room where floats a young man with a plug in his throat, stoppering a surgical incision. Pushing the boy's face up and out of the way, he pulls the plug and jams his mouth onto the pulsing hole.

pitching "Monopoly" in an attempt to restore his image as the once and future king of game shows. "You played it," he continued, "your dad played it, your mother played it—in fact, 250 million people in the world know this game and have played it and love it. Well, it's the biggest project I have ever worked on [conveniently forgetting the embarrassing Resorts]. It's the most magical game and we've kept it all there. You'll recognize the board, you'll recognize Uncle Penny Bags—rich Uncle Penny Bags."

The social mores have changed since the Depression. The greed and competitiveness of the game players are hard to reproduce on a television set. Money, instead of having a physical presence, was presented as lighted ciphers on a lectern in front of each contestant. Merv thought to have solved the translation problem—from board to screen—by superimposing a quasi–crossword-puzzle gimmick. To buy property and collect rent from houses and hotels, you had to solve a rudimentary crossword puzzle where you were given only the initial letter of the answer. This wasn't "Monopoly," it was an electronic crossword-puzzle game. "Those of us who sneaked a look were laughing at him," Frank Swertlow said. "It was pathetic."

His inspiration seemed to have faltered. The pilot had to be redone at the end of 1989. The market research carried out by Parker Brothers, owners of the game, forced Merv out of his red sweater into a power-statement suit by Fred Hayman. Potential licensees found the casualness off-putting, as if the lack of vestimentary rigor were contaminating the product.

And out went the midget, Uncle Penny Bags, who advanced on the board on the roll of the dice. Dressed in top hat and tails, she nevertheless looked more like a court jester than a millionaire. Sporting an enormous white mustache, doubly cross-dressed, her face was something between a death mask and a circus clown. "Everybody hated it," Bob Murphy, the current president of Merv Griffin Enterprises, told me, and "the little person," as Merv called this grotesquerie, is now gone. "I'm looking for a new Vanna, but new Vannas are hard to come by," Merv said. "I may go with a laser instead." And gone are the huge foam-rubber dice that whirled in a giant punch bowl, as if thrown by God himself. Merv didn't inform me what would take their place. "Monopoly," once scheduled to debut in the fall of 1990, was meant to be broadcast from Atlantic City. "You must understand, you're dealing with the man who actually owns Boardwalk, North Carolina Avenue, Atlantic Avenue—I own so much real estate there, I own all the streets." The success of "Monopoly" would mark Merv's game-show comeback, but after two years' preparation and over $1 million spent on development, only twenty-plus stations in the entire country signed on for the show as of spring 1990. When I last took a look, the show was nonexistent. Merv's luck, she doesn't seem to be running good.

"It was 1980, right after my father was elected," Patti Davis is telling me in that yuppie spaghetti house. "I went on 'The Merv Griffin Show' to promote *For Ladies Only*, this very controversial television movie about Chippendale guys. Plenty for Merv to talk about. I said, 'Don't ask me about the Secret Service.' It was something I didn't want to talk about; it was new and so awful to me to be followed around by his [Reagan's] people. I felt like it was a perfectly logical request," she snaps disingenuously, her long brown hair swaying, almost beautiful as she looks straight at me, her eyes the only made up feature in her bony face. "And Merv's first question was: 'And you're here with your Secret Service agent, and there he is right in the front!'" she laughs heartily. "And I thought, you son of a bitch—you know, I mean, he was just sort of nasty."

But not on the night of August 29, 1986. It was Merv's last television talk show, highlighting 23 years on the air. Pink, fat, patriarchal, he walks into his control room with his 60 years and 240 pounds to launch into the crown jewel of his career. "The greatest privilege we ever had was my personal invitation from the President of the United States, Mr. Reagan, and his beautiful first lady, Nancy, to come to the White House," he pauses, slightly gasping for breath. It was Reagan's only interview after two months of silence that outraged the press. "Probably the greatest honor of my life, not a Sam Donaldson chat—*what d'ya say about that!*—but a look at the presidency in a most unusual interview."

Dressed by Fred Hayman (formerly Giorgio of Beverly Hills) in a blue pin-striped suit and red tie and red breast pocket hankie, Merv Griffin is the only boiled pink face in a yellow room. "After the assassination attempt on your life, Mr. President, did your personal priorities change?"

"Well," the president takes his time, "no, I can't really say. . . . I think I had them pretty well in line. Later, I had to realize that any time I've got left, I owe to Him," and the president looks up with his moist Irish eyes.

"You know," Merv hesitates, "it was a tough question and a tough answer." Again he gasps for breath. "We had to go to the commerical right after that."

"Merv looked as if he was just about to jump in his lap and kiss him." Patti tells me. "There's nothing hidden in my father. It's all out there when he's with you. With Merv, on the other hand, you always have the sense of the manipulator, you feel uneasy. There's the part of him that's with you and the other part that is scheming behind his Irish charm." Merv introduced Nancy to the Nation's Astrologer, Joan Quigley. When Nancy withdrew her support from L.A.'s Phoenix House, Merv withdrew a $40,000 pledge of aid. Merv, as many of us would but none of us can, made himself useful to power . . . shall we say, played piano for his friends of long years, the Reagans. Merv's mythic longevity as America's Boychik has earned him a place in the ruling circles—an evidence for it, his standing invitation to the Bohemian Grove, a summer resort of male political and corporate leaders near San Francisco. There, free of their women, able to urinate on the ground and swim in the nude, they have made a place for our entertainment blob—who thanked them in this aside to me when he greeted me as his biographer: "Their jobs are so boring, they line up just to be spearbearers in the final show." They were pathetic to him. Merv bears an anger (when I just met him, he struck the lunch table so hard while talking about Brokaw and the other anchors, my silverware rattled), and he takes it out on the extras and the little people . . . like the radical novelist daughter of the forty-first President of the United States.

"When I was on his show I felt he was listening, but I didn't know in what way and from what angle," Patti tells me. "I always felt an angle there. Just like that glint in his eyes that made me nervous."

It's unlikely that the glint in those eyes made Donald Trump nervous eight years later when the mogul né entertainer pitted himself against the (maybe then, not now) billionaire master of the art of the deal. So Merv came onstage with a surprising line. Because Trump was offering $22 a share, "I made a huge jump to $35," Griffin said at the time. "I knew that if I was going to make any impact on the shareholders, or the media that are going to monitor all this, I couldn't come in at $24 or $25 a share." Said one Trump executive, "I mean, we couldn't believe it. If he had bid $22.50, it was his. What's the difference? $80, $100 million? He wouldn't have gone into bankruptcy if he hadn't bid so high. He impressed the media—did he impress the media now that he went bankrupt? He certainly got good coverage."

Having caught the attention of the media, Griffin walked into Trump Tower in New York for the showdown. "Against the best wishes of his advisors," the *Los Angeles Times* wrote, "Griffin agreed to meet Donald Trump at Trump's office. This is a delicate business negotiation, the advisors warned, and delicate business negotiations should not take place on your opponent's home turf." Griffin ignored the advice, on a high from a film experience.

"The night before I first met with him, I saw *Wall Street,* " said the gun from the west, "and I thought, 'Oh God, I'm in with a sea of sharks.' I was watching Michael Douglas [he had heard that Douglas's character was based on Trump], and I thought, 'Is that me? No, I must be the kid. But no, I can't be the kid. I must be the other one.'" He felt like the British billionaire visiting Douglas's character at his home in Long Island and locking horns with him.

He was confusing fantasy and reality. Merv Griffin arrived at Trump's office on the twenty-sixth floor, according to an eyewitness, covered with makeup, as if he were walking onto a set. When he opened his briefcase on the southwest-red-marble table, a copy of Trump's *Art of the Deal* fell to the carpet. Griffin had read the book, hoping for insights into the deal, and claimed to have studied Trump's body language. "What did he understand?" Trump told me, rejecting any semiotics of The Donald. "I said that *I want this, I want that, I want that, and I want that.* What's to understand?" What's to read? I'm all out there. A surface of greed and demand.

In a six-minute confrontation (real time apes movie time), the deal was done. Trump kept some land and the then unfinished Taj Mahal (the $1 billion hotel and casino that Trump calls "The Eighth Wonder of the World"), and Merv got the rest of Resorts International—the Resorts hotel and casino, some undeveloped New Jersey real estate, and Paradise Island, a casino and four hotels in the Bahamas. Soon after Merv came out apparently on top on the deal, the press screamed. "MERV GRIFFIN'S OUTRAGEOUS FORTUNE," went the *Los Angeles Times,* quick to single out the successful son about town. "When Millionaire Griffin Took on Billionaire Trump, They Said It Was a Mismatch. They Were Wrong." Even the more circumspect *New York Times* praised the smiling Sidney Greenstreet of the 80s. "THE UNDERSTIMATED MERV GRIFFIN. The Former Band Singer Enters the Ranks of the Corporate Raiders." Even the magazines, like *Manhattan Inc.,* were spotlighting the new financial star. "REVENGE OF THE MERV. Two Years Ago, He Was A Talk Show Host Without a Swivel Chair. Now Merv Griffin is a Mogul and Donald Trump's Adversary. How did Merv Get the Last Laugh? Ooooh, It's Fascinating. . . ."

The headlines annoyed Trump, who insists that Merv broke the golden rule of the art of the deal. "It made me very angry, because it was something that shouldn't be done. You shouldn't be trumpeting. He should have focused on running the company and not getting worked up about what a great deal he had made against Donald Trump. I mean, I've made more great deals than anyone, but I don't tell everybody, making somebody else look foolish, because I'm going to have to deal with that person again in the future, and what goes around comes around. It was a very difficult period for me, because I'm not used to getting horrendous publicity. [The interview took place before the marital Saint Valentine's Day massacre and its fallout.] He billed it as the man who came in from California and took on the big guy from New York."

Be that as it may, things changed quickly. It turned out that stately, plump Merv Griffin, like Sidney Greenstreet in *The Maltese Falcon,* had gotten hold of a phony bird instead of an exquisite, jewel-studded work of art. After the Resorts deal went through, on closer inspection, Griffin's Resorts company discovered that it had failed to look under the hotel elevators at the frayed cables, hadn't grasped the state of disrepair of the heating and cooling system, and, to cap it all off, had found that 50 percent of those in the pathetically small data base on prospective gamblers were dead or had moved away. "We knew there was a problem," Griffin said. "We didn't know how deep the problem was—that the building really had been put together with Scotch tape."

The Tomb

"Well, I always loved the Taj," Trump told me. "I thought the Taj was going to be something really spectacular, but the question by many people was whether or not it could be built. Had Merv kept the Taj, that company would have been bankrupt a lot sooner. I know how to build. No one else would have been able to build the Taj because of the incredible complexity of the building, because of the massiveness of the building, because of the construction of the building, construction crews—I mean, literally the numbers of men needed just to build it."

Not once did Trump refer to the architect of the building, the style, the esthetic appeal of the casino, as if bigger were better, unqualified. The Taj, appealing to a timeless oriental mythology of pleasure, has still to find its place in the 90s. One must bear in mind that unlike Monte Carlo, Las Vegas, and Atlantic City are for the broad American middle class. They are not where princes and captains of industry go to play baccarat, but a Disneyland of fortune where middle-American millionaires, retired couples in polyester, and big spenders in brown leather jackets with golden girls at their sides go to bet and take in shows in a world without time and history.

"This is like building one of the great pyramids," Trump said of the Taj, equating size with artistic achievement and historical portent. "It's the largest building in the world on a square-foot basis, 4 1/2 million. It's the Eighth Wonder of the World," repeating what he tells everybody.

More a semiotic landmark, a communication wonder, than an architectural achievement, the Taj is a dream in the eastern megalopolis that goes from Boston to Washington. "It is hard to think of each flamboyant casino as anything but unique," writes Robert Venturi in his study of the esthetics of Las Vegas, *Learning from Las Vegas,* "and this is as it should be, because good advertising technique requires the differentiation of the product." The also bankrupt Taj will try to carve its sign somewhere between the 60s decadence of Caesar's Palace and the 90s environmental paradise of the Mirage, both of course in Vegas.

Although constructing the building was a monumental task, maintaining the success of the casino is another gigantesque feat. To have it inhabited by rollers, big and small, in a constant flux—this, to the figure of more than $1 million a day profit, is what makes—but isn't it breaks? broke?— the Taj. Either by creating new gamblers or by siphoning the Vegas market.

"It's not the same market," Mirage spokesman Allen Feldman told me. "Atlantic City is primarily the bus people, staying one or two days, playing the slot machines. Vegas is for vacationers, the average stay being four days. The Taj will not be a draw on our market."

"Unless Trump takes over Atlantic City and builds an airport there and eliminates the casino restrictions," John Schadler, communications vice president for the Mirage told me, "Atlantic City will remain the mature market that it is. It won't grow, and Trump will take the largest profit slice."

Vegas is a mirage in the desert, and the Taj will be a gambler's dream surrounded by overpopulation. The original Taj was a white marble mausoleum built from 1630 to 1648—Trump completed his in much less than a decade—in northern India by Shah Jahan for his demised wife Muntaz Mahal. The original had two sarcophagi in a vault beneath the floor. It's easier to fill a mausoleum than a casino.

One year later, the press sang a different song. Under the headline, "RISKY BUSINESS," the *Wall Street Journal* had a front-page article on July 5, 1989. "Merv Griffin Plunge Into Casino Gambling Could Prove a Loser. Resort's Big Debt Obligations May Top Its Cash Flow; But He Is Still Optimistic. Did Donald Trump His Ace?" Obviously, he had, and the next month, in Atlantic City, Merv Griffin's $1 billion debt-burdened Resorts International was unable to come up with its interest payment to bondholders and indicated that it had to default on its junk-bond debt service. Four months later, Resorts voluntarily took itself into Chapter 11 bankruptcy.

The press, to the surprise of those of us who trust its commentary when it doesn't pertain to our specific expertise, had failed to study the deal rigorously and had been carried away by the win-lose, up-down story, a continuing myth of this country.

The press, for the reasons just stated, enjoyed the East Coast–West Coast polarization. It loved the emergence of a new mogul and enjoyed deflating Donald Trump. Merv became the tribune of the little people—a bizarre, cynical turnabout, given that his giant fortune almost seems to come from his trickery, his humiliation of "little people" (see chapter 10). The Merv-Donald story took precedence over the proper scrutiny of the financial deal. "I don't think reporters take the time necessary," said Susan Heilbron, a Trump lawyer at the time I intersected these lives. "I think they take canned news, I think they do quick and dirty—what's going to sell? Merv's story sells. Donald sells."

"*People* magazine, *New York* magazine, every magazine," Donald Trump tells me, "everybody with the single exception of *Business Week*, which turned out to be perhaps prophetic—hundreds of articles reported how Merv took on Donald and won. The PR that Merv got initially—obviously not now, now it's a disaster—was the best job I've ever seen. [A salute, given in hatred, to Warren Cowan.] It was incredible."

What no one seems to have noticed, even after the second round of headlines, was that for Merv Griffin it was mostly an image, not a financial, disaster. The small investors who put up the $1 billion in junk bonds—and had to "take haircuts," according to Heilbron—will doubtless in the end suffer more than Griffin. "The press doesn't understand that my company is compartmentalized," Griffin says blithely. "Resorts is only one corporation out of many, and the press keeps saying, He's going broke. Haven't they got any brains?" About Merv's financial losses, Eva Gabor told me that her friend—whom she calls a "typhoon," not a tycoon—doesn't really care. "It's true," Merv says in Atlantic City. "What am I, here for eternity? I'll be sixty-five in July [1990]. At this point in my life, am I going to cry over lost revenues or lost deals? When you're forty-three years old [like Trump], then it's meaningful."

Nope, in America it's meaningful till you die. Merv is on the dark side of the American success dream, a has-been, something we fear as much as getting old. "I think it's because he was out a talk show, chafing for a couple of years, that he went after Resorts," an old ex-friend of his told me. Merv may not know it, but he'll be an asterisk of the late 80s, a comic appendix to the spectacular catastrophes of the Milkens and Boeskys. And when you've fallen, your public face doesn't wail or spume. It's not that it would be bad manners to spit out your rage (this country isn't Britain); but it would be too hot, it would show too much of the interior, in a land that despises the inside. And besides, Americans don't want just to survive, as the Citibank ad goes, they want to succeed, and they can't bear the sight of too much hobbling. It would slow our run up the staircase of success.

So when you're down and blue, the code of success, which also governs failure, gives you positions to assume, so as to be *inoffensive* in failure. Failure with a tear—you can repent, as Boesky did (growing a beard to so signify, as John Ehrlichman did before Boesky). Or failure with a smiling face—you can pretend to shrug it off, as Merv now does. But he is hurting. "I promise you," Mike Dann told me, "that as much as Merv dislikes Donald Trump, he envies him because Trump and Murdoch and Marvin Davis, these people want to acquire the world." In December '88, on a rush from the acquisition, Merv is playing piano at Marvin Davis's annual Christmas party for Hollywood's mega-rich and famous. Suddenly Merv turns on the piano stool, and according to his ex-friend, tells the assembled millionaires, "I bet this is the first time you've seen a billionaire play the piano."

His ego was as big as his body. It still is. Merv is telling me that all his homes are on hills. "Carmel Valley [his home there] is 1,700 feet high in the sky, it's like a mesa on ancient oak trees. When I gave Walter Wriston his birthday party up there, all he did was walk around and just say, 'Oh, my God.' When Barbara and Cary Grant came up, they held hands all the time, the three days on a weekend, they never spoke to any of us, they just walked the property. And when I said, 'Come on, Cary, we're going to John Gardner's for lunch, he looked at me and in his Cary Grant voice said, 'Why would you ever leave the mountain?' And you know me, I said, 'Come on, Cary, we've got to go eat.'"

"Why are they all on hills?" I ask.

"I told him, 'We're coming down,'" Merv says, ignoring the question. "That place is so stunning to people. They're all beautiful and very different pieces of property. You've got desert, mountains and sea." Merv bursts into song: "*From the moun-tains . . . to the prair-ies.* That's the psychological thing," he lectures me in normal voice, answering my question. "It's the song 'God Bless America.'"

"And the Bahamas," Cowan adds.

"*God bless . . .*" Merv blares.

In his fantasy he overlooks and owns the continental land mass. Merv Griffin, for a number of months, did his best (or worst) to turn a parcel of that fantasy into reality. And so would most of us, I hazard, if adequate capital or fame came to unleash what the 80s called forth and what the 90s now mask. And that is monstrosity. Of the self and of the corporation.

"You're sitting there, having quite a good time," novelist Martin Amis says of the Mervs and smaller Mervs of America. "And then a terrible thought comes in. About success, failure. Hit, miss. Make, break. And you have to get up off your chair, as it were mentally, and show this thought to the door. And then you come back in and the thought is back, doing something bananas outside the window."

There he was, our same old Merv, kneeling on Boardwalk, when Morris Orens called. Orens clicked off and an invidious thought— "Buy Resorts"— came to Merv's window, its thumbs in its ears, wiggling its fingers. Appetite and agitation crowded in on Merv. Unbearable agitation, which he now swallows inside his huge chin with the rest of his crow.

Now Merv and Trump, the two former adversaries, both failures at gaming, need each other and have managed to forge a meaningful alliance. Together, they have to try to make a tattered Atlantic City thrive again. Trump opened the Taj, as it were, to place it in bankruptcy; Merv has remodeled Resorts and tried to revitalize it with his wholesome image and skills as an entertainer. "It is still a contest," Merv says, playing wild capitalist, "but we are next-door neighbors. I will do whatever I can to promote his new, exciting, and beautiful—it's quite different—Taj. And they'll come over to Resorts and they'll have fun there too."

Trump also agrees it's a collaboration of sorts. "I think Merv is going to be very much of an asset both to me and to Atlantic City and to himself as time progresses. As Merv rebuilds and renovates his hotel, it's going to be a great adjunct to the Taj Mahal. Merv brings a certain style with him that's good. It's polished, it's smooth, it's popular, and I think ultimately it's going to make him successful in Atlantic City."

"I'm going to be a parasite operation," Merv tells schlock novelist Sidney Sheldon as if nothing were the matter with this, in Merv's suite at Resorts. Sidney's new "bride" (Cowan calls her), Alexandra, seems edgy in this group of scotch-holding males telling Milton Berle and penis jokes. But that's Hollywood East, as they say. "There's a covered bridge between Taj and us, and I'm working to remodel Resorts so we can get his overspill." Glancing at me, Griffin realizes what I've heard. Later, he says, "I have to come up with another word for 'parasite.'"

So the love-hate relationship between Donald Trump and Merv Griffin continued. For a time, a fraudulent conveyance lawsuit

hovered over the Resorts deal before Merv bought off the bondholders by giving them back 78 percent of his equity. He also, as a
part of the settlement with the bondholders, gave them $5 million
to go sue Trump, doubtless under the theory that splitting the Taj
Mahal off the package left Resorts International insolvent. (Of
course, Merv was a party to the split, but he got the bondholders'
releases.) One issue raised by such a suit might have been Griffin's
failure to exercise "due diligence" in investigating the condition of
the properties before the deal went through. Merv himself admits
that his team didn't look at the elevator cables or much of anything
else. A player in his team was the aforementioned car salesman
Fedele Scutti. There were no seasoned hotel people aboard during
the protracted closing time during which Merv could have backed
out. "It was a race against time and against the seller," someone
from Griffin's camp told me, swearing me to secrecy trying to
exonerate the wounded boss. "We'd be looking for that list and
we'd hear, 'Well, it's not available right now,' or 'We've got a big
tour group coming through.'"

For more than a year the Trump Organization lived under the
cloud of being accused of obstructing Griffin's due-diligence search.
Which was fine for the bought-off bondholders since it was Trump's
deep pocket that they most wanted to get into. "Listen, we're not
talking about babies here," Trump told me. "All they had to do is
give the security guard three dollars [three hundred?] and he'll take
them through the entire building. You yourself, Marshall, as a
reporter, could check it out."

"Forget the security guard," Heilbron told me. "For several
months after they signed the deal and before closing, they had an
office there and in that office was a team of experts, including
lawyers, accountants, appraisers, and the like."

"Would I do the Resorts deal all over again?" Merv said, survey-
ing the wreckage. He sighed. "Probably not, had I known then what
I know now."

I wouldn't trust Griffin's sincerity: Isn't it better to play the
schlemiel than be the malfeasant?

Eva Gabor, the much-married Hungarian, says she "begged" Merv
not to buy Resorts. She has been Griffin's close friend and permanent social companion since the early eighties—"I've never dated
since I got my divorce," Eva tells me as we sip orange juice in the
living room of her Holmby Hills estate. She is wearing a pink-and-
white jumpsuit that accentuates the pink of her face. Pink. Blotchy
pink, not baby pink. Every power person that I have met in this
town—from Fred Hayman to Marvin Davis to Merv and now Eva—
has a face that displays this hue.

"I have my darling Merv, I love and adore him, we're the best
friends in the world," Eva flourishes. "Men in Hollywood think

today that they are God's gift to women. They turn out to be a bloody bore, so why bother. I mean, it takes them longer to do their hair than me. I mean, they blow-dry. Now there's this terrible plague which I call AIDS. You've got to check out a man to go to bed, not to mention to go out to dinner. Who knows?"

After her last divorce, seven years ago, when she had what she calls a walking nervous breakdown, Merv nourished her back to life. "I was ninety pounds and I really was a mess. Every Thursday he came to pick me up and took me to his ranch. He spoon-fed me and stuffed me and brought me back to life. I'm very lucky because he's the best friend anybody can have, and I think he's a fine man and he has a wonderful sense of humor."

When I mentioned to Merv that I got the feeling from talking to Eva that she wanted to marry him, he replied, "I'm sure. And I would like to marry Eva."

?!

"Only why? Is it in my interest? If I love somebody and want to be right next to them the rest of my life, I probably would. But, I think, aren't we at that stage where the marriage really is to raise children, and, I mean, I did that."

Eva participates in Merv's need to play a role in a multiplicity of farces. And they have, or did have, a lot of fun. "I remember we were at Matteo's one night," she says, "and I wore this little leather skirt. He always table-hops. This time I was table-hopping. I was leaning forward and I'm talking to somebody and I have this leather skirt on and he does like this." And she gestures an open-hand slap on the buttocks. "It made an enormous noise. I stood up and I said, 'Woman beater!' At this point we started to laugh, and we laughed so hard we were crying in the car. And then an hour later, he called me back and said, 'I can't go to sleep, I'm crying.' And I said, 'I can't go to sleep, either.' I mean, we laugh about the dumbest things."

For Merv G., Eva G. is part of his ongoing performance and ongoing fantasy. She's involved in many aspects of his life, including coming up with a name for his new, 160-acre ranch in the La Quinta desert: "I was sitting with Eva one night and I said, 'Now, Eva, we've got to name this place. It is Moroccan and there are some wonderful Moroccan names—Marrakech is wonderful, Tangier is great.' Now, Eva is not a vulgar person and does not use bad language, and she just looked at me and said, "Why don't you just simply call it the fucking Palace?"

"Now it's not because I think of myself as a pasha" [although he may *see* himself as one]. "It is the most fantasy place you've ever seen in your life."

Merv Griffin lives in fantasy. "The 50s are his roots," says Jean Plant. "It was his first national exposure. The orchestras then were like night-club acts today. They were the stars of the show. People, from their late twenties to their fifties, would dress up in their finery, pay a cover, and spend three hours in those lovely rooms in the hotels. You made an evening of it, fine food, dancing, partying, spending a night out with friends, and standing up to listen to Merv." And he's done everything in his power to recreate this past. If he couldn't sing in a ballroom, he wanted to perform under its turning, glittering, mirrored globe. And, if possible, to own it. His roots in the 50s drove him to design fantasy game shows and buy fantasy hotels that are islands out of time. He wanted the Beverly Hills Hotel, the symbol of Hollywood, but the Sultan of Brunei got it, so he had to content himself with the Beverly Hilton. "It's everything I love," Merv says. "Ballrooms, bands, singing, entertaining." In one of our interviews, Merv leaned foreward and began to sing, *"Dancing in the daaark . . . ,"* and I had the craziest image of Merv Griffin whirling me around the ballroom. For Merv, show-business heaven is still a ballroom, and in his ballroom fantasy he moves from one dream to another, and, as with our own dreams, they're always incomplete, inchoate. He ends up disillusioned and immediately begins a new fabrication. Failure is the end of the dream and the driving force to change again.

"He's a good singer," George Burns says, cackling, at the Scopus Award cocktail party. "And he plays the piano." He cackles again, and draws on his El Producto. "He's made a lot of money, but not singing. He's in the money business. I've never been in the money business; I'm in show business, I'm an entertainer. I'm lucky if I can fix my bathroom. To be 94 years old and get out of bed and like what you're going to do that day, you must be very lucky. In other words, tell your readers to fall in love with what they're going to do for a living."

Like Joe Bfstplk in "Li'l Abner," the black cloud of second best keeps following Merv. Back in '48 with Freddy Martin, "he used to slip into the second piano seat and play second piano," Jean Plant remembers. As a crooner in the early 50s, he wasn't Eddie Fisher, Perry Como—not even Julius La Rosa. "On the day he issued his only solo single," says Peter Barsocchini, "Elvis Presley came out with 'Hound Dog.'" Among the few movies he made, one was "released the very week of the first CinemaScope film." And the highlight of his Broadway career was playing a supporting role in a revival of *Finian's Rainbow.*

Merv has always been ambitious, but his ambitions lack specificity. He didn't choose to polish and perfect the crooning, as Sinatra did by studying the violin phrasing of Jascha Heifetz; nor did he starve for a few years in Greenwich Village until he found a role on Broadway that would propel him to stardom. Instead, he moved on to game shows, and then talk shows, the only thing he stuck with for a long time. But even with that, his prince was still second to Johnny's king, just as he used to play second piano back in '48 with

Freddie Martin. Now, it's clear, Merv Griffin and his Resorts are going to be second piano to Trump and the Taj, scarcely a reliable first piano any more. "Merv just can't tolerate being number two," said friend Bob King. Yet there is a world in which he remains number one. Heeeere's Merv Griffin and his orchestra under the slowly turning blue neon moon of Atlantic City. His arms flap like albatross wings, leading the Mervtones in white jackets, two on either side of him, shuffling their feet in a little dance step. Merv, a carnation wound in his lapel, intones "Jukebox Saturday Night" with the boys. *"Moppin' up the soda pop rickies,"* they croon to the crowd that stands and watches Merv. *"Goodman and Kaiser and Miller,"* Merv snaps his fingers, *"help to make things right."* On the dance floor they're jitterbugging in forgotten time. That is the tragedy of Merv's success.

12 Ted Koppel: America's Grand Inquisitor

And here is the tragedy of Ted's.

Ted Koppel has just surprised me—it's two hours to show time—by telling me he doesn't have a clue how he's going to start his program. It's 9:30 P.M. on Thursday, June 30, in the ABC "Nightline" conference room in Washington. Koppel and I, alone, are eating a typical "Nightline" dinner. Last night it was pizza, tonight it's Chinese delivery. The host asks perfunctorily if I'm enjoying the meal. "It's not so good," I tell him, to elicit something beyond the niceties. "Marshall, as we age our taste buds deteriorate," Koppel, 48, ripostes. Later I find out that he smokes heavily.

The relationship from the outset was bipolar: hostile-friendly, soft and tough, soothing and irritating, cold and hot, off and on. It was far more personal than the usual relationship of interviewer to subject, portraitist to model. In 1988 I spent three weeks at "Nightline," arriving at 3 P.M. when Koppel did, watching and listening as the staff reported on the Communist Party conference, on Angola, on the downing of Iran Airlines Flight 655; as the "bookers" lined up experts, "blew"—in their language—some and put others on the show; as Dukakis and Meese (names from a distance, deep down a memory hole) "blew" him, refusing to come on. Ted Koppel, during my brief tenure, was testing his power and limits, and I was watching his profile emerge as he fashioned, night by nightline, the seemingly smooth image that everyone who watches thinks is the real Ted Koppel.

I had more access than anyone before, his producers told me. I got it by researching an early version of this chapter, which was published in the *New York Times Magazine* on August 14, 1988. Koppel was not happy with the article; given that he denounced me on National Public Radio. I could not return and reinterview him. The reader will judge whether what I saw endures in "Nightline." While he tolerated me, Koppel let me in to his thoughts and meetings by fits and starts. He measured out welcome. He was gracious, giving as much as he deigned, never putting anything off the record, playing Dr. Jekyll while letting his staff play Mr. Hyde: "You've got to GET OFF OUR CONFERENCE CALLS!" This ambivalence was kept alive to the very end. Near the end of my visit, about to leave for the Metroliner because the show would be redundant, I saw Koppel turn toward me outside his office. He came my way like an Amtrak locomotive. Putting his arm around my shoulders, he said: "Marshall, haven't we seen the last of you yet? Get *out!*" he smiled. Aggressive language, friendly body language was the leitmotif of my time with Ted Koppel.

I had come to his Washington headquarters to get my own reading on the man five to seven million American households tune to every weekday night for their final reading of what happened that day. Ted Koppel of the curious haircut, the man straight out of Archie comic books, Alfred E. Neuman without the tooth gap (as he is often perceived by his audience) is the day's last decoder. He sends his viewers off to sleep, as Seneca recommended, examining their consciences and probing those of their leaders.

Pre-Mandela liberation, he managed to bring South Africa's former Minister of Foreign Affairs, R. F. Botha, and Archbishop Desmond M. Tutu into American homes on the same program, if from different cities, Johannesburg and Capetown. He startled the country with a new objectivity and nightlight on the Israeli-Palestinian nightmare when, in April 1988, he spent a week broadcasting "Nightline" live from Israel, giving both sides a forum in which to present their case.

In Israel:

> *Koppel:* Joining me on the stage of the Jerusalem Theater, a panel of four Palestinian community leaders and four leading Israeli officials. It is just after six-thirty in the morning here. What you are about to see is live. . . . You may have noticed this little fence that I'm sitting on here. It has been suggested to me and it is perhaps symbolic of the delicacy with which the negotiations proceeded just to bring this audience together, but it has been suggested to me that we need a symbolic divider between our Israeli guests on the one hand and our Palestinian guests on the other. . . . I will try and spend as much time on one side as on the other. Let me, in fact, as I move across our fence right now . . .

He sat on the division; he turned his legs to the one side of it, then the other; he stood up and crossed to the one side, then to the other. He was able to vitalize a piece of wood that the Palestinians had insisted be on stage and be a barrier. Koppel had made their symbol *his own.* He had succeeded in standing—and sitting—for American fairness. That was why the *Times* wanted his profile: he seemed a new breed of journalist—part statesman.

He was the first to get Jim and Tammy Bakker, after their fall from televangelism's pinnacle, because, as Jim told Koppel on the show: "I guess we had invitations just to about every program . . . but I felt that you're not only tough but I felt that you would be fair. . . ." Later, Koppel cut through their pietism, challenging Jim, who hoped to return as the head of the Praise The Lord ministry, with, "But you know, you're a lousy manager." To which the Reverend admitted, "Yes."

It's Thursday, June 30, and Koppel is briefing me on tonight's "Nightline." Jonas Savimbi, the then Angolan rebel leader, will be Koppel's live guest in two hours and Ted, as everyone calls him, hasn't yet figured out his opening salvo. He tells me he's going to look into Savimbi's face on a studio monitor as his guest watches the five-minute background report—it will show an atrocity, protestors—that will precede the questioning. "He may frown, he may scowl, he may smile, he may shrug his shoulders," Koppel says. "That will give me my first clue as to where the points of vulnerability are."

How does he read a face, revolutionary or otherwise? Koppel won't say.

So I say, "Read my face, read my physiognomy." Show me how you do it.

"Look, you want me to read your physiognomy?" Koppel's voice is tenser, tough.

"Yeah."

At last I have a chance to find out what lies behind the screen, behind the questions Koppel asks. I want to do nothing that he himself doesn't do to his guests, to break through the mask of the person many people consider to be the greatest interviewer/inquisitor on television.

"You had a predisposition," Koppel begins. "I think that's a dumb way to do a story. You came in and you told me, 'Look, I regard you as the most intellectual among the television journalists.'"

As I sit there wounded, he continues. "At the moment, I've challenged you. You're a little bit hurt. Not much, but a little bit. It's all going through your head right now—does he think I'm a fool? That's all in your body language. Attention: rigid, not wavering, not moving, trying to be in absolute control of yourself, wanting to know where your head is, where your eyes are, where your hands are, steepled, no fluidity, none at all. Now I've got your attention because I'm talking about you. And if I were interviewing you, I'd know that I had you *right now.* I got you off balance.

Figure 12.1 Under the lights: Ted Koppel, alone as usual in front of the monitors, prepares to go on the air with "Nightline." How frail he looks.

"That's when I'd move in, and that's when I'd hit you with two or three hard ones."

So that's what it's like to be a "guest" on "Nightline," the rubber clown who's punched and (sometimes) springs back for more. It is a breakthrough, not of communication, but of aggression, in which I accept the punch. In order to read you, Koppel first wounds you. He plays picador to his own matador, and what that does to fairness, I leave it to others to decide.

Koppel understood the odd success of this moment. He's telling me now: "Please don't misunderstand. You asked me to engage in a parlor game with you"—he's pulling back—"and do something I don't normally do." He's telling me he doesn't demonstrate and analyze his method for interviewers. He *does* use it to edge out his guests every week night on television.

Throughout my "Nightline" stay, in a previous presidential campaign, Koppel tried to hold yesterday's Tsongas, Dukakis, to a promise made on the night of his New York primary victory. Dukakis later conditioned his appearance on a face-to-face interview with Koppel. Appealing to fair play, Koppel refused to grant him a privilege that then Vice President Bush, appearing just after the California primary, had never made a condition. (Bush had asked for, and received, a return monitor—rarely permitted—on which to see Koppel; Dukakis would have been given the same privilege.)

Why the struggle? What is the advantage of apprearing face-to-face with Ted Koppel?

When you're interviewed on "Nightline," normally you sit in a studio, in Washington or anywhere else in the world, a listening device in your ear, facing a camera. You don't even have the comfort of seeing the image of Ted Koppel. The producers do not provide a monitor for you to watch the likeness of your inquisitor. Richard N. Kaplan, "Nightline" executive producer during my stay, explains: "If you watched that monitor, you would see yourself a second later than you speak. Let's say you're a guest in Cincinnati. The signal comes from Cincinnati to New York. It's fed down to Washington, where Ted sees it. He talks to you. The signal is mixed in New York and fed out to the network, and that's what you see coming back on the monitor. That takes a second. You would see yourself coming back a second later. You . . . would . . . start . . . talking . . . like . . . this. To watch yourself talk out of synch is mind-boggling. You can't do it."

Or "Nightline" won't let you.

Kaplan suggests another reason for the absence of a monitor: "When people are real comfortable, that makes them more easily able to ignore the questioner. When everybody's listening to an earpiece [and] all of a sudden a voice cuts through and says, 'Wait a second!' it stops you. Ted maintains control because they're dealing with an earpiece and not seeing the other guests or Ted."

And Koppel needs this edge, Kaplan says. "Most people who come on the program certainly know more about the subject than Ted does. They've been picked because they're experts. So Ted needs any edge you can give him."

"We do Bush," Kaplan continues. "Bush doesn't do very well." Several times he called Koppel "Dan," referring to CBS's Rather. Soon after the Bush interview, Kaplan says, "We get a call from the Dukakis campaign saying: 'Now, you know, with Dukakis, Dukakis wants to sit in the room with Ted.'" For if Dukakis can sit next to Koppel, he can gain eye contact, "and eye contact means gaining control," Kaplan explains. But if your "umbilical cord" (his phrase) is the earpiece—not a physical presence, not your eyesight and your ears hearing an unmediated voice—then, Kaplan says, "you are going to be real sensitive" (shall we say, subordinate?) "to any voices that come across that earpiece."

So there is no eye contact, not even your eye to image-eye, no instantaneous recognition of the interlocutor; rather, a sequential passage of words through your ear. In fact, it places the interviewee in a foreign perceptual world where the guest no longer has the benefit of two dimensions—spatial/instantaneous as well as temporal/sequential. The novelist Yukio Mishima once said that language explains but reality has nothing to do with language. When you use language, it's as if you were in a space sheltered from the bustle of the throbbing street; you are abstracted from immediacy. Using language, you possess the power of analysis, but you cease to react automatically, as the human animal. By removing his person from you, Koppel cunningly deprives you of your animal instinct.

When you are picked up in a limousine, when you're withdrawn from your personal space, when you are made to sit in a studio and when what amounts to a telephone plug is stuck in your ear, it's then that Koppel has willfully deprived you of the will *you* could muster in the eye-to-eye, mano-a-mano exchange, were you permitted it. I now realize why the gracious and deadly Jonas Savimbi looked so rigid on the control room monitor—he had been shrunk, so to say, to an ear and answering mouth.

Stuck before the camera, attentive to that earplug, you can't think to answer back to the physical Koppel. Eye-to-eye, if he interrupts you, you can ignore the aural channel and keep addressing the visual, thereby completing your rhetoric that he wants to cut short. If there's nothing to see, you have to stop immediately when he interrupts—'What's wrong?' you think.

The emotional is constrained by everything coming in your ear, by the verbal sequence you listen for that makes you rational. You are fair, you are . . . British. Before whom? A British-born-and-disciplined orator who knows all too skillfully how to use fairness to get away with murder. Little did I know, when I asked him to dissect me, that I was enjoying a privilege few of the greats ever get.

The months of tug and pull between the man who then would be president and the Alfred E. Neuman who worries a lot only seemed to be about fairness. It was about power, the power to impose the lethal ''Nightline'' format.

Koppel rufused to concede the edge. On Friday, July 1, irritated that Dukakis still hadn't agreed to come on the show, Koppel walked into the office of producer Richard Harris at 10 P.M., bearing a sheet of paper. Harris read it. ''Strong,'' he said, and I knew what it was—an exposure of Dukakis for reneging on a promise. ''You tell 'em, I'm prepared to read it on air, and I will. And I expect to hear from Dach [Dukakis's communications director] by Tuesday with an answer. And you tell them''—he is pointing a forefinger at Harris—''no live interview on any of the other networks 'til then.''

''He *said* that?'' a surprised Kaplan later asked me.

The document he handed Harris was an ''either you come on or . . .'' To a man who, day by day, had strengthened since his casual ''sure'' on the night of the New York primary victory.

I thought this crossing of a green line of fairness, if published, would unduly harm Koppel, so in that hot moment, I kept silent.

''Governor Dukakis wanted to do 'Nightline,' said Leslie Dach disingenuously, no more moral—neither he nor his boss—than Koppel, ''but it's better to do it with him sitting across from you, to see each other without any artificial separation, instead of being

Figure 12.2 In a standard interview, Koppel could see Jesse Jackson, but Jackson could only hear Koppel. Koppel is reading that down-turned face.

asked to go down the hall." Absurd image of shamefaced Dukakis, as it were in high school, marching down a hall after some dressing down. Stripped of the rhetoric of pathos, what Dach meant was that the nominee of his party would be uncomfortable obeying ear logic, weakening still further his noncharismatic image—uncomfortable being edged. As moderator from 1971 to 1973 of "The Advocates," a show pitting contentious sides against each other on issues of national concern, Dukakis had learned how to incite and manage controversy, and to appreciate the advantages of direct confrontation.

During the Democratic Convention, Richard Harris, a "Nightline" producer, approached Leon Kelly, a Dukakis liaison, offering the Governor a face-to-face interview with Koppel "any night that week"—not a substitute for the long-sought hour-long companion to the Bush interview, but a separate opportunity. Dukakis's people declined. When asked why, Leslie Dach answered, "We were making a lot of news and we were happy with it."

Earlier, Kaplan had stressed that Dukakis would be offered the chance for a "Nightline" appearance again, under the usual ground rules. And so would Bush. "You know," said Kaplan, "you can certainly be elected President without appearing on 'Nightline.' But we have very high standards on this program—we intend to always live up to them."

A muffled version of the struggle leaked to the press. *Time magazine* reported that "Dukakis aides wanted their man seated next to Ted Koppel, as Gary Hart had been"—a rare exception, granted for his first interview after his initial withdrawal from the Presidential primary race.

Also an exception was Jesse Jackson, who on the night of his triumphal speech at the Democratic National Convention sat next to Koppel in the ABC booth.

"Forgive me, I got a little distracted," said Koppel.

"I didn't know you could get distracted, Ted."

"I didn't either," said Koppel, and then reached out to touch Jackson's arm.

Jackson had the advantage not only of a face-to-face interview, but also of the tactile dimension. Koppel had surrendered more than his edge.

Four days earlier, when Jackson was still en route to the convention, Koppel had interviewed him long distance on the question of the hour: "What does Jesse want?" Addressing Jackson, Koppel said, coughing: "Just before you left Chicago, you put it in very bitter terms. You referred to yourself and your followers like the field hands out there, you know, bringing in the harvest while Massuh Dukakis and his aides are sittin' up there in the Big House. . . ."

Figure 12.3 Look at the eye, like a trembling wound in that armored face.

"Now, Ted, wait a minute," Jackson interrupted. "I, I think it's a bit unfair. I did not say 'Massuh' Dukakis."

"No," Koppel said, effectively admitting he had exaggerated.

"You, you, you are suggesting . . ." Jackson seemed about to define, and reject, the racial issue. But again Koppel interrupted: "I said *like* that."

"No, but you see, even to say that," said Jackson, "is to suggest a racial issue as opposed to the basic arrangement. I am expected to register more Democratic voters than any other Democrat. And I have."

Jackson had seized the monitor edge from Koppel and answered as if he were face-to-face, piercing and nullifying Koppel's technological advantage.

Once when Koppel himself graciously nullified it, his interlocutor cunningly or not turned the tables on him. At a New York town meeting broadcast on "Nightline," Nelson Mandela refused to look at Koppel seated next to him on a stage at City College. Koppel was forced to turn his head to the side while a rigid Mandela stared straight into the audience. Trained as an orator, Mandela had also been trained in the stentorian rhetoric of Communist internationalism. Twenty-some-odd years in prison had deprived him of the ability to speak in the contemporary rhetoric of sound bites. Paradoxically, this time warp was on his side. Koppel mistook Mandela's phrastic pauses for periods, started to talk, then stopped in little hiccups, realizing his mistake, on the alert for the elusive periods. Communist rhetoric and South African jail had put Ted Koppel in the position of his interviewees. His eyes were useless, he was straining his ears.

A couple of hours after demonstrating his face-reading technique on me, Koppel puts it into practice.

It's 9:10 P.M., Thursday, June 30. Jonas Savimbi is in Washington, doing public relations for his Angolan rebel cause, and I ask Koppel, "What will you look for in his face?

"Have you met Savimbi?" he asks. "He's going to be in the studio tonight because he's attending a dinner here in Washington." Koppel suggests I meet him. "He's a very tough piece of work. I mean, you will have no trouble looking at Jonas Savimbi and imagining Jonas Savimbi killing a man."

Two hours later, Koppel, having put on his makeup and his earpiece, its wire running down his back, goes into the greenroom to greet Savimbi, who is waiting to go on camera.

"Marshall, come on over." Koppel, now friendly, summons me inside and introduces me to Savimbi.

Koppel: "Marshall is only masquerading as a journalist—he's normally a professor. Journalists don't look this distinguished."

Savimbi slowly laughs, perhaps seeing the barb in me. You can hear every syllable: *ah hah hah hah hah hah.*

Koppel, the gracious host, asks Savimbi, all the while studying him: "Is it my imagination or have you lost weight? You look slimmer than when I saw you."

Savimbi drily: "Yeah, because of the war." And laughs.

Koppel: "It doesn't help for gaining weight."

Koppel is looking into Savimbi's face and I am, too. And I look at Koppel, who is gathering an impression that will generate his first question. Savimbi could kill, Koppel could wound, and I am the wide-eyed pedant in wonderland.

It's almost air time. Koppel is behind a desk on a stage at one end of a vast, almost empty ABC newsroom. His scuffed tan briefcase is at his feet, off camera. He brings it from his office every night; maybe it's a security briefcase, for he never opens it on air. From my vantage point below and behind him in a chair at an unused desk, I can see his jaw working and his left hand toying with his fountain pen. His cough, continual while he smokes, is mastered now, and I think to grasp the duality of the man. He is powerful but alone. He seems to control his guests but lives on the edge of rejection. He appears smooth but he is rough. All is being masked now.

On air:

> *Koppel* Mr. Savimbi . . . as you know, Governor Dukakis has already indicated that if he's elected, then U.S. aid . . . to you and your forces will end. Would it be fair to conclude, therefore, that you are here in kind of a last-ditch effort to change as much public opinion as you can before the elections?
>
> *Savimbi* We are here in order to present our program of peace. . . . What is . . . at stake now, it is the peace in the country."

He never wavers from the peace line.

After the show, Koppel dismisses the staff—"I need 10 minutes with Marshall."—fills a paper cup with ice to use as an ashtray, and asks me, "Well, what did you think?"

Before I can fully formulate an opinion, he treats me to self-critique and a critique of Savimbi: "The show never really caught fire, but you know that's really up to them [the guests]. My job is not to be pouring gasoline on it until finally something ignites."

Koppel is generous in his post-mortem on Savimbi's lack of fire. "From Savimbi's point of view, banality is exactly the protective cloak that he needed. All he had to do was come across as a man of utter reasonableness, committed to the peace process, reacting

Ted Koppel:

America's

Grand

Inquisitor

more in sadness than in anger to these ridiculous charges that his troops engage in atrocities or plant land mines.''

Ordinarily, Koppel crowds his guest. When I first met him, he told me, ''Once you recognize that the person has just handed you two or three really disingenuous answers in a row, then you have been authorized, in a sense, to say 'bullshit.' But you've got to say it in another form. There is another code for that. And that code can be the raised eyebrow, the look of astonishment, the 'Do you mean to tell me that . . . ?' or 'Maybe I haven't really understood what you've been telling me, but. . . .' ''

But the ''but'' didn't seem to come for Savimbi. Not only had Koppel been unaggressive and Savimbi unforthcoming, but Koppel also felt he had made a wrong choice for the night's subject matter. He said he felt blindsided (by whom, I didn't learn): the big story of the day wasn't Savimbi; it was, Koppel said, the first Soviet Communist Party national conference in 47 years, one of the early indicators of Soviet devolution. My *Times* editor and I had hoped that Koppel—and thus I—would have been in Moscow, but one of the bookers told me Ted was tired after Israel.

Koppel's only coverage of the conference had been on the first day, when Pierre Salinger, ABC's chief foreign correspondent, had appeared from Moscow with 27-year-old Artyom Borovik, foreign editor of the Soviet weekly *Ogonyok*. Like Vladimir Pozner, Borovik had been made a sort of hero of ''Nightline,'' one of the usual suspects to be collected by the bookers. ''A nice lad,'' Moscow TV's Vladimir Dounaev slyly said at home over a boisterous Russian dinner in which I lost myself for relief from Koppel.

For tomorrow, the last day of the conference, Koppel hoped to get high-level Soviet bureaucrats who could decode the events of the day. He had to settle for Salinger from Moscow, and only by telephone; plus a couple of American sovietologists.

Koppel had told me at the beginning that he would close only one door: that of his private life. Ted Koppel's basic biography, nevertheless, is in the public domain. Edward James Koppel was born in Lancashire, England, in 1940. His father, an industrialist, had fled the Nazis in '38 with his wife. Koppel went to a boarding school. ''It was all considered part of toughening you up, learning self-control and becoming more self-contained.''

At 13, he came to New York with his family. He went to Syracuse University, later earning his master's in communications at Stanford, where he met his wife, Grace Anne. He became a United States citizen in 1963. He got his first job at ABC at 23 and has never left. He covered the Vietnam War and was the network's chief diplomatic correspondent from '71 to '80, during which time he met and fell under the influence of Henry Kissinger. ''As much credit as I'm willing to give him for having taught me things,'' Koppel has said,

"I'm still more liberal than he is, but I'm much more of a pragmatist when it comes to foreign policy than most of my colleagues."

"Nightline" evolved out of "The Iran Crisis: America Held Hostage," the late-night 1979 Koppel show that helped keep the hostages in the American conscience after the Iranians had captured the United States Embassy in Teheran and boosted ABC's then-low ratings for that time slot. From the outset, Koppel earned the admiration of many of his peers.

All of this, with the exception of these few secrets, is part of Koppel's growing marble monument, even his reticence in talking about his wife and four children, his year as a part-time house-husband while Grace Anne studied law, Koppel working occasionally as an anchorman and on special assignments. Whenever his wife called during my stay, he always took the call, and whoever was in his office scuttled out.

Koppel attributes part of the success he has atained to what he calls the "Vanna Factor," a reference to Vanna White, the letter-turning mannequin who wondered aloud in my presence if Koppel was mocking her.

You'll recall that Koppel told me something I mentioned in the introduction: "Vanna leaves an intellectual vacuum, which can be filled by whatever the predisposition of the viewer happens to be," Koppel told me. "The viewer can make her whatever he wants." And so, too, make Ted Koppel. "In theory, I am equally tough on everyone: therefore viewers can project on me their own politics, their own views, their own predispositions. That makes me the beneficiary of a certain public acceptance that I would not have if I were, let's say, a commentator who expressed his own views on subjects, or a politician."

Vannafication is a fundamental principle in the understanding of political and media success—and failure. Koppel believes the Vanna Factor now exists in all aspects of American public life. "The more successful you are in leaving a certain uncertainty in the mind of the voter [the interviewee]. . . . You would think that the voter would be frustrated by that, but on the contrary he has become acclimated to the notion that you just fill in the blank. He watches me and he chooses to believe that I believe what he believes."

On Jackson's night at the convention, Koppel applied the Vanna Factor to the detriment of Jesse. "It's the very level of passion generated by Jesse Jackson that carries a price." Koppel says. "It is the dullness of a Bush that contributes to his acceptability across such a wide spectrum."

So Koppel, in his own view, is a void, a vessel, filled with millions of viewers' questions, expostulations, and concerns. When he approaches his different guests, and he turns to the right and the left, the right and the left alternately identify with him, he thinks. (In fact, the left abhors him.) Like the exalted politicians to whom he compares himself, he answers to fractious constituencies when he voices the different questions. Like an elected politician, he is the winner who takes all the brimming content of the vessel he is and runs with it to score his own goal.

Every morning at 11, the "Nightline" producers, whether at home, in their offices or in their cars, participate in a conference call to hear and discuss the day's bulletins and decide on the night's story. You get on the call by dialing a special ABC Washington line, as I did for three weeks; you ask the network operator to put you on the "Nightline" bridge, giving the unchanging password. Although ABC News's headquarters and main technology are in New York, Koppel dislikes the city; hence, he and his staff have to be bridged from Washington to New York, and to London, the show's European link. As each person joins in, a chime sounds, as if a magic wand had brought another fairy onto the ethereal bridge. No matter how grim the content, the conversation is pleasant, like a brunch of angels. And always:

"Is Ted on yet?"

"Good morning."

"Hi, Ted."

Let the conference call begin.

It's Wednesday, July 6, three days after the United States cruiser *Vincennes* downed Iran Airlines Flight 655. As they talk, Koppel decodes his producers' discussion about both sides' anger:

"Behind all this breast beating I sense they're still trying to continue a diplomatic discussion." A remembered detail from yesterday is configured into planning for tonight. After last night's program, off air, the Iranian Ambassador to the U.N., a guest, had admitted he went out of his way to be moderate. The signal is duly noted. Koppel lectures the staff: For nearly a decade, both sides have been looking down the barrel of a gun, and they know it and have impulse for normalization.

Later, at 9 P.M., as we tackle another Chinese call-up dinner, he elaborates. "The immediate expectation is that a devastating accident like this can only lead to disaster. Not necessarily. It all depends on how the leaders of both countries use it. They can be screaming bloody murder about each other on one level and still be dealing on another level to establish contact. This town specializes in balloon floating, and that's what you're seeing right now."

The program topic decided, the only thing left to do after the conference call was to fill in the content, decide the guest list, which was to have included Jimmy Carter. Koppel liked the idea. Someone tells him Carter is on a fishing-book tour. "If he's beginning a book tour, the idea of appearing on TV will not appear alien to him," Koppel says drily. "Speaking of fishing and outdoor wildlife, let's talk about the gulf," correspondent Jimmy Walker also drily says. "You would like a chronology of hate"—for the opening documentary that sets Koppel off. Quickly, the rest of the guest list was decided: the balloon-floating ambassador and the "Baby Shah," the son of the late Shah of Iran.

"That'd be neat," said Koppel, like a boy planning his first party to which . . . girls are invited. Unhappily, the guests, except for one, didn't come. Not Jimmy Carter, who doubtless didn't want to be remembered all over again as the Hostage President. Not the Ambassador who, I'm sure, thought it a mite dangerous to float balloons from a government in factional disorder.

"Put yourself in the position of a poor Iranian diplomat who doesn't even know who's running the show back home now," Koppel explained later as we ate.

The Little Shah, on reflection, was too little, and he was blown away very soon. The "Nightline" producers—typical situation—scrambled all day for substitutes.

The episode made me viscerally realize that no matter how conceptually dramatic Ted Koppel is, he cannot control events. People come on "Nightline" to serve their own ends, not Koppel's. He is always having to struggle to get good guests.

The day before, Koppel hadn't been available until late afternoon. The entire "Nightline" staff seemed at a loss, unable to advance the night's program. The program was suddenly headless. The staff, mostly in their 30s and heavily augmented by college interns, can follow orders, but as Koppel becomes more of a self-centered star—one of his staff has said it used to be that you had a 30–70 chance of winning an argument with him, now it's nil—it can contribute less to "Nightline."

For a time there was excessive talk in New York and Washington of a Koppel-turned-public-servant. Henry Kissinger has suggested that Koppel could have a high-ranking position in the State Department. Koppel himself has talked about the limits of his "Nightline" tenure, of the possibility of choosing a different course. He has already made his mark on television by adding depth and range to news coverage. For seven years by the time I met him, every weekday night at 11:30 P.M. EST, he had put his skills on the live line and often as not had emerged victorious.

Koppel reluctantly saw me because, at the time, he was negotiating a new contract with ABC, and an ABC key executive asked him to grant the interview. As a result of the new contract, he created his own, independent production company, ABC having the right of first refusal. By now, this should have considerably augmented his reputed $1 million-plus annual income. This guarantees his freedom to introduce new ideas in a medium that he considers a victim of the Vanna Factor.

He is a front-runner among the anchors. But it seems unlikely that any of the anchors will step into the shoes of Cronkite and become supreme; except of course for Jennings, because, notwithstanding his educational lack, he *is* the intellectual of anchors. The media is so rich in variety, so highly competitive, so democratic in its fragmentation, there is no space for Bonapartism or, should we say, Cronkytism. There will simply be a division of territories.

During my journey into "Nightline," Koppel was generous and aggressive. He was always ready to give me an answer or explanation but consistently ignored my modest analysis and opinions. When *I* was a nice lad, I was trained at the *Saturday Evening Post*—the very one that spawned Pete Hamill and Lewis Lapham—*not* to ask questions. Live with the celebrity, converse with him or her, stay long enough to become part of the entourage and see everything, I was taught. Carson, Dylan, Belafonte, a bunch of others were amiable, chatterers, maybe because they were young when I met them. Koppel chafed at my being and being there. In the Pantheon of the press, he is not comfortable being the goal of the press, namely to be pressed and ex-pressed—his insides pressed out onto the page of the reporter. This, I think, is because he is made, as the wise guys would say. The achieved person, whether godfather, captain of industry, artist, political leader or entertainment celebrity, often has an element of the monster within him- or herself, I think. Merely flip through the pages of this book for evidence. Koppel is no exception. This "monstrosity" is the other face of his smooth, precise, and polite television persona. In a high school publication, Koppel arrogantly reminisced: "I honestly don't remember anyone I went to school with."

In the address to the Duke graduating class referred to in my introduction, Koppel warned of "false gods of material success and shallow fame," saying "their influence is magnified by television." His hero that day was Moses. "Our society finds truth too strong a medicine to digest undiluted. In its purest form, truth is not a polite tap on the shoulder. It's a howling reproach. What Moses brought down from Mt. Sinai were not the Ten Suggestions. They are Commandments. Are, now were."

So a man who invokes Moses would prefer not to be muffled by television, not to be Vannafied. Behind the screen, Koppel is not impartial. He has a strong moral bias, a position on politics and life, but knows he must mask it to survive as an electronic journalist. He must resign himself to being not Moses but a television priest. That is why he is tough and smooth, principled and self-effacing, restless and content, successful and dissatisfied.

While We're on the Topic of Fairness . . .

Several months before meeting Koppel, I concluded six months intermittently spent at NBC's "Nightly News," which had agreed to let
me watch it watching the turbulent end of the Reagan regime, when
the Pope came here, when we went to Washington for the first
Reagan-Gorbachev summit, and when Reagan took more than a fall
on the contra aid vote in February 1988. During all this time, before
the Russians lost their external empire and the Evil Emperor became, for a time, The World's Darling, I had a desk beside then executive producer Bill Wheatley's (or when ousted by a production
assistant, a chair beside his). I was free to ask and did ask, "Why
did you do that?" whenever I wanted.

It was the "lineup," the daily, late-afternoon, closed-door meeting
of "Nightly News" writers, editors, and producers in which the executive producer gives the order of that night's stories, followed by
their length in seconds. Tom Brokaw was in a trailer at the makeshift
NBC studio at the Ellipse opposite the White House. A semiotic discussion was about to take place.

> *Wheatley* Tom, hot off that a series of voice-overs. Arias getting the
> Nobel Prize, fifteen. Wipe off that to West Bank violence,
> fifteen. Wipe off that to South Korea violence, fifteen.
> Then South African mutiny, fifteen, and a bump.
>
> *Brokaw* The nightly newsreel [his dry voice suggesting distaste].
>
> *Wheatley* It really is. [He reads a news bulletin:] "A contingent of
> South African black police mutinied against their white
> commander and fired on riot police sent to stop them."
>
> *Brokaw* I think West Bank violence, which is kind of generic vio-
> lence, is something we don't need. Like wallpaper.
>
> *Wheatley* [Referring Brokaw to a detail he didn't know:] You do
> have a death on the West Bank.
>
> *Brokaw* It happens once a month.

A Palestinian boy throws a rock. An Israeli shoots him. His mother
weeps. Real events, wet with blood and emotion. But not on television. What is large with life in the Mideast and isn't even known yet
as the *Intifada* can be an expected set of signs on the small screens
of America. That is what Brokaw is saying. And now he and Wheatley have to make a decision: to take these signs and make them tonight's news or leave them behind. Was this death simply more of
the same—moving wallpaper? Or was it a difference, the death that
burst through the paper? The newsman or -woman is always being
confronted with such "take it or leave it" moments—except when
events overwhelm, and these had not. (The Palestinian uprising

was, however, mere days away, and Wheatley, perhaps, was sensing it.) Nothing went on the air that Wheatley, for a time, and Brokaw, who is managing editor as well as anchor, didn't agree on. Each, while I did my time, had a veto and each, this day, was applying a different code to the event. Brokaw, that of information theory: information is only what's new—if it's not new it's not news. However, Wheatley was thinking rhetorically, was attracted by the relationship of the three—Korea, South Africa, the West Bank. The West Bank joins the newsreel of death, makes a contemporary metaphor of violence.

Is it a bulletin? On the night of the contra aid vote, February 3, 1988, ABC News reported from the lips of Blandon, Noriega's confidant, that if you weren't with Noriega you were his target for death. "This had been reported before. This didn't seem to me like a bulletin," says Wheatley. "Whereas our report reported not from Blandon but from our sources that the C.I.A. had been bankrolling Noriega." A dramatic death report is old and therefore not dramatic; the seemingly tamer fact is theater on the stage of the news.

Is it a bulletin? When "Gorby," as we all called him, gave his final, late-afternoon press conference, I think I was the only one watching. All of us had TV sets on our desks. The producer next to me was watching "The Buddy Holly Story." Why? Gorby was an hour into his "conference"—he hadn't said anything *we* didn't know. To make matters worse, he was making a speech—he had doubly broken the code of the conference.

Bulletin or not? It was shortly before 9 P.M. in April '88. The Democratic presidential polls were just about to close in New York. Wheatley was talking with Brokaw about updating the West Coast "feed," one of six transmissions the network makes to its affiliates on a typical night. They were discussing the question that Brokaw would ask John Chancellor during his commentary on the primary.

> *Wheatley*   Tom, just a thought. John is going to pretty much say
> what he said in the first show. He's going to add the business about so many New Yorkers being upset with [Mayor Ed] Koch. For the question, do you want to ask him—there's that statistic about Dukakis's . . .

Brokaw picked up on this mention of the fact that many Dukakis voters were saying they'd rather vote for Mario Cuomo. "Soft vote," Brokaw remarked, signaling that his on-camera question to Chancellor would focus on this aspect of the primary's apparent outcome.

> *Wheatley*   Then it will work.
> *Brokaw*   Right.

That would be the central message for NBC's wrap-up of the primary: A big—but qualified—victory for Dukakis; a rebuke to Koch, who in Chancellor's words, "savagely attacked" Jesse Jackson, the New York City winner. CBS that night let Koch speak on its news feed. NBC let the voters speak instead: "Pretty dirty," one voter told the cameras. "The mayor should go back to school to learn something about how we live together in this city," said another. Koch broke one of America's basic rules—we play fair. And if we don't, we pretend to. In America we mute racial difference. Indeed, we mute all difference, inasmuch as it involves the risk of conflict. In the age of excess, Koch provided a bulletin, all right. And more sensitive than CBS, NBC put its foot down.

Are we, the newscasters, being fair? This, too, is part of the rules of the news game. The pope would never dream of being fair—it would amount to giving the Devil his own five minutes. Preposterous! But in America, a Wheatley worries over the question of balance. It is 6:47 on the night of the contra vote; Congress hasn't voted yet, and our sources tell us the vote won't be until 8:45. We'll be off the air by then. Ed Rabel for Managua is on the screen, narrating as we look at one, two, half a dozen, more Sandinistas hobble on artificial limbs (Fig. 12.4).

> *Rabel* More than two thousand Sandinista soldiers have been maimed for life in the six-year-old civil war. They come into this center on the average of one a day to be fitted for artificial limbs.

"Strong," Wheatley had said to me earlier when we first saw it. A few seconds later in the spot, we watch a good-looking contra pull up his shirt and show off diagonal white stripes over a modest square patch (Fig. 12.5).

> *Rabel* This twenty-three-year-old contra rebel has been fighting for six years. He's been in at least a hundred fire fights with the Sandinistas—has been wounded three times. He vows to go on fighting even if Congress cuts off aid.

Later, I tell Wheatley I think I saw a binary system of wounds: the clean small wound of the contra (making me wonder whether he was a prop, a PR contra); the ghastly, unfakable sign of the absent limb, those pink prostheses telling me how they had lost their limbs. Contral land mines. The connotation: The contras ambush. By American standards they don't fight fair.

Wheatley is troubled by my analysis. "If you think that was selected that way to try to make the point, the Sandinistas are suffering more than contra soldiers, that is certainly not the case," he says. "To some extent it was the pictures we had. On another day it might have been that the contras looked that way and Sandinistas looked like the contras." The newsman giving the contra his share of suffering.

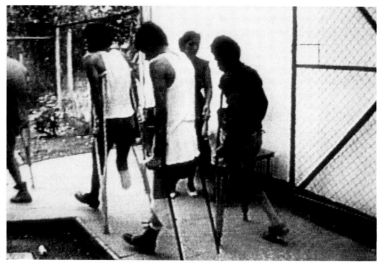

12.4

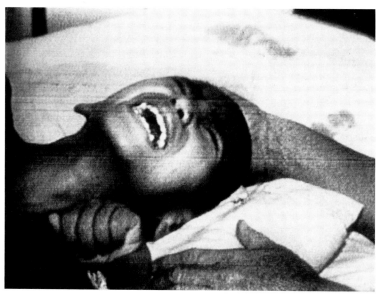

12.5

But it wasn't "another day," it was the eve of the contra aid vote. And even if Congress were evading the nightly news, or the next day's newspapers (the vote was finally taken at 10:45); even if Congress sought to decide but decide *quietly,* the code of news coverage required an epiphany. That night's imbalance of wounds was, in my judgment, part of the epiphany. Also the image you see, a Nicaraguan infant whose head is being caressed. The Rabel voice-over is ending—the child raises its head into the hand. It wails softly, the voice rising. "The tape was running out and you freeze it so you don't go to black," said Wheatley. Freeze and cut to Brokaw, who abruptly lowers his entire head. He makes of the head a punctuation mark. Unmistakably, and with the aid of chance, this has been a symbol. The child is little as Nicaragua is little—and Americans feel guilty destroying the small. The *New York Times,* four days later: "The difficulty in coming to terms with Central America is aggravated by a deserved sense of guilt. This is a region where the United States has acted inexcusably in the recent past and Americans know it." Suppose the image had been that of an adult, already defined as a Nicaraguan. Identification would have been minimal. But that child is a universal child. It is a helpless infant hurt in a hospital before it is a Nicaraguan.

Immediately, incongruously after the framed shot of the crying Nicaraguan child, came an image of weeping Mary Beth Whitehead. The voice-over from Brokaw:

> Also coming up here tonight . . . Cassandra Clayton on Baby M. Her surrogate mother, Mary Beth Whitehead, today lost the custody battle.

Mary Beth's outpouring had found its appropriate place. The tiny wail of the Nicaraguan infant had been almost too much for comfort-conscious viewers. (And besides, Nicaragua is too difficult for me to understand, thinks the average viewer.) So we shift from the little—but symbolically charged—wail to a nice, down-to-earth wail. Americans easily understand mothers, troubles with children, and romantic and other tragedies. So now we watch the "weeping and wailing by Mary Beth Whitehead," as someone had called the footage. The networks present their themes not surreptitiously but in little flashes. From Nicaragua, an outburst of universal pain and then an alternance, with Mary Beth, of comprenhensible individual pain.

Talking later about the footage of the Nicaraguan child, Wheatley told me: "I'm sure that when they put the piece together, they decided that would make an appropriate closing shot. It wasn't happenstance that that shot was the closing shot." But our conversation left something unresolved for him. "In making judgments about our fairness, our impartiality, our perspective, particularly on major issues, you have to make them over a period of time." In short, am I being fair about NBC fairness? By analyzing why that closing shot was "appropriate," we come to a subtler understanding of network fairness. That shot was appropriate now not because the networks wanted to stress to us, the viewing public, the horrors of the contra war, but because we in America had already reached a consensus that we no longer wanted to support that horror. It was "fair" because it accorded with the consensus view.

"We who write or take pictures or who broadcast things do have influence, but we do not have power," *New York Times* military correspondent Richard Halloran said several years ago at a Dartmouth colloquium on the media. "We cannot order the United States to go to war but the people we talk to, and write about, can." Another speaker, *The New Republic*'s Morton Kondracke, described the relationship between media and public this way:

> The press does not set the national agenda, it helps set it. It is, after all, one of the elite institutions of the society. The people who run the media tend to be friends with and share the values of and have gone to school with the major influential figures in the society. . . . When elite opinion in the United States changes on an issue, you will see it amplified by the media.

By amplifying the voices of business, government, academia—the news organizations hear and help shape what is called the mood of America. American mood wasn't for this war. This, in my opinion, is why NBC chose to illuminate a minor happening that day when anti-contra demonstrators in the public galleries interrupted the debate. The image showed men spread-eagled against a wall. The image is there to signify that common Americans are against the contras.

"I don't believe that social or political change can originate with journalism." NBC News senior commentator John Chancellor told me. "All that journalism, at least in my lifetime, has been able to do is to amplify social change and to accelerate it." He calls attention to Civil War days when there were newspapers and some magazines but hardly any other kind of media and certainly no electronic, no quick communication. The War was obviously replete with happenings—blacks running away to fight for the Union, etc.—having very little to do with any sort of media influence. A Civil War NBC or CNN would have facilitated, have swelled the defection.

Said Chancellor: "In the late 50s and early 60s we saw great social change in the U.S. because of desegregation of schools and other institutions. I covered a lot of that and it's my belief that what we put on TV, on the radio and the wire services made that whole movement proceed at a faster pace. The pictures of young blacks marching or trying to desegregate lunch counters in the south prompted other young blacks in other towns to do the same thing. Of course the politicians on the wrong side of change tend to hate this because they find that at some point the media begin to move more or less in the same direction as mass opinion."

Whereupon that opinion seems to take on the force of nature. When Walter Cronkite uttered his famous doubt about the Vietnam War, it became nationally memorable, attracting more and more news organizations to the negative aspects of the war and to the demonstrations against it at home. Effectively, the government could no longer wage the war. "But understand that news organizations themselves did not reach any kind of community or collegial judgment on the war's morality or lack of it," said Chancellor. "That came from young people who were going to be drafted and killed in the war and from others who thought war was wrong."

But even when the news-gathering institutions lock onto social change, they do so more on a reflexive than cognitive basis, and here perhaps is a novel way of understanding news gathering. "Some people think that news people operate on a kind of a neural network," said Chancellor—"that there's a brain and that instructions go out from a central headquarters. This is one of the dangers in the easy tossing around of 'Well, the media will do that or 'The media are . . .' as though we were all on some sort of bionic wavelength of some kind. To understand journalism in its deadline mode, you have to compare it to basic elemental things like fire, water, flood, earth, air."

And at first I do not understand when he starts telling me a story . . . "A forest fire burns all on its own because of reasons of oxygen, of combustible material—there is no neural network directing the flames. They go where the oxygen and combustible materials are, they do not move because somebody says, 'Let the flames all go north today.' The press on a big story is much more like a forest fire than you might have thought."

In fact, upon hearing a few days later a little lecture of the postmodern philosopher, Jean-François Lyotard, I realize that both the commentator and the philosopher are sketching a possible organization of the future, the very one perhaps capable of solving complex and intermeshed problems like massive immigrational flows, regional wars, and environmental damage control. It is as if the world were too complex for any other than complex forms of organizing energy. The hero of such an organization will not be the human subject, the ego, but energy itself, obeying the blind rules of necessity yet leaving a space for chance itself to play a part. To speak of energy says only that there is strength, energy knows nothing of differential systems.

Chancellor: "I don't know where Ed [Rabel] was on the day you saw that child. Since he's a reporter out in the field, you could think that he probably would have been in the field. I did this for a long time and sent in narrations and pictures knowing that these pictures would be made into television news stories by people I maybe hadn't even met. And then you'd come home and there'd be a tape or in the old days a kinescope of the program, and you'd sit and watch your work and say, 'Gee, that's wonderful,' and half of it was the strong visual images that were put together by a good editor who probably didn't read anything more complicated than the New York *Daily News* on his way home on the subway."

13

Dapper
Death

I don't think John Gotti's dissatisfied. He's quintessentially American, he's obscenely successful, and in this culture we worship the obscene, the thing so big you don't even know what it is any more. Here's how big John is.

At 2:15 P.M. on Friday, February 9, 1990, right on time for the weekend, the jury in the Manhattan assault trial of Gotti found the alleged chief of the Gambinos not guilty of ordering the shooting of John O'Connor, a union leader who had trashed a Gambino restaurant refusing to pay him homage. "Gotti doesn't pay homage to anybody," prosecutor Michael Cherkasky said. "It was a classic show of retribution and demonstration of power in a very public way, the head of the union walking into his building on Fifty-first street, shot four times in the back." Cherkasky's chief witness was the shooter, Jimmy McElroy, who told the court that he had broken the Ten Commandments, every one of them, many times. "Gotti's using people who are mad dog killers, who chop up bodies," Cherkasky said in post mortem of himself. "So we have people who are liers, who are cheaters, who are killers on the stand testifying against John Gotti." And for the defense: John O'Connor. "As I said in my summation: 'After you've been shot, having broken up a Gambino location, imagine what happens if you had testified against him?' Our problem was, we had a victim, John O'Connor, who is among the denizens of the deep. We had the evidence but we didn't have an emotional appeal." And so the two-time offender (manslaughter, hijacking), who could have drawn life had Cherkasky won, remains a salesman for something called Arc Plumbing, drawing a salary in the 60 thousands, and also, according to law enforcement, the boss of the largest crime family in the country, some 300 wise guys, good fellows, good guys, button men, made guys—sworn members of the family—and 1,000 to 1,500 associated members. "They involve themselves in pornography or narcotics or the traditional gambling, loansharking, labor racketeering. Basically, they're a supermarket of illegal activities," Cherkasky said, low-balling their annual gross as a meager $100–$150 million (others with less venom have estimated as much as $500 million). "I think he is a second-rate punk who by outrageous conning of the news media is called a dapper don," Cherkasky says. But Edward McDonald, former head of the Justice Department's organized crime task force, disagrees: "Sal Palissi—I put him in the witness protection program—Palissi and a lot of people have said the same thing about Gotti. If he had an education, he could be chairman of General Motors. He is an extraordinarily charming guy."

A Rug Rethink: Daily during the trial, Gotti's barber reportedly went to the modest house in Howard Beach for a primp and a brush, each bluish-gray streak being brushed back and up to make the entire head of hair looked capped. "What's the right word that would describe his appearance? Finesse?" Vito Politierri told CBS anchor Connie Chung after the trial. "He's a great guy, so I'm honored that he picked me and he likes me to do his hair." To spray it, too. Gotti's so arranged, he's untouchable. You don't want to muss this perfect do. Roberto Duran, before the *no mas* that humanized him, gave himself the aura of a statue, promoting his *manos de piedra,* his hands of stone. Compliments to Duran, John Gotti's rug looks terrific—*pelo de piedra,* hair of stone. Fifty-one years old, he could still butt your face with it, show you the sheer joy of being young again, on Mulberry Street. In 1973 when he was 33, he dragged one James McBratney out of a Staten Island bar—McBratney was supposed to have kidnapped a Gambino associate—and shot him in the head. Dead. Manslaughter. "He's a legitimate tough guy," says Lieutenant Remo Franceschini, commanding officer of the Queens D.A.'s Squad, who claims that he and Gotti "respect each other. Gotti was the type of guy that could take charge while he was in prison, and evidently that was observed by the upper echelon of the mob, and that's why he got his position as *capo* at a relatively young age," four years later, when he left state prison. Neil Dellacroce, underboss at the time, a huge man, physically intimidating, took a liking to the young John—"and Gotti tried to emulate him," Franceschini remembers. "This is a world where the nicknames frequently are important," Cherkasky reminds me. "Sammy 'the Bull' Gravano, 'Big Paulie' Castellano"—Gambino boss before Gotti, executed December 1985, allegedly on order of Gotti. The prosecutor and the lieutenant are evoking a world of such crude power that "your ability to knock someone out

13.1

cold," says Cherkasky, "to take him out with a single punch is terribly important, and your ability to stand up and be a man in face of attack by the police, incarceration, and your willingness to use a gun and to use violence to get what you want at the drop of a hat when commanded—these are the benchmarks of progress in the association." John Gotti comes from the blue-collar wing of the Gambinos, as Big Paulie, literally his predecessor, emerged from the white collar. The Gotti side did the truck boosts, the robberies, the murders, and now that bunch is calling the shots. "In New York State we're required to give the names of the jurors to the defense," Cherkasky told me. "So every one of those jurors knew that John

Gotti had their name. If you have family or if you're looking at your life, are you going to say: 'If I convict, God, I'm walking out there and looking over my shoulder for the rest of my life?'" By the hair atop that sturdy body, John Boy (his nickname) is writing himself bigger than life. Making myth of himself. Which? That of the human become statue, looming in stature. Neck extended, head erect, eyes like beacons, he shows himself to jury and press like a temple god. South of Rome somewhere.

Exchanging glances across the crowded room, his brows arched, widening his intelligent eyes, Gotti's gaze as always is thoughtful, sensitive. Shrugging here, brow furrowed, lips about to open, he is making of his face a surface concealing nothing, all the while pointing to the vestimentary surface. John Gotti wants you to know that what you see is what you get, like skin cancer. "Giv'im some money, Pete . . . Pete, some money," Gotti croaked as a panhandler staggered up to him while leaving court one day. "Why don't they fight crack dealers and people that are hurting the people. This poor guy hasn't hurt anyone," says barber Politierri, expressing popular sentiment. Here is a good man whose intention is as limpid as ours: to get unjust government off his back, as if he like us were victim of just and yet another IRS audit. "The government zeros in on people and if they want you they will get you," Bruce Cutler, his lawyer, says in slow, mellifluous cadence. "And they will ruin your life and they will send you to jail and they will destroy you." He thinks the public is fascinated with his client "because he stands up to the government; also because he's always come to the aid of the little man." His supporters stood before the courthouse bearing handlettered signs—FREE GOTTI NOW—as if he were a political prisoner. The FBI, which along with other law enforcement agencies has brought yet another case against him, in which, as of this publication, John languishes in jail, denied bail, is angry at the press, refusing all interviews. "Every paper carried that photo—the bedsheets strung up: 'GOOD LUCK, JOHN,'" FBI spokesman Joe Valiquette told me, dismayed that the press didn't take law enforcement's side. But what Valiquette may not realize is that the feds aren't the good guys anymore. Many of the post-Irangate, post–Gulf war, downwardly mobile working people are soft dissidents, and they don't care where John Gotti got his money. And if, as Frank Sinatra sings, he did it *his* way, all the better. He's their tribune, a symbol of dissidence against a government seemingly indifferent to their quiet cries against crack, homelessness, and racial diversity that shredded, they believe, the quality of their lives. "You have to remember that people who are engaged in organized crime don't commit crimes every waking moment," says McDonald, himself an actor, playing himself, in Scorsese's *Goodfellas*. "They have to think about committing crimes. They spend 99.9

*Dapper
Death*

13.2

percent of their time hanging around social clubs or restaurants or bars socializing with other organized crime figures.'' Because in the mob it's the same as any other walk of life: you have to network. ''You work your connections and you work your contacts to the best that you can,'' says former Gotti intimate Palissi, somewhere on the West Coast after testifying against his friend. ''He deals with dum-dums, idiots, and do-dos and they are drawn, they are attracted, they have an affinity for John Gotti because he is everything they can't be.'' A lot of wise guys earn a lot of money; a lot are intimidating and violent. But the leaders are leaders because they add to that, personality; they get ahead because they are popular. ''They can be charming, witty, they're raconteurs,'' said McDonald, ''because they spend all their time sitting around schmoozing—they don't work.'' And there we are near the heart of John Gotti's appeal. He earns his money the new-fangled way, he doesn't work for it—the dream of Leona's little people. ''We're taken up by him, we're fascinated by the high life, the fast life, the quick money, the easy way, the best route,'' school teacher and trial foreman John Golen told CBS after Gotti's acquittal in February. Golen's sworn obligation was to come to a conclusion based only on the evidence, not to read the mythic meaning of a luminary who never put himself into evidence by taking the stand in his own defense.

Gotti is a child of the mid-80s, when men became peacocks again, began lavishing attention on their appearance. His suits are custom-made by local tailors in Little Italy, each $1,200 to $1,800. The wide lapels italicize his chest. The peak lapels sprout like wings, pointing to his shoulders. Here is the inverted pyramid, the uplifted shoulder—recalling the epaulette of the soldier—made famous by Armani. ''The jacket shot out from the shoulder,'' Armani told me not long ago, critiquing his own *griffe,* his signature shape. ''That's not something that goes with man. We became too hard.''

No such thing as too hard for wise guys. Listen to this capo in praise of an elder statesman on a D.A.'s bug: ''The guy's 80 years old—he can still put a girl on her back!'' Furious, Cherkasky says: ''Gotti's a throwback, a troglodyte.'' But McDonald, better accounting for the boss's media success, calls him ''an attractive man—he's a handsome guy, he grooms himself very well. He has an attractive smile, a charismatic manner, something some people find formidable.'' A mere six years ago, the media hadn't heard of John Gotti. Then, on December 16, 1985, not even allowed a last supper, Big Paulie took a bullet in front of Spark's Steak House in midtown Manhattan at rush hour. ''The mob didn't feel that Paul shared equitably,'' said Cherkasky. ''John came in and it was a new regime.'' The audacity of the execution brought the new don instantly to our attention. Within a few months he was in federal court in Brooklyn, defending himself against racketeering charges prosecuted by Diane Giacalone, an assistant U.S. attorney, then bringing her first major organized-crime case. "We were doing Abscam, we had neglected organized crime, she jumped into the vacuum," said McDonald. "She was an idiot. The indictment was so broadly drawn it was going to have profound consequences regarding double jeopardy. Now the Justice Department wouldn't consider going back before '86 because of that." To boot, there was insufficient evidence, he told me. "Here this guy is, now available day in and day out walking into court. He became a media monster." In March 1987 Gotti was acquitted on all counts. "He feeds on acquittals," McDonald said. Unwittingly, Diane Giacalone had done her part to inflate him to mythical proportions.

John Gotti wants the armor, the jacket so close to the chest you think that massive thorax will crack through the armor, but it doesn't crack. And thus he presents an oddly unpostmodern sight. For no longer is a paunch or a barrel chest acceptable in a man as a sign of *ventripotence* (belly/chest power). But John Gotti sits a lot. He's out of the Howard Beach house by early afternoon, proceeding to various clubs in Brooklyn, Queens, or Manhattan where he holds court. By 5:30 he's at corporate headquarters, the Ravenite Social Club at 247 Mulberry Street, schmoozing for another four hours. Then it's off to dinner at one of the finer restaurants in Little Italy; also uptown, midtown, up and down Manhattan. "He has very very big meals with his associates," says Cherkasky. In Giacalone's trial, when he was in jail, he managed to persuade the judge to let him have his lunches catered in. "All afternoon you'd have the smells of tripe, calimari, and red sauce in the courtroom," Giacalone told me. "The *Daily News* called me ugly, very thin. We were losing weight, they found it." In Cherkasky's trial, a columnist found it surprising that the prosecutor, of "slight physique," would dare to point his "bony finger" at Gotti. In the Age of Schwarzenegger, Gotti's got bulk and his prosecutors are, well, nerds to the press. Says Cherkasky: "He's smart, he plays games with the press. We always turn over the tapes to the defense. Well, the defense leaks them to the reporters, who're going to portray them a certain way. They're talking to him, they're laughing and chatting and want to have lunch with the guy. They would never associate with another criminal convicted of murder." But after years of Mustache Petes secluded in Long Island estates, John Gotti's the Gorbachev of the mob, big and buoyant. Radiating gloss and good humor, he's Hyper Man in the hyperreality of America. The press couldn't care less about the deeds he's done, the sights he's seen, the shouts he's heard. He's a wonderful special effect, he's a meal ticket. He's not just the father of the Gambinos, he's the father of *cosa nostra,* too.

And then, after the crunchy woven ties, after the retro, deco, and the geo came the flowered ties, hot c. 1989. He is pretty nearly cutting edge, trying too hard, and that is vulgar. The tie is the most individualistic utterance in the language of men's fashion. The tie is the site from which the wearer sings his individuality. And as flowers have been considered effeminate, too decorative for men and thus the subject matter of an interdiction, it is a defiant gesture to bear flowers, a willful return of the repressed that says: "I have so much surplus masculinity, I can afford, as others cannot, to appropriate the most brilliant colors in nature, the sufficient sign of femininity." During the O'Connor trial, Gotti had his arm around WCBS-TV reporter Barbara Nevins. At the end of her *Vanity Fair* profile on Gotti, Marie Brenner is sitting, waiting with his capos for him to join the table for dinner. Women are magnetized to him. And men respect him. John Gotti's like a gunslinger with a reputation. 95 percent of the time his image suffices to command fear. But occasionally the testosterone has to be used. And that's why he's supposed to have ordered the *public* shooting of O'Connor. "Voices are revealing," a source close to the Giacalone prosecution told me. "His is deep, raspy, violent. He's like a silent movie actor—he understands that he mustn't speak in court." After his recent victory, a reporter asked in front of the Ravenite: "Are you happy?" *"We're Happy If You're Happy,"* the doorkeeper answered in a primeval voice, as if unable to take a full breath. From inside: "We're All Happy." Hoarse monster voices. *"The Whole City Should Be Happy,"* repressing ferocity, just as the source said.

There are three ways to wear a pocket hanky (oops, "square" if you want to be in fashion). You can square it off and show a quarter-inch to complement the cuff. Or you can soften it, make a little puff come out of the pocket. The third, the histrionic, way is John Gotti's: make the cutting edge show. It's a shark fin he shows, made of the very flowers of the tie. "A jury isn't supposed to be focused on the demeanor of a man who doesn't testify," says the source in the Giacalone trial, still nursing hurt over the outcome. "But there was a feeling in the courtroom, a lot of things happening besides the words of the witnesses. I remember just the way he moved through space." Skin, muscle, bone, nerves like a single silent instrument. McDonald remembers the subsequent Cherkasky trial: "Gotti packed the courtroom with guys with gold chains and sunglasses." The ancient orators used a trope called *antiphrasis:* by saying X, you could say its opposite. John Gotti isn't hiding his power. The very fastidiousness of the dress against that sternum of stone lets the violence shine through. Dapper death. "His concern was the jury," says the Giacalone source. "He was communicating to those close to the jurors. They would talk to the jurors in a favorable way even though the judge had instructed the jurors not to talk. And I've just undermined a very important assumption: a jury's not supposed to recognize symbolic conduct that is not evidentiary. That because they were fearful a jury did not fulfill its sworn obligation, that they violated an oath . . ." he said, trailing off in bitterness. "It's guttural taste, the clothes he wears," says Cherkasky, whose two good suits ($500 each, on sale) are from Paul Stuart. Yes, John Gotti may have made a sartorial mistake. A stylist would make tie and hanky identical in order to give a fashion shoot impact, but a customer isn't supposed to go to Saks or Paul Stuart and buy the very thing displayed in *GQ*. That's a Platonic ideal. Gotti, in the rush to invent himself down to the last finicky detail, got it too literal. He bought the fashion spread. So what. Guttural or no guttural, it worked. He saved himself by inventing a unique system of sleek signs.

The quintessential New York Exec, concerned that in public his double-breasted jacket never be flapping. "The first thing that struck me about Mr. Gotti was his self-assurance," trial foreman Golen remembered. "He seemed very at ease with himself, almost to the point of feeling that he had trust in the jury, that he did not see it as an enemy of his. An extremely manicured look to him. Very stylishly dressed and ready to have people decide his future." One is tempted at first to admonish the schoolteacher: It's a costume, an imposture (and besides, it's a violation of oath to be thinking this way). Indeed, donning the uniform made Gotti uncomfortable at his trials. "His jackets were so tight he was always unbuttoning and then buttoning first the inside, then the outside button," the Giacalone source told me. "It was a production." Instead of deciphering this production of signs, Golen seems to be responding to its dynamics. But his salute to the boss is perhaps imposture also—I wasn't fearful—a way of acquitting and feeling comfortable about broken oaths. "The goods were damaged in shipment," Golen said of Cherkasky's surveillance tapes. "Damaged goods. Can't sell 'em to anybody. Better take them home," he said, in full contempt of the D.A. "Every day the defense was talking to the press," Cherkasky recalls, "putting out an image of sweet John Gotti, never involved with drugs, faithful to his wife, being picked upon by the big bad government. They weren't doing it for that trial because our jury was sequestered. They were doing it for the next trial." Gotti has marketed himself to New York City as a Runyonesque rogue—with a less comic side showing to his jurors. The FBI doesn't know the good guys don't exist anymore. The press needs its Gotti playing De Niro playing Capone for the 90s. America needs its icon of dissidence.

As of this writing, Gotti is on trial again—racketeering and murder—in Brooklyn federal court. "He's become the Holy Grail," says novelist Stephen King. "The prosecutors are going to get him, they're going to get him, nothing else matters. 'We have to have John Gotti!' It won't matter that the streets are flooded with crack. And it won't matter that AIDS is rampant in this country. And it won't matter that organized crime has taken over different aspects of American life from insurance to the rental car. 'We've got to have John Gotti because he's thumbed his nose at us.' I think it's because he's too good-looking."

"Do you think he'll get off?" I ask.

"Not this time. Not this time. And if they don't get him this time, they'll get him next time."

14 A Tourist Guide to a Nightmare

And here are a few it doesn't need, the refuse of the system. These are headlines from another country, an underground socio-economic nation we read about in our morning papers, visit only as transit tourists, and suffer in our nightmares.

The beggars for dope, the Bellevue killer, the tight-lipped, lily-livered Bernhard Goetz, Cardinal O'Connor waiting for a phone call of surrender from the subway stalker, the nasty, brutish, and short trips we take in the wintry subway—they have brought to life and death the hallucinations lurking in the wrinkles of our mind when we think of the dirty, lousily run, decrepit old New York subway sewers. I decided to take a trip into the nightmare of the subway system and determine where horror ended and reality began. In our nightmares, fantasy and reality are one.

This is one tourist's guide to this cavernous country, with its 700 miles of railroad tracks, its 460 cities and towns, its 3.5 million inhabitants (mostly in transit), its vistas, laws, customs, traditions, internal security, and foreign policy. This guide also includes interviews with government officials from both the subway's State Department and its Defense.

Crossing the Stygian without Beatrice

I walk down the subway steps, at the bottom of which a black man is waiting, a styrofoam cup in his hand. That is a fact. I walk down the decline of an enclosed gangplank, at the end of which a black with a poleax waits for the steer that I am. That is my nightmare. One day years ago, in Kansas City, walking in the meatpacking district, I looked up and saw a gangplank in the sky, its sides and top wood slats, along which cattle walked. The dark men, of course, had the duty of meeting them.

"I'm enclosed by people, I'm penned in," Jane King, twenty-four, told me when I asked her—on the platform, Lexington and Fifty-first Street, Friday-evening rush hour—why she feared the subway more than the street. A luminous blond, wearing candy-pink lipstick, this graphic designer, who clutched her white fur closed while talking, considers the derelicts to be hunters. "They hang out down here because they are catching the people coming in from New Jersey, Long Island, and Westchester."

The trains, the passengers, the bums press forward. They are like a drive, recalling Freud's metaphor of the drive. The drive has no day nor night, neither spring nor autumn—it is a constant force. Like the subway itself, artifice of neon above and filth below. On the subway you confront the fat, the glum, the ghetto-tonsured, the readers, the studiers, the unpretty, the unaerobicized, the foreign backpackers, the coughers, the huge but oddly misshapen, those who spread their legs too wide, the going-fast-but-going-nowhere youth—in short, the all-too-human without benefit of Bloomingdale's cosmetics. To the above-ground New Yorker who rushes about in a distinctly different way—from party to pumice-faced woman to shining car to *bon mot* and *bonne cuisine*—everything about this Third World in our guts wounds our esthetic, deflates our ambition, offends our sweet whiteness.

The subway is a jungle without pity, without law, we upper-dwellers think.

We are wrong.

But it's the idea I *had* of Subwayland, an idea where I mixed my daily need to travel, my knowledge of a certain code of behavior, and the nightmares that keep pusillanimous New Yorkers from the underground caverns.

Fear is an unfamiliar pattern. As soon as the pattern of the subway system became familiar, explicit to me, my fear and loathing abated. Once you visit the cities and meet the inhabitants, Subwayland becomes just another Paris, Beirut, or Bangkok.

As I spent more time in the subway system, I discovered how automatically we all fall into a different behavior pattern in unknown territory. We begin to observe codes that help us avoid misunderstanding and danger. If a man is seated on the stairway, we don't ask him to remove himself; we simply sidestep him. If we see a man trying to steal a token from a fare box or half-cocking the turnstile, we don't exclaim: "What the hell are you doing?" Once in the train, if we see a space next to a man whose legs are open like scissors, we don't try to squeeze in—we remain standing or move to another empty space. These are codes for beginners, codes we all observe, often unknowingly. In Subwayland we must respect the indigenous, accept their values and (to the tourist) strange customs. In the subway, the man with the open legs, the sleeping body on the bench, and the turnstile evader are the permanent residents.

If all you know about the subway is what you read in the morning papers while sipping your Jamaican Blue Mountain, you'll only see the subway as the land of tight-lipped, pistol-packing Bernie Goetz playing Dirty Harry—"Make my day!" as he shoots four black youths. Or the land of the man who recently, confronting closed doors, sighed with relief as he jumped onto the platform between cars and proceeded to peruse his newspaper just before the train turned brusquely, giving him a turn for the worse and carving him to death. Or the dark forest of the stalker with the moonsilver gun about to force you to expose yourself and kneel against a trainstopping chopping block.

These are the nightmares of the working—and low end of the—privileged class, a subway mythology that people hallucinate across the country from Topeka to Pasadena, across the ocean to Tokyo, and around the world to Dublin and Palermo. Not to mention another nightmare: that the undermen are spewing up out of the hole to confront us at greengrocers and ATMs with those styrofoam cups inside of which lurk, the more edgy among us think, tuberculosis bacilli or worse. The cup is a monster defying our promenade. It is a premonition that above and below can no longer be kept separate. Hell is here.

In the First Circle with the Panhandlers

In my Katharine Hamnett mac, I am sitting on the concrete steps at the Bloomingdale's subway entrance listening to a day in the life of William Sanchez, thirty-something, who came from Puerto Rico a couple of years ago in search of a job above the minimum wage. At first he was a maintenance man in a hotel on One-hundred-third Street and Third Avenue. After a few fights with competitors for his job, he had to leave, and since then he's been homeless. "I wasn't getting any help, so I said 'Let's see if I can make some money.' I've been out on the streets since then," Sanchez tells me, the passersby looking down at us with distaste. "I'm making plenty of money," he says. "On a good day I will make about $60. There's people over there"—he points up toward the surface—"that will make $50 or $60 a day working in the office. Bad days I'll probably make $30"— more than the minimum wage, he reminds me.

I was skeptical about the income of a panhandler and surprised at his cordial manner as he explained to me the ins and outs of the Bloomingdale's city station. As I was beginning to forget I was a foreigner in this strange land, losing my apprehension about the system after several days of interviews and traveling through the underground tunnels, a woman named Agnes Sweeney stopped, abruptly towering above me. She declared: "Outrageous! This is a disgrace! Cardinal O'Connor spending all that money on the president the other night—it makes me sick. You know who was paying for that? The Catholic Church," as she drops her tingling token offering in his cup—"It's only fifteen cents," she apologizes, "I just work, myself, for a small wage." At the River Club, "a club for millionaires. And then Reagan said there's no poverty in this country. What's the matter with these bastards?"

Her liberal nightmare brought me back to the surface.

"I go out, let's say twelve o'clock at afternoon," said Sanchez, conducting me back into the quotidianity of Subwayland. "I'll stay in the streets walking back and forth trying to make a little money, you know, panhandling, until one or two o'clock in the morning. I be going to sleep like twelve o'clock at night, sometimes at one o'clock. It depends how I do. Sometimes I do good. If I do good I just keep on going." The American work ethic—right down to trying not to go to bed too late.

Immediately I thought of my above-ground values. "Aren't you afraid that they will tear your blanket off or go through your pockets and steal your well-earned income, or someone come and kick you awake?" I asked, imagining myself living in his world.

"Oh no, no. I never had that problem at all. Never," he said. "My bag and my blanket and things like that, I take when I go down below to sleep. If you leave it there's a lot of people who are homeless who are going to take it."

Sanchez is half at work as we talk. He jiggles his coffee cup, the coins inside resounding.

Another question out of my nightmares of destitution came forward, and I asked: "And what about your biological urges?"

"What?"

"I mean, when you have to go, you know."

"Ohh. Usually I go to the Metropolitan Hospital, no, Mt. Sinai, they'll let you take a bath there, a shower. I clean up and come back. But sometimes when you really have to do it badly, you have to find a place real fast to do it 'cause you can't go to the Metropolitan Hospital holding that. You have to find a secret place to do it, downstairs where there's no trains working. You go all the way back somewhere in the tunnel where you just do it. There's a lot of secret places."

Sanchez has a friend who sleeps next to him whom I had previously met. I ask his friend's name. He doesn't know. "He got a strange name," Sanchez said. "I always forget about it. He's sleeping downstairs but I don't know where." In this country, names are not important. You don't have an address or a telephone number. You're just a face by which to be recognized and to bond with. You may not have a name, but there is cooperation here and friendship.

Among the twelve to fifteen men for whom Bloomingdale's station is home, Sanchez is allied with "a few guys that I used to be with a lot. I just stay here with them. We will help out each other, you know. Like a little family, you see."

And, as a family has a place to call its own, so the little subway families enjoy more or less secure territoriality. When asked if the homeless displace the homeless, Sanchez answered: "Sometimes when we not here, they'll come and lay down there. Then they'll try to say that this is their place, you know. Then we have to tell them: 'Hey, you better just get out o' the place 'cause that's our place and we been sleeping here for a couple 'a years and you can't come and take our place. They don't come up with no problems." His colleagues—"the fellows"—have had different experiences. "Sometimes [the newcomers] get a little uptight and they don't want to get out. And that's when it comes to a fightin' matter," said Sanchez.

When you have to leave your lair to bathe or beg, "the fellows" protect your sometimes not-so-meager property. Ray Colombo, a friend of Sanchez, opened his epaulet-shouldered plaid overcoat to try to show me the label ("100% Virgin Wool" is all we could find). "A customer leaving Bloomingdale's, carrying a big box, gave me this coat off his back."

In the Merchants' Circle

At the Astor Place station, redesigned in the postmodern vein by Milton Glaser, William Wheeler told me the penny loafers he had on were a perfect fit, a $10\frac{1}{2}$ E. Wheeler and his friend, Lincoln East, sell on the cheap, for a dollar or two, "nice stuff," says Wheeler, "especially stuff we find that people throw away, and it'll be in excellent condition"—watches, copiers, toys, pairs of pants, calculators, the nearly new refuse they find on the street of a city so rich its garbage provides the raw material for the entrepreneurial class among the estimated seventeen hundred homeless in the subways.

There is wealth even in scavenging the refuse of the city.

"Even though we ain't got nowhere to live or nothing like that, when we leave, this place is spotless," said Wheeler of his Astor Place showroom. "And every morning we get up a certain time— they come wake us up, right? And we leave"—to spare the sensibilities of the commuters. "You know what I'm saying? It's cold, they giving us a break. And then we come back later. This is our home."

It is a singular town, one Wheeler starts to sell me as if I were a possible investor. "We got some nice people that come down. They say, 'You don't seem to be spending so much energy but here's anyhow a dollar or two for something to eat.' That's the one thing about the Village—everybody helps each other." Wheeler tried to live in other towns but they were harder than the Village. "I love it down here better than any place in the world," he added, "because down here there's no races, no prejudice thing. If I recommend any place in the world to live it's down here in the Village." Mayor Dinkins should hire Mr. Wheeler to sell the system to the world.

Uptown, in the tonier city of Bloomingdale's, William Sanchez doesn't like to eat in the neighborhood. "Over here the things are very expensive," he says. He likes to eat Chinese food, hamburgers, hot dogs, pizza. Late at night, he frequents a place on Third Avenue at Fifty-second Street where they sell fifty-cent hot dogs with mustard, onions, and sauerkraut. "They're beautiful," he tells me. Sometimes, when he has enough money, he goes to McDonald's— "Forget it! They're very expensive. That's why I say, when I have enough money I go and buy me at least a Big Mac. That's one of my specialties. That's when I have money, you know?" (If Mr. Sanchez made at least $30 a day, he would be earning $210 taxfree a week, since he works on weekends. That's $840 a month, $10,080 a year. Does he have a checking account at Citibank or does he send money back home?)

Most dwellers sleep late, often until midday, harrassed by the transients. "Sometimes when we're really sleepy, really sleepy sleepy"—said almost as a child would say it—"they'll come over and start banging their feet just to wake you." The residents live reduced lives—a hot dog with lots of sauerkraut while on the floor above, the shoppers eat *biftec garni* at the Blue Train in Bloomingdale's. Let us say the lives of the homeless are less metaphoric than those of the high consumers who, while dining at Bloomingdale's, think themselves Parisian.

In the Hot Circle of the Addicts

Kathy Weinberg, who lives in Broadway–Lafayette City, whose mother wrote a French textbook, whose husband abducted their eight-year-old son, who looks forty and says she is twenty, who has a $100-a-day heroin habit, who is on the prowl for money "twenty-four hours, seven days," who is driven in a way Sanchez is not, gently thanked me for two cups of hot chocolate I bought her. To sleep a lot, to sit a lot, to drink hot chocolate and feel the release of smack—you may not like this life but a life it is, stripped to basics. Twenty-four hours, seven days—it means you're on a track you can't leave, you'll never grow, you are doomed to repetition. And since the American dream is to succeed and not only survive—as the Citibank slogan tells us—these permanent residents I met are not American, for they only survive.

14.1

14.2

Figures 14.1, 14.2, 14.3 Isn't this your nightmare? My own?

14.3

Clinging to Paradiso

When I visited the Subway Parliament in Coney Island, in a goals-setting session at former P.S. 248, decorated with a nineteenth-century, wrought-iron subway station medallion, I sat in the back of the auditorium, hearing a politician, Transit Authority president David Gunn, addressing some six hundred middle managers, sketching his idea for a "removal process" directed at the homeless:

> *Gunn* Unfortunately, what's happened is that the type of laws that were used to control this kind of behavior, vagrancy laws and the like, have all been struck down in court. So you've got somebody on there [on the train] who smells not too bonnie.

Laughter from the managers, many of whom are wearing red-and-black pins received by the T.A. for its outstanding record in something or other.

> *Gunn* You cannot go up and say, because of that you're off the system. We're trying to do some research on who they are, where they're coming from, where they're going to, what their ridership patterns are. On Sunday you find them in one area and then during the week that same population goes somewhere else, and if you can sort of figure that out, you maybe can close the slam gates, so to speak, where they've gone out. You can then start setting up your defenses in a logical fashion so that when they try to come back in, you can stop them unless they pay the fare.

"We don't really pay tokens," Sanchez is telling me. "The clerks know us, they don't tell us nothing, we just go past. You just imagine how many times I walk through that gate—how many tokens I'd have to pay." Absurd! he's telling me. Unthinkable. The clerks know it, the homeless know it, but the middle managers laughing for Gunn pretend not to know it.

The T.A. developed an experimental program called Outreach in which teams were to go out at night, seeking to persuade the underworld homeless to leave the system and go to the universally despised shelters. The aim of the program wasn't hortatory, however; government urging a regime of health on its citizenry. The aim was intelligence.

For T.A. managers don't know who the homeless *are*, as if their lives in the shadows had precluded any knowledge of them. Michael Noonchester, marketing assistant vice president, opens his interview by telling me definitively that there are two types of homeless—"the economically homeless, who will accept shelter, and the emotionally homeless, who will not." I mention Kathy Weinberg. "That might be a third category," Noonchester says, "the drug people." All the categories you want, he's telling me. Help yourself to some more unrigor.

331

In the Commedia dell'Arte Circle

Back to the real.

That night, in my underworld time, I wanted to discover how the homeless pass their leisure time. Their entertainment is immediately evident as you approach some (but not all) of them—talk in the strong breath of spirits. Sometimes they have free performances to attend—the guitar player at Seventy-second Street, the soul singer at Fifty-ninth Street, the soul-searching Andean group playing the kena at Grand Central. I was given a special circus audition in a tunnel below Broadway and Lafayette where, in a corner, I saw half a dozen people, including a child, sitting, lost in the shadows.

Echoing coughs in the distance. A train whistles.

I approached the group and greeted them. "I'm writing about you."

One of them approached me.

"Are you Truman Capote? Are you over eighteen? Are you Jewish?

"Yes." Warily.

"You ashamed of your little willie?"

?!

"I got a trick for you."

And he pulled a pink balloon out.

"What's your name?" I confronted him.

"Balloonatic. Out of this one balloon I'm going to give you two balls, a penis, a vagina, and a stand for your coffee table. Are you ready?"

Artfully he shaped his balloon into a baton and orbs, twisting them. "You forgot to say ouch," he said as he bent the shapes around.

"I made a mistake," he said. "You know the mistake I made?"

"No."

"I made it as long as a black man's. I'm sorry, brother."

I was amused by the intercourse of balloons. Obviously he had once been a street performer in another country. I was intrigued to see how everyday life and good cheer flowed in a country with such meager resources. The homeless were so agreeable precisely because they are ignored, on the way to being invisible, and want to see themselves in other people's reactions. The subway as a dirty and dangerous country is more nightmare than actuality. There isn't much to steal: no jewels, minks, or PCs to heist. There's not a lot of property, not many goodies available to tempt you. Only bodies and personalities. The most valuable thing you bring to the subway is your body, a body that can be shoved, squeezed, rubbed against, made to cower in its seat, change cars in a hurry at the sight of youthful storm troopers; that can be offended, humiliated, thrown onto the tracks, or raped—most of this happening in our imagination.

There are two basic archetypes of fear, subway syndromes. The Bernhard Goetz syndrome—a male nightmare. This complex, which often takes the form of an obsession, sees in every inhabitant an enemy to castrate you, deprive you of your manhood, and turn you into a whining wimp. It's not so much the five dollars he might demand of you at the point of a begging threat. It's the impotence that pervades the male mind in such a confrontation. Above, your gender role is accepted without question. Underground, you feel threatened, vulnerable. In the psychotic stage of this complex, you see yourself as a Charles Bronson vigilante.

The other archetype is the Rape of Sabina syndrome. This female complex takes the form of undergoing sexual harrassment. The scale of fear goes from look to pinching and erection against you to violence—ending in rape. "You always get remarks," says Jane King. "They say, 'Ooh, baby, you look good. You have nice eyes, mama, ooh.' They try to talk—'Can I talk to you?' I try not to touch anybody if that's possible on the train. I don't look at anybody. I never have eye contact, and I always feel followed and pinned down by eyes."

With the Defense Department

The government of Subwayland, like most governments, deals with people as abstractions, as concepts to juggle around. The subway stalker became public news as a result of the police work of *Newsday*'s Jim Dwyer, who, by putting two and two rapes together, forced the Transit Police to admit the existence of the apparently first serial rapist in subway history.

From September 1988 to January 1989, a slightly built Hispanic male between five-two and five-four, 18 to 22 years old, brown eyes, dark hair, with a thin mustache, forced seven women out of trains and off platforms, into tunnels in the most forsaken corners of the subway system, where he robbed and raped them.

In one of the most publicized rapes, the attacker pulled the brake cord on an almost-empty M train and forcibly led his victim out of the car and into an abandoned area that had been carved out of the rock in the nineteenth century, the site of an experimental subway that had been outfitted with a charming waiting room for ladies, complete with grand piano and plush velvet sofas, now sunk in darkness, traveled by rats and only sparsely illuminated every forty feet with sixty-watt bulbs. "He forced her to walk across the tracks to an entranceway and up some stairs to a catwalk," said a police spokesman at the time. "Then he went downstairs to another catwalk. Then she was taken into a tunnel. She was bumping into the walls, causing injury to her face and her nose. She broke her eyeglasses."

"Finally, he halted in a spur track area used to reverse trains, behind a stopping block, out of sight," wrote Jim Dwyer. "Piece by piece"—Dwyer's narrativizing the event—"he stripped her clothing, hiding it on the ground. 'Kneel down,' he ordered. Announcing he needed to relieve himself, he urinated on her clothes. Then he instructed her to perform a sex act. At one point, she tried to pull away. 'If you do that again, I'll kill you,' said the attacker."

The subway rapist was only one more of the demons of the underground Hades. "There were four sexual attacks completed—it sounds like a football game," Al O'Leary, transit police spokesman, informed me, reading from a list of the victims. "We got a rape. We got a rape/sodomy/robbery. You got another rape/sodomy/robbery—I sound like a short-order cook: 'Give me two rape/ sodomies! On a platform to go!'—and a sodomy/robbery." I was sitting across from O'Leary and Captain Roland Rowland— honest—wearing a pistol in his ankle holster. We had been discussing the press and television coverage. I pointed out how events had been mythologized by the media.

"You're telling us we completely missed what the press was doing to us," said Rowland.

"You're not looking for a rapist, you're looking for a monster," I insisted. "The media, word of mouth, they've mythologized the rapist. He's the stalker, remember the Nightstalker movies? He's Jack the Ripper. New York is London, New York is Paris. It isn't *fin-de-siècle* twentieth-century, it's *fin-de-siècle* nineteenth. Our subway tunnels are sewers inhabited by *clochards*, rats, and dim lights. It's a tale told by Victor Hugo."

"Ohhh, Barry Civilo, Channel 4—rat-infested, filthy," said O'Leary, his professional cool broken temporarily, admitting reality was nourishing the subway mythology.

Precisely because they are the contemporary London *Times* or Victor *Les Misérables* Hugo, the media tell the ancient tale of the city as corrupt and its nether parts as the womb of evil. And in this city of New York, widely believed to be the most corrupt on earth, the media were spreading the signs of horror (and will, again and again in their never-ending poetics of urban despair). That is why, when *Newsday* broke the story Sunday, January 15, 1989, under the terse title "Subway Stalker," an image of an empty tunnel loomed large, darkness everywhere except at the end from which came a stark light. When New York's Channel 7 reported the rapes, the graphics showed a black hand, spider-taloned, with knives for fingers. It was the hand of Freddie in *Nightmare on Elm Street.*

"Why did you wait so long to admit seriality?" I asked.

"It didn't reach the point where there was a conscious decision where I as the press officer . . . it never got to the point where I was informed that we got a serial rapist [heh heh]," said Al O'Leary.

On the wall a grinning Mayor Koch shakes his hand ("To Al"). "There was not a conscious decision not to give this information out," O'Leary chuckled.

Expecting a rejection, I nevertheless requested a part in the pursuit of the rapist. I asked to spend a little time with one of the detectives trying to trap the stalker. "The chief of detectives told me," O'Leary grinned, "that a reporter would be in more danger today if he were in the vicinity of a transit police detective than any woman riding alone on the subway."

I froze, feeling myself threatened by the dictator's macho police force of a banana republic.

"You don't see the humor in that, do you?" O'Leary laughed.

I understood too well and held my discomfort—a reporter is to a detective as a woman is to a rapist, or so I felt. Disgusted with what I assume he thought was a wimp, Captain Rowland left the room without even an excuse to me or a glance in my direction.

That was my brief encounter with the Defense Department of Subwayland, which, like all governments, like business, like the public at large, treats the media as the scapegoat when the heat is on. "They're beatin' us over the head," Captain Rowland said of the media. But the media never uttered a peep while the rapist was notching his victim list.

Isn't it better if the publicity sends the stalker into hiding? I wanted to know of O'Leary. "It may chase him to another area. He may go above the ground. Who knows where he'll go? Our goal and our intention is not to displace this problem," he said.

"How does that make me feel, that they've known about it since fall?" Jane King said when I told her about the police attempt to black out news coverage. "I'm very angry slash upset. I feel very disrespected."

"He'd have gone into hiding?" I said, quoting the police.

"I don't care. Let us go into hiding, too, then."

The stonewalling reminded me not of what was happening underground, but of what had happened in the skies over Scotland, when another branch of government, the State Department, had failed to require Pan Am to inform the passengers of a terrorist threat to Flight 103.

"He's a very sick man who has a lot of anger," Diana Kaplan, a recommended psychologist, told me when I requested a profile of the subway stalker. I wanted to get an expert opinion as to whether the press coverage would encourage or discourage the rapist. I got the textbook gobbledygook that mainstream journalism uses to validate its stories and appear knowledgeable and fair.

"The sex impulse is expressed in aggression in a primitive way," Dr. Kaplan continued. "By urinating there is an anger towards the woman. For him, probably the vagina is something terrifying so it shows also homosexual impulses. There is probably a gender confusion, probably he is a polymorphous pervert. If he reads the paper and knows English, he will take the articles as a narcissistic gratification. He has a compulsion to rape so probably he can do it again—sure. He won't be satisfied with one."

She didn't help. Although many people confuse semiology with psychology, one thing is certain: semiology doesn't pretend to reveal inner motivations or foresee future behavior. There lies the difference. When last I gave myself to this chapter, the subway rapist was still at large, still a god in the subway mythology of New York City, haunting the news-fed nightmares of women riders.

The Budget Deficit of the Underworld

I also visited the government's Treasury Department, where the officials were considering market strategies to get new riders. The marketing department, only a few years old, didn't have a clear idea of who are and aren't its customers and why and why not "and what are the characteristics of segments we might want to go after," adds Carlos Diaz, development vice president. The department was in the process of bidding out a market segmentation study to determine its target, in an absurd attempt to introduce private marketing techniques to public service or disservice.

Patrick Fowler, director of marketing research, treats me to a Byzantine study about how many angels are riding the subway system. He tells me the department wants to get more of the Broadway theater crowd to travel on the subways. Then Michael Noonchester, assistant vice president, breaks in, telling me: "Ideally, off-peak is always going to be a target market." He gives the example of the Macy's Thanksgiving Day parade, during which the system gorges on Snoopy-loving, rubbernecking revelers. These gentlemen are dealing with the subway system as if it were Budweiser or Kellogg's cornflakes. Their only serious task should be to get the delinquent riders to cough up their tokens. There's even a plan, they tell me, to cause the new immigrants, who are doomed to travel the subway, to appreciate and enjoy the Big Apple's bloodstream, since supposedly they are unaware of the sinister mythology of the subway. Being new to the country, uneducated in Americana, they will take their logical place alongside the rest of the wretched to whom the system has ceded the subway. For that, in the best of American traditions, these marketers planned to accentuate the positive. "We're going to try to position ourselves as the heart of New York, more convenient transportation, good places they can go to by subway, and Broadway," said Fowler.

When I asked him and Noonchester about the rapist who might be damaging the targeting effort, Noonchester said: "I haven't even read the stories. I enjoyed my three-day weekend, you know [heh

heh]. I didn't open my papers," he said in an offhand Ronald Reagan fashion. "There's probably two or three other serial rapists going on in this city right now."

When I visited Subway Parliament, the aforementioned former P.S. 248, the representatives were discussing the budget deficit due to the turnstile delinquents and how to rid the system of the homeless. Since vagrancy and loitering are no longer crimes, the parliamentarians were trying to find a way to send the not-so-illegal aliens back to their country, no matter where.

"You said they smell bad," a black member of Parliament exclaimed, addressing the House speaker, T.A. president Gunn.

"I didn't say that," he answered, protecting himself against an innuendo of discrimination or racism. "I said you can't throw them off *because* they smell bad."

"I understand, I know, that's what I'm leading up to," said the member. "You said they smell bad and look bad—you can't throw 'em off. *It's got to be against* some kind of health code the way some of these people look."

Laughter on both sides of the aisle.

You've got to believe me. The New York subway system is a country just like ours.

That's the problem. It *is* ours. Every time we come across a homeless one, it's an accusing finger, a counter-myth, an invitation to question a fundamental myth, that of progress. The "idea" of progress is, more properly, a narrative, that of the Unseen Hand, analogous in this respect to the role played by master-fantasies in the Freudian Unconscious. Our politically correct behavior is a symptom, a trace, an outline of a story in which the American collectivity interrogates its oppressions and triumphs over them, its hope of an amicable multiracial, multiethnic, bi- or multi-erotic society realized. But if the unseen hand *isn't* . . . that is why homelessness is so threatening. (And Jean Baudrillard who, in these pages, says you barely see the homeless, may be, very simply, utterly wrong.) On crutches, with a cane, a shopping bag, enclosed in a blanket, hobbling, running to keep pace with you, inside your ATM sanctuary, the Homeless One invites you to question your subtext of progress. One or two, okay. But two on a block? Thousands? *Black?*—the word never used in the press to refer to them. It's the legacy of slavery that is subverting our master-myth, our organizing principle of society. In chapter 17, on Russia and the ex-Soviet Union, we sense what happens when the content evanesces from a master-myth. What about ours? What effect is created when a middle class shrinks, when income is reduced, when the society produces insane people on the streets?

Do believe me. The New York subway system is a country just like yours.

15 Horror: the Last Stand of Hell

And horror is another one.

"Last night before I went to sleep, I had an idea for a story and I think it's a good one," Stephen King said to me as we sat sipping iceless ginger ale in his memorabilia-filled office in Bangor, Maine. As the plot unfolded, my eye moved from King dressed in work shirt, jeans, and sneaks to the *Creep Show, Pet Sematary,* and *Skeleton Crew* movie posters on the wall.

"The story begins with an airline pilot who gets home from a trans-Atlantic flight," King continued, "let's say from Japan to Los Angeles. He goes back to his apartment—there's a message on his answering machine, his ex-brother-in-law telling him his ex-wife has been killed in a car crash, let's say, in Boston. Can he come right now? He calls his airline and gets a seat on the red eye to deadhead, to Boston. He's flying first class and he falls asleep for I don't know how long and somebody's shaking him. He wakes up and it's this woman and she's very frightened.

"'I see your white shirt and your black tie,' she says. 'I see your jacket with the epaulets on. For God's sake, please, can you fly this airplane?'

"He looks around and everybody in first class is gone. He gets up. The plane's flying along. He looks back in the main body of the airplane and there are three or four people there, but everybody else is gone. He goes to the cockpit. It's empty. Everybody except four other people have disappeared while he was asleep. Because he is a pilot he can fly the plane, and he lands at Boston. Everybody in Boston is gone. Everybody in America is gone. Everybody in the world is gone, apparently, except for these few people on the plane. The one common element is that when all the people disappeared,

339

these few were asleep. And now they hear these chewing noises from all over the city, as though something were chewing through the very fabric of reality towards them. And I know what this means and I know where the story goes.''

"Oh, that's the sealed jetliner, he's two chapters into it," Chuck Verrill, his editor, told me, laughing at the coincidence. It was an idea for a story that has now become the plot for his new novel. "What he's working on now occurs in a sealed airplane, that claustrophobic atmosphere where evil has either leaked into or out of a closed room." Verrill agrees with me, this is one of King's success formulas—"icky things infecting, invading, and wasting the whole landscape of America." The story sketch I had heard was an earlier version of his "about to become a bestseller" novel. "He's very excited about it," Verrill said. "Interestingly, of all who disappeared, their material belongings remain behind: watches, rings, wallets, purses, gold and silver fillings, metal pins that had been placed in mending limbs, wigs, toupees—which makes you wonder whether they've been transported to heaven or to hell."

Up in Maine, just below the desolate timber forests, Stephen King elaborates the dark side of our technologic infatuation. He is the figurehead of horror, a commodity that is taking over a serious portion of American book publishing, films, and the very fabric of the country's mythologic thinking.

Stephen King, after thirty-two books and six screenplays, is probably America's best-read novelist, although his work is often derided by belles-lettres critics. Singlehandedly, he keeps his publishers, Viking and New American Library, highly profitable houses; they have printed more than 85 million copies of his books.

King's office in Bangor is in the midst of a desolate, defunct Air Force barracks. When I walked inside, he was in his small sanctorum, earphones on his large head, writing something in longhand to the blast of U2's "Race Against Time." "I'll see you in there," he said and I lip-read—I could barely hear him—pointing to the secretary's larger office next door. Entering, in those casual clothes looking like his own farmer-in-the-dell character in the film *Creep Show,* he offers: "Want some ginger ale? Best vintage!" he tells me. "We have two hours; then my wife will jump from one foot to the other." He starts to boogie—his term for getting serious—and as he begins the two hours, I put my ginger ale on the Danish modern table on which are *US, Avon Fashions,* and other magazines supported above a beige wall-to-wall carpet next to the couch—black Indian geometric figures on orange background—on which we sit. A carpet, a couch, a coffee table very like the ones I had at Yale about twenty-five years ago. Big Stephen King, who likes rock to roar into his ears, is like a mega-student who still has the freshness of just being out of class, about to write a term paper.

From a bastard genre in traditional European literature, horror has gained a prominent place in American culture as we approach the end of the century. Beginning with the films of the 30s, which popularized European myths of the werewolf and the Frankenstein golem to broad audiences, and followed by a whole generation trained to devour comics like *Tales from the Crypt*, horror today has become a genre as important as, if not more important than, poetry. Just walk into a video shop and see the film categories: Drama, Romance, How To, Action/Adventure, Adult X, Adult R, Fine Arts (very small), and broadly represented, Horror, oozing out of the shelves, the titles often preceded by the awesome *The*.

Why does horror have such a claim upon the American imagination? In 1968, the European semiotician Tzvetan Todorov, in his book *The Fantastic*, described the social function of horror (and the fantastic in general) as "a pretext to describe things [horror writers] would never have dared mention in realistic terms." The genre "permits us to cross certain frontiers that are inaccessible so long as we have no recourse to it," he wrote, and he offered a horror list, categorized into themes of the self and themes of the other. Themes of the self were: psychosis, the collapse of the limit between matter and mind, the multiplication of personality, the confusion between the perceived and the imaginary, the destruction of limits central to the drug experience. Themes of the other were: incest, homosexuality, love for several persons at once, necrophilia, excessive sensuality. "It is as if we were reading a list of forbidden themes, established by some censor: each of these themes has been banned as a matter of fact, and may still be so in our own day." More than a mere pretext, horror is a struggle against censorship, Todorov thought. Sexual excess, for example, would more easily pass the censor if attributed to the Devil. "The function of the supernatural," he concluded, "is to exempt the text from the action of the law, and thereby to transgress that law."

Yet Todorov ended by believing that the genre had been rendered useless due to the social and sexual liberation of the 60s and before it, the modernity of which psychoanalysis was so large a part. He wrote:

A change has occurred in the human psyche, a change of which psychoanalysis is the sign; and this very change has revoked that social censorship which forbade dealing with certain themes. . . . Psychoanalysis has replaced (and thereby has made useless) the literature of the fantastic. There is no need today to resort to the Devil in order to speak of an excessive sexual desire, and none to resort to vampires in order to designate the attraction exerted by corpses: psychoanalysis, and the literature which is directly or indirectly inspired by it, deal with these matters in undisguised terms. The themes of fantastic literature have become, literally, the very themes of the psychological investigations of the last fifty years.

Todorov was wrong in his rationalistic arrogance. The human psyche doesn't change because of a new pseudoscience that is closer to fiction than to fact. (The very name, in German, of a great Freudian "discovery" could as well be the title of a horror book or flim, *Das Es, the id, the It.*) Neither did the 60s erase repression in society. Witness the return to romance and the increase in horror during the 80s.

Horror seems to have occupied the place that the nether world had in the past. A survey of recent surveys, reported in *The Economist,* found that the same 72 percent of Americans who believed in heaven in 1952 still do, whereas the proportion believing in hell had dropped from 58 to 53 percent. Protestant preachers, even Catholic preachers, have reduced the presence of hell and the Devil in their sermons. Only fundamentalists still preserve the concepts of brimstone and hell fire even among the televangelists, "cool" religion, finding hell irrelevant, carries the day now. Perhaps the best known of the Southern baptists, Jerry Falwell, never approaches the edge beyond which lies religious fright, ecstasy, possession. Hell would be unsavory to this CEO of preaching exuding reason, even tolerance. A major Texas-based evangelist, Kenneth Copeland, targeting the down-market of poor farmers, displaced workers, and country folk, waves his arms and, cackling gleefully, kicks a ghostly Satan in the pants in one segment. He proclaims: "I don't have any past! The blood of Jesus has eradicated it!" In a stroke of insight, redemption is equated with the obliteration of history. No sense of sin need burden his target market. During the offertory, an attractive blonde in a blue dress with red epaulets proffers euphoric hermeneutics. When the Bible prophesies "wealth" to the cheerful, she essays, the big book means rich in material things. This Christian soldier knows her product: religion, the American way—heaven on earth and that's all, folks! With utterly altered meaning, the expostulation attributed to William Lamb returns in our time: "Things have come to a *pretty* pass when religion is allowed to invade the sphere of private life."

And it's with old friend Pat Robertson that I find how pretty is media religion today. A Yalie in law and divinity, his Christianity never smacks of irrationalism or excess. When I had breakfast with him before his presidential run, he told me that he'd been a womanizer on three continents before his rebirth. Stumped on the third, I watched him broadly smile and tell me: "Why, Asia, doctor!" Utterly charming, this Ronald Reagan of televangelism looks you right in the eye on "The 700 Club," his show, intoning: "You are special, you are unique. God has a plan for you, a destiny of happiness and joy. Faith in Jesus Christ is the only way that you and I can know lasting peace. Sure, God doesn't mind giving us some of the toys of life along the way, but that's not the issue. He wants to be Number One." A little human acquisitiveness, that's okay, too.

After the theology lesson, the reverend prays, "Lord Jesus Christ, I'm a sinner and Lord, I have not lived my life for you. But Jesus, I know that you died to save me from sin, that you love me just like I am. So I turn away from selfishness and sin and toward living your way." He invites you to call him up. Right now. And if you do, you'll be able to say, as he says: "I've just prayed with Pat and now I've given my life to the Lord today." One call does it all (with apologies to the sex lines). Pat Robertson has graven the image of the good-natured, reassuring, strong yet tolerant Father of American fantasy. I hazard he's the only God many of us can imagine.

All of which leads one to believe more strongly that horror has taken the place of hell in the American psyche. American media and to some extent our personal behavior are an immense enterprise to simulate happiness, welfare, communication, human rapport. Why horror, then? Horror is the image of the danger of losing this material world that Americans so highly cherish. Recall the little story that begins this chapter. King told it very mildly, but I didn't ignore its aggression. As if he were a wrathful god, King hurled the jet passengers out of this world, all their *stuff*—unto their silver fillings—littering the plane's seats and aisles. Starting his yarn for me, the demiurge of horror was fabricating an anti-myth, as if to shout (and he loves to shout): "You've lived with so much shit, now see what it's like *with nothing!*" Horror films and fiction are thus the dark side, the other face, of America; not apple pie but the oozing monster, not the American dream but the American nightmare.

It is this nightside that blind-sided French critic Jean Baudrillard when, in Paris, I asked him to read America. It turns out that, with the aid of Stephen King, we can read Baudrillard reading America and better understand the renascence of our horror in the present. First, Baudrillard. He thinks America is a society that seeks to surmount "the division of the subject"—Parisian for the fracture of the self into ego and unconscious. Americans cherish an image of themselves given to them by advertising—happy, cool, easy. Ego without id. In Paris where it was "they . . . they," he told me that Americans don't seek to resolve, let alone live with, this contradiction but to reconcile themselves with the "happycooleasy" image of themselves; they do everything they can to identify with it. And in as much as the happyeasycool one (think of Camel's Mr. Penishead) wouldn't hurt a fly, the Americans have imaginarily effaced social division, disquietude, contradiction in general. "It's an attempt to put an end to conflict," he told his seminar of one as an opera singer practiced arpeggios on the other side of the cobblestoned rue Ste. Beuve. "And so in the United States, there is a kind of euphoria," he said. "I call that utopia, they've made a realized everyday utopia."

He thinks we're drunk on ads. He thinks their voices (as chipper as tour guides'), their music (as upbeat as a Sousa band's), their smiles and coyness *carry over*. When we do our wash, our dishes, deal with the kids, feed the dog, start the car, we whistle ad tunes while we work. Word phrases, too. And at least one famous American has a similar idea. Look for Stephen King to start his books with an America dawning "clear and bright and flawless: a postcard summer day with just enough breeze to make the bugs keep their distance," to take *The Tommyknockers* (1987) as an example. Roberta Anderson, a tough, young middle-aged recluse poet in Maine, having just discovered a buried flying saucer in chapter one, starts chapter two in this homey way:

> Anderson pottered around the house until almost ten o'clock, conscious of the growing pressure her mind was putting on her to dig it up, already.

New Yorkese, as in some Federal Express spot, has occupied her thoughtways.

> She could feel herself consciously pushing back against that urge (Orson Welles again—*We will dig up no body before its* . . . oh, shut up, Orson).

Oh, shut up, Roberta, who can't stop repeating tag lines—here, Gallo's.

> Her days of simply following the urge of the moment, a lifestyle that had once been catechized by the bald motto "If it feels good, do it," were over.

Every cliché virus that's out there, she's got. In the 60s, when it felt good, she got that one. In the 80s, when you forswore all that jazz, she did that.

> It had never worked well for her, that philosophy—

Oh, sure.

> —in fact, almost every bad thing that had happened to her had its roots in some impulsive action. She attached no moral stigma to people who did live their lives according to impulse; maybe her intuitions just hadn't been that good.

She's the beautiful American *sans* superego. You can carry over pot from the 60s—she'll never judge you. If she has a beer too many, she'll even mercy fuck you. A good heart, good times, good folks, as the spots say.

> She ate a big breakfast. . . .

Someday we'll do the semiotics of that. What do you digest with your Wheaties and wife's/husband's/kids'/dog's groggy chatter?

. . . added a scrambled egg to Peter's Gravy Train (Peter [the dog] ate with more appetite than usual, and Anderson put it down to the end of the rainy spell), and then did the washing-up.

If her dribbles would just stop [she's having a "leaking" period], everything would be fine. Forget it. . . .

The way we cut the other short, our impatience with what we call bullshit but is in fact discourse—

. . . we will stop no period before its time. Right, Orson? You're fucking-A.

You repeat dear Orson. You're encrusted with his clichés. Also America's ("fucking-A"). And all in good conscience. What a happy chatterbox, culture repeater, are you. This is what Stephen King, alongside Baudrillard, is saying.

And incongruous in the civility of the Ste. Beuve, a street named for the famous author, the man with the status of guru quietly lamented our postmodern paradiso: "It's an attempt to go farther and farther into a kind of pacification. I don't know," he paused and then regained vigor: "Historical divisions, psychological divisions, finally . . . *bon* . . . the problem of the subject with the famous mirror stage [a reference to Jacques Lacan]—if you want, the problem of identification, of projection—well, at bottom it's an attempt to resolve all that into a kind of happy indifference, which is not a *joie de vivre.*" Telling us "fucking-A" while feeding Peter his Gravy Train, Roberta/Everywoman would seem to flutter into her nest of indifference that Baudrillard calls euphoria. He doesn't even think it's proper to man. He doesn't conceptualize it as an emotion. Well, what is it, then? It's factitious, a product manufactured by our images, an effect of living, as supposedly we all do now, in a "semiosphere," a dense, suffocating atmosphere of signs triumphantly permeating all social, political, and imaginative life and constituting our desiring selves as such. Advertising—and film, which has become just like it, and ditto the art world, in short the entire culture of advertising—not only moves products but has become a constitutive element of the contemporary imagination.

When you no longer care about reality, Baudrillard said, "from that moment on, one is in a situation without passion, without depth. And thus one is simply happy, like a being under the influence, as if you had absorbed a sort of drug, eh? Which disconnects you from reality." (Which sounds like Costa-Gavras in the chapter you've read—I hope—on advertising.) "Thus at that moment, you float. That's our situation, superficial, floating, aleatory. But that's the source of a happy indifference. And America is a society which seeks the least difference, okay? The least difference, because every difference truly is the risk of a conflict of position"—

conflict being at odds with pacification. "It's a kind of regulation, a psychosocial regulation."

Words like these have made him a *casus belli,* polarizing the American cultural establishment. Suffice it to remark a devastating attack by critic Robert Hughes in the June 1, 1989 *New York Review of Books.* (I saw Baudrillard that very week in New York, prodding had he seen it? He feigned not to have.) "Here we all are in America," Hughes wrote, "260 million of us, passively caught in the webs of electronic maya, as incapable of discrimination as of skepticism. No one is smart or willing enough to see past the image haze of media. It's hard to say which is worse: Baudrillard's absolutism, his sophomoric nihilism, or his disdain for empirical sense."

Poor Jean—who's right, of course. You don't show your hand in America. Remember Koppel's Vanna Factor (p. 301)? You're an empty vessel. What befell Baudrillard is an operative version of what I endured when I let another Frenchman, Louis Marin, talk me into specifying my position vis-à-vis NBC. Americans seeking to efface conflict? Robert Hughes, general in the Thought Police, showed him a happy indifference or two:

> Baudrillard, who taught sociology at Nanterre from 1966 to 1987, is regarded, as the jacket copy puts it [Hughes is reviewing Baudrillard's *America*], as "France's leading philosopher of postmodernism." As such, he has the badge of a distinctive jargon. Jargon, native or imported, is always with us; and in America, both academe and the art world prefer the French kind, an impenetrable prophylactic against understanding. We are now surfeited with mini-Lacans and mock-Foucaults. To write straightforward prose, lucid and open to compre-hension, using common language, is to lose face. You do not make your mark unless you add something to the lake of jargon whose waters (bottled for export to the States) well up between Nanterre and the Sorbonne and to whose marshy verge the bleating flocks of poststruc-turalists go each night to drink.

Heady stuff.

A week to the day after I saw Baudrillard, I went to the Elysée Palace to interview Jacques Attali. He continued the anti-American line: "In terms of intellectual concepts, there are none coming from America. It is very strange in view of the numbers, mass capacity, the amount of money made, and so on. I cannot name one American social thinker." You've heard it already and it's not strange.

Disregarding the venom, Attali has touched something like a nature of American thought, whose beginnings are at least as early as Francis Bacon. In the *Novum Organum,* published in 1620, Bacon sneered at the collected works of Plato, Aristotle, and Homer. All of their work and everything based on them were nothing but

346

contentious learning, he said. The Greeks have that which is characteristic of boys: "They are prompt to prattle but cannot generate, for their wisdom abounds in words but is barren of works." That is what the Anglo world is telling the Mediterranean; that is what America tells Europe—and Hughes, Baudrillard. For all its theory and pompous claims, Europe has not adduced a single experiment that stands to relieve and benefit the condition of man, Bacon said. It is science to which Bacon refers—and thus began empirical thinking.

Tell Americans the system works this way, that way; present them with ideology and they will say: "So what do you do with that? What do you do with Aristotle? But if you invent a loom, you change the world." Europeans, like Baudrillard, still believe that a theory can be beautiful, is important. An American tells you: "What can I do with it?" Or, "God, you guys invented Communism!" Or, in Hughes' case, "Go to hell!"

But the American on whom this chapter is focused is different. And if Baudrillard had ever investigated Stephen King, who also knows the extent to which, as a culture, we're frivolous, he might have partially saved himself from execution for the crime of absolutism. Because what Baudrillard misses is how *thin* is the euphoria, how fragile the simulated happiness. Horror, King told me, is psychological and social actuality knocking on the partition of the euphoria. It is a reactive response to hilarity, a way of thinking the urgent, the catastrophe America tries to efface. And this figural way of thought is always now-sensitive, an appeal from the present. In the late 80s, Hollywood released *The Fly,* an AIDS movie, Jeff Goldblum's man/fly character Brundlefly being a figuration of the body turning against itself under the influence of an invading virus. Before greed became unfashionable, Michael Douglas suffered a *Fatal Attraction,* a yuppie-horror film where "they" come and take your stuff: your husband, even your child. At the recent turn of the decade when fear of child abuse became hysteria, *The Guardian,* your own nanny, can kidnap your kid and serve it up as tribute to the gods in the form of a tree. William Friedkin, the director of this film, also gave you the first *Exorcist,* a feminist, antireproduction film in which the demon-child will spit and befoul your house and life. In those early 70s during the advent of feminism, Friedkin's little diabolical was joined by *Rosemary's Baby,* who literally sucked the life out of the pregnant Mia Farrow, an *Omen* (also of that time) of the dangers of motherhood. By the early 90s, when economic decline has made necessity out of motherly work and not nurture, when crime became demonized, the corrosiveness of crime in film reached even to the nanny, the *au pair,* the day care center, the grandparent, who allow the freedom of spending only quality time with the offspring. "There's a superstitious, knock-on-wood feeling of a lot of horror fiction, the idea that we've lived so well for so long that there must be dues to pay," Stephen King told me. "We have a puritanical, Calvinistic side to our nature that suggests that if we do very well we must be doing something wrong and there will be dues. A lot of horror provides us with this secular vision of hell."

Giving the example, in film, of *The Amityville Horror,* King told me that it was "a kind of spiritual experience for people who don't really believe in spiritual matters any more. That house is hell on earth for those people. And audiences accept it because in America the miracles are on sale." In America we buy not only happiness, we buy heaven, we buy miracles.

So we have hell, although we haven't bought hell. We thought we could uncouple a millennia-old binary system, that of heaven and hell. We thought we could feast on the first forever, having cast the despised other into the refuse. In the most absurd hypertrophy of this ideology, James Cameron, director of *Alien,* a legitimate horror film, in 1989 released the horror simulacrum called *The Abyss.* At the bottom of "the abyss," the supposedly bottomless pit of that film, we find not the Devil but an E.T.-lookalike, neon angel who raises the dead hero from a watery grave, pointing a finger at his corpse to the accompaniment of an angelic chorus of hummers. Even in the canonical *Batman* of the period, a comic horror film, Jack Nicholson as the Joker is a very friendly devil. Shaking hands with a recalcitrant *capo,* Jack, the Joker sends 40,000 volts into his body with a "joy-buzzer." "Got a little hot under the collar," he chortles as he stands over the charred corpse.

Why should the American way of well-being welcome in horror? I had just asked. "Because there are two sides," King answered. "One side is: 'Have a nice day.' The other side is: 'Go ahead, make my day!' We're not happy and sad. We're happy and violent. Violence is something that unites us. We have violent tastes in entertainment, as the success of pictures like *Alien, Aliens, Pet Sematary* shows. Think of *Caddyshack:* we love to see people fall down. Even our taste in humor is violent. I don't think that Woody Allen movies play much outside of the New York–Chicago–Atlanta–San Francisco circuit where the audience is urbane and civilized. But what they like in the neighborhood theaters in the sticks is Burt Reynolds in fast cars, and they like *The Texas Chainsaw Massacre.* What's the number-one American sport? Stock-car racing. The number-one small business? The gun and weapon shop. Ammo. We're a tremendously gun-oriented, violence-oriented culture. We have a lot of frontier left right under the surface. Thank God that with the exception of pro boxing, which has a huge following, and also pro football, most of our culture is now symbolic violent entertainment, horror pictures, chase movies, suspense novels, that sort of thing," including car crash sequences. How invariant is this subgenre, the violence we do to cars. For 25 years, from the mid-60s until now, from Dirty Harry's debut behind a San

Francisco wheel to any Schwarzenegger sci-fi phallomobile, American cinema has consecrated the joust by car. Carapaced in car—from the slickest Japanese to the crummiest post-apocalypse Mad Max wreck—you tilt on the road with your stranger neighbor. And let the best barbarian win, as if we endangered Romans will need well into the twenty-first century our symbolic Huns and Goths, formerly in the South with Fidel, the Medellin lords, the Mexican aliens, and now, with the end of the Cold War, dispersed in a diffuse horror of revanchist Arabs, AIDS-bearing Africans, and starving subdevelopeds gouging out the ozone layer. In California occasionally, the combat isn't symbolic any more: the other fellow will electrically roll down his window and shoot you.

Stephen King, who taught high school English before typing into his destiny, is a 1947-born baby boomer avant garde who has a mild taste for social theory and popular culture. From the evidence of his fictional writing alone (forget his critical books, of which there are several), he grew up steeped in postwar American culture. "He identifies with the landscape of postwar American culture," said Verrill. "He's a voracious reader and a reader of all kinds of fiction, but also steeped in television and movies, B movies in particular." King told me that not a week went by that he and his wife Tabitha and three teenage children didn't go out to a movie or bring in cassettes for the VCR. "He's someone who's been a sponge all his life," Verrill continued. "His novels are laced with references to the world my generation grew up in. Because popular culture is more popular now than it ever was before—it's television, it's now been *broad*cast—it's how we identify ourselves."

Stephen King is the new writer for publishing as big business. This is not the kind of writer that gave prestige to Scribner's or became a candidate for the Nobel Prize. King is the kind of writer who justifies the takeover of prestigious publishing houses by corporate America. He is probably the most fecund of writers. He has broken a publishing rule: he can publish two books a year and both will become bestsellers (hitherto, it was a rule in publishing: space your novels by at least a year). "You're a goddam industry," an interviewer once told him. "How do you expect some people to take you seriously, if you keep turning out a book a year?" Judged by the traditional, cottage-industry standards of publishing, King would be considered a hack writer. But books as *belles lettres* are disappearing. Books aren't cultural events any longer, they are commodities. "Look at *Publisher's Weekly*'s wrapup of 1991," Bill Sisler, Harvard University Press director, told me. "Its bestseller list is dominated by the few, surefire, known quantities. Nobody's breaking through this monopoly. People know the formula: Steele, Clancy, King, very cinematic books, people can see these things as miniseries even as they're reading."

"What was once conceived as purely mass market has passed over into front-list hardcover," said Daphne Merkin, novelist and former associate publisher of Harcourt Brace Jovanovich. "In the 80s the mass market"—the paperback—"audience was leveraged into hardcover, through the late twentieth-century wonders of marketing and promotion. And it preempted the serious, the literary writers. A perfectly good-enough novel that would have once sold three to five thousand copies and would have made everyone happy, no longer has a place. Mid-list fiction—the proverbial nice third novel—was effectively killed."

In terms of modern production and turnover standards, King, alleged midlist killer, is more than a highly productive writer. He is an executive in charge of a production that happens to be in words. He is perhaps the most appropriate of writers to the revolution under way in marketing and publishing as conglomerates buy up large and small artisan-like publishing houses. These new mega-companies—allied with the bookstore chains—have more money to invest in their product than ever before. They can produce mass demand, but what they demand from writers is the big, popular novel—the entertainment, as novels increasingly are called.

In order to compete in this brave new marketplace, the once mildly literary Book of the Month Club was recently forced to acquire the entertainers, formerly the downmarket niche of its chief competitor, The Literary Guild. An early and apparent beneficiary of this eye newly open to market reality was King, whose novel *It* (remember Freud?) was a main selection in 1986. The author quickly became convinced that book-club sales were gouging a disproportionate share out of his retail sales. Thereafter withholding his product from the clubs, he demonstrated his monstrous powers: he has access to the broadest outlets, not only to the airports and commuter stations, but to the 7-Elevens and K Marts, to the drugstores and supermarkets, to everywhere the "trash" book is sold, to the periphery of the book empire. Any teenager on a trip for acne medicine can buy the latest King. Who needs the mail then? Who's got patience to wait for it? His personal marketing empire is at the furthest remove from the traditional publishing-house concept of literature and bookstores—and because of this, he sells millions. When, in 1988, he was prepared to return to Book of the Month, his four-book contract with Viking sold for a reputed $1 million a book, the bulk of which (estimates run as high as 80 percent instead of the usual 50) will go to King, not Viking. To the critics who associate quality with time and the careful shaping of a masterpiece, King answers: "Any writer who only produces a book every seven years is not thinking deep thoughts. No, a writer who only produces a book every seven years is simply dicking off." (Jesus, this book took four years.) In the management textbook genre, King has been used as an example in the category of "star," along with high-mileage, low-cost cars and audio-disc players. A star has a large share of a growing market. At the other end, in the category of "dog," you'll find the poetry of Allen Ginsberg and the novels of Harold Brodkey. A "cash cow" has a large share of a stagnant, nongrowth market—look for the works of Susan Sontag there as well as the novels of Norman Mailer.

King writes fast and you read him fast. You don't have to imagine anything—it's right there in your warehouse of ready-made images. Look at the end of *Pet Sematary:*

> Louis turned and was greeted by the sight of his wife, to whom he had once carried a rose in his teeth, lying halfway down the hall, dead. Her legs were splayed out as Jud's had been. Her back and head were cocked at an angle against the wall. She looked like a woman who had gone to sleep while reading in bed.
>
> He walked down toward her.
>
> *Hello, darling,* he thought, *you came home.*
>
> Blood had splashed the wallpaper in idiot shapes. She had been stabbed a dozen times, two dozen, who knew? His scalpel had done this work.
>
> Suddenly her saw her, really *saw* her, and Louis Creed began to scream.
>
> His screams echoed and racketed shrilly through this house where now only dead lived and walked. Eyes bulging, face livid, hair standing on end, he screamed; the sounds came from his swollen throat like the bells of hell, terrible shrieks that signaled the end not of love but sanity; in his mind all the hideous images were suddenly unloosed at once. Church [the cat] coming back with bits of green plastic in his whiskers, [the son] Gage's baseball cap lying in the road, full of blood, but most of all that thing he had seen near Little God Swamp, the thing that had pushed the tree over, the thing with the yellow eyes, the Wendigo creature of the north country, the dead thing whose touch awakens unspeakable appetites.

It's a comic strip turned into language; a smaller part is advertising imagery and street language. Louis with the rose in his teeth: a Spanish stereotype, cliché of passion, the Spanish senorita seen in commercials. The wife's head cocked at an angle: street language as in "Don't be cocky." That wallpaper splashed in idiot shapes: A debased adolescent form as in "Idiot face!"; impossible to think of Joyce, Kafka, or Proust using this adjective. Stabbed a dozen, two dozen, who knew?: not how the knife entered, how much it hurt. Eyes bulging, hair standing on end: children's imagery, comic book panels. Bells of hell: any bells in hell? The bits of green plastic: Glad bags. Gage's baseball cap: advertising icon. The yellow eyes: a monster movie. The touch of unspeakable appetite: what you read inside the comic strip balloon.

King has written: "I recognize terror as the finest emotion, and so

Figure 15.1 When Stephen King was a boy, he was reading comic books like these. "Knowing Stephen, he probably started in the cradle," said his editor Chuck Verrill. "They were a great influence on him. Look at *Creepshow*. It followed the format of these comics." *Collection of Dorothy Blonsky, my personal crypt-keeper and mother.*

I will try to terrorize the reader. But if I find I cannot terrify him/her, I will try to horrify; and if I find I cannot horrify, I'll go for the gross-out. I'm not proud." King deploys the gross, the supraliminal imagery of ads and the comics; and, as he told you, he screams at the top of his lungs like an adolescent on the street, thereby to fix the imagery in the discourse. He wants never to let the reader pass by without overwhelming him or her with explicitness. The opposite is the formula of literature. One fleetingly cites, surreptitiously and discontinuously states themes. One gives the reader a role, that of active participant who smiles privately on grasping the world connoted by the words. Think of Apollinaire's famous line: "The sun is a cut throat." A beat for the imagination to work (assuming you're educated); then you "get it" (and with all the pleasures of the paradox): looking up at the sun, in fact you're looking down into the neck of a headless torso. Perhaps you'll never see the sun the same way, but no matter for King, Penguin/New American Library, or Hollywood. They aspire to nothing of this sort, for if they did and King could execute it, he would hemorrhage his readers by the millions. King and NAL want automatic readers, and to generate this automatism they press the lowest common buttons, a technique all the bestselling novelists have used. When Ian Fleming wrote *Dr. No*, about to describe a beauty walking from surf to the sand, he didn't mention Olympia or the demoiselles d'Avignon; he called her Botticelli's Venus. Anybody with the most minimun education has seen that blond on Botticelli's half shell.

The thoroughness of his banality even eluded Umberto Eco, in his youth a specialist on Fleming. One evening, eating steak in the Midwest contributing to chapter 16, Eco told me that he had been tricked by an apparently beautiful Fleming opening line: "I quote it by heart," the novelist né semiotician offered bravely. "'James Bond was sitting in the Miami airport lounge with two gin martinis inside him and thinking of life and death.' Fleming is trying to present him not only as a brute machine—sex and war machine—but as a person able to reflect about a philosophical idea. But is not so extraordinary. He spent all his life in shooting people and risking to be shot, so obviously he was thinking about life and death."

Which tells us why those critics who praise King for his subtextual philosophical themes miss his method. His underlying ideas are usually so general as to be true and false at the same time. Life is a tale told by an idiot, life is strange, King shows. Fine. People are born and die and love each other and kill each other—even husbands, wives; fathers, children, as in *Pet Sematary*, which King could hardly bear writing, he says. To put it cruelly, so what? He doesn't tell you or me anything new. You can never avoid the philosophical implications of a narrative about even the simplest events; but in the case of commercial fiction, these characters and actions are much too simple to attract sophisticated readers. No more than Fleming can you rescue King—as some now attempt, given his mega-readership—by finding oppositions between life and death. Or any other opposition. Cutting his carbonized steak, Eco told me: "It's obvious there is always an opposition between life and death, because we are animals born on the verge of dying, and so we always speak of life and death, even when we speak of a steak, because it concerns the death of the cow and the life of ourselves for a little. And Fleming is a clear case of kitsch literature giving you the impression the page is telling you something sublime, while it's telling you something very very normal."

And King even more so. His novels are choked with images of stupidity, vulgarity, vanity, mundanity, nationality, normality, alas, the images by which so many constitute themselves as persons and ask their little worlds for approval. His novels are replete with the image bank *in me* (if not in you)—therefore I recognize the image-man I am and skim without the slightest pause for pondering or return to a past page. The novels are banal films in words, full of zooms, close-ups, and special effects that turn night into day and men into monsters, cross-cuts, and montage, and diverse other techniques of today's addictive cinema.

Shirley Sonderegger, his secretary, told me that King, at home, writes every morning, every day of the year except Christmas and his birthday. Working from eight to twelve or nine to one before coming to the office to handle business, he produces perhaps eight pages of real narrative—unlike his Jack Nicholson alter ego in the Kubrick film *The Shining,* who produces a ream of pages, every one differently formatted but every one telling the same tale: "All work and no play makes Jack. . . ." It's a snap for King, who seems all work and no play, who thinks horror even as he falls asleep, to produce 2,904 pages a year, that is to say, two 500-plus book-page bestsellers, easily translatable into film because they already are a version of film—the elaborated film treatment.

I have already indicated that King reaches a broad market by sharing and using a vast common ground with his readers. The novel has always appealed to a large part of the population, but to that you must add the audience gained by radio and television, plus the enormous amount of images and expressions that create a new code for listeners and viewers. Today, our consciousness is encrusted with the cornucopia of objects thrown into the stream by television—weapons, detergents, fashion, pizzas, presidents, wilding adolescents, joggers, celebrities, serial killers, wine, and faraway places. The novels of King—through his voracious consumption of media objects—are imbedded with the multiplicity of objects and situations that inhabit our lives, the lives of all the strata of America.

Withal, the reader may not realize how radical are King's politics. When I update, *uphour* him on New York's homeless, their ever more grotesque postures of beggary, the rush of the middle class past them, as if they were cardboard figures, King raises his voice: "Well, man, I wrote an essay about it. I call it 'The Aquarian Closet.' My generation was going to change everything, you know—peace in our time, an end to racism, an end to sexual inequality. And what I see now are a lot of people in Volvos going around: 'Nigger, nigger, nigger.' It doesn't have to be that blatant. It can be as simple as an insurance agent who was a war protestor in the 60s—who was smoking dope, talking 'Off the pigs'—who's talking now about how black baseball players can hit the ball harder. Or saying stuff like, 'How many people on a basketball team? There's six—you know, five to play the game and one to carry the ghetto blaster.' These people were in the streets in '68, but all that stuff's gone in the Aquarian closet."

The bitterness of this language may help explain the odd convergence of Stephen King and Jean Baudrillard. Both are men of the apocalyptic left, convinced, as critic Fredric Jameson has said, that every bit of once free space and time is on the way to being sold back to you as so many pieces of material junk to lie among all the other rusting and superannuated vehicles and appliances that litter the commodity landscape. In *The Talisman* (written with Peter Straub), King depicts another America, the Territories, an analogue land of long grassy plains, aching green under a transparent sky. "They have magic like we have physics, right?" says villain Morgan Sloat on first learning of the Territories. "We're talking about an agrarian monarchy, using magic instead of science," a despotic regime of sparse population, one for every hundred thousand in our America. On his first "flip"—trip—into the Territories (the month is September), the novel's hero, Jack Sawyer, sees the ocean he was standing near before he drank the magic juice; "now it was a darker, richer blue—the truest indigo Jack had ever seen." When he turns away from the sea—its "foam as thick as whipped cream"—this is what our Travellin Jack sees:

> Clustered amid the thorns were the fattest, darkest, most lush-looking blackberries he had ever seen. Jack's stomach, apparently over the indignity of the 'magic juice,' made a loud *goinging* sound.

Blackberries? In September?

> . . . They were amazingly sweet, amazingly good. Smiling (his lips had taken on a definite bluish cast), thinking it quite possible that he had lost his mind, he picked another handful of berries . . . and then a third. He had never tasted anything so fine—although, he thought later, it was not just the berries themselves; part of it was the incredible clarity of the air.

And intensity of the sun:

> He paused a little way from the blackberry tangles to look up at the sun, which seemed somehow smaller and yet more fiery. Did it have a faint orange cast, like in those old medieval pictures? Jack thought perhaps it did.

Get it? (Like you got Jack Sawyer?) It's the Middle Ages or before—before the capitalist conspiracy reached into every corner of our daily lives to sing its siren's song in praise of buying, deodorizing our bodies, subduing our perception, emptying us of needs and desires to be replaced by standardized commodities that blast the land and deform its inhabitants. So there's Jack and his Huck, the villain's son Richard, on the road or rather rails to California, on a little battery-powered train crossing America at twenty-fives miles an hour, entering the Blasted Lands:

> From this starved dry soil grew the wretched trees. Looked at directly, these were much as they had appeared by night, so stunted they seemed to be straining over in an attempt to flee back under their own coiling roots. This was bad enough—bad enough for Rational Richard, anyhow. But when you saw one of these trees obliquely, out of the side of your eye, then you saw a living creature in torment—the straining branches were arms thrown up over an agonized face caught in a frozen scream. As long as Jack was not looking directly at the trees, he saw their tortured faces in perfect detail, the open O of the mouth, the staring eyes and drooping nose, the long, agonized wrinkles running

down the cheeks. They were cursing, pleading, howling at him—their unheard voices hung in the air like smoke. Jack groaned. Like all the Blasted Lands, these trees had been poisoned.

So much are we junkies for junk—and who cares about the ecocide—that at the beginning of Jack's sojourn in the Territories:

> He wanted to get the hell out of the Territories altogether.
>
> Speedy's magic juice was the worst medicine he'd ever had in his life, but he would gladly have taken a belly-choking swig of it if someone— Speedy himself, for example—had just happened to appear in front of him and assure him that, when he opened his eyes again, the first thing he would see would be a set of McDonald's golden arches—what his mother called The Great Tits of America.

It's precisely those tits—plus of course what they stand for: modern technology—that Jack's fat uncle, Yalie Morgan Sloat, plans to introduce into the Territories:

> "I think we could put ourselves into a really synergistic situation over there" [he's telling Jack's father]. Our energy can feed their energy and come up with stuff we've never even thought of, Phil. . . . Of course I don't have a total window on this situation, you know that, but I think the synergy alone is worth the price of admission, to tell you the truth. But Phil—can you imagine how much fucking clout we'd swing if we gave them electricity? If we got modern weapons to the right guys over there? Do you have any idea? I think it'd be awesome. *Awesome.*"

"Peter and I wanted to conjure up that image of unspoiled country," King is telling me, "of a different place where a lot of the options were still open and then put a threat in place to that land, which amounts to industrialization, commodification, suburbanization. We never discussed whether or not in themselves things like suburbanization, industrialization, commodification are bad. We just assumed that they are, because these changes are bad for us, that's part of the American Romantic ideal, it's part of the American myth. My own reaction to it is to assume that these things are bad, that they isolate people, that they break down community and that community is the thing where people gather together, they shed light, they keep the horrors away in the dark, that the real horrors come from isolation and fragmentation."

So the threat is in place, the American Territories are poised on the brink, ready to fall into Sloat's hands. And among the interesting little changes he plans—"And then watch the money roll in, Sloat thought"—he may have to reorganize the labor force:

> Thick, choking vines of smoke rose from the depths of the Pit. Its sides were veined with thick lodes of some poisonous green metal. It was perhaps half a mile across. A road leading downward spiraled its inner

circumference. Jack could see figures toiling both upward and down-ward upon this road.

It was a prison of some kind . . . and these were the prisoners and their keepers. The prisoners were naked, harnessed in pairs to carts like rickshaws—carts filled with huge chunks of that green, greasy-looking ore. Their faces were drawn in rough woodcuts of pain. Their faces were blackened with soot. Their faces ran with thick red sores.

The guards toiled beside them, and Jack saw with numb dismay that they were not human; in no sense at all could they be called human. They were twisted and humped, their hands were claws, their ears pointed like Mr. Spock's. *Why, they're gargoyles!* he thought. . . .

The monstrosity who was guarding them—a twisted creature with a breechclout twisted around its legs and a patchy line of stiff hair growing from the scant flesh over the knobs of its spine—brought its whip down first on one and then on the other, howling at them in a high, screeching language that seemed to drive silver nails of pain into Jack's head. . . .

The men wailed and leaned forward even farther, their blood the deepest color in the yellowish murk. The thing screeched and gibbered and its grayish, plated right arm flexed as it whirled the whip over the slaves' heads. With a final staggering jerk, they yanked the cart up and onto the level. One of them fell forward onto his knees, exhausted, and the forward motion of the cart knocked him sprawling. One of the wheels rolled over his back. Jack heard the sound of the downed prisoner's spine as it broke. It sounded like a track referee's starter-gun.

The reader can have no hesitation. Every detail fits into a stereotypi-cal descriptive system about ore extraction in ancient Egypt, such as we have seen in the movies where George Sanders, or another evoking similar *Weltschmerz*, plays Pharoah's Master Builder, sadly overlooking the necessary whipping of recalcitrant slaves. The scene is the answer to every schoolboy's question: How on earth could they extract the stone for the pyramids without the help of cranes or mechanical power? But the scene isn't just about Egypt. Stephen King is reproducing some of the history of pre-capitalist modes of production, the very ones that Marx sketched in his *Pre-Capitalist Economic Formations.* The Gehenna of the Pit stands for Asiatic production, as Marx called it, a pyramid that subjects everyone to the paranoid despot at the apex, a motor ruling through a bureaucratic apparatus as its lateral surface and transmission gear, with the villagers at its base serving as the working parts. As in Kafka's "The Great Wall of China," power presents itself as a transcendent authority that separates and harnesses workers un-able ever to assemble, discontinuous fragments that turn around a hidden unity, an unknown law as if at the top of a tower—as distant from them as they are from one another. This is an astronomical construction.

But if Morgan Sloat wants to make money, he'll have to break up the despotic machine and replace it with a civilized one—the capitalist machine. "'Hey, be fair,' Morgan broke in," warning his partner not to side with the king against certain rebels. "'They also wanted to bring some kind of political order to a crazy inefficient system—sometimes you have to be tough, starting out. I can see that.'" To make a modern bureaucracy, he knows he'll have to change the archaic forms. Conjunction not disjunction: he'll need moles, scurrying in bureaucratic contact with one another, almost as if they were underground. And the splendors and decadences will have to go. The extravagance of the despot and his agents has to be decomposed—decoded. And recoded. The excess consumption of a class, consumption tied to enjoyment, luxury itself, has to become a means of investment. The age of cruelty has to become the age of cynicism. The only torture will be that of extracting surplus labor.

Sloat himself is tempted away from capitalism to a hyper-despotism. Near the end of the novel, on the brink of capturing the Territories, he's high on the will to power: *"What does it profit a man? It profits a man the world, and the world is enough . . . or, in this case, worlds. Two to start with* [the Territories, you see, have their Territories], *and more when and if they play out. I can rule them all if I like—I can be something like the God of the Universe.''*

From Stephen King's oeuvre we know how this crisis in the fable of capitalism will end. Sloat will settle for CEO of the Territories. Capitalism will become late capitalism: consumer society. Indeed, the American Territories have already become consumerist. Recall the ocean foam? Thick as whipped cream, doubtless Velveeta. Those fat blackberries were "amazingly sweet, amazingly good"—how good's that, Jack? The cliché is already in Eden. As Jack and Richard poop-poop their little train through the Blasted Lands, Richard unpacks an Uzi, "the terrorists' favorite toy," he says. Jack asks, "How do you know that?" Richard says: "I watch television. How do you think?" Already the image has replaced the thing. The toiling slaves are from a movie lot; their demon guards—why, they're the gargoyles later used in *Ghostbusters*. Jack's been given a dose of special effects. He even knows it: the snap of the spine sounded like a starter-gun. Pretty scary.

Everyone has a Twinner, an analogue in the Territories. When you flip there, you "migrate"—take benign possession of your Twinner. And he or she can take possession of you here. When Orris, Sloat's Twinner, migrates to Springfield, Ohio, he cruises his Hertz into a Fat Boy Drive-in and orders a hamburger, french fries, and a chocolate shake. Orris's first bite of the hamburger is tentative . . . then he gobbles the rest. He crams the fries into his mouth with one hand, dialing the radio with the other, picking up Perry Como, sucking the shake down, ordering more of everything. So much for the amazingly sweet blackberries. In America, not the Territories, they do berries and burgers right. And then, "halfway through the second burger he—Sloat as well as Orris—began to feel sick. Suddenly the fried onions had seemed too strong, too cloying. . . . His stomach lurched, he leaned out the window, and even as he puked into the tray that was fixed there, he had felt Orris fleeing from him, going back into his own world." Hey, it takes practice to digest the real thing. In the Territories he only got simulacra.

The odd couple, King and Baudrillard. Far from Bangor on the rue Ste. Beuve, Baudrillard is continuing his seminar. "Video is everywhere and we are tele-spectators, even on the street. We all bear an incorporated screen, eh? And that means that everything and everyone we see in the city is seen on screen. Which means there is no consequence to perception. It's always something you can disconnect, connect, disconnect." As with your remote. He thinks real life is something you can choose to see or not see. You zap the homeless, but you also zap all human relations. And when you don't zap, what is seen isn't the real, it's a flatter version of it. "Things thus become a surface, and one is no longer in a behavior of implication, of responsibility towards what one sees. That's to say that everything is superficialized." Which is what Costa-Gavras said, and what Pozner said (pp. 143–144).

Baudrillard calls this simulation. Simulation isn't a lie. To simulate isn't to hide something. It's to substitute something for something else. Abboud's pee-green jacket is a simulation. So is the color palette (red and blue) of TV spots (p. 142). Now, John Gotti's clothes are *not* a simulation. He wants you always to keep thinking that centimeters from that 100 percent superfine wool is the thorax of a killer. But a Big Mac *is* a simulation (sorry, Orris, you wimp). And the Walkman is a simulation, stopping your ears from the cries of the city (p. 493). And Japan is a simulation of China (p. 184). And the taxicabs of Tokyo are simulations as well. When their doors open and close automatically, when you cannot use your hand, it's the doors over there that simulate your hand. "Simulation is to substitute," Baudrillard drills his listener. "As, for the body, one has prostheses. It's like that, a proliferation of prostheses. We've got prostheses everywhere. All technique, all technology are prostheses." It's that *all* that infuriates his American critics. Simulation, for this thinker, is a system of substitution for the function of the body, for the function of man, and so on. Substitution by techniques, machines, images. ''*Bon*''—no, it's not good!—"the world of televisual images, that's an immense prosthesis also. And we, we live inside it, with our prosthesis system all around, okay?" It's not okay. That simulations, like leeches, cover our ears, our whole bodies—that TV images breach our minds, like traumas—that our very unconscious is wired to the media—that we can't find any space between signs, any Territory—this contention *drives-us-up-the-wall.*

"And that's where you are," he perorates. "One no longer knows where one is, okay? You no longer know what you think, you no longer know what you want, you no longer know what you desire, you no longer know what your identity is, you no longer know where your body is. Because all that has been ventilated, dispersed by all the prostheses."

At this very moment in his discourse, upon exposing it to my students recently, one nearly shouted: "What do you mean, I don't know who I am, I don't know what I want. I know damn well!" He thought Baudrillard was saying it like this: *You* no longer know what you want—because the "you" that wants something was produced by the tube. The real you, he thought, doesn't get a chance to have its say. I had to tell him, Baudrillard's more radical. Yes, he's saying that, but he's also saying: You no longer know what you want—said in soft monotone—there isn't a *you* to do much wanting. You no longer know who you are; there isn't much of an identity there at all. Baudrillard is saying we're mush inside, content as if drugged. "That's truly our situation. It's floating, superficial, aleatory. It's the source of our happy indifference." What, me worry? Alfred E. Neuman redux.

A final word on simulation. When something gets substituted, you forget there was an original. I remember explaining the TV spot color palette to Baudrillard, asking him what he thought happened after years of watching the televisual happiness coded as blue, red, always blue, red, very glossy.

"When one looks at one's 'real' life, when one goes into the street, let's say in America, and sees the poor people, sees the black people, in a city like New York or Chicago where you walk the streets, what happens to the simulation in your head when you hit the street?"

"One sees everything as on a screen at bottom."

Get it? You don't see the gray sky or wan complexion. You colorize the real.

"It isn't only when one is before the television that one is before a screen."

And, astonishingly, a month later, on my next trip to Europe, when I asked film director Stephen Frears—who was showing me a clip from *Sammy and Rosie Get Laid*—why, in a mob scene, there were beautiful pools of yellow where the bonfires were, he answered me *à la* Baudrillard. "I've never been in a riot," he said, "but if I were, I imagine it would look like it does on television. Gorgeous yellows from the fire." I am sure that Frears had never read Baudrillard. Obviously, simulation's in the air. Like a virus, the American critics would say.

So we live superficialized, among all these simulacra, forgetting there ever was real sky, real food, real anything, it would seem. "There are only effects," says Baudrillard, "special effects as in cinema. Effects which don't exactly have causes any more. That's the problem, that we're in a system where we can no longer find the origin or the cause, because in a way it's been devoured by the image. The system destroys its own causes. That's the problem. The image imposes itself on a surface. There is no longer depth, no longer origin," he repeats. "No one today can say, 'Why that?'" Nor does anyone want to, in the bad news according to Baudrillard.

I remember spreading the word in Moscow, talking about the superficial with one of the world's great animators, Yuri Norstayn. Sitting in Dom Kino (Cinema House), drinking tea, I had just shown him in my *On Signs,* animating the Lauren Hutton face, at the time in print ads for Revlon's Ultima (*On Signs,* p. xlvii). Once, the little space between her teeth was her signature of subjectivity. "Now, there are no teeth," I said; "the photographer made her close her mouth. You see a subjectivity being stilled. She's made to wear lace, hold a flower. There is an aspect of the grave to her. Super-ficialized."

"There is a Japanese allegory," Norstayn tells me. "A man is walking along the road. Suddenly he sees a woman sitting on the edge of the road, with her back turned to him, who is crying. When she turns around and faces him, he sees a flat, egg-like form, not a face. He is frightened and runs away. And in the distance he sees a campfire around which people are sitting. He runs up to the fire and, breathing heavily, he begins to tell the people about the woman he saw whose face was nothing more than an egg. And one of them turns around and says, 'You mean, like this?' And that very traveler died from a heart attack."

A horror story is what he told me. So much concentration on fashion, on superficializing, on cosmetizing the face and effacing the inner that, in this allegory, the effacement worked too well. There is no face, the horror breaches the euphoria.

And this, King thinks, is the way of horror. "It's screaming at the top of its lungs: 'Aren't you afraid that your normality is in itself a lie? That there is no such thing as normality? Aren't you afraid that you're . . . a freak?'" and drops his voice. "Any kind of horror story, when you set out, you immediately go to war with your audience." He is at war to rip the smile, the face, the surface off his audience. He is at war with the myth of superificiality itself. "I am screaming at the top of my voice most of the time in the fiction," you'll recall he told you. "Even the setups are just setups so that I can start to really scream and speed rap, and when the fiction succeeds on this emotional level, it's off the scale emotionally."

The setups are America the Banal, scenes and characters into which the average American can easily slip.

"We all lead these mundane, boring, essentially dull lives—we're

Figure 15.2 **An American Allegory.** You'll recall that photographer Eric Boman was telling what he thought was a secret about Avedon. He had pulled the September 1985 *Vogue* from between his sofa cushions and said to me: "Something about that cover struck me instantly, and nobody else noticed it, and I want to see if you can see."

Something about Rossellini's eye was grabbing my gaze. "Right away, I realized that Avedon had gone so far in retouching that he had taken away this whatever it's called . . . this red thing everybody has on the inside corner of eye." That fleshy pink thing is the lacrimal caruncle. "Well, he just plain got rid of it—he just cut it out," Boman says indignantly.

"Actually, it doesn't do much of anything, it just happens to be there," said my ophthalmologist, Dean E. Stetz, M.D.

As if he were a wise plastic surgeon, trading vestigial tissue for beauty, Avedon enlarged Isabella's eye, placing it right in the center of the page. "It looks like a hard-boiled egg," Boman says. He isn't certain whether Avedon employed a computer or worked by hand in this instance, but he cites this cover as one that would set an example for the computer retouching to come. Roland Barthes once saluted Avedon, writing that by his artistry he made you look right and deep into the eyes of his subjects.

(*caption 15.2, continued*) He sure does—here, by special effects artistry. Lila the porn people, Avedon cheats.

"I'm doing a series of baby pictures now," photographer Hiro is telling me. "I tell you, babies have the most beautiful eyes. Even when the eyes are semi-shut, there's an incredible clarity. They look at everything, everything is information going in there. As we get older we lose that desire to observe. You can almost see through their eyes," he returns to his theme. "So you see, the magazines are simulating baby eyes."

Eyes so big they do what all baby eyes do: snap you up, make you tumble into love. Not black but white holes on pink skin so smooth—first, because it's that of a thirteen- or fourteen-year-old model, then because it's computer retouched—that it looks like roseate writing paper. "The magazine face today is all surface," Hiro says, "with all its flawed features, the lines and wrinkles gone." It is a surface perforated with an entrapping hole. This is the only facial type tolerated. If you don't have it, your looks are dubious. In ways large and small, your life will be disciplined, if not wholly annulled.

"It's an unobtainable stage of the human being," says Hiro.

It's, the face of horror, Russian animator Yuri Norstayn told me. *Courtesy Vogue. Copyright © 1985 by the Condé Nast Publications, Inc.*

---

all dorks," said Verrill. "King puts people like ourselves, who are fairly ordinary, and then suddenly trips them into the extraordinary, the supernatural and the horrific."

His techniques are as valid as those of any other literary genre. "If Stephen King is a writer, then Thomas Mann is a pineapple," as critic Edmundo Desnoes said, and added: "If *The Talisman* is a novel, *Madame Bovary* is a restaurant menu." That's not the point. Whether belles lettres or hack, whether realistic or Baroque, writing has always been artificial, a technique. Even the so-called realism of Hemingway is not real. It's a formula, a rhetoric, as artificial as García Marquez.

The point is that Stephen King is entertainment that you effortlessly skim through with the plot supported by the lowest common denominator of American English. Metaphors do not refer to high culture but to consumer society. King indulges in brand-naming and American descriptive metaphoric slang to the extent that even onomatopoeic resources that one associates with the grunts of the Cro-Magnon are used in his writing. *Ouch, ooh, hah, gosh* grace his pages. As he powerfully states in *The Talisman* in an emotional crescendo: "Hee-yah! Heee-yahhh! HEEEEE-YAHHHH!" Or else he uses subtle philosophical statements: "Bobby Terry, YOU FUCKED UP!" When I was able to accurately quote this line from the Devil, Randall Flagg, in *The Stand*, King was elated. And he gave me the key to the use of this literary device. Again: "Even the setups are just setups so that I can start to really scream at the top of my voice, and that experience is antithetical to critical analysis. It almost defeats critical analysis. It's hard to go in on an academic level."

As an academic attempting to domesticate popular culture, I feel that King is a bridge between northern European gothic writing and the creation of original American myths. His stories go from traditional vampires (*Salem's Lot*) and werewolves (*Silver Bullet*) to more original American obsessions such as cars (*Christine*) and adolescence (*Carrie*). I asked him: "What do you think the American horror writers have contributed to horror? Simply new versions of old horror themes?"

"I said so in *Danse Macabre* [his horror criticism]," he answered. "There are archetypes, we depend on them: the monster theme, werewolf theme, vampire theme. But we've been able to give it a sense of humor. It's there in Hitchcock. I've been able to do some of that." King, like the best of American enterprising genius, is an intellectual in action, finds it rather difficult to intellectually analyze what he has done and what he will do. Because of the pragmatic nature of American life, he discovers things as he goes along and doesn't start with formulas or rely on theories. He has created American myths but seemed not to recognize this until I pointed it out to him.

"What about *Christine?*" I said.

"Yeah, well, that's it. I guess you'd say it's a monster story. But it's also a story about cars and girls and guys and how cars become girls in America. It's an American phenomenon in that sense. *Christine* is a freeway horror story. It couldn't exist without a teenage culture that views the car as an integral part of that step from adolescence to adulthood. The car is the way that journey is made."

And suddenly, King is talking to me, grasping and discoursing on the idea that the horror factor in films and fiction is no longer the romantic id of Shelley's Frankenstein, but the manifestation of mass anxieties over disease, ecological catastrophe, wars (planetary and spatial), and quotidian lurking dangers. The range goes from the foreign virus occupying our organism (*Aliens*) to the outer-space mythology of Darth Vader and the Tommyknockers of King's novel by that name. Stephen King is the genius who has liberated the Olympus of American monsters and mythologic thinking.

When we wrap ourselves in Phallomobiles, we have made ourselves mythic. Recall Giugiaro on the American car (p. 175). When we're inside one, no matter what our gender, we've given ourselves the penis of a porn star, the buttocks of Robocop. That's the American car. And it's the American way of myth: add on, bulk up. "American myth has these huge characters that cast these long Gary Cooper shadows," King concurs. Often they're mutilated shadows, often they're grotesqueries, like those shootings on California highways. But there's no question they are there, presented pure and distinct as a letter. Precise, complete, definitive, there is no arguing with myth. It is meant to make you gape. "We love machines in this country," says King. "I love machines, too, and I love to write about machines, particularly when they don't work." He wrote a story called "Trucks," which he made into a movie called *Maximum Overdrive.* In that film, the big rigs become sentient, demanding gas of the citizens they terrorize. "The best touches in the movie are the little ones," King tells me. "There' a dead pet lying in a gutter in the movie, a dog with a radio-controlled car in its mouth. Apparently, the toy killed it. Machines run amok. There's a story I wrote called 'The Mangler,' about a laundry machine, an ironer out of control. *Christine* is another story about machinery out of control. We love our machines in this country."

"Do you understand machines?" I ask.

"No, that's why I'm afraid of them."

King asks me to think of himself as a caricaturist and myth as a face. "If there's an American face, then it's fun to exaggerate one of its features and see what happens. If I were a humorist, the results would probably be funny, but because I write the kind of things that I do, they're usually horrible." If we love to bang the other guy with our cars—if we haven't the foggiest how we get all that power—why, let's give the combative auto even a tad more power and . . .

It kills you. Horror for King is mythoclasm.

In his story "Apt Pupil," the "hero," a boy, holds an ex-SS man prisoner for five years, "just locks onto this guy, sucks up every detail," says King, "and finds out after he's been holding this guy for five years that it's the other way around and the guy's been holding him. It's the horror of American persistence. If there's an American ethic, it's Can Do. The difficult we do at once; the impossible, it takes us longer. And this kid, by God, has made up his mind. He's an American boy, he's always the top speller in his class, he's got the paper route that the collections are always up on, he's going to find out all about the Nazis, he's going to find out all about the death camps and how they worked. And he does, doesn't he? It's an American success story."

Another American mythology: Nothing succeeds like excess. "If there's ever been a nation that believed in take it as far as it can possibly go, it's this country. So I did this story called 'Quitters, Incorporated' about quitting smoking. At that time I was smoking about three packs of cigarettes a day and thinking, 'I'll never get clear of this habit.'" He is smoking as we talk. "'I just will never be able to stop smoking at all'—how could I stop it? And then I thought, Well, the ultimate stop-smoking clinic would be run by the Mafia, and you would go to them and they would say: 'You're not going to smoke any more because if you do smoke, we'll take your wife and break her arm, and if you continue to smoke, we'll break her other arm, and then we'll hurt your kids, and finally, if you just can't learn, we'll shoot you and you won't smoke any more.' So I wrote this story and it's part of a movie called *Cat's Eye.* It's just a case of saying, the American way is Can Do—we can do anything. The American way is, it's no good until you do it as much as you can. It's not enough to masturbate, you have to beat it until it bleeds. You can't kill it, you've got to stomp it, you've got to dismember it, you've got to scatter the pieces, you've got to burn 'em and then you got to nuke the ashes."

Because I see King as a big adolescent, because I see him in the line of Twain, Hemingway, and Salinger, I tell him, thinking of John Belushi in the film *Animal House:* "You can't just puke, you've got to puke all over the dining table." And King, confirming my surmise, writes a better *Animal House.* He says excitedly: "And then you've got to get a spoon and gobble it back up again." And laughs, delighted. "It's never enough, it's never enough. The horror film celebrates these excesses. The horror story says: 'Come right in, I'm going to show you everything your mother didn't want you to see.' And in you come."

In the novel and film *Pet Sematary,* Lewis Creed, the protagonist, buries his daughter Ellie's cat in the cursed Indian burial ground, "because he doesn't want Ellie to miss her cat, he doesn't want her to be sad," King said utterly straight-faced—America the euphoric. The cat returns undead, the catalyst for the rest of the deaths to come. Not learning from his mistake, Lewis buries his son to atone for the lapse of attention that saw the son run onto the road, to be squashed by a trailer. "That's the American way, do anything to make it up," said King. The son kills his mother; the father, the son. The novel ends with the husband burying the wife, then embracing her on her return as she plunges a knife into his back. "American persistence," King told me—"do it and do it and sooner or later, you'll get it right. You'll have the whole goddamn town up there before the end."

In his attempt to explain himself, King has tried to relate his structural horror to specific historical moments and trends. It is what he calls the subtext. The subtext of the short story "Children of the Corn" (1978) is the Vietnam War. The bridegroom in the film is a Vietnam vet, and the children take over the town of Gatlin in the politically restless year of '68. In *Firestarter* (1980), the historical connection is with the C.I.A. In *The Dead Zone* (1979), it's presidential politics. "I'm able to build the story on top of the subtext. And people will take the subtext up. It's there to be taken up. But it shouldn't interfere with the pleasure of reading the story. All I know is, it just about has to be there for me because it gives the story a lot more resonance." Thus when the errant wife in *Creepshow 2* (1987) makes red hash of the black hitchhiker, it's impossible not to think of another hit-and-run offender—Sherman McCoy in his black

Mercedes fishtailing into the black kid in the Bronx in Tom Wolfe's *Bonfire of the Vanities* (1987).

A little embarrassed with too much theory, he said: "Excuse me, I got to go to the john." And while he was there I reflected on horror. He insisted to me that the cult of horror is part of the violence of the system, but King—who came to maturity in '68, the year of the bullet and the days of rage—wants to save the genre by stressing its cathartic aspect. He tells me that horror subverts basic American myths, "the family in the home, Mom making cookies, big glasses of milk with chunks of apple pie, Little League. I don't think you can use the myth very well if you don't value it yourself. I do. I *love* my family." His voice now rises. "I love the image of me *in* the family. I like to think of myself as good old *Dad,* and when good old Dad was writing the good old *Shining,* part of the reason he wrote it was to discover that underneath the Donna Reed overlayer, there was this guy inside saying, 'Sometimes I could just KILL THESE GODDAMN KIDS!'" Revealed to you, your emotions under the overlayer are relieved: "I think it's such a relief for my reader to know that 'I'm not the only one who feels that way.' People say, 'I always knew that I was uneasy about the family and I'm glad somebody finally came out and said what I don't dare to say.' It's so great to be able to say those things in a supernatural context, because it takes the burden of guilt off people." In *Danse Macabre* King sought to position his nihilism in the academic theory of horror's social function. Lecturing his enormous class of readers on Nietzsche and the conventions of the horror genre, he proposed that horror returns you to Apollo. Translated into social terms, its "main purpose is to reaffirm the virtues of the norm by showing us what awful things happen to people who venture into taboo lands," King writes. It's King as academic, Americanizing European horror theory. Tzvetan Todorov: "In the fantastic, the uncanny or supernatural event was perceived against the background of what is considered normal and natural; the transgression of the laws of nature made us even more powerfully aware of them." Far from being a praise of the imaginary, the literature of the fantastic posits the irrational as the exception that illustrates the virtue of the rule.

But as King signaled to me by his repeated outbursts, horror, at least in America, may not respect the courtliness of the classroom. He screamed at me; in *Danse Macabre,* he theorized that scream:

> But below all this, hidden by the moral conventions of the horror tale (but perhaps not all that hidden), the face of the *real* Werewolf can be dimly seen. Much of the compulsion I felt while writing *The Stand* obviously came from envisioning an entire entrenched societal process destroyed at a stroke. I felt a bit like Alexander, lifting his sword over the

Gordian knot and growling, '*Fuck* untying it; I've got a better way."
. . . The worst is now known; we are in the hands of an authentic
madman.

In this frame of mind, the destruction of the WORLD AS WE KNOW IT
became an actual relief. No more Ronald McDonald! No more *Gong
Show* or *Soap* on TV—just soothing snow! No more terrorists! *No more
bullshit!* Only the Gordian knot unwinding there in the dust. I am
suggesting that below the writer of the moral horror tale (whose feet,
like those of Henry Jekyll, are "always treading the upward path")
there lies another creature altogether. He lives, let us say, down there
on Jack Finney's third level, and he is a capering nihilist who, to extend
the Jekyll-Hyde metaphor, is not content to tread over the tender bones
of one screaming little girl but in this case feels it necessary to do the
funky chicken over the whole world. Yes, folks, in *The Stand* I got a
chance to scrub the whole human race, and *it was fun!*

King thinks that he creates worlds of affect in the expressionist
tradition of Tod Browning's cult film *Freaks*, which summarily
ended Browning's career by exposing real freaks—real alienation,
interior pain, and desperate communication—to a disgusted America. "Horror fiction is screaming at the top of its lungs, saying: 'This
is what you're afraid of.' And down underneath it's saying: 'Isn't
this what you're afraid of: aren't you afraid that you're not normal?
Aren't you afraid that your normality is in itself a lie, that there is no
such thing as normality? Aren't you afraid that you're a freak?'"

Freaks, however, is the world, and King, as Borges said about
literature, is something added to the world. American horror,
contrary to King, is a simulation. As he himself said and won't fully
accept, horror is symbolic violence. You always see the zipper up
the zombie's back. Which also is why so many of King's films add
comedy to the horror. Were it otherwise, his outrageous defiance of
all the social mores would be anathema. Only as literature, that is,
as simulacrum, is horror acceptable. The cult of horror is part of the
violence of the system, but the violence is only metaphoric, and
King no more than any other practitioner of horror bursts through
normality.

Among the ways we drug ourselves in America today, horror can
seem almost a religious experience. When, inside a story, we are
lost, trapped, and abandoned, we are thrilled by the idea and the
feeling of impending doom. "You see the same cycle of reaction,
particularly if you've been in the game as long as I have," King said.
"If you scare them, they'll scream and then they'll laugh. The
scream says, 'I'm scared.' The laugh, which is what you're left
with—the real punctuation mark—says: 'But not really.'" King
insists that film, a hotter, more visceral medium than novels,
especially has to build in the laugh, the zipper, the simulation—
hence the growth in importance of special effects.

In "The Hitchhiker," a segment of *Creep Show 2*, directed by George (*Night of the Living Dead*) Romero and written by King, a woman, still high after a session with a male prostitute, hits and runs over a black working man. He keeps returning—on the sunroof, on the passenger's side, on the hood. She shoots him, runs over him again and again, always evoking this response from him: "Thanks for the ride, lady." As he suffers her indignities, looking ever worse for wear, what he nevertheless finally resembles is nothing more frightening than raw meat.

So King's ordinary people get tripped into the supernatural "and by dint of necessity they become heroes," says Verrill. "Not for individual gain but for the group." Like game shows, like standup comedy, horror gives Americans a sense of transcendence, going beyond the quotidian limitations of their lives and making a part—but only a part—of their dreams or nightmares come true.

In America today the possibility of Aristotelian catharsis is in crisis. The catharsis that for millennia ruled western esthetics caused the consumer of the work of art to expend an energy applied to nothing and which, spent, *purged* and *purified*, the very meaning in Greek of catharsis. I have written an evil book [*Moby Dick*] and I feel as clean as a lamb, Melville once observed. Writing a monster book had cleansed him as he expected the reader to be cleansed. Joyce thought that true art freed you of the pornographic or didactic function of lesser art; freed you of the will to possess (an amorous object) or to learn (moral lessons). You could be like God, Joyce thought; detached, watching while paring your fingernails. In his book on Japan, *The Empire of Signs*, Roland Barthes beautifully described the process:

> Take the Western theater of the last few centuries; its function is essentially to manifest what is supposed to be secret ("feeling," "situations," "conflicts"), while concealing the very artifice of such manifestation (machinery, painting, makeup, the sources of light). The stage since the Renaissance is the space of this lie: here everything occurs in an interior surreptitiously open, surprised, spied on, savored by a spectator crouching in the shadows. This space is theological—it is the space of Sin: on one side, in a light which he pretends to ignore, the actor, i.e., the gesture and the word; on the other, in the darkness, the public, i.e., consciousness.

Absolved. The other's sin was your salvation; his or her torment, your peace. The ritual of tragedy was like a figure of speech, meant to shift your attention to a domain other than death, whose literalness is terrifying. The play of tragedy, its monumentality, its mourning and rhythms, all this hidden artifice performed a redemption; it recuperated the character's death, made it sacrifice. But in America the tragic element of death is lost. As King told you, the artifice—the zipper—isn't hidden. We hide little in America. In our tabloids and celebrity-bashing media—which, themselves, seem to pertain to the horror genre—we have dispensed with this cumbersome word "tragedy" and with the silliness of its operation. Undoing tragedy, we have literalized and trivialized death, producing the following. In the old world you felt cleansed upon leaving a church or theater. In the new and in its theater of advertising, you feel aroused: American advertising has transformed catharsis into desire. We are a pumped up, pulsating, dangerously high-voltage society.

The esthetic experience today, dominated by advertising, leads you to want to possess and to do. The most extreme extent was perhaps that of John Hinckley, who upon seeing *Taxi Driver* was driven to an assassination attempt to attract Jody Foster. Hinckley couldn't stop that film and her photos from resonating with one another. The face of Foster—its chubby cheeks and bedroom eyes—never stopped referring to other things; to a fragment of Yale, the White House, the gun De Niro straps to himself as he shaves his head in *Taxi Driver,* about to search out his victim. This signifying arrangement prepared for the moment, subjective and passionate, in which the jealousy, quarrelsomeness, and erotomania of Hinckley developed (calls to Yale, violence with father, descent into subjectivity with his psychotherapist). The Foster face, far from granting Joycean calm, was a despot, seen head-on by a person who was snapped up by the eyes. Hinckley in Love, the extremity and aberration of the "reach out and touch," get-up-and-buy culture.

Violence and horror are sometimes believed to lead to crime, but as King writes about a violent ABC drama called *Fuzz,* in which teenagers doused a wino with gasoline: "If it had not been shown, stupidity and lack of imagination might have reduced them to murdering her in some more mundane way." Crime is not created by fiction. Only the form of crime might follow fiction.

By introducing advertising art into our consciousness, America has pushed catharsis into a corner. But catharsis has to find a space in culture. Part of the eternal mechanism is the need for ritual that substitutes for reality. Even in the most advanced of capitalisms, we can't conceive of a person so snapped up by images, so vibrant in consumer power, that he or she never lives vicariously. And even in America, there are a few things you shouldn't be able to buy or do; a few things best left in the closet of the vicarious—like the narratives of all horror fiction.

Horror is the last stand of hell in America, but that stand takes place in the closet of simulated catharsis, a closet in which you are lightly dusted, if not cleansed, but surely not driven to action. Neither hell nor catharsis fit into the positive-thinking, outward-going, upward-mobility culture of this country. But horror, nevertheless, defanged as it is, has assumed a *midly* purifying role, like some over-the-counter medicine. Horror is the new and perhaps only space for catharsis—for what passes for catharsis—in American culture. The old Aristotelian principle returns with a pseudo-vengeance in the form of monstrosity and terror, full of humor and gore, delivering us from our nightmares. And we are clean and ready to go shopping.

And never escape the suffocating semiosphere? In the 1950s, the Polish writer Stanislaw Lem wrote a science fiction story in which the thoroughly human inhabitants of a distant planet were forced to live under water. Breathing under water, as impossible for them as for anyone, is the spiritual equivalent to living under Communism, wrote the emigré Polish literary critic Stanislaw Baranczak (*Breathing Under Water and Other East European Essays*). Folded one upon the other, Stephen King and Jean Baudrillard write their own *Breathing Under Water and Other American Essays.* "I was well trained for two things, and by two very different coaches," Baranczak wrote. "The Immovable History of my nation taught me that in my part of the world nothing ever changes. The Recalictrant Literature of my nation taught me that having no hope does not preclude demanding change and, more generally, behaving as a human being should." To imagine such behavior, I did not go to any of the collaborators in this book. Many of them make the signs that drown us; others utter our eulogy. I went instead to my old teacher. Toward the end of his abruptly terminated life, Roland Barthes began to sketch a behavior protected from the euphoria and the triumphalism of signs. In 1978, two years before being fatally hit by a laundry truck, he gave a packed seminar in Paris called "Le Vivre Ensemble," Living Together. Drawing on utopian literature, the anthropology of monk societies, and the writing of Friedrich Nietzsche, Barthes sought to establish several principles of a domestic utopia, all the while sensing he was producing a quasi-novelistic fiction of living together.

By the time of writing these words I had found some of my books and my Barthes notes and tapes, and it is impossible to reproduce here what I see was the subtlety of Barthes' prescriptions, the respect he showed for what he called the subject (the self) in his individuation, in his "sovereign worth." At the end of his life, Barthes wasn't deconstructing, he was reconstructing, attempting to find for the self a place *between signs.* And at a distance from the other, conceived as stuffed to the eyeballs with banal signs. What strikes me now, in this HIV age of generalized paranoia, is a Barthesian concept drawn from ethological studies and all the more relevant today. "Critical distance," Barthes said, "is that distance beyond or short of which there is produced a crisis." Perhaps these words can suggest why some three hundred students and auditors hung on that baritone voice:

The problem of crisis is linked to place. In our industrialized world, place is dear, place costs the most today. Formerly what cost were fabricated objects, the fabrication of mirrors in the eighteenth century, for example, and these could make an essential gift. Today, neither a mirror nor any object is proper for a gift. An object is too easy to manufacture, to give; it is too cheap to be a consecrating gift. What costs today is place, not object, and it becomes most precious to give someone place, a place. That is the absolute good, place . . . to have around one people, but not too many; to have around oneself place, but not too much. This is a utopian rule: The essential gift is the gift of space.

This critical distance is endowed with worth; Nietzsche gave it a rare value. It is not a simple step back, a reservation. It is the distance of a pathos. What is desired is a distance which doesn't break the head, a distance irrigated with tenderness. Eros and Sophia. And, yes, delicacy. To live together in delicacy would mean to live toward the others at once at a distance and with a certain free play. It would mean an absence of weight in the relationship and a lively warmth of this relationship. It would mean not managing the other, not managing the others, not manipulating. One actively renounces images of one and another sort. One avoids everything that can feed the register of images that weighs the relationship. Utopia: What can lighten the images of the relationship, this is utopian. A relation of love without image would be perfect and eternal.

In such an enclave you would have your space; the other wouldn't leave there the slime of stupidities drawn from mass myth. As for you, by the simple fact of not having a nearby other to overwhelm, the stereotypes within you would grow wan, no longer nourished by stifling gregariousness. For we all know we erect the torso and tell the other our little stupidities, lifted from the great and small media, in order to establish an imaginary identity. Our torrential and copycat words act as mirror: they are the varied, reflexive, always disappointing ways in which, to cite Barthes, we imagine ourselves and by which we want to be loved. First, to find from the media and then to tell the other, our Image becomes a distraught, exhausting pursuit (you never get there), akin, as Barthes once said, to the obstinacy of someone who wants to know if he has reason to be jealous. In order to achieve immortality, the Tao recommended an abstinence from cereals. Barthes wished, he sighed, for an abstinence from images. Critical distance would then be the act of love in which you give the other and yourself this abstinence. This book itself is the attempt to offer a propadeutics perhaps leading to abstinence.

As for the video games, the evening news, the game shows, the Stephen King on VCR, the night's porn jolt, the John Gotti flash, and all the rest out of which you can stuff your space and substitute for the other at a distance, well, all that's up to you. This book is my way to start getting rid of them, remembering always Italo Calvino, who, in *Invisible Cities,* told how difficult this was:

And Polo said: ''The inferno of the living is not something that will be; if there is one, it is what is already here, the inferno where we live every day, that we form by being together. There are two ways to escape suffering it. The first is easy for many: accept the inferno and become such a part of it that you can no longer see it. The second is risky and demands constant vigilance and apprehension: seek and learn to recognize who and what, in the midst of the inferno, are not inferno, then make them endure, give them space.

16

The Cutting Edge of Eco's Pendulum

Not many take the second way. Umberto Eco is one who did, in the midst of hell performing a literary high-wire act.

There is Umberto and there is Eco. He is the author of *The Name of the Rose,* an experimental whodunit that overnight became an international bestseller, but he is also professor of semiotics at the medieval University of Bologna. In November 1989, Umberto published *Foucault's Pendulum,* a novel that seduced the American literary establishment but that was at the center of a heated, yearlong critical debate in Italy. Some Italian critics believed it was a plotless distortion of history written by a buffoon who used his semiotics and knowledge of publishing ways to manipulate the market. Others considered it the first novel of a new, global, collage culture. The American critics deepened the ambiguity: Some refused to consider *Foucault's Pendulum* a novel, but praised it as a dazzling philosophical entertainment.

Eco, reverberating with the past, is a medievalist; Umberto, the first in his family to attend a university, loves Flash Gordon and ribald jokes about Wonder Woman. Eco—the name means echo—is inextricable from his native Italy, his memories of hunger during World War II, and his old school friends. He's also the first Italian writer of his generation to produce a truly worldwide blockbuster of a novel: *The Name of the Rose* has sold 9 million copies in 36 countries.

Although the *Pendulum* fell short of the *Rose,* readers went along with the critics' largely favorable verdict. Shortly after the book was published, there were 280,000 copies in print; it went halfway up the bestseller list to number six and stayed on the list for 15 weeks. In just seven years, Eco had gone from a $4,000 advance for the *Rose* to more than $1 million for the *Pendulum,* from an erudite semiotic scholar to a mega-celebrity on the cultural scene.

He is an outrageously imaginative writer who, in the second novel, saw such great monuments as the Eiffel Tower, Stonehenge, the towering Christ in the Rio harbor, and the Empire State Building constituting a gigantic, invisible communication network for the Knights Templar preparing to take over the world in the year 2000. As Umberto, he is well into the 90s, but as Eco he is still caught in the hood of the feudal monk.

Creative contradiction affects both his life and his work. One night, during a publicity tour in 1984, after an occasionally barbed dialogue with Susan Sontag before almost a thousand people at New York University, Eco sat, withdrawn and silent, in a Greenwich Village restaurant, unwilling to participate in the flushed conversation of the Harcourt Brace Jovanovich editors and publicists around him. The paperback *Rose* had been published a few months before. He pulled from his breast pocket a French article about himself, handing it to me without a word. He wasn't bragging. It was simply a gesture to connect with someone from his past (I've known him for eighteen years), rather than push ahead or be pushed ahead into the publishing industry blitz and glitz. Ambivalent about the attention, he would sometimes freeze, and Drenka Willen, his editor with a strong hand, helped him move around the publicity circuit as if he were a knight on a chess board. At the age of fifty-two, he was famous and he was scared.

All summer, before the publication of his second novel, Umberto Eco had been air-hopping the Atlantic, traveling from Milan to New York, Indiana, Chicago, away briefly for vacation in Spain, and then back to New York and Boston. Along the way, he rejected a special invitation from French president Mitterand to attend the Bicentennial of the French Revolution, preferring instead to shore up his academic base by giving scholarly lectures at several American universities. All the while, he was agonizing with his publisher, Harcourt Brace Jovanovich, over last-minute decisions about the launch of the novel.

"Please don't sell it as soap," Umberto Eco told HBJ publisher Peter Jovanovich in August. "Don't exploit the book as bath foam," he demanded over the phone from his country home in Monte Cerignone, Italy. "It's not by chance that I publish the novel as a Helen and Kurt Wolff Book, which is a respectable imprint." He wanted to have his million-dollar cake but not be forced to devour it with the media promoters that make bestsellers today.

In early July, when he arrived in New York before traveling to the Indiana University campus in Indianapolis, where he would deliver the keynote speech at the International Institute for Semiotic and Structural Studies, I picked him up at the Gramercy Park Hotel and took him to the bustling Trattoria dell'Arte. The restaurant, designed by Milton Glaser, is nicknamed "Il Naso" because of its giant nose in the window and its noses of famous Italians from Dante to Jimmy Durante on a painting behind the bar. "Yours should be there," I offer in pleasantry, noticing his receding hairline, his salt-and-pepper beard and full waistline.

"Hmmph," he says, contemplating the two icons of Italian culture, as if trying to figure out where he belongs.

He won't be cheered up. He's not just in the sag of jet-lag but worried about what he calls the Cape of Good Hope part of his novel. He thinks the middle sags like the Cape—"The characters no longer undergo events," he tells me, "they undergo fantasies, and the reader has to circumnavigate this cape."

Over antipasto, he sighs: "The Alitalia stewards know me and they spoil me—too many martinis." Even the Italian stewards are part of the Italian mama complex, members of the extended Italian family about to enter the nuclear family of federated Europe.

He brightens briefly when he notices on the wine menu a Gavi di Gavi Soldati la Scolca. "Ahh, I know the man who makes it—my neighbor in Piedmont." Another instance of the Italian national network.

Over the mixed seafood grill, Eco informs me he's about to buy a pied-à-terre in Manhattan, now that Italian law permits moving money out of Italy. He's buying his son Stefano, the twenty-nine-year-old president of a small New York publishing house, a two-bedroom apartment in Greenwich Village. "And now I will have a room of my own instead of these impersonal, sterile, anodyne two-hundred-dollar-a-night hotel rooms," Eco says. "And thankfully my new outpost is not an American city, is a European, Mediterranean city that just happens to be on your side of the Atlantic. That's why *I* love New York—it's cruel and refined." His owlish eyes sparkle behind his big glasses.

This is the same Umberto who, soon after, turns into Eco at New York's medieval Cloisters museum, and his voice echoing against the stone walls, proclaims to Bill Moyers, interviewing him for public television: "I *hate* Renaissance, I cannot *stand* it!"

"Why?" Moyers asks.

"Because I love Middle Ages."

"A monogamous lover," Moyers says drily. "Now that's a rare feature of the modern world."

"I can't stand those Renaissance people when they start being crazy making Cabala! I want a good medieval devil!" he spouts like a Neptune fountain.

Eco is a cultural curiosity, equally mobile in the old world and the new. He had shown up for our "Naso" dinner still dressed in his transcontinental uniform—jeans and a blue-checked Italian sport-coat. "I began wearing blue jeans in the days when very few people did," he wrote in *Travels in Hyperreality* (1986), "but always on vacation. I found—and still find—them very comfortable, especially when I travel, because there are no problems of creases, tearing, spots. . . . It's only in the past few years that I've had to renounce this pleasure because I've put on weight." He's less a victim of fashion than of the new middle-class esthetic of moderation, which frowns on any sign of *embonpoint*. The days when a bulging waistline was an expression of European *joie de vivre,* the image of a successful bourgeois man, are over.

Eco's worldy manner belies his scholarly vocation. The world traveler drinking martinis on Alitalia—Eco flies business class—is a world-class scholar who was deeply influenced by Charles Sanders Peirce, the late nineteenth-century pragmatic philosopher whose work anticipated modern semiotics; Eco's doctoral thesis was on "The Esthetic Problem in St. Thomas." Brought up as a devout Catholic, who couldn't even learn how to ski because he was too busy doing church work, Umberto, when he brought the *Pendulum* out in Italy, was accused by *L'Osservatore Romano,* the official Vatican newspaper, of "profanations and blasphemies, bufooneries and filth, held together by the mortar of arrogance and cynicism in which the man of letters in his lofty dignity delights." In December 1988, the pope himself, two months after the Italian publication of *Foucault's Pendulum,* condemned Eco before an audience of five thousand pilgrims as "the mystifier deluxe," telling the pilgrims that human life "does not move inevitably toward death and nothingness," a phrase taken almost verbatim from the *Pendulum.*

"We—are—not—as—those—that—believe," Eco slowly pontificates, satirizing the pope's pseudo-excommunication, "that—there—is—no—truth, no fixed point in this world." He laughs. "It was his job to say that, okay, okay. The whole affair was nothing but an invention of the newspapers that needed to have an Italian Salman Rushdie," he says, attempting to reconcile God and the Devil. "I received calls from English newspaper asking if the Catholics was hunting me and trying to kill me. They believed that the Catholic church is like Khomeini, so I was obliged to defend and protect the Catholic church against those Anglicans."

It's a love-hate relationship, more love than hate, that has characterized the relationship of continental Europe toward England, and Europe as a whole toward America.

Slightly overweight, Eco is caught in a double bind, physical as well as psychological. Psychologically, he is fascinated by the abundance and variety of contemporary lifestyles, while at the same time carrying a European guilt and abhorrence of waste and lack of discipline. He was born in 1932 in Alessandria, a medieval fortress city in Italy's Piedmont region, "a city completely submerged in fog in the winter, by comparison to which London is Miami," Eco says. "To be born in the fog, which is a sort of maternal womb, helps you to elaborate an attitude of introspection and prudence."

Eco came of age in the postwar years. During the war the family fled to the countryside to escape the bombing. "We were not poor," he said, "yet it was impossible to find food. I am preoccupied with the new generation who do not know what war is, who do not know what does it mean starving during the war, starving, with my mother crying because she couldn't have flour, could not find the *farina* with which to make . . ." The memory is too much, and he can't finish his sentence. Even at this emotional moment language is paramount in his mind. On the verge of tears, he stops to ask: "What is the difference between 'flower' and 'flour'?"

This cutup, this actor who manipulates pathos and sophomoric comedy, watches a woman at the next table telling of her indecision in the face of silicone implant prices. "My mother cried because she failed to find . . . yes, something to eat," he repeats. "And then the day after, she found *maron,* chestnuts. Flour. And so she made beautiful pie and we ate. And we were not poor," he adds. Having been cast by the war into the bottom ranks wounds him.

Sixty years ago, Eco's grandfather, a foundling, set books in type by day and toiled at night binding them. "And so my father, who was the first of thirteen children, read many books as a boy, and this was an important element in my youth, because my father told me many stories and gave me the taste for narrativity. Beyond this, my infancy was the most normal in the world."

Not so of course the boyhood spent looking for *marons* while dodging bombs. "The generation older than me was blasted by the war," he tells me. "Destroyed. And we arrived on the scene—at the end of the war we were thirteen, fourteen years old—young and innocent. We were starting again a new world, and people were interested in us because we were all that was left, so we were spoiled."

Brought up as a devout Catholic—"I belonged faithfully, strong-ly, dogmatically, passionately to the Catholic organization"—Eco dates the loss of his faith from the moment when, honored as a national Catholic youth leader, he was summoned to Rome to meet Pope Pius XII, "white, pale, very supernatural. He looked at a friend of mine wearing a medal. 'Oh, what's that?' And the young man said, 'Is the first prize for the national Ping Pong championship.' And the pope asked, 'Ping Pong, what's that?' And somebody said, 'Is table tennis. Ah,' he said, 'tennis, beautiful sport!' The young man said, 'It's not tennis—*table* tennis.' 'Ho, ho' the Pope smiled, 'is not so tiring.'

"And so I discovered that in this moment, Pius XII heard for the first time about Ping Pong"—the center of all parochial activity in Italy, the instrument every priest uses to attract young people to the parish, and thus a symbol of Catholic organization. "Pius XII, born Prince Pacelli"—Eco's voice is hushed—"had never in his life, not even in his youth, been to a parish. It was like discovering that the pope didn't know what a cross was, or a rosary. It was a religious crisis, an epiphany of disappointment."

But not so was the secular world. "We were the first generation that could take a flight to Paris. And once I used the expression: 'We are the avant-garde in *wagon lit,*' sleeping cars, because we went to our conferences by sleeping car, by airplane. It was so easy for us to be in touch with everybody. I remember at twenty-two I went to the Sorbonne. I met Etienne Surieau, Gabriel Marcel"—he growls the names, icons of a lost time—"Henri Mareau, the great giant in esthetics. At the age of twenty-three, I met Stravinsky. It was only 'Nice to meet you, sir,' but I met him. We were not people at the margins, we were in the center. And being there, in the university, the publishing house, we were criticizing the system. If I have remorse it is exactly on this point—it was so easy for us."

Eco feels he was blessed by another catastrophe. "You understand, I am fifty-seven years old and I still hold power—a small power—in my university. If the generation younger than me had prospered, the generation of '68, I would be retired now. But they were destroyed by confrontation. Some of them became terrorists, some of them escaped to the east with an Indian guru. It was a tormented, tortured, disgraceful generation. So I am privileged because those ahead of me were destroyed by the war and those behind me self-destructed. I feel I have been a filthy opportunist."

We meet again a week later at the president's house at Indiana University in Indianapolis. It's a twenty-room mansion, formerly the home of the pharmaceutical tycoon Eli Lilly. Eco, alone in the house that he calls a memorial, feels uncomfortable and regrets that the campus is dry—"a typical Anglo-Saxon bigotry, not only in Indiana University," he says, "but in all America except New York, which means that prohibition has never really ended." He also regrets that there are no ashtrays in the house. Before going to a cocktail party, he steps out on the balcony to sneak a smoke. "The housekeeper doesn't let me smoke," he says in a warm, throaty Italian accent, drawing on his cigarette and contemplating the campus lawn in the vastness of middle America. "And there's only a single beer in the fridge."

A few minutes later, martini in hand, he's doing his Eco-shtick (I heard it 11 years ago) before an audience of charmed academics on the terrace of the chancellor's house next door. "The French have admitted at last that the Gauloises are pure poison," he says. Aware of the course that smoking has traveled in the last 50 years—from dreamy sexiness and intense intellectual discussion to foul air and cancer—Eco talks with the yellow cigarette hanging from the corner of his mouth, eliciting gleaming eyes and ho ho's from the twenty or so professors clustering around him. "You see, it's *papier maïs,* corn paper. You don't need fingers to hold it. You can talk

Figure 16.1a One day, I received a phone call from a Charles Cleveland, president of Questor, Inc. of Des Moines. He advised me that I could continue using the word "semiotics" for journalistic and of course teaching purposes; commercial ends would be another matter. He had just trademarked the word and it was his firm's. Apparently the trademark office published the word, as you publish the bans, once, twice, going . . . Since academics don't read trademark office monographs, no one informed the feds the word was in rather common circulation. Sold to the gentleman (or lack thereof) from Des Moines. Who was in the delighted audience at Eco's speech on fakes.

around it, blowing smoke all the while in front of you." He demonstrates. "And from behind the smoke comes French philosophy, comes *la sémiologie,* and some of them actually rolled the Gauloise around the entire mouth as they lectured. Sartre, Barthes could do it." For Eco, Sartre and Barthes are still alive, side by side with Madonna and Indiana Jones.

Eco was in Indiana for the fourteenth annual meeting of the Semiotic Society of America, an organization he had helped found in Tampa, Florida, in 1978, alternating discussions about signs, codes, and messages with visits to Disney World in Orlando. That contradiction caused him no conflict—he revels in paradox—but when, 11 years later, it came to applying semiotics to the marketplace, he was distressed. He was surprised to discover that his keynote speech—"The Semiotics of Fakes and Forgeries"—was to be an address, not only to the final session of the Semiotic Society, but an address also to the overlapping, opening session of something called the International Institute on Marketing Meaning, with

Int. Cl.: 42

⭕

Prior U.S. Cl.: 100

United States Patent and Trademark Office

Reg. No. 1,299,992

Registered Oct. 9, 1984

SERVICE MARK
Principal Register

SEMIOTICS

Communication Development Company, Inc. (Iowa corporation), d.b.a. Questor
2222 Grand Ave.
Des Moines, Iowa 50312

For: COMMUNICATION ANALYSIS TO AS-
SIST IN FORMULATING STRATEGY AND
LANGUAGE FOR HUMAN COMMUNICATION,
in CLASS 42 (U.S. Cl. 100).
First use Jun. 16, 1983; in commerce Jun. 16, 1983.

Ser. No. 432,177, filed Jun. 27, 1983.

R. M. FEELEY, Examining Attorney

16.1b

an audience of marketing types from Japan and France as well as Americans.

"I don't like it and I feel embarrassed," he tells me a few hours before his speech. "Personally, even in my country, I have always avoided meetings like this. I prefer to feel free to criticize certain phenomena without being directly involved with their production. Mr. Nader does not sit down with Mr. Ford, and I sit with Nader and not Ford."

It wasn't only principle disturbing him, it was politics. From the first days of its importation in the early 70s, semiotics had been controversial in America, rejected by the marketplace and scorned by the traditional academy. Only in recent years, partly through Eco's scientific works, had it begun to be accepted by philosophers of language. In the hope of consulting contracts, the Marketing Institute seemed about to jeopardize the negotiation of two decades.

"Not to be too much scholarly, let me start with a small treatment for a science fiction story that I imagined," Eco tells his mixed audience, following a brief nap in his room. "Follow me. In 1921 Pablo Picasso asserts that he has painted the portrait of Honorario Bustos Demeq. Fernando Pessoa writes—"

Sitting there, I imagine that he's lost a quarter of the two hundred or so audience by now. I couldn't have been wronger. He is creating a state of fascination all the way to stupefaction. Try to follow him.

—that he has seen the portrait and praises it as the greatest masterpiece ever produced by Picasso. Many critics look for the portrait but Picasso says that it has been stolen. In 1945 Salvador Dali announces that he has rediscovered this portrait in Perpignan. Picasso formally recognizes the portrait as his original work. The painting is sold to the Museum of Modern Art under the title *Pablo Picasso: Portrait of Bustos Domeq, 1921.*

In 1950, Jorge Luis Borges writes an essay ("El Omega de Pablo") in which he maintains that: first, Picasso and Pessoa lied, because nobody in 1921 painted any portrait of Domeq; second, in any case, no Domeq could have been portrayed in 1921 because such a character was invented by Borges and Bioy Casares during the 40s [laughter]; third, Picasso actually painted the portait in 1945 and falsely dated it 1921; fourth, Dali stole the portrait and copied it masterfully and immediately afterward he destroyed the original [giggles from the woman next to me]; fifth, obviously the 1945 Picasso was perfectly imitating the style of the early Picasso and Dali's copy was indistinguishable from the original. Both Picasso and Dali used the canvas and colors produced in 1921. Sixth, therefore the work exposed in New York is the deliberate authorial forgery of a deliberate forgery of an historical forgery which mendaciously portrayed a nonexistent person.

The crowd roars. It's outrageous: meta-discourse to the fourth power.

In 1986 there is found an unpublished text of Raymond Queneau asserting that: first—

Here we go again:

Bustos Domeq really existed except that his real name was Schmidt.

Huge laughs. It's something like "blockhead" the crowd hears, and it hears aggressivity in the concision of the name after all the French and Spanish names.

Alice Toklas in 1921 maliciously introduced him to Braque as Domeq, and Braque portrayed him under this name in good faith imitating the style of Picasso in bad faith.

The crowd is laughing at the most elementary of semiotic constructs he is deploying: contrariety.

Second, Domeq-Schmidt died during the blanket bombing of Dresden and all his identity papers were destroyed in those circumstances. Three, Dali really rediscovered the portrait in 1945 and copied it. Later, he destroyed the original. A week later—

It's the breathlessness of journalism.

Picasso made a copy of Dali's copy, then the copy by Dali was destroyed.

Ho, ho. As if the concept of copy of copy, of abstraction squared, had never occurred to the audience. As if, lapping up his language, the audience reveals how new to it are imbrications, returns, ruses, in short, complexity.

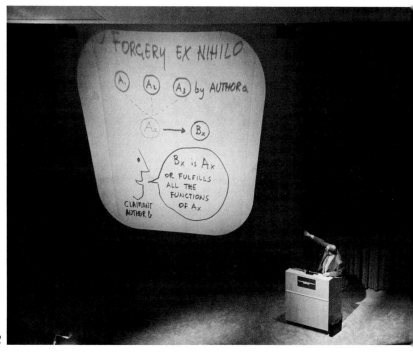

16.2

The portrait sold to the MOMA is a fake painted by Picasso imitating a fake Picasso painted by Dali [*ho ho*] who imitated a fake Picasso painted by Braque.

Paroxysm of meta-language, language combing the hair of language.

Fourth, he, Queneau, has learned all of this for sure from the man who has discovered Hitler's diaries.

Eco ironically revisiting his own novel which, recall, deploys Hitleriana. The most vicious history defanged, made icon. The postmodern response. And that is why the audience is hooting with abandon.

All the individuals involved in this story are by now dead. The only object we have at our disposal is that hanging in the MOMA? Is it the real thing or not? End of my story.

I think the poor marketers—even the *moyen* academics—were exhausted, dazzled by Eco, given a glimpse of a culture they never dreamed they didn't have by a pseudocultural discourse they couldn't possibly have understood. His speech on fakes, lasting forty-five minutes more, is to these marketers and academics as the *Pendulum* will be to America. He is a one-man culture industry.

Now come the questions and now a final questioner, a professor. "I happen to know that the real Umberto Eco is in Paris at the moment. I think we should congratulate this actor in his place." *Rhubarb, rhubarb,* as Eco in his novel describes crowd cheering. The applauding audience is delighted he has validated *them* in place of Mitterand. Happy he has not left them behind.

Most of the two hundred circulate at the reception after the closing (or opening) speech. Waiters hand the guests white wine and blush. Eco relaxes after his labors, sunk in a deep armchair. To the scholars drinking wine, he is Umberto, He Who Made Semiotics Happen. To the newcomer marketers, he is this Name, his books to be scoured for useful insights. He is a lord to many in this room, and the ten or so people standing around him have to bend down to hear. Others kneel at his feet. His academic publisher shows him his new contract. "Do you want me to change it? I can give you—"

"Put twelve months," he answers. He returns a pen: "This is yours, but my. . . ." He pats his jacket for his lighter.

"It's not mine," the man says.

"No, no, I mean that this"—Eco points to the pen—"and this"—he has found his lighter—"are the only two examples of real communism in the world." A micro-lecture, *avant la lettre,* of the triumph of the West. "There is no private property in pen or light. Everybody takes the one of somebody else."

A scholar Eco knows says, "What about Thursday? Maybe we can have lunch or dinner."

"Thursday I have the TV interview."

"Well, let me put it to you this way. . . ."

"No, no, look," says Eco, "I have maybe a seminar but if you come, we find time, okay?"

Now a stranger, a Swiss marketer trying to hire him from the kneeling position (Eco declines), gives him a brief theology lesson: ". . . a woman for whom the essence of life is procreation remaining a virgin—" Eco is staring at the man's glistening eyes. "—until she says, 'Yes, I accept you as a co-bearer of our children and only now are we allowed to have relations.'"

I vaguely fear for Umberto.

"But the church is the one that says it's the woman who is in the driver's seat, and the church is acting as a caretaker, a proxy for a virgin about to become a mother. Do you follow what I'm talking about?" the Swiss patronizes.

"Ah, yes, but"—Eco grabs a friend's hand—"heh, heh, he is my spokesman in Catholic matters: Father Dinnes," dressed in mufti. "Yes, do you think we have absolutely to go?" he turns to me.

"Quick question," from a student.

Life imitates Lodge—David, that is. The brightest star of academe has come into the small world of these scholars and opportunists.

Through broken-field walking, we evade the student and a Japanese marketer who materializes, and are in Mary Ann Carter's Honda (she is Eco's photographer), driving in the countryside scouting locations. Eco toys with a huge wristwatch.

"It says it's Saturday, which is wrong. It says it's February, which is wrong. It says it's the year 2000, which is wrong."

During the conference, executives of the Citizen Watch Company, Tokyo, presented him with a gaudy wristwatch that goes from the phases of the moon to what day of the week Eco's birthday will fall on in the year 2000. The watch was accompanied by a letter: "We would be happy if you share with us any thoughts symbolic of time or time measurement."

"Son of a bitch," he says, putting it on the dashboard, "I'll give it away."

This rejection of trade and profit reached a high mark in Eco's life during the student movement of the late 60s. Like most intellectuals in Europe and America, Eco was radicalized during this decade. "I was thirty-six, no more a student or a young person. It was a shock to me. In a way, I believed in them, I believed that they were bringing out some new ideals of purity. Probably it is due to this fact that I never acted as an adviser for advertising, for a corporation, because I felt that it was a way to prostitute my intellectuality. After the collapse of '68, most of them became either terrorists or tycoons. But they taught me the lesson of purity, which I never forgot and they betrayed."

As the speech on fakes—and his discomfort—made clear, Eco has not neglected his academic life and pursuits, in spite of his success as a novelist. No matter what happens to his fiction, his nonfiction life is a marriage he will not endanger, regardless of whatever quarrels may arise. Yet I've witnessed his impatience with traditional academics.

"They eat semiotics, they make love to semiotics, they sleep semiotics—enough semiotics," he grunts after an importuning husband and wife leave our table in a student bar.

Semioticians are sign-struck. To them, everything can be endowed with meaning—a sign. "Man moves in society through the use of signs," Eco wrote in the *Times Literary Supplement* in the fall of 1973. "Not only are words signs," Eco continued, "but also gestures, images, non-linguistic sounds like the chimes of Big Ben. Obviously devices (such as flags) created by man in order to indicate something are signs, but so are, in ordinary language, the thread of smoke that reveals a fire, the footstep in the stand that tells Robinson Crusoe a man has passed along the beach, the clue that permits Sherlock Holmes to find the murderer." Revealing his mania for meaning, Roland Barthes confessed in his autobiography (1977): "If I observe . . . that in the country I enjoy pissing in the garden and not anywhere else, I immediately want to know *what that signifies.*"

To get across the full meaning of semiotics, Eco used an efficient didactic recourse. Beginning a seminar at New York University in 1978, the professor balled up a piece of paper and threw it at a startled student. It bounced off her shoulder. "Is that a sign?" he asked. Eager not to offend, she nodded.

"No, is not a sign," he boomed, starting to make another paper projectile. "That was stimulus-response. Step on a dog, he barks. A stimulus is something present clashing with something else present. It's not a sign situation. This paper now"—showing the ball, raising his arm as if to throw at the hapless student—"is a sign. I am looking around with a menacing gesture"—this time she lowered her head and raised her arm in front of her face—"but I do not throw the ball," he told the class. "All of you have associated a possible consequence. The consequence didn't happen, therefore the presence of my body is a physical presence sending you back to something expected but absent. My body is a sign. The society here in this room informally coded a previous experience: 'Crazy man going around room to project paper on students'—the meaning of the sign."

Years later, during one of our last interviews for this book in New York, Eco recalled the class. "We are not always interested in things insofar as they are immediately consumable—to throw them, to eat them—but insofar as they can stand for something else," Eco explained to me one afternoon, his novel having just been blessed by the critics. "You see here behind us old books." We were sitting in the lounge of the Stanhope Hotel on Fifth Avenue.

"It gives you the impression you are sitting in the library of an aristocratic mansion. Yesterday I had a look at the books. They're interesting books, but not so rare. The poems of Longfellow, the writings of Lord Chesterfield. You can pull out a book and read it, but that is not the function of this small library. The management wants you to consider yourself a sophisticated traveler and not a tourist on a budget.

"You don't need a semiotician to understand this. The management understands it better than I do. The guests in this hotel read these signs perfectly. Everybody knows how to make love, but sexologists study and classify and define the way people make love. A semiotician tries to find the laws of the universe of signs."

Eco attributes his semiotic passion to a professional vicissitude. Because an academic post wasn't instantly available after his graduation from the University of Turin in 1954, he accepted an offer from RAI, the Italian state broadcasting network, to work on cultural programming for the nascent TV industry. In the RAI corridors Eco became friends with the avant-garde musicians Luciano Berio, Pierre Boulez, Karl-Heinz Stockhausen and John Cage, then experimenting with post-serial, post-Webernian, electronic music. "Although I was only earning fifty dollars a month," he remembers, "it was like a grant in which I was paid to see what happened around me. We met every day in the bar of the network, drinking capuccino, and my meetings with them meant a lot to me, not only in order to understand all the problems of contemporary music, but my personal copy of Ferdinand de Saussure's *Cours de linquistique générale* is the one I stole from the office of Luciano Berio. At that time, they were studying structural linguistics in order to understand some of the problems concerning sounds and voice, so Berio introduced me to Saussure and I introduced him to Joyce"—Eco's university specialty.

"RAI was a turning point in his life," said Furio Colombo, Eco's friend of 40 years, now chairman of Fiat USA and then Eco's colleague at RAI. "Everything was possible in many images at the same time, near and far away, in real time and in delayed time. I am persuaded that the basic concept of his first relevant work, *Opera Aperta* [*The Open Work*] was born in a TV studio when we were alternating between brilliant things, boring things, educational things" and where, Colombo adds slyly, "Umberto had the incredible privilege of being in charge of the *annunciatrici,* a group of beautiful girls who were in charge only of appearing and saying, 'Ladies and gentlemen, you are going to see. . . .' Every one of us knew where to go."

In *The Open Work,* published in 1962 when he was thirty and recently published by Harvard University Press in English, Eco argues that the avant-garde artist uses an "open," or indeterminate, form that encourages the creative collaboration of recipients of the work. "Probably I was among the first to focus on the activity of the receiver, the reader, the addressee, rather than on the activity of the author," he reminisced about his contribution. "I was pulled that way just because those musicians at that time were conceiving of works that had to be in some way manipulated by the receiver in order to be understood."

From the beginning of his semiotic career, Eco took seriously Saussure's belief at the beginning of the century that there could exist "a science that studied the life of signs in the heart of social life," a general discipline that researched systems of communication from the most apparently natural, spontaneous, and least cultural to the most complex cultural processes; from zoomsemiotics, the lower limit of semiotics, passing through natural languages all the way to visual communications, cultural codes, and esthetic messages. In 1974, when he organized the First Congress of the International Association for Semiotic Studies—and was known in the congress halls of Milan as "M. Cardiaque" for his perpetual motion on behalf of the conferees—he closed the proceedings of the semiotic nobles and commons to a standing ovation: "It is not only semiotics which wants to put its nose into everything. Since a few years, everybody wants to put his nose into the semiotic mysteries. Well, gentlemen, you are welcome. Provided we are the gate-keepers." Before him in the front rows were Roland Barthes, Roman Jakobson, Jacques Lacan, and Eco imperiously—to the delight of us all—sought perhaps the impossible. He wanted a new epistemology, a new university department.

"He was from the beginning in this core of intellectuals, Gruppo 63, whose semiologic approach completely changed the history of design and architecture," recalled Germano Celant, curator of contemporary art at the Guggenheim Museum in New York. "In '62 Umberto was already a public hero with *Opera Aperta;* in '64 he published *Apocalittici e integrati,* in favor of or against the mass media. *Integrate,* integrated, means you accept; apocalyptic, you refuse. There was incredible flame of discussion." Obviously, Eco was *integrati.* "People started to understand how to analyze architecture; it became a kind of scientific language. Whatever had been considered *arte minore,* second art, design, architecture, fashion, everything changed after Umberto. Naturally, after Roland Barthes, too. It is not by accident that Armani came along in the 70s. I know the owner of Armani—he came up through a background of reading Umberto. Armani perfectly understands that clothing is semiotic. Attention to the meaning, to the language of fashion, this is the meaning of the boom called 'Made in Italy.'"

Obviously, Eco wasn't a theoretician for Made in Italy, which was, rather, the by-product of his research. Celant's first encounter with the young scholar reveals a root of the semiotic impulse. "I was a student when I first heard of Umberto, who was just starting to do cartoon research, analysis about Mickey Mouse and that kind of stuff," he recalls. "I was involved with Portuguese, with the people involved with art at the time, Panovsky, so I was interested naturally in iconography and iconology, and I invited Umberto to give a talk in Genoa. He was twenty-nine, and I remember it was a very academic moment in Italy, around 1964. Comics were not considered a serious subject, not allowed, only art history, only Titiano or Raphaelo and those people. It was a big, very serious symposium, and he arrived by himself with a big bag and the bag had in it all the cartoons of the 30s and the 40s. 'Flash Gordon' fell out, 'Superman.' It was a shock for everybody, everybody became a kid, also the professors. He started this kind of analysis that was so precise that everybody went wild. At that zero time in the 60s it was revolutionary."

Celant finds the origin of this radicalism in Eco's everyday life as a cartoonist in speech. "He has an incredible memory for jokes and languages," said Celant. "He can translate the *Divina Comedia* of Dante into any kind of dialect from Venetian to Sicilian. It wasn't just that he knew incredible stuff about cartoons—how you make a gesture, the symbolic aspect of gesture, the sign. At the same time he gave us the pleasure of a cartoonist; he was an actor."

Talking as pleasure, the pleasure of the sign: Celant thinks (and I, too) that this is the instrument by which Eco reaches millions. He deals with the light-hearted, with the banal—banal in the German sense, as Celant reminded me: "who has the power, who has the money to give to you, banal as the ban. In Italian is *dotte,*" he tells me, "the hereditary value for someone who became a new prince or a new husband. When a light subject becomes very heavy—that's what is important for Umberto." The Eco of the 60s fought for the right to see power in the banal; even the Roland Barthes of the time was publishing the canonical *Mythologies,* on everyday myth, everyday domination by myth. They both were born of the pop movement, shared the historical moment of Lichtenstein and Oldenburg, all of them revealing the light irony and sexuality of quotidian artifacts. Driven by pop, the *Pendulum* and the *Rose* have an aptitude for seduction, according to Celant. "They are so morbid and sensual they seduce. The comic part, the irony, the humor suck you in, and then the books knock you down with banality. That is their strong meaning, their power."

"Eco has always stuck to semiotics, he never adulterated it, never tried to combine it with anything," Yale professor Geoffrey Hartman assesses him. "He is a scientist, he is too good to be considered a popularizer; he is a very high-level populist. All his scholarly life, he has been like a king making alliance with the people against the nobles."

The Ecos are gracious hosts (Renate Eco is an art education teacher). When, a few years ago, I went to Milan to research chapter 7, on Italian design, they facilitated my task by hosting an at-home dinner for leading architects, designers, and writers in a dining room so filled with books (the apartment has 20,000) that it was like eating in a library. They introduced me to Giorgio Armani, Rosita Missoni, and Mariuccia Mandelli (Krizia). It is difficult to imagine equivalent American designers agreeing to meet an academic. But these Italians are intellectuals, are validated by ideas— and by Umberto, who still believes more in the power of ideas than in fame and fortune.

And that very night in Milan he proudly displayed to his guests the just-finished version of "Fakes and Forgeries," the very lecture he would deliver in Indiana. One of his recurrent themes is the fakery and flakiness of our world and the excessive crust of wrong interpretation that prevents us from direct appreciation of things. In *Foucault's Pendulum,* once the bark of interpretation is removed—a bark elaborated by the three maniacs who contrive the novel's monumental hoax—one is left with a laundry list.

Umberto, who could socialize with anyone in Europe, prefers the company of intellectuals, the older the friend the better. "Monica Vitti called me," he says as we three, the photo session finished, drive to a mall to see the most recent *Indiana Jones* film. "Antonioni is very sick, cannot speak. I would like to speak to him. Do you know, he wanted to make [the film of] *The Name of the Rose?*" Eco had only perfunctory interest in meeting the stars of the film, joking that "I don't go to the set because usually authors go to make courtship to the actress, but in my movie there are only eighty monks and so I had no interest."

At the theater, he is reluctant to pose in front of the poster for the movie. "Why should I make advertising for *Indiana Jones?*" he tells Mary Ann, who shoots him anyway. Two hours later, crunching gravel in the parking lot, he is jubilant: "With the *Pendulum* I burn out all the . . . all the"—breaking up in laughter—"topics for the next two sequels." At the restaurant, flavoring his martini with an olive on a toothpick, he is discursive. "You cannot make a narrative situation composed exclusively of *coups de théâtre:* pow! pow! If everything is pow is the same as if everything is boring. A meal made exclusively of caviar is not enjoyable. You have to have caviar and then a little soup."

"Saussurian difference," I say. A couple of white guys sitting around boring Mary Ann.

"Is the ABC's, is impossible they don't know it," Eco adds. "Probably they know that their audience is now so spoiled that they want much much much much much and so, okay, give whistles, two thousand snakes, one lion, one after the other, okay? Like the coffee in the stations that is not hot, is boiling, is burning your throat"—he reads our myth—"in order to give you the impression that you get value for your fifty cents. At a certain point the audience wants some beautiful film in which nothing happens. A great Antonioni movie."

Three-inch-thick, blackened steaks appear. "In this country, they are afraid of tobacco but eat grilled steaks in which the burned part, which is the best one, is very very very dangerous," he says by way of benediction.

Mary Ann's and my cutlery are suspended in faint disgust.

"Go on, go on," he says to us.

"Eat it, eat it," Mary Ann goads him. "Do you cut the burned part off?"

"No, I want it," he cuts. "Once you start sinning you have to finish."

Chomping, I mention that Lévi-Strauss says we love the well-burned meats because of the luxury of wasting them. We eat meaning.

"It's the way our ancestors for some thousand years cooked meat," Eco retorts. "To have a meat cooked without burning it you have to wait until the end of the Middle Ages with the invention of the oven. So we like burned meat"—rejecting the semiotics—"because it was the first meat our ancestors ate. It's the most natural way to cook meat. It's also the way you die, carbonized in a car crash." Eating with this European, I realize that we Americans are probably the only people on earth that think meat is removed from the steer without hurting it. Mary Ann grimaces.

"In Italy we have a marvelous series of racist, anti-feminist, anti-everything jokes," he soothes, "one more cruel than the other. And they are told only by very liberal people, very open-minded, otherwise it wouldn't be possible."

"What is that?" says the waiter, pointing to the miniature mike on my Sony recorder.

"He is from FBI," Eco says. Back to us: "Superman is late to meet Batman at a bar." I know you heard it in the introduction. It's good enough to repeat. "Batman says, 'Where were you?' 'I was flying along when I saw Wonder Woman lying naked on her back on a hillside. I did what any gentleman would do. I flew down and made love to her.' 'Was she surprised?' Batman says. 'Not as much as the Invisible Man,'" Eco flourishes.

"When I first met him in Turin, he was very similar to what he is today," Furio Colombo told me: "strong personality, extremely entertaining, center of attention, in love with paradox, *calembours,* playing with words to a level and a quality that was drawing admiration but difficult to match."

Eco is a master at table because he has not only the power to stun you with word and culture play; he can upend you into the unconscious through witticism. For the amusing effect (Eco can induce hundreds) involves a factor of surprise: you feel yourself overcome, and it is in this way that we first encounter our unconscious.

"Listen," he says. "There's a transvestite wants to change sex and they tell him that in Casablanca there is a special clinic in which they make an operation and he can become a woman. Then he comes back as a woman and he talks to a friend. 'How was it?' the friend says. 'It was terrible, terrible, such a suffering, such a torture.' 'When they cut off your penis?' says the friend. 'No, no, no, they made an injection and I was . . . ' how do you say? narcotized?"

"Anesthetized?" Mary Ann offers.

"Anesthetized. 'When it was terrible?' the friend asks. 'When they put silicones in your breast?' 'No, no, you don't feel anything.' *'When?' 'When they cut you off half your brain!'"*

392

Rather than repressing, European intellectuals use jokes as an excellent way of expressing feelings regarding sex, class, race, nationality, etc.—in a word, social feelings. Years of feminist gains notwithstanding, one of the common stereotypical reproaches of women is that they are illogical and undiscursive. In the unconscious, many still belittle women and assign them to a lower social class than men. Because we don't talk about it, that unconscious produces unchallenged social effects; however, the joke is a way in which a social practice is mediated by a symbolic practice. By partially raising prejudice to consciousness, the Italians—and Eco here—are blunting it.

"Do do do . . . out my backdoor," Patsy Cline is singing on the car radio. Eco and I are driving in the darkness back to our hotel. *"I'm crazy for try-ing. . . ."* Swiftly we pass building facades, their signs and billboards: SPAGHETTI ALREADY . . . BIG SUR . . . WATERBEDS: BYE BYE, BACK PAIN . . . OLIVE GARDEN . . . GRINDSTONE CHARLIES . . . BIG MAN.

"Bi-i-i-g ma-a-an," Eco singsongs the signs. It is like a ghost town. Even though we pass houses, not a soul is around. It is as if there weren't any houses, only facades. And Eco who is whistling in the dark to the tune of "Jingle Bells" makes me oddly think there is faint danger here. "Taco bell . . . Taco bell . . . Taco taco bell," he sings.

"That was the baroque part of Umberto," Celant told me later, laughing. "It's the baroque part of European culture that America hates. You say, 'Don't let me get lost in the labyrinth.' We are for the labyrinth. You want the circle with its stable center. We are, from Boromini to Bernini, interested in two centers, thus the ellipse with two foci. We are always interested in deformation, and we look at America as a big garden." For Europeans, America is a vast Bomarrzo Park whose symbolic foci are Las Vegas and the Grand Canyon. Two monsters, the artificial and the natural.

Earlier that day, during the photo shoot, the three of us walked through a corn field looking for an appropriate background for a portrait. We found ourselves in a field whose deep green but oddly shabby corn stalks were more than six feet high. Behind them, a gothic barn formed the background. Eco was playful as he walked beside the corn. "I am something between Faulkner and Louis L'Amour," he said. "He died, didn't he?"—referring to L'Amour. "I remember him because when they published the paperback of the *Rose,* for a while I was on the top of the list ahead of him and they were so happy, my publishers"—his voice becoming singsong with remembered pleasure. Gnats darted in the air; occasional mosquitoes, too. "Your mosquito is our *zanzara,* which is more onomatopoetic-*z-z-zan,"* he buzzed. "I have a privilege that the mosquitoes usually don't bite me. There is something in my skin or in my blood that they don't like." The afternoon light was soft and mellow. Nonetheless, I felt a grayness gathering in the sky. It might rain or blow away. I hoped the gray cloud would go away and suddenly realized it was a premonition: his novel would be sunk. Etymologically, monster means premonition, something to surprise you. Obviously I wasn't psychic. I was seeing the corn field—as later I would see the buildings—through European eyes. I was baroque.

Joke time: another cocktail party in Indiana. "A man dies and he feels alive but he died," Umberto warms up the adoring audience. "He says, 'Okay, there is another world and I was an atheist so probably I have to go to hell.' He looks around. There are some signs: HELL. There is a beautiful valley with trees, fruits, some girls dancing on the meadow. It cannot be hell. There's a man, a guardian. Our hero says, 'Where is the hell?' 'Here.' 'What shall I do?' asks the hero. 'Do what you want. There are some ponies, you can horse ride, if you want.' So he rides a pony through beautiful valleys with a delicate breeze. He says, 'This is not possible, there must be something. . . .' And beyond the hill . . . he listens . . . horrible horrible cries and he climbs up on the hill with the pony: clop, clop, clop."

Eco the cartoonist, *pasticheur*.

"He arrives on the border of a flaming swamp where horrible devils are putting people into shit until the mouthful and with forks they are tormenting them. So he approaches a devil and says, 'Should I enter there?' 'If you want.' And the man says, 'If not?' 'If not, I am not the Red Cross. Go around. continue your walk.' 'But who are they?' 'Ah, they are Catholics, they like it like that.'"

Although *Foucault's Pendulum* spent more than three months on the bestseller list in America and has sold over 750,000 copies in Italy (the equivalent of more than 31 million in America), Eco is still very much a product of Italian intellectual remorse and contraction. "My success, if any, allows me to stay with my friends, with young students," he tells me back in New York to explain his misgivings, the launch of his book very close now. But after a seven-digit advance, Eco can no longer remain parochial. He has become an investment, his book is a property.

Eco is the only European in the last 20 years to command such a sum. Of all the books published every year, only 4 percent are translations, and of those 4 percent, "one or two books, if that, are bestsellers," Leigh Haber, Eco's publicist said, and even they are successful books, not star books. Marguerite Duras' *The Lover* (1985) sold a more than respectable 50,000 in hardcover; Gunter Grass's *The Flounder* (1978) sold 40,149 hard, 110,647 soft; and the most successful novel of Italy's most prestigious writer, the *Italian Folk Tales* of Italo Calvino, achieved a success of only—by comparison with Eco—25,504 hardcover and 84,419 soft.

"I want to be taken seriously," he says. "I can be taken seriously

The Making of the Rose

Neither critics nor publishers could—or would—explain the 1983 success of *The Name of the Rose.* Overnight, the novel became a bestseller in every country of Europe as well as in America, selling 303,000 hardcover copies here plus 1,546,000 in paperback. It was chosen one of *Newsweek*'s ten best novels of 1983.

Some considered it a freak. Others called the author a "literary engineer," saying that he had read the marketplace and given it back what unconsciously it wanted. Eco himself at the time told Susan Sontag, in a public debate, that the Ecomania came from a "cocktail of causes." He and his Harcourt Brace editor, Drenka Willen, remarked that chance had thrown a major splash in that drink. "I had no competition," Willen told me drily at the time. "There was no other 'big book' that season." At $24.95 a copy, its colorful jacket taken from a Spanish manuscript of the apocalypse, *The Name of the Rose* met its happy destiny and made Eco a celebrity whose Milan phone rang every few seconds, forcing him to get an unlisted number just to dial out. "Umberto Eco" became the answer to crossword puzzles.

"I don't think Harcourt Brace did all that much to position the last one," said an executive at Warner Books, the mass publisher of the *Rose.* "They were caught by surprise by the way it took off. The real positioning was done a year later when the book went into paperback and we applied our mass-market skills to a literary book. We recognized the college as a big market, did a lot of advertising in college newspapers," and niche-marketed it to the college students fresh from semiotics courses "who had the whole summer to read it. Semiotics was the hot topic then, SRO in the colleges. Also, people were dying for an intellectual read—that was the period of gross jokes. Rmember *Tasteless Jokes* and *Tasteless Jokes 2?*"

Remember Barbara Tuchman's Arthurian *Distant Mirror* of that time? Remember the appearance of "Dungeons and Dragons" then? Eco himself has written that "we are witnessing, both in Europe and America, a period of renewed interest in the Middle Ages." In a visit, at the time, to a New York bookstore the bibliomane Eco found in the "neomedieval" shelf: *A World Called Camelot, The Return of the King, The Sword is Forged, The Lure of the Basilisk, Dragonquest, Dragonflight, The Dome in the Forest, The Last Defender of Camelot, The Dragon Hoard,* not to mention in a nearby drugstore, comic books offering the following smorgasbord: *Conan the King, The Savage Sword of Conan the Barbarian, Camelot 3000, The Sword and the Atom*—"these last two displaying a complex intertwining of Dark Ages and laser beams"—*The Elektra Saga, Crystar the Crystal Warrior,* and *Elric of Melibone.*

"There is no special reason for amazement at the avalanche of psuedo-medieval pulp in paperbacks, midway between Nazi nostalgia and occultism," he continues in *Travels in Hyperreality.* "A country able to produce Dianetics can do a lot in terms of wash-and-wear sorcery and Holy Grail frappé. . . . Modern ages have revisited the Middle Ages from the moment when, according to historical handbooks, they came to an end." As for our own time, "the recurrent themes of nuclear holocaust and ecological disaster . . . are enough to indicate strong apocalyptic currents."

Insecure in the face of the millennium, dreaming of the Middle Ages in a quest for roots, a million and a half Americans in drug store and airport reached for the Warner cover of the *Rose.* Beckoning them, replacing the complicated medieval fresco of the hardcover jacket, the paperback showed a single graphic image, the embossed, brown-cowled head of a monk resembling a death's head. "It was crude," Drenka Willen told me. But close-ups of body parts that seem to leap off the page or screen are the way of life of today's graphics. Americans who love excess, according to Eco, demand the bold and crude and consider anything less, wimpish.

Realizing that it had a triply-hot product—not only medieval and semiotic, but "made in Italy"—Warner altered the usual two-for-one distribution ratio (two books to 7Elevens and drugstores for every one book to quality outlets like airports) in favor of a "half/half" distribution, targeting the traveling college population. "We had been afraid of a lot of books coming back," said the Warner executive, "but we had a big backlist section supporting him at the airports—the Sidney Sheldons, Louis L'Amours, Tom Clancys—and the sell-through was amazing, 60 percent." The price point of $4.95 still hadn't been breached then (now the price point is $5.95 and the market has softened). "Unlike the present, people weren't investing in hardcover," said the Warner executive. People hadn't been leveraged, as Daphne Merkin told you, to hardcover. "People had been waiting for it and we all got lucky. Everything worked for it."

"The publisher's rep, who is probably the most important ingredient in promoting a book, told us of the advance sales from Europe and that it was very well reviewed there," said Virginia Valentine, backlist buyer for Denver's 44,000-square-foot independent bookstore, The Tattered Cover. European success enhanced its value.

"The university community was behind it," Valentine continued. "It was also a good mystery and everybody said it was hard to get into but rewarding to read. Those are two factors that help sell a book." A book like the *Rose* also has a built-in guilt factor. "An awful lot of people love to buy books," Valentine added, "and then they have a guilt pile next to their bed, and if they don't read the book they feel guilty about it. People loved it once they got into it, so you'll try harder, you'll try it at least two or three times."

Word of mouth was also a factor. It was the book that everybody was reading, and people wanted to be socially in. "The so-called difficulty of the *Rose* and the summer worked together," Willen speculated. "It was the book you took to the beach—fifty pages every weekend."

"And it looked great, spread on the sand, cover up while you were tanning," said an executive of the Book-of-the-Month club. It told the then yuppies and their elders what an upscale person you were.

"The idea that I engineered a bestseller came about because the critics couldn't explain why a work of literature like the *Rose,* or like Calvino, could get a big audience," Eco says. "The critics speculated about a new formula, failing to understand there is a new audience, the girl of the evening school that now reads Kafka. I find that very beautiful, that a person of continuing education reads Kafka—probably not as Max Brod, but what happened the first time I read Kafka?

"There is a new sociocultural situation in which the cultivated publishers are a sort of avant-garde appealing directly to consumers and suggesting the new trends. This changes the role of literature in society. I am not saying that a million and a half people appreciated the *Rose.* I'm saying that a million and a half people started putting among their purchases even books. Years ago, they would have conceived of buying records, Coca-Cola, but not books. Now they also buy books."

"Don't sell the *Pendulum* as soap," Eco told his publisher—all the while grasping, I am sure, that, if bought in any numbers over 2,000—or what? 3,000? 5,000? 8,000? it would be another upscale recording. "Umberto Eco" had become, for the "girl of the evening school," a sign of culture and entertainment.

selling two thousand copies but with good criticism or two billion with good reviews, it doesn't matter." He was worried that his critical success would not cross the Atlantic.

"Success in America," Gian Carlo Ferretti, a professor of contemporary Italian literature at the University of Sapienza in Rome, told me, "is fundamental for an Italian writer. It consecrates him. It strengthens his mass media image on an international level and relaunches him all over again on the Italian market." Based only on Eco's name, his Italian editor Carla Tanzi has received a score of movie offers for the *Pendulum,* among them an offer from Dino de Laurentiis for 600,000,000 lire ($400,000) and a 5 percent royalty, given as a rule only to the happy few. "And they're calling from Los Angeles," she added, "and they haven't even read the book."

"I'm not selling it to the movies, I want the book to stand on its own." Eco believes that economic success taints one's claim to seriousness. "We are a Catholic civilization, which is exactly the opposite of what Max Weber told of the Protestant civilization," he says. "For the Protestant civilization, economic success is a sign of the benevolence of God, while for our civilization, poverty and suffering are proofs of his benevolence. Success, on the contrary, is the proof that God is ready to send you to hell."

In which case the shit is being prepared. Because Eco may have read the near future as we approach the millennium. "I started the novel when I realized," he tells me, "that in many European and American bookstores, in the same shelves in which in the 60s were the works of Marx, Gramsci, Marcuse, and Adorno, now there were books on the Age of Aquarius, on the New Age, on Indian philosophy, tarots, and so on. After an excess of political and economic interpretation of life, the so-called radicalism or Marxism of the generation of '68, there has been a collapse of such utopias, and many of these people went in search of something mysterious, supernatural, and occult. There has been a turn of a whole generation, looking for the holy, for the sacred."

In human history, there have been two ways to turn toward a supernatural explanation of the world. One is the way of the positive religions possessed of theology. In Christianity, from the Middle Ages on, theologians sought to explain the mysteries of faith in a rational way. Says Eco: "A monument like *Summa Theologica* of Thomas Aquinas is a way to explain even un-understandable mysteries in a way that our reason can control or at least analogically understand. But then there are the esoteric religions in which the revelation is always postponed. Nothing expresses the final truth, but everything is a symbol for something else and for something else and for something else. Always an escape toward a final secret that cannot exist because the real secret, in order to be kept secret, must be empty."

Eco sharpens the contrast between Christianity and Gnosticism.

"The gospels say everybody can understand, even the illiterate one. Sometimes the illiterate can understand better than the wise and the cultivated one. The Gnostic religion says, 'No, the truth is so arcane, so difficult, that only a few selected ones, the *pneumaticoi,* those who have the spirit in themselves, the initiates, only they can know the secret, and their duty is not to tell it.' In the Gnostic perspective, the truth is so difficult because the world is the effect of a mistake, and only the initiate, by repudiating this world, can approach the secret. Well, I think that today the yearning for mystery, for revelation, for illumination is more, for the masses, on the side of Gnosticism than on the side of the positive religions."

Which permits understanding why the pope and Vatican denounced the *Pendulum.* Eco suggests that it was because of a misreading. In his syntactically awkward yet powerful English he says: "I discovered that the critic of the *Osservatore Romano* was taking my book as a dangerous one because, being not enough cultivated, he didn't understand that my target was their enemy, the eternal heresy of Gnosticism, which has become mass Gnosticism. You know, there is a typical paradox of any advertisement that implicitly suggests only a few people can be so distinguished as to buy this product, so come everybody to be part of this happy few. Gnosticism was a mystery for the happy few, but in this Age of Aquarius, mass Gnosticism says everybody can become members of the happy few secret sect."

"The reaction of Khomeini against Rushdie was in another culture, but it was the same story here," Carla Tanzi, Eco's Milan editor, tells me. "It was a *censura,* the reinvention of the Index." Explaining the church's fury, she takes a somewhat different tack from her author. She acknowledges that the Vatican response was "a silly, dangerous reaction of power against disorder"—the very one Eco revealed, a massive hemorrhage of believers at the precise moment that the pope was seeking to control the Latin American bishops and augment the flock. She also reads the book as conflating the church and Gnosticism, exposing the roots of their power as "the plotting around history, the deception with history, the rewriting of history." To me, Eco is illumining a postmodern inferno, another country full of soft lunatics beyond church or state control, a wild card in the socially turbulent 90s. By the intellect of decipherment, not the collection of intelligence, he recounted, let us say, a Vatican embarrassment, giving the pope perhaps his very own *Satanic Verses.* "A few centuries ago, Eco would have been burned at the stake," a Milanese newspaper critic wrote at the time.

The relentless practicality of our times seems to have driven the masses into the irrational, into reading confabulation around them. "If you want to make a comparison with the *Rose,* let's say the characters of the *Pendulum* are all Williams of Baskerville who got crazy, who lost their intellectual lumen," Eco says. He discovered a wild semiotics abroad, a cancer of connotation. "I was prepared to see symbols in every object I came upon," Casaubon, the novel's narrator, says. "Our brains grew accustomed to connecting, connecting, connecting everything with everything else."

"I call this connotative drift, connotative neoplasm," he tells me. "You used another term, metastasis. We cannot control any longer the game of associations. That's what *Foucault's Pendulum* is about." And Eco is about how a man rooted in the old world is able to branch out to the new.

Once the novel's concept was clear in his mind, Eco went scouting locations, like a film director. He made a pilgrimage, as he puts it, to centers of Templar esotericism in France and Portugal. "And I spent nights and nights walking alone from 2 A.M. to 4 A.M. through Paris." To acquaint himself with the mental geography of his characters, "I pillaged all the bookshops in at least ten cities in Italy, France, and America." He bought some fifteen hundred books on occultism plus four hundred or so rare books—"more than I used for the novel, but at this point I was caught by this new mania."

"My diabolical editors are paranoid obssessives," Eco explains. They are also an amalgam of the leading poststructuralist philosopher Jacques Derrida, *Foucault's Pendulum* being a *roman à clef*. Eco in Indiana—we had moved on from Indianapolis to Bloomington—gave a polemical lecture on Derrida and afterward impishly asked his host: "It was wise then to rain all over these Derrideans?"

"Especially because you did it in a very discriminating way."

Derrida leapt to fame in 1967 when he insisted that a writer cannot control his writing; that, as Plato said, writing is orphaned, and as the word is separated from the word maker, it can metastasize into other words and meanings. "Once the text has been deprived of a subjective intention behind it, its readers have no more the duty or the possibility to remain faithful to such an absent intention," Eco explains Derrideanism to the packed theater in Bloomington. "It is thus possible to conclude that language is caught in a playing of multiple signifying games, that a text cannot incorporate any absolute, univocal meaning, that the signifier is never co-present with the signified, which is continually deferred and delayed, and that every signifier is related to another signifier so that there is nothing outside the significant chain, which goes on in infinitum."

Several times, while we were in the midwest, Eco asked me if I had a recent publication of Derrida's "Telepathy." Unhappily, I didn't acquire it until later. Unhappily, because it would have provided a marvelous rain source. In it, Derrida publishes what appear to be his own love letters—that somehow become also Freud's. Letters in which Derrida/Freud demonstrates how slippery is the field of meaning, how words change their forms. Here is what Eco was lusting for:

> I reread the Forsyth–Forsyte–von Vorsicht–foresight–Freund–Freud business in the *New Introductory Lectures.* . . . Often I ask myself: how are *fortune-telling books,* for example the Oxford one, just like fortune-tellings, clairvoyants, mediums, able *to form part of* what they declare, predict or say they foresee even though, participating in the thing, they also provoke it, let themselves at least be provoked to the provocation of it? There is a meeting here of all the *for, fore, fort's,* in several languages, and *forte* in Latin and *fortuna, fors,* and *vor,* and *forsitan, fr, fs,* etc.

> Then I dozed off . . .

Can you imagine the gleeful *prononciato* Eco would have brought to his critique? Doubtless also reading this Derridiana:

> Why, in my reveries of suicide, is it always drowing which imposes itself, and most often in a *lake* [*lac*], sometimes a pond but usually a lake? Nothing is stranger to me than a lake: too far from the landscapes of my childhood. Maybe it's literary instead? I think it's more the force of the word [*lac*]. Something in it overturns or precipitates (*cla, alc*) . . .
>
> Here we go:

> . . . plunging down head first. You will say that in these words, in their letters I want to disappear, not necessarily in order to die there but live there concealed, perhaps in order to dissimulate what I know. So *glas,* you see . . .

Glas, deathknell, is the title of a major Derrida work.

> . . . would have to be tracked down thereabouts (*cla, cl, clos, lacs, le lacs, le lais, la, da, fort, hum*).

Derrida is brilliant. But if you aren't in his camp, you can construe him as the greatest free associator in the world: cla, cl, closed, lakes, snare, trap, gin the silt, there, gone—now evoking Freud's famous *fort da*—a world-class free associator passing himself off as the model of all of us.

Even without this epiphany of Joycing, Eco rained on the Derrideans' parade by linking the father of deconstruction to Renaissance madness. As Eco and others have written, Renaissance hermeticism based itself on the principle of universal analogy and sympathy, according to which every item of the furniture of the world (to talk like Eco) is linked to every or to many other elements of the world below and that above. The basic principle was not only that the similar can be known through the similar but that from similarity to similarity, everything can be connected with everything else. Said Eco: "The main feature of the hermetic drift seems to be the uncontrolled ability to shift from meaning to meaning, from similarity to similarity, from a connection to another. One is reminded of that game that consists in shifting from one term, let's say, 'bed,' to another, let's say, 'Plato,' in no more than six steps. If the game allows for every possible connection, be it metaphorical, metonymical, phonetic, or other, one can always win. Let's try, 'Bed,' 'b,' 'bristles,' 'brush,' 'mannerist,' 'idea,' 'Plato.'"

And the rhubarb of these nearly five hundred students and professors is as strong as any shouts heard a few days before in Indianapolis. The game is still seduction; only now it's at a world-class level.

"The meaning of every symbol being another symbol more mysterious than the previous one, the consequence is twofold," Eco continued. "There is no way to test the reliability of an interpretation; and the final content of every expression is a secret." And Derrida has thus fathered the very diabolicals who people the *Pendulum,* who comprise the Nazis, one of whom "makes the supreme goof, confusing Ismail with Israel," says Casaubon, one of the editors. The Holocaust is the result of a minor deconstructive drift, a consonant change (in Italian it's Isra*i*l). Eco is playing for keeps. He wants not only to be taken seriously (read: perceived as a Writer); he wants to participate in a polemic that roiled in the wings of this lecture hall. Derrida's American career had been guaranteed by the famous and infamous Paul de Man, chairman of comparative literature at Yale, author of antisemitic journalism in Nazi-occupied Belgium. When, in 1988, the U.S. and European press discovered and condemned the deceased de Man, it was not primarily to ruin his reputation. The intellectual establishments on two continents were engaged in the more vital business of vulgarly trying to destroy living deconstruction. Eco in Indiana was subtly nuancing the image of Derrida. Welcome to academic superstar politics.

In an audacious comparison, Eco is saying that Derrida's model of word movement is like cancer. Words become other words in your head in the way cells metastasize. Think about it, it's terrifying.

"In cases of neoplastic growth," he continues, "no contextual structure holds any longer. And the interpreter is entitled to shift from one association to another where there is a first sign function"—a word like *Forsyte*—connoting the second one"—*foresight*—"and then a third one"—a sign means something, and that something means something else, and that something else means yet another something else—"and suddenly by a mere phonetic association between two expressions, you establish this sort of cancerogene link with another content, which has nothing to do with the previous one." Not only does such a way of mind permit every connection; not only is it unremitting; for Eco, the cell growth of connotations yields nothing. You can find something in common between an A and a B, and then the B and a C, and so on to E or beyond, Eco remarked. You can make the series continue ad infinitum, everything seeming linked to everything. "But in such a chain, at the moment we know E, any notion about A has vanished. Connotations proliferate like a cancer, and at every step the previous sign is forgotten, obliterated, since the pleasure of the drift is given by this shifting from sign to sign, and there is no purpose outside of the enjoyment of the travel."

Eco's breakthrough into America came in 1976 with his "Theory of Semiotics," and it was to Charles Sanders Peirce that Eco turned for a theory to counter Derrida. "There is a fundamental principle in Peirce's semiotics," Eco remarked in that auditorium in which only rarely were there coughs. Everyone knew something big was happening. "The sign is something by knowing which we know something more. . . . There is a sort of growth of the global content. . . . At the end, one knows more about the origin of the chain as well as about the chain itself." And Eco reminded his listeners of Peirce's famous definition of lithium as a packet of instructions aimed at permitting not only the identification but the production of a specimen of lithium. "It is a definition one page long. It tells you what the word 'lithium' denotes by prescribing what you are to do in order to gain a perceptive acquaintance with the object of the word."

Wrote Peirce: "—if you search among minerals that are vitreous, translucent, grey or white, very hard, brittle, and insoluble, for one which imparts a crimson tinge to an unluminous flame, this mineral being triturated with lime or witherite rats-bane, and then fused, can be partly dissolved in muriatic cid; and if this solution be evaporated . . ." all the way to: "will yield a globule of a pinkish silvery metal that will float on gasoline; and the material of this is lithium." The word "lithium" has been interpreted by other words; only through the interpretation are we able to see, to use lithium.

Eco is saying, we may not realize it but we utter encyclopedia entries when we listen and read. And we do this because we are compelled to by something that is not a word. An apple is green like greens which are good for me, and it's round like the earth things of the earth being good for me, and it's round like the earth, and the earth turns, and I can turn it in my hand to get another bite, and I grasp this concept, and concept in German is *Begriff* and so what? I am through with grasping and I've been a little bit hungry all along, so I chomp on the apple. To have understood a sign through the series of its associations—Peirce called them "interpretants"—means to have acquired a "habit," an aptitude to act in the world. We talk, write, read, listen in order to stop all that—in order to do things.

And since these actions constitute the business of life, the community we inhabit constrains and shapes the meaning of language, the growth of its connotations. Only the autistic don't require the society to approve their interpretations. "From the moment in which the community is pulled to agree with a given interpretation, there is," said Eco, "if not an objective, at least an intersubjective meaning which acquires a privilege over any other possible interpretation spelled out without the agreement of the community." If signs don't access the real, the thing itself, nevertheless the process of connotation produces, in the long run, a socially shared notion of the thing, which the community takes as if it were in itself true. Leaving ambition aside, Eco rained on the Derrideans because their French father seems to have suggested we all evanesce as subjects, never able to cohere into mental might. To a scholar like Eco, Derrida's model of us is a tad pathetic: we're linguistic dribblers, drifters, a word of one meaning passing to an altogether different meaning, as if we were drunk.

Eco wants to anchor the self. We produce expressions, signs, because we are compelled to by something that is not a sign. For Eco, that something is going to be the world in the form of the community. He's going to borrow from Charles Sanders Peirce, in whose theory is the final logical interpretant, the habit, a disposition to act on the world and the possibility to act as well. Peirce says we talk, we write, in order to do. We enjoy a capacity to act protected by communitarian thought. Eco in summation: leave language that slips from word to word. Language all alone. Ever the reader of the times, Eco aligned himself with new European philosophy stressing the reasonable play of the self anchored by law and community.

"I am not against interpretation," Eco said at New York's Jewish Museum, where he launched the novel. "Interpretation is a very serious human job. My story is a caricature of the paranoia of interpretation." The reader today, although ignorant of the diabolical and occult machinery of the book, much less Derrida, has been both the victim and the practitioner of over-interpretation. *Foucault's Pendulum*, like most literature, is figural. "The reader will recognize that my story only occasionally concerns three editors who publish occult books, and could actually be three politicians trying to understand what happened in their country, three agents of the C.I.A., three philologists trying to decipher an old parchment, three archaeologists trying to figure out where a stone came from, three psychiatrists dealing with paranoid people, three lovers obsessed by jealousy and constantly suspecting each other, or two lovers.

"There's a Wall Street crash and interpretation runs wild. People say: 'Oh, who at our shoulders, behind our backs, *decided this?'* " He is shouting, aping the terrified brokers. " '*What kind of plot against us is it?'* They are unable to recognize they are responsible for the phenomenon." This infinite interpretation, this metastasis of meaning, concerns every aspect of our life and the life of the culture.

Foucault's Pendulum is a thriller inside a tale of lunatic obsession. Like a detective story, the plot begins with the Milanese narrator awakened by a phone call from Paris. (Here are the Cliff Notes for the many for whom the book is a brick, unread in their guilt pile.) "They're after me. . . . They found me." A shot is heard. The narrator rushes to Paris and hides in a periscope in the Conservatoire des Arts et Métiers in order to keep an appointment that he made with his friend before he heard the shot. The rest of the novel is a monumental flashback explaining their predicament. They and a third colleague have concocted a gigantic hoax, explaining how the Templars, whom Eco likens to Green Berets, beginning in 1307 conspire to take over the world with the aid of the Holy Grail, possibly a meteorite but in any case an enormous power source, the very one Hitler was seeking on the eve of World War II, and which will not mature until the year 2000, at which time the Templars will surface from their underground hiding places and take over the world. (You can see why Eco didn't want to be photographed next to Harrison Ford.) The world's subways, the Eiffel Tower, the Christ in the Bahia Harbor in Rio, Stonehenge, the Empire State Building, and Mount Rushmore constitute a secret, planetary intelligence agency. The subways are spy nests for esoteric channeling, and the architectural monuments are a world broadcasting system for the Templars.

The Eiffel Tower is "the celestial probe, the antenna that collects information from every hermetic valve stuck into the planet's crust: the statues of Easter Island; Machu Picchu; the Statue of Liberty, conceived first by the initiate Layfayette; the obelisk of Luxor; the highest tower of Tomar; the Colossus of Rhodes, which still transmits from the depths of a harbor that no one can find; the temples of the Brahman jungle, the turrets of the Great Wall; the top of Ayers Rock; the spires of Strasbourg, which so delighted the initiate Goethe; the faces of Mount Rushmore—how much the initiate Hitchcock understood!—and the TV antenna of the Empire State Building."

It all ends with the hoax become real, in a monstrous Walpurgis Night, which includes the captured editor's trial, his judgment by all the world's Grand Templars, ectoplasmic accusers mispronouncing Hebrew, chanting Dervishes, a vestal not-so-virginal sacrifice, and an execution from Foucault's Pendulum, the nineteenth-century mechanism for proving the earth's rotation, which is housed along with other tributes to science in the Conservatoire.

When I asked Eco why he blended high culture and kitsch, he reminded me that we had gone looking for comic books the night before we dealt with the marketers. Eco calls this register jumping: "from the low register of everyday sophomoric bar conversation to the high register of archaism and very philosophical meditation. In *Portrait of the Artist as a Young Man,* Stephen Hero and Lynch or Cranley can make a conversation about Aquinas and philosophy and then jump suddenly to an obscene allusion. If we enter a newsstand, if we open a magazine, we can find an article on the Tienanmen Square or on severe ethnic problems and then we turn the page and we have an ad—maybe advertising *Playboy.* Our life is made by the Bible and *Indiana Jones.* We see in the street the cathedral and the red light district, the porno shop and the antiquarian shop. The way I tell my story outlines a sort of new realism. I tell life exactly as it is today.''

Nevertheless, one publishing giant was less than moved. The bidding for the paperback rights took place soon after publication. Given the high advance for the hardcover, Harcourt originally requested a floor of almost $1 million, a price that Warner, Eco's previous softcover publisher, did not feel tempted to pick up, doubting the book's chances. Ballantine Books, betting on Eco, paid more than $1 million. The bet paid off. The paperback sold . . . let Umberto tell you. We're walking recently in New York to B. Dalton in the Village to buy him some computer books. We pass piles of the *Pendulum* on the steps to the second floor. ''A million copies,'' he says softly, ever so noticeably shaking his head.

''It's tough, your second book,'' a hapless Warner executive told me, ''when people look at you and say, ''What's this?' The first time, he was this great literary find, supported by the publicity tour in which he was charismatic. The critics were afraid to say they didn't like the book. It would have showed them up. I don't think they're going to fall over themselves to love the new one, like they had to the first time,'' thus justifying Warner's pass.

But the critics were once again overwhelmed. In a barrage of positive reviews, only the *Boston Globe* and the *Kansas City Star* were negative. In England, however, more thumbs were down. Even Salman Rushdie, from his safe house somewhere in England, blasted the book: ''*Foucault's Pendulum,* the obese new volume from Umberto Eco, is . . . humorless, devoid of character, entirely free of anything resembling a credible spoken word, and mind-numbingly full of gobbledygook of all sorts. Readers: I hated it.''

''It looked like the Ayatollah's attack on him,'' Eco laughs it off. ''He did the same to me. But some months ago, I belonged to a group of writers invited by the *New York Times* to defend the right Salman Rushdie had to express freely his opinion, and I keep going in the same direction.''

Eco, who has written about possible worlds, imagines one in which England and America are reversed. ''It should have been the contrary,'' he says, ''not understood in America and loved in England, the fatherland of Joyce. But they were shocked by this novelistic form which is not a novel.''

England is dismissed. "America was my first important test, and all but two of the reviews were from enthusiasm to respect, so I'm very grateful." He chuckles, the angst of the summer dissolved in critical love. "The next test is France, the book is being published there in February. And after that, Germany. The atmosphere in Paris is very friendly." And remained so. Ditto, Germany.

"In Italy they published a dictionary of all the strange names and quotations of the novel [*Dizionario del pendolo di Foucault*]," he adds more seriously. "I don't think that the reader of the book should know the exact meaning of everything. Suppose I am a filmmaker and I show you a character walking in the dark in a castle holding only a candle, and you see only a few things, and you come to ask me: 'Would you put a lamp on the scene to illuminate the others?' But why? If I wanted the scene to be dark it's because that darkness has a meaning. So if I want to overwhelm you with a lot of mysterious magic spells and names it's not because I presume that you are a scholar of the Warburg Institute. I want you to feel this unbearable, suffocating accumulation of strange and exotic and magic spells. The reader has to understand I am making puns of ideas and so I use an enormous amount of material some of which even I don't know."

Foucault's Pendulum is the painful pseudo-encyclopedia explaining everything you wanted to know but were afraid to ask about European culture and history. It gives you never-before-known names, dates, events—signs of history and culture you can flash at home or work, proofs of your participation in the brave new upscaled world of the 90s. "I'm referring to Otto Rahn," says a character in the *Pendulum*, "an SS Obersturmbannführer who devoted his life to rigorous, scholarly study of the European and Aryan nature of the Grail. I won't go into why and how he lost his life in 1939. . . ." You yourself become Harrison Ford in *Raiders of the Lost Ark*.

The paperback floor was to have helped Harcourt Brace break even, were guilt and New Age readership found insufficient. Now the house will not only survive, as the Citibank ad goes, it will succeed—at least with respect to Eco.

But the problem is that Eco doesn't want to succeed now, but wants to survive, be an immortal. He was in pain when he realized, during the summer, that Harcourt was maneuvering to place him on TV shows like "Today" and "This Morning." Most writers would have rejoiced at a $250,000 promotion budget—three times what the best European writers get as an advance. Eco thwarted it.

"I am an author who is a mass mediologist," he says, "an author who knows that exaggerated, commercial boasting can have a negative influence on critics. So I am a novelist fighting against publicity. I told them, I reprimanded them, I was severe with them."

"When he came into the office his voice was booming—he was ordering them around," an HBJ editor said of Eco's final visits to his publisher before the book was published. The professor who, six years before, had been a piece on a chessboard in the hands of his discoverers, now came to life as a king and instructed them to mount the entire promotional campaign as an intellectual pursuit.

And as he wished, so it was done. *Foucault's Pendulum* was co-launched in New York at the Jewish Museum, where Eco debated Moseh Idel, the world's leading Cabalistic scholar, and in Washington at the Smithsonian with "An Evening with Umberto Eco." Umberto Eco, who is his own best publicist, was juggling fame now for immortality tomorrow.

"Not for modesty or for Franciscan heroism that I oppose big promotion," he tells me, "but because I know publicity is negative. Publicity is good for selling Coca-Cola, but not good for selling books. I am an author who doesn't want to have a TV launch. I don't want people writing and speculating about the book before it's published, as they did in Italy. It sold a lot but it hurt the critical reception.

"Maybe my position is conflicting with the position of the publisher, because the interest of the publisher is to sell immediately. But the interest of the author is to sell for the next 2000 years."

"As Benedetto Croce once said," Eco told me after he swept across a shelf reading the titles at the Strand in New York, "the duty of youth is to age. I am 57 years old with two children and I like still to make love. If the genie of Aladdin arrived and told me, 'You have to choose: You can make love all along the rest of your life with the most beautiful women of the world, but you cannot have more children. Or you can make still a child, but you are condemned to make love only once more in your life.' Probably I would—even at my age, after two kids—select the second option." He paused. "And for the rest, masturbation."

The Eco that wants the option of being a patriarch talked of his past in a soft voice. "I remember that after graduating with my friend Furio, one evening in Milano at the age of twenty-two, we said: 'We have finished university, we are starting new jobs but what do we really want to do with our lives?' And I remember to have answered: 'I want to make a book and a kid, because they are the only ways to overcome death, a paper thing and a flesh thing. Lovemaking alone, for all its pleasures, is stupid; nothing comes of it. But my death can have a sense if somebody survives me and continues. And I write a book, not to have a success now but with the hope that in the next millennium, it will be still at least in a bibliography or in a footnote. And if I like the success now, it's because probably it helps the book to survive."

Eco still clings to the traditional concept of the great writer who produces a masterpiece for posterity, a concept that the last 30 years seem to question. Fewer and fewer of our contemporaries are discussed as geniuses. Young writers no longer endeavor to write "the great American novel." They are content with writing the novel of the season, the book of the year. Eco, however, wants to be a demiurge in full control of his work as father of the text, absolute possessor of form. "I have done to the signified what Joyce in *Finnegans Wake* did to the signifier," he said jubilantly when I first greeted him at the Gramercy. He believes he is in the mainstream of the great European novel, the novel of ideas, and his other point of reference is Thomas Mann.

"In a world of mass communication in which narrativity becomes more and more narrativity about facts, facts, facts, literature has to come back to the great model of the *romanzo d'idées,*" he tells me. "I think that readers look for a story of ideas because they have too many stories of brute facts—J. R. marries, J. R. cheats, J. R. kills."

He is relaxed, sitting on a temporary cotton couch in the new, still unfurnished apartment in New York. His son's electric guitar and keyboard are on the floor by the window, and the books are still in boxes. King Kong is climbing a kitsch Empire State Building. "Until a few years ago," Eco says, "I thought that I wanted to remain in the memory of mankind for my theoretical work and the rest was divertissement. Now this divertissement has taken on a certain visibility, which means a lot to me, and I ask if by chance, all the theoretical work was not a sort of long, long preparation for my works of fiction." The success of his fiction, the *Rose* and now the *Pendulum,* has cast him in the role of the creator, which is romantically much higher than the prestige of a thinker.

"Listen," he says with energy, "someone accuses Woody Allen, in one of his films, of taking himself for God. And Woody Allen says, 'Everybody has to choose his own models.' Okay, every writer has to choose models but that doesn't mean that one pretends to have matched the model." Eco has moved into a space that other writers of fiction have abandoned, the great master of western literature.

Yet, as a communications expert, Umberto is aware of the transitory nature of our cultural objects, aware that the modern world lacks a center and has shattered traditional hierarchy. Modern industry, of which book publishing is a part, relies heavily on the new and not on the traditional concept of "a classic."

It seems that both Eco and his publisher are going to have their way. He might not become an immortal, but he has been recognized as a great writer by the intellectual community here and abroad. "If you place him where he should be placed, among his American peers," literary agent Georges Borchardt told me, "he belongs in the company of Updike, Styron, Irving, Bellow, half a dozen American authors who are not writers of potboilers but who are considered literary novelists who have become successful." At the same time, Harcourt Brace Jovanovich and later, Ballantine, despite Eco's fears about the literary dangers of massive promotion, rode high on the bestseller list.

We are probably witnessing a cultural phenomenon, a change in the role and form of literature. Eco is probably not the last of a tradition of belletrists but the first in a new tradition of collage, anything-goes writing. Alberto Moravia, a traditional novelist, aware of the clash, called the *Pendulum* "a university lecture with a short novel inside." But in the United States, the reviewers decided not to apply traditional canons to *Foucault's Pendulum*. They accepted Eco lock, stock, and barrel. "It's a brilliant piece of research and writing—experimental and funny, literary and philosophical— that bravely ignores the conventional expectations of the reader," Herbert Mitgang wrote in the daily *New York Times* on October 11, 1989. The following Sunday, Anthony Burgess proclaimed: "You may call the book an intellectual triumph, if not a fictional one. No man should know so much. It is a work not of a literary man but of a man who accepts the democracy of signs."

"Umberto Eco has reinvented the novel," Eco's friend Furio Colombo stated at the Jewish Museum launch. "In his novel, what was sentimental, interior, passiónate in the typical classical novel has turned into an adventure of the mind, an adventure of knowledge. We keep hearing: 'Is literature still alive? Who will write the next great novel?' *Foucault's Pendulum* is the answer."

The division between literary value and bestselling potential is being eroded by a new democracy of culture. "I never thought *The Name of the Rose* was bad," Viking publisher Elizabeth Sifton remarked, "but I don't tend to think: 'Is this literature or is this not literature?' If you're trying to force a distinction between commerce and literature, I refuse to collaborate with you." Highbrow and lowbrow will also merge into each other. Durante and Dante: It's the postmodern choral style.

Living in contradiction might have placed Eco on an eternal pendulum, but from our persepective he is a synthesis, a meeting point between the old and the new, Europe and America, guilt and appetite, traditional and popular culture, logic and fantasy, anonymous scholarship and center-stage celebrity.

410

17   *Jingling*
B*ells*
with
Y*evtushenko*

Meanwhile, back in the F.S.U. [former Soviet Union], Yevgeny Yevtushenko performs a different sort of high-wire act. Like others of his countrymen in the throes of perestroika, he may have lost the wire.

I called him when I arrived in Moscow. 593—whoops, sorry about that, comrade. He's the intellectual all Americans want to see. The official dissident—licensed by Khrushchev—the neuralgic point in the communication between East and West.* He was a face to give you all the faces of the once Soviet Union. He is the screen supposed to be the Soviet Union. He'll tell me about the *Splendeurs et misères* of his Union. As he wants us to see them. I said, "Mr. Yevtushenko?"

"Yah."

"I'm Marshall Blonsky. I write for Oxford University Press and I'm in Mos—"

He cut me off: "You don't write for eternity? Then I can't see you," he said in Dostoevskian Slavic transcendence. A Russian way of vowels and history seemed to come through his voice.

He must have heard something in *my* voice, choking slightly, and he said: "I hear something. Now you are sad"—he recognized he had given me an American guilt trip—"and you have made me guilty." Another Dostoeveskian guilt—quite different from my American guilt. "Now I must give you an interview."

---

*He is the man routinely denounced by U.S. press and politicians—his sin, that he survived. He collaborated—with regime after regime. In the great cold war days of Nixon's time, Pat Buchanan, then White House speechwriter, reportedly called him the Politburo's "house nigger."

We come from two different worlds, are on a trajectory of contact, and we are going to experience this clash all along. Why? Because even when people from the same country communicate with each other, they are not fully aware that words are only a part of the communication. Assumptions and premises always guide us. Jean-Paul Sartre called this the context. Yevtushenko lived within a context, the Soviet Union and the intellectual life of the Soviet Union—and his incomplete awareness of the western way of performing (even though Yevtushenko has often visited the West). And my context? Different from his, as you shall see; my premises, also different. Our entire discourse was governed by difference. And only in one moment or two did Yevgeny Yevtushenko transcend this with his poetic gift: metaphor that both of us grasped and could understand. Then there was something like a transcendence in a more universal code. Through it, we became, if not more real to each other, less polemically coded.

The instant I phoned him, I found myself entangled in the old question: can we get to things from words? Yevtushenko will speak of Chernobyl, Hollywood, Pasternak, and terror. Like a symptom, his words will seem to mark out places, states, people. In learned terms, we call this the referential function, the text saying: "I am the referent," setting up an urging toward place, toward that extratextual real from which we think the words came and to which they send. Like those naifs who read Magritte's words—"This is not a pipe"—we nevertheless have the impression we shall imminently touch a pipe. We seem bound by a drive for place and the gliding away of that place, state, referent. And who but perhaps the wisest among us does not keep whining: As creatures for whom signs and symbols are of central importance, must we always speak in codes? Can't there be something veridical that is obscured by code? The great artists and demagogues suffer less reality-ache than their fellows; are better able, let us say, to live with code. Observe the cunning Yevtushenko. He will demonstrate how consciously to manipulate the codes.

A week after the guilt-tripping phone call, Keith Livers, my interpreter, dressed in a forbidden costume for Moscow—*very* short shorts—Keith, who is six-foot-something and also part black—yet again an oddity in Moscow, as if he were an African attending Lumumba U., or a reincarnation of Paul Robeson, or a character out of *Porgy and Bess*—Keith and I extend the territory of our visa. We bend fences to please Yevtushenko and leave Moscow proper. We direct the cab twenty-one kilometers on the Minsk Highway, tell the driver: turn left, now go straight, look for the pond, now turn right on that second street—is it Gogoli? We're in Peredelkino, the writers' colony.

I had visited the Cloisters in New York a week before I left. There the trees seemed friendly and a symbol of summer. Here, even in the days after Gorbachev has won the West, when the branches bend low over the path, they seem to be listening. Each leaf seems to hide a microphone or an eye, to be part of a KGB—or whatever it's called now—organ. The code of the Soviet Union has entered even its trees for me.

We pass what had been Boris Pasternak's dacha, the *Literary Gazette* dacha . . . suddenly I think: what wealth is here after the fumes and little blue cars and green trucks and (to me) gray-faced Muscovites in grim Moscow. Foliage everywhere, green-yellow. A cornflower-blue sky and steady sun, but quite the opposite from Oklahoma, where the corn grows high as 'a' elephant's eye. We find our way to a discrete shack . . . he had called it. This is no shack.

I knock on the door. No one had prepared me for Yevtushenko, dressed, all six-plus feet of him, in a gray-brown shawl.

"Marshall Blonsky?"

I say, "The one."

He says, "What tragic eyes you have!"

Again the Dostoevskian digging into me. The searching into eyes for soul and transcendence. He performs as a Slav. He knows the code, he lives it.

Let me borrow format from my supposed Donor: In no way shall I claim to analyze a reality, this being a major gesture of western discourse. Instead, I can isolate far from us (in the troubling East) a certain number of features, and out of these features form a system. It is this system which is my (and your) Russia.

The F.S.U. and America in this chapter are not to be taken as realities, to be compared and contrasted historically, philosophically, culturally, politically. I am not a Kremlinologist reasoning toward a Soviet essence. To me the phantom Union, merely as a political entity, is a matter of indifference; rather, it provides a reserve of features whose manipulation, whose invented interplay, allows me to entertain the idea of a symbolic system detached from our own, with a lesson for our own.

What can be addressed in the consideration of the corpse of the Union are other symbols, another wisdom, an alien mythology whose decay suggests an affliction in our own—supposedly— triumphant mythology. Someday we will write the history of our own obscurity, manifest the destiny of our narcissism, tally up the several appeals to difference we have occasionally heard, the ideological recuperations that have infallibly followed and that consist in always acclimating our incognizance of Russia by means of certain known languages, the Russia of Dostoevsky, of the foreign-affairs experts, of Pasternak or of Intourist magazines. Today there are doubtless a thousand things to learn about this vast region, although if we won't reconstruct it, what need have we of learning? Nevertheless, about to hear Yevtushenko tell me of Russian Soul and Soviet ideals, I am going to hear a fundamental reason why the Union will soon, with a rapidity and finality not even he can imagine, collapse.

Yevtushenko is one of the talking heads of the system, and a major poet, a fount of symbol. He has roots in Russia but is the one who, all these last years, has interpreted *Sovietsky Soyuz* for us, the West. It's through his poetry that we have understood, or tried to understand, the troubling East. This man uses language the West seems to understand, yet his premises are different from ours. To be in front of him is to watch a screen that is supposed to show the Soviet Union. Place yourself before Yevtushenko.

"What tragic eyes you have!" I am Little Red Riding Hood in Moscow and this bear might eat me up.

He leads us in, limping, and says, "I have poisoned myself. My doctors don't know what it is. But it happened in Italy"—the eternal myth of the North corrupted by the South (see Thomas Mann, *Death in Venice*). Yevtushenko, back in his cold, pure land, sits, places his leg, hurt down south, on a hassock, and tells us he must keep the foot high "or I might lose it." The Anglo would underplay the leg—"it's not important," he'd say. For the Slav it's another tragedy.

Here, indeed, is a poem Yevtushenko composed in this period:

Oh God, how I suffer!
I wouldn't wish for my enemy.
I can't take any more—
I can't take less either.

Poverty and nonpoverty torment me,
tears torment, laughter torments,
both nonrecognition torments
and success torments.

Give me a break.

Barely are we ensconced when Keith says, "I'm hungry"—playing *Porgy and Bess*, Hungry Southerner. Keith, you see, is not a student at Lumumba University, a Third World person grateful for Second World cuisine. He's an American student from the U. of Michigan now at Pushkin Institute—where, he has informed me, breakfast every day is a hot dog floating in tepid water and an egg nearby, wobbling. Keith hates the Soviet Union because they won't feed him well. What must Yevtushenko, seeing a black, think: all the preconceived ideas about our country!

Ever the gracious host, Yevtushenko, although gimpy, brings us jams and cakes. The interview is on.

"You know, I've been in America many times, so I think that probably nobody from Russia knows America as I know." He

414

makes the assumption that America is vital but Russians are intellectually superior. How European: instinctual America and pondering Europe. Another cliché. Another code. No matter what I do, I am an American, ergo culturally inferior.

Yevtushenko continues: "I know the whole geological slice of American society. I met your presidents, the candidates, your police people, your C.I.A. people, your diplomats, your bankers and your so-called movie stars, your *vedettes,* your writers, your journalists, newspaper journalists—your doctors, because I was sometimes ill in America, your thiefs, your whores, your students, your reactionalists, your fascists, your Zionists, your anti-Semites—because you have anti-Semites, too—and so-called ordinary American farmers, workers, lumpens, unemployed."

The abundance, the reiteration of it, the opposite of Hemingway or the Swiftian Anglo code of the right word in the right place. This is the poetry of the endless naming of things to overwhelm you. Like Stalin's buildings, like Soviet firepower. The Russians believe in numbers.

I taped the interview, of course, and when I gave it for transcription back in New York, the transcriber was offended, listening to this deep voice that millions love, this voice reading poetry that can fill a Soviet stadium with twenty thousand—unheard of in America! "He really doesn't speak English that well," the transcriber told me, "and in keeping with his inflated posturing, he spoke loudly whenever he thought he was being particularly brilliant!" She reacts to the code of overwhelming. But instead of taking his words as the code of a culture, she judges him with assumptions: People who are intelligent are discreet, well mannered, simple—anyone like Yevtushenko is a farce! Not only did he speak loudly, "he talked with his mouth full," she said. In short, triple violation of the Anglo code: he didn't keep a stiff upper lip, he moved it as he ate (and talked), and he flapped it in the breeze—*did he brag!* But the transcriber got him wrong: Yevgeny Yevtushenko doesn't obey Brit codes, he talks and walks to a different drummer. Which? That of the Artist. Which? The Soviet PR Man. Again: the Court Jester.

And I, dressed in khaki Armani pants (Armani's gift), in Armani blazer, I, whose sin to Yevtushenko had been . . . *to be sincere* ("I write for Oxford"—*who cares!* he had answered back), I too obeyed codes. Mine? They produced the Nice American. The Intellectual, Fount of Ideas, clichés all. And Keith obeyed codes, too. Became the Black Who Dared the Russians, who, by the way, didn't faze Yevtushenko. He asked Keith, a bit later: "You have black blood, yes?" Keith was shocked, I think. He needn't have been. The words were nothing but one of Yevtushenko's archetypes again: the Outrageous Poet. Images met images that day and the real was far away. I had an idea of Russia. Yevtushenko had an idea of America. Keith had *his* idea. (He had met me a week before, on my first night in Moscow, at the Hotel Belgrade. He wanted supper. Food at the Pushkin stank. He couldn't wait to get out of Russia—for where? Hungary, where he could eat. "And don't go with the whores," he told me, referring to the shinily dressed women waiting for escorts at my Belgrade Hotel's dining-room door. "They have loose connections with the K.G.B.," Keith told me. Keith, need I say, was anti-Soviet that summer.)

In short, we three met in a world of coded reactions. When Yevtushenko told me I wasn't writing for eternity, he was in the guise of poet posturing in the romantic way—as if, at the heart, all Russians were romantic. I, from a society competitive for success image, felt my own, of Author, slip away.

The codes (more than selves) had a meeting in Moscow. A meeting of codes that *didn't* meet, didn't acknowledge one another. Yevtushenko, had he thought about it, I am sure, would have said his behavior and language were less coded than mine, more real than this pallid Anglo. He acted as if he were more authentic than I—he writes for eternity, he lives with one leg on the existential edge. The Russian strives for feeling, expressiveness in rich language. But in the rarefied and Anglo air of my publisher, the transcriber considered all of that buffoonery. Realism, honesty, simplicity, and concision constitute the valid code—never perceived as code—over here.

I, fresh from meeting Armani in Milan (see chapter 1), had an image of myself. And an expectation of Yevtushenko. At his door, I had expected that unelectronically, he would be uncharismatic unhistrionic, the Man Behind the Declaiming Head and Hand. Yevtushenko, fresh from blood poisoning in Italy, had an image of himself. And of me. American Writer (Maybe Useful) to Toy With. Keith, too, played his image like a musical instrument. *I'm hungry!* he moans. He's the Spontaneous American demanding food. Yevtushenko instantly saw a hierarchy break down. The man who is translator suddenly had a personal voice, needs of his own. He broke the Loyal Assistant code. No problems: The host, being Artist, deftly accepted the transgression of codes. Out came the jams and the bread for the student. Ah, but the host felt violated. And being the artist, therefore licensed to deploy the entire cuisine of emotion, he soon enough showed Keith aggression. In a short time he will shout at him: "Find ways [to eat]! I don't know how. But I survived even in this country in Stalin's time! *Goddamn! Huh? Don't ask me how to do it!*"

And again, still later in our three-hour . . . chat and chatter more than interview: "You have black blood, eh?"

Keith, aghast at being called a mulatto who passes. The Romantic Russian knows he can break any known code he wants (the hidden ones he doesn't break, true suffering, et cetera). The code of the Interview—it's nothing to Yevtushenko.

What were we three? Three code clusters unable to know ourselves as we were and are. I'm sure each of us thought himself to be authentic: Father Russia, Nice Guy, and Take No Shit. What a trio we'd make! In fact, we spent three hours at a lovely June lunchtime, eating jam and jabbering and later eating what the Russians call *okroshka** probably without sixty seconds of "authenticity." It's the modern way, maybe it's always been thus. We slipped out of one code into another as the struggle—let us say, of East against West— required. It was rhetoric that we blared at one another that day.

And, oh yes, not to forget the Anglo transcriber—disgusted, because of her code, at our codes. She foamed at the mouth—she was rabid, when I gave her the tape. "Exposing this great quote unquote man as a poseur and a buffoon will make a good read," she said. "It may also get you a free excursion to Siberia next time." As if an American visitor had ever been sent to Siberia! More codes: The Americans expose—Watergate, Irangate, et cetera (a little secret: the age of serious investigative reporting has been over some twenty years). American glasnost is her code. And another one: gulags over there.

And if all our relationships were Kafkian code confusion, clashings of codes? And if we never saw the other?

"Nobody from Russia knows America as I know it." And we're off on our—let's not be too quick to call it an interview. An interview presupposes representation—that the subject's words bear some relation to reality. The encounter with Yevtushenko was of an entirely different sort. A war of codes.

Yevtushenko is telling me about the big difference between Russians and Americans:

We Russians, we have one defect. That's a kind of masochistical confessionalism. For you could meet one Russian, you could formally ask him, "How are you? *Kak voy pozhivaete?''* That chap will grab your neck and during three hours . . . how you say *neet'?* Whine. Whine. Yeah, he'll *wh-i-i-i-ne.* About editors, about his bosses—three hours could do it. The Russian people very easily transform their own sufferings, what seems in their eyes as a suffering, into kind of toy. They like these toys. They like to suffer. They admire their suffering, digging into their own kidneys with their dirty nails, their own dirty nails. They bleed in your presence, vomit into your bread, as they say.

But in America you could be a friend of one American, but, only till certain level. It's very difficult to penetrate to the bottom. Why? Not

---

*"OKROSHKA. Most any sort of meat—game, beef, lamb, boiled ham, etc.—cut into triangular pieces, onto a large plate. Add peeled cucumbers (salted or fresh), hard boiled eggs, finely-cut onion, dill, tarragon—serve in a soup dish, add sour cream and KVASS (a peasant drink, a cross between beer and cider, made, usually, of dry bread), and also add salt, pepper and a piece of ice. Meat, 2–3 cucumbers, 3 eggs, 1–2 tablespoons of sour cream." Helen Molohovetz, *A Gift to Young Housewives* (St. Petersburg, 1881).

because this chap is a liar or insincere. No. He's just . . . most of Americans think that to be unlucky, that's shameful. They trying to hide it. They try to hide their unhappy personal life, their frustrations. They trying to squeeze it down as deep as it is possible. Squeeze it down because it's man who is speaking how he is unlucky or unhappy, he who speaks always is a weak man. So I think weakness of American society is to avoid speak openly about their weaknesses. That's main weakness.

He's a master rhetorician. He loves the paradox. Talking with public television's Robert MacNeil:

Russian people always were—even in Stalin's time—whispering sometimes but they were always discussing about the most painful problems. After Stalin's death we were discussing openly, but unfortunately inside our houses. It was very difficult to publish. It means in some circles of society we had kind of openness, kind of glasnost. But it was unfortunately glasnost which was not open.

Unopen openness for MacNeil. For me it's the weakness not to show weakness. Yevtushenko feeds you language, not just jam. He gives the thrill of vertiginous and phony exactness. He short-circuits reality. Americans "avoid speak openly about their weaknesses"? No, they can't wait to double for you what they just told the therapist. Michel Foucault's entire last years were devoted to the confessionalism at the heart of western life.

Yevtushenko tells me a story:

Old friend of mine, American. He was born in Salt Lake City. And once, we visited with him his native city, Salt Lake City, Mormon city, where he began his work selling ties, ties, *cravattes, les cravattes.*

It was *vedettes* and now it's *cravattes,* French in Russia, removing our poet another instance from reality.

Now it's a big store. He was deeply touched. He wasn't about eighteen years in his native city. He found that store now the big one. The owner of shop recognized him, embraced him. . . .

This is coming from Russian literature, not American life—men, need I say, aren't licensed to cry over here.

And I said to my American friend: "Okay, give me . . . I would like to buy for you a tie in this shop, in this section where you were selling ties. And I did it, in presence of owner.

When we left his shop, I said to him: "You know, I couldn't imagine such situation in Soviet Union. How the owner of shop permitted to me to *pay* money for . . . he must to . . . just to give you like this."

And he became very gloomy and very sad, my friend. So I hurt, I wounded him with my remark because it was a place of his childhood.

418

Figure 17.1 Yevtushenko in aspic. In the Yale Club library with the Claude Montana tie he coveted. *Courtesy Catherine Smith.*

Next day we were leaving Salt Lake City very early, and he said: "Genya, could you wait. I just would like to say goodbye to owner of shop." In fifteen minutes he came back with a . . . bouquet of ties in hands. And he said: "That's generous. You know, you don't understand us Americans," he said. "You think we could be mean." I said: "That chap—I didn't say that he was mean, he just didn't guess that he could be more generous." And my friend say: "Because he was so excited he forgot that he could be generous. You remember he was crying yesterday, so he just forgot, he didn't notice that you were buying. But now he gave these twelve ties to you, Genya, and to me, so you choose what you want, I'll choose what I want."

"And he was very excited, my American friend, shining eyes, slightly, a little bit too much nervous, too much happy. That's American culture—do you get it?"

This is what I get. That nobody talks any more about selling ties, except when you think of Harry Truman. How did he get his start? He was the little haberdasher from Missouri. Yevtushenko is mythologizing us again. His long, detailed, perfected tale, told in a land that still loves language, comes from another century, the nineteenth, and from a Russian tradition of telling. In our land we speak in bullets, we come to the point—where's the beef? The beef was six paragraphs up!

All of us are generous, in different ways. We all confess, for different reasons. A code of the Russians requires confession because of suffering. Ours, because we want a nice day and don't have

419

one. The American ideology of well-being always makes us fall off the mark.

We live in a world of codes in which, each carapaced in a way of talking, behaving, we knock against each other; sometimes, for an instant, there can be a spark of coincidence; then we go our different ways. We, after all, inhabit different, coded, that is, exclusive worlds.

Yevtushenko tried to tell me this wasn't so—look at Chernobyl.

> I think Chernobyl was very good, very good reaction—Americans, they reacted for Chernobyl very well. Americans, their first reaction could have been indifference: "Ah, it doesn't matter what happens. They're so far away." Second reaction could have been: "My God, that's good. Punish them. They deserve to be punished." Third reaction: "Oh gosh, they are so uncapable, those Russians. They are so back wooden. Even without any kind of war, they will blow up themselves. Better to blow them up first.
>
> But I haven't seen in America neither first reaction nor second nor third. No. I was incredibly touched. Sympathy for the victims. Real, real feeling, very sincere, without hypocrisy. And real concern, concern not only about American future, but real concern about our common future. And Americans themselves, when they call to radio, they began themselves to speak about explosions in some American nuclear plants, too, about the general possibility that everything will explode. Do you know that Soviet Union, our government, got a lot of personal letters by Americans? Do you know about it? Giant number, giant— personal letters to Gorbachev, just to Soviet girls, Soviet people, from children, from housewives, workers, different kind of people.
>
> So it was wonderful response, it was wonderful response by American people.

I try to temper the praise. I tell him of our mood during Chernobyl and of a powerful press line that heard—encouraged—it. "The press was nasty," I tell him. "In New York, the press of Rupert Murdoch at that time, the *Post,* was nasty at the beginning. What they stressed was: The Russians lie. The Russians would never have told if it hadn't been for the Scandinavian countries. Why, the Russians were shooting their own people who wouldn't do rescue duty in Chernobyl.'

I am trying to break this code of the good American people underneath the ideology of their rulers. But Yevtushenko thinks he knows better. Passionately:

> What it means? It means that hatred, so-called hatred for the Soviet people has no deep roots in American hearts. That's not hatred. That's fear of unknown animal.

He thinks he has a deeper knowledge of a depth of self over here—generous, transcending ideology. It's the Russian press that is speaking. Sometimes Yevtushenko talks like his country's press. It sought to split the (good) American people from its (aggressive) rulers. I have to insist: It has been years since we harbored love toward the Russians. Is it returning in the wake of their tragedy? I don't know. But the career of Sylvester Stallone surely wouldn't have been possible without a roiling well of hatred for things Soviet. Where is that well now? And I don't even bother to mention the success of Tom Cruise in *Top Gun*. Or Sean Connery in *Russia House*.

Sure, we burst forth in sympathy for the Chernobyl victims. Before that, we did it for the starving Ethiopians (remember them?). And we used to mourn missing children as we skimmed our morning milk cartons. Then the homeless caught our interest. We flit from one sympathy object to another. Americans like to feel sorry. For a while.

And Russians like to suffer. Yevtushenko told us this. Thus, to prove his point about Chernobyl, he adds:

> When John Kennedy was killed . . . being killed, I haven't foreseen such a kind of response of Russian people. Taxi driver was driving me and he was crying. So many people, Russian babushkas lining up to their shop with their *yoshkas,* with their transparent cane bags, they were crying.

But he has told me, the Russians like to suffer, to cry. Here, a big cry:

> So many people came to American Embassy to sign. Unexpected people, it was the first probably days when the American Embassy gates were open for everybody. That's real. Which means more reserves which we don't count, don't calculate sometimes, inside our peoples.

He's not describing an authenticity of Russian sentiment; rather, a coded reaction. Describing it within his own code of metaphor, of hyperbole. This is to say that we linguistically leaner Anglos easily read Yevtushenko as rhetorician. When it comes to rhetoric closer to home, such as honesty, simplicity, generosity, it is harder to perceive them as rhetoric. Nevertheless, most of what we say probably *is* rhetoric. Yevtushenko's is so obvious to us because it is strange. And this is why many have called him a poseur—simply the cruel, crude name hurled by those who demand of language that it reveal the Truth instead of delighting us.

Anecdote: A friend, the Cuban novelist Edmundo Desnoes, was taken aback when, in 60s Cuba, he heard Yevtushenko read. "This tall guy was like Mayakovsky thundering," he remembers. "I thought to myself—I was scarcely the only one who thought it— God, I'm listening to someone who wants poetry to sound like a river, like the bells, bells, bells of Edgar Allan Poe. It wasn't in good taste to us who were trained in modern poetry, in the subtleties of Eliot, in the value of the idea."

The rhetoric of Yevtushenko serves ideology: it is confrontational of the West. In the three hours we talk and eat lunch, we talk of many things, including American theater and cinema:

> Just to make conclusion, my friendly conclusion. I think America now is in very dangerous isolation from world culture. We have a Russian expression: *Kashy Katoroy Sam Zavaril,* steaming in his own juices. That's what's happening now in American culture. Because I saw some American so-called shits, Broadway hits. They're miserable. *Cats,* it's miserable. I saw *Les Misérables*—still is miserable. Such a comfortable version of French Revolution because you couldn't see red flag on American stage now. That's not real art, that's gimmick, you know. Gimmick. I'm not hypocrite, man. I liked old American musicals, for instance like *My Fair Lady, West Side Story, Fiddler on the Roof*—

What a cliché! "The great thing about America is the musical comedy." I have heard this from intellectuals a million times now! Every intellectual enters this role: I love your musicals! When I first came to know Umberto Eco in the 70s in New York, he asked if I wanted to accompany him to a Broadway show—to watch tap dancing. *No, I don't want to see tap dancing. I don't care about Fred Astaire* (I wanted to tell him but didn't dare). *Look, to me the only interesting thing about American shows are the porn parts.* I wanted to shout something like that to break this accumulated cliché of intellectuals.

Yevtushenko's is a historical society and ours is not. Therefore we have no business staging history, he is telling me. When we do, as in *Les Misérables,* of course he objects, mocking us for talking about the French Revolution: "The people who suffocated the French Revolution applaud with crocodile's teeth to little Gavroche in Broadway version." Our business, for him, is to be ahistorical, to idealize the world as we did in the 50s, in what for him was the essence of Broadway. This is not a gimmick? It's Yevtushenko Agonistes. Who is good and who is bad in our bilateral relations—this he calculated for our three-hour lunch. Your Broadway hits are shits, your film today is shit: "We see so many bad American films. You create such a terrible commercial censorship that very difficult just to get through for real good films. Because they suffocate them in cradles." I get the example—of course—of *Platoon.* And "Milos Forman many years was trying to find money for *Amadeus.''* And Yevtushenko *même* is an example:

> When I went to America in Hollywood, I was trying to sell my script, *The End of Musketeers.* I wrote script based on the last parable in Dumas' story, about the oldness and death of musketeers.
>
> Now Kirk Douglas, he's absolutely in love, he wants to be, to play. But it's very difficult to get money. Because they don't believe in commercial success. They are very sincere with me because they know that I'm not petty journalist [A reference to me?] but they insult—I

never insult America like they insult their own country, these Hollywood sharks, who are just saying to me: "Eugene, that's too clever,
your script is too clever for our mob." As a polite guest, I said: "You call
it, American people, what we said 'mob'?" The producer tells me:
"They like Rambo"—

The transcriber wrote "Rimbaud"—she's a literary type, the conversation has to be lit chat about Rimbaud.

"They like Rambo, they like stupid," the producer tells me. And I ask,
"Who created their taste?"
"We, of course," says the producer.
"But that's a vicious circle," I say. "You create their taste. Afterwards,
you accuse them that they are mob. Above all, you don't know, because
even so-called mob could love such films like *Amadeus,* like *Platoon.''*
"But that's Russian roulette," the producer says. "We can't bet on
such films."
So I think America now in spiritual crisis in arts, in politics, too. You
have no new outstanding people who could speak from the name of
American nation.

This isn't my style of discourse. I am trying to understand the
Soviet Union, but he is trying to establish a vis-à-vis America. Even
the few times he praises America—how good we were during
Chernobyl—even when he throws me a flower—in order later to
attack—I don't catch it. I didn't come to Russia to accuse the Soviets
or defend my own people. I had no stake in defending America as
Yevtushenko is defending Russia—the real subject of this conversa-
tion. He is on the attack and the defense, and at the same time wants
to be loved by Americans. And their money.
"You never hear of such people?" he asks me, referring to
nonexistent outstanding Americans.
"Who?" I say. I am listless, a ghost at the conversation.
"You have no such people." Aggressive.
"That's what I was asking," I say.
"That's what I'm saying. You have none."
You, we, you: it's the cold war again: who's good, who's bad? I
am lost in the Russia of Eugene, exemplary at this moment of so
many of his and of my people. Both sides relate through images and
coded ideas. Tragic.
And marvelous. Here is Yevtushenko in Hollywood, arguing with
the producers who won't produce his Three Musketeers because
Kirk Douglas is old and no one cares about death here. "So I think
America now in spiritual crisis in arts. . . ." No, he admires us. He
attacks us but he wants this America. His presence in Hollywood
shows his respect for our cinema. Counterproof: No important
American would take a script to Russia!
Further proof: He brings up "James Dean, *Rebel,* and now, uh,
Jay MacWorth . . . Jay Fox . . ."

Blonsky	Michael Fox.
Yevtushenko	Michael Fox, social climber. *Secret of My Success.*
Blonsky	You know . . .
Yevtushenko	(*"impolitely ignoring Blonsky,"* types my transcriber) No, he's a good actor. I mean, energy. He creates energy.

Our cinema in crisis? Except for Michael J. Fox? He doesn't know what he's talking about.

Our crisis? The Americans see Russia in crisis always—but the Russians used to see us in constant crisis, too. We were about to crash. This crash would be the Disaster. American art still is bankrupt. So, too, our sexual mores. But, remember, Gorbachev can't last. And what about the resisting Baltics? (Not to mention the sharpened-shovel-remembering Georgians.) Two sets of crises? Or two codes through which neither side sees the other? We're chatting away. I tell Eugene about my interview with Peter Ueberroth. What values was he trying to strengthen with the L.A. Olympics?— his big shot at fame. His answer: I wanted to restore volunteerism to America. I tell Eugene I was surprised. Volun—what? All the money was raised privately, Ueberroth was saying. And I thought— I tell Eugene—volunteerism is a word from the America of the past. America of den mothers. Of the Jerry Lewis Telethon that let you know it was Labor Day weekend. Of buying savings bonds in school. Of trick-or-treating for Unicef. Of planting trees in Israel. Not only was father to be found at home, but he also knew best.

It was of course the 50s, the confident Pax Americana. Ueberroth (I tell my new friend, Eugene) was one more nostalgist for America, the home of the brave who were simply—quoth the raven, never more, never more.

Whereupon—poetic outburst being new to me—I accidentally (on purpose?) drop my raspberry jam on the tan Armani pants I have just brought from Italy. "I invent a new word," Eugene says, looking at my red thigh. "Past-riotism. Your country in the Ueberroth years was delicious. Now as well."

And I say to this august man: "Can I put some water on my pants? I just spilled that jam on them."

Yevtushenko	Yeah, just use cold water.
Blonsky	Yeah?
Yevtushenko	Uh huh.
Blonsky	(*getting up*) I've heard it never comes—
Yevtushenko	Would you like *okroshka?*
Keith	(*sighing for some reason*) Sure.
Yevtushenko	Well, let's go, let's go. I don't suggest you want any kind of feast but we'll try.

Genya's Dictionary
of Invented Words

DEMOCKERACY n [Gk demos, people + Gk kratos, rule + ME mok-ken, of mocquer, to ridicule by imitation of speech or action, from a root mok- imitative with residue of laughter; by rhetorical trope tmesis with a little help from a friend (see etymology for "pastrio-tism"), the insertion of the virus of an almost silent "k," causing the "mock," like some parasitical monster, to exit the wordbelly, making it gape.]: 1. Government utterly not by the people. 2. That form of government in which the sovereign power feigns and imitates res-idence in the people and whose exercise by them is hollow form. 3. Imitation of democracy with an ulterior motive, pseudo-democratic discourse in a venomous language, replete with laugh-ter. "The composite elements of a demockeracy were described in a conversation with Bill Moyers by linguist Noam Chomsky: In a cap-italist democracy, you have the problem that the general population participates in the decision-making by participating in politics. The state is not capable of stopping them. You can't shut them out, you can't put them in jail, and you can't keep them away from the polls. It's striking that this has always been perceived as a problem to be overcome. It's called 'the crisis of democracy'—too many people or-ganizing themselves to enter the public arena. That's a crisis we have to overcome. . . Even the mainstream democratic theorists have always understood that when the voice of the people is heard, you're in trouble, because these stupid and ignorant masses, as they're called, are going to make the wrong decisions. So, therefore, we have to have what Walter Lippmann, back in 1920 or so, called 'manufacture of consent.' We have to ensure that that actual power is in the hands of what he called a specialized class—us smart guys, who are going to make the right decisions. From a point of view which perceives democracy as a problem to be overcome, and sees the right solution as being farsighted leaders with a specialized class of social managers—from that point of view, you must find means of marginalizing the population. Reducing them to apathy and obe-dience, allowing them to participate in the political system, but as consumers, not as true participants. You allow them a method for ratifying decisions that are made by others, but you eliminate the methods by which they might first, inform themselves; second, orga-nize; and third, act in such a way as to really control decision mak-ing. The idea is that our leaders control us, we don't control them. That is a very widespread view, from liberals and conservatives. And how do you achieve this? By turning elected offices into ceremonial positions. If you could get to the point where people would essentially vote for the Queen of England and take it seriously, then you would have gone a long way toward marginalizing the public. We've made a big step in that direction."

PASTRIOTISM n [late ME paste, from the Gk pastos sprinkled, + L patris fatherland, from pater father; by + tmesis, when the orator refuses to utter a word in its proper way, instead splitting it and inserting a foreign element in the gap, here "s"; a father sprinkled everywhere (his stature annihilated), then moistened and kneaded, make into smooth dough spread over the land, suggesting a fatherland as a gigantic baked tart exuding sweetness, the citizenry melded into one another to form a smooth, creamy mass without bones, sticky to the touch]: The character or passion of one who hurls himself at national ideas and imagery like an animal jumping at a lifelike rag waved in front of it. "Pastriotism was first uttered by the poet Yevgeny Yevtushenko in his dacha at Peredelkino, after this chronicler, dishing semiotic dirt on Peter Ueberroth, accidentally spilled jam on his Armani pants. Chronicler: Ueberroth told me he raised the . . . Jesus Christ, look what I've done . . . he . . . fuck it, he raised all the money for the '84 Olympics privately, by volunteerism, a word from the 50s, trick-or-treating for Unicef, get it? planting trees in Israel—Jesus, just one more nostalgia ploy.' Yevtushenko (observing the raspberry stain on the thigh): 'I invent a new word. Past-riotism. Your country in the Ueberroth years was delicious.'"

   1. "Charles shudders and stares at the screen from which the president is still smiling . . .
   "'O-O-' O-GH! What was in that speech?'
   "Loosening his bow tie, Howard smiles, too . . .
   "'A subliminal imbed I developed, Charles! It is RATHER POWERFUL!'
   "Charles rises, grasps the table for support! His body goes limp . . .
   "'We call it PASTRIOTISM. Rather clever, I think. It DISSOLVES CALCIUM and PHOSPHOUROUS salts! You know. . . What BONES are made of!'
   "'UUUGGNNN!'
   "Suddenly the rigidity leaves Charles' body and he collapses to the floor . . . a mass of flesh . . .
   "'We thought we should test it here in the Company first and you ARE past retirement age. WELL past, you know.'
   "'GLLAGHH!'

"'Now I am not the SPINELESS, BACK-BONELESS ONE, Charles! YOU ARE!'"

"Howard gazes at the mound of quivering flesh before him! His thoughts go back to the days when he was a child, at the beach . . . when he would accidentally crush a slimy jelly-fish under his bare foot! He shudders as he thinks of the patriotic duties ahead, then dismisses the thought, clenches his fists and . . .

"'Now YOU are a jelly-fish, Charles!'"

And we three go to his kitchen, whose little bathroom I now enter, rubbing my pants with a wet washcloth, while Yevtushenko and a woman who has suddenly appeared make *okroshka*.

"I like to invent new words," his voice resounds in my little space. "When I read about Gary Hart affair, I rushed immediately and said: 'It's not democracy, it's de*mock*eracy.'"

I leave the bathroom, a large water stain on my right thigh, and I spot a small picture of a young woman. "Is that your wife?" I say.

"Yah," he goes.

"Will she be joining us for lunch?" Ever the gracious American.

"Nah, she takes her exams now. In Moscow."

"Oh, she's going for another degree?" I, Innocent, say.

"What you mean another degree? It's college degree." And: "You see, I'm married"—with relish he rolls the *r* of the next word—"criminally young."

I have no idea what narrative connections took place. My tape recorder was off during the pants rubbing. I sat down at a round wooden table, watching as Yevtushenko directed the *okroshka* making. I turned the machine on again, and this is what Yevtushenko is saying:

"I think they're tired, Russian prostitutes."

"They look bad, they're not well dressed." I say. "And the Finns! Last night one of them at my table—"

At my Belgrade Hotel table, I was placed next to Finnish construction workers, one of whom said: "Look at me."

"And see what?" I said.

"I am not a handsome man," he said.

I told him I thought he looked fine.

"No, I am not a handsome man, and in Finland, the sex is free, and because it is free, there are no ladies like these." He gestures in the direction of the score or more of shinily dressed, makeup-coated prostitutes in green and red and blue dresses evocative of the 40s. "No women like me so I come here for the ladies. Very nice ladies."

One of whom shortly slides next to me, saying: "I want to dance only with you." Her hand on my thigh.

I am telling Eugene all this:

Blonsky	He said, "I am not a handsome man."
Yevtushenko	You?
Blonsky	(*a bit agitated*) He. *He* said pointing to himself. "I am not a handsome man."
YEVTUSHENKO	Ah, poor thing. Poor thing.

It's absurd. Here I am talking to one of Russia's greatest poets with my pants stained and we're talking of:

Blonsky	So all the while he's telling me this, his friend is negotiating with a—
Yevtushenko	(*interrupting*) How much do they cost now?
Blonsky	This is what he does. The woman is at another table. He puts—

And I show him. Two fingers up, then forefinger in the mouth, then that forefinger out of the mouth points up.

Blonsky	Two hundred Finnish marks—
Keith	(*interrupts*) He probably meant get her drunk and you can get her down to two hundred—
Blonsky	(*exasperated*) Two hundred—vodka—in my room upstairs.
Yevtushenko	Two hundred Finnish marks—that's how much? In dollars?

How pathetic: Here is my breakthrough in which he becomes the ignorant and I, the idiot savant. He who has pronounced, now hearing about prostitutes, does an about-face: how much they cost now? He is interviewing *me* about the Soviet Union. He doesn't know the price of a whore!

Blonsky	It's about sixty dollars.
Yevtushenko	Of course I did it when I was very young.

Trying to recover his authority.

A couple of white guys sitting around. Yes, sexists all around.

As we eat he asks me (I being partially Russian), did I have this in my childhood?

"We were totally assimilated. My parents forgot their Odessan background."

The transcriber typed Odyssean.

Yevtushenko	(*talking, yes, while eating*) Canteens on the road are so terrible in America. They always put pepper on everything.
Blonsky	(*confused*) Pepper?
Yevtushenko	Everything. Instead of salt.
Blonsky	Why?
Yevtushenko	Because there is religion. They are saying that salt is very harmful and pepper is progress.

What is he talking about? This is lunacy.

Blonsky	I bet you don't know this one—Arthur Treacher's Fish and Chips. You never heard of it, did you?

By no means is it lunacy. Genya (if I may) Yevtushenko is a jester at the court of the General Secretary. I, for this book, was a jester at the court of Pat Robertson, the Elysée Palace, the house of Armani, NBC "Nightly News," and "Nightline." Yevtushenko paid me the honor of treating me as a similar. For three hours in Peredelkino, we jingled the bells on our conical hats at each other. Courtiers, especially the witty kind, have to stay in practice.

> *Yevtushenko*   (*taken aback*) No, I . . . look, I was many times in America.
>
> *Blonsky*   The *New York Times* reviewed it and they said that as you cut into your fish, it bled.
>
> *Yevtushenko*   (*to Keith*) How long time you learn Russian?

He cannot bear it that he doesn't know a datum about America.

> *Yevtushenko*   Best readers which I have met in America. You couldn't find such kind of readers of literature in Europe. Impossible. In Europe you could find all snobs. So called connoisseurs. Or ignorant. Or arrogant. In American provincial you could find people with spiritual life—sub-clerk, little clerk in bank or just pharmacologists.
>
> *Blonsky*   Pharmacists.
>
> *Yevtushenko*   Pharmacists. They publish their own work, very honestly.

It's a theme dear to Europeans. It is from Chekhov, from his little village in which there is a teacher, a pharmacist who reads, who talks in the village inn, the *botecario* in Spain, the *apoteke* in Russia.

Broadway is shits and only the little people, the pharmacists, carry on the spiritual life here. In a little town in America, after one of his readings, "one of them asked me, was pharmacist—he asked me: 'What do you think about my idea that Stephen Crane short story "Blue Hotel" was the cradle of Ernest Hemingway style?' And 'Goddamn!' I said. 'Goddamn! That is what I was thinking once. Hemingway before Hemingway.' It was only place in America where I found connoisseurs of Thomas Wolfe. Nobody reads him but he's one of the greatest American writers. Oh, I love it, he's a great writer." Yevtushenko and one pharmacist, bearers of a tradition we have abandoned.

So I jingle about our new, our callow, writers:

> *Blonsky*   Have you read some of the stuff coming out, *Bright Lights, Big City, Sex Tips for Girls, But Enough About You?* Ghastly stuff.
>
> *Yevtushenko*   No.
>
> *Blonsky*   Trashy novels.
>
> *Yevtushenko*   What are names?

Blonsky	Jay McInerney, Cynthia Heimel, Bret Easton Ellis.
Yevtushenko	Could you write down before you leave?

He wants to read them, has to keep up with everything American.

"He doesn't like to be left out," Edmundo Desnoes is telling me. "I met him in Havana when we both were young. His skin was resilient. There were no wrinkles. He was tall and didn't have a little pouch as he has now. He was staying at the Havana Riviera, and there is a modern sculpture there which is the typical thing you find in Vegas. Like a pasta sculpture without any structure, something like the shape of a woman. He said: 'I love modern art. I love to walk out of the hotel and see the sculpture the Revolution has done.' But it wasn't done by the Revolution. It was done before, by the people who built the Riviera. Just a decorative thing of a cheap, Jewish, Renaissance hotel." Oops.

Yevtushenko survived because he played jester, poseur, buffoon (as some, not I, call him). Robert MacNeil in Moscow introduces him with—"He has survived . . . just on the margin of official approval/disapproval, occasionally chastised but permitted extraordinary freedom to publish and travel." Playing the jester, he is at times the one who must tell the king the truth. Or tell the court, including ambassadors to it, what is moral.

At the first Reagan-Gorbachev Moscow summit, when he spoke to Robert MacNeil, he bore something like state responsibility. The codes, to which I was treated and which I relished, had a lesser, or at least different, place in the dignity of a summit. Introducing his partner MacNeil, Jim Lehrer sensed the less coded quality of Yevtushenko:

Lehrer	We begin tonight with [MacNeil's] first report. It features an extraordinary interview with an extraordinary man about the new Russian Revolution called perestroika.
Macneil	You said that you're a man who has hopes and fears. Is fear, the sensible fear of . . . getting into trouble, is that fear being dispelled by perestroika?
Yevtushenko	I think it ten times less fear than before. But I mean . . . you know, extermination, abolition of fears, that's very slow process. Very slow. Because fears, they are running in our *blood* (he exaggerates the vowel), together with—how you call it?—red and white balls you call them.
Macneil	Corpuscles.
Yevtushenko	(*struggling*)Cor—
Macneil	Corpuscles.

431

Yevtushenko Corpuscles . . . yes . . . together with white and red corpuscles inside our veins are running *gray* (he draws the vowel out) corpuscles. That's corpuscles of [pause—lowered voice—drawn vowel] *fear*. Because fear doesn't permit us be too colorful. Fear trying to force us to be [his voice lowers] *gray*. Fears, they produce grayness in society. But grayness produce [somber] brown color. If you remember history, you know what meaned German history of German brown color. And I mean we have, for instance, now very strong Russian chauvinist groups. And some of them really behave as fascists in relationship with our minorities, for instance. They behave as fascists when they trying to accuse in all defects of our society Jewish people.

With your hat and your bells, once in a while you puncture the pretense of the crown. Some of us are fascists and (marvelous metaphor) fear is so deep we have a third corpuscle!

You stand and make your little flourish with honesty. As, after lunch, mellow, Zhenya tells me this untranslated story of his fellow writer, his contemporary, Prestovkyn:

To Russian kindergarten from central Russia came to the place Chechens. And some Chechens, they are hiding in cracks of mountains. You can translate this, sir.

He says to Keith.

I help you.

Keith demurring.

I'll say to your American publisher: "Look, it's a great book." Now I speak as the publisher: "But Prestovkyn, who's he?" He isn't known in America. You know why not? Pasternak became known in your country only after political scandal—he deserved Nobel Prize already in early 30s. Your American publishers only after scandal, because you always saying to us: "Yeah, but we need publicity." So Russian writers, to be published in America, they must squeeze into mental hospital, into prison, they must rape Kremlin tower. Preferably from the backside. That's really true, sir."

To a dubious Keith who's just been offered a career. But Keith will later snarl after we've left: "I can't wait to get out of this fucking country. I want to go to Hungary." You see, in Hungary, you eat better.

Sine die, Genya calms himself and finds the narrative thread:

From central Russia came Chechens to Russian kindergarten. They are hiding, these Chechens, by day in cracks of mountains.

The Chechens, in the eighteenth century, in the days of Catherine the Great, were a Caucausus Mountain people, obstacles to Russian expansion. This is a story about the collision of two peoples. It is of course intended allegorically for me.

And in the night, Chechens are coming down from the mountains to make massacre with Russian childrens who slept now in their school, kindergarten, how you call? . . . *sirotsky dom*, orphanage. And so one Chechen opens blanket, and he killed one Russian child, nine years old. Afterwards he opened more blanket. He saw absolutely same Russian, same face. They were twins, but he was like a stone, petrified. Is a horror. And his son, little Chechen, was biting his hand. Didn't give him to kill the second one.

Afterwards came Russian soldiers. Russian soldiers became punitive expedition. They began to kill all these rest of Chechens. They found them in cracks. And this Russian boy . . . I'm in love with this story. If I could speak English I could translate it. This Russian boy, one of twins, he decided to fulfill the dream, last wish of his killed brother. Because his dream was to see the sea. And he's carrying his dead brother on his shoulder, carrying to the train which goes to the seaside. And on the way he met this little Chechen. He's like little animal [Whispers:] He's hiding . . . from Russian soldiers . . . in one crack mountains.

And he recognizes little Chechen because he saved his life. So they began to carry his dead body together. Chechen shoulders. And they put him with dead body of the child under the train carriage, with rocks. They weighed. Moscow-Sukhumi, it's the port [on the Black Sea]. And afterwards they came back and Russian secret police, army police came to the orphanage.

''You have some *Chechens*—amongst you!''

''No, no Chechens here.''

''But they, they, they are killing your children. You are trying to hide Chechens!''

[Soft voice:] ''There is no Chechen. There are only children.''

''*But this one. He has no Russian eyes. Black eyes. Huh? Say me something in Russian?*''

He couldn't speak. He's . . . how to say it? . . . deaf mute.

''*Who is he?*''

''That's my brother,'' another chap answered. ''That's my brother.''

''He have different eyes.''

[Softly:] ''That's my brother.''

''*Could you affirm that he is his brother, really? Let me document.* Kouznan-sky, Kouz-na . . . yeah, two brothers. [Softly, slyly:] Are you really brothers? Are they really brothers?'' he asked all children.

All children knows that Chechens killed [shouts it] *his brother*. This is Chechen.

''Yes, he is his brother.''

At the end, a Chechen according [to a] very ancient rule, with his little dagger cutting his hand and hand of his Russian brother. They changed blood.

It's beautiful. It's not political but it's such a beautiful book.

Yevtushenko is trying to tell me something about our two countries. He is telling me about solidarity that transcends tragedy. These two children represent the new world of the future where differences and hates will disappear. It's a socialist realistic story done with all the gushing emotionalism of the Soviets. Suddenly the one who kills part of you becomes your brother. You protect him and found the future on forgiving mutual hatred. The police come, the solidarity. Even the blood exchange, which is a cliché. This complex tragedy and love merge into the situation where the two opposites survive as friends. The one who kills you and then saves you is your friend and you protect him.

He went back to his old code. There is tragedy in the kitchen. There is a tragedy of misunderstanding between the two countries. For a moment he seems to break the code with corpuscles, then he becomes a soulful Russian all over again, brimming with solidarity, which doubtless would be effective on a Slavic stage. Perhaps, however, we would not feel that this is a metaphor for forgiving your enemy as you forgive. . . . This is a Christian metaphor.

He reached a point where he became universal, then recoiled into Russian code. Is it possible that we can reach an understanding between the two of us? And is this the way the Russians could see this as metaphor? Will Americans see that they kill my brother and I'm going to save him and become his friend, transcending the most horrible murder possible, that of a child, to create a solidarity for the future? Is this possible in the world? This is almost a Dostoevskian metaphor. Can we survive after killing each other? After you've killed my young? Can we be friends and create a new world? Yevtushenko says yes. Here again, I think we are living in two different worlds. Can we break these two codes? Break them in order to aid and live with our enemy, achieve a transcendence through tragedy, which the Slavic mind understands and the American mind does not?

There were two and the father killed only one of them. That's another metaphor. The father killed half of the identity. The son then assumed the other half. He became the brother. Through his father he killed one brother and placed himself in the brother's position. They became brothers. It is a metaphor of salvation. Could we in this world understand this tragic image? Could it be understood in our culture?

I am sure that Yevtushenko wanted me to take his story figurally; as a way to think the morass of languages, codes, images, and stereotypes that underlie the clash between east and west, between the Slav and the Atlantic experience, between the world of heavy engineering and big battalions, on the one hand, and micro-electronics and pluralism, on the other. But you'll recall that sometimes figuration doesn't work; metaphors don't transport us, tragic narratives don't redeem us. Back in America, not long after I heard this tale, I read in my distinctly unliterary *New York Times* of yet another vote of no confidence in Mikhail Gorbachev by Parliament. Sazhi Z. Umalatova, a woman from the Chechen-Ingush Autonomous Republic, called for the vote. "Having disrupted the country and divided the people, [Gorbachev] goes to the world with outstretched hands," said the conservative. "Perhaps you favor this kind of charity, but I am deeply insulted by it. In all the applause from the West, Mikhail Sergeyevich has forgotten whose President he is." When Umalatova sprang into life as metaphor for Soviet devolution, just at that moment was the tragic element of Yevtushenko's story lost. His tale had become literal. Really chilling. (And not even to mention Yeltsin's near invasion of the Republic.) And I grasped that Yevtushenko's Chechens and Russians weren't debating administrative tinkering, or market reform, or even economics. The debate was about their soul, about what metaphor they would choose by which to tell the world: "This is how we wish you to designate, to identify us."

The debate is far from over, but one thing can be known: whatever the metaphor that will come to these suffering peoples, it will be of the soul. Russians want to act in conformity with that which is Right, with the Historically Grand; in doing so, they are the tools or instruments of God. It is this that destroyed communism—which had become so corrupt and decadent, so enfeebled, that Russians lost their faith in it. Their myth remains: They must be Right, must be in the vanguard of History and Truth; in the name of which one can suffer, can impose suffering. The myth remains but its content evanesced. The conditions of Russian lives ceased to be congruent with Russian mythology. When it was plain that their lived experience was not that of the vanguard society; that instead they were blunderers; then all the icons of communism fell, down to Gorbachev, who, on his post-putsch return from the Crimea, would not, in his haste to resume his Kremlin throne, stop to embrace the man who had saved his life and saved democracy, Boris Yeltsin. God's instrument does not act so . . . unsoulfully. And that is why the once World's Darling is as of this writing a columnist for *La Stampa*.

The putrescence of communism tells us again that cultural meaning is primary. If you want to assess where a people is headed—how vigorous they are—don't look at their figures for GNP. Understand, instead, whether their lives are in tune with the meanings—the myths—that matter to them. But while, from the security of the remaining superpower, you're looking at the corpse of the other, you might want to ask yourself: "To what extent may our lives be out of joint with our cherished myths? Is America really the home of the brave and the free?

We take the electric train home from Peredelkino. Russian soldiers are everywhere in our car, sleeping, mouths open, *zzzzzz*. And this crazy thought comes to me: I've been captured by the enemy, *I'm* the Chechen. It looks to me like a scene from a spy film. It has come to me from the books I've read, from *Gorky Park,* from Le Carré. I am an American spy surrounded in a Hitchcockian train by these snoring bastards. Who are they? Doubtless poor, conscripted peasants, their mouths open—on the seats beside them, baskets full of food—whom Americans through their old prejudices used to see as the Red Threat. Probably hungry, they snore, perhaps dreaming of home.

Is this the imposing goose-stepping enemy marching in Red Square presented only a short while ago in our media? In our love affair with perestroika—now our sympathy for its victims—have my code and theirs really been broken to become one?

436

18 *Why Stop Now*

Because I'm tired after four years of travel and the solitary pleasures of pixels on the night of my screen. And because I'm a bit afraid of the machine I made in the last seventeen chapters. And the machine I made of myself. Let me explain.

I hit the road and met the Attalis and Yevtushenkos, the Armanis, Costa-Gavrases and Kings (you get my drift—truth is, they're all unique: there are no Yevtushenko*s*). All right, I received their discourse, and now I know two or three things about the near twenty-first century. Meanwhile, much that Theodore Zeldin told me would happen did. The "high supereducation" (his words) I got made me cosmopolitan, a bit French, a bit Talmudic, a patchwork of this and that, inevitably not an American. I came to like certain people (you'll have told it from prose) and dislike others (the same), and now I know why. Because the Bellinis of this book made a contact with me. Which? They gave me a place at the table of their knowledge and irrigated the short distance between us with tenderness, eros, and sophia. Costa-Gavras sitting on the sofa cradling his sleeping son—take it as the metaphor of the good part of my trip; it was a relation of love without image, without posturing. An *epithymia,* as the ancient Greeks called it, an epithymics, if we had the word in English, a desire without vulgar object, desire in its pure state, the stretching forth of erectile life itself.

It was the Europeans and the Japanese with whom I accomplished this more than the Americans. Why? Because being foreign, their very sentence structure and physiognomy began my alienation from America, the condition of my reading it. Maybe I found in their homes what I've always wanted to find, a *dépaysement,* as the French say and we cannot: an uncountrying, taking leave of your country. I only know that, as Zeldin on the road predicted, now I miss these intellectual friends; less the flights to see them, the hotels that received me, the minor luxuries of interviewing than the warm conversation. It's conversation itself in the age of image—conversation drifting into silences unsupported by music (and need I add, conversation glowing with desire for ideas)—that has seemed absent in America all during the writing of this book. This isn't a truism about the solitude of writing; nor, I hope, is it naive anti-Americanism. I found Mark Goodson talking game show theory in a windbreaker, nursing some inner sadness, as strange a bird as animator Yuri Norstayn comparing me in Moscow to a secretary bird (it, too, is bald). Stephen King blasting the room with rock, describing a ghost he saw, is . . . not American, shall we say in delicacy. Far from happy, cool, easy. I think my observation—I miss the conversation—amounts to saying: I want to be estranged. I want out of the jackets I wore before undertaking this book. Out of Parisian velvet as much as Poughkeepsie tweed. Out also of Armani slouch. To let none of the foreigners, either, straightjacket me in silk—that was a postulate by which I tried to live on the road and in the writing. "It is necessary to have the courage to show oneself a little as one is—inside," Armani told me. It was not only a moral precept, it was also a marketing concept. Knowing that turns of decade radically question ideology, write The End—before others see an end—to the culture of appetite and agitation. And as he foresaw, so it transpired.

Greed, business, Reagan, Giorgio of Beverly Hills, all of it became retro. The newly discovered—the turn-of-the-decade discovered—excess of yesterday now props up the normality of the supposedly gentler present. That is what Armani's about-face means. That is why he sketched for me his "schlep" suit. That is why, when he finally unveiled it in fall 1990, his models walked the runway in loose, shambling, even apologetic gait—postures of humility. Having been near consecrated by the *New York Times* fashion page:

> MILAN, Italy, Oct. 11—Giorgio Armani showed a four-star collection Wednesday night, bringing the spring and summer ready-to-wear openings to a rousing conclusion.
>
> The presentation was swift and pointed. Within half an hour the designer had suggested a way for women to look cool, confident and elegant for the new decade. . . . Retailers looking for a new fashion direction were attentive. Nostalgia for the 1960s, which has blanketed many shows, is not enough, they believe; what fashion needs is a road to the future. Armani has provided it.
>
> In blazing his new trail, he has also changed his own direction. Armani shot to fame in the late 1970s with the oversized jacket that younger designers were reviving as the "boyfriend" jacket a year ago. He made

the pants suit a staple. More recently, he has reduced shoulder pads and elminated construction in his jackets.

BERNADINE MORRIS

—he greeted admirers at the door of New York's Fashion Institute of Technology, retrospecting his work, dressed how? I was behind him, he who could flawlessly tailor his own jacket, make it wrinkle and fold free. Navy blue, it was slightly overlong, emphasizing a plummet, a descent. At the right shoulder blade was a deep fold, surprising me. A sloppiness, I crazily thought. Nothing in Armani is sloppy. He was slouching his own way to Bethelehem. Fashion for an age of uncertainty. A rhetoric like others, but glorious.

"I want to be estranged"—it means I want to think from within my own system, not be armored in Armani's or any others. And obviously, for that, one needs a foreign interlocutory power, be it a person or compelling idea. I would hope that this book could function as the latter for you. But an idea, truly to be foreign, must ultimately come from the friendly mouth of another, the Other. Therefore I offer the book to the reader in a relationship (of friendship, love, education, whatever). Porn addicts won't want it.

That said, I wish to pose an outrageously American question about the "supereducation" within these covers. *So what?* When Jacques Attali told me—

> In terms of intellectual concepts, there are none coming from America. I cannot name one American social thinker.

—you remember the put-down (p. 9); when he said those words over coffee in the Elysée, he wasn't only sneering at our culture, an upper-crust equivalent of some bad-tempered Parisian waiter bad-mouthing one's accent. He was alluding to our penchant for the practical. What can I do with your idea? Can I sell with it? Enhance my life? And by the way, what can I do with your American mythologies?

I have tried to show that connotation today—far beyond the advertising phenomenon—is no longer merely "hidden persuasion" but is in fact a semiosphere, a dense atmosphere of signs triumphantly permeating all social, political, and imaginative life and, arguably, constituting our desiring selves as such. But you can say to me: You have seized a sign artifact, you have dissected it, dispersed it according to a different order from the logico-temporal order to which initially it was submitted. You have succeeded in making a theoretic discourse about American mythology—SO WHAT (so emphatic, there's not even a question mark). That is what Francis Bacon told Aristotle and Plato—so what.

Here's what. And it's a story about the enunciation of those mythologies, the different modalities in which I can tell my knowledge. The first one, the following, is unacceptable.

439

The semiosphere we imbibe is so vulgarly rich (I trust you'll grant me this now), it would seem to demand a semiotic perpetual motion, a ceaseless simultaneous translation of the social rhetoric into its connotations. Fine. All the while the world speaks to me I can speak and spit back its spectral messages. My mental arteries may be clogged, but following the principle that curiosity is a beautiful virtue, at least I know my state. This turns me into a raconteur of my arterial mind disease, offers me a life's work, and jails me in perpetuity. I am as dependent on the jabber of culture for my identity as John Gotti's persecutors and prosecutors depend on him for their prestige. The semiotician is sign-struck.

This is why the critic Christopher Ricks greeted the publication in London of Barthes' *Mythologies* and this mythology—

> I think that cars today are almost the exact equivalent of the great Gothic cathedrals: I mean the supreme creation of an era, conceived with passion by unknown artists, and consumed in image if not in usage by a whole population which appropriates them as as a purely magical object.

—with the wisecrack: "What a copywriter." You utter your myth-ologies, among which one or two or three are about advertising; you think that advertising is an epiphenomenon, that you've performed a Brechtian *Verfremdung,* an alienation from the stu-pidities you've dissected; lo and behold, your book, your seminar, your life's work is a form of advertising. You know, going in, you're all tangled up with the Other—ideology inside you—but you think that by your decoding, your mythoclasm, your deconstruction, you've freed yourself. Only to realize that you're entangled all over again. You're not a manipulee. Fine, you're a pitchman for the system. It's a nightmare that ought to shadow every critic worthy of the name (to criticize: put one's object in crisis). But the stresses and strains of consumerism on thought—rarely is this itself thought.

What to do?

Not to return to the academic chamber, to its spare prose whose marks, since free of subjectivity, are supposed to be free of social coercion. "If you want to produce a scholarly book," Zeldin told me in Oxford, "it means you want to produce a book like other books. That's what 'scholarly' means. Scholarship is an agreement about the form in which books should be presented." And form is decisive. Blustery Yevtushenko wouldn't have been Yevtushenko if he had greeted me at his door with "hello" instead of "what tragic eyes you have!" The man of two countries, survivor Vladimir Pozner, wouldn't be Pozner if he had merely agreed with Yev-tushenko on the glossiness of our superficial imagery. "An injection for the eyes!" Yevtushenko had exploded. And the canny Pozner: "Remember the ending of Fosse's *All That Jazz?* A beguiling foreground while in the back, Roy Scheider . . ." An encounter with Pozner is like being in a constantly moving turnstile that presents alternately a Russian and an American. He is like two computer images folding on one another, moving through and around each. His existence whispers: "I am not the Russian you think I am; I am someone other than this American you think I am." Back in America, two months later, he tells someone in my hearing—it's a vast US-USSR political exchange in Chatauqua, New York—that he's been offered $800,000 a year to become an American anchor. He's tempted, he says, but we won't leave his country. His form *is* the man, and so my trip taught me to respect form. What form for me? For you?

Why

Stop

Now

Zeldin the scholar had also told me: "I think it is a diminution of your talents to produce something which bows to scholarly conventions. It says, 'Put a tie on, put a jacket on.' You've got to behave, when you appear in public, the way we have always behaved. Scholars have always tried to expel the personal from their books. And they failed. They fool themselves. You cannot expel the personal—because books are written by people."

So I desire to go farther from the Barthes of the world and into the personal. I have a story in this connection.

The day before I left Moscow, I flagged a gypsy cab to take me to the Beriozka, a hard currency store, across the street from the Novodevichy Cemetery. I had final gifts to buy for friends in America. Along the way (like a proper Soviet, I am sitting in front; in back would be aping the plutocrat); the driver—"I am Alex," he said—and I talked in English. He gestured to me to put on my seatbelt, but as I started to buckle it, he said leave it, it's okay. This had happened to me before in taxis. In Moscow you just put the belt across your lap—a simulacrum for the police eye.

Alex's daughter, married to an American, lives in L.A. No, he's never visited and never will, he says; his job is "hush-hush," he won't be allowed out (this was before the collapse of Communism; perhaps things would be different now). We are crossing a channel of the Moscow River and I tell Alex, to make conversation, that a side of my family is from Minsk. "I hope I am not impudent," he responds, "but please, what religion are you? Protestant, Catholic, Jewish?" After a beat because I am startled, I answer: "Jewish." "And I also," he says. And we talk of Pamyat, the right-wing nationalist group let loose by perestroika. Pamyat, Alex tells me (the word means "remember"), has insinuated that Jews have destroyed ancient Russian churches. Pamyat staged a demonstration in Moscow; to placate its members, then Moscow party chief Boris Yeltsin met with its leaders.

"Can you imagine Yeltsin meeting with Jews?" Alex says with asperity. "Could the Jews make themselves a group?"

Because I want to reduce the heat in his voice, I make a little joke. "Ah, but if there were, you could call it Zakhor," I say—"after Pamyat."

He is impassive.

"Zakhor means remember in Hebrew," I say. "You didn't know that?"

"How could I know that?" Even more asperity. "I didn't go to Hebrew School. There isn't a Hebrew School in Moscow. There is one synagogue in all Moscow. It is hard to be a Muscovite and it is harder to be a Jew."

We have arrived at the Beriozka, and Alex agrees to wait for me. A limousine is parked outside. A Mercedes saloon is nearby. A Latin American family idles near its car, a BMW. Inside, I roll my shopping cart past Hunter's Vodka, Courvoisier, caviar, cheeses. I am struggling with a decision I must make. On the second floor now, bottles of vodka in a bag, I buy seal and marmot hats for friends in New York. I say to the Intourist saleswoman: "Is it permitted"—we have already exchanged a few words in English—"is it permitted in the Soviet Union to give a gift from a Beriozka to a Muscovite?"

"I . . . don't . . . speak . . . English," she mumbles.

"Est-ce que je peux vous aider?" A man is next to me speaking French. *"Bien sur, c'est possible,"* he says, *"mais ça, c'est fait avec delicatesse ici,"* it's possible but it's done quietly over here. But his lips are moving in French, and the sibilance of *delicatesse ici* seems at that moment a warning hiss. The very question, "Is it permitted?" tells of my fall into a structure of fear—real? Imagined?

On the way home to my hotel, I ask Alex about the alcohol ban. Is it a matter only of queues, of just a few hours a day they give you to buy vodka? He smiles ruefully. "Vodka is hard," he says—he means hard to get. Embarrassed by my plenty, thinking the craziest thoughts, that perhaps he'll rip me off, I and this little man who looks edgy, a tad undernourished, a bit like a younger Charles Aznavour, drive to the Hotel Belgrade near the Foreign Ministry. In the driveway, I who had thought Russia so strange that perhaps one couldn't give gifts there; I who in New York, laden with packages, have seen and easily passed people eating from trash cans . . . there in Russia, where there is supposed to be justice . . . I felt guilty. In the Soviet Union, having more than others used to be not ideologically legitimate.

So you hid it before perestroika became market economy. Or you placate it. So there I am, already turning Russian, leaving two bottles of vodka, wrapped in simple paper, on the floorboard of the front seat. Alex bends to retrieve my parcel—"You forgot it," he says.

"I didn't, it's for you," I say.

And this wizened man whose face had seemed to me gray with

442

his lot extends his hand, the face opening like a flower. "Thank you," he says, grasping my hand. "Just thank you."

Perhaps I have succeeded in producing evidence about America; that was my first task. But as the reader by now can tell, I experienced moments of warmth and discovery (also, displeasure and animosity). This second process should not be thought an obstacle to reading America—it is the means by which I accomplished my first task (well or badly). I met a man called Alex, who either is or isn't leading an aberrant life; who would like to come to L.A. A moment of warmth passed between us; in it, I *knew*—how hard to live in Russia, be it Jew or non-Jew; the compensatory pleasures of conversation. The gift was, for me (for Alex it was different), a way to say, I am talking to you: you exist for me, I want to exist for you. In that moment I said to myself, really affirmed it: this is how I'm going to write my book. I'll try to paint a picture of America in collaboration with a little community of quirky, talented people. Maybe it'll be a good picture, but I'll never believe that it shows "reality." Some talents will make an American picture but not in the classical mode; rather, in the impressionist. Composed of many small dots, the vision will be misty in order to signify: this is a vision of America, perhaps even a hallucination. It is art more than truth. Thus we return to an epithymics: I desire to read America through my interviewees' desire and my own, which is produced by theirs. I value all of it, from the stirring of interest to the flutter of anxiety and the tremolo of fright.

So what? So this: you can take the knowledge of this little band I assembled, and out of it fashion language in which the one who writes acknowledges himself; more than that, assumes himself as subject, the human subject of what he writes. At the moment you do this, you're not writing sociology, or any kind of treatise; you are . . . writing. And at such a moment, you rediscover the value of style. It is in the style that the subject of the enunciation is present, and it does not suffice to say "I" or "told me" to contact one's subjectivity. Style is play with language, and if one is successful at it, at that moment one is a writer, no longer obeying grammar but cosseted in discourse, which is a species of energy, of the *energon* of the Greeks. This energy dialecticizes language and is, as Stéphane Mallarmé said, the supplement of the language, which is always fascist because it obliges saying things. All of us are caught by language, made to be soft-spoken executors of it until, in drink or drugs or raucous party-going, we burst its bonds. Playing with language is another—if not better, a more lasting way. It is an almost revolutionary appeal to the patrimonial tongue. It is a force that resists the nature of language, language as nature, its historical weight, anteriority, coextension with authority, all its traits that make us monotoned utterers of it, clerks of its systematicity. But play—real play, not the office and bedroom jokes to

443

which we are prey—is a permission to say in another way. To be different.

It is difficult to find style. It may even require the intervention of chance. As the following. This entire book was written with amber pixels on a black background, as I said earlier. I only discovered the meaning of this event here in this chapter, and the meaning, I think, is this. I used an IBM computer, not a Mac. Not for me, therefore, the Mac's gregariousness, its black font on bright background, bright enough to resemble an interrogation light in your face. Despite its faintly punitive lighting, the Mac can appear to be friendly; the IBM, never. To me, it was scary, the black of my screen recalling solitude and night. Maybe this is why my preferred time of writing was the night.

My Princeton Max-12 monitor sits atop the IBM AT black box (which is gray). And it came to me suddenly, writing this End, that for the entirety of the four years of logging itineraries, making 4 A.M. transcripts of Martin and Merv, of writing drafts and chapters, of F8-ing (external copying) Martin into McDonald's, causing unknow-able secret travels of byte armies, the screen has been *too high*. No wonder my neck has been aching so long. I have been looking up at my black, my fingers hurling orange bursts into the sky, and I think I know what that hour-of-the-wolf experience has been for me: something like the sublime. The only sublime I will ever know, that of mind-language become visible before me through a digital code of fingers quietly tapping.

The sublime of nature as described by the great eighteenth-century writers was that of an astral dazzlement. Here, first in the original German and then in English, is Hegel on these thought-annihilating stars—less a poem than a philosophical meditation:

> Mein Aug erhebt sich zu des ewgen Himmels Wölbung,
> zu dir, o glänzendes Gestirn der Nacht,
> und aller Wünsche, aller Hoffnungen
> Vergessen strömt aus deiner Ewigkeit herab,
> der Sinn verliert sich in dem Anschaun,
> was mein ich nannte schwindet
> ich gebe mich dem unermesslichen dahin,
> ich bin in ihm, bin alles, bin nur es.

> My eye rises to the eternal Heaven's arch,
> To you, o glittery stars of the night,
> And of all wishes, all hopes
> Forgetfulness streams downward from your eternity,
> The mind loses itself in its contemplation,
> What I myself named disappears
> I give myself over to its immeasurableness,
> I am in it, am all of it, am only it.

Hegel is writing about literature, which "always contends with a star-system of some kind: with foreign inheritances, native debts, or an overhead of great works whose light still pulses though they existed long ago" (Geoffrey Hartman, *The Fate of Reading*). The literature of the sublime—the sublime experience—puts the stars in their place. Thus Hegel:

Why

Stop

Now

> Dem wiederkehrenden Gedanken fremdet,
> ihm graut vor dem unendlichen, und staunend fasst
> er dieses Anschauns Tiefe nicht.

> The returning thought feels estranged,
> Shuddering before the infinite, and astonished
> It does not grasp the depth of what it contemplates.

Inside the vortex in which the stars have drawn the mind, thoughts struggle back alienated, "until imagination intervenes," writes Hartman of this poem. "This return from apocalyptic feelings to mortifying thoughts, this vacillation between nothingness and nothingness, becomes sufferable and even strengthening when it elicits, as here, a counter-assertive, inward, humanizing power" (*Fate,* 115).

This is something of the power I sought from play with language, a sublime not of nature (impossible today) but of mythology. I have tried to make those pixels humanize the stars I saw, put them in their place, master them into mind; make them linguistic and no longer divine beings. Koppel, to me, was a glittering night star, and he imploded me inside himself when he snapped: "You had a predisposition. I think that's a dumb way to do a story." He knew he had mortified me when he continued: "You're a little bit hurt. Not much, but a little bit. It's all going through your head right now—does he think I'm a fool? That's all in your body language . . . Now I've got your attention because I'm talking about you. And if I were interviewing you, I'd know that I had you *right now.* I got you off balance. That's when I'd move in, and that's when I'd hit you with two or three hard ones." And so I hit him.

The sublime of mythology: This for me is the meaning of capturing Merv at his piano bench; fat Merv who turns to Marvin Davis's guests and announces it's the first time they've seen a billionaire play piano; capture him there making *his* mythology and send him floating through the air in *my* mythology; Merv, so rich he doesn't have to diet, although he does diet, deflating and inflating like a bladder, 220, 190, 240, God knows how many pounds of entertainment blob floating through air to unplug his living vial of blood. This is the kind of artificial mythologizing I have sought and you can do.

And yet I said that it frightens me a bit, what I have done in these chapters. Because I have tightened the rhetorical skein entrapping me. All of us are tangled up in rhetoric, sliding along the glissade of our words, penetrating what is real much less than we think. The search for a style may even increase this distance from reality. For skipping across the comic surface of his words, the subject of the writing is devoted less to truth than to his or her own magnification.

This amounts to simultaneously buoyant and troubling news from Europe. The buoyant, first.

You'll recall that long ago in this book's introduction, Naohiro Amaya asked the question: what is the social software most compatible with our telematic age? But we can invert the question: What is the telematic organization that will fit the social system that is developing? I don't think technology is first and the soft society second. They are interacting forces. Society is selecting technologies, and technologies are selecting among different possible soft societies. Be that as it may, Amaya said that people are still searching for the answer to his question; for himself, he said, he knew neither what the software would be nor who would elaborate it. I've always thought he was being discreet. Jacques Attali told me he thought it would be Japanese in inspiration and Euro-Japanese in execution, a social organization producing "hyperindividuals" in quest of ever greater autonomy. You'll recall Attali's idea that the Japanese culture is oriented toward a notion of self-control of individuals, a self-mastery related to the nature of Japanese society, "based on piling individuals one upon the other." Because Japan is a small, narrow country, it has been obliged to value self-mastery and to elaborate around it an ethics, etiquette, esthetics, literature, mythology—in short, a self-disciplinary cosmology. But to discipline the self, you constantly have to scrutinize it.

Which led the Japanese to esthetics, Attali observed. "Monitoring your own aspect can be understood as a kind of first degree of esthetic practice." Because if you're always looking critically at yourself, you'll have a natural interest in perfecting it. Inside and outside. Makeup and emotional mastery. The Japanese give esthetics a rare value, "and esthetics is more and more one of the main characteristics of the rules of the future."

Invoking this old category, Attali is giving it a twist that distances it from its regressive, idealist background and that makes it approach the body and the world. But Attali's estheticized self is all too bound up in the world and its codes. In *Lignes d'Horizon*, his 1990 *Horizon Lines*, he writes:

> Little by little the citizen of the democracies must convert his autonomy into liquid funds. His liberty bought and sold. To live longer, to more easily find work, he'll be taught not to count too much on society, to keep in shape, to eat better, do gymnastics, run, maintain himself, scrutinize himself, in short *stay formed* and *informed*. If he refuses he

shall pay the price for it: he'll be paid to be in form; he'll pay for the right not to be.

To be in form and informed is to resemble a model, a "star" such as cinema shows. What began in music and wardrobe—hit parade and fashion laws—becomes a much more general social phenomenon. Little by little everywhere we find defined the abnormal to hunt down, the dangerous to exclude, the violent to eliminate. The scapegoat is no longer the one who has no money but the one who isn't "in shape": the gross, the deformed, the lazy, the sick, the ignorant, the unemployed . . .

Doctors and professors notably have the function of verifying for the account of society that each is conformed to the norms thus specified, suggested or imposed."

A chilling premonition (God forbid I were that professor) of the administered society he predicted in his 1977 book *Noise.* Subtracted from such administration and its injunction is the less muscular vision of Alain de Vulpian, president of Cofremca, the prestigious Parisian market research firm, and who along with Jacques Séguéla of chapter 3 helped elect Mitterand president of France. De Vulpian locates the nascent esthetic order in a generalized revulsion vis-à-vis postmodern culture and its producers. "A number of our people in France, Spain, Germany are longing for an esthetic that is not produced by estheticians," he said. I called him in June of this year, disturbing him in his summer home outside Paris in Chalmaison. But, exhausted as Wim Wenders by postmodernity, I was eager to hear, from someone I think I trust, what might be the shape of this esthetic *thing* coming from Europe. "Most of the furniture the designers produce doesn't at all respond to our people's needs," de Vulpian said—"strange chairs that don't really mean chairs, buildings that borrow from different centuries and combine their appropriations artificially." The movement he is observing is toward a mix of esthetic and meaning, "a meaning that is authentically felt within oneself," he added.

Because of the brutal *décalage*—unwedging or rupture—between culture makers and consumers, the evolution is taking place at a quotidian level. De Vulpian gave me a simple model for the everyday made esthetic: "People have this experience they're longing for when they have the feeling that everything is going fine, that there is no blockage, that people are getting together in networks, pushing one another in a good direction. In French we say, *ça baigne dans l'huile,* it's bathing in oil. Or again *ça marche au doigt à l'oeil,* it works from finger to eye." There are current products that have brought that feeling, he informed this New Yorker who needs no car; European cars like those of BMW and Volvo, "very big and very

447

smooth cars that are the contrary of the sports car—they go very fast but it's not necessary to go fast. They are not very far from the ideal, which would be a car that responds immediately to the brain without movement.''

You see? You and the BMW, a cyborg of style, a magnified subject of easeful motility. Remember Lacan (whom I have made a secret, sacred object of Eco's interdiction)? In his, yes, brilliant seminar of '73, he wrote that bliss, *jouissance*, joy, orgasm, coming could be sort of said in language this way: If there were an Other of this moment, I wouldn't have to be there. In De Vulpian's evocation of Lacan (the French market researchers conjure with this stuff), I don't have to go fast in my BMW (but I bet, it being Europe, they're going more than 65 mph). So it's writing for some; riding, flying etc. for others; country weekends spent in old houses ''you yourself have restored''—Roman architect Annamaria Cassini is informing me of Italian quotidian esthetics. The fashionable Italian is the one who doesn't make a gaudy display of the home, or anything else for that matter. This is why Eco, writing in his *Espresso* column, ''*La Bustina di Minerva,*'' recently heaped scorn on the new *nouveau riche* who walk the streets of Milan with their portable phones, exhibiting extravagant signs of their avant-garde affluence. In ''The One Who Uses the Portable Phone Has No Power'' he accomplished a little assassination on the wild capitalists who wouldn't die:

> The division between classes is an atrocious mechanism. It produces the fact that the new *nouveau riche*, even when earning an enormous amount of money, due to an atavistic proletarian stigma, doesn't know how to use the fish fork and sticks a monkey on the rear window of the Ferrari, not to mention a St. Christopher medal on the corporate jet window. Or he says ''manAGement'' and so is not invited by the Duchess of Guermantes. And he asks himself why he isn't invited, even though he has a boat so large that the deck reaches coast to coast. Those people don't know that Rockefeller didn't need a portable phone, because he had so large an efficient secretarial staff that, at the limit, if his grandfather were dying, the driver would come and very quietly whisper in his ear. The man of power is the one who is not obliged to answer every phone call and indeed, is the one, should he pick up, who says he's not available. Even at a low level, the two symbols of success are the key to the private bathroom and a secretary who can say, ''The doctor is out of his office.''

The ''*Bustina*'' that week was an attack, by someone who ought to know, on signs that flaunt glittery surface, Eco acting as a kind of point man on behalf of a European movement, almost like a huge sigh, if De Vulpian were correct; a mass desire for a ''deepening of personal and life emotional experience,'' in his words. He gave me some of the traits of the new esthetic sensibility developing: ''It is not artificial, nor mannered; ''it's near the body and sensations; it functions without being rationally, visibly functional; it has meaning authentically felt, without imposing the meaning: it is polysemic." Charles de Gaulle airport is an example of the sensibility. It is large without appearing large, in that sense *"proche du corps,* near the body," he observed. "Curve and undulating without being cocoon. Readable without being rectilinear. Extremely easy to use without appearing functional; sensorial, notably sonorous ambiance, calming and pleasant. You traverse it without rushing."

Something we can scarcely say of John F. Kennedy airport in New York. You're traveling in psychic steerage there. Dysfunction, demonstrations, lines, hustling. Whereas De Gaulle is about comfort, affluence—De Vulpian is invoking a society no longer straining to find its place in modernity, a society that assumes modernity and a comfortable modernity, one in which laughter plays a part, it being vital to esthetics. "There's a point of humor but humor which isn't destructive or provocative"—one might compare our Dice Men and Murphies—"and which discharges the authoritarian, the closed," De Vulpian told me, adumbrating the sensibility, adding a rather different trait: "It awakens primordial emotions; at the limit, sacred. The Grand Louvre, for example." Its glass pyramid intellectually contradicts the palace by its visible modernity, but it completes it on the emotional plane, for it is order *à la française,* hierarchical, monarchic. "Simultaneously," said De Vulpian, "with the great hall that it illuminates, it is timeless and awakens a primordial and sacred emotion. The combination of styles and meanings is neither genre-citational nor artificial; rather, humorous and open to diverse interpretations."

"It's not a coincidence he's using architectural examples," Annie Cohen-Solal, French Cultural Counselor in the U.S., told me. "Pei, De Gaulle, all these projects took place during the Mitterand years. Mitterand's been a good builder and he's completely changed the face of Paris. In the last ten years the French have the impression of arriving at a new harmony, and a concept expresses this—*mobilier urbain,* urban furniture." Not to upset the reader too much, in Paris are structures where one waits for the bus protected from the rain and from which one can telephone; public restrooms are there; columns where one finds advisories, including news of concerts and performances. "The streets are taken care of as if they were houses," said Cohen-Solal, "maintained as if by a good housewife putting flowers in a little corner, ashtrays everywhere, decorating. It's the opposite of New York. When I come back from Paris I feel destroyed by the violence of New York, the ugliness of the streets, the fact that everybody has given up. Not only in New York but in the big cities, there's a leitmotif, a poetics of despair about the city itself. People talk of nothing but the city and the catastrophe of the city. But in a fatalist way."

She remarked the 1991 Biennial at New York's Whitney Mu-

Figure 18.1 The glass pyramid intellectually contradicts the palace by its visible modernity, but it completes it on the emotional plane, for it is hierarchic, monarchic, it is order *à la française*. Simultaneously, with the great room that it illuminates, it seeks to awaken a primordial emotion, sacred even.

seum of American Art. There were three floors used, each exhibiting a different generation of American painters, each exhibiting a different atmosphere. On the second floor, those who came of age in the 60s, Lichtenstein, Rauschenberg, Johns, Stella, the artists of pop exhibiting technology, modernity, the social critics. On the third floor, those who came of age in the 70s and 80s, Salle, Fischl, Halley, Bartlett, neoexpressionists, *auteurs* returning to painting. On the fourth, those in their mid-twenties, Glenn Ligon, Carlos Alfonza, Nayland Blake, Jessica Diamond, Sally Mann. "It was very violent and very political," said Cohen-Solal of the fourth floor, "race issues, social issues. And I thought the three floors were pretty symbolic of a new order in the States, a coexistence of three generations expressing contrary proclivities, hesitations, and estheticisms. This is what is not yet arrived in Europe, America being ahead by two or three years, a very confrontational society. Not to forget Spike Lee. All of it is a new frame for deciphering the world.

So here's the troubling news from Europe: All along, Attali, De Vulpian, Séguéla, Cassini, Eco have been talking about privilege. "Mitterand's been a good builder, he's completely changed the face of the city"—there it is, the face, a *prosopopeia,* the trope that fools us that the thing we're struggling with is as stable as our own reassuring faces. Paris is not wholly stable, to mention only its *banlieux* where Algerians struggle to become an emergent group. But the Good Housewives of France, not to mention the rest of Europe, are trying to centralize things, to master them, rationalize them and place them under control. *Per contra,* the United States is split into so many Madonna Nations, Queer Nations, Pro-lifers, Pro-choicers, Multi-culturalists, Plurogenderers, Camille Paglias, emergent groups ("so many new markets for new products," observes critic Fredric Jameson, "so many new interpolations for the advertising image itself . . .") of such bile that *New York Times* columnist Russell Baker, recently wrote:

> Take your stand and shout until your jaws beg for mercy. It's this year's big fun slanging match for intellectuals, probably because it offers such rich opportunity for venting your most beastly animosities on race, sex, and ethnic issues while sounding so utterly, so absolutely, so unbelievably civilized.

Thinking of New York, of the Big City here, shall I remember my Wordsworth somewhere in a box still:

> Rise up, thou monstrous ant-hill on the plain
> Of a too busy world! Before me flow
> Thou endless stream of men and moving things!

The subject of my thesis, known still by heart:

The wealth, the bustle and the eagerness,
The glittering chariots with their pampered steeds,
Stalls, barrows, porters; midway in the street
The scavenger, who begs with hat in hand,
The labouring hackney coaches, the rash speed
Of coaches travelling far, whirled on with horn
Loud blowing . . .
Here there and everywhere a weary throng,
The comers and the goers face to face,
Face after face; the string of dazzling wares,
Shop after shop, with symbols, blazoned names . . .

—that mean nothing. The word as degraded inscription, as advertisement. *The Prelude* describes an allegory of degradation, ours. Borrowing from European sensibility, however, you can seek to rationalize your patch of the anthill through style whose major figure, in my eyes, is language.

"Why do you hate stories so much?" asks Haroun, the hero of Salman Rushdie's children's book, *Haroun and the Sea of Stories*. Haroun is addressing Khattam-Shud, tyrant of Chup, "a place of shadows, of books that wear padlocks and tongues torn out."

"Why do you hate stories so much? Stories are fun," says Haroun.

"The world, however, is not for Fun. . . . The world is for Controlling," replies Khattam-Shud, monopolist of speech, metaphor of the media, that grand monologist, "silencing drives, deodorizing the body, emptying it of its needs, and reducing it to silence," in Jacques Attali's jeremiac words (*Noise*).

It's to capture speech back in the form of fun that I suggest hurling yourself across your own language, should you choose the linguistic option.

But we all know that such hysteria eventually exhausts itself, whereupon you face this question. What to do when you've laughed at the joke of life and the robust *Ha Ha* dribbles off into its spittle of *heh*

heh?

I propose that one stop the entertainment before it stops on you. I want to borrow a concept from the beginnings of conceptual art. In 1969 the artist Joseph Kosuth announced the project of producing consciousness by stripping away the formal properties of the work of art. In the magazine *Arts* under the pseudonym Arthur R. Rose, he said: "A few years ago I became increasingly aware of the fact that the separation between one's ideas and one's use of material, if not wide at the inception of the work, becomes almost uncommunicatively wide when confronted by a viewer. . . . I also began to realize that there is nothing abstract about a specific material. There is always something hopelessly real about materials, be they ordered or unordered." In aid of abstracting from cloying materiality, in aid of abstraction itself, of ideation, Kosuth made war on the materials of art, borrowing a page from the structural linguists around him at the time. "Obviously then the art wasn't *in* the materials used no more than the *meaning* is *in* the phoneme in a spoken sentence," he wrote in 1971. Five years later, the great Russian linguist Roman Jakobson would publish—and had already been telling his students—that speech sounds as a whole are an artifact built precisely for speech, precisely to be differentiated from one another, and not for the gross, raw phonic matter as such. The idea of words as motor and acoustic phenomena is therefore a fiction, he pronounced (and it's not necessary here to probe the doubtful side of his polemic). The idea of art materials as esthetic phenomena is a fiction, Kosuth declared with the force of the period. As Arthur Rose, he remarked: "I wanted complete art and wanted to remove even entertainment as a reason for its existence. I wanted to remove the experience from the work of art."

Which teaches us that like Glaser's Falstaff, the Great Non-Dupe, you can know the inferno and laugh at it from deep down inside it . . . and stop. Take a dose of Kosuth—stop entertaining yourself. And the following can happen.

First, this idea. Just *don't* do it.

You might just want to stop ogling Vanna. Or going "bullshit" with Ted. Stop slouching (nor preen) and stay the hand that reaches for the Mac. And the eye for Bedford's blue and Annie's boobs. The next time you glom porn, to say to yourself: "That . . . is . . . only . . . image."

(Only it's hard. I recall in greater specificity Lacan's depiction of the pleasure of coming: If there were an other of this, it wouldn't be necessary that this be that other. *"S'il y en avait une autre,* if there were an other, *il ne faudrait pas que ce soit celle-là,* it wouldn't be necessary that this be that. Freed of necessity, freed of drive, I float here. The porn state, no? In an irony Lacan never imagined, we can say of the porn fans: If there were an other of what they're doing, it isn't necessary they do it. That's how content they are.)

Just don't do it: It's a kind of "So what, who cares?" you hurl at the world. A *"Je m'en fiche,"* a "fuck it!" A walk away.

I know. I hear the reader saying: "I'll stop when you do."

It's an ideal. A value, a notion for the times. It's something to debate with.

And another one is this. I build it from the encounters with Glaser and Baudrillard. Glaser told you he most feared simulation. Not to be a part of the semiurge of America: happiness, simulated of course. He fears that enormous American enterprise, the simulation of happiness, welfare, communication and human rapport. When I was with Baudrillard in Paris, I brought up Terry Bedford, his admission that the Bedfords of advertising, all of them simulate happiness, coding it blue and red. I asked Jean Baudrillard: "When one looks at one's real quote, unquote life; when one goes into the street, let's say in America, and sees the poor people, and sees the black people, the ethnicities—I'm talking of a city like New York or Chicago where you walk the streets—what happens to the simulation in your head when you see the real poverty in the street? Does one carry the simulation with one?"

At first he stumbled: *"Là, je pense qu'il y a* . . . there, I think there's . . . *"qu'on la voit"* . . . that one sees it . . . *elle est vue*, it's seen." Then he found himself:

> There's always a sort of screen now, that's to say that one sees all things, everything as on a screen at bottom. It's not only when one is before the television that one is before a screen. I think that when one is in the street, when one is in the city, one is also on screen, eh? We are always tele-spectators of reality, no longer even spectators, eh? Implicated like them, responsible.

Surprised at his audacity, I asked: "Before real life?"

> Before real life. One has a screen incorporated, okay? To employ another image, we're a little like an integrated circuit, okay?—with a computer in a sense. Do you see? So there's a way of seeing everything on screen in a sense eh? It's no longer the theater of everyday life. It's no longer even the cinema of everyday life, it's the screen of everyday life, all right? And a screen always more or less televisual, so that one is protected by this televisual distance.

Joining the apocalyptic fun, I goaded: "And when one says televisual, one says 'little screen' and 'screen without depth'—he interrupted me: "Without depth, of course." Continuing, I said: "And the implications of that are—"

> That there is no consequence, all right? That's to say that it's always something that one can disconnect, connect or disconnect.

Reminding me that most of us don't tap the buttons of the tube with our hands, we use the remote.

> That's to say real life is always something that one can choose to see or not to see.

Not even hearing the pathos of his parody of *Hamlet*.

> And it suffices us to connect or disconnect. That's to say we act with reality as with the television apparatus, we can change, we can zap, even in the street or even in human relations. It's a behavior which is like . . . like . . . ludic in the aleatory sense of the word. We're no longer in a behavior of implication, of responsibility for what we see. For myself, what I thought was that in effect things become a surface, okay?

There it is. Baudelaire's painter of modern life, the *oeil flâneur*, is finished. Walking in the street, zapping each other, we don't even zap humans, that is, beings in three dimensions. We two-dimensionalize everything, as if all those in our field of vision were like the cardboard Reagans and Bushes next to which we're photographed. For Baudrillard, we have flattened the city and everything in it into an image.

Why Stop Now

And if he were right. . . . Let's say that we want visibly to be struggling with all the mechanisms, the intricate relays by which we disconnect. Remember the Japanese allegory—the woman with the egg face—that Yuri Norstayn told (page 361)? When I met him he showed me an unfinished animation of Gogol's *The Overcoat*. There was Akaky Akakievich, the copyist, whom he drew to look like a fetus. "Akaky Akakievich is similar to an animal," he told me, "in the same way each of us is like an animal in some way. In the course of casual conversation we sometimes say: 'This person looks like cat, he has a duck's gait, he has a bear's gait.'"

He told me he had been looking into my eyes and wondering what sort of animal I was most like. Now he has decided that I must look at a book of birds. "Birds have eyes and look to the side," he told me. "When I see you looking at your translator, I see the animal in you. There's a bird called the secretary bird. It's bald but it has a little tuft of hair."

And as I protested, for it isn't pleasant to be called back to the

Figure 18.2 Yuri Norstayn. Sketch of Akaky Akakievich for his animation of Gogol's "The Overcoat." *Courtesy Yuri Norstayn.*

animal you may be, much less a fucking bird, Norstayn tried to soothe me by comparing me to his own Akaky Akakievich: "After he's born he hopes that his head will look somewhat like that. The animal side of us, the animal instincts and so on, are often forgotten and we're that much poorer for it. A human face, if it doesn't in some way reflect the inner workings of the person, if it's not somehow intense or tensed, no matter how beautiful it might be, it's not worth looking at."

"But in the west, it goes exactly the other way," I told him. "If you reveal the inner person, the animal inside—"

"It's not only in the west but also here," he interrupted.

"—you're not worth looking at," I ended.

"It's a horrible thing."

You can value the secretary bird in you; and the lemur in the other—Norstayn's wife calls him a lemur, pointing to his slow, methodical movements. Let's say I came to identify with the Akiky Akakieviches of the world; that I tried to reconnect to the animal within. In doing so, one strips away the rhetoric (for it's rhetoric that removes you from the body)—as I failed to do when I met Yevtushenko; as I succeeded in doing when I met Alex.

I don't know if I was seeking—but I found—the nodes, the contact points on the net of my travels and intercommunication. I think I value most what shook, what fissured the symbolicity I brought to the encounters. (Honestly, then, did I value Koppel's blow?) Or the emotional certainty. This is why I value Alex, who with asperity and a wan face let me feel Russian *deficit*. I value Armani, who let me watch him sketch the future, favoring me with telepathy. Value founds everything on taste or distaste, and I feel the latter for Griffin who armored himself in bonhomie and yes-men.

Finally, this idea. As with Griffin, as with Yevtushenko, as with Koppel after the "face reading," as with so many of the people who loom large in our path with their myth, we cannot always connect. So let's coldly read them. Turn *their* rhetoric into idea, description, brutal interpretation. We cannot efface them, so we deface them (with or without telling them). It's a practice you can craftily engage when the other isn't just a person but a thing, the media or any other sign artifact. Unlike Griffin's dork hollering "Dork!" at the game show contestants, you softly say: "I know what you mean and it's . . ." and you fill in the blank. The fewer words, the better. The more savage. You cease to entertain yourself in order to *know,* as we say, really know the inferno.

This amounts to a notion of pedagogy borrowed from the un-published Barthes, to whose memory a salute. The ideal course is the one in which the professor is more banal than his students; in which what he says is behind what he incites in his listeners. A good proposition must be incomplete, a little weak, the teacher obeying a law of non-exhaustivity. If he does not, then his pedagogy is a position, a kind of phallic occupation of ideal space. The other teaching, "weak" pedagogy, is a non-oppressive banality, aerated by an ethics of delicacy.

Why

Stop

Now

So the professor I am chooses to end this book in a kind of silence with a partial alphabet for the nineties. Each letter I have chosen becomes a sketch of what could have been written, a sketch cast now in this, now in that voice of style, austerity, intellection, reportage, as discussed above. They are a few letters for thought—yours. Finish the sketches, if you like. Substitute your own. Add the other letters. *Se produire,* as Lacan said of the unconscious; it produces itself, wells where no one thought it was, producing itself.

Make yourself.

"But into what, dear author? And what if I must be confrontational?"

There are one, two, three paths . . .

19 *Sort of an ABCs for the Early 90s*

A: *Abode* The new nature of contemporary man and woman. We live in our houses and apartments as primitive man lived in the jungle. But more blessed than he, we enjoy twelve seasons—every month, the glossy leaves of magazines fall on chairs, the floor, tables, even by the toilet bowl. We eclipse at will the sun in our Tizio lamp. The moon: candles for two. The ocean: the gurgling waves of a jacuzzi. If we don't like our landscape, we redesign the path between our rooms, the trees in the living room, the season on the walls. Presto, we proceed to redecorate—with or without the protection of a contractor to neutralize foreign tribes carrying pipes and electrical bolts to rape our women and empty our granaries. These are the risks of city warfare. We stand before our windows as the poet on a mountaintop, waiting for an economic quake, a nuclear thunderstorm, or the assault of millions of unfriendly eyes.

B: *Bookseller* (c. 1991): Next to the dog doo-doo, near the beggar softly crying she has cancer, on the New York sidewalk by the feet of joggers and *boulvardiers* are the books, scores of them neatly arranged in rank and file. We boulvarde a single block, passing two competitors who offer *The Doctor's Dilemma* (Shaw), *Tristram Shandy* (Sterne), *The Snows of Kilimanjaro and other stories* (Hemingway), *A Cannibal in Manhattan* (Janovitz), *Trump: The Art of the Deal* (guess), *Select Letters of Voltaire*, *The Godfather* (Puzo), *The Paris Review* (Keith Haring number), a Currier and Ives catalogue raisonné, *Firestarter* (King), *Future Shock* (Toffler), next to *Nuns in Jeopardy, Woman in Sexist Society, Conjoint Family Therapy, Looking Thin, Fighters for Freedom*, a Spiegel catalogue, *High Heels, Hamburger Sex Illustrierte, Prison Evangelical Magazine, Soldier of For-*

tune, Madonna "Blonde Ambition Tour" album, "The Immortal Otis Redding," "The Best of Bill Cosby", et cetera. The written word in the dumps, the same scene repeated all over the city, all over Chicago, L.A., every cosmopolis. Enterprising blacks and Hispanics, the refuse of society, no? have perused the refuse of the city, finding the old culture there. They have laid it to rest on the sidewalk. When people throw their "Blonde Ambition" album away, it's to replace it with a higher-fidelity CD. (Better start perusing these sidewalk record stalls: By the year 2000, the record will be a collector's item.) But when they throw their books away, it's not to replace them with a library in a box of diskettes. The book is replaced with television shows, tapes, barbecues, beer, and hang-gliding. Girls (and boys) just want to have fun and fun isn't reading. Formerly, the bookcase gave the house respectability. Mom and dad filled it up with the *Encyclopedia Britannica,* a history of literature (Byron, *The Thousand and One Nights,* Shakespeare, Homer), a history of art (Michelangelo, Raphael, the Greek miracle), a treatise on psychology, a Bible, a Bullfinch. After supper, the patriarch read, mother knitted, the tots listened (and, grown older, read, too). Today, reading is for the birds and absolute beginners. Every adolescent comedy tells the same story: The classroom is for flirting; pay some nerd to read the lesson and brief you. But but but but but . . . the nerd has made his comeback, is having his revenge. In the new esthetic order of which Attali speaks, brains have their place.

Peter Heath, music video and television commercial director, asks the author (a little before the Berlin Wall came down) to play a cameo in a music video. Fine, comes the answer. The role: to be the father of the star; to greet her as she comes home—post–World War III London—after school; she, dressed in ripped kilt, a quiver at her groin, filled with pencils, not arrows; dad (of bald head) wearing hair curlers, pink housedress, green apron, pink moue-moues; daughter throwing down her books on the floor, singing. People no longer accumulate books—a book isn't the sign of education any more. Booklovers, console yourselves: Now you don't have to go to a second-hand bookstore. It's all out there on the street, a dollar a copy, Janovitz next to *Jane Eyre* and to hell with library science. Books, with their linear, sequential thinking, have been replaced by the warmth of videotapes. Videotapes, which almost have the same shape as the book (it has to be by design), have taken over the bookshelf and exiled books to the sidewalk. Now is the culture of the videoshelf. Now is visual culture.

E: *Energy* The new name for God. Whether you crave it or not (but you do), whether you believe in it or not (but you do), it's there. It's a force to create supermarkets or destroy religions. It's packed into atoms, money, and brain cells. It can cover the earth with warm hamburgers or heat the planet to death. It can put

460

McDonald's in Moscow, Disneyland in Paris, and (sputtering) revolution in Central America. It can patch the ozone hole with a layer of yen. It can fuck the brains out of religion and crash the head of communism against the head of capitalism. It is the Force. $E = MC^2$ is no bullshit. It has no ax to grind. It cleanses with filth, it soils with light. Everything on the planet is its mask.

F: Fanuc also *Fuji, Mt.,* site of the Fanuc robot factory. ". . . then they are sent to first floor through warehouse and then sent to final assembly," the plant manager is telling me as we walk in rubber sandals into the delivery room for robots at the Fanuc factory at the foot of Mount Fuji. The lights are dim here, a few humans in yellow jumpsuits, yellow robots. Some, the unborn, are utterly still; others, the assemblers, insert pins in them, cut wire, fix chips. Robots are making robots in this final assembly room. The plant manager continues in English: "And then some will be test given to control room." Faint sliding sounds, hissing, otherwise silent.

A robot brings an unborn down and gives it a little nudge to move it left. Clackety clack sound.

"We're not fully automated," apologizes as we leave the holy of holies for a room in which robots merely make motors. "80 percent of our production is under human control, 10 percent under robot control."

Two hundred humans are in this building (there are five others), producing some 4,000 "control devices"—components for motors —a month. Acting the perfect touree, I inquire: "This operates twenty-four hours?"

"No, not yet," he says, "because they need human help," and laughs apologetically. He adds compensatorily: "About five years ago we used five or six pieces of circuit board, but now one circuit is enough for control."

Fanuc is one of the five or six Japanese robot manufacturers, at the top of the industry; Sweden and Switzerland also support robotics; the Swiss firm, Aseea, houses its plant "even in Japan," he tells me a bit proudly. I had traveled by bus from Tokyo to Fuji Fanuc to take a first-hand look at Japan's highest-tech growth sector. On the way my Japanese guide and I had passed light industrial sites, gray and brown fields, more factories and industrial parks. Idly I inquired the name of one.

"I don't know what it means," he said.

What does it say in letters? I prodded.

"I can spell in your language: *L . . . a . . . f . . . o . . . r . . . e . . . t.*"

"That's not my language," I said. "It's French. *La fôret,* forest."

"That's the name of the owner, he's Mr. Forest," the guide exclaimed.

So prestigious is French, and English, in Japan that even if ordinary Japanese can't read it, owners exalt it high. Simulation signage.

We were an hour late to our appointment. It had been lunch with the plant manager, and, erring, my guide had taken me to lunch in a Mt. Fuji robata. Angry, the manager, has banished the poor guide, and now is telling me of further Fanuc developments, "technological development in new technological dimensions." What I'm seeing now is embarrassingly manual labor, he explains, but, pointing behind him to the entrance and beyond it the parking lot where we left his car, he says: "That car combined into robot would cause some social confliction." He laughs. "Gradual drop in humans would be most desirable."

"You think people would be upset if a robot suddenly could do too much."

"That's right," he says.

Shrieking sounds where we are now. We have to raise our voices to be heard.

"Do they ever make mistakes?"

He laughs. "Yeah, almost perfect. But some parts of work are still performed by men. Simple work for human but complicated for robot. Many up to now used in automobile industry in small job shops because it's hard for them to employ young workers, so they rely on robots."

"Why not young workers?"

"Because young workers are not willing to work in job shop, because the treatment is not so good in that kind of work."

So the robots are slaves in the auto industry. Slaves that sometimes rebel. We are standing in the testing room. A newborn robot extends its arm up, absurdly resembling an elephant, its trunk raised high. The handler underneath it watches. It is being put through its functions. It will undergo 100 hours of test.

"Each robot has girl's name," he says, "the employees give nickname. And I don't think they are ugly. They are rather wild and so we have to be careful not to be bitten. There are some risks, people have to be careful, have to be careful," he sighs. "Even girl might bite us. Even she," he pointed upward to Mr. Fuji, smiling.

Back in Tokyo, my humiliated guide refused to accept his 150,000-yen fee (in another era, in a different institution, he might have self-immolated). "Go see Detroit," the plant manager had urged; leaving Tokyo, I went. "Detroit" meant GM-Fanuc, a joint venture to sell Fanuc robots programmed by GM to American industry.

It was a full court interview—six Americans and not a single Japanese executive. "Couldn't make it" . . . "not available" . . . was the excuse the Americans gave in the name of their Japanese colleagues. Strange, a venture dependent on Japan, and robots, robots everywhere and not a Japanese to be found. Stranger still as I listened to a rant about black youth in Detroit. "Over there," the executive said, pointing out the window at the ghetto. "Incorrigibel uneducable!" Other epithets. They had a dream, these GMmen—a robot for every worker. Part proselytizers, part salesmen, they had been going around stumping for a man-by-man, woman-by-woman replacement of worker—no matter the industry—by robot. This will be the stopper of deindustrialization.

"But what about the workers?" Meaning, the workers fired to make room.

"We upgrade them to engineers."

My, what a robust economy, a chicken in every pot, a robot for every worker, and every factory dad or mom a shining new engineer.

F: *Fax* Deathknell of writing. No attraction of the surface, no fantasm of the stroke or the tool. Graphic thought itself has withered. Stationery holds little interest. How ancient an idea, that of tracing the raised characters of ingenious logos and precise company names. How precious to send papers hinting in their texture of fibrous origin. Easily we have sloughed the luxury of surface for that of telematic mind. The fax is binding word. We even come to hallucinate its shiny paper that passes the finger quickly over its surface. The text is gray with tiny nicks in the letters, like a scene that shimmers a little in a crystal ball. As if you had, after all, to pay a price for communication at such distance.

As early as the end of the 60s, conceptual artist Joseph Kosuth had demanded the right for meaning to exist separate from its material conditions, signified from its signifier, content from the substance expressing it. Predicting the age of the *tele-matos,* of mind over matter, will over distance, conceptual art was perhaps prologomena to the fax age, the age of absolute transitivity. Time? No perceptible duration, Bergson's *longue durée* inexistent, derisory. Space? Like a stage set, as if you were acting at being *in situ.* Bent over the fax watching the shiny tissue come forth, you are coupled with another mind as near as next door, as far as the antipodes, it scarcely makes a difference. Forgetful of your body, scorning space, you are atopic. It was utterly fitting that when the department store Barney's opened in Shinjuku, Tokyo in late 1990, Kosuth should curate a fax show in the gallery on its top floor. Six artists, Kosuth included, faxed a single work from Barney's New York to Barney's Tokyo: 011 81 3/225-9784, a number set up for the show. In Tokyo the works were received on acetate acting as a photographic negative from which, in the last step, the image was printed as a large photograph. Look at Barbara Kruger's fax, reproduced 70 x 54 inches. Her original English message read: "We are not your maids." To everyone's surprise, when translated into Kanji the

Figure 19.1 Barbara Kruger wanted her message, faxed from New York to Tokyo, to read: We are not your maids." Her translator into Kanji made it: "We are not your maidservants." Feminist venom exacerbated in translation. *Courtesy Joseph Kosuth.*

message became: "We are not your maidservants." Because of the surplus in translation, because the Japanese hadn't heard of her and had only a nascent feminism, she sprang onto the Tokyo scene a Fury, nothing lost in transmission, as much venom on the Tokyo seaside as the New York shore. More, in fact. In New York her edge is dulled, given she's a commodity, already consumed by the market. The fax gave her back her edge. She didn't politely, traditionally, flying JAL, install a show in Tokyo—bodiless, instantaneously, she hurled her war cry there.

And look at Haim Steinbach. "The words he chose are nominally

English," Kosuth told me. "They function in the sea of international commerce, entirely in the language of the Japanese with their total logoesque relationship with English." The Japanese speak their language, our language, write theirs and ours as well. They show the way, Kosuth is saying, to a soft technology—the language of a global market economy—utterly appropriate to instantaneous intercommunication.

Discharging the fetishism of originality, dispensing with aura rooted in ritual and place, Kosuth sent a network of minds to Tokyo. His own work, these words in Kanji:

> One of the foremost tasks of art has always been the creation of a demand which could be fully satisfied only later.

Absent quotation marks, it doesn't even signal that an attribution is missing (Walter Benjamin, *The Work of Art,* etc.). The Japanese spectator who may speak the new *lingua universalis* by no means necessarily speaks Benjamin. What does that mean? he or she is urged to ask of the Kosuth, which is intended to be opaque, a reference but to where? Kosuth never gives citations to the enig-

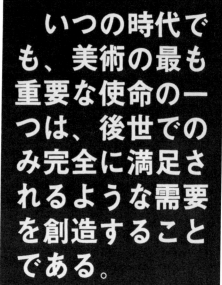

Figure 19.2 "The energetic new hardware entails a new software, a language not English or Japanese but global." *Curator Joseph Kosuth on Haim Steinbach's "Yo. Beep, honk, toot." Courtesy Kosuth.*

Figure 19.2a Appropriating Walter Benjamin for his work in the Tokyo Barney's fax show, Joseph Kosuth declares: "One of the foremost tasks of art has always been the creation of a demand which could be fully satisfied only later." *Courtesy Kosuth.*

matic language he employs. You cannot pin him down, fix his meanings. And herein we approach perhaps an essence of contemporary art, its deferral of meaning, told guilelessly to us by the little pseudoquote. Kosuth faxed the Japanese the news that even in the age of the instantaneous, there's still a place for deferral, which is to say art.

G: *Greenaway, Peter*   In New York's Plaza Hotel, about to launch his November 1991 film *Prospero's Books*, director Peter Greenaway mentioned that when he started making films some 20 years ago, he was annoyed by the fact that cinema was predominantly actor-based and seemed to be little but an excuse for actorly virtuosity. "On the second level," he continued, "it seemed to be very much concerned with this tiresome, supermarket, Freudian, psychoanalytic approach to phenomena. I wasn't alone in this, a lot of people felt the same. I had some no doubt ridiculous *cul de sac* beliefs that we shouldn't use actors, people who pretend to be somebody else." As a painter at that time, he also felt that 2000 years of European image-making concerned the image being slave to text, its retelling; only in the mid-nineteenth century and of course the twentieth becoming free to be autonomous of text. "I distrusted narrative a great deal," he said.

Doubtless his mistrust was also born of a certain facility at narrative. "If you see some of my early films like *The Falls*, there are 92 narratives in three hours. In other movies like *A Walk Through H*, there are also 92 narratives—in about 40 minutes. I remember feeling a godlike authorial power, able to create projects which had 3000 characters or only three; I could put them on the moon or on Mars, I could kill the heroine off in the first act or wait till the end." Narrative sickened; it became "in some peculiar way very anecdotal and ephemeral. I find it unsatisfactory as an explanation of the world."

Its credibility, he thinks, has been destroyed by its overuse for commercial purposes. "The world now is full of soap—not soap in terms of bubbles, in terms of soap dramas—and you know how Borges says every literary phenomenon creates its own precursors. There's a way that looking back after seeing 30,000 episodes of 'Dallas' and 55,000 episodes of 'Twin Peaks,' narrative itself is somehow debased. *Bouvard and Pecuchet* is diminished because of its retrospective narrative cross-connections to the soaps. The image, the same. Think, for example, of that Victorian image of the robin on the log at Christmas time. Audubon probably drew the first robin with perfect empirical observation, and it had an esthetic value as well, but now you cannot ever look at a robin without somehow having this Christmas card connotation. I feel in a peculiar way that's also happened to the whole narrative process, certainly because of the psychodramas."

Given such a clot of animosity against narrative, he sought to substitute for it a taxonomic talent. "I tried to find what could be described as universal systems to run alongside the narrative. Witness the concern for the alphabet in *A Zed and Two Noughts,* the number count in *Drowning by Numbers,* and indeed the color coding in *The Cook and the Thief* (red for carnivores is the color of the dining room, green for vegetal fecundity of the kitchen, etc.)." When an intellectual precursor, Barthes, wrote *A Lover's Discourse,* to discharge the possibility of a love story, he chose and thought he chose the "absolutely insignificant" order of the alphabet as the structure of the book (*absence, adorable,* etc.). To Greenaway, the necessary recourse to the alphabet is entirely preposterous and ridiculous:

"Under the letter H is *holiness, happiness, hysterectomy, heaven, hell*—absurd. Although I want to use these constructs, there is always a sensation that they should be regarded with utmost diffidence because they, too, are essentially ephemeral and insubstantial." They are tools by which he tries to organize, to understand the chaos. "I use these systems but also mock them whilst using them."

His taxonomic gift seems extraordinary; witness his ancillary career as curator. By the end of 1991 he had been invited to curate four exhibitions at European museums. At the Louvre, in a show to be called "The Unseen Seen," he will organize fifty or sixty Botticelli, Rembrandt, and other drawings hitherto kept in the basement, unseen. His concept: the metaphorical, metaphysical attempts of the artist make the unseeable seen. "Imagine the concept of elocution," Greenaway said. "How do you demonstrate elocution? Well, there's a superb drawing by Titian where one of the ancients, perhaps Galen, is standing on a podium and there are these words coming out of his mouth, which as they come forth become chains which are wound round the necks of his audience. Beautiful concepts like that." For the Reichs Museum of Amsterdam, he chose to discuss death as a technical problem, how artists and artisans portray death, the conceits, metaphors, and emblems they use.

The taxonomy of *Prospero's Books,* his adaptation of *The Tempest,* is precisely the books that Gonzalo threw into the bottom of the leaky vessel that took Prospero out onto the sea, away from Europe and into exile. Although Shakespeare does not elaborate their number or identity, Greenaway imagines 24 of them. "There would need to be books on navigation and survival; there would need to be books for an elderly scholar to learn how to rear and educate a young daughter; how to colonize an island, farm it, subjugate its inhabitants, identify its plants and wild beasts. Twenty-four volumes might be enough to cover the information needed—bestiaries, an herbal, cosmographies, atlases, astronomies, a book of

Sort of

an A B Cs

for the

Early 90s

languages, a book of utopias, a book of travellers' tales, a book of games."

To frustrate narrative and thereby its naive claim: I am the referent. When Magritte paints a pipe and writes underneath, *Ceci n'est pas une pipe* [*this is not a pipe*], he demonstrates how inexorable is our urging toward the thing and not the text that posits the thing. This is perhaps the most basic semiotic proposition. I first encountered it in 1971 in the teaching of my master Paul de Man. Greenaway has turned it into film. He never lets you forget you are staring at a construct, a film; his obsessive metaphor for it is the stage. Ariels (there are four) are always parting curtains. It's the proscenium arch, the artificiality of theater he exhibits. "I deliberately tried to create a vocabulary for myself by which to tell an audience that they're only watching an artifice, this isn't a window on the world. At the end of *Prospero's Books,* we bring down something which almost looks like a safety curtain. The freed Ariel is running towards us and Prospero's audience is applauding, picking up their cue from Prospero's epilogue: 'If I have satisfied you, you may now applaud me'—a signal to you out there, the audience looking at his audience, to continue that clapping. The safety curtain falls and Ariel is on our side of it, running toward us. You're about to pick him up with all tenderness and then he eludes us, escapes and goes over the tops of our heads." Greenaway made Ariel appear to be with us, in the audience, therefore making everything behind the safety curtain nothing but actors. If you will, *ceci n'est pas une tempete:* "Cutting us off, reminding us that we have only been watching an artifice perpetrated by Shakespeare, Prospero, Gielgud [the major actor] and finally Greenaway."

To Greenaway, as to my old master De Man as to the others who taught me semiotics, the most successful works of art—let Greenaway say it: "not just in the cinema but anywhere, always have a full acknowledgment of their own artificiality so that *Hamlet* is very much a piece of theater about theater. And Rembrandt's *The Night Watch* is very much about painting. But this desire to acknowledge one's materials, people obviously find very difficult in the cinema because I suspect that most people go to cinema for the deliberate wish to escape, to be swept up by illusions."

"Boatswain," *The Tempest,* and *Prospero* begin. Gielgud says the word again and again, "he experiments with it to see how it sounds and what sort of characters should he make of it," says Greenaway. Gielgud is imagining the master of his enemies' ship, who, about to sink, cries out for his b'osun. But to Greenaway the signifier itself, the word in its sonorous materiality, is what fascinates Gielgud. "It's a joke to him, a conceit," Greenaway says, "like one of those masques put on by Inigo Jones. We know it's a cheat, a piece of stage machinery."

Hence the little ship and the nymphs above. "I didn't want to

468

19.3

make the ship concrete," he says. "Conventional reproductions of the stage play *The Tempest* usually go to great lengths to try to convince an audience that a storm is happening on stage whereas this, I think, is much more interesting because it's going on in his head as part of his revenge drama. It's much more akin to an Eisenstein theory of montage as well. You have the bullet being fired and you have the crowd coming toward you and you put the two together and you believe that a crowd is being slain. That's what's happening here, the nymphs and the boat, a collage montage by association."

Miranda speaks . . . or rather Gielgud, who speaks all the parts because he can only populate his island with signs which are not things . . . so Gielgud speaks, Isabelle Pasco as Miranda doubling his voice:

"O, I have suffered
with those that I saw suffer! a brave vessel
(who had no doubt some noble creature in her)
dashed all to pieces!"

Greenaway intended a kitsch origin of this image. "Do you know the expression *pompier?*" he asks. "Salon, rather kitsch imagery of the French middle nineteenth century, a vulgar image in some ways but one of great peculiar eroticism." One of the deities just flicks her leg and we're in trouble. "It comes so appropriately on that line: "dashed to pieces" and on the "dashed" onomatopoeically, that boat is struck," he says.

Greenaway is called obscure, overwhelming by his critics. He is adored by his constituency, who more or less unconsciously, live and relish a *fin de siècle* phenomenon: the art of signs, semiotics become art (don't forget Unberto Eco of many pages ago). I leave this odd matter to the reader to interpret.

H: *Health* What God was for our forefathers—something distant, mysterious, inaccessible. Yet worth running after. If health is youth, it's an illusion. If it's balance and harmony, it's impossible. After it ceases to be whole, every step, every flexing of a muscle, every blink of an eye creates imbalance, entropy. Our forefathers wanted to make God a living reality—we are turning health into toxic ideas. We are throwing our bodies into a burning bush.

H: *History* Something to plunder. Knowing it conditions you to repeat it. Only when we ignore it are we free of its fatality. (Do you believe this? Careful careful careful.) Today (but for how long?), it is an endless source for new fashions, from shoes to headgear, an endless reservoir of styles, problems, outfits, language, masks.

K: *Kansas City, my home town* When Jacques Attali told me that Europe wasn't really being Americanized:

> We have to build a word which would be "New York—Hollywood-ization," because we are not Americanized in the sense that we are not going to be closer to St. Louis, Missouri or some place else. These countries are far from us and we are far from them. They are less in advance, less influencing than New York and Hollywood.

—I thought I might catch a glimpse of one of the "less influencing" countries; if not the dreaded St. Louis, then Kansas City, my natal site. It was spring and oblivious of the scornful comment of the sharp-tongued Frenchman, I found myself at Royals Stadium on opening day of the baseball season—my host, former sports writer of the *Kansas City Star*, Joe McGuff, now its editor-in-chief. Easterners aren't liked, he's telling me, because "everything east is viewed as good by easterners and everything anywhere else is viewed as hickish, unsophisticated, and so there's a sort of built-in antagonism. Going back to sports, the Yankees are an absolutely wonderful opponent for the Royals because there's a lot of natural animosity on the part of these fans"—pointing around him—"before it ever starts."

The Royals didn't do well but it was only the first day and they weren't playing the Yankees, and by the All Star break the regional hatreds would be in symbolic bloom. Other sports are organized by city, "but baseball's been there longer," McGuff reminds, and baseball's the master way in which regional and ethnic frictions are mediated and mythically resolved. "I think probably sports is as much of a cohesive factor as we've got in this country," said McGuff. "You talk about economy and all that, but there's nothing in our economic structure that ties everything together the way a baseball league does, and there's nothing in entertainment . . ." He trails off to watch George Brett fly out. Because all of us, hicks and snobs, zone out with Cosby, all the hatred repressed. "There's no other field where you have this firm structure that you have in sports that involves the whole country," McGuff returned. "Perhaps it *is* a safety valve of some type."

I gave up on baseball when my beloved Yankees stopped winning. In the great old days—"when you used to crush the yokels," McGuff smiled—when Munson was alive and Goose was young and Reggie was vital, every one of them fractious, I was bananas. My Yanks were a metaphor of New York. "No, Thurman was not a nice guy," McGuff was saying, "he was an interesting guy, a great interview if you put up with all the bullshit." But he died in his plane crash, and the Yanks broke my heart every weekend, and inasmuch as Yogi never called *me* from the dugout phone to assess such and such a move in advance, why should I curse and stomp when he lost? For the sake of equilibrium, I taught myself not to mistake myself for the Yanks or the Mets, or the Knicks or . . . "If everyone thought like you, there wouldn't be cities and civic consciousness," McGuff gently chided.

After foodless lunch at Wendy's I visited a man who happens to share some of my name. His KCMO radio show was already in progress:

> And so let us stride forward into this exploration of why people do what they do and how they get to be the way they are. Let's talk psychology stuff. This is Dr. Marshall Saper.

He's on a billboard above I 435, a demigod to the little and large people who call in from eight states. He takes 20 calls a day, that's 100 calls a week, it's 5,000 callers a year for 11 years; that's 155,000 years; that's 55,000 callers—barkeeps, grocers, doctors, professors telling Saper troubles he can't remember the next day. "Marshall, in 11 years they've all blended together," he'll tell me. Now in the KCMO studio, he's ending his monologue:

> It was a sad situation indeed, the sick father saying his son never came to see him, how did he deserve this, oh woe is me, woe is me. Then I happened to talk to the son, fairly successful young man, 25, nothing aberrant or peculiar about him on the surface, very personable fellow as a matter of fact. When I came out and said—"How is your father doing? I understand he's been ill"—the young man became frosty. "I guess my father is all right, I don't know," he said. "Did you feel you'd lose him?"

471

I prompted. And this young man said: "I couldn't care less, I don't care whether my father lives or dies. I don't wish him ill, I simply don't care."

The show's over for another day and Saper and I are sitting in the office in which he counsels patients. "What I notice from the phone calls and what I notice from my private practice is, I don't think you can separate American culture from sick Americans. If you listen to a cross section of people calling in to talk about their personal problems, keeping out those that are hard-core psychotic, which is a very small minority in the population of the country and a small minority of the population of my callers, what you hear crying out is social despair as much as individual anguish."

"Some of the traits of this despair?" I said.

"A lack of identification of self. Who am I? A lack of grounding in any strong tradition that has clear definition to it."

Here we go again. I had come to Kansas City to meet civilians, consumers of Goodson and Glaser, Bedford, Koppel, and Yevtushenko, the taste-makers I had traveled halfway around the world to decode. Naively or not, I had half-believed my old prof De Certeau, who had written in my own *On Signs* that we "play within the labyrinth of city signs (street names, advertising slogans, historic landmarks, commercial, political or academic identities) in the same way in which the voice wanders, delinquent, stubborn, through the networks of the linguistic system, tracing pathways foreign to the meaning of the sentences." I didn't come to Kansas City to hear of unpretty little women suffering agoraphobia to force to their bedsides relatives with as little concern for them as that 25-year-old for his sick father. Baudrillard got it wrong, sort of. The Kansas Citians calling Saper don't know who they are or what they desire, but they're not Baudrillard's happy, easy, cool crowd. Baudrillard's America is pieces of the big cities where the Armani-clad boys and girls have refined experience-denial to an art. They don't know who they are and that's fine. In Kansas City it's rawer. Anguish unbound. I asked Saper to profile them:

A sizeable number of them are like little children that have gotten stepped on in a crowd, and they don't know who to blame for it or where to go for help or how to evaluate it as just a temporary thing. They don't know how they got there or how to get out of it or why it happened to them. And so the pain they feel in their toe at that moment is not what an adult would feel with temporary inconvenience. Rather, the pain in a child who's stepped on is intense, accompanied by fear, because he doesn't know where the pain came from or what's going to follow. There's no context to evaluate the pain.

And then getting into your field, I attribute it to the pretty general breakdown of social institutions that used to be able to comfort people by establishing predictable patterns, not just the breakdown of churches but everything, including the moguls, the politicians, the stars, the anchors, all these creatures of the media that have no context and no history in our lives. So then we get into another aspect of what I hear from callers and that is, "Tell me how to fix it now," the famous American how-to, the four ways of solving a bad marriage, tell me, doctor, the six techniques for raising a happy child. People call from roadside pay phones, I hear trucks going by in the background, truckers call: "I got my big rig here, doc, and people are waiting to use this phone." And I hear the truck engine in the background—he's stopped off to take a piss and to call me to solve a problem in his life.

AIDS people are starting to call now. They want to know how to deal with dying, what are the ten steps to deal with your own death that's looming in front of you? They know enough from the media to know what they got is fatal. The question then is, what do I do now to feel better? People seek their information in easily digestible capsules, very few people go to a book for it, nothing matters except the pain that I feel now and how do I get it fixed now. Buddy, you know the kind of books they're buying? Diet books and psychology self-help books. So Marshall, whatever you write in your book, I hope you'll put a title on it that implies media and weight reduction, and don't forget to use your doctor label: *Doctor Blonsky's Media and Weight Reduction Book*, because the doctors are the secular priests now. They're the ones the people are looking to to fix them. Hell, even the Baptist preachers call themselves doctors now. And they have as much right as anybody else.

So now we got another myth, the assumption that whatever ails you, some expert somewhere will fix, absolute blind faith. I think part of that one comes from the electronic media. Everything that happens is presented in a tight capsule with a beginning, a middle, and an end, then you forget about it and you go on to the next tight capsule. In my practice one of the first things I have to do is educate the patient to the fact that what happens in a psychotherapy session is different from a ten-minute telephone conversation on the radio. Because even though we come to an end of the conversation and the caller hangs up and says thank you, that doesn't mean we've come to the end of the caller's problem. But to the person listening, accustomed to the vignettes and the half-hour soap operas the one-hour dramas, there was a beginning, a middle, and an end to the call, the caller hung up and said thank you, therefore it's fixed.

The narrativity of the radio call feeds the myth of the Fixable and Fixed. But nothing's been fixed, and Saper is woe-weary. He's been on-air a decade, and all the cases have blended together. He can barely remember yesterday's callers. "Remember my monologue this morning? I got a call from a woman . . ."
Priceless!

> Woman   I disagree with how you feel about children and spending so much time with them. I think when fathers are working, if they spent as much time playing with kids as you seem to suggest, they wouldn't have enough on the table.
>
> Saper   Does your husband work so hard that he doesn't have much time to spend with the children?
>
> Woman   We don't have children but my husband works all the time and—
>
> Saper   Did your father perhaps work so hard he didn't spend much time with the children?
>
> Woman   He certainly did and I loved him dearly!
>
> Saper   That's good.
>
> Woman   Never did I resent it.
>
> Saper   That's nice. Except I wasn't talking about how much time is spent working, madam, I was talking about how much time is spent interacting with the children when the husband is there.
>
> Woman   But I think kids are sort of like cats. Their loyalty just goes to whoever gives them the most attention. They really don't care if they get it from one person or another.
>
> Saper   You don't have children?
>
> Woman   Not in this marriage, no.
>
> Saper   Okay, kids are like cats. I hadn't heard it put quite that way but it does get to the point of your opinion, doesn't it?

I think we've transferred our previous relationships to others into relationships with things. "Get away, kid, I'm watching, I'm playing with my damn dish." When I was growing up there just weren't as many objects to buy as now. Can you believe it, we didn't have tape recorders, forget about the satellite dishes. I remember my youth vividly, and each day, you know what I did? Man, I'm prehistoric. I went out of the house *and played.* Life was primitive, there weren't many things around, so you related to people, you played imaginary games. We were just hanging around. I think now when kids hang around it's for the purpose of stealing hub caps. It's for the purpose of getting things.

Little things. For the little people of the plains and the little people who love the Yanks and call them yokels.

We're talking about the media [said Saper] and the media exists largely to sell products, which means to shape consumers of those products. And you can't sell a product until you get someone to want the product and so one gets reduced to being the perfect model consumer for the mass-produced products like your creepy little hamburger at Wendy's today. You and I are old enough to remember what life was like before Wendy's. You and I eat that dreck and we say, "Yuch!" You talk to any kid who's under 25 and this is heaven and they go out of their way, businessmen in their 20s or early 30s going out of their way to go to Wendy's for lunch because that's what they're used to. So we're talking about molding the consumer to fit the product. You and I look at a Wendy's meal or McDonald's and think how petty, how mass produced, how without form and identity and without worth. My father owned a store downtown, so when I would go to visit him one of my treats was to go to the café in the area. I found a selection of the meals I got at home. It was real food and there were cafés in every neighborhood on every corner as there are now fast food joints. We only have one or two in the whole city left.

And as he drives me to my next appointment, I ask if he likes KC. "Today is a big day for Kansas City, you know. We got the basketball tournament here. I mean, that's it, pal. Do you know what our local politicians and civic leaders are saying? They're saying this is going to put Kansas City on the map. It's a joke, it's pathe—"

Whereupon something behind me fell.

"See, you jumped like a New Yorker," Saper said. "Sounded like a gunshot, right? You anticipate the worst. And in New York you're usually right. It's another reason you wouldn't fit into Kansas City."

Early Sunday morning, November 3, 1991, Marshall Saper fired two shots into his chest in the driveway of a medical office building near Humana hospital in Kansas City. On the following Monday he was to have gone on trial to defend against a former patient's charge that he had seduced her.

M: *Madonna*   Blessed by a name that ignites a binary opposition ("or whore"), she has exploited the system of choice since her beginnings. At the 1986 Live-Aid concert, after the vulgarity of Bette Midler's introduction ("a woman who has pulled herself up by her bra straps"), she shouted: "Today I'm not taking shit off" . . . while dressed in the prettiest mint-green long coat (*Playboy* and *Penthouse* had just run nude photos of her 19-year-old self). And there she is at the end of her early video "Material Girl," in the cab of Keith Carradine's homely truck, having chosen his love and daisies over wealth . . . she smirks, an ugly contortion to the face. But her all-white dress dazzles the eye. "She's appealing to the mass public through the sentimental channel," director Susan Seidelman said, "giving up all those jewels [offered her by suitors in the earlier part of the video] for that sweet guy."

I wish you could have heard the irony in Seidelman's voice. Keith Carradine is anything but sweet. The role he's playing is that of film director watching Madonna on video . . . as the video *we* watch completely closes up on what he sees: Madonna as Marilyn, an ornament lavishly handed around by Busby Berkeley, Cordon-rouged, tuxedoed chorus boys. Here are the 40s and 50s commingled, no one cares what signs are thrown in with what. Jewels or daisies, a choice at every moment. And smirks while holding daisies, and 40s boys court 50s girl—the present itself can be split. In "Like A Virgin," in a Bob Guccione-like chateau of soft focus, making sure to keep her bridal gown on, she slithers across the parquet floor, singing "Oh, oh, oh, oh, oh, oh, oh, oh, oh/Ooh, baby—" The overly simple percussion is precisely that beat known so well as the soundtrack of porn.

"Madonna combines ideas that shouldn't be able to be combined," said Seidelman, her first director (*Desperately Seeking Susan*). "Her candy-quality voice makes this a sweet, little-girlish song, perfect for sentimental Americans who love Halloween and big-eyed doggies. Oh? Feels so good inside?" But the dress is full, it performs fashion's function of erasure. The dress deconstructs the "oh, oh"; the slithering deconstructs the dress. The matrix not a simple 0/1, a binary scansion that passes across the bar from one stable term to another. No theme she proposes is stable. She never poses anything, even when she vogues. Don't even try to answer the question: what does she believe in now? As if her changes were part of some artistic evolution. In her 1990 "Rock the Vote" video, she literally wrapped herself in the American flag: "Freedom of speech is as good as sex!" Whereupon, as exclamation mark, one of the chorus boys slapped her flag-draped, protruded buttock. "And if you don't vote, you're gonna get a spankie!" she ended. Pro vote? Pro spankie?

The fashion system dominates our clothing, hairstyles, lifestyles, music, not only all our artifacts but our behavior as well, all of it hooked up to styling changes. Commodities, goods, values have to be instantly understandable, thoroughly enjoyable, utterly forgettable. They enter laughing like a genial actor and exit the stage, as it were, in mid-speech and mid-pitch to make room for another. In Jean Genet's *Funeral Rites,* it's morning, Genet having made love all night to a boy whom he tells now to leave. But all those things you said last night, the unfashionable boy remonstrates. Genet: It was last night, it was a sandcastle of words. What Madonna understands deep down inside is that to beat the fashion game (which raises you up only to dash you down), you have to play the change game. Change yourself before fashion changes you by finding your replacement. Madonna is therefore not this role or that, she is not Madonna or whore, she is the will to power, the will to endure. Exalting option, offering the illusion of freedom, she is a parody of the fashion system itself.

"Express yourself," she sang in a Marilyn dress, in a slip bumping and shimmying, in a man's suit flashing bra and grabbing her crotch, collared and chained, crawling in leather skirt, bathing a slave in milk, and utterly nude. Be motherly, sultry, subject or object or utterly degraded or capitalist pig, anything goes, be my guest, she affirms. When Forest Sawyer, subbing for Koppel, interviewed her on "Nightline," he asked her where she drew the line in sexual representations.

Madonna   (blinking unable to see him): I draw the line with violence and humiliation and degradation, okay? And I don't think any of those issues are evident in my video. That's where I draw the line. That's what I don't want to see.

Sawyer   Well, I guess then one woman's art is another woman's pornography. I'm thinking of the "Express Yourself" video. I mean, there are images of you chained—

Madonna   Yes but I am chained—

Sawyer   —there are images of you crawling under a table, and there are a lot of people who are upset by that.

Madonna   Okay, I chained myself, though, okay? There wasn't a man that put that chain on me. I did it myself. I was chained to my desires. I crawled under my own table, you know. There wasn't a man standing there making me do it. I do everything by my own volition. I'm in charge, okay?

And you can be, too. More than okay, it's a thrill to be alive in America. One, two, a million choices await.

"I think it's bullshit but I still want to watch her video." Why do we hear it over and over? The speaker will say: "I guess I really got interested when someone said, 'It's the first time there's been breasts on network TV.'" Even Madonna was excited to tell Sawyer:

When I did my "Vogue" video there's a shot of me where you can . . . I'm wearing a see-through dress and you can clearly see my breasts. Now they [MTV] told me they wanted me to take that out but I said I wouldn't and they played it anyway. So I thought that once again I was going to be able to bend the rules a little bit.

We're fascinated with haecceity, thisness, the event, what's never happened before, what will never occur again and thereby seems precious. Your city breaking a temperature record, Daryl Strawberry beating his home run record, stat craziness in general and the first breasts on TV—who cares! The whole country cares, and Madonna has to keep coming up with a first for the rest of her public life.

477

Figure 19.4a and 19.4b Madonna, "Justify My Love," 1990.
Stephane Sednaoui.

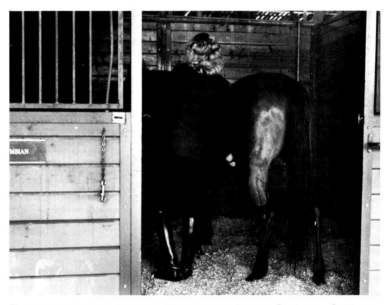

Figure 19.5 Helmut Newton, *Woman and Horse, Burbank, California 1987.*

478

19.4b

Figure 19.6 Helmut Newton, *Kiss, Los Angeles 1985.*

N: *Newton—revisited*   So none of her roles is substantial. Even if a video costs $1 million to make, the parts she plays have to be superficial and look it. In "Justify My Love," the video that MTV banned for fielding a bestiary of erotic isms, the S&M is so good humored, one wonders what was bothering MTV. "We're dealing with sexual fannies . . ." her tongue slipped on "Nightline"— ". . . fantasies," she corrected. "And being truthful and honest with our partners, you know. And these feelings exist and I'm just dealing with the truth here in my video." No, her images aren't your fantasies, they are too polite. She kneels in a hotel corridor, undressing, legs spreading to flash bare thigh and garter belt. The camera, about to veer into her crotch, turns away, slides up and over the thigh, respectful of the surface. Had that camera been the eye of fantasy, the hand of fantasy would have reached right in.

Passing quickly by a room, the camera sees a man behind a leather-clad woman, his pelvis at her buttocks—with a space inbetween. Her lover strips, she in bra and panties. "I want to know you," she sighs, he descends. "I want it like that"—pushing his chest back. But you can't do it like that—too far away. "I don't want to be your mother"—now a woman descends on her. "I don't want to be your sister, either," she intones. "I just want to be your lover." On a chair next to the bed, holding his head as if tired, her male lover. This isn't voyeurism, a voyeur has to hide. It's that rarity, a bedside visit from a doctor.

Madonna knocks off Newton. Look at the real thing. I mean, if you've got a crotch nearby, you go for it ("Woman and Horse, Burbank, California 1987"). If you've got the opportunity to hump, then you grind ("Woman and Cadillac, Hollywood 1987"). If you're going to descend on someone, put your back—or your tongue—in it ("Kiss, Los Angeles 1985"). Inside the head, we are not polite.

But Madonna can't make images so strong as to make you invest in them; how could you leave them next month when the new scandal breaks? No role she produces can be profound or stable, and her S&M is obliged to be simulacral. Obliged by her logic, not the network's. Look into the eyes of that woman humping the tail fin: look at the diabolism of cunning, the exuberance of the subjectivity. It gives you ideas, as we say. That image is a force grafting onto you, swelling you. Jacques Lacan used to say of the image: "It makes you walk on your foot," affects you. Stuck as a change artist, Madonna, unlike Newton, is weak.

Remember Koppel's Vanna Factor? Make yourself an empty vessel, don't go on the record. It would be the death of Madonna to make strong signs.

N: *Nudity*   The female body comes to life when contemplated. Male visual investment traveled (c. 1950–1980) from legs to breasts to derrière and finally to the pubic area and the opening into interiority. The hustler pinkness became a surface, interiority becomes exterior, labia majora and minora assumed the same value as facial lips. The search for interiority merely created more surface. (Remember Annie on page 107.) The search for more revelation, more intimacy, made the copper circle and the pink jewels artificial adornments. Private areas became like garments to a point, proving, as Eliot said, that "man cannot take too much reality." We are buoys that cannot sink, go deep. All attempts at depth end up in surface.

As for the other, the male body, it too has traveled: from the aggressive actor to a slithering adornment of the female. He is now the *déjeuner* male surrounded *sur l'herbe* by dressed females. Muscle in man is pure apparel instead of a coil of strength. The dangerous phallus (because it could fecundate) has turned into a floating anemone in the Jacuzzi. The buttocks have become domestic pets. And facial hair has become pure Miami makeup.

Whether male or female, you'll have to look as if you have on flesh-colored spandex or you won't cut it in the 90s. Nudity has become dress, one glistening part leading to the other, a wash of skin, the final adornment of the body. And dress is nudity, the skin of desire, the shape of pleasure. The buttons are crowning lozenges. Zippers are the promise of coyly crossed legs. Soft ties are anticipation of warmth and ripeness. Fabrics are resilient and shapeful. A $1000 Ferré cashmere jacket falls from shoulders to hem—your eye can't resist treating it like nude skin: I want it all, at once, now! An Armani $1500 coat moves as you move, capturing the eye of the other that darts hither and yon upon it as on a hostile beast. Your skin is buttoned at the navel. The breasts are padded. Your body hair is your tassels. Skin itself has become a product, a texture like silk or cotton. It is something you can modify by stretching, reducing, an entire process of re-creation through exercise, odor, injection, or silicone or suction of fat. Freedom as never before, and the sculptural possibility of molding, producing yourself as your own sculpture. The body has lost its depth. The nude as the ultimate surface: no shame, little excitation. And if you're naked, forget it.

O: *Obsession* Also Eternity. Also "I am Shalimar: Always." The opposite of postmodernity, because of postmodernity. In a world that seems to be constantly changing, where quiescence is a virtue, to call things "eternity" and "obsession" is religious thinking; a religious idea turned toward sexuality for those who can't abide the age. Calvin Klein and his colleagues are trying to give the perfume a sense of the absolute, of intense passion. As eternity is forever, obsession is exacerbated desire. On the face of it, ridiculous: a thrust toward the absolute by something so evanescent as perfume. If there isn't religion or desire in the world, just say there is. Splash it on your body. That's postmodern.

O: *Optima* If you've got the card in your wallet, I'm afraid I helped put it there. When Jacques Attali told me, "America is only a marketing network anymore," I decided to test him. I went into the market, discovering that Lester Wunderman, chairman of the direct marketing agency Wunderman Worldwide, had been reading Umberto Eco. Not what everyone read, the seductive *Name of the Rose;* rather, the scientistic *Semiotics and the Philosophy of Language.* Having played Dark Doctor to poor Pat, it wasn't hard to become part of the secret "Companion Card" team, it was called. Companion Card was the code name for what American Express would call Optima, its revolving credit card to compete with Mastercard and Visa. AmEx's problem: the bank cards, more aggressive than ever before, were trying to cast AmEx as the narrow, "special occasion" card; moreover, AmEx was vulnerable from a utility point of view, the bank cards linked to more numerous merchants. AmEx had learned through research that its cardmembers actually charged more of their personal purchases on these lesser competitors than on the company's own instruments. AmEx was worried that the competitors would achieve perceptual acceptability ("It's okay to use my Preferred VISA where I would have used AmEx before"). Since the competition was going to encroach on the AmEx cardholder base, Wunderman felt it necessary to "bond" with the existing American Express cardholders. The card that became Optima was to be the glue in the process.

So one Sunday with nothing better to do, I joined Mr. Wunderman and one Joel De Tucciarone, Wunderman's vice president and senior idea man, and Wunderman told the two of us to "gift" the consumer with the new card. Write me a glossary for this gifting, Wunderman told us. And Tucciarone, whose schtik was "customized persuasion," uttered the words "personal needs," "difference," "dialogue with the target."

Now I once had a friend Roy Jackson, a millionaire in his twenties when it meant a lot more than it does now, who told me: "Don't worry about your liabilities, build the asset side. Debt isn't something to be afraid of." Tell that to the former Trump. But it being Sunday—and brainstorming for them and experiment for me—I uttered a phrase taken from Eco (forgive me, Umberto): "signification system." Signification system is a way the culture has cut up your world for you, made it pertinent to you, made it matter. The Eskimo have many different words for snow, we have one, I quasi-lectured. Eskimos see, perceive, and think of many different things there where I see and name one. Pertinence is a function of practice, Eco taught, the Eskimo's practice or profession obviously being snow-bound and mine not at all. Eco gave his students—and I, mine—the model of a room in which on a table are a large crystal ashtray, a paper cup, and a hammer. I can organize these pieces of furniture of my world of reference into at least a double system. If I'm a thirsty man I'll reach for—see, speak about—the cup and even the ashtray. If I'm aggressive, it'll be the hammer and, as the occasional psychotherapist has learned, the ashtray. Practices select pertinences; pertinences direct gaze and speech. "My friend Jackson was inducting me into a hidden signification system," I ended. "For the rich."

From which came the following two glossaries, a piece of cake:

	MASS SYSTEM	ELITE SYSTEM
"Credit"	Equivocal concept: know you need it, fear it	Pure instrumentality: a tool for leverage
"Revolving Credit"	Not well understood; socially coded as "low"; a few steps from layaway; always fools you: you feel you can pay off more than you can	Taken for granted; many more sophisticated credit options open
"Debt"	Fear word: door to the poorhouse; in a relation of tension with "credit"; one wishes to be out of it, into the black; embarrassing	Viewed in productive relation to wealth accumulation and/or business growth
Etc.		
SUM OF WORDS	CREDIT CREATES LIABILITY	CREDIT CREATES "ASSETABILITY"
	Credit as weakness, as embarrassment	Credit as power, as vital instrument

Here was a pool of supposedly elite language, available to the "creatives" who with word and image could connote this new class into which Optima would induct its holder. The first headline, the master headline these creative ones wrote was this: "The Optima Card: The perfect complement to the world's most respected Card." Perfect? I thought that in the elite world, nothing is perfect.

Oh, from the Wunderman side.

And so the headline became:

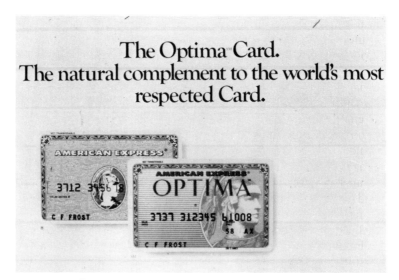

The Optima™ Card.
The natural complement to the world's most respected Card.

Figure 19.7 Can you spot the error in the headline? This ad plus supporting mailings are supposed to constitute a myth of elitism, but to an elite today, nothing is natural. The myth is deconstructing. *Courtesy Wunderman Worldwide.*

THE OPTIMA CARD

The natural complement to
the world's most respected Card.

Forgive me, Roland, for whom of course nothing in our time is natural. Except Optima, now in—I didn't go back to ask—how many pockets?

Did I tell you what fun the marketers had (save for the creatives)? What a robust experience of jokes and electronic "white boards" and breaks for send-up Reubens and pastas (no Koppel frugality here)? The little experience taught me that the people in that room that Sunday and subsequent days only thought they were working for American Express. They weren't selling Optima so much as selling consuming. They were selling selling, they were selling buying, they were creating the sensorium. If Optima turned out to be a good ad it would be like a trauma, as Freud in his theory of trauma describes it: Trauma breaches the skin of your mind, it falls right into you. Traumas, the effective ads just go into you. You don't remember them but you end up buying.

I had participated in a pseudo-myth: the signs would only seem to make the world intelligible. Reading the Optima language, looking at its imagery, you would scarcely be able to perform the elite acts they hinted at. As Barthes might have said, the Optima discourse had no responsibility vis-à-vis the real; the advertising "real" is not operable. Unfortunately, managing a true credit card business, as opposed to their traditional monthly charge-and-pay (a zero-sum game), layed the ax to the roots of the myth. As the constrained economy of the late 80s and early 90s hit, the need to manage, not myth but the reality of bad credit performance, struck. But Optima managers, perhaps seduced by the myth of the elite system, did not put in place the tools to closely monitor and take action to manage the bad debt—into the hundreds of millions. I would assess the Optima myth as a short-lived myth, permitting the following note about myth. The dynamic and restlessness of the culture creates an impulse not only for long-lasting myths but short-lived ones, too. Temporary values—here, being "in on" elite codes of finance.

All the while consuming more than one saves—in the name of the immediate and the dream of material pleasure. Sorry about that consultation: I may have put you more in debt, but I had to test Attali. Why not send it back to AmEx?

P: *Passion* It's something you've gotta have. Although it has been gutted of its rancid, redolent, porous, nineteenth-century flavor. It's not throbbing loins or crackling neurons. It's not hidden between soft sheets or in a closet universe. It is simply a calculated risk—maybe even worth illness, exile, or death. It's something you've got to keep doing over and over. Yes, it could be a man or a woman, another body, but it's also ice cream, crack, hot tubs, cornflakes, buttocks, or sodas. Periodically Marlon Brando overdoses on ice cream and has to be hospitalized. Cornflakes are Arafat's favorite cereal, soaked in tea and covered with honey. And T. E. Lawrence, in spite of his medieval asceticism, always had time for soaking in a hot tub. It's a calculated risk, but it's something you've got to have.

S: *Sunglasses* Death of the soul. Sunglasses hide the windows of the self, the wet, viscous pool of intimacy. The dark discs wipe out the fluid, restless, vulnerable, revealing core of your identity. They turn the head into an absolute surface where the only movable part left is the devouring mouth. The empty discs can be filled with anything or everything. Sunglasses turn the face into an empty vessel to be filled with your own makeup or someone else's imagination. Sunglasses are no longer to protect you against the harmful rays of the sun, but to protect your eyes from the voyeurism of the world.

The eyes, for so long the exhibitionist element in your face, the revealer of desire, tenderness, and fear, are concealed as safely as your inner thoughts. The glasses are no longer a practical, functional object tied to a specific hour of the day or season of the year. Polarized, placed within fashion frames, they have become an arbitrary, universal warning sign ("noli me tangere") you can wear at night, indoors. They are a facial garment. It is better to have two black holes where other people can place their fantasies than be a blue-eyed boy or girl. In the words of e. e. cummings, "What do you think of your blue-eyed boy, Mr. Death?"

T: *Tom Cruise* also *Paulina, Eddie Murphy, Robert de Niro*. Early in the research, I made a mistake when I called Tom Cruise's publicist in L.A. "Not your ordinary journalist," I told her, "a semiologist . . . sensitive to his words." *The Washington Post* was prepared to preprint the Cruise chapter, we wanted an empty vessel kind of star—recall the Koppel chapter—Rob Lowe (too soft), Dennis Quaid (maybe), Tom Cruise (ideal: hard edge encircling nothing).

"Then we don't want you," she devastated me. "Profile him in that newspaper and all the other journalists will follow you. And if you define him on the pages of that newpaper, it'll happen to him what happened to Travolta. He died." Because defined. "But . . . but . . . but"—the reasoning phase. "*Outlook,* the Serious Page, the *Post,* the prestige"—just blah blah to a good publicist. "I hope you won't feel offended, we want dumb journalists," she said. And boy, did I learn it's a two-tiered press system today: the serious press the publicists won't let near the stars; and the other press. For stars, scandal, gossip, lifestyle, whatever you want to get drunk on.

Michele August
Elite Models
111 East 22nd Street
New York, NY 10010

Dear Ms. August
This is to consolidate our phone conversation.

The Washington Post is interested in my writing a profile of Ms. Porizkova for the Sunday *Outlook* section. I would like to do something quite different from the interviews with Ms. Porizkova that I have read. I have seen other possibilities, a fresher perspective on fashion and beauty, given her European background, her early years in Czechoslovakia, and her cultural interests. I would like not only to interview her but to accompany her for a day of her professional activities. I think she would be very helpful in giving an insight into a world that is usually presented either as esoteric or trivial and I believe that by interviewing and witnessing her at work a more serious understanding and appraisal can be achieved. The piece would obviously reflect her views on American culture.

Not a word about semiology, definition although in hindsight I can see that awful word "different" again. But she's supposed to be an iconoclast, she doesn't give a damn what she eats, she's the Lauder lady in public and a hellion in private. Maybe she'd like a nice forum to speak out.

Forget it. A cold August declines, no reason given.

Eddie Murphy
c/o Terrie Williams
The Terrie Williams Agency
250 West 57th Street
New York, NY 10107

Dear Mr. Murphy

You are caught between the devil of conservative white thinking and the deep blue sea of traditional radical thought (the White piece in *The City Sun*).

I have been asked by *The Washington Post* to approach you for a profile for its *Outlook* section. This letter is a request for an interview.

You have positioned yourself at the cutting edge of a new space being created for blacks in this country, an area that I think will expand during the 90s.

I would like to show a mainstream audience the identity and humor system you have created that give you a role in a completely new game. You have established a model without any subordination, unlike the Rochester (Eddie Anderson) of the 40s or even the Sammy Davis, Jr. of the 50s. You are *an* American character, a character that is another traditional Hollywood role model (like the Irish-Cockney W.C. Fields, the Jewish Groucho Marx and the Italian Frank Sinatra—once perceived as ethnic stereotypes that have been incorporated into the American pantheon).

I would like to have your response one way or the other, whether positive or negative.

Best regards,

Now we're cooking. I had given up on empty vessels, I had gone to the other extreme, approached the brimming-with-subjectivity De Niro, whose producer Irwin Winkler said no ("he doesn't give them"), and now here I was in the field of racial strong signs, Eddie Murphy. He was in the middle of a dogfight over *Coming to America,* and optimist me, I would give him a *Post* platform.

DOCUMENT: Murphy PAGE: 1 LINE: 29

ceived as ethnic stereotypes that have been incorporated into the American pantheon).

I would like to have your response one way or the other, whether positive or negative.

Best regards,

Civil rights had opened the way for integration. Minority of skillful blacks took advantage, leaving rest behind. Two populations: black bourgeoisie and the rest as in French *reste,* leftovers, The Black Nation. Use Jesse as contrast: a foot in each system, speaks to poor and tries to integrate the bourgeoisie—call it the Democratic Party. Always ambiguous, half bourgeois, half oppressed. Not so Eddie Murphy. Think of him as tribune of the bourgeois black. Loves Armani. But needs legitimacy, wants the oppressed to like him. He'd be in deep shit if the blacks as a whole rejected him.

So addresses the nation through black newspaper, *The Sun,* as a byproduct legitimizing it. Never before spoke through black press for fear of alienating the system. Intellectually, trying to have his cake and eat it, too, astute, and hypocritical.

His vision of black identity very white. Uses authentically black phrases and style within white myth. Don't forget the "Half!" slogan. Audiences love it. But his mythology not totally white. When he inserts himself into white vision he uses aggressivity that before wasn't allowed. Thinks that validates him.

His burning problem: those that died. Without Malcolm and Martin—without white guilt vis-a-vis blacks—he wouldn't be where he is. The two M's created the political situation that made his M possible. He is reaping the benefits of people who really were about roots and blackness, leaving most of his fellow blacks in the gutter. I'm black like you but I have millions and you're begging. Exploit this tension.

Remember what got Koppel mad? I had a predisposition, I thought he was an intellectual. I thought I had hidden my DOCUMENT: Murphy—hidden my predisposition—from Murphy. For when you approach celebrities, you yourself are an empty vessel, a tape recorder to let them register. Their strong signs on your blank tape or page of a mind. To get them to agree, or rather their publicists, you write them upbeat letters, mention a few of their success traits, predict the profile—"It's gonna be good." You might think it's called bullshit. It isn't. The publicist has already pulled your clips, assessed your image. The letter you fax him or her is nothing but a handshake, a confirmation you're what you've always been, will do what you've always done, flatter, flatter, flatter the star. The "giving an insight" you write in your letter, or "fresher perspective," is nothing but your part of a contract that you're in the dumb tier that doesn't decode.

Terrie Williams called back. Eddie's too busy for now but in the future, well, and let's have a drink and last year she sent a Christmas card. A final salute to Koppel: Williams had made herself Vanna.

V: *VCR* Liberation from the programmers—you watch when you want, what you want. Want to network more? Get in some squash? Complicate your dangerous liaisons? Then (heresy) skip the nightly news. Let your VCR do the watching. Get a week's worth, all at once, when, late Friday night, pleasantly exhausted from intrigue and ambition, you find a time slice to play catch-up with Brokaw. And who says, Saturday, you have to watch looney toons? Look at horror, if you please. Sunday, when you wake, you don't have to listen to a preacher—you can put on some porn. Tapes are control over time. They are graffiti on monuments. You defy the stations by covering Dan Rather with a half hour of *Creep Show.* And don't worry that you're avoiding reality. You're avoiding the recreation of reality, courtesty of the media. You yourself concoct your own reality stew: a severed head walking upside down, maybe a laugh at the improv, even a peek at a favorite porn star. There you are, three times removed from reality, loving it, a child of Andy Warhol—who made art not from live models, recall, but from photos. Since the game shows make dorks into heroes; since the improv comics let the little guy shout his grief and think it's heard; since the nightly anchors smile at, ponder, and carefully enunciate the nightmare of history; since TV subtracts you from the real, why not slide that plastic cassette in the slit and have the choice of *your* lie? Or . . . artifice, to be more precise. The triumph of Burger King: reality—had your way. And if you're a klutz at channel programming, we can even offer freedom from the VCR. Just buy a VCR plus remote by Gemstar, ($160), press "clock," enter year/month/date/hour/minute, press "cable" and do a couple of things more (you can do that much, and if you can't, they'll do it for you at The Wiz), and now you're ready. Want to record a week's worth of "Nightline"? Just turn to your TV Guide or daily paper, punch in the number at the end of each listing, and now with my 58975 on the tiny screen, I hit "Daily (M–F)," lay my plus on the VCR and that's it. The VCR will come on when Ted's on, and I don't even have to be in the room. Koppel stockpiled.

V: *Vogue*   Fashion killer. When Anna Wintour came to *Vogue,* she and Alex Liberman set about refocusing the character of *Vogue* photography. Let Liberman tell you:

> I think there are sort of unspoken recognitions between the woman reader and fashion magazine pictures that perhaps reveal to her moments that she suddenly recognizes as having lived through, and I think this hitting of correspondences is a very interesting challenge for modern editors. I think that men should not edit women's fashion magazines because, more and more, editing requires this instinctive recognition. The editor becomes the reader and only a woman, in my opinion, can do that: identify not only with her concerns but reveal her own recognitions and communicate them through instants caught. Unfortunately, most photographers are men and most of them, I think, are not quite capable of doing this. The interesting ones, like Arthur Elgort, capture these moments in spite of themselves, through chance.

Usually male photographers are authoritarian, they impose images as they conceive them, they're not willing to let go of their superiority.

Look at Penn and Avedon. They always imposed, they pose their concept, their look. "Turn your head, look up," they commanded their models, and you could almost hear it on the surface of the picture. Liberman again:

It was artificial. Most male photography continues in the sculptural tradition, three-dimensional objects definitely portrayed like a painting by David. With the introduction of really modern art, the static image has dissolved—it disappeared in abstraction. I've always believed that women photographers are even more capable of the shift from the definite to the so-called weaker image, to the *instantanes*, snapshots, but they haven't been given the chance because photography for a long time was this strong image. Today it's the weak image that is the real communication and that is the interesting change.

Basically until very recently fashion was really artifice, and in many ways fashion is dead and what exists is envelopment of the body to a certain extent. All these loose clothes, they're part of a freedom. It has to do with women's liberation, and that's why models have cut their hair, they practically have men's haircuts. There's the other extreme of long haircuts but the real revolt and desire is for the boy cut. The boyishness of a look, Armani or Chanel, affirms a certain liberated woman, and "liberated woman" means she's ready for anything. As the French say, *elle n's pas froid aux yeux.* She's not afraid of her eyes getting cold, of being shocked. She's willing to dare.

Hence, requires her comfort.

Comfort is anti-fashion—fashion conceived in the traditional sense. I remember Diana Vreeland saying to me when looking at a French collection: "How do you bend down to a file cabinet?" Well, of course ladies who buy $50,000 dresses don't bend to filing cabinets!

Liberman is sitting with me in his Condé Nast office. He has called for some back issues of *Vogue* and as we wait, he gives me a theory of "weak" photography:

It's women caught off guard as if unobserved. In art, Degas did women in their bathtubs, sometimes from behind, wiping themselves, as if nobody were watching. I think, more and more, the good photographers in fashion are the ones who establish an intimacy with the human being where the fashion doesn't count but what does is the unobserved instant. There are an infinity of unobserved moments in our behavior. The interesting photographers catch a certain moment where time, life, movement all come together. Most men are voyeurs. You walk in the street or ride in a cab—you see suddenly a moment of flash of hair, legs—you turn and are attracted. It's not by accident that the majority of *Vogue* pictures today are taken in the street. The women in the pages could be passersby. I'll show you what I mean.

The magazines have arrived.

More and more—and this is something that I predicted—the paparazzi approach, journalistic approach, would be and is the future of fashion photography. When Anna Wintour came to *Vogue* . . . could I have the October issue?

—he says to the assistant.

You'll understand the change. The October issue was one of the last Avedon covers (Fig. 19.8), a stylized studio image of a very pretty woman evidently smiling, conceived as an advertising image, selling *Vogue*. Now Anna Wintour's first cover was this (Fig. 19.9)—a casual snapshot of an attractive new face wearing blue jeans. This is Talisa, who's also a young actress; she's in a James Bond film. She happens not to be as famous yet because she doesn't sing, because music seems to be the way to contemporary fame, but the approach is extremely similar.

Figures 19.8, 19.9 A portfolio selected by Alexander Liberman. These are some of his favorite things.

 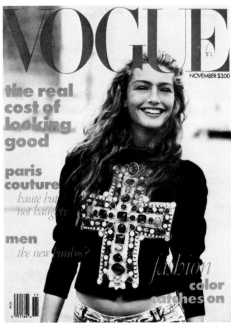

florals and fragrance

BLACK AND BLOOM
A flowery complement: florals worn
with black. This page: A rose-
covered cotton jacket paired with
cotton knit stretch pants.
Jacket, Butterick Pattern #6759.
Fabric by Cyrus Clark. Leggings,
Butterick Pattern #3507. Fabric
by Charter Fabrics. Opposite
page: A jersey top and silk
sarong. Both by Genny. Viscose
top, about $240; sarong,
about $345. Betsey Bunky Nini,
NYC; Knit Wit, Philadelphia;
Greta, Beverly Hills. Bouquets
come in bottles as well:
Wind Song by Prince Matchabelli,
L'Air du Temps by Nina Ricci.
Details, more stores, last pages.

19.10

I've always praised the amateur, always praised the paparazzi, I have resisted the slickness of finish, of estheticism, and I have always admired what I call the bad pictures, the photo *rate*. I've always looked in contact sheets for something beyond the plan of a so-called concept of the photographer. Now I find this enchanting (Fig. 19.10) because it's throwaway. It doesn't take fashion to the three-button clarity. The photographer catches a certain femininity, and ideal, and ideals, to come back to your mythology, don't apply to one woman, they apply to the essence of women. A picture like this applies to essence. Most editors will not publish a picture like that. Only *Vogue* will. Why? "Has he got three buttons in front? Has it got lapels?'' most editors will worry. But an intelligent, modern woman will say, ''Who cares?'' These pictures are the essence of modern photography. You are able to catch an aura that emanates from a total feeling of a woman's presence, which includes movement, includes of course hair, a certain coordination—everything is there between the photographer and the human being that is a momentary ideal. I'm purposely taking these pictures which seem to be very ordinary, but they are beyond natural. What was previously considered natural was a portrait in daylight in repose.

They are hypernatural, the figure caught in the interstices between poses.

> Previously, nobody would have thought of publishing dresses out of focus where you don't really see the dress. You get an illusion of the dress in most cases, and readers are accepting it. Ten years ago, even more recently, the editors, as I told you, wanted to see every button, to show the fashion. I think women today don't really want that. I think they're afraid of being the victims of influence, so they want sort of fleeting, inspirational glances. This is to allow them the freedom to have the illusion that it's their own choice and their own creation. Thus the fashion magazine is no longer looked upon as authoritarian advice, it's advisory advice, so the editorial function doesn't become dictatorial but becomes exposure to choice. And choice is, I think, the new secret of success today because it's flattering to the woman to be given the opportunity to choose, to have her self-esteem, her confidence in herself. The choice is good both ways, the game is rigged. She may have two choices given to her, black and white, two fashions for the same moment of the day, but they're both approved by the editorial staff, so she really can't make an error. This is one of the magics of fashion magazines.

Programmed difference. Like polling, elections, consumer purchases, the fashion magazine forms part of a system of binary regulation, stablized by choice. The option—between parties, products, life- and fashion-styles—closes the system.

W: *Walkman* In the towns of medievalism, in the cities of the Renaissance, the blacksmith forged, the crier exclaimed, and the street was all the time filled with very charming noise. Since the eighteenth century, since the rise of modern industry, our masters excluded the criers and every kind of human noise they could, introducing their own noise they called music (see Attali, *Noise*). Cut to now, to our latter-day master, Norio Ohga, president of Sony, who without market research said, Let there be Walkman. And Walkmen covered civilized earth, taking the control of city noise very far indeed. There's the instrument around my ears: In a zone that once was free—my ear and all the space it could reach out to—Sony and clones now speak to me, coo, and substitue for the city noise. It sings, I don't—it plays, I am silent—no matter I annoy my neighbor with the seepage of my noise, not music, with my hiss and vibration. Ohga music makes new noise all the while protecting his customer from other noise. It's one more nail in the coffin of Baudelaire's *oeil flâneur,* the *peintre de la vie moderne* buried by Sony. Freud told us of the joy of strolling in the motherland, not telling us so well why. The fun of walking the city? Think of Heidegger's promiscuous eye and yours. Yo!—something caught your attention, you identified with it. The head in the city was a subtly moving, bobbing head, casting glances everywhere, at a dandy, a slit in a skirt, a hairy athlete, a mouth uttering barbarism, altercation, arrest, the festival of life. (Your eye was omnivoyeur but not exhibitionist.) It's the Mirror Stage, Jacques Lacan would say; yeah, the city's the mirror in which we recognize ourself: "That's me," we say, "and me and me and me!" Added benefit: The eye as master of what it sees, its ego bubbling with jubilation. The city was the mirror. But injecting itself into our ears, the Walkman pulled the lid over the eye, slimming the pleasure of being out of doors and out of self. We are tamed by artificial sound instead of enjoying the sounds of nature. What if now our walking men and women were having accidents in greater abundance thanks to Sony? I bump in, I get mugged, I fall in a manhole, I drive my car with Sony at my ears and hit a cab. Can one imagine bringing a lawsuit against Sony? Our city life administered: its aim, to sanitize us, to subtract us from noise, which is to say instinct.

Z: *Zero* The culture's ill at ease with it, hates anything to do with negativity, be it death, sickness, fading of consciousness, the unconscious itself. Ask a person his or her sleep position and you'll be treated instead to the favored sex position. We're a society that seeks to renounce the division of the self discovered by Freud, that seeks to renounce all division, all contradiction. Race: we jump on our Andy Rooneys, our Jimmy the Greeks, admitting the accidental evil of a remark or two the better to conceal the principal evil of the civilization. We immunize the culture of racial division by means of a small innoculation of acknowledged antagonism. And cry horror when Al Sharpton takes on the effect (how can I use her?) instead of the cause (was she or wasn't she?) of Tawana Brawley. As with race, with all divisions. Driven by advertising we seek to resolve all contradictions, to reconcile ourselves with our own image, to efface social division, disquiet, contradiction. Efface them where? Why, in image. In irony we can call this kind of euphoria utopia. America as an everyday, realized utopia. Frege said that zero was invented to stand for the case of everything nonidentical to itself. What's in that class? Nothing. Everything in the world is homogeneous, through and through what it is, identical to itself. Because of zero I can start counting: one . . . The number one—homogeneity—is born from zero. And I'm always awake, always what I am, always conscious. Except that I'm out of here, ready for the release of tension, for sleep, for drunkenness. "Always be drunk," wrote Baudelaire. "That's all: it's the only question. Not to feel the horrible burden of Time which breaks your back and hurls you to earth, you must be drunk without respite. But with what? With wine, poetry or virtue, as you please. But get drunk."

Except that once you've awakened to the inferno, you can't so easily return to sleep. You're in the domain of truth, of *aletheia:* in my etymology, without sleep. Remember Calvino's choice: to accept or to know. And if it's *know* you can't go back to *lethe,* the deepest of sleeps. I'm sorry. If it's *know* . . . how difficult that shall be, Jacques Attali reminded me at the top of his bank opposite London's new architectural landmark, the Lloyds Bank near the Tower. All its entrails are on the outside, all its piping, its lifts going up and down full of executives. "You can judge a country through its myths," Attali said. "What are the American myths? Their heros are those of youth, very often children"—scarcely uttered in denunciation. To a European, America is a very young nation; two hundred years is nothing; the youth of our mythologies is perfectly understandable. "But youth very often look at a world without tragedy," he continued. "And the heros of America are without tragedy. Maybe I'm wrong, it's the idea a friend gave to me and I think it's a very profound idea: the lack of tragic hero in the national mythology, which pushes to optimism."

Treat the little idea as a heuristic. Call our myths those of youth or, if you please, those of freshness, of new beginnings; whatever your personal expression, we can revisit the mythologies of this book and go a ways with Attali or rather, his friend, a Danish surgeon. Think of Stephen King's apt (Can Do) pupil, who sucks up every detail of the death camps. Or the supposed adult Lewis Creed whose monomania in that pet sematary gives the lie to his size. Or the porn men who flee women for an image of them. Or the Little League enthusiasm of Merv's dork made pseudo-hero. Or John Wayne in Tokyo and Clint Eastwood or somebody else in Euro-Disney. Or the capriciousness that Madonna and *Vogue* teach. Or the acceleration anger of Gotti and Koppel, disguised in the first case by clothes and in the second by "Do you mean to tell me that . . . ?" A mega-myth whose burpable body and double face shall be Merv's: *"So much love feeling good!"* shouting *"NATHA!"* Have a nice day! and Make my Day! Of course what is missing in this gummy violent euphoria is the tragic, the play of mourning over the dead, including ourselves who will be dead.

From which it follows that—how could there be anything but— little feeling of threat in America, although as we go nearer the millennium great dread probably will break through the trompe

l'oeil Nice Day—as lesser dread already has in the name of recession. *From which it follows that—how could there be . . .* Can
one not hear the delay, the prolonging of the moment that introduces a difference, a Now that is the origin of all narrative and of a
narrative under my pen, as we used to say? I have begun to outline a
narrative movement in which many groups of the collectivity called
America might anxiously interrogate their fate; and do so with hope
or dread at this moment when many of us feel new, feel the sense of
a New Day, a Today after the collapse of Communism. Victory In
The Gulf, the global fantasy of an apostasy: Democracy. Ideology is
another name for the collective subtext I am about to sketch. The
semiotics of this book has arrived at a crossroads where it meets
politics and the possibility of something like a new ideology in a
country, ours, where fresh air seems impossible to respire and
where nevertheless is no vision for an alternate life. Having become
a bit of a stranger to my country (as Teddie Zeldin pages and eons
ago predicted); having come a bit close to some European states-
men fashioning ideology for a new Europe, possibly a Europe, I can
end this book wearing a different cap, suggesting an alternative
ideology for America. I can utter a narrative by means of which one
might hope a little.

I said that there is little sense of threat in our country. There had
been a widespread idea of decline perhaps a year and a few months
ago; an idea eroded now, given the Gulf War and the supposed
triumph of American will and arms it brought to the light of day.
The Victory, however, was the unforeseen effect of a mildly arthritic
strategy targeting a rather more formidable enemy than Iraq. ''The
only thing that made the American response to Iraq possible is the
fact that it had been in preparation for 30 years,'' says Berel Rodal,
former Director General of Policy in the Canadian Defense Department and now an international consultant. ''You can't put close to
two thousand combat aircraft and all that personnel into a desert
unless you prepared a very long time in advance. Operation Desert
Storm benefitted from unusually successful strategic planning. No
place on earth is more removed from American power than the
Persian Gulf.

Three decades ago, American planners had taken the decision to
prepare against a Soviet incursion somewhere in the Middle East, a
volatile region on the Soviet rimland bearing the major part of the
world's oil reserves. Without establishing how or from where an
incursion might come, the risk of one and the strategic rationale for
it was clear. Saudia Arabia was the base for these perparations. ''The
U.S. Army Corps of Engineers virtually paved Saudia Arabia,'' says
Rodal. ''All those state-of-the-art bases ready to accommodate
advanced fighters and equipment in such numbers''—never identified during the war because of Pentagon censorship—''were the
happy product of these preparations over many years to deter and

counter a Soviet invasion of some kind somewhere in the Middle East." It is because this contingency was so well prepared that the Americans were able to respond to Saddam Hussein in the way that they did.

All that being said, we now discover that Saddam Hussein was months away from the Bomb. From the elites to the "average American," we ask: what if he hadn't been so greedy and had waited a few months? We realize how by miscalculation we ended up as victors who might have been other than that. How little we knew and, shall we say, know. We went to extraordinary lengths to get rid of him and there he is. And who wouldn't let us get rid of him? The Saudis. Why? It would have destabilized Iraq and removed it as a bulwark against the threatening Shia territory on the rim of Saudi Arabia. There are faults, flaws, deconstructive doubts that run from the elites to the "common man" in the heart of the Reassertion of American Spirit, the Overcoming of Vietnam.

It is well and good to talk about American leadership, the end of the duopoly, no more superpowers, only Us and the rest. At the same time, no one's domestic base is as vulnerable as the Americans'. Out of a thousand or more instances, this example: New York Telephone needed to hire a thousand or so telephonists; had to interview some 50,000 people to arrive at this fifth. Example: If you are black, aged 15–35, what are your chances of being in jail, or dead? Recently, Allistair Cooke, answering the question, "Is America in decay? If so, will it endure some patchwork surgery, or weaken and expire?"; answering on the front page of London's *Financial Times*, he observed:

> The city crime rates are regularly beyond those of all but the worst previous years, and random street crime at night matches the jottings of 18th century diaries. Drugs are a pestilence afflicting all classes and every age. We have just wakened to the discovery that for a long time, maybe for several decades, public education in America has been setting such easy and dithering standards that, at the least, a large minority, perhaps a majority, of high school graduates are, in comparison with their European and Asian fellows, semi-literate.
>
> An even more recent discovery is that "flourishing" real estate in the big cities has meant mainly office skyscrapers and luxury high-rise apartment buildings. Within mocking distance of these are the open lots or scrubby bits of park where the homeless huddle and the drug pushers bargain.

Where the poor nomads, as it were, beg, bargain, and bludgeon for a few drops of what the rich nomads above, attached to their Walkmen, PCs, faxes, and other portable objects, have in so much abundance. Moved to answer the question he had sworn never to respond to—whither America?—this very sweet man exploded on the FT:

So what is the likely outcome, if we ever achieve a day, a season, which can be seen as an historical turning point? There appear to me to be three possibilities. 1. The second American Civil War, triggered by separate ethnic and regional uprisings. 2. The arrival of a populist dictator (under, as Burke predicted, the banner of liberty). 3. An emergency return to the benevolent form of national socialism created by Franklin Roosevelt in the first New Deal.

All the above seem to Cooke to be real possibilities if the social dangers and deprivations we paper over with mythology cannot be placated by the present political system; if they become too much for most Americans to bear. For my part, things are not forever or long going to continue as they are. Gibbon's fourth etiology of decadence, internal hostilities, will work its potent destructions. Here is a character worthy of Stephen King: someone coming in the name of Liberty.

The moment we are living feels to be one of uniqueness: America is the uncontested power, the powerhouse, the leader, yet on the other hand there's a keen, even haunting sense of vulnerability on the part of Americans.

This amounts to saying: Yes, our mythologies are those of youth, but they are tinged with bitterness, as if our youth wake each day old and fatigued, already exhausted. Think of Griffin, watching his bondholders take "haircuts." Think of Gotti, nurturing his flock in divisiveness. Think of Cohen-Solal, her ears ringing with New York's poetics of despair. Think of Balloonatic in the subway, his good humor a howl. Think of Armani, opening A/X for the almost-poor. The glossy dreams of luxury are shot through. The dream-makers are falling stars. In the spirit of irony, one could imagine a new soap opera, *My Bitter Children.* When I brought the matter up with Stephen King, he began to sketch a treatment:

> We sold everything including our own dreams and myths in order to support a shoddy instant culture—books, movies, MTV—that dies each day and we remake it again on the next day. But every time that we remake it, it's a little bit cheaper. I think that we probably know on some level that whatever we had that was lasting we sold off. On some level we know that there is a difference, let's say, between John Gotti and Kevin Costner as Robin Hood, or at least that at one time there was a difference; that at some point there was a society where King Arthur had more weight than, let's say, Elvis Presley. But that's not our society. I think there's a lot of bitterness when, having spent so much time trying to change the lead of daily existence into the gold of myth, you discover that what you've done instead with the popular culture has been to change what is gold into lead. You've achieved a kind of reverse alchemy, and that would make anybody bitter. It's the ultimate back-fire.

Take Magic Johnson. He was everything that's good, a mythic figure who had a disease, who went public and now everybody says, "Now, wait a minute, though, he got AIDS, he was promiscuous, he killed all these women. The guy's a rat." And then the next thing you know, people are telling jokes about Magic Johnson. So you've got this revisionist mythology, an impulse to take any mythological figure and tear it down. Everything has to be put in perspective by a sort of flow of alternate information, whether it's Magic Johnson who's seen as the quintessential good sports figure—all at once he becomes a poisoner. In another field, it's Bill Clinton who's supposed to be the standard bearer for the Democratic Party—all at once he's a sexual monster. Mike Tyson: from champion of the world to big bad black rapist.

When I mention that pol who came in from 60s, Jerry Brown, King can't help himself—the "tear it down" impulse is too strong:

> When he was in Maine, I came out and took a look at him and thought that he looked like a fraud with his plaid shirt that still had the creases in it from the rack in the store. And I thought that his face and posture were that of a man who was saying: "Get me home so I can get out of this fucking shirt and put on some Armani again."
>
> And the impulse works the other way, too. Hey, John Gotti's become Robin Hood, right? And look at this shit, Bugsy Siegel. They've turned him into this tragic mythological figure. Black is white and white is black. That's what Kevin Costner says in *J.F.K.* He says, "We're through the looking glass people." And that's where we are. Our own culture has no basic sounding chord anymore. We've lost the belief that there's anything in our culture that has any real validity. Whatever had value has been destroyed by a flood of cheap information and a total breakdown of moral standards.

Do you remember what Yevtushenko taught us? Until very recently, the Soviet Union was a potent military power. All the materiel, the science and technology, the military muscle was in place. Yet the Union fell. It was a major failing of culture.

Mythologically, we are at the vanguard, teaching the world how to live with the challenges of ethnicity, of multiracial society. But if it turns out that this isn't so, then the ideas of freedom and of market access are nonsense; that in fact this is a society of Dukes and Buchanans, of bigots and racists; that the middle class is destroyed as a viable concept, the underclass continually enlarged; if that be so, the content of our guiding mythology would be weakened, as was the Soviet content. The system then fails because what makes the system work is the belief that it results in progress. And it's worth repeating: The base of our leadership is wobbly.

When George Bush spewed Miyazawa in Tokyo, our old friend Amaya happened to be in Tokyo's NHK studio as commentator. His instant remark was widely reported here: "It's so symbolic," he said in the *New York Times*. "The superpower America is tired and everyone around it has to take care of it."

"Somebody said the U.S. Secret Service was looking for poison. At that moment nobody could see whether his fall was fatal or not. We were shocked by that happening," Amaya recalled from his home in Tokyo. "So when the NHK interviewer asked me, 'What's your impression?' I answered: 'I feel that symbolizes the present situation of the United States. The U.S. is tired but the disease is not fatal, so the U.S. will recover. However, Japan should help the U.S. when it is sick.' That was my answer. Perhaps it was abridged [in your press]."

Perhaps, or perhaps he is again discreet. He had literally seen the leadership fall and had instantly turned attention to the base. "The U.S. forgot how to make good things, it forgot the lesson of Carnegie and Ford," he said. "By transferring offshore your car, chip, computer, and telecommunications manufacturing, you are losing the capability of manufacturing good things. I feel that America is like a greyhound that missed its target to pursue. Suddenly the hare disappeared. Where to go? What to do?"

"And Japan? What kind of dog is it?" I ask.

"Japan is greyhound number two pursuing greyhound America. Japan is at a loss because United States is at a loss. The target was to catch up with the U.S. in terms of economy. Japan has succeeded, therefore the hare disappeared. The question is: Where now? What is the next hare to be pursued?" Amaya is now president of Dentsu Institute for Human Studies, leading scholarship to ascertain "what sort of hares the Japanese companies should chase from now on," he tells me.

The base, I insist, is cultural. Image of our culture: How many Americans feel they have any chance of living in the kind of house in which they were brought up as children? American mythology is now in transition from that of being a sense of a fresh beginning to that of looking back at a golden age. A new mythology is coming into being: Once we lived in a shining city in a time of perfection. This is why, taking a trivial example, our "business books" so emphasize quality, performance, all the sorry other signifiers. Citing Claude Lévi-Strauss, Roman Jakobson in my own last book *On Signs* wrote that " 'a mask is not primarily what it represents'—and how often and in how many fields must we take this into account— a mask is not primarily what it represents, but what it transforms,' that is what it chooses either to represent or to omit. Like a myth, it excludes and denies as much as it states. Diplomats have said that language exists not merely to reveal but, perhaps even more, to conceal." We always have to ask, Jakobson said, how a myth is able to deny what it is affirming while simultaneously remaining affirmative. *Let there be quality, excellence, all the positivities,* say the business books, meaning: *there was strength, there was vigor, there was coherence.* What America is losing, as everyone falls over everyone else to support yet another cause (call it the multicultural agenda), is coherence. Its continental force. America is a mishmash, once unified "from sea to shining sea," now become a fractious multiracial, multicultural pit bull arena, all the parties triumphant. On such a terrain, one might wonder, how do you shape strategy without a threat and mythology without strategy?

So I repeat that there is little threat now, but threat can be an asset for a country, especially a young one. Witness Sputnik and its effect of birthing the American space industry. To look to the past, in the Netherlands or Venice or London, it was the perception of threat that pushed those countries to find innovative solutions to economic and social problems. Amsterdam, for example, without adequate land on which to grow wheat, devoloped its dye industry in the seventeenth century. Most recently, analogously, Japan, a narrow, surrounded country without energy, developed telecommunications and computers, given their greater energy efficiency; in turn a necessity given that the Japanese have no energy. As they have an excess of population on a small territory, they were obliged to miniaturize, developing the portable objects on which so much of the world now depends.

The consciousness of threat can be an asset; nevertheless, we feel little given all of the above and this in addition: an excitation built into the American way. "United States feels no threat because of this fascinating reason: that democracy and market economy are creating the apologia for the ephemeral, reversibility being the core of everything," Attali told me. This is only a different formulation of his "amortization" idea: we change our cars, change our ideas, spouses, friends quicker and quicker. The words "market economy" mean that we can change goods—mean disposability, in a word. The word "democracy" means that we can change leaders; hence in both arenas, political and economic, the first principle would be that of reversibility. In fact, what may be announcing itself in this moment of market triumph is something like the end of politics; by which I mean that perhaps what we usually call politics, and of course the politics of democracy which implies a certain set of concepts (*polis,* state; *civitas,* city; *civis,* citizen), perhaps this is in the process of being dismantled. Perhaps none of these European, Greek, and Latin concepts are capable any longer of defining the essence of the current social experience in which democratic politics, without disappearing, plays a different rule in a newly structured space and time that are not *simply* apolitical or ahistorical.

Using a text of Jacques Derrida ("Democracy Adjourned," in the 1991 *Minuit; L'Autre Cap* [*The Other Cape*]), let me sketch this other scene. What is called public opinion is supposed to be a principle, an *arche,* an origin of democracy; it is supposed to be the forum of a permanent and transparent discussion and, of course, would be opposed to nondemocratic powers. Oddly, however, "public opinion" is held in low esteem; it is unpredictable, mobile and changing, difficult to govern, defying force and reason. Why? Because it can change *"from day to day,"* Derrida writes, italicizing the "day to day" because of its coming importance. "Literally *ephemeral,* it has no status because it is not held to stability, not even to the constancy of instability, for it sometimes has 'long times.'"

Precisely because of its arhythmic rhythm, as it were, public opinion and thus the public have a bad press, as we say. Nevertheless, society has given it something, something that is proper to it. Its quotidian, quicksilver rhythm supposes the massive diffusion of something like a daily, a newspaper. What is the Daily? "This techno-economic power permits opinion to be constituted and to be recognized as *public* opinion," Derrida continues. "Although its categories appear barely adequate today, the newspaper is held to assure a place of public visibility proper to *informing, forming, reflecting* or *expressing,* thus to *representing* an opinion which would find there the milieu of its liberty."

How does the newspaper accomplish such representation? What does it do to opinion, this ground of democracy? "Public opinion never speaks in the first person . . . one *cites* it, makes it speak, ventriloquizes it [*real country, silent majority, moral majority* of Nixon, *mainstream* of Bush, etc.]." Result: public opinion is not *expressed,* if one understands thereby that it exists in some inner heart before being manifested to the great day in its phenomenality. "It *is* phenomenal," Derrida writes; it is only appearance. "It is no longer *produced* or *formed,* even *influenced* or *inflected,* only simply *reflected,* or *represented* by the press." We do what we want, say what we want: utter severance from the "people."

It is fitting to revisit the acknowledgements page of this book. The reader knows that without the aid of certain newspapers and magazines this book would not exist. The prepublication was a subtle struggle to take advanced critical theories out of the academy and into, if not the world, then its Dailies. "Research called 'difficult,' rebellious to the stereotype of the image or of narration, scarcely submissive to the norms of culture thus represented in its average (in the singular, 'opinion' always signifies the 'average') are excluded from the scene: occulted, deprived of the *day. By consequence, they are judged* more and more 'obscure,' 'difficult,' even 'unreadable' and they *become* what one says they are and wants them to be: inaccessible." They are guaranteed an existence in small journals or small editions making them like confidential correspondence, quasi private, Derrida remarks.

Thus it is that the rhythm of the daily weighs on the "citizen," made only a fraction of a passive "public," a consumer. The rhythm of this daily is the rhythm of the day. You can't "take time," mull, ponder, ramify; you are obliged to live day to day, waking up *tabula rasa* with a slightly nauseous glance at yesterday's newspaper as if it were something unclean. The very rhythm of the daylight, of the New Day, of the New Fix undoes us. This is the press, the daily inculcates, the iron law of quotidian rhythm; this is the true capricious of which Attali is warning.

And our leaders are scarcely exempt from the Daylight. In their world, it is called the Quarterly Report, the Reckoning. The rules of the game require that the leaders of companies, of the universities, that the elites look only at the next quarter. Obiously, were I constructing something like a statesmanly ideology, I would try to tell the story of the importance of the long time, of a longer perspective; economically speaking, of incentives. A society merely looking at the short term—to put it in a public policy code—cannot save, cannot invest, cannot think about products that will be needed in twenty years. And we shouldn't snicker at the moral Attali whose speeches in Europe tell of the "good man." "To be a good man or woman in a modern society," he told me, "one has to be a forester, one has to invest knowing it will be someone else who will see the trees." One has to be a parent; and we can say that life is happening in our country as if parenthood had a low value. Attali reminded me that the wise man, according to the Indians, is the one who takes care of the interests of seven generations. Such a man may be Nicholas Brady, Secretary of Commerce. Attali's U.S. director, William G. Curran Jr. is talking to me in London about the man who appointed him director, Brady himself.

> Nicholas Brady is trying to change the laws of accounting so that a company doesn't have to, every quarter, show its financials. He's trying to get companies to think longer term, invest for the future. But they won't do it because by law they've got to have a quarterly report that states where they are regarding earnings per share each quarter. And if one quarter's down, because they've invested in something that hasn't paid off in thirty days, then they sell the bloody stock. The market doesn't want to know, the analysts say, 'The company's lost money this month or this week'; and they never say, 'The company is building." The Japanese don't give a damn about quarterlies. The Germans don't tell you what their earnings are; they can invest and plan and take the hits now to get market share, which we are unable to do. Now Secretary Brady is trying to change our mentality by hoping to change some of the technical aspects of reporting procedures. But he's having a lot of trouble with it; he's got to get through the trade associations, the banking regulators, the S.E.C. and the powers that be; and he may not succeed because those institutions want to Do It Now.

Brady's vision isn't our culture, which is that of the capricious. And very quickly when a society has no other culture than that of the ephemeral, one sees other values surging: fanatic, mystic, theocratic, even dictatorial (in salute of Cooke). Why? Ask the question, what you want, really want. To last in eternity; that was the religious feeling. To last by your heirs, giving your name to someone else. But if a fundamental value is to last, and yet society day by day builds an apology for something which is not lasting; if the civilization of ephemera destroys family, destroys names, destroys the very future, then men and women will desire to escape that civilization and find somewhere else to last. They will seek another way of lasting. And a place has been set for the theocrat, old friend Pat; for the charismatic, who unlike Pat will doubtless come in running shorts preaching EST. The place of the dictator; or for the paradise of an always dangerous New Man; or for drugs, the voyage of continents without projects, as Attali put it.

Thus if we want to leave the critical, even deconstructive mode, if we were obliged to deal with the real consequences of our thoughts, to live in a world of human effect with humane ends, we might understand that we have to inscribe the ephemeral society in the heart of something more durable, without abruptly abandoning the market or what passes for democracy. Simply speaking, that "more durable" would be what we call the constitution. A constitution is the original foundation of an institution. It is something not reversible, which lasts in all its originary force. "During the history of an institution, each time we refer to the constitution," Derrida has said, "we do not simply translate it in the sense of making a statement about the origin; we repeat the origin. When, as a judge, I say, 'Such and such amendment of the constitution is valid,' I don't simply quote or simply apply or simply translate. I'm reenacting, it is a second birth." And one would want to put in this constitution greater than any existing now; in this constitution in a democracy to be invented, one might place constructs important for endurance, environmental concerns, weapons control (happening already), prohibitions against certain genetic manipulations, "because it's in the laboratories where genetic fantasies are the last avatar of the western dream, the ultimate point of this double and dangerous ambition: purity of choice and descendance" (Attali, *1492*). But I fear the constitution, the law in the most fundamental sense, is not a basalt value—think of the Gotti myth, even Ted Koppel's breaking of *his* law, fairness.

Now that postmodernity has killed the charismatic, paradoxically we might say: to prevent great men we need great men and women, or at least rebels. Not to sound too much like Paul Simon, but in this year of the quincentenary, where are they? The Columbuses? (God forgive him for fulfilling the royals' command: *Descubrir y Gañar,* discover and gain.) Martin Behaims? Leonardos?

Or, more modestly, a Jacques Attali for 1992? Where?

End

Index

508

RENNER LEARNING RESOURCE CENTER
ELGIN COMMUNITY COLLEGE
ELGIN, ILLINOIS 60123